Dedication

This book is dedicated to the biologist Dr. rer. nat. Ulrich Baensch, the founder of the modern aquarium hobby and the inventor of the first natural fishfood produced under industrial methods.

Dr. Rüdiger Riehl
Hans A. Baensch

Cover photos:
Title: Burkhard Kahl
Black cover: Aaron Norman, top and bottom left
Burkhard Kahl, top right

Publisher:
Hans A. Baensch

Editor:
Dr. Rüdiger Riehl

Translated and revised by:
Hans A. Smith
Eberhard Schulze
Bob Behme

ISBN: 3-88244-050-3

Printed in Hongkong
First English Edition, 1987
Second English Edition, reprinted 1989
Third Revised English Edition, 1991
Fourth English Edition, reprinted 1994
Fifth Revised English Edition, 1996
16050

Distribution
USA: Tetra Sales (Warner-Lambert-Company) Blackburg, VA 24060
Canada: Rolf C. Hagen Inc., 3225 Sartelon Street, Montreal, Que. H4R 1E8
Great Britain: Rolf C. Hagen (U.K.) Limited, California Drive, Whitwood Industrial
                Estate, Castleford WF 10 50H, West Yorkshire, England.
Australia: Pet Pacific Pty Ltd., Lot 8 Leland Street, Penrith NSW 2750
                P.O. Box 481, Penrith NSW 2750, Australia

Dr. Rüdiger Riehl
Hans A. Baensch

AQUARIUM ATLAS

MERGUS

Publishers of Natural History and Pet Books
Hans A. Baensch · Melle · W. Germany

Contents

Contents

FOREWORD

With more than one hundred fine aquarium books available, some several volumes in length, you may ask, why offer another? There are at least two reasons:

1. With so many choices an aquarist can easily lose a broad overview.

2. A handy, current book, which deals, in one volume, with all of the important aspects of the hobby in an uncomplicated manner, still needed to be written.

Our book does that. It offers mega-doses of information, concentrated so that it is informative and interesting. We've included photos of 600 species of fish and 100 aquatic plants, yet this is not an encyclopedia of fish and plants but a practical guide on the keeping, care, breeding and adaptation of aquarium fish and plants. For both biological and aesthetic reasons, we feel live plants and fish belong together. An aquarium with living plants means healthy fish and though it requires more expertise than a tank with plastic plants, it is well worth the effort. The aquarium is pleasing to everyone who sees it.

Most new hobbyists know too little about fish. Many imagine that all fish are alike, that a discus is as easy to keep as a goldfish! Our book is broad enough in scale, yet with enough concentrated information, to be of interest and help to both the beginning and advanced aquarist. It is written for everyone who would like to gain more knowledge than can be found in the small, beginners' handbooks and is aimed at hobbyists who want practical, workable information without the unnecessary depth and complexity of text only a dedicated hobbyist would wade through.

We can say, with confidence, that the knowledge necessary to start and keep an aquarium successfully has been assembled in this modestly priced book. For those who care to go beyond this, to penetrate the subject of fish keeping in greater depth, we recommend:

Gunther Sterba: Freshwater Fish, Vols. 1 and 2.

Our book is written to fill the gap between the simple guides, those small books on special topics, and the big books only a few hobbyists need... and for which fewer have the funds.

When comparing this book with existing literature you may notice differences, particularly in nomenclature. This is due, in part, to a fresh look at the massive amount of available scientific literature, in another to utilizing the latest products of the aquarium industry, and finally, from our experiences which do not follow specific trends, but is broadly based.

Dr. Rüdiger Riehl
Hans A. Baensch

March, 1991

Living with Fish

The aquarium hobby is popular around the world. In the U.S. it has been described as the second most popular hobby (stamp collecting is first) with nearly 100 million fish in hobbyist's tanks. In Canada there are more than one million aquariums. In Germany there are nearly a million aquariums and some 36 million fish and the numbers are similar in Japan, Norway and half a hundred other nations. But is it a permanent hobby? Do aquarists remain fish-keepers for long periods?

Not as many hobbyists are as devoted to the long term as one might like. Each year ten to twenty percent of us leave the hobby. The reason most often given is that the plants no longer grew or a combination of fishes led to losses which could not be checked. A dead fish is reason for sorrow, as the death of any animal will disturb an animal lover, but the experience should not become so emotionally overwhelming that we cannot learn from our mistakes.

It is easy enough to buy an aquarium, accessories and fish but some knowledge is essential if the fish are to be kept alive and healthy for any length of time. Properly kept, many fish live five to ten years. Some even longer.

Fish do not breathe oxygen as we do nor do they have our unlimited atmospheric resources. They are limited to the oxygen the hobbyist puts into the tank – be it cleaned, filtered and fresh, or turbid and almost unusable. In an aquarium a fish must swim and breath in its own excretion unless the water is cleaned.

A place for an aquarium in every home

Aquariums are virtually ubiquitous and while there may be reasons for not wanting a tank, a lack of space is not one. A simple glass tank can fit any place and a larger or more complex set-up can be as attractive as the finest furniture.

A place can be found in every home. Something as simple as a window sill is acceptable, though not ideal – as long as any heating vent near by is screened at the bottom and the tank is protected from the sun at the top. A plastic sheet angled across the vent will work at the bottom and at the top an aquarium cover will protect the tank from sunlight but remember, water can be quickly heated to more than 100° F (40° C) in a window with a southerly exposure. Few fish can tolerate temperatures above 85° F (30° C).

The Aquarium

A living room or den is an ideal place for an aquarium. It should be placed so it can be viewed without intruding on other elements in the room. An aquarium can provide a lively, colorful, natural focus of attention and should be easily seen from the sitting area, preferably from the aquarist's favorite chair. It must not overpower other elements in the room. The stand and the tank should blend with the furniture and other decor.

Possible locations

1. As a room divider
   a. A custom designed aquarium
   b. A tank on a stand
   c. Built into a wall
   d. Tank on masonry Base
   e. Between two rooms
   f. A large tank at floor level

2. A free-standing aquarium
   a. On a pedestal, possibly decorated with carpeting that matches the floor
   b. On a support of wood, stone or concrete (possibly decorated with carpeting or painted and styled to match the furniture)
   c. On an aquarium stand
   d. On a chest, table or other furniture
   e. On a modern metal stand such as those used to hold television sets.

3. On the wall as a living picture
   a. On a special shelf
   b. In a custom-made alcove.

These are only a few of the possibilities and hundreds more come to mind. There are virtually no limits to the places one can fit a home aquarium.

In the next chapter we will discuss, in detail, methods for establishing your first aquarium. Regular water changes and proper filtration, which can be compared to cage or kennel cleaning for other pets, a little knowledge about proper foods, and the right combination of fish are the three secrets to a successful start. Half of all disaters result from an ignorance of these facts. Learn a little about aquatic plants and add one or two points about water quality and you are well on your way to successful fish-keeping.

In this chapter we will concentrate more on concepts of interior design. We'll offer hints on ways you can integrate an aquarium into any home, whether your style is modern, rustic or antique.

Some examples

The photographs which follow give you an idea of the vast potential for adding an aquarium or two in your home. Most often it is placed in the livingroom and our examples are concentrated there, however, you can effectively utilize a tank in an entrance hall, in stairs, between two rooms and even in an office or bedroom. Aquariums in public buildings such as banks, offices and restaurants are beyond the scope of this book.

An aquarium without a stand! It is dynamic, space saving, and brings freedom of movement. However, such an arrangement requires carefully construction. The support structures must be securely anchored to the wall and additional braces should be placed every 50 - 60 cm of tank length.

In this case, the external filter was placed in a separate box to one side of the aquarium - truly an attractive, elegant solution for interior decoration.

Constructed with black silicon, this aquarium rests on a sturdy stand. There is sufficient space for technical equipment such as a pump-driven filter and heating and cleaning apparatuses (caution: store feeds separately). The heat-generating ballast of the fluorescent tubes can be placed underneath the aquarium; this arrangement reduces the weight of the hood and provides plants with a warm substrate, much to their benefit. Filtration hoses are routed behind the aquarium, unless the tank has previously been fitted with drilled holes to install filtration inlets and outlets in an efficient manner. The use of clamps and valves should be obvious.

The complete setup on a pedestal integrates an esthetically and (almost) maintenance free aquarium into a focal point for any modern living room. Filter and pump are located in the pedestal, and the bottom pane of the aquarium has holes drilled into it.
With appropriate stocking, maintenance is limited to feeding and filter cleaning. Algivorous catfishes (e.g., *Ancistrus* spp.) will clean the glass panes. Likewise, the kissing gourami relishes algae.

Placing the aquarium in a linving room bookcase is one of the most popular solutions when situating the "living television". The considerable weight of the tank, however, should not be entrusted to just any piece of furniture. A good carpenter may be required to install additional supports; these supports should be firmly planted on the floor. After all, a 2 m tank, like the one shown, easily weights half a ton!

Lighting can be placed in the space above by a handy aquarist or your aquarium store dealer, and the filtration system can be housed beneath the aquarium.

This aquarium is almost a bog aquarium (paludatium). The emphasis here is on the plants in the landscape, not on the fishes - a pleasant arrangement for botanists. An aqua-terrarium of this type can readily be stocked with brackish water species (archer fishes, scats) as long as the roots of the plants don't reach the water (salt content). Humidity-loving (hydrophylic) plants like ferns, some bromeliads (tillandsias), orchids, etc., prosper in the area above the aquarium.

When freshwater fishes are kept, philodendron roots can be encouraged to grow into the aquarium water. These quickly branch, offering good hiding possibilities for fry. Caution: these roots mus not be injured, as they release a sap which can be toxic to some fishes.

This 75 gallon tank has been mounted in a wall and can be seen from only one room. The tank is serviced from the adjoining room through an overhead flap. In this design, there should be be at least one foot (30 cm.) of space above the tank and 15 inches (40 cm.) would be better. It is also useful to leave space beneath for a large outside filter. The tank can be supported by metal brackets, triangular shelf ends or metal "tees" counter sunk into the concrete.

When the owner conceived this room, with the chimney place in the foreground, the partial divider between the living and sitting rooms was designed to hold an aquarium. From the front, only the aquarium pane can be seen, but from behind, the recess in the dividing wall is appreciably larger as can be seen from the photo on page 19. The aquarium is slightly larger than normal, about 100 gallons, and four spot lights have been fitted into the cabinet to light it. The bulbs are easily replaced a space above helps cool them.

Supporting brackets are built into the wall and below is a cabinet with sliding doors. Accessories are kept in the left section and an outside filter is mounted on the right. The cabinet also contains water lines and a drain. Three electrical outlets are mounted above and three below.

A typical, species-correct cichlid aquarium with calcareous rocks and African *Anubias*. These vibrant-colored cichlids can certainly compete with the stunning hues found in marine aquaria, yet their care is simpler.

Blue, yellow, and orange cichlids can be kept, although undesired crosses may occur when congeners are maintained together. Resourceful persons can bypass the aforementioned problem by caring for a group of blue males with yellow females - or vice versa.

The Right Aquarium

The choice of aquarium will depend on several factors:
1. Size and cost
2. Space - the best place
3. Aquarium design
4. Needs of the fish

In many ways our fourth point, the needs of the fish should come first, but remember, you can change priorities by selecting the fish to fit your aquarium.

1. The size of an aquarium will depend on available space and, of course, cost.

The tank dimensions are of particular importance. When placed in a 200 square foot room it should not have more than 50 to 55 gallon capacity. In a room half that size a tank of about 25 gallons is better. For larger rooms the popular solution is to use a tank as a room divider, that is to separate a sitting area from the rest of the room with an aquarium. The tank can be placed on free-standing shelving and viewed from two sides. Aquariums thus seen are more difficult to decorate than those which stand against a wall because the decorations must be placed in the central axis of the tank rather than against the rear glass. For this reason the tank should be wider than one standing against a wall. We recommend a minimum width of 20 inch (50 cm.)

A larger aquarium is easier to maintain than a smaller one since it requires fewer water changes and less frequent cleaning. Your local pet shop can offer advice on both sizes and cost. If possible start with a 15 or 20-gallon tank (the closest comparable size in some countries would be one of $17^1/_2$ gallons [about 80 liters.]) If a particular species is to be kept, the dimensions of the tank will depend on the requirements of the fish. You'll find minimum tank lengths listed under individual species descriptions later in the book.

2. The best place. There are many places in a house or apartment to keep an aquarium. Some of our favorite locations were listed in the last chapter and other ideas will come to mind as you look around your own home. If you use existing furniture as a support for the tank, instead of a specially designed stand, it should be sturdy enough to support both the tank and the water. Water weighs about eight pounds per gallon and an aquarium is heavier than it looks. A 30-gallon aquarium, for example, (one about three-feet in length) will weigh in at about 250 pounds and an antique table or an unreinforced shelf could not support it. If you build your own supports measure the bottom of the tank beforehand. The shelf should be as large or larger than the tank bottom. One smaller will not provide adequate support.

The modern all-glass aquarium, assembled with silicone cement, is so simple it blends with any room and the selection of stands and cabinets, in wood or metal, combines tastefully with most furniture. There are few limits on personal taste and while the hints below are merely suggestions they should be helpful when setting up an aquarium:

a. Monitor the sun - Too much sunlight can cause the water to overheat in summer and will encourage algae. With the selection of fluorescent hoods available, aquariums can be independent of daylight.

b. Avoid heat - Never place an aquarium above or near a heat source, a radiator, heating vent or stove. Similarly, avoid the sudden drops in temperature you can find near an air conditioning outlet.

c. Easy water changes - While you can change aquarium water with a bucket, it is easier if water outlets and drains are close. Any within fifty feet are both convenient and usable. Aquariums which must be drained and filled by bucket are too often neglected – to the detriment of both the fish and plants.

d. Convenient power- Electrical outlets should be convenient and plentiful and are best when beside or behind the tank. Be certain to have enough: a network of plugs and adapters is hazardous.

e. Protect the furniture - Allow a safe distance between the tank and expensive furniture since splashing can hardly be avoided when cleaning a tank and changing water and accidents can happen. For example, a tank should not be placed near an expensive Persian carpet. The water may do little damage, but try to convince a housewife!

f. Be sure you're insured - The attitude may seem defeatist, but be wise, carry insurance to protect your furniture against water damage. Even the best-made tank can burst; even the finest hose can leak. If you live in a condo or apartment carry liability insurance to protect against damage to an apartment below.

g. Play it safe - If your stand is made of metal or if you have an older, metal-framed tank, never use it as an electrical ground. The danger of shock in an aquarium is minimal, but to attach electrical current to a direct ground is asking for trouble.

h. The proper support -Since water weighs more than eight pounds per gallon the larger the tank, the greater the need for adequate support. In older homes the feet of the stand or cabinet should be placed as close to floor joists as possible (you can find them by tapping the floor with a hammer or by visible rows of nails.) On linoleum and carpeted floors protect against depressions and punctures by placing furniture cups beneath the feet. The tank should be carefully levelled.

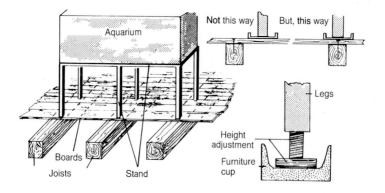

Sometimes an aquarium is positioned so that a nearby window is reflected in the front of the tank. Though distracting it can be avoided by angling the aquarium just enough to send the reflection in another direction. Tilting the front glass forwards ten to 15 degrees often does the trick, deflecting a reflection below eye level.

3. Selecting an Aquarium (Aquarium design)

A variety of aquarium styles are available from local pet shops. You can choose by capacity – from a small plastic or glass bowl through five gallon tanks to more than 100 gallon setups; by material – glass or plexiglass; and by shape – rectangular, square or hexagonal. Some, or all of the following may be found in your area:

a. All-glass, frameless
b. All-glass with plastic framing
c. Plexiglass
d. Glass with anodized aluminum frames
e. Glass with coated steel frames
f. Glass with chrome-plated steel frames
g. Fiberglass holding tank
h. Professional tank (Molded glass)
i. Custom-made aquarium and cabinet

We recommend styles a, b, d and i for breeding and h for quarantine tanks. Type g is suitable for coldwater fish. A, d and g are often built into custom-made aquarium furniture.

You can buy ready-made aquariums, you can build your own and you can have a hobbyist or a tank maker assemble one for you. Manufacturers of silicone cement, such as Dow Chemical, and General Electric (Marina) can provide plans and instructions, but remember, there are two types of cement, those with an acetic acid base and those with an ammonia base. Use only an acetic-acid base cement and, even then, only those specifically formulated for use with aquariums.

There are advantages and drawbacks for each type of tank. You'll find some of them listed on the following page.

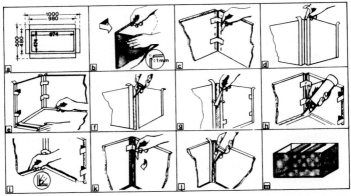

Selection of the Aquarium

Tank Type	Advantages	Drawbacks
a) Glass, frameless	Contemporary design fits any place.	Fragile. The edges easily broken.
	A manufacturer's guarantee is important.	
b) Glass, with plastic frame	An ideal tank if the frame is sturdy and the tank well-made.	Inexpensive tanks may leak. Buy only a well-known brand.
c) Plexiglass	Very light. Particularly useful as a standby or hospital tank. Can be styled in curved and free-form designs.	Plastic scratches easily. Vulnerable to grit, sand and jewelry. In a curved tank the view can be distorted. Sometimes the distortion is pleasing.
d) Glass with aluminum frames	Panes are easily changed if scratched or broken.	Leaking tanks are difficult to seal.
e) Glass with coated steel	Inexpensive	Frames may rust after a few years. Should not be used for saltwater. Obsolete in U.S.
f) Glass with chrome-plated steel frames	Inexpensive and good looking.	Chrome bleaches, then rusts. Not recommended for saltwater. Obsolete in the U.S.
g) Fiberglass Ponds	Stronger than glass. Ideal as a mini-pond for goldfish and koi. Fountains and other designs are available.	Some are unwieldy. Can be set into the earth. Some need a protective coating to prevent hardening of the water.
h) Molded glass	Handy. Ideal as a breeding tank for live bearers or as a tank for Betta. Inexpensive.	Some tanks more than 13 inches in length can crack - for no clear reason. Corners fragile.

4. Needs of the Fish

Fish are not concerned about a tank's design but the inside should be roomy, large enough for the species you plan to keep, with adequate space for swimming.

Catfishes and labyrinth fishes generally prefer a broad, deep tank with a large water surface.

Tetras and danios and most schooling fish, require a long tank with room for swimming – you might call them 'racing tanks'. The tank can also be deep.

Angelfish do best in tall tanks. Most other species or groups of fishes will be happy with whatever tank they are offered, but you should always pay attention to both the capacity and tank dimensions. In Europe tanks are sold according to their length but in the U.S. they are sold by capacity. The common sizes (in gallons) are: 5, 10, 15, 20, 30, 40, 50, 55, 60, 70, 80, 100 and larger. Some tanks are also designated as "L" or "H". These are either higher or longer than standard dimensions and are designed for display.

The wider and longer the tank, the more space for plants and the greater the water surface for oxygen exchange. Both are important factors for the health of fish. A shorter, wider tank is always preferred over a narrow, taller one.

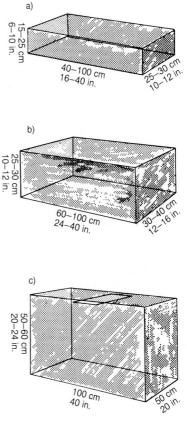

a) Aquariums for: Catfishes and labyrinthfishes

b) Tetras and danios

c) Angelfishes

25

Sand, gravel and the aquarium floor

If you are going to add live plants, as we suggest, you should pay special attention to the gravel used in the bottom of the tank. Its quality determines whether plants thrive or languish. Your fish are not concerned. They only require gravel without sharp edges. A few species prefer very fine "pea" gravel, about $1/4$ of an inch in size, in which to burrow, searching for food, detritus, decayed animal and vegetable substances. Sand is an inappropriate material for undergravel filtration.

For plants the gravel should contain neither metals nor too much calcareous materials (i.e.lime): while calcareous gravel is not harmful, it hardens the water. Many fish do not like hard water and some plants cannot tolerate it. The calcareous nature of gravel and rocks is easily determined. Add a few drops of hydrochloric acid to a small sample. If it foams, it is calcerous.

The most commonly available gravels in the U.S. are river and colored gravels, some with a quartz base. Most will contribute little to the water in the way of minerals but are easy to clean.

Recommended materials:

Coarse sand
(Quartz Gravel) (Top right)
Volcanic ash
Basalt chips (Center, right)
River gravel (Bottom, right)

Not Recommended:

Marble (calcareous)
Soil
Pumice (floats)
Dolomite (limestone)
Coral (calcareous)
Sea and beach sand (has a calcareous content)

Cleaning Gravel

A kitchen strainer can be used to clean gravel in smaller tanks, those to 20 gallons or so. Place two cups of gravel or sand in a strainer and rinse in running water. Larger quantities can be more easily handled by placing the gravel in a bucket, flushing away sediment and dirt with a hose.

Fill a bucket half full of gravel then turn the hose on lightly and push it to the bottom. Stir the gravel vigorously with your hands, flushing the dirty water gently over the rim (as if panning for gold), until the water flows clean. The more thorough the preliminary cleaning the fewer the problems with cloudy water later. We do not recommend cleaning fine gravel in a sink or laundry tub since it is impossible to prevent some from escaping and nothing blocks plumbing like fine gravel.

Gravel contains few nutrients and in Europe it is mixed with fertilizer to create an effective substrate for plant. This can be done in several ways if you can find the proper materials. They may not always be available here, but this is the approach:

1. Place a layer of coarse, un-washed gravel along the bottom of the tank about $1/2$ to one inch deep (1-2 cm). The nutrients may become de-pleted after a year or two and should be replaced. A layer of fine, washed gravel, $1^1/2$ to two inches thick (4-6 cm) should be placed on top.

2. Washed "pea" gravel can be mixed with a fertilizer and laid 1-$^1/_4$ inch (3 cm) thick along the tank bottom. A second layer, two inches in depth (5 cm) should be placed on top. The method is excellent for a new tank but difficult with an established one. In our opi-nion this system has enough value that you may even wish to try it on an established set up.

3. Ready-made substrates with added fertilizers are also available in some areas. Hobby, from Dohse, is imported in some places. This ready-to-use substrate should be mixed with washed gravel and spread evenly over the tank bottom. It is easiest when setting up an aquarium.

4. In an established tank the only method is to add fertilizer to the gravel bed. You can use round, dried loam pellets, pressed into the substrate in two or four inch diameter centers. These can be made at home from rich garden loam, formed and dried in an oven at a medium temperature (350° F) for one hour.

The time spent preparing the substrate will pay handsome dividends in luxurious plant growth.

Laying out the substrate

It is not easy to contour the gravel in the bottom of the tank. If it is level it will be monotonous. If it is lower at the front and higher in the back, to help plants spread their roots (as it should be when plants are grown in the back) the fish will soon rearrange it. Rear terracing is best but can be achieved only with help — by using long flat stones, glass strips, petrified wood, or bogwood and artificial plastic roots to hold the gravel in place.

Gravel is terraced with glass strips or flat stones.

The Aquarium

A little about Water Chemistry

There has been an increasing interest in water chemistry in recent years and the aquarist is faced with a growing number of products and processes which promise to keep aquarium water perfect. It is little wonder most of us become confused. The basics of water quality seem to be tremendously complex.

Through out this book we say that no one should keep plants and fish together without learning a little about water chemistry, but some hobbyists exaggerate the complexities of water chemistry. If you learn the few essential, tried and proven rules of fish-keeping, you can easily learn enough water chemistry to be successful.

Basics should include a little knowledge about water hardness, the carbonate system, pH values and the nitrogen cycle. Each will be explained below and an alphabetical list of basic technical terms, and their meanings, will be found at the end of this chapter. The list can help you quickly familiarize yourself with the essentials.

Water Quality & Total Hardness

All spring and river water contains calcium and magnesium in varying quantities. The most important elements are calcium bicarbonate [Ca$(HCO_3)_2$] and calcium sulfate ($CaSO_4$). Water rich in calcium salts is considered "hard": with little it is called "soft". Hardness is measured in "degrees of hardness", one degree being equal to 10 mg of calcium or magnesium oxide per liter of water.

Hardness caused by calcium bicarbonate is called temporary or transient hardness since it disappears when water is boiled. The hardness resulting from calcium sulfate is considered "permanent" since it remains. Together temporary and permanent hardness produce overall or "total hardness." Another term you'll hear is "carbonate hardness", explained in the next section.

dGH = dKH + PH (Sulfate)

GH = Total Hardness (dGH = German Total Hardness)
KH = Carbonate Hardness (dKH = German Carbonate Hardness)
PH = Permanent Hardness

This equation cannot be used with commercial hardness test kits. When measuring Total Hardness the cations, that is a positively charged ion, Ca^{2+} and Mg^{2+} are measured. While measuring the carbonate hardness the anions of HCO_3^- are determined. The carbonate hardness may be greater than the total hardness because of the presence of sodium, potassium and other cations in addition to calcium and magnesium. They do not cause hardness but may occur together with the bicarbonate anion to increase the quantity of bicarbonate. The following table shows the three basic ways of determining total and carbonate hardness.

	Cation	Anion	GH		KH
GH greater than KH	Ca^{2+} Mg^{2+}	HCO_3^- SO_4^{2-}	2 20°	: :	1 10°
GH equal to KH	Ca^{2+} Na^+	SO_4^{2-} HCO_3^-	1 15°	: :	1 15°
GH less than KH	Ca^{2+} Na^+	HCO_3^- HCO_3^-	1 10°	: :	2 20°

(based on Tetra's brochure, "Correct Water Testing"

Total hardness has a direct effect on the cellular functions of fish, plants and microorganisms. The most favorable values for aquatic life are between three and ten degrees, although these may be too low for Tanganyika- and Malawi cichlids.

Total hardness can be illustrated as follows:
DEGREES OF HARDNESS
0 - 4°	dGH = very soft	12 - 18°	dGH = fairly hard
4 - 8°	dGH = soft	18 - 30°	dGH = hard
8 - 12°	dGH - medium hard	over 30°	dGH = very hard

The Aquarium

Carbon Dioxide and Plants

Carbon dioxide (CO_2) dissolves readily in water and forms small quantities of carbonic acid. The salts of carbonic acid and simple carbonates usually account for the largest part of the electrolytes in aquarium water. This means the absorption of carbon dioxide by plants is closely linked to the complex system of aqueous carbonic acid and carbonates. The implications will be explained in greater detail in the chapter on Fertilizing Plants with CO_2 on page 72.

The Carbonate System

Carbon dioxide is about forty times more readily soluble in water than oxygen but diffuses some ten thousand times less readily from water than air. About 0.2% of the dissolved CO_2 is converted to carbonic acid (H_2CO_3). As you add CO_2 the quantity of carbonic acid increases and the pH drops. As CO_2 is removed the pH rises. Carbonic acid disassociates or decomposes gradually, in two stages:

1st stage: $H^+ + HCO_3^-$
2nd stage: $H^+ + CO_3^{2-}$

Two important salts needed in an aquarium are calcium bicarbonate [$Ca(HCO_3)_2$] and calcium carbonate ($CaCO_3$). Calcium bicarbonate dissolves easily in water and produces temporary or carbonate hardness. This evaporates or disappears when the water is boiled while calcium carbonate is practically insoluble in water and is largely deposited. One example: the deposits on the wall of a tea kettle. Calcium bicarbonate continues to circulate in an aquarium only if an amount of carbon dioxide is in solution. The quantity of CO_2 is called the "equilibrium CO_2" and when insufficient causes some of the calcium bicarbonate to decompose into barely soluble carbonate. It can be expressed this way:

$$Ca(HCO_3)_2 \xrightleftharpoons[\text{CO}_2\text{-surplus}]{\text{CO}_2\text{-deficit}} CaCO_3 + CO_2 + H_2O$$

There is an relationship between the carbon dioxide content, the pH value and the bicarbonate when one considers equilibrium and balance. One outward sign: various forms in which carbon dioxide combines (CO_2 + H_2CO_3, HCO_3^-, CO_3^{2-}) display a characteristic distribution dependent on the pH value.

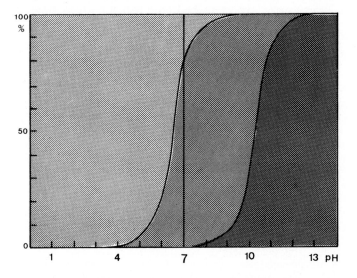

Relationship between compounds of carbon dioxide with the pH value (at 0° C). Light: CO_2 + H_2CO_3. Medium: HCO_3^-. Dark CO_3^{2-}. At a pH value exceeding 8 the amount to dissolve carbon dioxide is negligible (after GESSNER).

1. In acid water (pH of less than 6.0) free carbon dioxide is in solution and carbonates are negligible. (Example: Calcium deficiency in peaty water.)
2. In neutral and slightly alkaline water (pH 7.0-8.0) most of the CO_2 is found as bicarbonates. (Example: normal aquarium water.)
3. In highly alkaline water (pH over 10) most of the CO_2 exists as carbonate. Dissolved CO_2 is generally absent above pH 9.0. (Example: The sodium-rich water in which certain cichlids live.)

The carbonate system is a mixture of a weak acid (carbonic acid) and its salts and, in a chemical sense, is a typical buffer. Buffers have the special property of combining with moderate additions of acids or bases so that the pH value barely changes. When an acid is added to a buffer the H^+ in the bicarbonate is bound, producing carbonic acid which breaks down into carbon dioxide and water with the residue showing little tendency to dissociate. The H^+ concentration is increased only slightly and the pH value remains constant.

If a base is added to a buffer, the OH^- ions are immediately fixed by CO_2 and bicarbonate is formed. The loss of carbon dioxide has only a slight effect on the carbonic acid content (H^+-ions concentration) and the pH value rises very little.

As you add acid it diminishes since bicarbonate is not present below pH 6.0. As you add bases it also diminishes since carbon dioxide cannot be found beyond pH 10. The quality of the buffer depends on the water's mineral carbonate content. The buffer action of hard water is much better than of soft, peaty water and the more hydrogen carbonate aquarium water contains, the more free H^+-ions which can be caught up. This is known as the acid-combatting ability of carbonate.

There is a close interplay between the carbonate system or carbonate hardness and pH values. In most cases, the higher the hardness, the higher the pH value but at the same time the pH value is buffered or stabilized better. A carbonate hardness between 2° and 8° is recommended.

pH Values

pH assigns values to the degree of acidity in water and indicates a change from a chemically neutral point. Neutral water H_2O, contains equal parts of hydrogen ions (H^+) and hydroxide ions (OH^-). Hydrogen ions make water more acid and hydroxide ions make it alkaline. A pH of 7.0 indicates neutral water. Values above 7.0 indicate increasingly alkaline water while those below indicate increasingly acidic water.

Changes in concentrations of H^+ and OH^- can be measured in grams. pH 7.0 means that 10^{-7} (= one ten millionth) of a gram of H^+ is dissolved in one liter of water. A pH of 3.0 indicates 10^{-3} (one thousandth) grams. A pH of 10.0 indicates 10^{-10} (= one ten millionth) grams.

Since negative powers are cumbersome the pH scale is used. It runs from 1 to 14 as follows:

pH	1 2 3 4 5 6 7 8 9 10 11 12 13 14
H^+-Ion-concentration (g/l)	10^{-1} 10^{-2} 10^{-3} 10^{-4} 10^{-5} 10^{-6} 10^{-7} 10^{-8} 10^{-9} 10^{-10} 10^{-11} 10^{-12} 10^{-13} 10^{-14}

$10^{-1} = 1/10$ g H^+-Ions per litre of water etc.

It is also worth noting that a change of one unit in pH equals a ten times change in the acidity or alkalinity of the water. Two units indicate a 100 times change: three units 1000 times and so on. The optimum pH for aquarium fishes lies between a pH 5.0 and pH 9.0. Most freshwater fishes prefer a pH between 6.0 and 7.5 while most marine fish prefer values between 8.0 and 8.5.

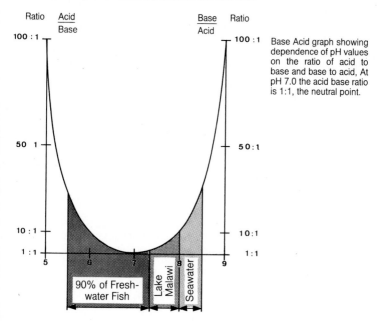

Base Acid graph showing dependence of pH values on the ratio of acid to base and base to acid, At pH 7.0 the acid base ratio is 1:1, the neutral point.

The Aquarium

The pH value is closely associated with bicarbonate anions and the buffering effect of the carbonate system. Make regular pH checks. All inhabitants of your aquarium, from fish to microorganisms, are sensitive to changes in pH. Abrupt fluctuations, often as a result of carbonate disturbances, can lead to serious problems with your fishes, acidosis, alkalosis and others.
(See the chapter on Fish Diseases.)

Nitrification

Nitrogen is one of the vital elements of protein and is absorbed by green plants in the form of nitrate. Along with ammonia both occur in small quantities in most natural waters. The situation differs in an aquarium where plants, fish and other animals are raised together. Nitrogen compounds can be created quickly by feces, urine and other excreta, plant remains and decaying food. When concentrated, the compounds can have a harmful effect on the tank's inhabitants. An aquarist must set up and maintain his tank as free as possible of harmful nitrogen compounds.
Organic nitrogenous substances decay in stages in the presence of oxygen, a process called oxidative breakdown. It produces various nitrogen compounds as follows:

Organic nitrogen compounds → Ammonia and Ammonium → Nitrite → Nitrate.

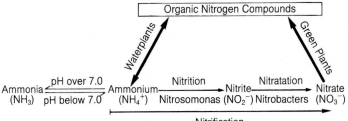

Toxic ammonia and non-toxic ammonium are produced in the first stage of the nitrogen cycle. The pH value greatly determines which of the two will predominate. Ammonia occurs at a pH of 7.0 and over: ammonium at a pH of less than 7.0. Ammonia build-up cannot occur in water which has the slightest acidity and from this one can understand the importance of regular pH checks.

Few plants utilize ammonium, nitrate being the chemical most can use.

The second stage of the nitrogen cycle is nitrite which is the result of the bacterial oxidation – some call it the 'combustion'-- of ammonia or ammonium. The bacteria which promote nitrification belong to *Nitrosomonas* sp. Nitrite is also very toxic and harmful to fish. Guppies *Poecilia reticulata* are susceptible to 1 mg/l and the threshold is even lower for other fish. The threshold of toxic ammonia is higher than that of nitrite.

In the third and final stage nitrite is converted to nitrate. This is promoted by the *Nitrobacter* bacteria and is much less toxic. Nitrate becomes harmful only in very high concentrations. Those above 150 mg/l should be avoided since denitrification, that is the reduction of nitrate into nitrite and ammonia, increases.

The nitrogen cycle cannot occur without oxygen. If the supply in an aquarium is poor, organic compounds decay more slowly and the water is enriched with interim toxic products – ammonia and nitrite. Bacterial denitrification can also occur. Some experts suspect the process can even occur within the bodies of the fish. Nitrite accumulates in the red corpuscles of fishes' blood and hinders the absorption and transportation of oxygen.

Nitrosomonas and *Nitrobacter* are not immediately present in a new aquarium and must develop and multiply over a period of time. The bacteria are primarily found in filter and substrata gravel elements of an established aquarium and can be transferred from one aquarium to another. It may take several weeks (up to 100 days) for them to reach the numbers where they can break down organic nitrogen compounds in a new tank. In the interim the quantity of bacteria in an aquarium will fluctuate widely.

Each water and filter change reduces the amount of available bacteria and affects the tank's equilibrium. For this reason we do not recommend changing the two simultaneously. Allow at least one week between changes.

Solving water problems

Reducing hardness

1. Make a water change using distilled or clean water. Never use rain water.
2. Use special equipment to soften water. A commercial water softener or an ion exchanger are suggested.
3. Filter water through peat.

Increasing hardness

1. Carefully add calcium or magnesium sulfate.
2. Make a water change with hard water.
3. Filter water through marble chips or coral sand.

Lowering the pH (acidulation)

1. Filter water through peat.
2. Make a partial water change.

Increasing the pH (alkalinity)

1. Add sodium bicarbonate ($NaHCO_3$) or sodium carbonate (Na_2CO_3).
2. Aerate water vigorously to expel CO_2.
3. Make a partial water change.

Reducing Nitrite and Nitrate

1. Regular water changes are suggested. (Intervals differ with the species of fish.)
2. Add a biological filter – an add-on tank filter, a corner sponge filter etc.
3. Add filtering material from an established tank. Gravel, filter media, etc. contain important nitrifying bacteria.
4. Regular cleaning of the filtering system.
5. Reduce feeding. Increases in nitrite and nitrate can often be traced to over-feeding.
6. Add live plants to the tank.
7. Clean the tank, removing dead fish, decaying plants, stems etc.

Common chemical terms

Acid
A number of sour, water-soluble compounds derived by a partial exchange of replaceable hydrogen; a substance in which an aqueous solution can form positively charged hydrogen ions (H^+). In testing acid colors litmus paper red.

Ammonia
A colorless, toxic gas with an irritating, tear-producing odor. In formula it is NH_3. It is easily dissolved in water at the rate of 700 volumes of ammonia to one of water.

Ammonium
Non-toxic, positively charged (cation) particles NH_4^+ or in salts. Its properties are similar to those of alkali metals sodium and potassium.

Anions
Negatively charged particles. Examples include (CO_3^{2-}, HCO_3^-, SO_4^{2-}). In an electrical field seeks the positive anode or pole.

Base
A strong alkali which, in an aqueous solution can form negatively charged hydroxide ions (OH^-). In tests it colors litmus blue.

Bicarbonates
Carbonic acid salts: one atom of hydrogen in the carbonic acid is replaced by an atom of a metal.

Brackish Water
A combination of fresh and sea water.

Buffer
Substances whose solution resists changes in pH.

Carbonate Hardness
Water hardness caused by bicarbonates.

Carbonates
Salts of carbonic acid (H_2CO_3). In these salts the two hydrogen atoms of carbonic acid are replaced by atoms of a metal.

Cations
Positively charged particles: (examples Na^+, Ca^{2+}, Mg^{2+}). In an electrical field cations seek the negative pole or cathode.

Denitrification
The reduction of nitrate to nitrite and nitrogen oxides (NO, N_2O) or molecular nitrogen.

Electrolytes
A non-metallic conductor of electricity in which the current is carried by the movement of ions. May be acids, bases or salts.

Ions
Positively or negatively charged particles.

Ion Exchangers
A number of artificial and natural substances with numerous acidic or basic sites. When an acidic ion exchanger is introduced into water hydronium ions (H_3O^+) are formed: Because of their charge they remain tied to the negatively-charged particles: In basic exchangers hydroxide ions (OH^-) are produced in a similar manner: used to remove salt from water. A distinction is made between cation and anion exchangers. Cation exchangers are **acidic** since their hydronium ions can be exchanged for cations (Na^+ or Ca^{2+}). Anion exchangers, in comparison, exchange for anions (Cl^- or SO_4^{2-}). Exhausted exchangers, those fully charged, can be regenerated with concentrated acid or base.

Nitrates
Salts of nitric acid (HNO_3), not as toxic to fish and plants as nitrite. Concentrations from 150 mg/l may be dangerous.

Nitration
The second stage in the oxidative reduction of nitrogen. Nitrite is transformed into nitrate by bacterial action.

Nitrification
The process of the oxidation of nitrogen, by bacteria, in the presence of oxygen; the steps are from ammonia or ammonium to nitrate via nitrite.

Nitritation
The first stage in the reduction of nitrogen by bacteria. Transformation of ammonium and ammonia into nitrite by bacterial action.

Nitrites
Salts of nitrous acid (HNO_2): Highly toxic to animal life. As little as 0.2 mg/l is harmful to most fish.

Nitrobacters
Bacteria which oxidatively transform nitrite to nitrate.

Nitrosomonas
Bacteria which oxidatively transform ammonia or amonium into nitrite.

Overall Hardness
Water hardness produced by calcium and magnesium salts as measured by the cations Ca^{2+} and Mg^{2+}.

Oxidation
The withdrawal of electrons and consequently an increase in the electro-positive valency of the substance oxidized: simply, a loss of electrons. Formerly defined as the combination of oxygen with an element or compound. Its counterpart is reduction.

pH Value
A measurement of the acidity of water; defined as the negative decade logarithm of a concentration of hydrogen ions: $pH = -^{10} \log H^+$. The scale of measurement extends from pH 1 (very acid) to pH 14 (very alkaline). pH 7.0 is neutral.

Redox Potential
The oxidation reduction potential; a measurement of the oxidizing or reducing effect of a redox system.

Redox System
Aquarium water; a solution in which a substance or substances are reduced while others are simultaneously oxidized by electron transfer.

Reduction
The absorption of electrons; such as occurs in a loss of oxygen from a compound; in an electro-chemical sense, the addition of electrons by a reducing agent; leads to a lowering of the positive valency of the substances reduced. Its counterpart is oxidation.

rH Value
Represents the negative logarithm of the hydrogen pressure with which a platinum electrode must be charged in order to produce a reducing effect corresponding to the solution involved: can be used for the easy designation of the oxidizing or reducing capacity of a solution. The scale is divided into 42 rH values. Aquarists are most concerned with the rH range from 27 to 32.

Sea Water
Water with a salt content of 3% (30‰) or more. The chief component of the dissolved salts is sodium chloride NaCl which is, literally, household salt.

Water
Basis of an aquarium: a liquid which, at normal temperature, commonly has no smell. It solidifies into ice at 0° C or 32° F; its boiling point is 100° C or 210° F. Consists of two atoms of hydrogen and one of oxygen (H_2O).

Two fighting cichlid males, *Pseudotropheus aff. zebra.*. The weaker fish must be removed to prevent injury or possible death from bites.

Aquarium Lighting

Types of Lamps

1. Fluorescent tubes

The luminescence (a measure of intensity) of fluorescent tubes depends greatly on the reflective qualities of the aquarium cover. A hood with a white or mirrored surface would be ideal but since few are made this way you can improve the reflection value of any cover with a little effort. If the inside is dark, glue aluminum foil to it. Foil can improve the reflective output by as much as 50%. Tubes with built-in reflectors are also available. A good tube will continue burning 5,000 hours though its intensity is reduced with age; so much so that those burned twelve to sixteen hours a day may need to be replaced within a year. After six months of intense use only half of the useful light may be available, one reason your plants may languish, only half-alive. Even with these disadvantages fluorescent lights are preferable to all other light sources: they consume less power, generate less heat and distribute light equally throughout the tank.

Fluorescent Lamp Table

Aquarium		Suitable Lamp Length in mm	Watts	No. of Tubes required
Length in cm	Litres Content approx.			
30	12	212	6	1
40	25	288	8	1–2
50	35	438	15	1
60	65	517	13	2
70	100	590	20	2
80	110	720	16	3
100	180	895	30	3
110	220	970	25	4
130	325	1200	40	4
160	480	1500	65	4

Color

Special tubes for underwater plants, such as the Grolux and Sylvania 77, were introduced 25 years ago. Their reddish-violet color spectrum creates a unique underwater world which can vary from the fairytale to the gaudy. Red-colored fish, for example, seem to glow but such spectacular effects may not be sufficient reason to use the lights. They also promote the growth of algae. Because the emitted light is primarily in the red and blue spectrums the tubes can be combined effectively with daylight tubes.

2. Filament bulbs

Conventional light bulbs are still the least expensive and can work well with small tanks. They do have one drawback: the spectral imbalance especially in areas of red and blue, does not promote plant growth.

3. Spotlights

You can achieve spectacular effects with the smaller filament-type spot lights but the bulbs are expensive and their life is short. They can be fitted into individual sockets, their intensity controlled by dimmers.

4. Halogen lamps

Low voltage halogen lights with 100 watt white spots are popular for special effects. The lights do require a transformer, which, though moderately expensive, is readily obtained from any lighting house. The safety of low voltage around water is a plus.

5. Mercury Vapor Lamps

Neither recommended for an average tank nor common in the U.S. these lights can be spectacular in the proper setting. Their great intensity at a relatively low wattage suits them well to larger aquariums where they can be used to generate a bright light at low costs. The bulbs will not fit conventional sockets and require special equipment. When the lights are turned on they barely glow but within a few minutes develop their full, glittering brightness.

For a tank with a 20-inch depth we recommend 4.5 watts per inch of tank length. For a deeper tank try 6.26 watts per inch of tank.

Mercury Vapor Lamps

Water depth in cm/inches	Tank Length in cm/inches	Wattage per Bulb	No. of lamps
40/15½	100/39½	60	2
50/20	130/51	80	3
60/23½	160/63	125	3
60/23½	200/80	125	4

6. Sodium Vapor Lamps

Basically in the red and yellow spectrum they are not recommended for aquarium use.

How much light?

Aquarium lighting should be used independently of daylight and the requirements differ for fish and plants. Fish can "get by" with 8 to ten hours of lights while plants need 12 to 14 hours. The longer period of lighting will not harm fish but less will inhibit plant growth. More intense lights, used for a shorter period, are not as beneficial as the right amount of light used for the proper time. Lighting which remains on too long or is too intense can encourage the growth of green algae and if algae develops in your tank the period of lighting should be reduced. The lighting can be controlled by a timer and to inhibit the growth of algae you can eliminate artificial light for an hour or two at midday. This will not harm either fish or plants.

Luminescence

The intensity of the light should depend on the kind of plants, the size of the aquarium, the type of lights and their location. As an example:
A 20-gallon tank, placed away from a window with fluorescent tubes and quick-growing plants: choose one watt for each half-gallon of water.

20 watt fluorescent tubes exist but are generally too long for the tank in our example. The next shorter available size is a 13 watt lamp about 20 inches in length. Two will provide 26 watts, more light than required, but too much light is better than too little. We should remember: the intensity will decrease as the tubes are used.

The meaning of Lux

Lux is a scientific measurement – specifically, the amount of light a one watt source placed a little over three yards away could cast on an area three-foot square. Tropical daylight measured at midday without clouds, would read approximately 100,000 lux. In shade or under cloud cover it can drop to 10,000. Depending on such variables as turbidity and depth, light beneath the water can measure between 50 and 5,000 lux.

Plants readily adjust to the amount of light available and while they can be given too little light it is nearly impossible to give too much.

Floating plants require a lot of light (2000 lux or more). *Eichhornia, Salvinia, Pistia, Vallisneria gigantica, Nuphar* and other water lillies require a lot of light – 2,000 lux or more – (excepting the water fern *Ceratopterus* which will grow in 1000 lux.)

Plants growing in middle levels do best in an aquarium with a light level from 800 to 1800 lux.

Low growing plants and cryptocorynes need a minimum of 100 lux and do better at 250 to 300 lux.

Measuring luminescence

A lux meter is the professional way to measure the quantity of light but they are expensive and few hobbyists have access to one. A photographic light meter makes an excellent substitute. The following table, based on readings from a **Lunasix** meter, can be used for comparison.

Lux: Lighting Times Table					
Lux	Shutter	Time sec.	Lunasix scale	Light value at 18° DIN 50 ASA	Suitability of light quantity for aquatic plants
19	2.8	2	8	2	Light too weak
38	2.8	1	9	3	
75	2.8	1/2	10	4	Cryptocorynes and other plants requiring little light, adaptable plants
150	2.8	1/4	11	5	
300	2.8	1/8	12	6	Plants in the middle tank range; lower light requirement limit
600	2.8	1/15	13	7	
1200	2.8	1/30	14	8	
2400	2.8	1/60	15	9	Surface plants in Aquarium
4800	2.8	1/125	16	10	
9500	2.8	1/250	17	11	Plants in Nature
19000	4	1/250	18	12	
38000	5.6	1/250	19	13	
75000	8	1/250	20	14	Daylight in bright Sun

A light meter can be as accurate as an expensive lux meter and simpler. A conventional meter cannot be submerged while an under-water light meter can, but you can make a conventional meter water-proof. Place the meter in a plastic bag, seal the open end and measure the light in the tank, underwater, at gravel level.

Light intensities can be approximated outside the tank, the light reflected from the tank to the meter by a mirror.

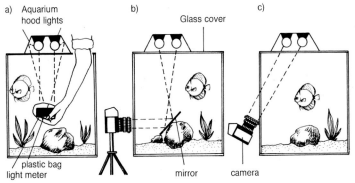

a) Aquarium
     hood lights

b) Glass cover

c)

plastic bag
light meter

mirror   camera

When using a mirror the indicated values should be divided by two or three, the higher value used with thicker glass. The method is not exact but provides a handy approximation of the intensity of the light reaching the gravel. (See drawing c.)

Quartz lamps and fluorescent tubes should be chosen for different situations. The tube is ideally suited to low tanks and the quartz lamp to tall ones, those measuring more than twenty inches (50 cm) high.

Controlling light

As mentioned at the start, tanks should be lit 12 to 14 hours daily and at least PAFFRATH recommends 16 hours. The lights can be controlled automatically by a timer. If you use one, adjust it so that the light turns on half an hour before the morning feeding and off on your own schedule. In every case, the lights should remain on at least half an hour after the final feeding. Some catfish feed only in darkness and thus, will not eat until the lights are off. Lighting controls can also be coupled to an automatic feeder, which can be a good investment for holidays.

Dimmer switches

Dimmer switches are also a sound investment. They can be used to vary light levels with filament bulbs and adjustable light levels create a pleasing effect. As you dim the light, fish which are active during the day will retire to their sleeping places and those active at night will awaken. Often, though a tank is not completely dark they can be enticed from their hiding places with food and observed.

The problem of heat

The ballasts required by fluorescent tubes generate considerable heat, which can affect the temperature of the aquarium water, in the summer sometimes heating it above 86° F (30° C) even though you turn off the heater. On the warmest days be certain to turn off the light. Heat will reduce the supply of oxygen in the air space between the water surface and hood. Some manufacturers solve the problem by mounting the ballast on the plug end but if it is mounted near the fixture you may need to do something. We often drill holes in the sides of our hoods to create a better flow of air and find one inch holes are best. Some aquarium covers are manufactured with punch-out holes for just this purpose. If all else fails, the ballast can be mounted in a remote location.

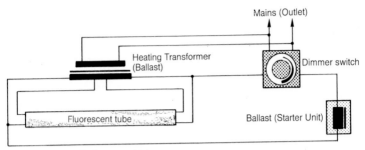

Mains (Outlet)

Heating Transformer
(Ballast)

Dimmer switch

Fluorescent tube

Ballast (Starter Unit)

Wiring diagram to dim fluorescent tubes.

An additional caution: the higher the nitrate content, the more light aquarium plants will require. A plant in a tank with less than 10 mg/l nitrate may do well with little light in one tank yet may not respond in another tank even though the lighting is increased. Fertilizers will not help. The nitrate (which is the real problem) must be removed by a water change.

For a deep tank such as this, a 30" high (about 80 cm), quartz lamps are recommended. The plants grow above the tank level since there is no cover to restrict them.

Heating in the Aquarium

Every living thing needs food and warmth: Some more warmth, some less. For example, tropical fish need more heat than native American fish since their bodies have been adjusted, over millions of years, to tropical conditions.

Unlike mammals and birds, fish are poikilothermal or cold-blooded. Their bodies adjust to the outside temperature and the explanation lies in the structure of their heart. The circulatory system of fish, reptiles and amphibians is not divided into arteries and veins as with humans. The need for food and metabolism is reduced as the temperature lowers.

For all species there is a "middle ground" in which they are happiest and they must, therefore, be kept within that 'vital range'. These are some "safe" ranges: 72°-78° F (24°-26° C) for tropical fish; 60° to 68° F (16°-20° C) for most goldfish and 64° to 72° F (18°-22° C) for fantails. Native European fishes are happiest at 53.5° to 68° F (12°-20° C). Trout and other fish from mountain streams are used to temperatures of 46° to 53° F (8°-12° C). Similarly, tropical fish from high altitude streams are most comfortable at temperatures of 59° to 68° F (15°-20° C.)

Temperature fluctuations in streams are less than is generally assumed. At less than one foot depth (about eight inches or 20 cm.) day and night temperatures vary no more than five degrees. The exceptions are unseasonably, unexpected cold weather when even wild fish can be disturbed. In Brazil, for example, there are periods of unpredictable, intense cold when millions of fish die.

In an aquarium we can provide stable conditions. A heater with thermostatic controls will keep the temperature even. The idea that the temperature should ideally vary with the time of day, is mistaken and the fact that fish may live ten to 20 years in an aquarium, is proof to the contrary. Similar species live much shorter lives in the wild.

Temperature requirements are an important consideration when selecting fish for a community aquarium. Temperatures too low are more harmful than those too high but an excess in either direction can have an adverse effect on lifespan, fertility and coloring.

Aquatic electricity

The combination of water and electricity is dangerous because water can be an excellent conductor. If you accidently touch a live wire while grounded you will receive a shock and while an aquarium is considered "safe", the combination of water and electricity is always potentially dangerous.

"Can" is the key word. In reality there should be little danger. Electrical equipment such as a heater or light, will rarely short circuit and be dangerous only if a tank is grounded. With today's designs, safety measures prevent trouble: a fuse will generally blow either in the aquarium or household circuit. With the older two-prong system the aquarium equipment such as a heater will generally break before a short is created. Soft water is a lesser conductor of electricity than hard.

It is a good idea to wear shoes with rubber soles when working around an aquarium. Rubber soles, wooden and plastic floors and a carpet all protect against possible shocks, but our best advice is to buy reliable electrical equipment, install it properly and keep it in good condition. The latest type of equipment, which operates on low voltages, is even safer and is recommended even though the required transformers are bulky and expensive. Because the power is low there is little danger.

Various heaters

The most popular heater in the U.S. is the glass immersion heater. Its heart is a nichrome heating coil, wound on a ceramic or glass insert, controlled by a thermostat either internally or connected with it. In European designs the tube is often filled with sand: that is not common in the U.S. Electrical resistance heats the wire so it is essential the unit always be immersed in water. Unplug the heater when you work around the tank. Disconnecting can also prevent heater problems – breakage, burn-out and more – in the event the water level drops.

It is important that the heater be properly selected for the tank. One too small may not heat properly in cold weather and one too large may overheat if the thermostat malfunctions. Most experts suggest 2 to 4 watts per gallon of water: we recommend $2^1/_2$. Since heaters are available in a wide range of wattages from 10 to 200 it is possible to buy exactly what you need. The primary advantage of a glass heater is its low price. A drawback is the relatively high surface temperature generated over a small area. There are two types of heaters, the "submersible", designed to be mounted entirely beneath the water and those whose top must remain above water.

The Thermostat

An aquarium thermostat is a simple device, reliable and long-lived. Several types are available from the expensive mercury contact type to the inexpensive bi-metallic strip. Either is a good choice.

How does it work? As the heater warms, a bi-metallic strip expands outward, the circuit opens and the electricity is "shut off". As it cools, the bimetallic strip bends inwards, the circuit is closed, the electricity flows and the elements warm. The strip consists of two separate sections of special metals which react to temperature, each expanding and contracting at a different rate. It is a concept common around the world. A thermostat separate from the heater has been available in North America at various times in the past. These were most often used to regulate multiple tank systems.

Submersible heaters are available in the U.S. but are more popular in Europe. Never place a heater under water unless it is specifically called "submersible."

The Combined Heater/Thermostat

The heating device most commonly used in the aquarium is a combined unit (heater core/bi-metallic strip thermostat). Most units are used in an upright position. The choices offered are usually in two distinct forms. The first type clips on to the aquarium with the controls kept above the water surface. The clip on heater is the least expensive heater on the market and not made to be water tight. Care should be taken when this is used to be sure there is no excessive splashing or strong aeration nearby. Water will easily get into the tube and cause the heater to stick (on or off), fill with water, or rust prematurely.

A bi-metallic control is extremely reliable, holding temperature variations within an extremely narrow range, generally just a degree or two. The bi-metallic thermostat turns the current off as the temperature rises above the selected value and turns it on when it falls. A variation of 5° F (1-2° C) will not harm aquarium fish. Most heaters have a pilot light which glows when the heater is operating.

A more expensive, but a better option, is the completely submersible heater. This heater is waterproofed and able to be located in any position in the tank. The only limitation is that the tube must not be placed in the gravel substrate. This would cause excessive stress on the heater tube and provide a good chance for breakage. The submersible allows great flexibility for placement in the tank and therefore allows the creative aquarist to effectively hide it from view. This is an advantage not offered by the clip-on types of heater.

Submersible heaters have developed the thermostat in two ways. The first is much like the clip on style where the thermostat is set manually to each tank. Once set, the temperature is held constant by the thermostat. The actual temperature must be verified by an accurate thermometer, and should be periodically checked as time goes by.

The following relates both to the clip on style as well as a manually set submersible heater. When first placed in the tank, let the heater sit in the tank without power to let the thermostat adjust to the water temperature. After a few minutes plug the heater into power and turn the heater on. This means that the pilot light will glow. Keep the pilot light on until the temperature reading is at the desired level. When this desired reading is accomplished, turn the knob until the light turns off, then turn the control until the light just turns back on. The heater now should be set. Check the temperature regularly over the next few days to be sure the setting was accurate.

Many clip-ons have safety caps over the control screw. They serve two purposes. First they are oversized to reduce the chances of water splashing into the tube itself. The second reason is to protect the heater setting from accidently being changed by the cat or inquisitive children and adults. These caps have saved many tanks from accidental boiling or freezing over the years. If the heater doesn't shut off or come on when you try to set it, remove the safety cap and turn the screw until the heater operates in the desired range. Be sure to replace the cap when the heater is working satisfactorily. Since the submersible has no controls out of the tank, safety caps are not used with them.

The newest innovation in the submersible heater is a preset scale built in. This can be either in Fahrenheit or Celcius. The unit has a scale calibrated on it that you can choose the correct temperature setting for the tank it is to be placed into. The heater must also be given a chance to adjust to water temperature before it is plugged in, but the heater's temperature can be chosen before it is placed in the water. Once plugged in and allowed to do its job, the water should gain the pre-selected temperature by itself. This type of heater is extremely accurate, some them keeping the water in the plus or minus 0.25 degree range for long periods of time. A thermometer is still a very good idea to have. This will make sure that the original setting was indeed accurate. More importantly, it is insurance that should the heater become accidently unplugged, become broken, or defective for some reason you will have a way to check the present temperature easily.

Both types of heaters are built to last for years but do occasionally require care. Do not strike the tank with the tube and never leave a heater connected when it is out of water. Be sure to disconnect the unit before you siphon water for periodic changes. The heater will try to heat any environment into which it comes into contact. If the temperature should change dramatically or unevenly on the glass tube, it will crack easily. This normally happens during a water change where the water level drops below the top of the heater core. Uneven temperatures between air and water on the tube while the core is still warm may cause the tube to break.

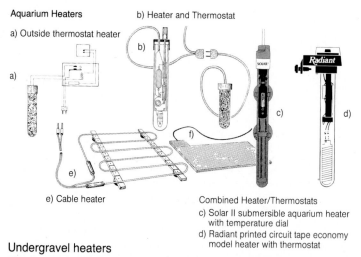

Aquarium Heaters

a) Outside thermostat heater

b) Heater and Thermostat

e) Cable heater

Combined Heater/Thermostats
c) Solar II submersible aquarium heater with temperature dial
d) Radiant printed circuit tape economy model heater with thermostat

Undergravel heaters

Those who have terrariums are familiar with buried cable heating: the cable mounted beneath the gravel bed. The method can work in an aquarium, too, if you install it when you set up a tank. It is obviously not worth the effort to install buried cables in an established tank.

Although glass is a poor conductor of heat, outside bottom heaters are available. They are more popular in Europe than in the U.S. but you do see them occasionally.

Electronic thermostat

Small electronic thermostats are sometimes used in aquariums. The design never wears and has both unlimited durability and great reliability. The temperature is read by a tiny electronic sensor no larger than a match head and automatically controls the heater via a semi-conductor. The installation is expensive and in some cases requires rewiring of heater-thermostat connections.

Heat Output

A tank in a home will require about $2^{1}/_{2}$ watts per gallon of water. In unheated rooms it may demand as much as five watts per gallon, and you may have to experiment to find the precise formula. It is a good idea to keep an inexpensive heater in reserve in case the main one breaks or when you need a back-up for a quarantine tank. If power fails a tank can drop to as low as 64° F (18° C) for a short time. If the outage lasts more than 15 hours something must be done to save the fish. A bucket of heated water can be poured into the tank as a temporary, warmup water change. Be certain to remove as much cold water as the warm you replace. This technique may not be practical in larger tanks.

54

Technology and Accessories

Thermometer

One of the least expensive but most important of all devices is the thermometer. It must be checked for accuracy and should either be the floating type or mounted where it is easily seen. The temperature should be checked daily and it is a good idea to place your hand against the glass as you check. You'll get a "feel" for the water temperature and, even if the thermometer breaks, you can check your tanks. Mercury thermometers are not recommended. If one breaks you'll find the mercury is poisonous to fish.

The choices available range from free floating types to the sophisticated liquid crystal thermometers. Most of the least expensive ones use mercury in tubes to register the temperature. They are not extremely accurate and normally it is a good idea to check them against one that you know is accurate. One of the greatest problems with most thermometers is that they seem to find the most inaccessable area of the tank to come to rest. To combat this, there are some which use suction cups or metal hangers to keep them in place. This usually obstructs the easy view of the fish. Often it is better to hang them on the side of a tank. This can be difficult to do when a standard canopy is used.

The liquid crystal types are a bit more expensive, but they are much more accurate and easier to use. The thermometer sticks with an adhesive to the outside of the tank and is put on permanently. Accuracy is very good and they can be put anywhere on the tank with ease. Just pick an easy to read place somewhere on the tank that doesn't obstruct the view of the inhabitants and apply the thermometer. It is there permanently for a fast check to be sure all is well.

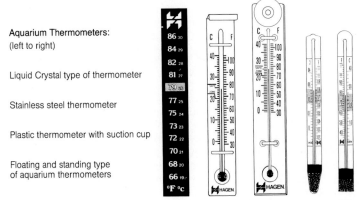

Aquarium Thermometers:
(left to right)

Liquid Crystal type of thermometer

Stainless steel thermometer

Plastic thermometer with suction cup

Floating and standing type
of aquarium thermometers

Filtration

A good filter handles a number of tasks:

1. Mechanical filtration (all types)
2. Biological filtration
3. Chemical filtration
4. Additional oxygen
5. Surface movement
6. Create tank currents

Mechanical filtration is so termed because it removes the particulate waste products as well as other suspended matter from the water. This is done by capturing the water and passing it through some form of sieve of filtering media. Water is purified as it passes through the filter and then returned to the tank. The finer the sieve produced by the media, the better the mechanical removal of particles from the aquarium.

Biological filtration depends on bacterial action to break toxic organic by-products into safer compounds for the fish. There is usually a four to six week delay before there are enough bacteria in the substrates to accomplish the task correctly. This is called "aging the water". Biological filtration actually refers to the action of two specialized bacteria which degrade toxic nitrogen compounds to safer substances as a source of energy. *Nitrosomonas* breaks down ammonia or ammonium to nitrite. The bacteria *Nitrobacter* then converts the harmful nitrite to the less toxic nitrate compound. The bacterial action works on by-products of urine, feces, respiration, and excess feeding.

Chemical filtration describes the active change of water properties. The chemical bonding of filter media with substances in the water can remove ammonia (ammonium), change the pH or hardness in the water. Discoloration by dyes or medications are also normally removed by chemical action with carbon or other filter media. Chlorine and chloramine removal are one of the most overlooked forms of chemical filtration. Proper removal of these common additives to the municipal water supplies is one of the most important chemical reactions for successful aquarium maintenance. Overdosing the proper chemicals to remove the chlorine compounds rarely hurts the tank or its inhabitants, but underdosage can cause death, loss of equilibrium, or at best, gill damage that will cause problems later.

The addition of oxygen and subsequent removal of carbon dioxide can also broadly be defined within the realm of chemical filtration. The exchanges are actively enhanced by proper surface agitation and water currents. Oxygen is a staple of life both under water and on the surface. If the active replacement of used oxygen is not occurring, or if carbon dioxide is allowed to build to stressful levels, the effects are not to the aquarium inhabitants' favor.

Filter size depends on the size of the aquarium, the number of fish in the tank and, consequently, the amount of detritus produced. As a general rule, the larger the filter the better. For most power filters, three to four times the tank capacity an hour is a very good rule of thumb to follow as a guide for proper output.

The function of a filter

1. Mechanical filtration

Nearly any filter material is suitable although the most practical is synthetic filter wool and, in larger filters, ceramic rings. The wool will remove particulate matter to clean or "polish" the water. The finer the wool the smaller the particles filtered. The ceramic provides a bed for biological bacteria as well as capturing larger matter before it can clog a filter. Foam blocks and cartridges have become increasingly popular for a number of filters and have begun to replace the filter floss in many applications. Foam blocks have the advantage of re-usability as well as providing a good location for bacterial buildup of the helpful bacteria.

Mechanical filter materials also include activated charcoal or carbon which, because of the porosity, can absorb or bind fine particles. Activated carbon also absorbs certain toxic substances so it should be removed from a tank whenever you treat with medications. It should be replaced when the treatment is complete. Certain large installations even use sand or gravel as a mechanical filter to trap the wastes as they flow through the unit. Often this substrate also doubles as a biological filter as well.

New filters, not yet "run in" work only as mechanical filters until the bacteria have an opportunity to take hold. High speed filters such as those charged with diatomaceous earth are only designed to polish the water, but most other types will offer biological filtration to some degree after a period of time.

2. Biological filtration

Urine and feces, the wastes of fish, will pollute an aquarium (see section on chemistry) though the fact is sometimes overlooked because it is something you cannot see. Toxic nitrogen must be removed by water changes or the proper filters with correct filter materials. These include the bacteria found in a biological filter. They do not "filter" nitrogen, but convert it as we have explained: *Nitrosomonas* convert ammonium to nitrite and *Nitrobacter* nitrite to nitrate. The bacteria must live in a suitable filter material with a large surface and an adequate oxygen supply.

Suitable filter materials include:

bacteria resistant foam
porous gravel (such as lava)
smaller sized commercial aquarium gravel
activated charcoal or carbon
inert ceramic rings

A gentle undergravel filter with pea sized gravel not more than $1/5$th inch diameter is the most effective because of its great surface area. It should cover the bottom of the tank and be at least two inches in depth. The shape of the gravel is best irregular as this provides the most jagged surfaces for the bacteria to attach themselves. Smooth pebble varieties or marble shaped substrates provide the least amount of surface area per given volume and should be avoided.

Power heads are now available which move a lot of water through the undergravel plate and increase the efficiency of the standard undergravel filter well beyond what was once only a hobbyist's dream. A power head is placed at the top of the return stack to pump the cleaned water back to the tank, this draws the water (with its oxygen) through the gravel. The water then flows under the plate. The filtered water is then output at the top of the tank to aid in surface agitation and to create useful currents throughout the tank. The good power heads are flow adjustable so that excessively strong water flows need not be a problem at all.

In the classic design, air stones perform the previously mentioned duties of the power head. The mixture of air with water by the stone causes a chimney effect. The flow rates, however are not as high with this type of water movement. The lower output doesn't provide as much current or surface agitation for the fish. Large power filters with chambers for ceramic rings and other materials also provide alternates for biological filtration. For more information see the chapter on chemistry, pp. 35-36.

3. Chemical filtration

Strictly speaking, chemical filtration belongs more in our section on chemistry but since the units are often used in conjunction with the filter, we will include them here. The category includes the ion exchanger which can reduce either carbonate or sulphur hardness. In some systems it may even bind nitrates.

A chemical filter should always be used in conjunction with a mechanical unit to protect the filter media. One of the newer materials in common use in many mechanical filters is ammonia absorber. It helps reduce excess ammonia from distressing the fish. It is especially useful where municipal water is treated with chloramine to produce safe drinking water. The result of proper dechlorination in this type of water releases free ammonia. Ammonia absorbers help to remove this byproduct before it has a chance to build to toxic levels.

Ultraviolet lights have been adapted to water sterilization because of the germicidal effects they produce. The light kills microscopic bacterial and other live disease agents. A protein skimmer removes organic materials from the water by a process called air stripping. The organic particles adhere to air bubbles in the skimmer chamber and are brought to the surface. The protein is trapped in a cup as the bubbles break, before it is able to return to the water in the tank. This could change the water chemistry over time. They have the potential of removing necessary trace elements as well as the harmful by-products of life, so normal water changes on a regular basis are highly recommended. This combination can provide the most disease free conditions for fish, but has found its application most often in the marine hobbyist's tanks or in the closed systems of comercial set-ups.

Peat is not a popular filter material. It is difficult to use and imparts a brownish tinge to the water but it does have its advantages. It uses humic acid, which most fish tolerate, to soften water, but does require patience. The harder the water, the more difficult it is to soften with peat and the process may require frequent changes of material. As a filter element it is most popular with advanced hobbyists interested in providing accurate native water conditions for difficult fish or for breeding applications where the water must be soft and acid to induce a pair to spawn.

4. Oxygen enrichment and
5. Surface movement

There is no need for an air pump when using a motor-driven external power filter. The beloved air stone, which produces such pretty bubbles and noisy pump vibration can usually be eliminated. The tank should be adequately oxygenated with a power filter, a stone is only needed in unusual or special cases. A filter's return is designed to keep the surface of the water in constant motion. This promotes the exchange of gasses. Oxygen is absorbed by the water and carbon dioxide is eliminated to the air. If the surface is disturbed too much, carbonic acid, an important plant fertilizer, may also escape. Flow adjustments have recently been added to modern pumps to tailor the output exactly to a tank's needs. This allows just enough agitation without creating excesses that are not required.

6. Create tank currents

The water surface should be moved in a circular pattern and the air bubbles should not be "forced" into the water. Surface movement will work only when there is sufficient contact area between the atmosphere and the surface of the water. There must be adequate space above the tank, in the form of vents in the hood or uninterupted open space, for the exchange to be made. If the filter is not strong enough to circulate all of the water in a tank an air stone should be added. It should be placed in a corner opposite filter output.

A noticeable direction of flow, "current", is important for many fish and plants. Many of the fish we keep in aquariums are naturally found in fast-flowing, oxygen-rich waters. You'll find such fish like to stay in the filter's current searching for food. In addition, swimming "against the current" keeps them healthier. The current also nourishes plants by carrying nutrients which are absorbed by the leaves.

Current also distributes the heat from the heater avoiding "dead spots". These can also be layers with more or less heat. In addition a current helps to reduce unsightly buildup on the glass which can be caused by an accumulation of bacteria or dust. With insufficient water movement the lower regions of the tank may be too cool. Fish may catch cold and plants may get "cold feet". A power filter will also prevent rapid temperature buildup.

Common filters

1. Internal filters
   a. undergravel
   b. foam cartridge
   c. inside corner box filter
   d. internal power filter
   e. power head

2. External filters
   a. power filter
   b. cannister filter
   c. diatom filter

Internal filters

Undergravel filters consist of a plate to hold the gravel above the tank bottom and at least one stack to draw the water up from below the plate. An air stone has classically been used to mix air and water to create a lighter water (aerated water). This rises up the return stack and tank water is drawn through the gravel to replace it. As water flows through the gravel it oxygenates the bacteria that live there. These bacteria are breaking down the organic wastes that are drawn into the gravel when the water is forced through. The foam cartridge and the inside box filter also use the aerated water principle to cause a current to draw the waste material into the filter media. This is inefficient, air is used to move water to a place where the wastes in the tank can be trapped.

The power head is used for two different purposes. First it can replace the air stone in an undergravel system. Good power heads also allow the opportunity to aerate the water with air drawn into the output stream that helps to agitate the surface. The higher flow rates allow a much greater amount of water to travel through the gravel. The increased oxygen in the gravel due to the water rate enables the bacterial population to grow more numerous and break the organic wastes much faster and efficiently.

The second use of a power head is to create currents in the tank. In essence, the water is freely pumped to make a desired current without any effective filtration being done. This can be quite beneficial for some fishes as they need fast flowing currents to simulate their natural habitats.

The power filter uses a motor to actively move the water through the chosen filter media. It moves a great amount of water per hour. Internal power filters are a relatively new innovation. The motor must be a water cooled, totally submersible pump. This frees the user from having to disguise unsightly hoses or placing filter cases between the tank and the wall. This type has become especially useful for limited spaces or built in applications where external filtration is difficult or impossible. It even has an option where air can be drawn into the filter and then expelled to send air bubbles to the surface to agitate it. The major advantage with this machine is that increased output is produced by an efficient water pump. The dirty water is moved through the foam or carbon inserts and keeps particulate matter to a minimum.

Most modern power filters have switched to the use of inserts, normally foam blocks and carbon inserts for ease of replacement. The foam blocks are re-useable and get less clogged than the filter floss of the corner filters. Gentle rinsing to remove trapped debris does not kill or wash away the beneficial bacteria so the biological cycle can remain active. Never do a full filter media change. Rather change a filter block one week and the carbon another week to allow proper seeding for the bacteria to proceed.

External filters

The standard power filter has become the most commonly used filtration device. The water is drawn from the tank, filtered through a series of media and then returned to the tank free of particulate matter. Often a cover is supplied to reduce dirt and dust from contaminating the system. The newer styles have radically increased water flow in recent years. The motors have become much simpler and energy efficient, some only having one moving part in the entire unit.

The outside power filter has become the filter of choice in most cases. It has become almost silent so it can be used almost anywhere. It moves amazing amounts of water through the filter media every hour. Its cost is well within most budgets and it comes in enough assorted sizes to be capable of providing adequate filtration in the smallest and the largest of tanks. Besides all this, the filter is easy to work with during cleaning. Accessability to the filter at the back of the tank makes the maintenance easier than most other filter types. One small drawback is that the filter must be cleaned quite regularly so extremely strong biological filtration is not common.

The cannister filter is becoming increasingly popular in North America. The cannister is a closed container where the water is siphoned into the filter, forced through the filtering material and then actively pumped back into the aquarium. A major advantage with this style is the large filtering area of the cannister. By design, the volume of the container is larger than the standard power filter. It can be as much as eight to ten times the filtering area of a comparable power filter. Coupled with the variability of media, this is a great advantage.

The cannister style is much better suited to biological filtering as the media doesn't need to be changed as often. This design often uses filter modules which allow separation of a number of different filter media in the same filter. Thus numerous filtering jobs are accomplished at once, which is quite popular in the advanced stages of the hobby. This is mostly due to the fact that many exotic media combinations can be tried with ease.

The cannister can be hidden in an inconspicuous place such as a cabinet. New technology has allowed increased water movement with reduced electrical usage. As well, there are water cooled units instead of the classical fan cooled types that had to be in airy spaces to keep the motor cool. Modern water cooled units can be put virtually anywhere as they use the tank's capacity for cooling, not atmospheric dissipation. Assorted return ends allow for the output to be a spray, a stream of water, or even to draw air into the tank with the returned water.

The diatom filters are used only for spot cleaning a dirty tank. The filter uses diatomaceous earth to form a fine screen on a bag. The particulate matter is forced against the bag and trapped. The more the bag catches, the finer the screen becomes. When the filter is dirty the bag can trap particles as fine as one micron. This is one of the few times where a dirty filter can be more effective than a clean one. It must be noted, however, that the flow rate of the filter drops dramatically the dirtier it becomes. Diatom type filters are used for regular maintainance jobs, not as a permanent single tank filter. It is normally used in multi-tank installations for required spot cleaning jobs, not the permanent filter for a given tank. Due to the short times that this filter is used, there is no chance to form any biological action whatsoever. This type of filter is the closest to a purely mechanical filter there is in the hobby.

Each of the filters listed meets one or more, perhaps even all, of the requirements for a good aquarium filter. Success does not depend on the filter alone. You must also consider the filter material and the fact that a biological filter often forms a part of the system. The biological materials may be found in many places, in the filter media itself, in the gravel bed, on the aquarium glass or filter sides themselves. It is to these places that the bacteria attach themselves. An undergravel filter really only supports the substrate (i.e. the gravel) where the actual filtering and biological breakdown occurs. It is very important to provide enough areas for this type of filtration, no matter what the size of the tank.

Filtration and tank size

Small tanks up to 10 gallons often use an air pump and corner box filter, alternately they can be filtered with the foam cartridges. The foam cartridge filter is especially useful in bare breeding tanks as the suction they produce is so minimal even babies can easily escape.

Medium tanks most popularly use power filters for filtration. These often are the first choice of the beginning hobbyist purchasing a medium tank. The ease of set up and operation, easily replaceable cartridges, and the ability to clean this style of filter thoroughly generally persuades a novice to opt for this method.

Undergravel plates with power heads or air drives are also in common use, but have not become as popular as the standard outside power filter mentioned above. Cannister filters, either located inside the tank or the more common ones that sit below are becoming more popular because of the biological and chemical filtering they make feasible. There is the added bonus of quiet operation as well as the possibility of hiding the filter from view with ease.

The larger tanks may require various combinations of filters depending on the organic load they will be carrying. If there is only one large fish, a single large outside power filter may be adequate. But, in most cases, large tanks require combinations of filters to get all the various filtration jobs done properly. Normally the large power filter is coupled with an undergravel plate for biological action.

Filter-Systems (examples)

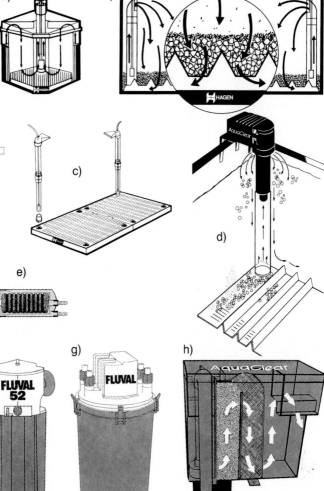

a) Jet Flow corner filter, b) + c) Two different types of undergravel filter systems, d) Aqua Clear undergravel power head, e) Spongefilter (Tetra), f) Fluval internal power filter, g) Fluval canister filter, h) Aqua Clear outside hanging type power filter

Summary and Hints

Mechanical and biological filtration are equally important. Dirt and other debris must be removed from the tank: turbidity makes water unhealthy as well as unsightly. However, a filter needs a run in period, from several days to several weeks, before it can function as a biological filter. It may take up to 100 days before it will reach optimum performance as a biological filter. This run in period corresponds directly with the creation of the nitrite cycle where the bacteria must be allowed enough time to multiply to great enough numbers to use all the ammonia or nitrite as soon as it is formed in the tank by the organic processes.

In this three month "run in" the filter may have been cleaned several times and the beneficial bacteria will have been disturbed. With this in mind never clean the filter or its materials with hot water. Even after the initial run in is over, it is important to remember that with all of the plastic now in use in the hobby, hot water often is warm enough to deform or even melt filter cases, siphons, or other important plastic parts. Rinsing in lukewarm water is a much wiser idea if you want the filter to work at its best for a long time.

Always return part of the old material to the filter to "impregnate" or stimulate bacterial growth in the new media. You'll find the biological system develops much faster in this way. A sterile breeding tank is the lone exception to this rule. Everything should be cleaned in this case.

FILTER CARE = WATER CARE = FISH and PLANT CARE

With a well maintained filter you are half way to your goal of successful fish keeping.

We want to remind you that many aquarium medications may reduce, or completely eliminate the action of the biological filter system. After using medications it is best to make a nearly complete water change, replacing as much as $4/5$ths of the water. Before adding medication remove some of the filter material and keep it wet. Later, you can use this to regenerate the biological system. See our chapter on "cleaning" starting on page 887 for hints in cleaning a filter.

Decorations

Suggestions for various tank "set-ups" are outlined in our chapter on "Community Aquariums" (pages 178-197) and we suggest that you study this before creating your first aquarium. You should also read the chapter on "Decorating with Plants" which begins on page 72.

Once you've determined the species of fish you will keep, along with the landscaping you want, it is easier to select the best decorations. In addition to stones, wood, slate and readymade plastic terracing, plants will be your main decoration. The exception: aquariums with fish that eat plants or with African Cichlids.

The following natural materials are particularly suitable for aquarium decoration:

Stone	Wood
Basalt	Roots from bogs and bayous
	We do not recommend other
Porphyry	woods: rotting wood
	uses oxygen and may harm fish
Granite	
Colored sandstone (if it does not	
contain chalk)	Imitation rushes (Tonkaing rods)
Lava	Slate Bamboo
	Xyloith Coconut shells (work
	well as breeding hollows)
Flowerpots and shards	
(as hiding and breeding places)	

Marble and chalk are not recommended.
Dolomite is not recommended:
use only under certain circumstances.

Materials which contain
copper, such as brass, are toxic.

Make a small sketch first. It can help you pinpoint the necessary materials and the routine for assembling them. Make a list. Without one you may purchase too much or too little or return home with elements which do not fit well together. Combine the materials for the best effect, namely, to create a tank with variety. Knowing how to create a unified, natural feeling which reflects your individuality is the mark of an "advanced aquarist."
You can find a lot of material locally. Beautifully colored and shaped rocks and gravel can be found on Sunday walks and much is available in mountain streams, gravel pits and quarries. Knotted roots found in local ponds may seem attractive but are totally unsuitable. Even if the wood is waterlogged and bleached it can rot and mold in a warm aquarium. The procedure consumes a great deal of oxygen and is bad for the tank. On the other hand, wood which has lain for years in acid soil, cut off from air, it is called bogwood in some places, is safe but must be boiled to drive out any air it may contain. Pieces too large for a pot can be treated by placing them in a bathtub, pouring boiling water over them several times.
Many larger pieces of wood never become fully waterlogged and thus tend to float. There are ways to anchor them. Drill a half-inch hole through the wood on the same plane as the tank then insert pieces of

dowelling just slightly wider than the aquarium itself. When the edges of the dowel are forced against the tank, pressure will keep the wood in place. The dowels must be placed below the level of gravel and can be covered.

a. Holding down a root beneath the tank frame.
b. Securing a root as described above.
c. Securing wood with a sheet of glass.

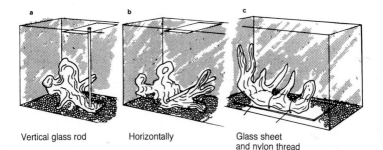

Vertical glass rod Horizontally Glass sheet
and nylon thread

Decorations

The basic premise of any decoration is to please those who see it but it is also a way to conceal equipment and provide hiding places for fish. The decorations should be scaled to the fish in your tank. A *Hypostomus* catfish needs a larger hollow as a daytime hideaway than Spiny Loaches and Dwarf Cichlids. Do not over decorate: fish and plants need most of the room in an aquarium. An over-decorated tank looks tasteless and crowded.

"Cute" decorations such as divers, seahorses and treasure chests are generally frowned upon but the back glass can be made interesting and appealing. It should be coordinated with the rest of the tank. A blue seascape, for example, should not be used on a fresh water tank. The best back panels are made of durable printed plastic. Painting the glass, as is sometimes done, is not recommended. Paint is difficult to remove. A homemade panel can be extremely effective and here is one idea:

Build a wooden frame the exact dimensions of the tank. Attach a mirror to the frame, then spread a little glue over its surface in an abstract pattern. Sprinkle colored "sparkles" over the glue, leaving patches of mirror showing through. When it is dry attach the panel to the back of the tank. It will add visual excitement and an illusion of depth. You can also add strips of bamboo, dried grass, stones and such between the outside of the tank and the mirror.

Your first aquarium

In the previous chapters the many steps required to set up an aquarium have been explained in detail. We will summarize the major points in the most commonly followed sequence.

1. Select the proper location. (Page 21)
2. Choose the kinds of fish you want, then be sure the tank is scaled to fit them.
3. Clean the tank, fill it with water, check for leaks then empty it.
4. If the tank will be placed on an uneven or cold surface such as marble, insulate the bottom with plastic.
5. If you plan to use a bottom heating mat place it on a piece of plastic, then add the tank. If you plan to use inside cable heating dry the tank and attach the cable with special mounts.
6. Add the undergravel filter plate and then the gravel. (See 7) If you plan to include live plants an undergravel unit is not advised.
7. Wash the gravel. (Page 27)
8. If you are using live plants add fertilizer to the bottom layer of gravel.
9. Place clean gravel on top.
10. Fill the tank half-full of water. To avoid moving the gravel or stirring debris, place a large piece of paper over the gravel and set a plate on that. Some aquarists pour water over their hand to weaken its force.
11. If an in-tank heater is to be used add it now. If it is the type which mounts with suction cups, do that but in either case do not connect the heater.
12. Even if a bottom heating mat is used, you will need to add a thermostat control in the tank. Once the heater and thermostat are connected and water added you can connect the heater.

13. Install the filter. Details on matching a power filter to the tank can be found in the chapter on "Cleaning" on page 888.

14. Add an appropriate quantity of conditioner to the water (Chlorine remover etc.)

15. Heat the water to 68° F (20° C). Check the temperature with a thermometer.

16. Use stones, plastic terraces, slate or similar material to conceal the equipment as much as possible. The focus of the tank should be the plants. The taller plants should be placed in corners at the rear. Bushy and smaller plants can be placed in the center and foreground. Fast growing plants such as *Hygrophila, Vallisneria*, Water Starwort and Sword Plants are recommended for new tanks. Do not economize on plants since they will not thrive if there are too few to achieve an equilibrium.

17. Add water to fill the tank, pouring carefully so you will not uproot the new plants.

18. Add a decorative panel to the back glass if you wish. You can purchase ready-made panels or design your own.

19. Connect the filter.

20. Check the heater. The automatic thermostat can be adjusted with a small regulating screw if it fails to settle-in at 75° to 78° F (24° to 26° C).

21. Check the water for pH, hardness and nitrite if necessary.

22. If everything seems right a few hardy fish can be added but do not add many since the tank needs time to develop its biological filter. The bacteria which develop in the filter and gravel need several weeks to culture before they can effectively decompose the nitrogeneous materials excreted by fish. To add fish float the bag which contains them in the tank for ten minutes or more so the fish can acclimate to the temperature. Then they can be set free. Fragile fish should also be given a taste of the water they are to enter. Do this by adding some of the tank water to the bag and wait a few minutes. You can repeat this step a few times if the specimen requires a slow adjustment to new water conditions. After this step you can release the fish to swim in the tank.

23. Add an aquarium cover, light hood or a sheet of glass. Do not leave open space for the fish to jump out. Covering a tank also prevents excessive evaporation and heat loss.

24. Switch on the lights.

Natural Plants

There has been a tremendous surge of interest in aquatic plants. More than 250 varieties are now grown in controlled environments and since there are 4000 varieties of bog and water plants it is obvious many more will find their way into home aquariums. The numbers include all plants which live or grow permanently or periodically in the water or at its edge. These are divided into three groups.

1. Floating plants may float freely, lie just beneath the surface or be rooted firmly, developing long stalked leaves which lie on the surface.
2. Aquatic plants start and end their cycle in the water, their existence depending on certain factors. They lack a supporting structure so that the body of the plant remains pliant and bends with the current. They are buoyant through air-filled hollows in the stalk which reduce the plant's specific weight.
3. Bog plants root in wet or damp soil. Their leaves and shoots grow in air forming a firm support which keeps the plants upright. Many amphibian species can survive submerged and frequently produce different, submerged forms of leaf which are better adapted to life underwater.

Growing plants in an aquarium

Growing a plant in a tank may pose problems, but success is assured if you avoid certain common errors. You would invite trouble, for example, if you placed a plant which needs soft water in hard water. Light and temperature should also be considered. There are two important points: First, an awareness of basics, the combination of gravel, water and light each plant prefers. Secondly, an awareness that success can be aided by certain techniques so that several varieties, not commonly seen together, can be grown successfully in the same aquarium.

Healthy Gravel

The gravel at the bottom of the tank is used to anchor plants, to help them form roots and to provide nourishment. Properly fertilized the gravel will promote plant growth and will absorb fallen foods, excreta and other detritus. Within limits, plants use the by-products from their chemical transformation as nutrients. Improper gravel and a lack of nutrients are a frequent cause of problems.

Proper lighting

Good lighting is essential. Its importance to the growth of plants is often underestimated. Too often the light level is too low and luxurious growth only comes with sufficient light. Light must be provided in adequate amounts, for a sufficient length of time and in the right combination. (See also the chapter on "Lighting an Aquarium" beginning on page 42.)

Water

Water is the basic substance of life for fishes and other aquatic vertebrates (newts, turtles), invertebrates (snails, shrimps) and plants. The substances dissolved and suspended in it are some of the most decisive factors governing life in the aquarium. For the proper growth and health of aquarium inhabitants there are ranges and values for the concentrations of these various substances which are considered desirable. Extremes, in most cases, should be avoided. Most aquatic plants, for example, do well in a pH range of 6.5 to 7.2, Carbonate water hardness (KH) should lie between 5 and 12 degrees. See "Symbols" on page 82.

Fertilizer

Just as with the more commonly known terrestrial plants, aquatic plants require certain nutrients for proper growth and health. In the community aquarium, where both plants and animals are maintained, there is a much reduced need for additional plant nutrients (fertilizers). There are circumstances, however, when extra nutrients should be added to the water.

While many natural waters have sufficient dissolved iron, most municipal water supplies are depleted. Since iron is an important element for proper plant nutrition (it helps prevent leaf yellowing) it should be supplied via fertilizer. Other elements required for proper plant nutrition include manganese, molybdenum, boron, magnesium, copper, nitrogen, phosphorus and potassium. These, and other elements, should all be present in well balanced aquatic plant fertilizers.

The main source of carbon for all plants, of course, is carbon dioxide, CO_2. Fortunately, in a community aquarium there is more than an adequate supply provided by the respiratory processes of the animals. Even in aquariums without fishes the carbon dioxide supply should be of little concern because of the millions of tons (most emitted by our industrialized society) normally present in the atmosphere. Routine aeration will insure that the aquarium plants have sufficient carbon dioxide. The only other requirements for the plants which must be met by the aquarist are those for heat, light and, on occasion, cooling. The factors can be summarized this way:

1. Iron fertilizer fulfills an important function in nourishment, particularly if iron is in short supply (as evidenced by yellow, chlorotic leaves.) It provides a basis for healthy, viable foliage and consequently helps existing nutrients to be assimilated. Iron fertilizers provide healthy, dark-green, luxuriant plants. Iron-rich compounds are available.
2. Fertilizers can help in other ways but should be used with care. Too much can be more harmful than none at all.
3. Carbon dioxide is another element important for optimum growth of water plants. It helps them grow, promotes root formation and reduces the shock of replanting. In addition CO_2 is needed more in hard water because it more readily combines in a bicarbonate-carbonic acid imbalance than in soft water. Carbon dioxide stabilizes the pH within the range which promotes growth. The added carbon is also an important nutrient.

Several firms offer complete systems. Success is virtually assured with CO_2 if you remember the basics, light, heat and fertilizers in the gravel itself.

Decorating with plants

You can create an exciting, lovely garden in any aquarium with the proper assortment of plants. We've described the basics and certain rules must be followed as you begin planting. You must seek contrasts and differences.

Backgrounds

When possible an exciting touch of green should be added to the back and sides of an aquarium. Long-lasting rhizome plants, that is those with root stalks, are recommended. The more common species include *Crinum, Echinodorus, Sagittaria* and *Vallisneria*. These are well suited to highlight levels and taller tanks. In shallower situations the tank should be planted with varieties of medium-height: in taller tanks, taller plants are an obvious choice. Fast growing, stalky plants which do not require much light are suitable, but should be chosen with care. Suggestions for their use appear in the information section, identified by the symbol AH (for aquarium height.)

Foreground plants

Low-growing plants, placed in the front, allow swimming room for fish and provide a clear view of the tank. When selecting smaller plants, luxuriant varieties which reproduce by runners are preferred. These include *Cryptocoryne, Echinodorus, Eleocharis, Marsilea* and *Sagittaria*. These plants require plenty of light and if the level is low you will need to make other choices.

Contrasts in shape

Still other plants can be used in the front and back for contrast since variety will increase the visual excitement. Contrasts can be highlighted by variety in the shape of leaves, growth or size. Plants with similarities should be separated. Examples of contrasting shapes are the round-leafed *Lobelia* contrasted with the pointed leaves of the *Ludwigia* or with the split leaves of the *Cabomba* against the undivided leaves of the *Hygrophila*. Plants with larger leaves can be pleasing beside those with smaller leaves.

Color contrasts

Red-leafed plants can be used to create a color difference beside those with traditional green leaves and when combined with varying shapes the effect can be specially pleasing. However, most colored plants demand considerable light. Their color can be intensified with iron fertilizer. The color should be limited in or to specific areas, contrasting against specific plants. Be sure taller plants do not shade smaller ones.

Group planting

Stalky plants are more decorative if you combine several of one variety. The number will depend on the size of the tank and the distance between each plant will depend on the size of their leaves.

A typical Dutch plant aquarium which leaves little room for fish. In the foreground is *Cryptocoryne willisii*, in the center Red Tiger Lotus and behind, *Lobelia cardinalis*. In the center, right, is *Heteranthera zosterifolia* with *Cryptocoryne siamensis* behind.

A nice visual trick is to stagger a group of stalky plants. Cuttings of different heights can be inserted in order of increasing height from front to rear.

Single plants

Larger rhizomes with rosette leaves are generally planted singly, displayed as solitary specimens. These should be selected according to the size of the tank and can form an important focal point. They should not be placed in the center, but to one side, at a point about one-third of the tank's length. Accompanied by contrasting plants (with either different leaves, color or height) creates an astonishing effect.

Reproduction

Plants can be propagated in several ways, some easy, some difficult: either way the procedure helps to reduce the cost of establishing tanks. It can be particularly rewarding with rare or difficult to propagate specimens. A brief explanation is found below:

Cuttings

Shoots removed from a stalky plant and thrust into a bed to root are called "cuttings". The floating tips, or "head cuttings" are preferred and can be obtained from unbranched stalks. The tip forms the cutting. The remainder of the stalk is untouched and will soon form new tips. These, too, can be removed when six to eight inches (15 to 20 cm) in length. Examples of suitable plants include *Ammannia, Hygrophila* and *Lobelia*. There are also "selfrooting" plants which, when they reach a certain size, naturally form side roots. These include *Didiplis, Ludwigia, Mayaca* and *Rotala*.

Daughter plants

New shoots which are formed on stems produced by a mother plant and root in the bed of their own accord are called "daughter plants." This is the simplest form of reproduction and is often prolific. The process can soon produce, many new plants. Examples are *Echinodorus, Sagittaria* and *Vallisneria*. *Nymphaea* will always produce one new plant per off-shoot and will separate on its own, producing five or six leaves. *Cryptocorynes* are similar but should be left undisturbed to multiply and form a colony or group.

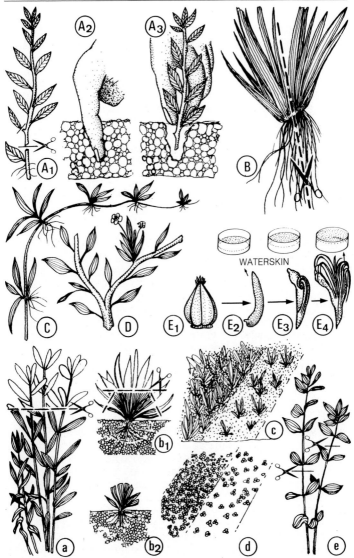

Types of Reproduction: A) Cuttings. B) Daughter plants. C) Adventitious plants. D) Sideshoots. E) Seeds. **Plant care** a) Pruning. b) Rejuvenation. c) Forcing. d) Thinning. e) Cutting back.

Reproduction

Shoots which form specifically from the mother plant are called adventitious plants. These produce on the leaves of *Microsorium, Ceratopteris* and *Eleocharis* and are removed when large enough. The submerged blossoming stalks of certain *Echinodorus* produce adventitious shoots from the Verticil and these are removed when they have developed roots and five or six leaves. They can be planted in and will grow into individual plants. With some varieties it is better to bend the stalk to the gravel, without cutting, holding the new shoot in place with small stones or plant clips.
The stalk will then root undisturbed. Once rooted, you can cut through the connecting stalk.

Rhizome side-shoots

The rootstock of *Echinodorus, Lagenandra* and *Anubias* can produce independent side-shoots. These can be be separated, along with a few leaves and some of the rhizome. To do this cut through the long root stock about half way along its length, allowing both portions to root. You can do the same with the two to four inch (5-10 cm) retrograde rhizome sections removed when transplanting older plants. The section is placed on the gravel, secured with a plant clip, and allowed to develop new side shoots. These will root.

Seeds

Plants with blooms can be reproduced by seed after floating though, as a rule, the blooms must be artificially pollenated. To do this the pollen is transferred from one blossom to another with a small brush or piece of cotton. Examples are *Aponogeton* and *Echinodorus*. Self-pollination is possible with such species as *Barclaya* and *Nymphaea*. Seedlings can be raised in small plastic pots in a mixture of three parts sand, one part loam and one of peat. Press the seeds, on one-inch centers, flush with the top layer of sand. Place the pot in an open area of the aquarium, above older plants on a stone or suspended by wire. Lower the container as the seeds germinate and the plant grows stronger. When sturdy enough young plants can be set in the aquarium.

Care

Timely and skillful attention is an important part of all aquarium care. When choosing plants you should be sure they suit your tank's environment taking into account the amount of light, water condition and temperature. The roots should be properly trimmed and the plants properly rooted and spaced. These requirements are outlined beneath each species.

Pruning

Certain taller stalked plants may eventually grow above the water. The leaves below the water line then die unless you prune the leader about half way. You can use the section removed as a cutting to propagate new plants. Among such species one can list *Ammannia*, *Hygrophila*, *Lobelia* and *Saururus*.

New growth

A stalk which is repeatedly pruned will eventually create new growth. The shoots can be removed and a new group created using the healthy tips; it will prevent the "tired" look often seen on older plants. The technique applies to plants which reproduce by runners, expanding until the growth is much too dense. To thin, remove the best specimens and replant. Discard weaker or superfluous plants.

Transplanting

Excessive cutting and handling weakens plants and should be avoided. Selectively remove about half of denser plantings, creating new space for growth. Examples include *Sagittaria*, *Vallisneria* and Dwarf Amazon Sword Plant.

Thinning

Thinning achieves the same result as replanting and applies to those stalked plants with intertwined shoots which eventually branch, becoming tall and dense. By removing longer stems half way along

their length, you can reduce the tendency toward new growth and improve the appearance of your tank. Among examples are *Hemianthus, Ludwigia, Mayaca* and *Rotala.*

Cutting back

Larger leafy solitary plants may stifle competition in the tank and may need to be cut back. Remove the outer leaves as required to open the aquarium to light. Cutting back is also required on plants with floating leaves such as *Echinodorus cordifolius* and *Nymphaea lotus.* These leaves should be systematically removed until submerged, short-stemmed leaves are produced.

The *Echinodorus grandiflorus* from Eastern Brazil growing above water. These leaves do not grow well under water. The plants are ideally suited to bog-gardens with approximately eight inches (20 cm) of water.

Symbols and Descriptions

D = Degree of difficulty.
The symbol indicates whether a species is easy or difficult to grow. Those categorized as a one or two are recommended for beginners. Plants in group three require more experience. Those in group four demand exacting water, generally soft, and should be considered only by experienced aquarists.

D: 1 Robust and adaptable, these species can stand hard water and relatively poor food supplies. They require weak to moderate light, approximately one watt for every gallon of water, and generally reproduce without problems. pH 6.0 to 8.0, KH to 20°.

D: 2 Robust and long-lived, these species demand more controlled water quality and moderate to average light... one watt per one half to one gallon of water. Propagation is reasonably easy. 6.0 to 7.5, KH to 15°.

D: 3 These plants do best in soft to medium-hard water with a balanced food supply. They can also survive in water with a higher carbonate hardness if you add carbon dioxide. They do best with medium to high light, about one watt to one to two quarts of water but are sometimes difficult to reproduce. pH 6.0 to 7.2 and water hardness to 10 KH.

D: 4 These plants are difficult to adapt and generally require soft water and more intense light, about one watt for every one to one-half quart of water. Reproduction is difficult. pH 6.0 to 6.8 and hardness to 4 KH.

KH = carbonate hardness
The portion of carbonate hardness in water is often a decisive factor in plant growth. Very soft water, that below 2° KH, does not often favor growth. A plant will also do poorly if the pH rises too much or if the carbon dioxide content is low. The best range can often be determined by trial and error and light fluctuations are generally acceptable. Plants with substantially different demands should not be grown in a community tank.

pH = relative acidity and alkalinity

A pH number indicates the amount of acidity or alkalinity. Most plants prefer a rather neutral range between 6.5 and 7.2. Some plants can accept water above or below these figures but other genera demand strict attention to pH. If a plant does not grow well in your tank, check the pH first.

T = Temperature

This measurement indicates the temperature at which a species does best and is usually slightly above normally indicated values. Some plants can tolerate up to four degrees more heat but, because of a change in metabolism, will require more food and more light.

AH = Aquarium height

This will give you an idea of the best tank height for a given species. Tall and leafy rhizomes and fast-growing stalked plants should be planted in taller, more spacious tanks. They would be out of place in a lower tank and could require frequent pruning. Shorter species can be planted in any aquarium but in à taller tank the added water depth may reduce the intensity of light at the bottom. Shorter and smaller-leaved stalk plants may receive too little light and will languish unless the output of the light is increased.

For the sake of brevity the three tank heights are shown here:
(need to measure)

AH = 1 smaller tanks, approximately ten gallons and height to 14 inches (35 cm).

AH = 2 Medium tanks, about 20 gallons, height to 18 inches (45 cm).

AH = 3 Larger tanks, to 50 gallons and 20 inches (50 cm) in height.

Groups

To speed up identification, species are arranged in groups and sub-groups according to their growth.

Group 1

Stalked with up-right stems

The plants have sturdy stems and full leaves. They are generally planted in groups, small or large, as decoration. They can be reproduced only by cuttings. Some 40 genera and 90 species are in the category. These can be further categorized by leaf arrangements.

1.1.
Eusteralis

Sub-group 1

Leaves in vertical form.

Three or more leaves grow from the same stem elevation. The leaf generally has several fine points though a few varieties may be undivided. There are 11 genera and 25 species.

Sub-group 2

Opposed leaves

Two leaves grow from one terminal. The shape is generally undivided, seldom pinnate and rarely forked. There are 15 genera and 45 species.

1.2.
Hygrophila

Sub-group 3

Alternating leaves

Leaves grow from individual terminals and often spiral around the stem. Leaf shape varies but is generally undivided or, if divided, seldom has more than one tip. There are 14 genera and 20 species.

Group 2

Rosette leaves

The leaves grow upward from a somewhat bulky rootstock. Prefers a gravel bed and leaves are rosette-shaped though varying in size. Smaller plants can be planted in groups; the larger ones, individually. There are 22 genera with 115 species.

1.3.
Lobelia

The sea-grass-leaved *Heteranthera zosterifolia* in a fastflowing stream in the southern Brazil Amazon. Water plants are seldom seen in Brazilian rivers since the level rises rapidly during the rainy season and bottom-rooting plants are deprived of light. Vegetation is restricted to the smaller streams with water levels less prone to fluctuation. Plants such as the floating *Eichhornia* are exceptions.

Sub-group 1

Smaller-leaved rosettes

These are generally taller growing with thin, non-petiolate leaves and are used in groups as a decorative background. A total of eight genera and 30 species are recorded.

Sub-group 2

Broad-leafed rosettes

Characterized by round, heart-shaped leaves and compact growth. They are usually planted individually. A number of similar plants can be found in other sub-groups.

2.1.
Sagittaria

2.2.
Nuphar

Sub-group 3
Amazon plants (*Echinodorus*)
A native of the American continent, it is found in 47 species and varying forms. 25 to 30 are common in aquariums and can be planted individually or in groups, depending on size.

2.3.
Echinodorus

Sub-group 4
Aponogeton (*Aponogeton*)
Common to Africa, Asia and Australia about one dozen of its 42 species can be grown in aquariums. These are fast growing corm types (with a thick rounded underground base and scaly or membranous leaves) which happily flower and fruit in an aquarium.

2.4.
Aponogeton

Sub-group 5
Cryps (*Cryptocorynes*)
A widely-distributed genus with more than 60 species, common in south east Asia. About 30, with varying leaf shapes, are suited to home aquariums. Cryps generally demand careful water quality.

Group 3
Mosses and Ferns
A small group with nine genera and 15 species, some are also listed among floating plants. The submerged varieties generally grow slower and prefer soft water. Species with creeping runners can be secured to rock or wood, on which they will continue to grow.

2.5.
Wasserkelche
(*Cryptocoryne*)

Group 4
Floating plants
There are two distinct groups. Some species float freely with a dry upper side to their leaves. Others float horizontally below the water line and in their manner of food intake are closer to true aquatic plants. Surface vegetation is usually avoided because it restricts light to the plants below but can be indispensable for certain fish. There are one dozen genera and 25 species.

3.
Hydrocotyle

4.
Pistia

Eichhornia crassipes, see page 142 for description.

1. Plants with upright stems
1.1 Vertical leaves

Ceratophyllum demersum LINNAEUS, 1753   Hornwort

Fam.: *Ceratophyllaceae*

Distribution: Worldwide.
A rootless plant, it floats beneath the surface and in nature its fairly fragile stems are anchored to the bottom by root-like organs (rhizoids). Whorls of rigid, dark-green, leaves are covered with soft thorns and are sensitive to pressure. Rapid growth and the production of side-shoots quickly produce thickets which serve as haven for fry. In an aquarium regular thinning will open the plant, allowing light to reach the tank bottom. Propagation: cuttings and side-shoots.

D: 1; KH: 5-15; pH: 6.0-7.5; T: 64-82° F (18-28° C); AH: 1-3.

Egeria densa PLANCHON, 1849   Argentine Acharis

Fam.: *Hydrocharitaceae*   Syn.:*Elodea densa*

Distribution: Argentine; Paraguay; Uruguay; Brazil.
An adaptable, fast-growing species, the plant prefers hard water and is particularly suited to cold water tanks. It will accept warmer water with adequate lighting. It has a fairly brittle stem and the long, non-pinnate, dark-green leaves $3/_4$-inch (2 cm.) long and $1/_4$ (0.5 cm.) wide, are seen in compact whorls. About 30 fine teeth mark the leaf edge and its long, floating skeins sometimes bloom above the water. The species is diclinous and generally only male specimens are grown in Europe. It differs from *Elodea* through a different development of its bloom and in pollination by insects. Propagation: cuttings from side-shoots.

D: 1; KH: 8-15; pH: 6.5-7.5;T: 68-75° F (20-24° C); AH: 1-3.

Hemianthus micranthemoides NUTTAL, 1817   Pearlweed

Fam.: *Scrophulariaceae*   Syn.:*Micranthemum micranthemoides*

Distribution: Cuba and southeastern United States.
A plant of medium-height recommended for the area between low growing foreground species and taller plants in the back. Its thin, pliable shoots with light green, pointed ovate leaves, $1/_4$ to $1/_2$-inch (approx. 1 cm) long and $1/_4$-inch wide are seen in whorls of three or four. The plant is not demanding in terms of either water hardness or temperature but needs quantities of light. Plant in small groups. The shoot ends root well and produce numerous side-shoots, quickly forming a thick cushion. Regular care is important. The plant is sensitive to preparations containing trypaflavine. Propagation: cutting and runners.

D: 3; KH: 2-12; pH: 6.0 -7.0; T: 72-82° F (22-28° C); AH: 1-2.

Limnophila aquatica ROXBURGH,1824   Giant Ambulia

Fam.: *Scrophulariaceae*

Distribution: India; Sri Lanka.
A fast-growing stalked plant, it is ideal for group plantings in deeper tanks. Leaf whorls can be found to five inches long though they are generally smaller. Normally seen with 18 to 22 finely divided leaves with an elongated tip. Its many segments are thin and threadlike without a central vein. The plant prefers soft water and is difficult to grow. New plants may not root easily. It does best in the presence of iron and responds well to ferrous fertilizers. The leaves become thicker and prettier with light. Do not cut stems too much. Propagation: cuttings, and side-shoots (after cutting back).

D: 3; KH: 5-12; pH: 6.5-7.0; T: 75-79° F (24-26° C); AH: 3.

Plants

Ceratophyllum demersum

Hemianthus micranthemoides

Egeria densa

Limnophila aquatica

1. Plants with upright stems
1.1 Vertical leaves

Limnophila sessiliflora VAHL, 1820   Dwarf Ambulia

Fam.: *Scrophulariaceae*

Distribution: India; Pakistan; Indonesia; Japan; Sri Lanka.
An elongated, stalked plant with leaves in whorls of 8 to 13. The pinate leaf is one inch long and $^1/_2$-inch wide with forked cuts and a forward-projecting segmented tip. The end does not extend over the previous segment. Shoots develop height, float and decorate the upper tank area. Older stocks will recondition themselves and the plant adjusts to hard water but will die without sufficient iron. Be sure to use iron-rich fertilizer. Propagation: cuttings, side-shoots and runners.

D: 1; KH: 3-15; pH: 6.0-7.5; T: 72-82° F (22-28° C); AH: 2-3.

Myriophyllum aquaticum VERDCOURT, 1973   Brazilian Milfoil

Fam.: *Haloragaceae*   Syn.:*M. brasiliense, M. proserpinacoides*

Distribution: South America as well as the southern part of North America.
Its feathery leaves and stalk make this the best Milfoil for an aquarium. Leaf whorls are generally seen in groups of five with three and six less common. Roundish leaves are one 16–18 mm ($^3/_4$ in.) long with 8 to 10 light-green, thread-like segments $^1/_4$ to $^1/_2$-inch long on both sides. The plant can tolerate a variety of water conditions, such as soft, low pH water. With light it may grow above the surface, producing coarse, crested leaves. While the plant produces side shoots it should not be cut back often. Propagation: cuttings from side-shoots.

D: 1; KH: 2-12; pH: 5.0-7.5; T: 72-82° F (22-30° C); AH: 1-3.

Myriophyllum mattogrossense HOEHNE, 1915   Red Milfoil

Fam.: *Haloragaceae.*

Distribution: Brazil and other areas of South America.
Brownish to rust-red stem and leaves are a unique feature of this plant. Two-inch long leaves are seen in whorls of five to seven with 10 to 12 thread-like "feathers" $^3/_4$ to 1 $^1/_4$-inch long (2-3 cm.) on each side. As with all plants with feathery leaves, the water should be well filtered to minimize algae and keep the leaves clean. It does best with plenty of light, and water of relatively high hardness. A fast-growing, floating plant, it produces many side-stems. Iron-rich fertilizers improves growth. If the leaves cast shadows the reduction in light may result in poor growth. Shoots should be separated by a couple of inches. Propagation: cuttings.

D: 2; KH: 5-12; pH: 6.0-7.2; T: 72-82° F (22-28° C); AH: 2-3.

Myriophyllum scabratum MICHAUX, 1803   Foxtail

Fam.: *Haloragaceae*   Syn.:*M. pinnatum*

Distribution: Eastern North America; eastern Mexico; Cuba.
Easily distinguished from other varieties in that the leaves do not form true whorls. The plant normally grows two or three leaves along the stem in pseudo-whorls, one leaf generally set higher than the others. It produces leaves to 1 $^3/_4$-inches (4 cm.) in the wild with more than 20 pinnules but in an aquarium it has smaller leaves, about one inch (2-3 cm.) with fewer and shorter pinnules. A cold-water plant, it has been adapted to tropical aquariums and needs medium-strong light and clean, well-filtered water. A "current" is an advantage. Propagation: cuttings and side-shoots.

D: 1; KH: 5-15; pH: 6.5-7.5; T: 64-75° F (18-24° C); AH: 1-3.

90

Limnophila sessiliflora

Myriophyllum mattogrossense

Myriophyllum aquaticum

Myriophyllum scabratum

Alternanthera "lilacina" (species not identified botanically).

Fam.: *Amaranthaceae*

Distribution: Central and South America.
A striking plant with red leaves and stalk, it needs plenty of light and can tolerate only a narrow range of conditions. Lanceolate leaves are 2 to $3^1/_4$-inch (5-8 cm.) long and one inch wide and brown to deep red olive tone underneath. The leaves are found in pairs. The plant will not tolerate floating plants overhead and needs room space to avoid crowding and shadows. The compact planting in the picture can be successful only with strong light. A staggered planting is not only visually attractive, but allows more light to reach the plant. Propagation: cuttings, and from side-shoots after cutting-back.

D: 3; KH: 2-10; pH: 5.5-7.2; T: 75-86° F (24-30° C); AH: 2.

Alternanthera reineckii BRIQUET, 1899

Fam.: *Amaranthaceae*   Syn.:*A. rosaefolia. (nomen nudum)*

Distribution: Tropical regions of old and new worlds.
A visually attractive plant recommended for larger tanks. It is the best of the genus, fast-growing and adaptable. Narrow, lanceolate leaves, $3^1/_4$ to 4 inches (8-10 cm.) long and $1/_4$ to $1/_2$-inches wide, are on short stems. The leaves are blood red, hairless and glossy, olive-green to deep red on the bottom, and blunted at the front. The color depends on the amount of light. Place the plants about four inches (10 cm.) apart to prevent shadows and allow light to reach the lower leaves. A similar plant, *A. sessilis var. orforma* is not recommended for an aquarium.

D: 2; KH: 2-12; pH: 5.5-7.0; T: 75-86° F (24-30° C); AH: 2-3.

Ammannia senegalensis LAMARCK, 1791   Red Ammannia

Fam.: *Lythraceae*

Distribution: South and east Africa.
An upright, stalked, ornamental plant, it is recommended for its decorative values. Opposing, sessile leaves are $1^1/_4$ to $1^1/_2$-inches long (3-5 cm.) and about $1/_4$-inch wide, olive-green to reddish in color. The leaf edges bend backwards and the tips point down. The plant is difficult to keep and may not adapt to hard water. It needs medium to strong light and does best in areas devoid of floating plants. Develop groups from cuttings and keep the sizes of individual plants unequal for more interest. Prune regularly when the shoots reach the surface. Propagation: cutting and side-shoots after thinning.

D: 3; KH: 2-10; pH: 6.5-7.2; T: 77-82° F: (25-28° C); AH: 2.

Bacopa caroliniana (WALTER) ROBINSON, 1908   Giant Bacopa

Fam.: *Scrophulariaceae*   Syn.:*B. amplexicaulis*

Distribution: Southern and central United States.
A fast-growing, stalked plant ideal for planting in small groups. Needs plenty of light – which it may not receive in an aquarium – but adjusts well to a variety of water hardness and temperatures. Coarse gravel and a lack of fertilizer will result in spindly plants with poor leaves. Opposing ovate, light-green leaves are without stalks and are one-inch long and about $1/_2$-inch wide. Propagation: cuttings.

D: 2; KH: 5-15; pH: 6.0-7.5; T: 72-82° F (22-28° C); AH: 2.

Alternanthera "lilacina"

Ammannia senegalensis

Alternanthera reineckii

Bacopa caroliniana

1. Plants with upright stems
1.2 With opposing leaves

Bacopa monnieri (LINNAEUS) PENNELL, 1891   Dwarf Bacopa

Fam.: *Scrophulariaceae*

Distribution: A wide area of the tropics and sub-tropics.
Its slender stalks are most effective when planted in groups of 15 to 20, graduated by height. Opposing, thick, ovate medium green leaves one-inch long and $^1/_2$-inch wide, taper toward the base. Is not demanding of water quality or substrate and with good lighting, remains compact. This is an important point in shallower aquariums where increased pruning may be needed with less light. The plant becomes ugly with too much pruning. Propagation: cuttings from side-shoots.

D: 2; **KH:** 2-15; **pH:** 6.0-7.5; **T:** 71-86° F (22-30° C); **AH:** 1-2.

Cabomba aquatica AUBLET, 1775   Yellow Cabomba

Fam.: *Nymphaeaceae*

Distribution: From northern South America to southern North America.
This ornamental plant is more demanding than many. It needs clean, clear water and plenty of light and planting in an open area results in a more compact plant. The species is easily recognized since each finely divided leaf forms up to 600 thin, elongated segments 0,1-0,4 mm across. In an aquarium the leaves are generally smaller with about 200 segments. Propagation: cuttings; self-propagation.

D: 3; **KH:** 2-10; **pH:** 6.0-6.8; **T:** 75-86° F (24-30° C); **AH:** 2-3.

Cabomba caroliniana GRAY, 1848   Green Cabomba

Fam.: *Nymphaeaceae*

Distribution: Central and South America.
Groupings are most effective in deeper aquariums. Compared with *C. aquatica* this species has coarser leaves with less obvious divisions. The 100-150 segmented tips are 1-2 mm with a clear central vein. The plant adjusts to a variety of aquarium conditions and can accept harder water. It is also less demanding about lighting. The water should not be aerated with an air stone since this removes carbonic acid, increasing the pH. Propagation: cuttings and side-shoots.

D: 2: **KH:** 2-12; **pH:** 6.5-7.2; **T:** 72-82° F (22-28° C); **AH:** 2-3.

Cabomba piauhyensis GARDENER, 1844   Red Cabomba

Fam.: *Nymphaeaceae*

Distribution: Central and South America.
While others of the genus have opposing leaves, this plant produces three reddish leaves at one height. The distinctive, decorative leaves are easy to identify though the plant is difficult to grow in an aquarium. It needs soft water, strong light and iron-rich fertilizers. At the surface the floating tips may turn yellow and become glossy but when the plant is happy it is extremely lovely. .

D: 4; **KH:** 2-8; **pH:** 6.0-6.8; **T:** 75-82° F (24-28° C); **AH:** 2.

Bacopa monnieri

Cabomba caroliniana

Cabomba aquatica

Cabomba piauhyensis

1. Plants with upright stems
1.2 With opposing leaves

Didiplis diandra (NUTTALL) WOOD, 1855

Fam.: *Lythraceae*   Syn.: *Peplis diandra*

Distribution: North America.

A group of ornamental plants able to tolerate a broad range of water and lighting conditions. Responds well to iron-rich fertilizers and develops problems only in very hard water or with poor lighting. Light green opposing leaves, resembling pine needles, ($^{1}/_{4}$ to $^{3}/_{4}$-inch long; 1-2 cm.) are found on a slender stalk. Closer to light they often become red at the tip. Brown nodules in the axils are submerged buds. Propagation: cuttings and self-propagation. Insert wellseparated, long cuttings in groups in soft sand. Side-shoots produce a thick bush.

D: 3; **KH:** 2-12; **pH:** 5.8-7.2; **T:** 75-82° F (24-28° C); **AH:** 1-3.

Gymnocoronis spilanthoides DE CANDOLLE, 1836   Spade Leaf

Fam.: *Asteraceae*

Distribution: Tropical South America.

Recommended for deeper tanks. Arrange as you would *Hygrophila* with which it is often confused. Has a heavy stem with opposing light green lanceolate leaves, 4 to 6-inches (10-15 cm.) long, 2 to 3-inch wide (5-8 cm.), set close to the stem. Above water the leaves become toothed with both ends pointed. Submerged they are smooth-edged and blunt. Three lighter main veins extend from the base and are reticulated. When new, the shoots grow quickly to the surface and should be cut back until the growth eventually slows. Propagation: cuttings and side-shoots which develop after cutting.

D: 2; **KH:** 5-15; **pH:** 6.5-7.2; **T:** 64-79° F (18-26° C); **AH:** 2-3.

Hygrophila corymbosa (BLUME) LINDAU, 1904   Giant Hygrophila

Fam.: *Acanthaceae*   Syn.: *Nomaphila stricta*

Distribution: India; Malaysia; Indonesia.

Perhaps the best known of all aquarium plants, it is fast-growing and adaptable and can be planted singly or in groups. It has an upright, brown stem with broad, medium-green lanceolate opposing leaves (3 $^{1}/_{4}$ to 5 inches; 8-12 cm. long and 1 $^{1}/_{4}$ to 2 inches; 3-5 cm. wide) pointed at both ends. While it can tolerate a range of water hardnesses it will not do well at a pH below 6.0 when the leaves become yellow, spotted and small. It is ideal as an "outline" plant and should be pruned regularly for optimum growth. Propagation: cuttings and from side-shoots which develop after cutting.

D: 1; **KH:** 2-15; **pH:** 6.5-7.5; **T:** 72-82° F (22-28° C); **AH:** 2-3.

Hygrophila difformis (LINNAEUS fil.) BLUME, 1826   Water Wisteria

Fam.: *Acanthaceae*   Syn.: *Synnema triflorum*

Distribution: India; Burma; Thailand; Malaya.

A loose-growing, stalked plant suggested for large groupings though its short-stemmed, pinnate, opposing leaves (to 4 $^{3}/_{4}$-inches; 12 cm. in length) contrast well in a tank. If the tank temperature is low the leaves will be smaller and lobate. As with others of the genus the plant requires plenty of light and without it the lower leaves will either fall or become sparse, creating unsightly open spaces. Propagation: from cuttings and side-shoot runners.

D: 2; **KH:** 2-15; **pH:** 6.5-7.5; **T:** 75-82° F (24-28° C); **AH:** 2-3.

Didiplis diandra

Hygrophila corymbosa

Gymnocoronis spilanthoides

Hygrophila difformis

Hygrophila polysperma ANDERS, 1867

Dwarf Hygrophila

Fam.: *Acanthaceae*

Distribution: India.
Not positively identified until recently, the plant is readily available and one of the best of all aquarium plants. It grows readily in a range of water conditions but is at its best in water of average temperature, with bright lighting and a loamy soil. Light-green, short-stalked, lanceolate leaves are $^3/_4$ to 1 $^1/_2$-inches long (2-4 cm.) and up to $^1/_3$-inches (1 cm.) wide. The tip is rather blunt. Prune regularly. Re-potting helps to rejuvinate older plants. Propagation: from cuttings, especially when pruning, and selfpropagating. A similar plant, longer, with brownish leaves (to 2 $^3/_4$-inches long (7 cm.) is also known as *H. polysperma*.

D: 1; KH: 2-15; pH: 6.5-7.8; T: 68-86° F (20-30° C); AH: 1-3.

Hygrophila stricta (NEES) LINDAU, 1894

Thai Stricta

Fam.: *Acanthaceae*

Syn.:*H. guianensis*

Distribution: Southeast Asia; Thailand; Siam.
A robust, upright, stalked plant first introduced in 1967. It has short-stemmed, pointed, lanceolate leaves 4 to 6-inches (10-15 cm.) long and to one inch wide and adapts well in home aquariums. With plenty of light the leaves grow close together. It can be used in groupings in a larger tank or planted alone, where it develops into a compact bush. The best effect comes when the plant sizes vary. It may not be a separate species but a narrow leaved variety of *H. corymbosa*. Propagation: cuttings and self-propagating.

D: 2; KH: 2-15; pH: 6.5-7.2; T: 75-82° F (24-28° C); AH: 2-3.

Ludwigia arcuata WALTER, 1788

Needle Leaf Ludwigia

Fam.: *Onagraceae*

Distribution: Eastern U.S.; Virginia; Carolinas.
The deep red plants are often used for contrast. It requires a strong light to maintain color and becomes green and sparse as the lighting diminishes. Its thinnish stem has paired leaves 1 $^1/_4$ to 2-inches long (3-5 cm.) and $^1/_5$ to $^1/_4$-inch wide (0.2-0.3 cm.) with a long, pointed tip. It requires good water with iron rich fertilizer to maintain proper leaf color. When first planting, the cuttings should be well spaced. It grows fast under good conditions and expands via side-shoots. Propagation: cuttings. It is a good self-propagator.

D: 2; KH: 2-12; pH: 6.0-7.2; T: 64-75° F (18-24° C); AH: 2-3.

Ludwigia repens FORSTER, 1771

Creeping Ludwigia

Fam.: *Onagraceae*

Syn.:*L. natans.*

Distribution: North and Central America.
Though the species is found in a variety of colors and leaf forms these are not considered as sub-species. The broad, round-leaved form illustrated is the variety most often available commercially. The leaves are brownish-green above and deep red beneath, stalked, broadly ovate and $^3/_4$ to 1 $^1/_2$-inch long (2-4 cm.) and $^3/_4$ to 1 $^1/_4$-inches wide (2-3 cm.). It adapts well to a variety of aquarium conditions, can tolerate medium lighting and is highly recommended. The fast growing stalks put out numerous shoots and form thick groups which are best planted in the center and side areas. Plants need regualar attention. Propagation: cutting and self-progagation.

D: 2; KH: 2-15; pH: 5.5-7.5; T: 68-86° F (20-30° C); AH: 2-3.

Hygrophila polysperma

Ludwigia arcuata

Hygrophila stricta

Ludwigia repens

Ludwigia palustris x repens

Fam.: *Onagraceae*   Syn.: *L. natans, L. mullertii*

Distribution: North America.
One of the most commmon species of the genus, it is considered a cross because of its characteristics. Olive-green, stalked, lanceolate leaves are reddish underneath, $^3/_4$ to 1 $^1/_2$ inches long (2-4 cm.) and $^1/_2$ to $^3/_4$-inches wide (1-2 cm.). A rarer, pure green form has narrower leaves. It grows well and adapts to a variety of tank conditions. A tendency to produce side shoots gives the plant a bushy look which can be encourged by trimming. Its dense growth provides hiding places for many fish. Propagation: cuttings and self-propagation.

D: 1; KH: 2-15; pH: 5.8-7.5; T: 64-86° F (18-30° C); AH: 1-3.

Lysimachia nummularia LINNAEUS, 1753   Creeping Penny

Fam.: *Primulaceae*

Distribution: Europe; Western U. S.; Japan.
A widely distributed, prostrate creeper with pale yellow flowers, it is generally found on the edges of ditches and damp, marshy pastures. Related to land varieties, it easily adapts to an aquarium. Submersed, upright stalks with opposing, short-stemmed, light-green, rounded, pinnate leaves are $^3/_4$-inch wide (2 cm.). The plant can adapt to a range of tank conditions but needs lots of light and should neither be shaded by floating plants above nor crowded by competing vegetation. It can tolerate the higher temperatures found in tropical aquariums but after a time will cease to grow and should be replaced with cuttings.

D: 1; KH: 5-15; pH: 6.5-7.5; T: 59-71° F (15-22° C); AH: 1-2.

Rotala macrandra KOEHNE, 1880   Giant Red Rotala

Fam.: *Lythraceae*

Distribution: India.
The red leaved plant is ideal for contrast and decorative highlight. It should be used in front of light-green plants. Its thin, supple stems feature opposing, unstalked, elliptical to oval leaves with short points and are $^3/_4$ to 1 $^1/_4$-inches long (2-3 cm.) and $^1/_2$ to $^3/_4$-inches wide (1.5-2 cm.). The color of the leaves depends on the amount of light provided and becomes deeper and more intense with iron-rich fertilizer. The stems are sensitive to pressure and must be carefully transplanted in soft sand. Do not use in a tank with active fish. Propagation: cuttings and self-propagating.

D: 3; KH: 2-12; pH: 6.0-7.0; T: 77-86° F (25-30° C); AH: 2.

Rotala rotundifolia (ROXBURGH) KOEHNE, 1880   Dwarf Rotala

Fam.: *Lythraceae*

Distribution: Southeast Asia.
Can be used in groups to create green backgrounds in larger tanks. Its thin stems and paired, short-stalked leaves can be sometimes found in whorls of three or four leaves. The green leaf is narrow, lanceolate and blunt at the front $^1/_2$ to $^3/_4$-inch long (1-2 cm.) and $^1/_8$ inch (0.3-0.5 cm.) wide. The color of the leaves may change from olive-green to a reddish tint. Medium strong light is needed for good growth. Eight-inch cuttings can be planted in groups. The plant will form side-shoots. Propagation: cuttings and self-propagating.

D: 2; KH: 2-15; pH: 5.5-7.2; T: 68-86° F (20-30° C); AH: 1-3.

Ludwigia palustris x repens

Rotala macrandra

Lysimachia nummularia

Rotala rotundifolia

101

Blyxa novoguineensis DEN HARTOG, 1957

Fam.: *Hydrocharitaceae*

Distribution: New Guinea.
The genus includes a number of very demanding plants. The species above is adapted to soft water and will not grow well in water with high carbonate hardness. It requires plenty of light. *B. novoguineensis* forms a stem to 12 inches (30 cm.) long with alternate leaves. The narrow leaf is unstalked, pointed at the front, 4 to 6 inches long and $^1/_4$-inch wide (0.5 cm.). The plant is brittle, sensitive to pressure and recommended for gentle fish. Propagation: Cuttings from pruned side-shoots.

D: 3; KH: 2-8; pH: 5.5-6.5; T: 68-82° F (20-28° C); AH: 1-2.

Cardamine lyrata BUNGE, 1835   Chinese Ivy

Fam.: *Brassicaceae*

Distribution: Eastern Siberia; northern and eastern China; Japan; Korea.
These small-leaved plants require plenty of light and generally find an aquarium too warm for comfort. Higher temperatures and weaker lighting produce thin stems and smaller leaves but given suitable conditions, which includes water of moderate hardness, the plant will prosper. Be cautious with medications and if it is necessary to add chemicals to a tank, put starter shoots in another tank for protection. Propagation: cuttings though generally self-propagating.

D: 2; KH: 5-12; pH: 6.5-7.0; T: 59-71° F (15-22° C); AH: 1-2.

Eichhornia azurea (SWARTZ) KUNTH, 1843   Blue Water Hyacinth

Fam.: *Pontederiaceae*

Distribution: Tropical and sub-tropical America.
Light-green opposing leaves are single-veined, linear and sessile 4 to 8 inches long (10-20 cm.) and $^1/_4$ to $^1/_2$-inch long (0.5-0.8 cm.). In the juvenile stages the leaves are arranged distichous and pinnate along the upright stem but as it reaches the surface the leaves change shape and the plant must be cut back. The cutting should be planted. The water should not be too shallow since frequent cutting weakens the plant. The plant requires plenty of light and will not adapt to water with much carbonate hardness. Propagation: cuttings, especialy those from trimming.

D: 4; KH: 2-8; pH: 6.0-7.0; T: 75-82° F (24-28° C); AH: 2.

Blyxa novoguineensis

Cardamine lyrata

Eichhornia azurea

1. Plants with upright stems
1.3. With alternating leaves

Heteranthera zosterifolia MARTIUS, 1823   Stargrass

Fam.: *Pontederiaceae*

Distribution: Northern Argentina; southern Brazil; Boliva: Paraguay.

A tall, bushy plant it is used mostly in background and side plantings. Opposing, linear-lanceolate light-green leaves have pointed tips, three thin longitudinal veins and are 1 $^1/_4$ to 2 inches long (3-5 cm.) and $^1/_4$-inch (0.4 cm.) wide. They are connected by a thin stem. The plant is easily grown with adequate light but requires regular pruning. Once it reaches the surface it develops many side-shoots and a low-growing variety may be considered an alternative. To plant, place short cuttings diagonally in an open, well-lighted area. These will produce creepers and develop a rich, cushion-like grouping. Propagation: cutting and self-propagation.

D: 2; KH: 3-15; pH: 6.0-7.5; T: 75-82° F (24-28° C); AH: 1-3.

Hydrocotyle leucocephala CHAMISSO et SCHLECHTENDAHL, 1826
                                                         Brazilia Pennywort

Fam.: *Apiaceae*

Distribution: Brazil.

Excellent for group plantings, the shape of its leaves and its light-green color contrast effectively with other plants. The submersed stem grows upright and its opposing, rounded, kidneyshaped leaves have a moderately sinuate edge 1 $^1/_4$ to 2 inches wide (3-5 cm.). It requires plenty of light but is otherwise tolerant of tank conditions. The fast-growing shoots must be cut back before it spreads to the surface reducing the light below. It should be planted sparingly, pruned often and can also be used as a low-growing bog plant. Propagation: cuttings and self-propagation.

D: 1; KH: 2-15; pH: 6.0-7.8; T: 68-82° F (20-28° C); AH: 2-3.

Lagarosiphon major MOSS, 1928

Fam.: *Hydrocharitaceae*   Syn.:*L. muscoides var. major, Elodea crispa*

Distribution: South Africa.

A true water plant suggested for aquariums with cooler water. The delicate stalk bears opposing leaves in tight spirals. The darkgreen leaves are linear, $^1/_2$ to $^3/_4$-inch long (1-2 cm.) and $^1/_{16}$-$^1/_8$ inch wide (0.2-0.3 cm.), with a finely-toothed edge. The leaves are bent back toward the shoots. It is often difficult to blend with other plants because of its rigid appearance. It does best in a shallow tank with bright lighting and is sometimes difficult to grow. In warmer water the leaves may be small and the stems thin. Cuttings should be reasonably spaced, planted in a group. Propagation: cuttings.

D: 2; KH: 5-12; pH: 6.8-8.0; T: 64-72° F (18-22° C); AH: 1-2.

Lobelia cardinalis LINNAEUS, 1753   Scarlet Lobelia-Cardinal Flower

Fam.: *Lobeliaceae*

Distribution: North America.

Its light-green, spatular leaves provide an excellent contrast with other plants and its somewhat rigid appearance can be softened by using plants of varying heights. It has a strong stem and the alternating leaves are 1 $^1/_2$ to 2 $^1/_2$-inches long (3,5-6 cm.) and $^3/_4$ to 1$^3/_4$-inch wide (2-3 cm.). The tips are blunted and the base extends into the stalk. Because it grows slowly it requires little attention. Shoots which reach the surface can be clipped and used as cuttings and will grow and produce still more cuttings. The cuttings should be well-spaced, planted in a brightly lighted area. The plant can be grown out of water and then produces large purple-red blooms. Propagation: cuttings and from side-shoots after cutting back.

D: 2; KH: 5-12; pH: 6.5-7.2; T: 72-79° F (22-26° C); AH: 2-3.

Heteranthera zosterifolia

Lagarosiphon major

Hydrocotyle leucocephala

Lobelia cardinalis

Mayaca fluviatilis AUBLET, 1775

Fam.: *Mayacaceae*   Syn.:*M. vandellii*

Distribution: Tropical and sub-tropical America.
A small, prostrate, fern-like recumbent bush found in bogs and shallow water. Its thin, submerged stem spirals tightly upward with alternating leaves. A loosely planted group looks well in the central and frontal areas of an aquarium but the plants should not be shaded since they require plenty of light. Prefers soft, salt-free water but can acclimate to harder water if carbonic acid is added. It is extremely sensitive to trypaflavine based medications. Propagation: cuttings and self-propagating.

D: 3; KH: 2-8; pH: 6.0-7.0; T: 75-79° F (24-26° C); AH: 1-2.

Potamogeton gayii BENNET, 1892

Fam.: *Potamogetonaceae*

Distribution: South America.
There are more than 100 species in the genus. Some are fully submerged and others have floating leaves. Only a few from warmer regions can be successfully kept in a tropical aquarium. The species above can tolerate a wide range of water temperatures and values though it needs medium to bright lighting. As the plant matures its thin stems will reach the surface and float. Alternating, linear, sessile brownish leaves are 2 to 4 inches long (5-10 cm.) and $^1/_{16}$-$^1/_8$-inch wide (0.2-0.4 cm.). They have short, pointed tips. Cuttings require time to root and settle-in but once acclimated grow rapidly and will spread via runners. Propagation: cuttings and runners.

D: 1; KH: 2-12; pH: 6.0-7.2; T: 68-86° F (20-30° C); AH: 1-3.

Proserpinaca pectinata LAMARCK, 1791

Fam.: *Haloragaceae*   Syn.: *Hottonia inflata* (Incorrectly identified)

Distribution: Southern United States.
A demanding group of plants recommended only for brightly-lighted tanks with the best of water conditions. The alternating lightgreen, pinnate leaves $^3/_4$ to 1 $^1/_4$-inch long (2-3 cm.) and $^1/_2$-inch wide (1 cm.) are found on a thin stem. Two rows of long, nearly equal crest like segments can be seen along the central axil. Bright light is essential and medium-hard water is preferred. Carbonic acid fertilizer is helpful if the KH is high. Its light-green, feather-like leaves make a nice contrast and a few small groups can be effective in the foreground of any tank. Plants should be topped regularly and the cuttings replanted. Propagation: cuttings, side-shoots and often self-propagating.

D: 3; KH: 2-10; pH: 5.5-7.0; T: 72-82° F (22-28° C); AH: 1-2.

Utricularia species   Tropical Bladder-wort

Fam.: *Lentibulariaceae*

Distribution: Southeast Asia.
This rootless species is one of several unidentified freefloating, finely-pinnate water plants. It is a fast-growing variety which can quickly take over an aquarium and thus requires regular thinning. Special organs, seen in the photo as light bubbles, trap miniscule pondlife such as infusoria, cyclops and daphnia and absorb the nutrients. The trapping mechanism is dangerous to fry and for this reason the plant is not suggested for breeding tanks. Occasionally the bladders may be missing for reasons not clearly understood. Propagation: side-shoots.

D: 1; KH: 2-15; pH: 6.0-7.2; T: 72-86° F (22-30° C); AH: 1-3.

Mayaca fluviatilis

Proserpinaca pectinata

Potamogeton gayii

Utricularia species

2. Plants with rosette leaves
2.1. Narrow-leaved rosettes

Acorus gramineus var. pusillus (SIEBOLDT) ENGLER, 1830

Japanese Rush-Dwarf Rush

Fam.: *Araceae*

Distribution: Asia; Japan.

While this is a popular choice for foreground plantings it does not do well submerged. Its dark-green, grass-like leaves 2 to 4 inches long (5-10 cm.) and $^3/_4$ to $1^1/_2$-inch wide (2-3 cm.) narrow to a point in the front and are arranged in a fan-like rosette. The plant, which can reach a height of 16 inches, will remain fresh for sometime if water temperatures are low but should be replaced eventually. The bog species found in the wild as well as the species above are well suited to a terrarium.

D: 4; KH: 2-10; pH: 6.0-6.5; T: 59-68° F (15-20° C); AH: 1-2.

Crinum thaianum SCHULTZE, 1971

Thai Onion Plant

Fam.: *Amaryllidaceae*

Distribution: Thailand.

A few plants provide a lasting green color either in the background or middle areas of a larger aquarium. The two-inch, long-necked bulb becomes a plant as tall as five feet (150 cm.), which limits its use. A well-rooted specimen can be cut back. The narrow, ribbon leaf is $^3/_4$-inch wide (2 cm.). The plant adapts well to an aquarium and is easier to care for than the Giant Vallisneria which has a similar appearance. Propagation: daughter bulbs a few at a time.

D: 1; KH: 2-15; pH: 6.0-8.0; T: 72-86° F (22-30° C); AH: 3.

Eleocharis parvula (ROEMER et SCHULTES) LINK, 1827

Hairgrass

Fam.: *Cyperaceae*

Distribution: Coastal regions of North America to Cuba; Europe; Africa.

An ornamental plant recommended for the foreground, it adapts well and does best in bright light. The slender rhizomes propagate by division and produce small rosettes at the joints of thin, thread-like, medium-green leaves $1^1/_2$ to $3^1/_4$-inches long (4-8 cm.). In time the numerous side-shoots will create a dense, "lawn-like" effect. Fading can be prevented by replanting. *Eleocharis acicularis* is a similar, but more angular plant with 10-inch (25 cm.) leaves. Propagation: runners. The plant grows fairly rapidly.

D: 2; KH: 2-15; pH: 5.8-7.5; T: 68-82° F (20-28° C); AH: 1-3.

Acorus gramineus var. pusillus

Crinum thaianum

Eleocharis parvula

2. Plants with rosette leaves
2.1. Narrow-leaved rosettes

Eleocharis vivipara LINK, 1827   Umbrella Grass
Fam.: *Cyperaceae*   Syn.: *E. prolifera*
Distribution: Eastern United States: Virginia; North Carolina to Florida.
A short plant with a rosette of thread-like stems 16 to 24 inches long (40-60 cm.) and less than $^1/_4$-inch thick (0.5 cm.). It has a tiny leaf producing an adventitious bud at the axil. These and young shoots occur frequently so the plant spreads quickly. Grows best in soft water with medium-bright light. When planted in groups it needs room for expansion. Propagation: from adventitious plants which can be separated.

D: 2; KH: 5-12; pH: 6.0-7.0; T: 72-82° F (22-28° C); AH: 2-3.

Sagittaria graminea MICHAUX, 1803 *var. graminea*   Grassy Arrowhead
Fam.: *Alismataceae*   Syn.: *S. eatonii*
Distribution: Eastern United States to Texas.
A variable bog plant with lanceolate leaves seen most often below the surface. The juvenile form is best for an aquarium. Rosette leaves are sometimes broad and spoon-shaped but more often blunt or pointed, between 6 and 10 inches long (15-25 cm.) and to $^1/_2$-inch wide (1 cm.). Five longitudinal veins extend from the narrow base, three ending in the tip. Under a bright light leaves near the middle will turn down; without it the leaves grow upright. Plants are best grouped loosely in the foreground or center of a tank. Propagation: runners.

D: 1; KH: 5-15; pH: 6.5-7.5; T: 72-79° F (22-26° C); AH: 1-3.

Sagittaria subulata var. pusilla (NUTTALL) BUCHENAU, 1903
         Dwarf Arrowhead - Dwarf Sag
Fam.: *Alismataceae*
Distribution: Eastern North America.
A particularly hardy plant used for scale in the forground. Its low rosettes are without a stalk and its linear leaves, 2 to 6 inches long (5-15 cm.) and $^1/_4$-inch wide (0.4 cm.) have three veins. The central vein ends at the blunt tip. It can do well even when conditions are less than perfect and will tolerate very hard water. Grows best with bright light but will do well with less. With adequate lighting it quickly proliferates to create a green, carpet-like "lawn". When planting allow room for growth. Propagation: numerous runners.

D: 1; KH: 2-15; pH: 6.0-7.8; T: 72-86° F (22-30° C); AH: 1-3.

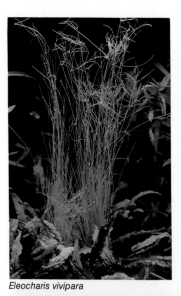

Eleocharis vivipara

Sagittaria graminea

Sagittaria subulata var. pusilla

2. Plants with rosette leaves
2.1. Narrow-leaved rosettes

Sagittaria subulata var. subulata (LINNAEUS) BUCHENAU, 1871   Floating Arrowhead
Fam.: *Alismataceae*   Syn.: *S. lorata*

Distribution: Coastal areas of the eastern U.S.
Many variations can be found. Its linear, full-edged leaves 7 $^3/_4$ to 11 $^3/_4$-inches long (20-30 cm.) and $^1/_4$-inch wide (0.4 cm.) have three veins, the outer two ending at the blunt tip. In an aquarium the leaves rarely reach the surface but do produce blooms, several whorls of white flowers on long, slender floating stems. This undemanding plant thrives in many types of water, and in moderate light. It is suggested as a background plant in areas where Vallisneria is either too tall or will not flourish. Propagation: numerous runners.

D: 1; KH: 2-15; pH: 6.0-7.8; T: 72-82° F (22-28° C); AH: 1-3.

Vallisneria asiatica var. biwaensis MIKI, 1934   Corkscrew
Fam.: *Hydrocharitaceae*   Syn.: *V. spiralis f. tortifolia*

Distribution: Japan; Lake Biwa; Yodo river.
These plants contrast well with others in a tank and can be used alone or to define and outline areas. A plant with rhizomes, its dark-green, corkscrew-like leaves are 11 $^3/_4$ to 16 inches long (30-40 cm.). The leaves, which twist tightly, need plenty of light and should not be shaded by floating plants. At low light levels the spirals become less pronounced and fewer in number. When planting use 8 to 10 plants spaced two inches apart. Keep them low. The plant adapts well but may not flourish in soft water. Propagation: runners and daughter plants.

D: 2; KH: 5-12; pH: 6.0-7.2; T: 75-82° F (24-28° C); AH: 1-3.

Vallisneria gigantea GRAEBNER, 1912   Giant Vallis
Fam.: *Hydrocharitaceae*

Distribution: New Guinea; Philippines.
These stately, long-lived plants look best at the rear of a large, tall aquarium. Dark-green, ribbon-like, fleshy leaves rising from a rhizome, have rounded tips, coarse, toothed edges and are more than 39 inches long (100 cm.) Sometimes difficult to grow, the plants do best in a mix of fine gravel. Yellow leaves indicate an iron deficiency and higher temperatures become a problem as the water becomes softer. The thin, floating leaves may reduce light below so watch the tank closely. Propagation: daughter plants.

D: 2; KH: 5-15; pH: 6.0-7.2; T: 64-82° F (18-28° C); AH: 3.

Vallisneria spiralis LINNAEUS, 1753   Straight Vallis
Fam.: *Hydrocharitaceae*

Distribution: Tropic and sub-tropical regions.
While the original habitat was North Africa and portions of southern Europe, the plant has been introduced worldwide. It has become one of the best known of aquarium plants and is ideal as a background in a larger tank. Its ribbon like leaves 15 $^1/_2$ to 24 inches long (40-60 cm.) and $^3/_{16}$-$^1/_4$-inch wide (0.4-0.7 cm.) often spiral. A fine toothed-edge and blunt tips differ from the spoon-edged leaves found on Sagittaria. The plant grows fast, adapts well and is suited to cold water. Problems which stem from being contained in the same space long can be avoided by repotting or replanting. Propagation: runners, daughter plants.

D: 1; KH: 5-12; pH: 6.5-7.5; T: 59-86° F (15-30° C); AH: 2-3.

Sagittaria subulata var. subulata

Vallisneria gigantea

Vallisneria asiatica var. biwaensis

Vallisneria spiralis

2. Plants with rosette leaves
2.2. Broad-leaved rosettes

Anubias barteri var. glabra BROWN, 1901

Fam.: *Araceae*   Syn.: *A. lanceolata*

Distribution: Tropical western Africa.
A robust, undemanding, long-lived plant, it has firm, lanceolate dark-green leaves 5 $^3/_4$ to $9^3/_4$-inches long (15-25 cm.) and 2 to $3^1/_4$-inches wide (5-8 cm.). The central vein has numerous capillaries. Under favorable conditions the plant may reach heights of 16 to 20 inches. Adults require moderate lighting and young plants need more. A slow growing plant, it takes time to acclimate and requires fertilizer. Fertilizing before planting is recommended. Propagation: division of rhizomes, side-shoots.

D: 2; KH: 2-15; pH: 6.0-7.5; T: 64-82° F (18-28° C); AH: 2-3.

Anubias barteri var. nana (ENGLER) CRUSIO, 1979

Fam.: *Araceae*   Syn.: *A. nana*

Distribution: West Africa.
Possibly the smallest of the genus, the plant reaches a maximum height of four inches in an aquarium. It is ideal for use in the foreground. The species can be identified by its short-stemmed, dark-green leaves about four inches long and 2 inch wide. Growing horizontally it produces side-shoots which give it a bushy look. It is not demanding but does require a moderate light. Propagation: side-shoots from the rhizome.

D: 2; KH: 2-15; pH: 6.0-7.5; T: 72-82° F (22-28° C); AH: 1-3.

Barclaya longifolia WALLICH, 1827   Orchid Lily

Fam.: *Nymphaeaceae*

Distribution: Burma; Andaman Is.; southern Thailand; Vietnam.
Features a small, cylindrical corm with leaves in a rosette. The long-stalked, lanceolate leaves, 4 to 8 inches long and $^1/_2$ to 1 inch wide (1-2 cm.), can be found in two color variations. An olive-green form will adapt to moderate light and grow to 16 inches (40 cm.). A deep red-leaved variety is lower and wider and does best under strong light. The latter will bloom easily in an aquarium. The number of flowers depends on the light and though they may open under water, the buds normally open above it. In a deep tank the flowers may not open but will produce seeds capable of germination. Propagation: easy from seed and from side-shoots separated from the rhizome.

D: 2; KH: 2-12; pH: 6.0-7.0; T: 72-82° F (22-28° C); AH: 1-3.

Anubias barteri var. glabra

Barclaya longifolia

Anubias barteri var. nana

2. Plants with rosette leaves
2.2. Broad-leaved rosettes

Nuphar pumila (TIMM) DE CANDOLLE, 1818   Spatterdock Dwarf Water Lily

Fam.: *Nymphaeaceae*

Distribution: Central and eastern Europe; western Siberia.
An aquatic plant with both floating and submersed leaves found in lakes, ponds and ditches in 20 to 60 feet of cool, clear water. It cannot stand the higher temperatures normal in an aquarium, but otherwise adapts well and is even suitable for a smaller tank, reaching a height of $7^1/_2$-inches. Its light-green leaves about $4^3/_4$-inches long (12 cm.) and to $3^1/_4$ inches wide (8 cm.) contrast nicely with other plants in an aquarium. Place in coarse gravel with the rhizome upright. Remove any questionable, soft or rotten parts of the rhizome before planting. It does best in an open area with moving water. Remove leaves as they reach the surface. Propagation: side-shoots at the rhizome.

D: 2; KH: 2-15; pH: 6.0-7.2; T: 64-72° F (18-22° C); AH: 1-3.

Nymphaea lotus LINNAEUS, 1753   Tiger Lotus

Fam.: *Nymphaeaceae*

Distribution: East Africa; southeast Asia.
A species with two submerged forms which varies in color and shape. It can be found with green leaves streaked with red or with red leaves streaked with darker red. The leaves, 4 to $7^1/_4$-inches (10-18 cm.) long and $3^1/_4$ to 4 inches wide (8-10 cm.), are on long stalks with their base deeply cleft. With bright light the plant growth is more compact. To keep submerged leaves healthy, remove those which float but leave floating leaves when you wish blossoms, sweetly-scented white flowers with yellow centers. Fruit may even form after self-pollination. Propagation: seeds, daughter plants on short runners.

D: 2; KH: 4-12; pH: 5.5-7.5; T: 72-82° F (22-28° C); AH: 2-3.

Nymphoides aquatica (WALTER) O. KUNTZE, 1891   Banana Plant

Fam.: *Gentianaceae*

Distribution: Florida and other areas of the southeastern U.S.
A popular plant, it does not survive long in an aquarium. The bushy, green, club-like plant has projecting roots which store nourishment and when propagating roots should not be buried but placed on top where they will root by themselves. The submerged leaves are heart-shaped to 4 inches in length (10 cm.) and on short stalks. At the surface floating leaves are larger, to 6 inches (15 cm.) across. Small, yellow blooms with fringed petals will grow from the stalk. Adventitious plants will appear without the "bananas". Leaves are sometimes available from suppliers. These may be floated on cool water and brought to bloom. Propagation: adventitious plants.

D: 2; KH: 5-10; pH: 6.5-7.2; T: 68-86° F (20-30° C); AH: 1-2.

Nuphar pumila

Nymphaea lotus

Nymphoides aquatica

Ottelia alismoides LINNAEUS, 1753

Fam.: *Hydrocharitaceae*

Distribution: Tropical and sub-tropical zones; Africa; Asia; Australia.
A rare, demanding plant which does not readily adjust to carbonate hardness. It does best in a rich soil with bright light. Yellow-green, stalked leaves can be seen in rosettes to 14 inches (35 cm.). The leaf is rounded to heart-shaped $4^3/_4$ to $8^3/_4$-inches long (12-22 cm.) with edges curving sharply inward. The leaf base is triangular and toothed. There can be as many as 11 longitudinal veins with the tissue between them convex. Fragile and sensitive to rough handling, it is suggested for aquariums with peaceful fish. Often blooms above water with inconspicuous fruit. Propagation: difficult even with seed.

D: 4; KH: 2-6; pH: 5.5-6.8; T: 75-79° F (24-26° C); AH: 2-3.

Samolus parviflorus RAFINESQUE, 1815/25   Water Cabbage, Green Water Rose

Fam.: *Primulaceae*   Syn.: *S. floribundus*

Distribution: North America; West Indies; South America.
A foreground plant growing to four inches (10 cm.) and recommended for group plantings. Though difficult and somewhat delicate, it provides excellent contrast in many aquariums. Light-green, spatular, stalked leaves $2^1/_2$ to 4 inches long (6-10 cm.) and $1^1/_4$ to 2 inches wide (3-5 cm.) grow in rosettes from the base. With bright lighting and warm water it grows well and remains healthy a long time. Does best in well fertilized medium-sized gravel and in an open, unshaded spot. When planted in groups allow space between plants. Can be grown out of water where it will bloom, bear fruit and produce seed. Propagation: not under water.

D: 3; KH: 5-12; pH: 6.5-7.5; T: 68-75° F (20-24° C); AH: 1-2.

Spathiphyllum wallisii REGEL, 1877

Fam.: *Araceae*

Distribution: Colombia.
Not everyone feels this is a plant for an aquarium since it is difficult to grow in a small tank. It can survive for as long as six months then generally dies though it may do better when wellrooted specimens are potted. The pots can be concealed with rocks or other decorations. Should be planted alone in tanks with large, active fish. Replace as necessary.

D: 1; KH: 2-15; pH: 6.0-8.0; T: 64-82° F (18-28° C); AH: 2-3.

Samolus parviflorus

Spathiphyllum wallisii

Ottelia alismoides

Echinodorus amazonicus RATAJ, 1970   Amazon Sword Plant
Fam.: *Alismataceae*   Syn.: *E. brevipedicellatus*
Distribution: Brazil.
A medium-sized loner about 16-inches in height and ideal as a decorative highlight. Light-green linear, lanceolate leaves have a slight sword-like bend and are 12 to 16 inches long (30-40 cm.) and $^3/_4$ to $1^1/_4$-inches wide (2-3 cm.). Three veins extending from the base to the tip are visible and two less prominent ones can be found which are closer to the edges. The plant is often confused with E. **bleheri** which is more widely distributed. It does not grow well in water with extreme carbonate hardness and prefers medium-bright lighting, well-heated water and a mediumfine gravel bed. When a plant becomes long-stalked it should be thinned. Propagation: adventitious shoots.

D: 2; KH: 2-12; pH: 6.5-7.2; T: 74-82° F (24-28° C); AH: 2-3.

Echinodorus berteroi (SPRENGLER) FASSETT, 1955   Cellophane Plant
Fam.: *Alismataceae*   Syn.: *E. rostratus*
Distribution: Southern North America; West Indies.
Though it is an interesting aquarium plant with a variable leaf, it does not live long. The immature form has stalkless, narrow, pointed leaves. The mature form has heart-shaped leaves $7^1/_4$ to 12 inches long (20-30 cm.) and $1^1/_4$ to $1^1/_2$-inches wide (3-4 cm.) with bright yellow veins. As long floating leaves appear those underwater may disappear. The incidence of floating leaves can be minimized by reducing fertilizer and restricting lighting to less than 12 hours daily. Regular thinning of the leaves will also keep the plant submerged. Propagation: moderately successful with side-shoots from rhizomes.

D: 3; KH: 2-12; pH: 6.5-7.0; T: 68-79° F (20-26° C); AH: 2-3.

Echinodorus bleheri RATAJ, 1970   Broad-leaved Amazon Sword Plant
Fam.: *Alismataceae*   Syn.: *E. paniculatus, E. rangeri*
Distribution: Tropical South America.
The most common plant of this genus, it is an excellent, durable, thickly-leaved selection for any aquarium. Can be used alone as a highlight in smaller tanks and, when there is space, in groups. Dark-green, lanceolate leaves are 12 to 20 inches long (30-50 cm.) and $1^1/_2$ to $3^1/_4$-inches wide (4-8 cm.). Both ends of the leaf are pointed and two inner longitudinal veins extend from a point near the end of the central vein with two other veins seen near the base. Numerous cross veins may be brown. A hardy plant, it will do well in hard water with medium-bright light. The leaves will become yellow when lacking in iron. Propagation: adventitious plants.

D: 2; KH: 2-15; pH: 6.5-7.5; T: 75-82° F (24-28° C); AH: 3.

Echinodorus maior (MICHELI) RATAJ, 1967   Ruffled Sword Plant
Fam.: *Alismataceae*   Syn.: *E. martii, E. leopoldina*
Distribution: Brazil.
A stately, imposing plant best used singly in a large aquarium. Light-green, short-stalked, lanceolate leaves 16 to 20 inches long (40-50 cm.) and $1^1/_2$ to $3^1/_4$ inches wide (4-8 cm.) have ruffled edges and blunted ends. Two lateral veins extend from a central one with two more at the base. Requires a medium-bright light, an open area and well-fertilized, loose, fine gravel. Keep the water temperature even. A rigid stalk may tower as much as 40 inches above the water when the plant is ready to flower. You will see a number of blooms and even fruit after artificial pollination. Propagation: can be done from seed or via adventitious plants planted in the substrata.

D: 2; KH: 2-12; pH: 6.5-7.2; T: 75-82° F (24-28° C); AH: 3.

Echinodorus amazonicus

Echinodorus bleheri

Echinodorus berteroi

Echinodorus maior

2. Plants with leaves in rosettes
2.3. Amazon plants (Echinodorus)

Echinodorus cordifolius (LINNAEUS) GRISEBACH, 1857   Radican Sword

Fam.: *Alismataceae*   Syn.: *E. radicans*

Distribution: Central and southern North America; Mexico.

An undemanding plant it is ideal when used singly in larger tanks. Its blunt-ended, heart-shaped leaves are 7 $1/4$ to 10 inches long (20-25 cm.) and 4 to 6 inches wide (10-15 cm.). The leaves can be a spotted, reddish color with a visible longitudinal vein extending from the base. Floating leaves should be removed to allow those under water to develop. As the plant grows you may want to prune its roots to reduce the intake of nutrients and limit the growth. The powerful stalk will produce large white blooms above water and fruit may form after pollination. Propagation: remove and plant adventitious shoots from the stalk as they appear at the surface.

D: 2; KH: 5-15; pH: 6.5-7.5; T: 72-82° F (22-28° C); AH: 2-3.

Echinodorus horizontalis RATAJ, 1969

Fam.: *Alismataceae*   Syn.: *E. guianensis, E. muricatus*

Distribution: Northern South America; Amazon basin.

A compact plant of medium-height recommended for use alone in a larger aquarium. Typical of the species, the leaves are held almost horizontally from the stem. Dark-green to reddish-brown, heart-shaped leaves are found on short stalks 6 to 7$1/4$-inches long (15-20 cm.) and 2 to 4 inches wide (5-10 cm.) with 5 to 7 primary veins extending from the base. The plant is easily distinguished from *E. cordifolius* by its pointed shape. With bright light it adapts well to most tanks. It does not produce floating leaves and may require time to become adjusted. Blooms are often seen just above the surface. Propagation: adventitious plants separated and planted.

D: 2; KH: 5-12; pH: 6.5-7.2; T: 72-82° F (22-28° C); AH: 2-3.

Echinodorus cordifolius

Echinodorus horizontalis

Echinodorus osiris RATAJ, 1970   Red Amazon Sword

Fam.: *Alismataceae*   Syn.: *E. osiris rubra, E. aureobrunata.*

Distribution: Southern Brazil.

A hardy plant suggested for use alone in very hard water. It reaches heights of 16 to 20 inches and makes an excellent decorative highlight. When immature the leaves are reddish, 12 to 16 inches long (30-40 cm.) and 1 $^1/_2$ to 2 inches wide (4-5 cm.). The leaves have noticeable longitudinal and cross veins and the edges are ruffled. The plant is not demanding about the intensity of light but with bright light needs fertilizing. No open blooms have been observed in an aquarium. Propagation: separate adventitious plants from the stalks, sideshoots from rhizomes.

D: 2-3; KH: 5-15; pH: 6.5-7.5; T: 72-82° F (22-28° C); AH: 2-3.

Echinodorus osiris

Echinodorus parviflorus RATAJ, 1970

Fam.: *Alismataceae*   Syn.:*E. peruensis, E. tocantins.*

Distribution: South America; Peru; Bolivia.
Popular with connoisseurs, the plant adapts well to many tanks. It can be used alone in smaller tanks or in groups in a larger tank where its medium-height helps conceal the stems of taller plants behind it. Thickly-leaved with compact rosettes, it does well in moderate light. It does not do well in coarse gravel. The dark-green, short-stalked leaves vary in size and shape but are lanceolate 6 to $7^1/_4$-inches long (15-20 cm.) and $^3/_4$ to 2 inches wide (2-5 cm.). Short, narrow, brownish cross-veins can be seen between five main veins which proceed from the base. The bottom of the leaf may be pointed or round. Propagation: adventitious plants. Reduce the water level when planting.

D: 1; KH: 2-15; pH: 6.0-7.8; T: 72-82° F (22-28° C); AH: 1-3.

Echinodorus parviflorus

2.   Plants with leaves in rosettes
2.3. Amazon plants (Echinodorus)

Echinodorus quadricostatus var. xinguensis RATAJ, 1970   Dwarf Sword Plant
Fam.: *Alismataceae*   Syn.: *E. intermedius*

Distribution: Brazil; Para, Xingu rivers.
An excellent plant for use in the foreground of all sizes of tanks. The height varies from 2 to 6 inches (5-15 cm.) depending on light and the plant itself. Light-green lanceolate, longstalked, pointed leaves are 2 to 6 inches long (5-15 cm.) and $1/4$ to $1/2$-inch wide (0.5-1.0 cm.). Several difficult to see lateral veins curve from a central vein. The plant adapts well to differing intensities of light but does not grow well in coarse gravel. The leaves become yellow with iron deficiency. Since the plant grows fast use only a few well-separated specimens at first. As these expand occasionally thin the grouping and trim roots. Propagation: from runners.

D: 1; KH: 2-12; pH: 6.5-7.5; T: 72-82° F (22-28° C); AH: 1-3.

Echinodorus tenellus (MARTIUS) BUCHENAU, 1869   Junior Sword Plant, Pygmy
Chain Sword
Fam.: *Alismataceae.*

A small plant recommended for a lawn-like foreground. Since this one sends out many runners the original plantings should be spaced well apart. Thin the plants as needed. It is a pretty plant with thin roots and narrow, pointed, grassy leaves with a single vein and can be distinguished from *E. tenellus var. tenellus* by dark-green to occasionally reddish leaves 3 $1/4$ to 5 inches long (8-12 cm.) and $1/8$-inch wide (0.2 cm.). *E. tenellus var. parvulus* adapts better to brighter lights and harder water. The latter's bright green leaves are 1 $1/4$ to 3$1/4$-inches long (3-8 cm.) and $1/8$-inch wide. It is a more demanding plant requiring brighter light and is not recommended for harder water. Propagation: numerous runners.

Echinodorus tenellus is seen in the left foreground. The plant in the center is a rare water orchid *Spiranthes cernua* L.C. RICHARD, 1818. It reaches a height of 6 inches (15 cm.).

D: 1-2; KH: 2-15; pH: 6.5-7.2; T: 72-86° F (22-30° C); AH: 1-2.

Echinodorus quadricostatus var. xinguensis

Echinodorus tenellus (left in the foreground)

2. Plants with leaves in rosettes
2.4. Aponogetons

Aponogeton boivinianus BAILLON ex JUMELLE, 1922

Fam.: *Aponogetonaceae*

Distribution: Northern Malagasy.

Generally used alone in the central area of a larger aquarium. The plant will outgrow a shallow tank. A round, disc-shaped corm with dark-green leaves 14 to 18 inches long (30-45 cm.) and 1 1/4 to 2 1/2-inches wide (3-6 cm.). Even in hard water it will produce many leaves. To reproduce, the corm should be placed level in loose, fine gravel. In a heavily-planted tank the size of the plant is reduced. Needs plenty of light. Propagation: difficult from seed. Produces a spike of sterile white flowers.

D: 2; KH: 2-12; pH: 6.5-7.5; T: 68-79° F (20-26° C); AH: 2-3.

Aponogeton crispus THUNBERG, 1781   Crinkled or Ruffled Aponogeton

Fam.: *Aponogetonaceae*

Distribution: Sri Lanka.

A well known, decorative plant which adapts well and grows rapidly. Its leaves, from dark to olive-green in color, have rippled edges and are 7 1/4 to 16 inches long (20-40 cm.) and 1/2 to 1 1/2-inches wide (1-4 cm.). A floating plant, it will grow toward a light source producing long-stalked leaves in weaker light. It flowers easily in an aquarium and can be artificially pollinated with a cotton swab or small brush or by submerging the single spike of white flowers with a feeding ring, allowing it to resurface. The fruit matures in two months. Propagation: easy from seed. The flowers are fertile.

D: 2; KH: 2-15; pH: 6.5-7.2; T: 72-86° F (22-30° C); AH: 2-3.

Aponogeton elongatus MUELLER ex BENTHAM, 1878   Elongated Aponogeton

Fam.: *Aponogetonaceae*

Distribution: Northern and eastern Australia.

One of the few Australian water plants which look well in an aquarium, this fast-growing, thick-leaved plant of medium height (about 16 inches; 40 cm.) is best when used alone. Its light green leaves with ruffled edges are 12 to 16 inches long (30-40 cm.) and 1 1/4 to 2 inches wide (3-5 cm.) and found on short stalks. Several varieties are available. The plant shown here is *A. e. forma latifolius*. *A. ulvaceus* is similar but not as brightly colored. The plant is easy to grow and can survive in hard water with the addition of CO_2. Propagation: from seed though difficult. A single, yellow-green flower spike is sterile.

D: 2; KH: 2-12; pH: 6.0-7.5; T: 72-79° F (22-26° C); AH: 2-3.

Aponogeton boivinianus

Aponogeton crispus

Aponogeton elongatus

2. Plants with leaves in rosettes
2.4. Aponogetons

Aponogeton madagascariensis (MIRBEL) VAN BRUGGEN, 1968   **Laceleaf Plant**

Fam.: *Aponogetonaceae*   Syn.: *A. fenestralis*

Distribution: Malagasy.

An odd water plant, the leaves lack tissue with only a network of veins visible which give it both a lacey appearance and its name. To grow well it requires soft, clear, moving water free of lime and within the suggested temperatures. It prefers a slightly acid pH and moderate to minimal lighting. The tank should be free of algae since it will destroy the leaves. The narrow-leaved variety survives longer in an aquarium. Propagation: difficult from seed. The white flowers are fertile.

D: 4; KH: 2-3; pH: 5.5-6.5; T: 68-72° F (20-22° C); AH: 1-3.

Aponogeton ulvaceus BAKER, 1881

Fam.: *Aponogetonaceae*

Distribution: Malagasy.

It is extremely decorative when used alone. The smooth, round, brown corm produces short-stalked, wavy light-green leaves 12 to 16 inches long (30-40 cm.) and 1 $^1/_2$ to 2 $^1/_2$ inches wide (4-6 cm.). A fast-growing plant, it prefers moderate lighting and increases height with brigher lighting. Periods of busy leaf and flower development are followed by a pause when nearly all leaves are shed. To propagate clean the corm and place it on the substrata. Replant in two or three months. A yellow flower spike is generally sterile. Can be propagated from seed.

D: 2; KH: 2-15; pH: 5.5-7.0; T: 72-82° F (22-28° C); AH: 2-3.

Aponogeton undulatus ROXBURGH, 1824

Fam.: *Aponogetonaceae*

Distribution: India; Bangladesh; Burma.

An unusual feature of the plant is its different manner of propagation. The stalk, which normally bears the flower, develops an adventitious plant in the form of a rooted corm. This can be separated and planted. When mature, the plant may reach a height of 12 to 16 inches (30-40 cm.). Its dark-green leaves are generally long-stemmed with ruffled edges. The amount of ruffling depends on the intensity of the light. The leaf is darkest close to the broad central vein. It adapts well to hard water but needs periods of "rest" when growth is slowed. Propagation: adventitious plants. Flowers are rarely seen.

D: 2; KH: 5-15; pH: 6.0-7.5; T: 72-82° F (22-28° C); AH: 2-3.

Aponogeton madagascariensis

Aponogeton ulvaceus

Aponogeton undulatus

2. Plants with leaves in rosettes
2.5 Cryptocorynes

Cryptocoryne affinis BROWN ex HOOKER fil., 1893

Fam.: *Araceae*   Syn.: *C. haerteliana*

Distribution: Malaysia.

For many aquarists this is considered the best known of the genus. It adapts well to tanks preferring moderate to low levels of light. Extremely decorative, it has lighter green leaves with velvety-green undersides. It grows quickly, the rate depending on light, reaching heights between 4 and 12 inches (10-30 cm.) and thus can be used in many ways in a tank. It is somewhat sensitive to changes in light, temperature and water conditions and is prone to cryptocoryne-leaf disease. Propagation: very productive via runners.

D: 2; KH: 3-15; pH: 6.0-7.8: T: 72-82° F (22-28° C); AH: 1-3.

Cryptocoryne balansae GAGNEPAIN, 1941

Fam.: *Araceae*

Distribution: Thailand; north Vietnam; Tonkin.

The plant has unusual, narrow leaves with a "drawn" and dimpled surface. Growth depends on lighting and the leaves are 7 $^1/_4$ to 16 inches long (20-40 cm.) and to $^1/_2$-inch wide (1 cm.) tapering toward the tip. The plant needs a loose gravel bed, medium bright lighting and relatively hard water to grow well. A well separated grouping should do well with the leaves emphasizing the shape of the plant. Propagation: from runners. May be difficult at first but becomes easier as the plant matures.

D: 3; KH: 2-12; pH: 6.5-7.2: T: 77-82° F (25-28° C); AH: 1-3.

Cryptocoryne ciliata (ROXBURGH), SCHOTT, 1832

Fam.: *Araceae*

Distribution: Southeast Asia.

It looks best in a group and since it grows slowly it should be planted heavily from the start. The medium-green lanceolate leaves have pointed tips with a wedge-shaped base, formed laterally on a round stalk. They are 11 $^3/_4$ inches long (30 cm.) and to 1$^1/_2$-inches wide (4 cm.). *C. ciliata var. latifolia* is a different variety with heart-shaped leaves 4 to 6 inches long and to 2 inches wide (5 cm.). The latter is a more compact plant about 7 $^1/_4$ high. It is not demanding in terms of water but does best with frequent water changes. Requires less light than many floating plants. Propagation: infrequent runners and occasionally from short shoots in the leaf axils.

D: 2; KH: 5-12; pH: 6.5-7.5: T: 72-82° F (22-28° C); AH: 2-3.

Cryptocoryne petchii ALSTON, 1931

Fam.: *Araceae*

Distribution: Sri Lanka.

A medium-sized plant, it is popular for group plantings in both the front and center planes of an aquarium. It adapts well to most conditions, grows fast and reproduces readily. Shortstalked, lanceolate leaves have ruffled edges with dark cross markings and are 3 $^1/_4$ to 4$^1/_2$-inches long (8-12 cm.) and to $^1/_2$-inch wide (1 cm.). The leaf color varies from brownish-green to dark olive with red undersides, depending on the intensity of the light. The leaves will not show a true green even with low intensity lighting so that the plant remains an excellent contrast against greener plants. Abrupt changes in lighting can bring on disease. Propagation: from runners.

D: 2; KH: 2-15; pH: 6.5-7.5: T: 75-86° F (24-30° C); AH: 1-3.

Cryptocoryne affinis

Cryptocoryne ciliata

Cryptocoryne balansae

Cryptocoryne petchii

Cryptocoryne purpurea RIDLEY, 1902

Fam.: *Araceae*   Syn.: *C. griffithii*

Distribution: Malaysia.

Beautiful underwater blooms make this crypt popular with many aquarists. The spike can be $7\frac{1}{4}$-inches long (20 cm.) with a reddish-purple flower. Plants hardy enough to bloom do best with minimum lighting over a shorter-than-normal period and in fertilized gravel warmed to water temperature. The occasionally long-stalked leaves, an elongated oval in shape, are reddish with purple veins beneath. Propagation: runners.

D: 3; KH: 2-12; pH: 5.5-6.8; T: 79-82° F (26-28° C); AH: 1-3.

Cryptocoryne crispatula ENGLER, 1920

Fam.: *Araceae*

Distribution: Southeast Asia.

Dark-green, ribbon-like leaves $\frac{1}{2}$-inch wide and as much as 24 inches in length are a unique feature of this plant and because of its obvious size it is restricted to larger aquariums. In shallow tanks the leaves will surface and float with little decorative effect. The plant is undemanding but requires a medium-bright light. It is readily propagated and spreads rapidly. It flowers best with less than 12 hours of light per day and also blooms above water. Propagation: abundant shoots.

D: 1; KH: 2-15; pH: 6.0-7.5; T: 77-82° F (25-28° C); AH: 3.

Cryptocoryne siamensis GAGNEPAIN, 1941

Fam.: *Araceae*

Distribution: Thailand.

When used in groups its red-brown leaves constrast effectively with greener vegetation. Its egg-shaped leaves $2\frac{3}{4}$ to 4 inches long (7-10 cm.) and $1\frac{1}{4}$ to $1\frac{1}{2}$-inches wide (3-4 cm.) are marked with dark-red veins. The plant resembles *C. blassii* though the latter has broader, heart-shaped leaves. It does best with moderate lighting, relatively low water hardness and a loose, fertilized, warm gravel bed. It will require some time to acclimate to a new tank. Well-rooted plants produce the most shoots and eventually create a decorative grouping. Propagation: runners.

D: 3; KH: 2-8; pH: 6.0-7.0; T: 77-82 ° F (25-28° C); AH: 1-3

Cryptocoryne purpurea

Cryptocoryne crispatula

Cryptocoryne siamensis

Cryptocoryne usteriana ENGLER, 1905

Fam.: *Araceae*   Syn.: *C. aponogetifolia*

Distribution: Philippines.

With its wrinkled leaves this plant resembles *Aponogeton* which accounts for the fact that that name is used as a synonym. Extremely hardy and adaptable, the plant produces long-stemmed leaves 20 to 40 inches long (50-100 cm.) and 1 $^1/_4$ to 2 inches wide (3-5 cm.). Because of its size and spreading roots it requires considerable space and is suggested only for larger, deeper tanks where it looks best at the back or sides. Propagation: shoots, which are plentiful on older plants.

D: 1; KH: 5-15; pH: 6.0-7.8; T: 75-82 ° F (22-28° C); AH: 3.

Cryptocoryne walkeri SCHOTT, 1857

Fam.: *Araceae*

Distribution: Sri Lanka.

Of medium-height the plant adapts well, propagates readily and is used most in foreground settings. Lanceolate green leaves 3 $^1/_4$ to 4 $^3/_4$-inches long (8-12 cm.) and $^1/_2$ to 2 inches wide (1-2 cm.) are sometimes found with brown areas near the center vein. They may be green to red on the underside. The plant is undemanding and new specimens do well after they are acclimated. A few well-spaced plants soon become an attractive grouping. Occasional thinning will improve appearance and promote growth. Propagation: numerous shoots.

D: 1; KH: 2-15; pH: 6.0-7.5; T: 75-86° F (22-30° C); AH: 1-3.

Cryptocoryne wendtii DE WIT, 1958

Fam.: *Araceae*

Distribution: Sri Lanka.

A tall plant 12 to 16 inches in height (30-40 cm.) it is effective in groups as a background. There are several varieties and the basic type has lanceolate leaves 4 to 6 inches long (10-15 cm.) and 1 to 1 $^1/_4$-inches wide (2-3 cm.). The base of the leaf is rounded, the end is pointed and the edge is often ruffled. The color of the upper side ranges from olive green to green but occasionally has brownish mottled tones. It is a popular aquarium plant and adapts well to many types of tanks and even to moderate lighting. Fast-growing runners quickly develop into dense growths. Be certain to avoid sharp changes in water temperatures and lighting since this can promote leaf disease. Propagation: numerous shoots.

D: 1; KH: 5-15; pH: 6.5-7.5; T: 75-82° F (24-28° C); AH: 1-3.

Cryptocoryne willisii REITZ, 1908

Fam.: *Araceae*   Syn.:*C. nevillii*

Distribution: Sri Lanka.

A hardy, low-growing plant suitable for most tanks, it is used mostly in the foreground. Its green lanceolate leaves are 1 $^1/_4$ to 2 inches long (3-5 cm.) and $^1/_4$ to $^1/_2$-inch wide (0.5-0.8 cm.). Several plants have a similar appearance but are not normally found in home aquariums (*C. parva, C. lucens*). When utilized as a grouping, plant a dozen or so close together. The plant is easily propagated and will grow well if it is not disturbed. Needs good lighting and can tolerate cooler water but does best within the suggested temperature range. The nomenclature was recently changed by the Danish botanist N. Jakobsen. Propagation: shoots.

D: 1; KH: 2-15; pH: 6.5-7.2; T: 72-86° F (22-30° C); AH: 1-3

Cryptocoryne usteriana

Cryptocoryne wendtii

Cryptocoryne walkeri

Cryptocoryne willisii

3. Mossy plants and ferns

Bolbitis heudelotii ALSTON, 1934   African Fern

Fam.: *Lomariopsidaceae*

Distribution: Africa, from Ethiopia to South Africa.

In its native country the plant is found along the banks of rivers generally close to the mean water average with its roots submerged. Its dark-green, pinnate fronds reach 16 to 20 inches in height and require that much depth beneath the water. It prefers fresh, clean, moving water but is not demanding about light and will do well in shade. The rhizome and roots must be submerged and the rootstock should be secured to a rock or other object. New growth will also attach itself to a base. Propagation: division of rhizomes and side-shoots.

D: 2; KH: 2-12; pH: 5.8-7.0; T: 75-79° F (24-26° C); AH: 2-3.

Ceratopteris cornuta (BEAUVOIS) LE PRIEUR, 1810   Floating Fern

Fam.: *Parkeriaceae*   Syn.: *C. thalictroides*

Distribution: Africa.

The nomenclature has been changed and the former designation, *C. thalictroides* now is used only to describe the finely-divided Indian fern. *C. cornuta's* pinnate fronds vary noticeably in description from wide and coarse to narrow and finely-lobed. A relatively coarse form is illustrated. It grows well with bright lighting and floats on the water. The fern can be grown beneath the water but generally demands too much room to be kept in a smaller tank. The rhizome should be planted shallow. Propagation: adventitious plants from the fronds.

D: 1; KH: 5-15; pH: 5.5-7.5; T: 64-86° F (18-30° C); AH: 2-3.

Ceratopteris pteridioides (HOOKER) HIERONYMUS, 1905   Floating Watersprite

Fam.: *Parkeriaceae*   Syn.:*C. cornuta, C. thalictroides f. cornuta.*

Distribution: Tropics.

A floating species, it is hardy and fast-growing. Numerous shoots can be seen near the edges of the blunt-lobed fronds and these can be separated and planted. Its spongy leaves shade all beneath them and should be thinned often. The plant is ideal for a breeding tank and is especially welcome as a site for the labyrinth fish's bubble nest. The pendant roots will protect the fry while the root tips offer vegetarians welcome nourishment. Propagation: numerous adventitious plants.

D: 1; KH: 5-15; pH: 6.5-7.5; T: 64-82° F (18-28° C); AH: 1-3.

Ceratopteris thalictroides (LINNAEUS) BRONGNIART, 1821   Indian Fern

Fam.: *Parkeriaceae*

Distribution: Tropics: America; Africa; Asia; northern Australia.

A relatively consistent plant, especially when compared with *C. cornuta*, its light-green fronds grow straight from the soil and are multi-lobed and deeply pinnate. The fronds are divided with tips more slender than those of the coarser floating fern. This species can be grown beneath the water or allowed to float. It grows fastest at the surface where it produces a dense cover. Beneath the water it requires more light and should be grown singly. It should be planted upright, in the position in which you wish it to grow. The point at which the rhizomes join the root should be above the substrata. Propagation: adventitious shoots at the leaves.

D: 1; KH: 5-12; pH: 6.5-7.2; T: 75-82° F (24-28° C); AH: 2-3.

Bolbitis heudelotii

Ceratopteris pteridioides

Ceratopteris cornuta

Ceratopteris thalictroides

3. Mossy plants and ferns

Fontinalis antipyretica LINNAEUS, 1753   Willow Moss

Fam.: *Fontinalaceae*

Distribution: North America; Europe; northeast Asia; north Africa.
There are more than two dozen varieties. Most have stems without true roots and dense, slender, slightly triangular dark-green leaves $^1/_8$ to $^1/_4$-inch in length (0.4-0.6 cm.) alternating in three rows. Suggested for aquariums with cooler water and bright light. The plant prefers fast-moving water and should be planted near the filter outlet. It will not do well in hard water and under even the best of conditions will need replacing from time to time. Varieties from slower, warmer streams are better suited for an aquarium. Propagation: layering and from shoots.

D: 1; KH: 2-12; pH: 6.0-7.2; T: 59-72° F (15-22° C); AH: 1-3;

Vesicularia dubyana (C. MUELLER) BROTHERUS, 1925   Java Moss

Fam.: *Hypnaceae*

Distribution: Southeast Asia; Malaysia; Java; India.
A versatile, undemanding moss, it will grow on nearly any surface. Lanceolate, light-green leaves 0,05 to 0,11 inches long (2-4 mm.) are found in two rows on a slender stem. A popular spawning plant it is recommended for the bottom of many breeding tanks. Secured to a stone or root, its rhizoids will adhere and grow. Heavily branched shoots will quickly create a thick cushion which may be thinned and cut back without danger. Fastened to bark or a rock it can also be grown near the surface. Propagation: by the division of side-shoots.

D: 1; KH: 2-15; pH: 5.8-7.5; T: 64-86° F (18-30° C); AH: 1-3.

Marsilea drummondii BRAUN, 1870   Clover Fern

Fam.: *Marsileaceae*

Distribution: Australia.
A low-growing foreground plant it quickly produces a "lawn-like" effect. Since it grows rapidly a few separated shoots quickly become a dense, lush area. It is a creeping plant with alternate stalked dark-green leaves generally in a single lobed frond though occasionally seen with multi-lobed leaves all about $^1/_2$-inch wide. It will tolerate a variety of water conditions and will even do well in hard water if it is given bright light. It needs less light in softer water. A typical *Marsilea* disease can attack an entire stand quickly decimating it. If this happens replant. Propagation: shoots from runners.

D: 2; KH: 2-15; pH: 6.5-7.5; T: 72-82° F (22-28° C); AH: 1-2.

Fontinalis antipyretica

Vesicularia dubyana

Marsilea drummondii

3. Mossy plants and ferns

Microsorium pteropus (BLUME) CHING, 1933   Java Fern

Fam.: *Polypodiaceae*

Distribution: Tropical southeast Asia: Java to the Philippines.

An amphibious fern, it lives at the edge of mountain streams either at the water line or attached to roots and stones which are periodically submerged. In an aquarium the rhizomes should be secured to rocks or roots with wire or nylon thread until they become attached. The dark-green lanceolate fronds are 4 to $7^1/_4$-inches long (10-20 cm.) and $^3/_4$ to $1^1/_2$ inches wide (2-4 cm.). Occasionally these will have two side-lobes at their base. The plant adjusts well to most aquariums and requires minimal light. Portions of the plant may blacken with age and these should be trimmed. Propagation: adventitious shoots at the leaves and roots.

The plant is well suited to tanks that contain herbivorous fish as they do not touch the fern. It has happened, however, that insatiable scats (*Scatophagus argus*) ate of the fern and died (see page 810).

D: 1; **KH:** 2-12; **pH:** 5.5-7.0; **T:** 68-82° F (20-28° C); **AH:** 1-3.

Azolla filiculoides LAMARCK, 1783

Fam.: *Azollaceae*

Distribution: South and central America; also found in North America and Asia.

A free-floating, ornamental fern which adapts easily and reproduces readily. The floating stems bear small, round hairy leaves which often overlap like roof tiles. The space within the two-lobed leaf is the only place one can find an oxygen-binding single-celled blue algae, *Anabaena azollae*. Brought to Europe in 1880 it was subsequently planted in malaria-infested areas to help control mosquitoes in a unique way. Mosquito larvae in the water directly beneath the plant suffocate since their breathing tubes cannot penetrate the plant. Propagation: side-shoots.

D: 2; **KH:** 2-10; **pH:** 6.0-7.2; **T:** 68-75° F (20-24° C); **AH:** 1-3.

4. Floating plants

Eichhornia crassipes (MARTIUS) SOLMS, 1883   Water Hyacinth

Fam.: *Pontederiaceae*

Distribution: Through tropics on the American continent.

A common floating plant found in many places, its leaf stalk thickens into a spongy ball which contains a fibrous tissue that retains air. The leaf, round to heart-shaped, reaches a length of 6 inches (15 cm.). Water Hyacinth is best in an uncovered, brightly lighted aquarium and can also be grown out of water in a sun-lit area. It is more likely to bloom there. Originally from South America the plant has spread to many other tropical and semi-tropical areas. It grows rapidly, propagating by shoots so quickly it has become a pest and in many places is controlled chemically.

D: 2; **KH:** 2-15; **pH:** 6.0-7.8; **T:** 72-79° F (22-26° C); **AH:** 2-3.

Microsorium pteropus

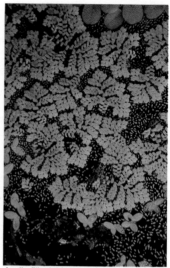

Azolla filiculoides

Eichhornia crassipes

4. Floating plants

Lemna minor LINNAEUS, 1753   Duckweed

Fam.: *Lemnaceae*

Distribution: virtually world-wide.
An undemanding floating plant which is often introduced into an aquarium by accident. Glossy light-green leaves, round to oval in shape and lighter colored on the bottom, are about 0,09 inches long (3 mm.). The plant adapts well and grows fast so that it often takes over an aquarium if not thinned. Thinning also insures that light will reach the lower reaches of a tank. Propagation: by division.

D: 1; KH: 2-15; pH: 5.5-7.5; T: 50-86° F (10-30° C); AH: 1-3.

Limnobium laevigatum (HUMBOLDT et BONPLANDT), HEINE 1968
         Amazon Frogbit, South American Frogbit

Fam.: *Hydrocharitaceae*   Syn.: *L. stoloniferum, Hydromistria stolonifera*

Distribution: South America.
A floating, adaptable plant with many hairy submerged roots and small rosettes of dark-green, short-stalked, round to heartshaped leaves $^3/_4$ to 1-inches long (2-3 cm.). The leaves are lighter green underneath with a visible spongy thickening. The plant needs more light than many but since it is a floater the aquarium light should be placed far enough away to prevent the over heating and burning of leaves. Initially the plant was described as *Salvinia laevigata*. Propagation: very productive using runners with shoots.

D: 2; KH: 2-12; pH: 6.5-7.5; T: 72-75° F (22-24° C); AH: 1-3.

Pistia stratiotes LINNAEUS, 1753   Water Lettuce

Fam.: *Araceae*

Distribution: Many tropical and sub-tropical areas.
A free-floating plant with a rosette of blue-green leaves. Velvety hairs and finely-branched roots are submerged. The leaf, spatulate to cuneate, is fleshy and to 6 inches long (15 cm.) and 4 inches wide (10 cm.). With time it may become slow growing producing smaller leaves ($^3/_4$ to one inch wide (2-3 cm.). In this condition it may be confused with *Salvinia* though the latter has a floating axil and opposing leaves. Be sure to keep the aquarium light some distance away. A cooling movement of air can also be promoted by placing the tank cover at an angle. Propagation: from shoots.

D: 1; KH: 5-15; pH: 6.5-7.2; T: 72-77° F (22-25° C); AH: 1-3.

Lemna minor

Limnobium laevigatum

Pistia stratiotes

4. Floating plants

Riccia fluitans LINNAEUS, 1753   Crystalwort
Fam.: *Ricciaceae*

Distribution: World-wide.

A spongy, floating plant, it can form a decorative cover in any aquarium. A dark-green thallophyte with a body 0,03-0,05 inch thick, it propagates through progressive forking to form a thick cushion. It should be thinned to allow light to penetrate into the tank. The plant is extremely hardy and can survive in a range of temperatures and does well even with subdued lighting. It dislikes soft brackish water. Propagation: by division.

D: 1; KH: 5-15; pH: 6.0-8.0; T: 59-86° F (15-30° C); AH: 1-3.

Salvinia auriculata AUBLET, 1775   Small-leaved Salvinia
Fam.: *Salviniaceae*

Distribution: South and central America; Cuba to Paraguay.

A free floating plant, it is suggested both as a decoration and in the breeding tank. Its horizontal axil grows to 7 $\frac{1}{4}$ inches in length (20 cm.) with leaves in whorls of three. Two round, floating leaves with up-turned edges have short, stiff bristles on their tops. The third leaf is submerged, hairy and root-like, clearly functioning as the missing root. The plant offers fry welcome protection and its soft tips serve as food for vegetarians. It is sensitive to the heat of strong light and should be protected. Leave the tank cover ajar to guarantee adequate ventilation. Propagation: by division.

D: 2; KH: 5-12; pH: 6.0-7.0; T: 68-75° F (20-24° C); AH: 1-3.

Utricularia gibba ssp. exoleta (BROWN) P. TAYLOR, 1810
Fam.: *Lentibulariaceae*

Distribution: Africa; Australia; Asia.

The plant forms a barely submerged floating cushion. An ornamental aquatic plant, it has a thread-like stem with needleshaped forked leaves $\frac{3}{4}$ to 1 inch long (2-3 cm.). The leaves from plants found in temperate zones are generally smaller and are forked just once. Small bladder-like organs on the plant catch and digest tiny aquatic life but do not develop if the water lacks nutrients or does not have sufficient albumen. Even so, the plant will continue to grow. Because of its small size it is ideal for use in breeding tanks. Propagation; dividing shoots.

D: 1: KH: 2-12; pH: 6.5-7.2; T: 72-86° F (22-30° C); AH: 1-3.

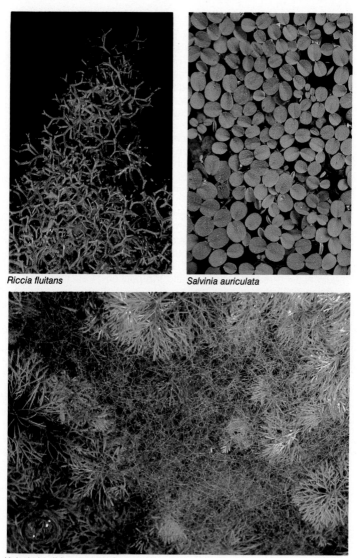

Riccia fluitans

Salvinia auriculata

Utricularia gibba ssp. exoleta

The Classification of Fishes

The many species of fish in this book are classified in a practical manner that is easy for an aquarist to use. We have divided fishes into ten groups and within these, orders or suborders. The fishes in each family are listed alphabetically. One exception are American Characins (*Characidae*) with its multitude of species. These are listed by closely-related sub-families so that species which are closely related are together. Hobbyists have been found to prefer this to a more scientific classification which would sometimes separate them.

Since the True American Characins have been classified by sub-families it would seem logical to do the same for Cichlids (*Cichlidae*) but many fishes in this order are under review, particularly the genus *Haplochromis*, and further changes appear likely. We feel an aquarist is better served if final placement in some sub-families is left until all questions have been answered.

Families and sub-families have been systematically classified on the following pages for the sake of their special interest to the hobby. With few exceptions, fishes are listed only when they are species of interest to hobbyists and when they are listed we have included information on sub-family, family, sub-order and order. This format should allow a reader to understand the postion of each species in the scientific systematics of fishes.

Nomenclature

The nomenclature of animals is governed by strict standards as outlined in the "International Rules of the Zoological Nomenclature". 87 articles deal with all aspects of selecting names. Two articles are of special importance to the aquarist, as they determine the official name of a fish and under what circumstances the name of the author and the year of first description have to be put in parentheses.

The most important articles deals with the regulation on priority. This regulation specifies that the oldest name that was given to a taxon is the official name; provided that this name has not been made invalid by the nomenclature regulations or has been suppressed by the nomenclature commission.

Example: In 1897 BOULENGER gave a description of a species of *Tilapia* as *Tilapia aurata*. Yet later research proved that this African Cichlid does not belong to the genus *Tilapia* at all but to the genus *Melanochromis*. Since the name of the species has to be retained (regulation on priority!) the fish nowadays must be called *Melanochromis auratus* (BOULENGER, 1897). The name *Tilapia aurata* is a synonym.

Another article deals with the use of parentheses for new combinations. If a taxon of a species had been described as belonging to one genus (e.g. *Tilapia*) and later been moved to another (e.g. *Melanochromis*) the name of the person who gave the first description and the year of the description have to be put in parentheses if both examples are quoted.

Fishes

General Classification of Fishes

Phylum:	*Chordata* (Chordates)
Subphylum:	*Vertebrata* (Animals with Backbones)
Superclass:	*Agnatha* (Animals without Taws)
Class:	*Cyclostomata* (Round-Mouthed Fish)
Superclass:	*Gnathostomata* (Animals with Taws)
Class:	*Chondrichthyes* (Cartilaginous Fish)
Sub-Class:	*Elasmobranchii* (Plate-Gilled Fish)
Order:	*Selachiformes* (Sharklike Fish)
Sub-Order:	*Batoidei* (Rays)
Fam.:	*Paratrygonidae* (Freshwater Rays)
Class:	*Teleostomi* (= Osteichtyes) (Bony Fish)
Sub-Class:	*Actinopterygii* (Ray-Finned Fishes)
Super-Order:	*Chondrostei*
Order:	*Acipenseriformes* (Sturgeons)
Fam.:	*Acipenseridae* (True Sturgeons)
Super-Order:	*Holostei**
Order:	*Amiiformes**
Fam.:	*Amiidae**
Order:	*Lepisosteiformes**
Fam.:	*Lepisosteidae** (Jars, Garpikes)
Super-Order:	*Teleostei* (True Bony Fish)
	(see separate classification on p.150)
Sub-Class:	*Brachiopterygii*
Order:	*Polypteriformes*
Fam.:	*Polypteridae* (Lobe-Finned Fish, Bichirs)
Sub-Class:	*Dipnoi* (Lungfishes)
Fam.:	*Ceratodontidae* (Australian Lungfish)
Fam.:	*Lepidosirenidae* (South American Lungfish)
Fam.:	*Protopteridae* (African Lungfish)

* Not discribed in this book

Classification of True Bony Fishes (*Teleostei*) based on GREEN-WOOD et al (1966) with minor alterations.

GREENWOOD, P. H.; Rosen, D. E.; WEITZMAN, S. H. & MYERS, G. S. (1966): Phyletic of teleostean fishes, with a provisional classification of living forms. – Bull. Amer. Mus. Nat. Hist. **131** (4): 339–456.

Super-Order:	*Teleostei* (True Bony Fishes)
Order:	*Anguilliformes*
Fam.:	*Anguillidae* (True Eels)*
Order:	*Osteoglossiformes*
Sub-Order:	*Osteoglossoidei*
Fam.:	*Osteoglossidae* (Bony-Tongued Fishes)
Fam.:	*Pantodontidae* (Chisel-Taw)
Sub-Order:	*Notopteroidei*
Fam.:	*Notopteridae* (Featherbacks)
Order:	*Mormyriformes*
Fam.:	*Mormyridae* (Mormyrides) (Elephant Snout Fishes)
Order:	*Salmoniformes* (Salmons, Trouts etc.)
Sub-Order:	*Esocoidei* (Pikes and Mud-Minnows)
Fam.:	*Esocidae* (Pikes)*
Fam.:	*Umbridae* (Mud-Minnows)
Order:	*Gonorhynchiformes*
Sub-Order:	*Chanoidei*
Fam.:	*Kneriidae* (Kneria)
Fam.:	*Phractolaemidae* (Phractolaemos)
Order:	*Cypriniformes* (Carps, Barbs etc.)
Sub-Order:	*Characoidei*
Fam.:	*Alestidae* (True African Characins)
Fam.:	*Citharinidae* (Citharinids)
Fam.:	*Characidae* (Tetras etc.)
Fam.:	*Characidiidae* (Bottom Characins)
Fam.:	*Crenuchidae* (Sailfins)
Fam.:	*Serrasalmidae* (Piranhas)
Fam.:	*Erythrinidae* (Trahiras)
Fam.:	*Cteneoluciidae* (South American Pike-Characoids)
Fam.:	*Lebiasinidae* (Lebiasinas)
Fam.:	*Gasteropelecidae* (Hatchetfishes)
Fam.:	*Curimatidae* (Curimatas)
Fam.:	*Anostomidae* (Headstanders and Leporinus)

Sub-Order:	*Gymnotoidei*	(Naked Eels)
Fam.:	*Gymnotidae*	(Knife Fishes)
Fam.:	*Electrophoridae*	(Electric Eels)
Fam.:	*Apteronotidae*	(Speckled Knife Fishes)
Fam.:	*Rhamphichthyidae*	(Mottled Knife Fishes)
Sub-Order:	*Cyprinoidei*	(Carplike Fishes)
Fam.:	*Cyprinidae*	(Carps and close relatives)
Sub-Fam.:	*Cyprininae*	(Cyprinine Barbs)
Sub-Fam.:	*Leuciscinae*	(Leuciscine Barbs)
Sub-Fam.:	*Rhodeinae*	(Bitterlings)
Sub-Fam.:	*Rasborinae*	(Rasboras)
Sub-Fam.:	*Abraminae*	(Breams)
Sub-Fam.:	*Garrinae*	(Garras)
Fam.:	*Gyrinocheilidae*	(Siamese Sucking Loach)
Fam.:	*Cobitidae*	(Spine Loaches)
Fam.:	*Homalopteridae*	
Order:	*Siluriformes*	(Catfish-like Fish)
Sub-Order:	*Siluroidei*	
Fam.:	*Ictaluridae*	(Bullhead Catfishes)
Fam.:	*Bagridae*	(Naked Catfish)
Fam.:	*Siluridae*	(True Catfish)
Fam.:	*Schilbeidae*	
Fam.:	*Pangasiidae*	(Asian Catfishes)
Fam.:	*Clariidae*	(Labyrinth Catfishes)
Fam.:	*Malapteruridae*	(Electric Catfishes)
Fam.:	*Mochocidae*	(African Catfishes)
Fam.:	*Doradidae*	(Spiny Catfishes)*
Fam.:	*Auchenipteridae*	
Fam.:	*Aspredinidae*	
Fam.:	*Pimelodidae*	(Many-Coloured Catfish)
Fam.:	*Callichthyidae*	(Armoured Catfish)
Fam.:	*Loricariidae*	(Evenly Armoured Catfish)
	Chacidae	
	Trychomycteridae	
Order:	*Atheriniformes*	(Silversides and similar Fish)
Sub-Order:	*Exocoetoidei*	(Flying Fishes, Half-Beaks)
Fam.:	*Hemirhamphidae*	(Half-Beak Fish)
Fam.:	*Belonidae*	(Needle Fishes)

* Not described in this book

Sub-Order:	*Adrianichthyoidei*
Fam.:	*Oryziatidae* (Ricefishes, Medakas)
Sub-Order:	*Cyprinodontoidei* (Toothcarps, Four-Eyed Fishes)
Fam.:	*Cyprinodontidae* (Egg-Laying Toothcarps, Killifishes)
Sub-Fam.:	*Rivulinae* (Rivulus)
Sub-Fam.:	*Fundulinae* (Fundukus, Killifishes)
Sub-Fam.:	*Cyprinodontinae* (Pupfishes)
Sub-Fam.:	*Aphaniinae*
Sub-Fam.:	*Procatopodinae*
Fam.:	*Anablepidae* (Four-Eyes)
Fam.:	*Poeciliidae* (Live-Bearing Toothcarps)
Fam.:	*Goodeidae*
Sub-Order:	*Atherinoidei*
Fam.:	*Melanotaeniidae* (Rainbow Fish)
Fam.:	*Atherinidae* (Silversides)
Order:	*Gasterosteiformes*
Sub-Order:	*Gasterosteoidei* (Stickleback and similar Fish)
Fam.:	*Gasterosteidae* (Sticklebacks)
Order:	*Syngnathiformes*
Sub-Order:	*Syngnathoidei*
Fam.:	*Syngnathidae* (Pipefishes)
Order:	*Channiformes* (Snakehead Fishes and relatives)
Fam.:	*Channidae* (Snakehead Fishes)
Order:	*Synbranchiformes**
Sub-Order:	*Synbranchoidei**
Fam.:	*Synbranchidae* (Synbranchid Eels)
Order:	*Scorpaeniformes**
Sub-Order:	*Cottoidei**
Fam.:	*Cottidae* (Sculpins)
Order:	*Perciformes*
Sub-Order:	*Percoidei*
Fam.:	*Centropomidae* (Glassfishes)
Fam.:	*Centrarchidae* (Sunfishes)
Fam.:	*Percidae* (True Perches)
Fam.:	*Monodactylidae* (Fingerfishes)
Fam.:	*Toxotidae* (Archerfishes)
Fam.:	*Scatophagidae* (Dung-Eaters)
Fam.:	*Nandidae* (Leaffishes)
Fam.:	*Badidae* (Badis)
Fam.:	*Lobotidae*
Fam.:	*Cichlidae* (Cichlids)

* Not described in this book

Sub-Order:	*Blennioidei*	
Fam.:	*Blenniidae* (Blennies)	
Sub-Order:	*Gobioidei* (Goby-like Fish)	
Fam.:	*Gobiidae* (Gobies)	
Fam.:	*Eleotridae* (Sleeper Gobies)	
Fam.:	*Periophthalmidae* (Mudskippers)**	
Sub-Order:	*Anabantoidei*	
Fam.:	*Anabantidae*	
Fam.:	*Belontiidae* (Gouramis)	
Sub-Fam.:	*Belontiinae*	
Sub-Fam.:	*Macropodinae* (Paradise Fish)	
Sub-Fam.:	*Trichogasterinae* (Pearl Gouramis)	
Fam.:	*Helostomatidae* (Kissing Gouramis)	
Fam.:	*Osphronemidae* (True Gouramis)	
Sub-Order:	*Luciocephaloidei*	
Fam.:	*Luciocephalidae* (Pike-Head)	
Order:	*Mastacembeliformes*	
Fam.:	*Mastacembelidae* (Spiny Eels)	
Order:	*Pleuronectiformes* (Place-like Fish)*	
Sub-Order:	*Soleoidei* (Sole-like Fish)*	
Fam.:	*Soleidae* (True Soles)*	
Order:	*Tetraodontiformes* (Triggerfishes, Boxfishes, Puffers)*	
Sub-Order:	*Tetraodontoidei* (Globe and similar Fish)	
Fam.:	*Tetraodontidae* (Pufferfish, Globe Fish)	

** This family is often included under the *Gobiidae*.

A little about collecting and importing

Only a small, select number of aquarium fish were bred in Europe prior to the end of World War II. Most were collected in the wild. Today nearly 90% of all aquarium fish are bred in Asia, particularly in Hong Kong, Thailand, Singapore, Taiwan, in Japan, or in the U.S., especially in Florida where large numbers of live-bearing Toothcarp are available. More than 300 million fish are captive-grown worldwide. Less than 30 million are collected from the wild.

Many wild-caught fish are difficult if not impossible to breed in an aquarium. The list includes the Cardinal Tetra, many *Corydoras* species, the Red-Tailed Black Shark, *Epalzeorhynchus bicolor*, the Clown Loach, the Asian *Botia macracanthus* and a range of rarer species appealing most to the specialized aquarist who is on the look out for novelties. Of the 10,000 known species of freshwater fishes about 4,000 are adapatable to the freshwater aquarium. In reality the figure is high when one considers that just 1200 to 1300 species are bred regularly. About 20 species account for 90% of all hobby sales and the large majority of fishes have no commercial importance.

The species included in our book are those which can be seen with some frequency in aquarium stores and it should be possible to find most of them in your area. In rare cases you may need to visit a well-stocked aquarium specialist and occasionally may even have to special-order a few.

Our descriptions include an indication (under "Habitat") of whether or not the species is commonly available. Beginners should concentrate on these fishes since the loss of one or two will not affect the environment as would the death of a rarer specimen.

Unlike many coral fishes, a large number of freshwater fish are plentiful in the wild. The Cardinal Tetra, as an example, dies by the millions during drier periods when food is scarce. In the wild the Tetra may live no more than one or two years while its life expectancy in an aquarium can top ten years. The fish breed so successfully in their environment it would be impossible to consider them "endangered" in their native waters of the Brazilian jungle. Exceptions to this may be the various types of

Discus which are caught at night by torchlight. Though it is advisable to leave two to six of every 20 to 30 fish caught to reproduce and multiply, uninformed collectors sometimes capture entire schools. There is little an aquarist can do to change the system in foreign nations and an ornamental collector is hardly likely to read this book so this comment is intended only to explain to a beginner why he should not start with wild-caught specimens such as the Discus. (Incidently, several American breeders are successfully breeding Discus.)

Because of improved transportation methods, better food, superior handling and display in pet stores, losses of wildcaught freshwater fishes have been cut by more than half. The average loss is now less than 10 percent.

Losses of commercially-bred fish from Asia are often nearly as high as those collected in the wild since fish kept in the restricted conditions one often sees in Asia are prone to disease. An importer who is not able to recognize these diseases and act quickly will experience similar losses. All imported fish must undergo two to three weeks quarantine so that only healthy specimens reach the stores. Only in this way can a hobbyist be certain of obtaining healthy fish from his aquarium dealer. There are many ethical and sincere wholesalers and importers who supply fish with just such a guarantee of good health. The fish may not have labels attached, but your retailer should offer livestock with some kind of replacement guarantee.

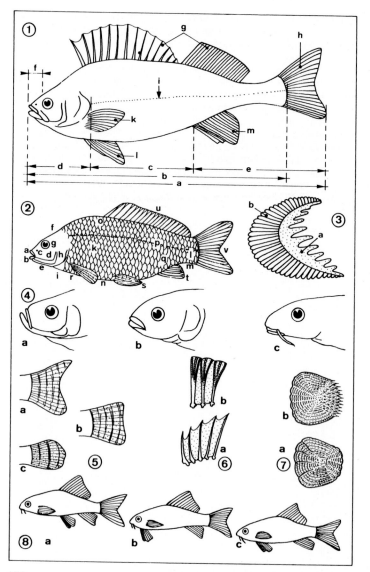

Ichthyology

Table of Distinguishing Features

Figure 1: **Main Body Measurements.**
a: Total Length. b: Standard or Body Length. c: Trunk Length. d: Head Length. e: Tail Length. f: Nose Length. g: Dorsal Fins (first, simple rays; second, soft rays.) h: Caudal or Tail Fin. i: Lateral Line (Linea Lateralis). k: Pectoral Fins. l: Pelvic Fins. m: Anal Fin.

Figure 2: **Morphology.**
a: Mouth. b: Lips. c: Nostril. d: Preoperculum (anterior gill cover bone). e: Throat. f: Brow. g: Eye. h: Operculum (gill cover). i. Breast. K: Body Scales. l: Tail Scales. m: Caudal Peduncle. n: Stomach. o: Back Scales. p: Lateral Line. q: Hemal Scales. r: Pectoral Fin. s: Pelvic or Basal Fin. t: Anal Fin. u: Dorsal Fin. v: Caudal or Tail Fin.

Figure 3: **Composition of a Gill Arch.**
a. Gill Rakers. b: Gill Filaments (membranes which absorb oxygen).

Figure 4: **Mouth Positions.**
a: Pointing Upward (e.g. Hatchetfish). b: Pointing Forward, (e.g. Tigerbarb). c: Pointing Downward (e.g. Armoured Catfish).

Figure 5: **Shapes of the Caudal Fin.**
a: Forked (e.g. Tigerbarb). b: Concave (e.g. Spiney Loach). c: Rounded (e.g. Mudskipper).

Figure 6: **Fin Rays.**
a: Hard or Simple Rays or Spines. b: Soft Rays.

Figure 7: **Types of Scales.**
a: Cycloid. b: Ctenoid.

Figure 8: **Positions of the Pelvic Fins.**
a: Ventral, located behind the Pectorals. b: Anterior, located in front of the Pectorals. c: Posterior , located beneath the Pectorals.

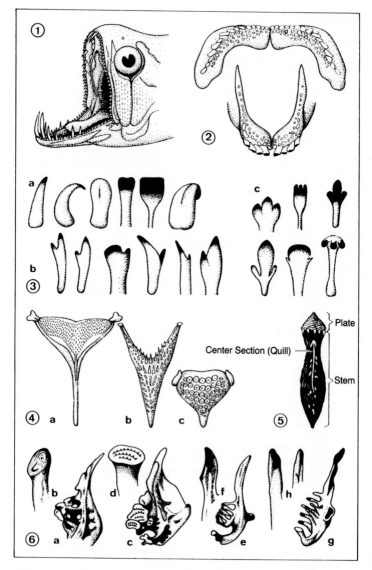

Table of Dentition and Tooth Shapes.

Figure 1: Jaws of the itharin *Distichodus niloticus*. Note the long canines or catching teeth in the Lower Mandible.

Figure 2:
Upper and Lower Mandibles of a young Cichlid (*Chilotilapia rhoadesi).*

Figure 3:
Variations in the Maxillary Teeth of some Cichlids:
a. Single-tipped (monofid) teeth.
b.Twin-tipped (bifid) teeth.
c. Triple-tipped (trifid) teeth.

Figure 4:
Teeth of the Lower Pharyngeal Bone of certain Cichlids. The shape depends on the natural food selection of each fish.
a. The tiny teeth of a Phytoplankton-eater (*Tilapia esculenta)*
b. The long, pointed teeth of a predator (*Bathybates leo).*
c. The molars of a Mollusc-eater (*Haplochromis placodon).*
The teeth are flat-surfaced and very strong, designed to grind the hard shells of snails and shellfish.

Figure 5:
The teeth on the vomer of a fish in the salmon family (Salmonidae). The bone consists of two sections, the stem and the plate. There is also a central or Quill section. Only the plate is toothed on certain salmonidae; on others only the stem; and, on still others, both the plate and stem are toothed.

Figure 6:
The Pharyngeal teeth of certain members of the family Cyprinidae. These were formed from the fifth gill arch and may have taken on the function of true teeth, which these fish lack.
a. Arulius Barb (vegetarian). b. Pharyngeal tooth of an Arulius Barb showing a spoon-shaped hollow. c. Carp (mostly vegetarian). d. A carp's molar. e. Bream (Omnivore). f. The pharyngeal incisor of a Bream with a chewing edge. g. Rapfen, a predator or fisheater. h. A predator's pharyngeal incisor.

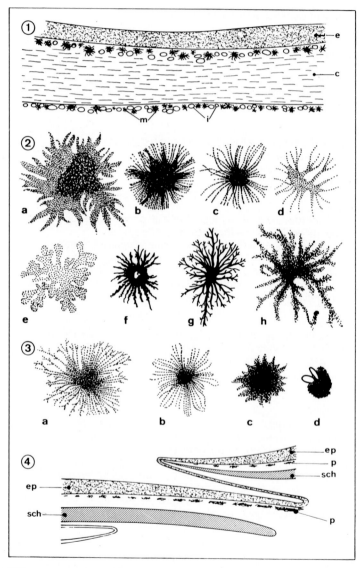

Table of Colors and Pigments

Figure 1:
A cross-section of the skin of a flatfish (Fam. Pleuronectidae).
c= Corium. e= Epidermis. i= Iridocytes (guanophores). m= Melanophores. Iridocytes give fish their silvery color, Melanophores their black color.

Figure 2:
Different types of Melanophore (the black pigment). For clarity the melanophores of marine fish are generally shown.
a. *Myoxocephalus scorpius*. b. *Agonus cataphractus*. c. *Scophthalmus maximus*. d. *Liparis sp.* e. *Anguilla anguilla*. f. Trigla sp. g. *Pomatoschistus minutus*. h. *Liparis reinhardti*.

Figure 3:
Melanophores in various degrees of pigmentation.
a: Maximum pigment. d: Minimal pigment.

Figure 4:
A cross-section of the skin of a species of Trachinidae. Large, heavily pigmented melanophores are located at the base of the scales. ep= Epidermis. p= Pigment (melanophores). sch= Scales.

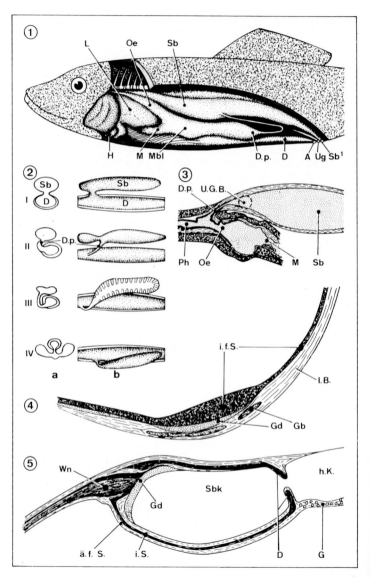

Fishes

Table of Swim Bladders

Figure 1:
The internal anatomy of a species of Herring (Order Clupeiformes).
A = Anus. D = Intestine. D.p. = Ductus pneumaticus (the duct connecting the intestine and swim bladder). H = Heart. L = Liver. M = Stomach. Mbl = Epithelium. Oe = Oesophagus (tube to the digestive tract). Sb = Swim Bladder. Sb[1] = Rear opening of the swim bladder. Ug = Urogenital orfice (opening of the reproductive and excretory tracts).

Figure 2:
An over-all view of the duct which connects with the Intestine.
a = Cross-section. b = Profile.
D = Intestine. D.p. Ductus pneumaticus. Sb = Swim Bladder. I = Sturgeon and fish with the duct. II = Predatory *Erythrinus*. III = Australian Lungfish *Neoceratodus forsteri*. IV = Lobe-finned Pike (Fam. Polypteridae).

Figure 3:
A cross-section of the swim bladder of a Dogfish (*Umbra krameri*).
D.p. = Ductus pneumaticus. M = Stomach. Oe = Oesophagus. Ph = Pharynx. Sb = Swim Bladder. U.G.B. = The gas-gland found on either side.

Figure 4:
A cross-section of the lateral wall of the swim bladder of a Crucian Carp (*Carassius carassius*).
Gb = Bundle of fibers. Gd = Gas gland. i.f.S. = muscles, a thickened area near the gas gland. l.B = surrounding tissue.

Figure 5:
Cross-section of the swim bladder of a Pipefish (Fam. Syngnathidae).
ä.f.S. = External tissue. D = Diaphragm. G = Bundle of fibers. Gd = Gas gland. h.K = Rear chamber of the swim bladder. i.S. = Lamellar or plate-like connective tissue. Sbk = Swim bladder sac. Wn = growth.

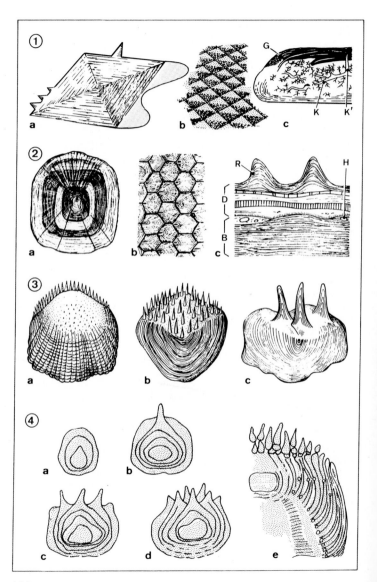

Table of Scale Shapes.

Figure 1:
Ganoid scales found in primitive bony fish (Sturgeon and Gars).
a: A single ganoid scale. b: A set of ganoid scales. The scales are linked by joints. c = A cross-section of the rear edge of a ganoid scale. G = Ganoin layer. K = Duct connecting the artery. K' = Artery branches.

Figure 2:
Cycloid or round scales found on most bony fishes.
a: A single round scale. The concentric lines are "year rings" which record growth. b: The placement of round scales on the side of a fish. c: a vertical cross-section of a cycloid scale.
B = Basal layer, D = Exterior layer, H = Hollow area, R = Ring

Figure 3:
Ctenoid or comb-like scales found on many species of Bass and Sunfish.
a-c: Several types of ctenoid scales.

Figure 4:
a-e: The development of a ctenoid scale.

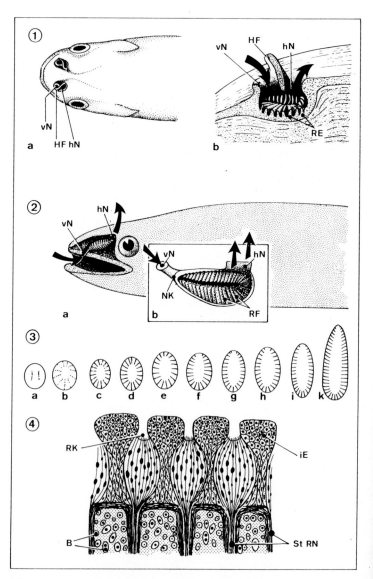

Table of Olfactory Organs.

Figure 1: a: The head of a bony fish from above. Note the position of the nasal openings. b: A longitudinal diagram of the nostril of a bony fish.
HF = A passage which guides water into the anterior nostril during swimming. hN = Rear nostril. RE = Olfactory epithelium. vN = Anterior nostril.

Figure 2:
a: Location of the olfactory organ on an Eel illustrating the inward and outward flows. b: A cross-section of the olfactory organ of *Anguilla anguilla* (Eel). The arrow illustrates the direction of flow. The intake peduncle can be raised. hN = Rear nostril. NK = Nose flap. RF = Olfactory fold. vN = Anterior nostril.

Figure 3:
A diagram of the olfactory cells of certain bony fishes. The number of folds are indicated in brackets. a: Stickelback, *Gasterosteus aculeatus* (2). b: Pike, *Esox lucius* (9-18 smaller folds). c: Rainbow Trout, *Salmo gairdneri* (13-18). d: Perch *Perca fluviatilis*, (13-18) e: Minnow, *Phoxinus phoxinus* (11-19). f: Gudgeon, *Gobio gobio* (19-23). g: Tench, *Tinca tinca* (15-29). h: Merlin, *Noemacheilus barbatulus* (16-24). i: Eelpout, *Lota lota* (30-32). k= Eel, *Anguilla anguilla* (68-93). Fishes a and b depend on their eyes, c through h on eyes and nose and i and k on the nose only.

Figure 4:
A microscopic cross-section of the olfactory membrane of a bony fish.
B = Connective tissue. iE = Secondary epithelium. RK = small bud. St = Stem of the olfactory nerve.

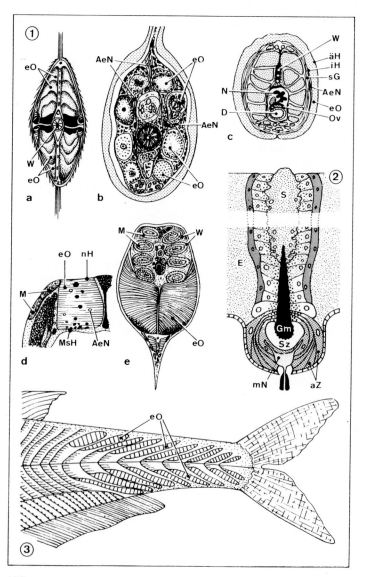

Table of Electric Shock Organs

Figure 1:
Cross-section of the electric shock organ in fishes illustrating their position. a: Mormyrid (*Mormyrus*). b: *Gymnarchus*. c: Electric catfish (*Malapterurus electricus*) d: Electric Stargazer (*Astroscopus*). e: Electric eel (*Electrophorus electricus.*)
AeN = nerves which produce electric current. äH = Outer skin. D = Intestine. eO = Current producing organ. iH = inner skin or corium layer. M = muscles. nH = outer skin. MsH = Membrane in mouth. Ov = Ovaries. sG = sub-cutaneous tissue. W = Backbone.

Figure 2:
A diagram of the Ampulla or electric receptor of *Gymnarchus niloticus*. Based on an electro-miscrope photo from DERBIN.
aZ = Secondary cells. E = Epidermis. Gm = Granules in the ampoule lumen. mN = Nerve fibers with a myelin sheath. S = Mucus. Sz = sensory cell.

Figure 3:
An exposed view of the electric shock organs of the Mormyrid (*Mormyrus*).
eO = Electric shock organs.

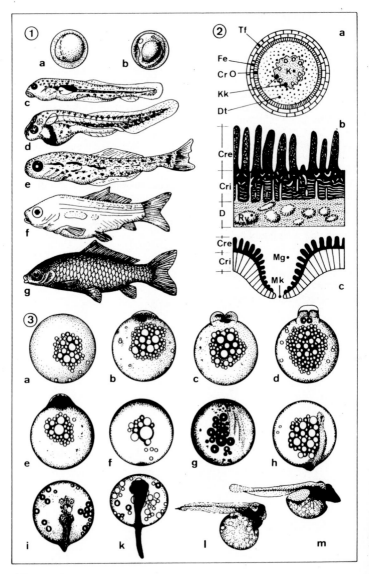

Table of the Development of Fish

Figure 1:
The life of a goldfish (*Carassius auratus*)
a-c: Embryonic phase. a = Ovular phase. b = Embryo phase. c = prelarval phase.
d-e: Larval phase. d = Protopterygiolarval phase. e = Pterygiolarval phase.
f: Fry.
g: Adult.
h: Old age (not shown).

Figure 2:
Diagram of a cell or oocyte. b: Oocyte cell cover of a Gudgeon (*Gobio gobio*). c: Micropyle – the opening through which the sperm penetrates the egg.
Cre- Cortex radiatus externus. Cri = Cortex radiatus internus. D = Yolk. Dt = Yolk platelet. Fe = Follicle epithelium. Mg = Micropyle groove. Mk = Micropyle duct. K = Core. Kk = Nucleus of cell. Rv = Cytoplastic vacuole. Tf = Follicle theca. The two cortex layers form the egg sac.

Figure 3:
Development of *Fundulus heteroclitus:*
a: Unfertilized Oocyte or egg cell. b: Single-cell stage. c = Double-cell stage. d: Four-cell stage. e = 32-cell stage. f = Blastule. g = Gastrula. h = Formation of ocular vesicles. i = First stage of heart movement. k = Formation of liver and related organs. l = Appearance of first rays in the caudal fin. m = Spawning stage.

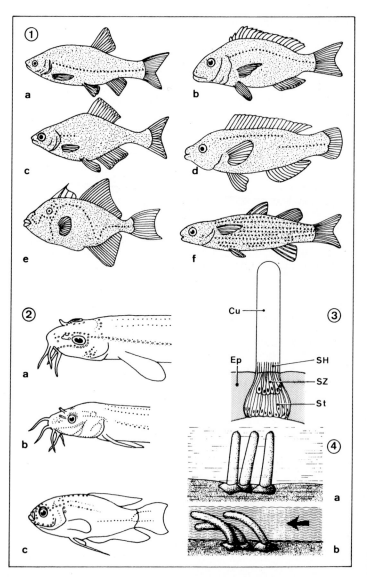

Table of the Lateral Line.

Figure 1:
Various forms of the Lateral Line.
a: Complete and nearly straight (Carp). b: Complete and curving upward (Perch). c: Incomplete (Bitterling, Leucaspius). d: In two segments (Cichlid). e: Irregular (Triggerfish). f: Multiple and interupted (Grayling).

Figure 2:
Lateral Line organs. a: *Noemacheilus barbatulus* as seen from above. b: Mudskipper (*Misgurnus fossilis*) with lateral canals missing. c: Paradise Fish (*Macropodus*) with lateral canals formed at the head.

Figure 3:
Structure of a typical Lateral Line organ: Free-standing sensory bud. Cu = Cupola. Ep = Epidermis. SH = Sensory hair. St = Supporting cell. SZ = Sensory cell.

Figure 4:
The Lateral Line organs of the Minnow (*Phoxinus phoxinus*).
a: A grouping of free-standing sensory buds at the body line with the cupolae in normal position. b: The cupolae sensing wave vibrations from the right.

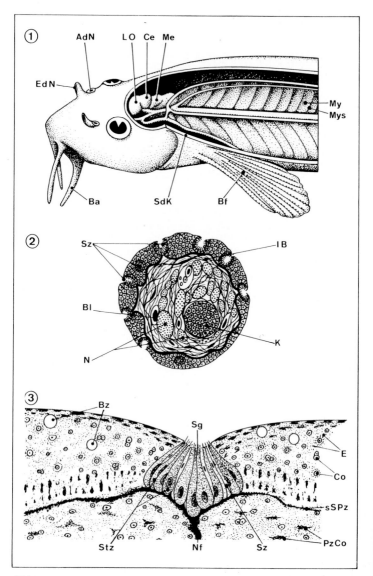

Table of the Organs of Taste.

Figure 1:
The barbels of a Loach (*Noemacheilus barbatulus*). The illustration is partially separated or exploded to show the position of the taste buds. AdN = Out-going nasal passage. Ba = Barbels. Bf = Pectoral fin. Ce = Cerebellum. EdN = In-coming nasal passage. LO = Optic lobe. Me = Medulla. My = Myomer. Mys = Myoseptum. SdK = Skin.

Figure 2:
Cross-section of a barbel on an Armoured Catfish (*Corydoras punctatus*). Bl = Blood vessel. IB = Free connective tissue. K = Cartilage. N = Nerves. Sz = Taste buds.

Figure 3:
A microscopic cross-section of the taste bud.
Bz = Beaker cell. Co = Corium or dermis. E = Epidermis. Nf = nerve endings. PzCo = Pigment cells in the corium. Sg = Sensory furrow. sSPz = Sub-epidermal layer of pigment cells. Stz = Supporting cells of the taste buds. Sz = sensory cells.

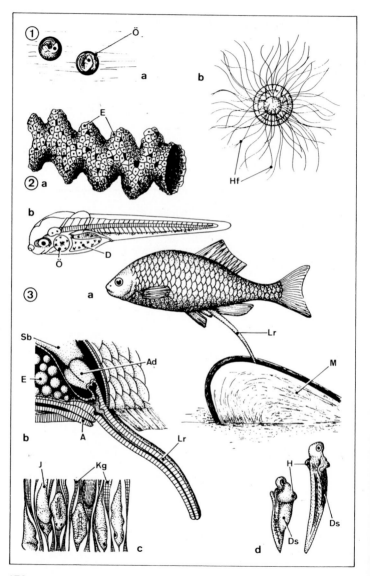

Table of Eggs and Care of Fry.

Figure 1:
The adaptation of eggs to varying ecological conditions.
a: Pelagic eggs which after spawning are left to hatch suspended in the middle regions of the ocean. They float because one or two globules of oil are included. b: The egg of a fish which spawns on the bottom. Very fine adhesive threads on the egg cover hold it in place. Hf = Adhesive threads. Ö = globule of oil.

Figure 2:
a: A cross section from the spawn of a fresh-water Bass (*Perca fluviatilis*). The eggs are laid in strips rather than individually and have a heavy coating of adhesive gelatin to hold them together. Female Bass secure these to water plants. b: Five day old fry of the Ruff *(Gymnocephalus cernua)*. The globule of oil and remains of the yolk are clearly visible.
D = Yolk. E = Eggs. Ö = Globule of oil.

Figure 3:
a: A spawning Bitterling. (A more complete description can be found under the species.) b: A cross-section through the ovaries and ovipositor of the female. c: Placement of the Bitterling young between the gills of a Pond Mussel (*Anodonta*). d: Bitterling fry seen at various stages. The adhesive pad and remains of the yolk sac are visible. The adhesive pad is a thickening seen at the head, which anchors the fry to the Mussel gills. Once the fry are old enough to swim freely the pad is absorbed and the fry leave through an opening.
A = Anus. Ad = Appendage gland. Ds = Yolk sac. E = Eggs. H = Adhesive pad. J = Fry. Kg = Gill tissue. Lr = Ovipositor. M = Mussel. Sb = Swim Bladder.

Community Fishes

The things fish require in an aquarium were discussed in the chapter titled "The right aquarium", p. 20 and since reading it you have probably selected a commercially-made tank. Its sizes and dimensions are standardized and readily adapt to both your needs and equipment available for it. The chapter which follows will give you an idea of how to establish your aquarium and select the fish best for it.

Fish which can live happily together in a community tank can be selected from the hundreds of species listed in this book though it may appear to be difficult for a beginner to quickly choose fishes from the more than 600 we have illustrated. To make it easy we have graded fishes with a "Degree of Difficulty in Keeping" indicator and those perfect for a beginner are marked, **D**: 1. The possibilities include many Livebearers such as swordtails, Guppies and Platies, certain Labrythinth Fish, a few Cichlids such as Angelfish, many species of barbs and Characins.

It would seem to be simple enough to put a mix of listed fishes in an aquarium, but without a little thought you would create nothing more than confusion. None of the species would be displayed to best effect in terms of color or behavior. As you begin it is better to choose just a few species and build an aquarium around several of each. The following points should be considered when establishing any piscatorial community:

1. The fish must mesh in terms of temperature requirements.
2. They should prefer similar water condition values such as hardness. Fishes which go best in hard water should be kept together and those which prefer softer water should be kept in a separate tank though compromises are often possible.
3. Be sure to provide the proper food, particularly for those which require live foods.
4. The fish should be able to tolerate tankmates in terms of personality and living habits. For example, you must not put a predatory perch in the same tank with smaller, peaceful Characins.
5. The species in a community tank should not inhabit the same part of the tank since one area would be heavily populated and other sections would be empty. A bottom-feeder such as *Corydoras* should be selected first, then a suitable schooling species for the middle region and possibly one or two surface dwellers as well.
6. Finally, when choosing fishes for a community tank, consider size. A species should not be selected which, when adult, will out-grow the tank.

The information you will need to meet each of the conditions above can be found in our descriptions of the various species.

When you have created your community tank according to this guide you will quickly discover that the fish come from a variety of geographic locations, though this is not important as long as the species are combined in accordance with the factors just discussed.

Only a perfectionist will establish individual tanks to reflect geographical regions, though the concept is interesting to consider, fun to do and lovely to view. For example, you could establish a tank of fish only from Southeast Asia or from the reaches of the Amazon imitating a small stream by means of decorations which come from the area. Some ideas along this line are given below and you'll discover there will be some overlapping. An all Asian aquarium, for example, may simultaneously be both a landscape tank and a home for one particular fish.

The list of possibilities below is not intended to be inclusive since the number of biotopes, species, types of underwater landscape and geograpical regions is so large it would difficult to list them all.

To consider just one example, look at *Eichhornia*, a floating plant known to all aquarists. A small variety of Characin, *Klausewitzia*, has adapted its life style and coloration to this narrow biotope and lives in the roots of the plant. If we were to keep the fish exactly as it lives in the wild, we would have to supply the tank with peat-brown, nearly opaque water and *Eichhornia*, adding the Characin in the proper number for the size of the aquarium.

And in the strictest sense, this would constitute three kinds of aquarium, a landscaped tank (a river scene,) a species tank (Characins) and a geographic tank (South American) though it should be noted that *Eichhornia* is quite cosmopolitan and can be found worldwide.

Because of such factors we have a large measure of freedom in the creation of a community tank and considerable latitude in both the design of the aquarium and the selection of the fishes. Among the possibilities:

1. Community aquarium
2. Landscape or biotope aquarium
   a. A stream
   b. A river
   c. A shallow thicket
   d. Rocks
   c. A bog
3. A species aquarium, which in some countries is called a family or genus tank. Examples: tanks with only Characins, Catfish, Barbs, goldfish or Livebearers.
4. Geographical aquariums
   a. Southeast Asia
   b. Africa, general
   c. African lakes (Tanganyika and Malawi)
   d. South America, jungles and pampas
   e. Australia
   f. North America
   g. Europe

In a general way most aquariums are a combination of these categories in terms of layout and species but to these possibilities we must add several other categories:

5. Selecting species by temperature requirements
6. Selecting species by water conditions
7. Selecting species by the limitations of tank size
8. A tank limited to plant-eating fish
9. A "Dutch" type of aquarium

There are very few hard and fast rules when establishing a community tank and the result usually reflects personal taste. Here is a typical American aquarium with a colored transparent rear panel. In Europe a tank with natural aquatic plants is more common and you can find numerous examples in our book.

Since we have discussed generalities, we will now consider specifics:

1. The Community Aquarium.

The term includes all aquariums stocked with more than a single species of fish and includes both variations in species and fishes from specific geographical regions. Particular attention is given to tanks which include a variety of fishes and every species suitable for combining in a community aquarium is noted.

2. Landscaped Aquariums

a. A Stream

Streams are home to fishes with a higher oxygen requirement than are found in standing and slow-moving waters. Normally there is a medium to strong current and the bottom is clean and covered with fine to medium-sized gravel with a few roots and rocks between. Currents can be simulated by a strong filter and aquatic plants which thrive in moving water should be used. Examples include Vallisneria for a brook of moderate temperature or *Heteranthera zosterifolia* for a tropical stream. Floating plants are out of place. Vallisneria will tolerate relatively hard water to about 20° KH. *Heteranthera* prefers softer water and grows best with a hardness of less than 10° KH.

The Nine-Spined Stickelback, *Pungitius pungitius* is particularly well suited to a **European Coldwater Stream** aquarium and, under certain conditions, so is the Three-Spined Stickelback, the Minnow and possibly the Alburn and Leucaspius.

For a **Moderate Temperature Stream** we would suggest the White-Cloud Mountain Minnow, *Tanichthys albonubes*, Danios, especially the Zebra Danio, and Rainbow Fish such as *Melanotaenia maccullochi*. The latter will also tolerate higher temperatures.

All types of tropical Characins and schooling fish can be selected for a tank which simulates a **Warm Water Stream.**

The **Cryptocoryne Stream**, typical of Southeast Asia and particularly Sri Lanka, Thailand and Indonesia, is extremely popular with aquarists. Experienced hobbyists will grow various Cryptocorynes which are native to the area – even though many are difficult to cultivate – in soft water together with species of Rasbora and more difficult Labyrinth fish such as the Honey Gourami, the Dwarf Gourami and the Croaking Gourami. Neons can also be kept though a perfectionist might not associate Asian Cryptocoryne with South American fish.

An Amazonian stream: a typical Brazilian "black-water" stream without vegetation.

A *Cryptocoryne* stream in southern Thailand.

b. A River.

Since the water flows slowly the fish require less oxygen and the list of typical species which could dominate the scene includes such carp as Barbs as well as Cichlids and Angelfish. When adding Barbs with Cichlids remember that Angelfish will not settle-in with the Sumatra Barb since it likes to nibble on the long pelvic fins of the former – and will attack the feelers of most Labyrinth fishes.

The bottom consists of fine gravel with many kinds of roots providing good cover. Vegetation is relatively sparse since most tropical rivers have subdued lighting due to the peat-brown water. As a result there is relatively little underwater vegetation and the surface is covered with a variety of floating plants.

c. A shallow thicket

This is a variation of river landscaping, a shallow section near a river bank thick with reeds. It can be imitated by inserting bamboo and similar thin woods vertically in a gravel bed though this makes it difficult to catch fishes which will hide between the rods. Middle-range plants are missing and you can use *Salvinia, Pistia* or even Duckweed for the floating varieties, if subdued lighting is called for. Vegetarian fishes such as *Abramites, Leporinus* and *Distichodus* are ideal for this kind of an aquarium.

d. Rocky landscape

Our first thoughts probably focus on the unique biotopes suggestive of Lake Tanganyika and Lake Malawi Cichlids. Many of these species live in cracks in the rocky bottom at depths of 10 meters. Enough light penetrates the clear water to allow algae to grow on stones and a few sturdy Vallisneria and Sagittaria can be used in the gravelly foreground.

Another possibility is the South American stream. Dark slabs of slate or basalt with cracks between form the basis of such a stream. It is water perfect for the Striped Anostomus (*Anostomus anostomus)* and related species such as Leporinus. With their upward-pointing mouths the fishes browse off the rich growth on stones, often dining in the nearly vertical cracks.

A thicket can be quickly imitated through the use of sections of Tonkin reed.

An underwater photo of a rocky landscape typical of Lake Malawi.

e. A Bog Aquarium.

This is a difficult biotope to imitate, but rewarding once you succeed. A mangrove swamp is one possibility with Archerfish and Scats swarming through the water with, perhaps, even a few Monos and Mudskippers included. The water is brackish and slightly saline and since mangroves are not seen in Europe and only in the southern tip of America, we can be dramatic by creating the flooded landscape typical of the Brazilian jungle. Various Cichlids and a few Tetras, and *Moenkhausia* is an example, can be kept in four to eight inches (10 to 20 cm) of water. The surrounding land will play host to Philodendron whose air roots hang into the water. With care Philodendron can be a beautiful and useful decoration in such an aquarium. Its roots quickly branch into the water, creating hiding places for smaller fishes.

The rear of an aquarium can be decorated with squares of cork or, better, with peat planted with bromelias. Bog terraria, called "Paludariums" in Europe, are also good projects for the plant enthusiast.

3. Species Tanks.

These are rarely kept except by specialists though the term does not limit the tank to one species of fish. Related species can also be combined though in the strictest sense it becomes an aquarium of a family or genus of fishes. Hobbyists who keep Egglaying Toothcarp often combine several species though only a single species and then only a pair may be seen in smaller tanks. The bottom of the tank will be lined with peat and suitable water plants are Cryptocorynes and others which tolerate soft water.

Most hobbyists will keep several of these tanks, one with delicate Tetras and another with smaller Cichlids for example. Still another could house *Apistogramma* while a fourth could contain livebearers. Another example of a species tank is a goldfish bowl. It may be unheated, since goldfish can tolerate lower water temperatures. Its bottom should include coarse gravel and plants at home in hard water – Vallisneria and Sagittaria with a few clusters of *Elodea* (*Egeria densa*).

A bog aquarium with a shallow water section. Land plants are above.

A species tank with Labyrinth fish.

4. Geographical Aquariums

a) Southeast Asia

Cryptocorynes, described in Section 2, should be mentioned again since this is a typical Southeast Asian biotope. Other Asian biotopes are similar to those in our description of a landscape tank and it is merely the choice of water plants and fishes that determine the character of the geographic aquarium. As an example, an aquarium with Labyrinth fish and Asiatic plants is an Asian aquarium even though we ignore the handful of Labyrinth fish found in Africa.

b) African Aquarium

There are only a few aquatic plants which are truly African and the list includes varities of west African Anubias (*Anubias lanceolata** and *Anubias barteri*) as well as the Dwarf Anubias (*Anubias nana**) which does not do well in most aquariums. On the other hand, many species of aquatic plants have become established in African waters so that one can almost say the community of fishes determines the character of an African tank.

We suggest a school of Congo Tetras, *Phenacogrammus interruptus*, though the handsome male with its extended dorsal and caudal fins requires a careful aquarist to look its best. To accompany the Congo Tetra we would add the related Yellow Congo Tetra, the Dwarf Distichodus, *D. decemmaculatus* and the Red-Eyed Characin, *Arnoldichthys spilopterus*. Those who would allow more latitude could combine the Congro Tetra with Cardinal Tetra although they would no longer have a species tank, but rather a community aquarium based on color. Both species require much the same kind of water.

---

* The *Anubias* is currently classified as a separate species, see page 114.

A swamp area in Thailand. *Labeo bicolor* is caught in bamboo tubes in this impenetrable underwater jungle. The Labeo uses the tubes as a hiding place and can be readily caught by skilled collectors.

c) An African Aquarium (Tanganjika and Malawi)

African Cichlids have been described in Section 2 (d), page 184, and also are at home in an African Aquarium. Since the species requires water with a relatively high hardness they are generally given their own tank. The brilliant coloring of these Cichlids, which is often compared with the splendor of saltwater Coralfish, explains why they are so popular. They are also hardy and aggressive. When several fish are combined care must be taken to provide each fish, or each pair, with an adequate hiding place to prevent continuous fighting over territory. If the fish fight, the weaker ones will eventually die.

Since few plants can survive in hard water only a few species can be suggested. The most suitable is the Java Fern, though it is not strictly in keeping with the theme of the tank and, more to the point, not particularly well liked by this plant-eating species. The fern will not grow if the nitrate level is too high and the water will need frequent changes. In any event, if the Cichlids are to be bred, regular water changes are indispensable so it may not be an issue. Additional information can be found in the descriptions of the species.

d) A South American Aquarium

One South American stream has been suggested in Section 2 (a) and a replica of the bank of a South American stream is probably the ideal of most aquarists. To create the scene we need South American plants such as *Echinodorus* – the Amazon Sword Plant, the Pygmy Chain Sword Plant, *Heteranthera* and others. Place either a bogwood root or a large rock with smaller rocks beside it in the middle area to create daytime hiding places for such nighttime-active fishes as *Hypostomus, Rineloricaria, Pterygoplichthys, Hemiancistrus* and *Peckoltia*. In addition to the catfish, Tetras, peaceful Cichlids and, possibly, a few Central American livebearers would be appropriate. The latter are recommended, however, only if the plants and fish do not require excessively soft water since livebearers prefer water from 20° dGH upward.

In a tank with African Cichlids, the rocky out-croppings determine the biotope.

A South American tank with Tetras and Central American *Poecilia*

e) An Australian Aquarium

There are only a few species of Australian fishes in the hobby and most are captive-bred in Asia. With few exceptions the fish we see are Rainbow Fish and can be combined with many other species since they are both peaceful and hardy.

f) A North American Aquarium

Fifty years ago North American fishes were the most popular choice for aquariums since, aside from a bunsen burner beneath each tank, there was no satisfactory way to heat aquarium water. While not demanding about temperatures North American species still require some attention in terms of water quality and food.

North American Perches and some smaller species can make a splendid tank though they are generally more difficult to keep than warm water fish. The first requirement is a reasonably large aquarium, one nearly three feet in length (unless you plan to keep such dwarf species as *Elassoma evergladei* and *Lucania goodei*. A typical tank would be filled with a three to four-inch bed (8-10 cm.) of medium-coarse gravel. The hardness of the water can range between 10 and 25° dGH. The water does not need to be heated. A number of European aquatic plants are suitable. The water should be carefully filtered and circulated and should be rich in oxygen. Some North American fishes make boisterous companions and not all species can be combined in a single tank. A few will not even tolerate more than one specimen of its own type. A small school of half-grown fishes may be the best compromise. As they grow, they will become used to each other.

The major difficulty is food. Most species will take only moving food and tend to ignore both flakes and freeze-dried offerings. On the other hand some frozen-foods are readily accepted. The large Perches are best fed on earthworms and small pieces of liver and heart. Such a tank could also be considered a "species tank".

Pseudotropheus spec. aff. zebra, see page 762

g) European Aquarium

Today few people take the time to establish a true European aquarium, that is a tank with native European fishes. What child today catches Stickelbacks in a stream and keeps them at home – even if we consider the fact that he now needs special permission? Indeed, where can one find Stickelbacks, Bitterlings, Bullheads and other cold water fish? They are rarely available from a pet store though occasionally we may find such small Whitefish as Roaches in angling stores. They are sold there as bait.

Stickelbacks are found in clear, clean meadow streams and in small ponds and drainage ditches on the outskirts of towns. They require live food and may be caught in a small eight-inch (20 cm) net.

When you find Bitterling you also see the Painter's Mussel, essential to the Bitterling for reproduction. The Painter's mussel is found only in clean waters with a muddy bottom. Dummersee Lake in northern Germany is an example, though you cannot catch fish there since it is a Nature Conservancy Area. There is an easier answer. Several cold water fish farms specialize in breeding fish for aquariums and you can often buy Bitterlings and other species there. If there is a problem with the European tank the cause is found in our homes. The rooms are generally too warm and European fish cannot stand either high temperatures nor the lack of oxygen that accompanies the heat. If you plan to try your hand at a European tank one could be established with such native plants as Arrowhead, Waterweed, Floating Crowsfoot and Vallisneria. Then, as the spring sun warms the waters you'll be able to observe the courtship and spawning of many European species in your cold water tank. It would be good if more aquarists were to keep at least one. A cold water tank demands more skill and expertise than a warm water aquarium, but is worth the effort. We can hope our cities will soon control water pollution for without it a cold water tank in our homes may be the only way to can save some of the species now threatened with extinction. Even today you can breed threatened fishes at home, returning them to their native waters. Obviously you should coordinate this kind of effort with other aquarium hobbyists, anglers and government fisheries experts – all familiar with local conditions. In Germany for example, a local "Red List" has been published listing the local species aquarists can help to save. Below are some examples:

1. Species which may be threatened with extinction at some future date: Two-Spot Bleak (*Alburnoides bipunctatus*).
2. Threatened species:
Miller's Thumb, Mudskipper, Merlin, Minnow, Bitterling.
3. Endangered:
Crucian, Three-Spined Stickelback, Ruffle, Leucaspius, Dwarf Stickelback.

All of these can be kept in home aquariums but other endangered native European fishes cannot because of their size, yet anyone who says European fish have nothing new to offer is mistaken. There is a lot of personal satisfaction in helping to protect these species for future generations.

A European river landscape: Hortobagi in Hungary.

5. Combining fish by temperature

    a) **Cold Water Aquaria 46-64° F (8-18° C)**
North American fish
European cold water fish

    b) **Fish for moderate temperatures 57-68° F (14-20° C)**
The list includes Macropods among others
White Cloud Minnows
Goldfish
Rosy Barbs
Varigated platies and other livebearers

    c) **Tropical fish at home in lower temperatures**
In general these are species found at higher elevations such as in tropical mountain streams. The temperature ranges from 68 to 75° F (20-24° C) or below.

    d) **Tropical fish requiring higher temperatures**
These include species from the lower areas of the tropics and are found, for the most part, in larger and deeper lakes in which the temperature remains uniformly high even during "cold spells" – 75-86° F (24-30° C).

When keeping fish it is extremely important to consider temperature requirements. Please read the comments in our chapter on "Heating" (page 50).

6. Combining fish on the basis of water conditions

    a) **Soft water, below 8° dGH**
The list includes most of the "blackwater" fishes.

    b) **Medium-hard water, 8-12° dGH**
Fish found in this kind of water are those most often recommended for a beginning aquarium.

    c) **Hard water, over 18° dGH**
Such fish as Rainbow Fish, African Cichlids and Livebearers are at home in this water.

    d) **Brackish water, over 30° KH and a 0.5% concentration of salt.**
Fish at home in this water include Archer Fish, Scats, Moons and Mudskippers.

7. Choosing fish according to tank size

While you can combine fish in the many ways we've listed above you must also consider the eventual size of the adult fish in relation to the size of your aquarium. Some fish are ideal for small tanks to 16 to 20 inches long (about 40 cm.) and there are others which demand tanks many times that size. The minimum tank length will be found in our descriptions of individual species.

8. Plant-eating fish

The species Leporinus, Abramites, Distichodus and many Serrasalmidae require a special tank, one without edible plants. There are many ways to solve the problem. You can decorate without plants using rocks and such, you can use plastic plants and you can add hardy plants which do not appeal to the fish. We'd recommend Java Fern and Java Moss.

9. The Dutch Plant Aquarium

Dutch aquarists are particularly keen on aquatic plants and create entire gardens of them. The fish are an after thought. The effects of the plants are of primary importance and each species has its place in the tank. The decoration is not based on the homogeneity of the aquatic species, but on the over all effect. Plants are positioned so they contrast with each other in shape and color. Such a tank requires a lot of work, as will any garden, and the taller, faster-growing plants must be cut back regularly.

This Dutch plant aquarium differs from the one seen on pages 74-75 with the addition of more swimming room for the fish in the foreground. The tank is longer and shallower and the foreground terrace achieved less by the shape of the gravel bed than by the careful placement of taller plants.

Symbols used in the illustrated section:

Fam.:	=	Family
Subfam.:	=	Sub-family
Syn.:	=	Synonym
		In the systematic classification of animals only the name adopted by the initial describer applies. Subsequent descriptions are known as synonyms.
Hab.:	=	Habitat; the place of origin.
Fl.:	=	First introduction. It is often interesting to discover where the hobby first learned of a species.
Sex:	=	Ways to differentiate between the sexes.
Soc. B.:	=	Social behavior.
M:	=	Recommended maintenance procedures. Indications of pH values and hardness (dGH) are often followed by figures in brackets. These indicate the range tolerated by the fish.
B:	=	Breeding procedure indicators. Complete breeding instructions can be found in technical journals and relevant textbooks.
F:	=	Suggested feeding procedures; types of food.
S:	=	Special notes.
T:	=	Temperature range.
L:	=	Length of the adult fish. A figure in brackets indicates the potential length in an aquarium.
A:	=	Recommended length of the aquarium.
R:	=	Region within the tank preferred by the fish. t = top; m = middle; b = bottom.
D:	=	Degree of difficulty to keep. Also see notes on page 203.

Further explanations

F: Suggested feeding procedures.
The abbreviations C, H, L and O can be seen under this heading. Their meanings are:

C=Carnivore or meat-eater.
These are generally predators and require live foods. The fishes have a short digestive tract and a large stomach which can hold an entire fish or other prey. These fish chase their prey and eat an entire animal

or a large chunk once or twice a day. Larger fishes may only eat once or twice a week spending a significant period of time, from several hours to several days, digesting. Such fishes include the predatory *Hoplerythrinus*, Snakehead and several perch.

When young these fishes can easily be fed with flakes. The larger flakes are suggested.
Included in this group are carnivores which are not necessarily predators but which feed on such live foods as freshwater shrimps, insects and larvae. The list includes small Tetras for which we recommend Tetra FD Menu, Tetra Growth Food, TetraRuby and F/D Bloodworms.

H = Herbivore or vegetable-eater.

Fish in this classification are the opposites of carnivores. They have adjusted to a different ecological niche in terms of nourishment and it may be said they are not as advanced in their development. In their native habitat the fishes live on fruit, plants and algae. Many will also eat live food but truly active predators are not found in this category.

Herbivores do not generally have a stomach but possess an expanded small intestine. The fishes must eat often and cannot satiate themselves at one feeding. They must, therefore, be fed frequently in an aquarium, quite probably three or four times a day. The fry prefer a vegetable-based flake food such as Tetra's Conditioning Food and similar formulations. These will generally prove inadequate for an adult who should be given cooked lettuce, cress, chickweed, and frozen spinach. Precise recommendations can be found in the feeding plan.

L = Limnivore or mud-eater.

Mud-eaters feed on such vegetable matter as algae and detritus and on the micro-organisms which live in them. The fishes will also take an occasional worm from the bottom as well as other food found there. The fish continually investigate the bottom, including plants, rocks and roots, in a day-long search for food. In an aquarium they may have to be fed a special diet if sufficient food is not available naturallty. Food tablets are their best substitute. The species generally have a small stomach and a long intestine and prefer to eat their foods leisurely. This is an advantage for the tablet.

O = Omnivore; fish prefering a general diet.

The list includes many carp-like fish, many Tetras and many Cichlids. None are either predators nor vegetarians, but prefer a diet that offers a little of both. Because of this Omnivores are the easiest to feed and all accept commercial flake foods. Adults should be fed two or three times a day; the fry more frequently.

In some cases the letters C, H. L. and O are not used alone. They can be combined when the precise mix of food for a species cannot be precisely catagorized. The first letter is always characteristic of the food found in the wild and the second is an indication that, in an aquarium, the species can be trained to consume other foods. An example is *Nematobrycon palmeri* for which we suggest: C, O; flake food, live food (*Artemia, Daphnia* and *Cyclops*). C means that in the wild the fish feeds mainly on live foods. The O which follows indicates that in an aquarium the species will accept flake foods formulated with vegetable and animal matter.

When flake foods are listed first it indicates the species can be fed exclusively on flakes. The foods which follow are recommended for supplemental feedings. When a good supply of live food is available it would be recommended since it is the closest to the species' natural food and there is, of course, no objection to using it. Where live foods are listed first it means the species must be fed predominantly with live foods, even in an aquarium. The foods which follow should be used only supplementary.

The Degree of Difficulty, indicated by the symbol D, can also be related to the foods a fish requires.

D: 1 Beginner's Fishes
The fish are generally omnivorous and have no specialized food requirements. A variety of flake foods are suitable.

D: 2 For slightly more experienced hobbyists
Flake foods are suitable. The letters under category "F" indicate the type of food recommended.

D: 3 For advanced aquarists
In general flake foods are still recommended but often need to be augmented with other types such as freeze-dried, food tablets and live foods, the selection depending on the species and our suggested feeding plan.

D: 4 Species recommended for aquatic epicures and experts
Included are fish with highly specialized diets: predators which require live foods, vegetarians which need algae and wilted lettuce and sensitive species such as Discus which present the dual problems of food and water quality.
The number indicating Degree of Difficulty is often followed by letters which explain why a species has been assigned to class 4. The following letters are used:

H = Herbivore
Vegetarians which cannot be kept in a tank with live plants.

Ch = Chemistry

Requires water of the highest quality or needs particular water values.

C = Carnivore

Predators which cannot be kept in a tank with smaller fishes though they may often accept tankmates of their own or differing species if of the same or larger size. C also indicates the fish must be fed live foods and that a constant supply will be needed.

S = Size

The species needs a large tank with plenty of space for swimming. When you purchase young fish you should know, in advance, the size it will attain as an adult.

To avoid a complicated rating system we have not always indicated every factor which could be evaluated. For example a predator indicated by "C" may also reach a prohibitive size. We have not always indicated this and the letters included underline the most important aspects in evaluating our Degree of Difficulty rating.

Pseudo-Osteichthyes and Chondropterygians

We have listed these apart from the True Bony Fish because, though they are very interesting in terms of aquatic evolution, they are of less significance to an aquarist. In an evolutionary sense, the fish are much older than True Bony Fish.

Paratrygon sp. from Venezuela. The upper picture shows the almost colorless underside of a Stingray with its mouth and gill slits exposed. The lower picture shows its unusual swimming pattern.

Group 1

Fam.: Acipenseridae (True Sturgeons)

Acipenseridae, a family of fishes with such primitive characteristics as heterocercal tail fins and a continuous spiracle, are found only in the Northern Hemisphere. They can be identified by five rows of angular, bony plates inserted in the skin of the body. The mouth is at the bottom and can be extended forward like a nose. There are four barbels or feelers in front of it. The family includes four genera and the roe of almost every variety is prized as caviar.

Fam.: Lepidosirenidae

The family is composed of two genera, *Lepidosiren* and *Protopterus*, and are found throughout west and central Africa as well as northern and central South America. These Lung-Fish have an eel-like body, a dichotomous lung, four gill arches and small, round scales. The eggs are laid in muddy holes and guarded by the male. The young, tadpole-like, breathe through external gills. Five species are known.

Fam.: Paratrygonidae (Freshwater Rays)

The fish are found in the fresh waters of South America and have a flagellate tail with a barbed stinger on the upper side. Their body is disc shaped and flattened. The species are live-bearers and the female concieves internally, the sperm transferred by a thick, finger-like organ on the pelvic fin of the male.

Fam.: Polypteridae (Lobe-Finned Pike)

Lobe-Finned Pikes have an elongated body covered with smooth scales, and some are so elongated they are virtually snake-like. The dorsal fin has five to 18 lobes and the pectoral fins, which are used for forward movement, are pediolate and fan-like. The fish has a dichotomous lung which is linked to the intestine and serves as an accessory respiratory organ. Certain of the young have external gills. When breathing is inhibited, the fish die. They are found only in Tropical Africa.

Acipenser ruthenus
Sterlet

LINNAEUS, 1758

Syn.: *Acipenser ruthenicus, A. dubius, A. gmelini, A. kamensis, A. jeniscensis, A. pygmaeus, Sterlethus gmelini, S. ruthenus*

Hab.: Europe and Siberia: tributaries of the Black Sea, Sea of Azov, Caspian Sea; Polar Sea from Ob to Kolyma ; also in such tributaries of the Baltic Sea as Duna.

Fl.: A European species.

Sex: Unknown.

Soc. B.: Harmless and peaceful, the species is a burrower. Though it is hardy and undemanding, it should not be kept with very small fish.

M: Recommended only for large aquariums, the fish need a soft, sandy bottom. Avoid sharp stones. Needs lots of space and clear, cold water, 15-20° dGH at pH 7.5. Create a current with a filter and keep fish only to 6 inches long in an aquarium (10 to 15 cm.)

B: It is not considered possible because an aquarium is too small. In the wild *Acipenser ruthenus* spawns in May and June on gravel beds. The fish are prolific, producing 11,000 to 135,000 eggs. The young hatch in four or five days.

F: C; live foods; such water insect larvae as Day-fly larvae; Snails; small fish.

S: The name Sterlet refers to the small bony stars found in the skin. Because of its unusual body shape the species is considered a highly uncommon fish for an aquarium. Despite their size the young are easy to keep.

T: 50-65° F,   **L:** 39″,   **A:** 39-60″,   **R:** b,   **D:** 2-3.
    10-18° C,   100 cm,   100-150 cm,

Protopterus dolloi

BOULENGER, 1900

Syn.: None

Hab.: Africa; lower reaches of the Zaire.

Fl.: 1954

Sex: Unknown.

Soc. B.: A predator, the species is intolerant of others and will bite. The male looks after the eggs.

M: Needs a tank with a muddy bottom and heavy vegetation. The water can be about ten inches (25 cm.) deep and there are no special requirements in terms of water. Only the younger fish are recommended for a home aquarium. The fish should be kept alone.

B: The species has not been bred in an aquarium.

F: C; live food; fish; tadpoles; snails; earthworms; insect larvae.

S: *P. dolloi* has the most elongated body of all the species. Their unusual lungs play an important part in survival during dry periods. If a stream dries the fish buries its body in the mud, rolls into a ball and excretes a slime which hardens the exterior. A hole in the capsule allows the fish to breathe. Thus buried the fish can survive for six months and when the rainy season returns it is ready for another year of life.

T: 75-86° F,   L: 34″,   A: 47″,   R: b,   D: 4 (C).
  25-30° C,   85 cm,   120 cm,

Potamotrygon laticeps
Freshwater Stingray   (GARMAN, 1913)

Syn.: *Paratrygon laticeps*

Hab.: South America; Brazil; Paraguay; Uruguay; Argentina.

Fl.: Probably after 1970.

Sex: ♂ is more colorful and has finger-like inspissations on the pelvic fin.

Soc. B.: A peaceful, lively bottom-dweller.

M: Does best in a species tank with the largest bottom area and little water, about 12 inches (30 cm.) in depth. Use soft sand on the bottom with lots of swimming room and floating plants above. The fish are fastidious and sensitive to water pollution. Use medium-hard, neutral to slightly acid water, 10° dGH and pH 6.5-7.0.

B: Has not been bred in an aquarium.

F: C; live or frozen foods; *Tubifex*; earthworms; shellfish; shrimps; mosquito larvae; chopped fish meat; frozen crab.

S: The fish have a barbed stinger on the upper side of the tail. When carlessly handled it can cause painful abrasions. The stinger is replaced two or three times a year.

T: 72-78° F,   **L:** 27″,   **A:** 39″,   **R:** b,   **D:** 4 (C).
23-25° C,   70 cm,   100 cm,

Erpetoichthys calabaricus   (J.A. SMITH, 1865)
Snakefish

Syn.: *Calamoichthys calabaricus, Calamichthys calabaricus, Herpetoichthys calabaricus*

Hab.: Fresh and brackish waters of West Africa; Nigeria and Cameroon. The fish is particularly common in the Nigeria Delta.

Fl.: 1906, F. E. Schneising, Magdeburg, Germany.

Sex: The caudal fin of ♂ has more bars (12 to 14): ♀ has but 9 and the fin thickens during the spawning season. The male's fin is olive, the female's is a light ochre.

Soc. B.: A peaceful nocturnal fish, it is especially good with its own species. It should not be kept with smaller fish as they will be taken.

M: Needs a substrate of soft, fine sand with thick vegetation and many hiding places among roots and rocks. Suggest a slightly acid, medium hard water 10° dGH and pH 6.5-6.9. Keep in a community tank only under certain cases.

B: Has not been bred in an aquarium.

F: C; live foods only; fish; frogs; shellfish; crabs; insect larvae; chopped heart, beef and horsemeat.

S: Food is located by smell: Snakefish have poor eyesight. The fish can leave water for several hours, breathing air with a lung-like swim-bladder. Because of this the tank must be covered. *Erpetoichthys* differs from the related genus *Polypterus* by the absence of pelvic fins.

T: 71-85° F,   **L:** 15¹/₂″,   **A:** 39″,   **R:** b,   **D:** 3.
    22-28° C,   40 cm,   100 cm,

Polypterus ornatipinnis   BOULENGER, 1902
Syn.: None

Hab.: In fresh waters of central Africa; Upper and Central; Zaire.

Fl.: 1953.

Sex: Uncertain. Anal fins of ♂ are said to be larger and the head of ♀ is reportedly larger.

Soc. B.: Fish may bite when placed together, though they seldom fight if adequate hiding places are available. The species is rarely hostile to larger tankmates.

M: The tank does not need height and 12 inches of water is adequate. Suggest lots of hiding places such as caves, rocks and roots. Add plenty of vegetation and open swimming room. Needs a sandy tank bottom.

B: Only occasionally bred in an aquarium. According to ARMBRUST the ♂ initiates the courtship and is the active partner. Spawns on clumps of vegetation. The anal fin of the ♂ is spread so that it resembles a hollow hand and is pushed beneath the anal orfice of the ♀. 200-300 eggs are laid and fertilized in this manner. The young hatch in four days at a water temperature of 77° F (26° C).

F: C; only live food; such chopped meats as beef and beef heart.

S: ARMBRUST initiated spawning with sodium iodine (KJ) adding one drop of a 1% solution to 25 gallons (100 liters) of water. (But no more!) Be sure to cover the aquarium since the solution causes the fish to become restless, often leaping about the tank.

T: 77-83° F,   **L:** to 17″,   **A:** 39″,   **R:** m,   **D:** 4 (C).
    26-28° C,   to 46 cm,   100 cm,

Erpetoichthys calabaricus

Polypterus ornatipinnis

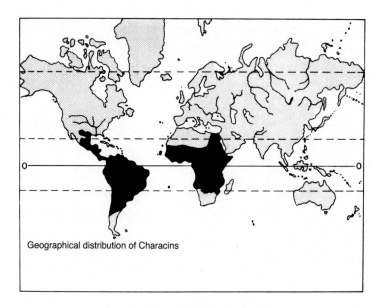

Geographical distribution of Characins

The sub-order Characins and related Characoidei

WEBER (1820), BOULENGER (1904), GERY (1977) and other writers have assumed that Characins represent some of the most ancient, if not the oldest, fishes in the order of Carps or *Cypriniformes*. BOULENGER considers them the ancestors of Naked Catfish, Barbs, Eels and Knifefish while other writers feel the Catfish is the oldest Bony Fish extant.

In 1820 E. H. WEBER described the "Weber's apparatus" which, in the case of Characins and related fishes connects the organs of hearing with the swim bladder where it operates as a sounding board. Characins have a particularly keen sense of hearing, are very alert and also have a "chemical warning system" which enables them to sense danger and form schools. The parallel development of the various families of Characins in both South America and Africa is considered proof the two global continents were once joined. The implication is that Characins originated before the land masses split, in Mesozoic times, some 80 to 150 million years ago.

212

Hyphessobrycon socolofi, see page 284

By any yardstick Characins are prolific. Some one thousand species have been identified in South America and another two hundred in Africa though BOULENGER had recorded but half this number in 1904. GERY feels many species remain to be discovered.

Externally, the most visible distinguishing feature is an adipose fin of unknown purpose. It is lacking in several genera – *Macropoma, Erythrinus, Lebiasina, Pyrrhulina, Corynopoma* and *Hasemania*. The fin can also be found on certain Catfish, *Corydoras* and Salmonidae are examples. They are not related to Characins.

According to GERY (1972) there are 14 sub-orders of Characins. Most Characins are schooling fishes and are particularly suited to this through their ability to receive environmental stimuli. As an example, if food is scattered across the surface of a jungle stream, Characins are inevitably the first to find it. They also seem to sense trouble before it happens.

Apart from such predatory Characins as Piranhas (Pike), the species are peaceful even though most are carnivores. The genera also includes such notable herbivores or plant eaters as *Distichodus* (Africa), *Prochilodus* and *Leporinus* (South America).

Species which live mostly on the algae and micro-fauna found in their habitat are known as Limnivores or mud-eaters. Omnivores or fishes which eat nearly anything and includes several Characins although the best known fishes in the group are Barbs.

Characins, a hardy fish with elongated bodies, prefer clear, running water. In South America they are found in clear, blackwater regions as well as turbid white-water rivers though populations tend to be larger in fast-moving water because of the plentiful supply of food. The fishes need a lot of oxygen and because of it fare the worst when the wetlands dry under sizzling hot summer suns. Then oxygen is in its shortest supply. The fish will also succomb to rough netting or too much time in a phototank. They cannot tolerate stressful disturbances and the oxygen depletion which often results.

Therefore, when Characins are kept they should be given a long tank with room in which to swim, a strong filter with a continuous "current" or flow and plenty of oxygenated water obtained through surface movement. Most species appreciate the "familiarity" of brown-colored, softened water, made slightly acid through peat filtration. The water should always be clear though colored. Unless herbivores are kept, fine, feathery plants can be added since they too require clean, clear water. Since most characins are not burrowers, the water should remain in good condition.

According to GERY several hundred Characins remain undescribed. One example is this *Hemigrammus sp.* for which the name Signal Tetra has been suggested.

Arnoldichthys spilopterus
African Red-Eyed Characin

(BOULENGER, 1909)
Sub-Fam.: Alestinae

Syn.: *Petersius spilopterus*

Hab.: Tropical west Africa: from Lagos to the Niger Delta.

Fl.: 1907, C. Siggelkow, Hamburg, West Germany.

Sex: The anal fin is convex with red, yellow and black stripes on ♂ and nearly straight with a black point on ♀.

Soc. B.: A peaceful, schooling fish.

M: Needs a roomy, shallow tank not more than 12 inches in height. You can add a light planting, but leave room for swimming. The gravel bed should be dark and the water well filtered through peat. Try a hardness to 20° dGH and pH 6.0-7.5. Partial water changes should be made every three or four weeks.

B: Suggest soft, slightly acid water. One pair has laid more than one thousand eggs in a single small tank. Those fry hatched after 30 to 35 hours, surfaced on the fifth day and were swimming by the seventh. The fry are especially timid and when frightened flee head-first to the tank bottom-- so this should be soft, of peat or very fine sand. The fry grow rapidly and are nearly 2 inches long ($4^1/_2$ cm.) within seven weeks. They should be first fed finely ground food then, from the second week, brine shrimp, finely ground flake, egg-yolk, Liquifry and *Cyclops* – all foods easily obtained.

F: C, O; live food; large flakes.

S: While it requires a larger tank, this is one of the finest of African Characins and a species everyone should try at least once.

T: 73-82° F, **L**: 3″, **A**: 39″, **R**: m, **D**: 2-3.
   23-28° C,   8 cm,   100 cm,

Brycinus imberi

(PETERS, 1852)
Sub-Fam.: Alestinae

Syn.: *Alestes imberi, Brycinus bequaerti, B. curtus, "B. fuchsii", B. jacksoni, "B. lemairii"*

Hab.: Cameroon; Zambia; Stanley Pool, Zaire; Lake Malawi.

Fl.: Unknown.

Sex: Unknown.

Soc. B.: A peaceful, schooling species.

M: Similar to suggestions for *Phenacogrammus interruptus*.

B: Not described. In its natural habitat a ♀ lays as many as 14,000 eggs.

F: C, O; live food, flakes.

T: 72-79° F, **L**: 4″, **A**: 31″, **R**: m, **D**: 2-3.
   22-26° C,   10 cm,   80 cm,

Arnoldichthys spilopterus

Brycinus imberi

Brycinus longipinnis
Long-Finned Characin

(GUENTHER, 1864)
Sub-Fam.: Alestinae

Syn.: *Alestes longipinnis, Bryconalestes longipinnis*

Hab.: Niger Delta; Ghana; Sierra Leone; Togo.

Fl.: 1928.

Sex: The rays of dorsal fins are greatly extended on ♂.

Soc. B.: A peaceful, schooling fish suggested for a large community tank.

M: These lively, nimble swimmers need a lot of room. Sunlight, strong artificial lighting and a dull-colored bottom are appreciated. The species will not damage plants. Suggest a water with a hardness to 25° dGH and pH 6.5-7.8. Good filtration is essential since the fish will not do well in a tank heavy with nitrates. Suggest water changes of one third the tank on a regular basis.

B: Has not been accomplished.

F: C, O; large live foods; large flakes.

S: A fine, lively species for a larger tank.

T: 72-79° F, L: 4¹/₂",   A: 39",   R: m,   D: 2.
   22-26° C,   13 cm,   100 cm,

Hemigrammopetersius caudalis

(BOULENGER, 1899)
Sub-Fam.: Alestinae

Syn.: *Petersius caudalis*

Hab.: Stanley Pool, Zaire; other tributaries in Zaire.

Fl.: 1954.

Sex: Pelvic fins are tipped with white on ♂ and are clear on ♀.

Soc. B.: A peaceful, schooling species recommended for a community tank. Keep with peaceful tankmates.

M: Keep a group of five or more to prevent fish from becoming timid. In a school group behaviour is noticeable. The species is not a plant-eater. Suggest water with a hardness to 20° dGH and pH 6.5-7.8.

B: Follow recommendations for *Phenacogrammus interruptus.*

F: C, O; live food; flakes.

S: A species recommended for the connoisseur.

T: 72-79° F, L: 3",   A: 31",   R: m,   D: 3.
   22-26° C,   7 cm,   80 cm,

Brycinus longipinnis

Hemigrammopetersius caudalis

Lepidarchus adonis
Adonis Characin

Syn.: None

Hab.: West Africa.

Fl.: 1967, M. Blair, Scotland; 1969, E. Roloff, Karlsruhe, West Germany.

Sex: ♂ has numerous purple spots on the tail fin and rear of the body. ♀ has a nearly transparent, glassy body.

Soc. B.: A peaceful, gentle species which should be kept only with such smaller fishes as *Nannostomus*.

M: Does well in a small, heavily planted tank. Use extremely soft water to 4° dGH and pH 5.8-6.5. Peat filtration is recommended.

B: Can be easily bred in soft water, about 2° KH at temperatures between 24 and

26° C. Though not prolific the fish will lay 20-30 eggs in the smallest tank on fiber or soft plants. The fry hatch in 36 hours and become free-swimming in seven days. They will accept newly-hatched brine shrimp. Be sure to darken the tank since the fry prefer dark places. The feeding corner should be lighted. If the young do not eat, make the area brighter during feeding and reduce the water level.

F: C, O; fine live food; FD Menu.

S: One of the smallest species kept in an aquarium, it is a gem for the specialist. Since breeding is easy more aquarists should try keeping the fish.

T: 72-79° F,   L: ¹/₂",   A: 8",   R: b,   D: 3.
   22-26° C,   2 cm,   20 cm,

Ladigesia roloffi
Sierra Leone Dwarf Characin

Syn.: None

Hab.: Yung River, Liberia; Sierra Leone; Ivory Coast; Ghana.

Fl.: 1967, Roloff, Karlsruhe, West Germany.

Sex: ♂ has a floppy, extended anal fin; on ♀ it is straight.

Soc. B.: A timid, peaceful, schooling fish which in nature, coexists with *Neolebias unifasciatus*, *Epiplatys annulatus* and *E. bifasciatus*. Recommended only for community tanks with peaceful tankmates.

M: Since the fish will jump whenever disturbed, the tank should be tightly covered. Needs a dark bottom, peat filtration and

water with a hardness to 10° dGH and pH 6.0-7.0. A floating cover such as Water Lily or *Nymphea* are essential.

B: The fish spawn immediately above a peat bottom in fairly soft (pH 6.0), fresh water (less than 4° dGH). The very small fry will accept only extremely fine foods. The species is not prolific.

F: C, O; fine live food: fruitflies; Grindal worms; brine shrimp. Also flakes and FD Menu.

S: Adults are brightly colored and the species deserved more attention through effective breeding.

T: 72-79° F,   L: to 1¹/₂",   A: 23",   R: m,   D: 2-3.
   22-26° C,   to 4 cm,   60 cm,

Lepidarchus adonis

Ladigesia roloffi

Micralestes acutidens

(PETERS, 1852)
Sub-Fam.: Alestinae

Syn.: *Alestes acutidens, Brachyalestes acutidens*

Hab.: Nile; Niger; Zaire; Zambesi; Togo; Ghana.

Fl.: 1932, W. Schreitmueller.

Sex: ♂ has a differently-shaped anal fin and a slenderer body.

Soc. B.: A lively, peaceful, schooling fish recommended for a community tank.

M: Does best in a long tank, planted along the back and sides. Needs room for swimming but is not demanding about water. Suggest a hardness to 25° dGH and pH 6.2-8.0 with good ventilation.

B: Unknown.

F: C, O; flakes; all types of live foods.

S: It is rarely imported though the species is abundant.

T: 72-79° F, **L:** 2¹/₂″, **A:** 31″, **R:** m, **D:** 2.
    22-26° C,   6.5 cm,   80 cm,

Phenacogrammus interruptus
Congo Tetra

(BOULENGER, 1899)
Sub-Fam.: Alestinae

Syn.: *Micralestes interruptus, Alestopetersius interruptus, Hemigrammalestes interruptus, Petersius codalus*

Hab.: Zaire.

Fl.: 1950, "Aquarium Hamburg", Hamburg, West Germany.

Sex: ♂ is larger and more colorful with extended tail and dorsal fins.

Soc. B.: Though a peaceful, schooling fish, it should not be placed in a tank with aggressive tankmates since it is easily frightened.

M: Needs a large tank with room for swimming. Recommend a dark tank bottom with floating plants to reduce the light. Lower levels of light shows off their colors better. As are most Characins, the fish are sensitive to noise. Do not tap on the glass.

Suggest a light-brown, peat-filtered water with a hardness of 4-18° dGH and pH 6.2. The fish may eat softer plants and young shoots.

B: Courtship can often be initiated by bright lighting, artificial or sun. A pair will spawn in the shallows, allowing up to 300 eggs to drop to the bottom. The fry hatch in six days. Feed such small live foods as Infusoria and, from the second week, brine shrimp and small flakes.

F: C, O; live food; large flakes. The fish are timid eaters. They accept food only after the keeper has gone and may nibble plants when not watched.

S: One of the finest of African Characins, the fish will not do well in a small aquarium nor in water high in chalk or nitrates.

T: 75-81° F, **L:** ♂ = 3″, ♀ = 2³/₄″, **A:** 31″, **R:** m, t, **D:** 2-3.
    24-27° C,   ♂ = 8.5 cm, ♀ = 6 cm,   80 cm,
R: m, t, **D:** 2-3.

Micralestes acutidens ♂

Phenacogrammus interruptus, top ♂, below ♀

Distichodus decemmaculatus
Dwarf Distichodus

PELLEGRIN, 1925
Sub-Fam.: Distichodinae

Syn.: Unknown

Hab.: Central Zaire basin.

Fl.: Possibly 1970.

Sex: Unknown.

Soc. B: A peaceful fish suitable for any aquarium with small, quiet tankmates. Needs plenty of vegetation.

M: Keep only in a tank with such hardy plants as Java Fern, Java Moss, Indian Fern or plastic duplicates. Recommend water with a hardness to 20° dGH and pH 6.5-7.5.

B: Someone should concentrate on breeding these beautiful Characins.

F: H; vegetable flakes; food tablets; lettuce; spinach; chickweed; watercress.

S: The smallest and easily the most attractive of the species it, unfortunately, is a plant-eater. Adults are more brightly colored than the photo indicates. The bottom half of the body is mossgreen from the side-line to the stomach. The fins, particularly the pelvics, are red.

T: 73-81° F,   L: 2³/₄″,   A: 23¹/₄″,   R: b, m, D: 2.
    23-27° C,   6 cm,   60 cm,

Distichodus fasciolatus

BOULENGER, 1898
Sub-Fam.: Distichodinae

Syn.: None

Hab.: Cameroons; Stanley Pool, Zaire; Katanga; Angola.

Fl.: 1953.

Sex: Unknown.

Soc. B.: Though it is a peaceful fish, it is recommended only for larger species tanks.

M: Treat as you would others of the genus but because of its high intake of vegetable food (as ballast), it pollutes the water. A strong filter is needed and should be cleaned regularly. Suggest water with a hardness to 25° dGH and pH 6-8.

F: H; a hearty plant-eater. The young will accept flakes.

S: Not recommended for an aquarium.

T: 73-81° F,   L: 12″,   A: 56″,   R: b, m, D: 3 (H).
    23-27° C,   30 cm,   150 cm,

Distichodus decemmaculatus

Distichodus fasciolatus

Distichodus lusosso

SCHILTHUIS, 1891
Sub-Fam.: Distichodinae

Syn.: None

Hab.: Zaire basin; Angola; Cameroon; Katanga.

Fl.: 1953.

Sex: Unknown.

Soc. B.: A peaceful fish with a great love for plants.

M: Requires a larger tank but follow suggestions for others of the genus. Will be "true to the genus" only in a species tank.

B: Probably impossible in an aquarium.

F: H; plants. See recommendations for *D. sexfasciatus*.

S: Not recommended for aquariums: grows too large. Can be distinguished from *D. sexfasciatus* by its longer nose.

T: 72-79° F, L: 16″, A: 56″, R: b, m, D: 3 (H).
  22-26° C, 40 cm, 150 cm,

Distichodus affinis

GUENTHER, 1873
Sub-Fam.: Distichodinae

Syn.: None

Hab.: Lower Zaire.

Fl.: 1911, Fritz Mayer, Hamburg, West Germany.

Sex: Unknown.

Soc. B.: A peaceful fish similar to the Dwarf Distichodus.

M: An excellent choice for community Cichlid tanks in which you cannot use plants because the other fishes are also burrowers. In juvenile form the fish is not appealing. Follow recommendaions for *D. decemmaculatus*.

B: Unknown.

S: Of the 30 or more known species of the genus only a few are suited to the hobby. This is easily the finest, however they are infrequently imported and difficult to find.

T: 73-81° F, L: 4¹/₂″, A: 31″, R: b, m, D: 3 (H).
  23-27° C, 12 cm, 80 cm,

The three similar *Distichodus* with red fins and black spots on the dorsal can be distinguished as follows:

D. affinis (photo)
Rounded tips to the tail fins, anal fin is longer than the dorsal. A 19-21 scale count; 37-39 scales on the lateral line. Lower Congo.

D. noboli
The tail fin is rounded, the anal is shorter than the dorsal. A scale count 14-16; 38-45 scales. Upper Congo.

D. notospilus
The tail fins end in a point, otherwise similar to the species above. The body coloring is more uniform than *D. affinis* but has less checkering on the sides. Found from Cameroon to Angola.

Distichodus lusosso

Distichodus affinis

Fam.: Citharinidae

Distichodus sexfasciatus

BOULENGER, 1897
Sub-Fam.: Distichodinae

Syn.: None

Hab.: Zaire basin; Angola.

Fl.: 1953.

Sex: Unknown.

Soc. B.: A peaceful, schooling fish, exclusively a vegetarian and a loner. Suitable for community tanks without plants.

M: Not recommended for an aquarium since only the young are attractively colored. Adults become yellow-grey. The conspicuous red tail fades, changing to grey. Decorate the tank with rocks and roots and possibly plastic plants. Java Fern will not be eaten if sufficient food is offered in other forms. Recommend water with hardness to 20° dGH (though 10° is better) and pH 6.0-7.5.

B: Unsuccessful.

F: H; plants; stewed lettuce; corn; salad; spinach; watercress; chickweed; vegetable flake; large flakes.

S: Suggested only for specialists; keep in a tank without plants.

T: 72-79° F, L: 10″, A: 47″, R: b, D: 3 (H).
  22-26° C, 25 cm, 120 cm,

Nannaethiops unitaeniatus
One-Striped African Characin

GUENTHER, 1871
Sub-Fam.: Distichodinae

Syn.: None

Hab.: Widely distributed throughout Africa; from Zaire to the Niger in the west; to the White Nile in the east.

Fl.: 1931.

Sex: ♂ is slenderer and more brightly colored. Portions of the dorsal and the upper lobe of the caudal fin are colored during spawning.

Soc. B.: A peaceful, schooling species which is best kept in a species tank. Only under these conditions will it display its fine, copper color.

M: Needs a bottom of fine sand with sparse planting and a lot of light. Use water with peat filration, hardness to 12° dGH and pH 6.5-7.5.

B: Not difficult to breed in a species tank. Morning sun promotes a desire to breed. Use clear, soft water, pH 6.0-6.5 with peat filtration and with a good conditioner added. A free-spawner, the eggs are dropped among plants and stones and hatch after 30 hours. The fry are free-swimming in five days. Raise with micropond food and brine shrimp. The breeding tank should contain at least 15 gallons (50 liters).

F: C; all types of small live food; freeze dried foods after acclimatization.

T: 73-79° F, L: 2¹/₂″, A: 23¹/₂″, R: b, m, D: 2-3.
  23-26° C, 6.5 cm, 60 cm,

228

Distichodus sexfasciatus

Nannaethiops unitaeniatus

Nannocharax fasciatus

GUENTHER, 1867
Sub-Fam.: Distichodinae

Syn.: None

Hab.: Cameroons; Volta; Niger; Gaboon; Lower Guinea.

Fl.: 1969.

Sex: Unknown.

Soc. B.: A peaceful loner, well suited to a community tank. Should be kept only with other small, peaceful fishes.

M: The fish can do well in a small tank but require oxygen-rich water with good circulation. Suggest a hardness to 15° dGH and pH 6.0-7.5. Use only a few plants and plenty of light to correspond to its natural surroundings. We recommend the addition of peat extract.

B: Not successful thus far.

F: C; all types of small live foods; freeze-dried food; after a time individual flakes will be accepted in moving water.

S: Similar to the South American genus *Characidium* though the latter rests on the bottom on its pectoral and pelvic fins. *Nannocharax* relies on its pectorals, anal fin and the lower lobe of its caudal for this purpose. The species is curious and not at all timid. It swims with its head upward at an angle of 45°.

T: 73-81° F, L: $2^1/_2$-3″, A: $15^1/_2$″, R: b, D: 3.
23-27° C, 7-8 cm, 40 cm,

Neolebias ansorgei
Ansorges Neolebias

BOULENGER, 1912
Sub-Fam.: Distichodinae

Syn.: *Neolebias landgrafi, Micraethiops ansorgei*

Hab.: In boggy pools of central Africa; Cameroons; Angola; Chiloango.

Fl.: 1924.

Sex: The male is finely colored. See the color photo.

Soc. B.: Though peaceful and timid, it should not be kept in a community tank. It will always feel intimidated surrounded by tankmates.

M: Does best in a small, darkened aquarium about 20 inches long. (See Killifish.) Use a good water conditioner to improve "aging" when changing the water. The species does not respond well to fresh water. Keep the depth of the tank water

about 8 inches. A filter is not essential. Decorate the tank with *Myriophyllum, Nitella, Cabomba* and *Nuphar.*

B: Spawn as you would Killifish. Lays to 300 eggs which fall to the bottom (on moss or peat fiber). The fry will hatch in one day and lie suspended at the surface for some time. Feed very fine food such as Infusoria. The fish mature after seven months. Recommend a water level of 6 to 8 inches.

F: C, O; small live foods; mosquito larvae; flakes.

S: This is the most common of the ten species. The genus is without an adipose fin.

T: 74-82° F, L: $1^1/_2$″, A: $19^1/_2$″, R: b, m, D: 2-3.
24-28° C, 3.5 cm, 50 cm,

Nannocharax fasciatus

Neolebias ansorgei

African Characins
Fam.: Citharinidae

Phago maculatus
African Pike Characin

AHL, 1922
Sub-Fam.: Ichthyborinae

Syn.: See notes under S.

Hab.: West Africa; Niger delta.

Fl.: 1913, von Hase, Hamburg, West Germany.

Sex: Unknown.

Soc. B.: A predator which can only be kept alone or with larger fishes (from 4 inches or 10 cm.). See F.

M: The fish prefers quiet and will not eat if upset. It needs hiding places between branches, roots and similar vegetation but makes few demands in terms of water. Recommend a water hardness to 20° dGH and a pH between 6.5.-7.5. A dark, peat-colored water meets the species need for concealment.

B: Unsuccessful in an aquarium.

F: C; smaller fish will eat live foods and, as it grows, entire fishes. In the wild they will even nibble the tails of larger fishes.

S: Seldom imported, GERY (1977) says the name is not secure. The fish may be identical with *Phago loricatus* GUENTHER, 1865. The sub-family are mostly known as tail-biters.

T: 73-82° F,   **L:** 5¹/₂″,   **A:** 31″,   **R:** m,   **D:** 3-4 (D).
     23-28° C,   14 cm,   80 cm,

Abramites hypselonotus
High-Backed Headstander

(GUENTHER, 1868)
Sub-Fam.: Anostominae

Syn.: *Leporinus hypselonotus, A. microcephalus*

Hab.: Amazon and Orinoco basins.

Fl.: 1917.

Sex: Unknown.

Soc. B.: Though the young, to 4 " (10 cm.), are peaceful and suited to a community tank, the adults will not tolerate others of their species.

M: Similar to suggestions for *Leporinus*. Needs a tank with roots and stones but without vegetation. Suggest medium-hard water to 18° dGH and pH 6.0-7.5 with strong filtration.

T: 73-81° F, **L**: 4¹/₂", **A**: 31", **R**: b, m, **D**: 2-3.
  23-27° C,   13 cm,   80 cm,

B: Unsuccessful.

F: L, H; will browse on algae and will nip new shoots. Suggest lettuce, watercress, vegetable flakes and small live foods.

S: A very interesting loner. In addition to *A. hypselonotus hypselonotus* there is one other sub-species, *A. hypselonotus ter netzi* (NORMAN, 1926).

Anostomus anostomus
Striped Anostomus

(LINNAEUS, 1758)
Sub-Fam.: Anostominae

Syn.: *Salmo anostomus, Leporinus anostomus, Anostomus gronovii, A. salmoneus, Pithecocharax anostomus*

Hab.: Amazon, from Manaus upstream; Orinoco; Venezuela; Guyana, Columbia.

Fl.: 1924, W. Eimeke, Hamburg, West Germany.

Sex: Unknown.

Soc. B.: Will become aggressive if kept in a small school but will tolerate each other better in larger groups, say seven or more. Single specimens can be kept in a well-cared for community tank where they will seldom bother tankmates.

M: Can be kept in a well-planted tank if there is sufficient algae or if it receives adequate vegetable foods. Do not keep with fishes which demand the same foods as *Hemiancistrus, Gyrinocheilus* and *Epalzeorhynchus* since it may not fare well in competition.

B: Has been accomplished though details are not available. See *Chilodus punctatus.*

F: L; many writers feel the up-turned mouth is intended for browsing on algae and stalked vegetation. It is true that virtually all *Anostomus* live in nearly vertical rocky fissures in the faster-moving portions of shallow rivers and streams where the algae is at its best. The fish will accept plants and leaves as a substitute, but live foods – mosquito larvae, *Daphnia* and small worms – are also eagerly sought after. Will also accept vegetable flakes, stewed lettuce, watercress and chickweed as a supplement. Smaller fishes will happily accept FD tablets.

S: Anyone who has not kept this fish cannot be called a true aquarist. The fish makes the customary demands of any South American Characin in terms of water: a hardness to 20° dGH and pH 5.8-7.5 (with 6.5 preferred). To decorate the tank use layers of rocks (or plastic substitutes). Weight is the primary problem since a layer of rocks may weigh more than the tank bottom can support. (See page 24.) If you have tried most everything in terms of species and landscape aquariums, *Anostomus* will provide a new challenge. Much is still to be discovered about their breeding habits. Be sure to use a strong filter to simulate the currents found in the wild. Circulate the tank water at least twice per hour. Strong lighting promotes the growth of algae on the rocks. Individual fishes will mark out territories.

T: 72-83° F, **L:** 7″,   **A:** 39″,   **R:** b, m, **D:** 2-3.
    22-28° C,   18 cm,   100 cm,

Anostomus taeniatus

(KNER, 1858)
Sub-Fam.: Anostominae

Syn.: *Laemolyta taeniata*

Hab.: Central Amazon; Rio Negro.

Fl.: 1913, C. Kropac, Hamburg, West Germany.

Sex: Unknown.

Soc. B.: A peaceful, schooling species.

M: In Rio Moiocu and the Tapajos the fish live in gently flowing water beneath thickets of such plant as *Eichhornia* together with Discus, *Osteoglossum, Klausewitzia* and Cichlids. The fish are hardy in an aquarium and can easily be kept with peat filtration. When making changes use a good water conditioner. Recommend zero hardness and a pH of 6.

B: Unknown.

F: L, O; flakes; algae; live foods; FD tablets.

S: See *A. anostomus.*

T: 74-82° F, **L:** 8″,   **A:** 39″,   **R:** b, m, **D:** 3.
    24-28° C,   20 cm,   100 cm,

Anostomus anostomus

Anostomus taeniatus day coloring above, young in night-time colors below.

235

Anostomus ternetzi

FERNANDEZ-YEPEZ, 1949
Sub-Fam.: Anostominae

Syn.: None

Hab.: Brazil; Orinoco; Rio Araguaia; Rio Xingu.

Fl.: 1965; possibly imported earlier under another name.

Sex: Unknown.

Soc. B.: A very peaceful fish which can be easily combined with its own and other species.

M: Similar to recommendations for *A. anostomus* but is less sensitive to general tank conditions.

B: Unknown.

F: L; flakes; algae; small live foods; FD tablets.

S: Not as colorful as its larger cousin, *A. anostomus,* though more peaceful.

T: 75-82° F, L: 6″,   A: 39″,   R: b, m, D: 3.
   24-28° C,   16 cm,   100 cm,

Anostomus trimaculatus
Three-Spot Anostomus

(KNER, 1858)
Sub-Fam.: Anostominae

Syn.: *Schizodon trimaculatus, Pithecocharax trimaculatus, Anostomus plicatus* (not EIGENMANN), *Pseudanos trimaculatus*

Hab.: Amazon; Brazil; Guyana.

Fl.: 1913, W. Eimeke, Hamburg, West Germany.

Sex: Unknown.

Soc. B.: A peaceful, schooling species.

M: In the wild these fish live in deep water in schools of 12 to 50, often with species of *Leporinus* (*L. frederici* and *L. "maculata"*). Needs well oxygenated water and likes plants.

B: Unknown.

F: L; O; algae; soft plants; plankton; FD tablets; vegetable flakes.

S: Is much like *A. plicatus* in appearance.

T: 73-81° F, L: 4″,   A: 31″,   R: b, m, D: 3.
   23-27° C,   12 cm,   80 cm,

236

Anostomus ternetzi

Anostomus trimaculatus

Leporinus affinis

Syn.: Leporinus fasciatus affinis

Hab.: Venezuela; Paraguay; Brazil; Columbia; Peru.

Fl.: 1912, J. Kropac, Hamburg, West Germany.

Sex: Unknown.

Soc. B.: A peaceful herbivore though occasionally preditory toward its own species.

M: Needs a large tank with clear water (hardness to 20° dGH and pH 5.8-7.8), a gravel bottom, roots and such hardy plants as Java Fern or, for less care, plastic plants. The fish live in clefts in sandy bottoms of streams formed by currents and are rarely kept because they are plant-eaters. In the wild they eat anything which floats by, preferring plants but accepting fruit and fallen leaves. They even

(GUENTHER, 1864)
Sub.-Fam.: Anostominae

"browse" on fallen trees. Since they become very large, care must be taken when buying one.

B: Unsuccessful.

F: H; large vegetable flakes; watercress; lettuce; chickweed.

S: The fish is most often imported from Belem and differs from *L. f. fasciatus* by the rounded tips on its caudel fins (in comparison with normally pointed ones) and nine cross stripes (in place of ten on the former). The fish remains greenish in color while *L. f. fasciatus* has a brick-red throat. *Leporinus* means "little hare" and the species was named for its hare-like mouth and two prominent teeth.

T: 73-81° F,   L: 10″,   A: 39″,   R: b, m, D: 3.
   23-27° C,   25 cm,   100 cm,

Leporinus fasciatus fasciatus
Black-Banded Leporinus

Syn.: *Salmo fasciatus, Chalceus fasciatus, Leporinus novem fasciatus, Salmo timbure*

Hab.: Central South America; Amazon tributaries; Venezuela.

Fl.: 1912, Vereinigte Zierfischzuechtereien, Berlin, West Germany.

Sex: Unknown.

Soc. B.: Though it likes to nibble at the fins of tankmates of its own species, it is a generally peaceful fish.

M: Keep in a tank with a sandy bottom but without plants. Add roots and large stones for shelter. Needs a strong current created by a powerful filter. The tank should be covered since the fish are excellent jumpers. Use soft, slightly acid water with a hardness to 20° dGH and pH 5.5-7.5. The fish can adapt to other waters.

(BLOCH, 1794)
Sub-Fam.: Anostominae

B: Unsuccessful.

F: H; fruit; leaves; lettuce; watercress; chickweed. Smaller fishes will accept vegetable flakes.

S: Five sub-species have been described: *Leporinus fasciatus affinis* (GUENTHER, 1864); *L. f. altipinnis* (BORODIN, 1929); *L. f. fasciatus* (BLOCH, 1794) and *L. f. tigrinus* (BORODIN, 1929). The status of a final sub-species, *L. f. holostictus* (COPE, 1878) is in doubt.

T: 72-79° F,   L: 12″,   A: 47″,   R: b, m, D: 3.
   22-26° C,   30 cm,   120 cm,

Leporinus affinis

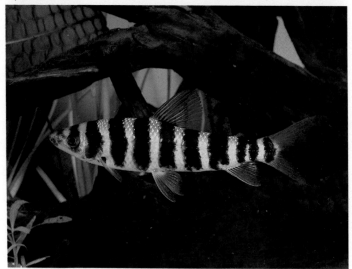

Leporinus fasciatus fasciatus

Leporinus nigrotaeniatus

Syn.: *Chalceus nigrotaeniatus, Leporinus margaritaceus, Salmo biribiri*

Hab.: Brazilian Amazon; Guyana.

Fl.: Unknown.

Sex: Unknown.

Soc. B.: A peaceful fish though it sometimes becomes agitated when kept with its own species.

M: Though undemanding the fish is rarely offered to hobbyists and is included only so aquarists can see the very attractive young. Follow suggestions for other large *Leporinus*. Water hardness to 25° dGH and pH 6-7.8.

T: 73-79° F, **L:** 15¹/₂″, **A:** 60″,   **R:** m, b, **D:** 4.
 23-26° C,   40 cm,   150 cm,

(SCHOMBURGK, 1841)
Sub.-Fam.: Anostominae

B: Considered impossible in an aquarium.

F: H; all types of plants; fruit; Cassada roots.

S: Not recommended for an aquarium because of its size. The photo may not be typical of the species.

Leporinus striatus
Striped Leporinus

Syn.: *Salmo tiririca*

Hab.: Bolivia; Columbia; Ecuador; Mato Grosso; Paraguay; Venezuela.

Fl.: 1935, "Aquarium Hamburg", Hamburg, West Germany.

Sex: Unknown.

Soc. B.: A peaceful, schooling species suggested for larger tanks.

M: Keep without plants, as one would other *Leporinus*. The fish need a strong current and the writer has seen them more than 24 inches long in the very strong currents beneath waterfalls. Its size is one reason the fish are not bred in captivity though *L. "maculatus"* is bred abundantly in Japan.

T: 72-79° F, **L:** to 10″,   **A:** 31″,   **R:** b, m, **D:** 3 (H).
 22-26° C,   to 25 cm,   80 cm,

KNER, 1859
Sub-Fam.: Anostominae

B: Unknown.

F: H; vegetables; fruit; lettuce; watercress; chickweed.

S: *L. arcus,* from Venezuela is similar, reaching 16 inches or more in length. The latter species has more red coloring and three black stripes along its body. (See lower picture.)

Leporinus nigrotaeniatus

Leporinus striatus in the middle, *L. arcus* below

241

Aphyocharax alburnus

(GUENTHER, 1869)

Syn.: *Chirodon alburnus, Aphyocharax avary, Aphyocharax erythrurus*

Hab.: South Brazil; Paraguay; Argentina.

Fl.: 1934.

Sex: Unknown.

Soc. B.: A peaceful, schooling fish recommended for a community tank.

M: Needs a roomy, shallow tank with a variety of plants. It requires more oxygen and more precise water values than some of the genus: a hardness to 20° dGH and pH 5.5-7.5.

B: Unsuccessful.

F: O, C; flakes.

S: May be distinguished from the better known *A. anisitsi* by the pale coloring of its caudal fin and a conspicuous blue body line.

T: 68-82° F, **L:** 3″, **A:** 31″, **R:** m, t, **D:** 1-2.
   20-28° C,   7 cm,   80 cm,

Aphyocharax anisitsi
Bloodfin

EIGENMANN & KENNEDY, 1903

Syn.: *A. rubripinnis, A. affinis, Tetragonopterus rubropictus*

Hab.: Argentina, Rio Parana.

Fl.: 1906, Oskar Kittler, Hamburg, West Germany.

Sex: A small hook can be seen on the anal fin of ♂.

Soc. B.: A peaceful, schooling fish recommended for any community tank.

M: The species is most interesting when kept in a school. Plant *Vallisneria* and *Sagittaria* along the edge and back of the tank.
The fish can be kept in an unheated tank though its coloring will pale. Use a dark tank bottom. Suggest water with a hardness to 30° dGH and pH 6.0-8.0.

B: Spawns freely on the surface and indiscriminately between plants, laying 300 to 500 eggs. The eggs will be quickly eaten unless the adults are removed. Raise the fry with fine flake and brine shrimp.

F: O, C; flakes.

S: Very hardy, the fish can live for a decade or more.

T: 64-82° F, **L:** 2″, **A:** 23¹/₂″, **R:** m, t, **D:** 1.
   18-28° C,   5 cm,   60 cm,

Aphyocharax paraguayensis, page 284

* Because of the size of the family, the True American Characins are additionally arranged in alphabetical order by sub-families.

Aphyocharax alburnus

Aphyocharax anisitsi

Brycon falcatus

MUELLER & TROSCHEL, 1845

Syn.: *Brycon schomburgki*

Hab.: Guyana; Rio Branco, Brazil.

Fl.: 1923, probably Eimeke, Hamburg, West Germany.

Sex: Unknown.

Soc. B.: A peaceful, schooling fish, it tends to become a predator as it grows.

M: Easy to keep when small, to 5 inches (12 cm.) and can be combined with hardier Cichlids. At home with such hardy plants

as Giant *Vallisneria* and *Echinodorus*. pH 5.5 to 7.5 and hardness to 25° dGH. A fast swimmer and an agile leaper.

B: Not reported.

F: Omnivorous; flakes, food tablets and, as they grow, live food.

S: Larger fish not recommended. Should do well alone in a display tank. The dorsal and pelvic fins become orange.

T: 64-77° F, **L:** 10″, **A:** 48″, **R:** m, **D:** 3 (Si).
    18-25° C,   25 cm,   120 cm,

Chalceus macrolepidotus
Pink-Tailed Characin

CUVIER, 1817

Syn.: *Brycon macrolepidotus, Chalceus ararapeera, Pellegrina heterolepsis, Chalceus erythrurus*

Hab.: Guyana; Amazon.

Fl.: 1913, W. Eimeke, Hamburg, West Germany.

Sex: Unknown.

Soc. B.: A predatory fish which should be kept only with fish larger than itself. Not a recommended aquarium species.

M: Not difficult to keep in a large tank and is not demanding about water conditions. Needs room: will not do well in a small tank. Will not bother plants.

B: Not thus far.

F: C; a predatory omnivorous; fish, fish meal and meat. Smaller fish will also take flakes. Can be adapted to tablets.

S: Has reached 19 years of age (at the Hellabrunn Zoo in Munich, West Germany.) In South America it is a food fish.

T: 73-82° F, **L:** 10″, **A:** 60″, **R:** m, **D:** 4 (C).
    23-28° C,   25 cm,   150 cm,

Triportheus angulatus

(SPIX, 1829)

Syn.: *Chalceus angulatus, Chalcinus angulatus, Chalcinus nematurus, Salmo clupeoides, Triportheus flavus, T. nematurus*

Hab.: Very common in some areas of the Amazon Basin; Peru, Paraguay, Orinoco (Venezuela).

Fl.: 1934.

Sex: Unknown.

Soc. B.: Generally a peaceful fish, it does best with others of its species. May attack smaller tank-mates.

M: Is sensitive to atmospheric pressure and needs plenty of oxygen. Once accli-

matized, can be easily kept in a sunny, well-lit aquarium if there is adequate swimming room and substantial water surface. pH 6.0 to 7.5: hardness to 15° dGH. Cover the tank since it is a very agile fish. The fish can become airborne for several feet and, in South America, are common prey for surface predators.

B: Not known.

F: C; Insects, FD food and flakes.

S: An attractive fish, but not yet popular with many fanciers.

Brycon falcatus

Chalceus macrolepidotus

Triportheus angulatus

The fish in the photo is 4 inches (10 cm.) in length. According to LUELING, Triportheus prefers midges which, during the insects breeding ritual, carpets the surface of local rivers.

Five sub-species of *Triportheus angulatus* have been described, *T. a. angulatus* (SPIX, 1829), *T. a. curtus* (GARMAN 1890), *T. a. fuscus* (GARMAN, 1890), *T. a. signatus* (GARMAN, 1890) and *T. a. vittatus* (GARMAN, 1890).

T: 72-82° F, L: over 4″, A: 31″, R: m, t, D: 2.
    22-28° C,   over 10 cm, 80 cm,

Exodon paradoxus
Bucktoothed Tetra

(MUELLER & TROSCHEL, 1845)

Syn.: *Epicyrtus exodon, Hystricodon para-doxus, Epicyrtus paradoxus*

Hab.: Rio Madeira, Rio Marmelo, Rio Branco, Brazil; Guyanas.

Fl.: 1935.

Sex: ♀ has a more pronounced stomach.

Soc. B.: Individually or in small groups. One of the most predatory of fishes, if it cannot swallow its prey, it may tear the scales and flesh from any fish it attacks. Not recommended for a community tank. When kept in groups of ten to 15, *Exodon* is relatively harmless. In smaller groups the fish will frequently attack tank-mate's eyes.

M: A jumper, the tank must be covered. Use peaty, brownish yet clear water with a pH between 5.5 and 7.5. (6.0) and a hardness between 0 and 20° dGH. Does not eat plants.

B: Possible. Spawns between plants. Fry hatch in one to $1^1/_2$ days. Difficult to raise since they will attack each other.

F: C; fish, worms, and large flakes.

S: Since the fish is a predator, you must be cautious. The young are often considered the most attractive of all freshwater fish. You should try keeping these at least once.

T: 73-82° F, L: 6″, A: 40″, R: m, D: 3.
    23-28° C,   15 cm,   100 cm,

Gnathocharax steindachneri

FOWLER, 1913

Syn.: None

Hab.: Madeira river, Brazil.

Fl: 1970, Dr. Geisler, city unknown.

Sex: ♀ has a black pregnancy patch.

Soc. B.: Peaceful, schooling fish. Very easily combined with many gentle Characins, Catfish and Cichlids.

M: Easily kept with no special requirements. Water: pH 5.5-7.5 and hardness to

20° dGH. Does well in a roomy tank with floating plant cover. The lively fish need swimming room, prefer darker areas in the bottom of a tank and like water movement at the surface. Choose a filter system which accomplishes this. Cover the tank.

B: Unknown.

F: C, O; flakes, live-food.

S: Good jumper.

T: 74-81° F, L: $2^1/_2$″, A: 31″, R: m, t, D: 2.
    23-27° C,   6 cm,   80 cm,

Exodon paradoxus

Gnathocharax steindachneri

Roeboides caucae

EIGENMANN, 1922

Syn.: None

Hab.: Cauca River, Colombia.

Fl.: Possibly after 1950.

Sex: ♂ more extended. ♀ has an arched back.

Soc. B.: A predator. In the wild it subsists mainly on the scales of other fish. Not recommended for community tanks.

M: Although seemingly placid, this Characin can clean out a community tank in a few days. Closely related to *Exodon paradoxus*. Needs clean, oxygen-rich water and plenty of food. Other aspects of water quality are of secondary importance.

B: A surface spawner, it lays eggs between plants and roots. The fry hatch in one to two days and will consume large quantities of Infusoria. If not available, they may attack each other.

F: C; small fish, larger live food and flakes.

S: Although a predator the species is of interest to aquarists who want something new. The species is frequently found in Brazil and parts of northern South America.

T: 72-79° F, **L:** 2$^1/_2$", **A:** 24$^1/_2$", **R:** m, **D:** 3.
22-26° C, 6 cm, 60 cm,

Asiphonichthys condei

GERY & KRÖPPEL, 1976

Syn.: *Epicyrtus microlepis, Anacyrtus microlepis, Cynopotamus microlepis, Roeboides microlepis*

Hab.: Venezuela; Asuncion, Paraguay.

Fl.: Unknown.

Sex: ♂ has a slender body, is a brighter yellow and has a broader anal fin. ♀ has an arched back.

Soc. B.: Predatory. Sometimes a schooling fish, sometimes a loner; should not be placed in a tank with smaller fish.

M: Since these fishes like to swim, they need open space. Low, bottom vegetation and a few floating plants are all the decoration required. Peaty water enhances health and color but otherwise not a demanding fish. pH 6.5 to 7.8; hardness to 20° dGH. Darker gravel makes the best tank bottom.

B: The throat of the ♂ turns orange-red during spawning. Little is known about breeding and rearing, but the pattern is thought similar to that of the species above.

B: C; large live food and, on occasion, flake food.
May bite tank-mates when feeding.

S: Older adults swim with the heads slightly downward.

T: 73-77° F, **L:** 4", **A:** 32", **R:** b, m, **D:** 3.
23-25° C, 10 cm, 80 cm,

Roeboides caucae

Asiphonichthys condei

Corynopoma riisei
Swordtail Characin

GILL, 1858

Syn.: *Corynopoma albipinne, C. aliata, C. searlesi, C. veedoni, Nematopoma searlesi, Stevardia albipinnis, S. aliata, S. riisei*

Hab.: Rio Meta, Columbia.

Fl.: 1932, Otto Winkelmann, Altona, Germany.

Sex: Long pectoral fins, paddle-like on ♂.

Soc. B.: A peaceful, shoaling fish, ideal for community tanks.

M: A good quarantine period is essential since the fishes are prone to disease: Sturdy, once acclimated. Water: pH 6.0 to 7.8 and hardness to 25° dGH. Requires swimming room and floating plants need protection.

B: Milt is implanted in the oviduct and as the eggs are laid, they are fertilized without a male present. The fry hatch after 20 to 36 hours. Feed *Artemia* (i.e brine shrimp), finely ground flake-food and liquid foods.

F: O; flake and all types of live foods.

S: In earlier days their distinctive breeding behavior made them favorites, but now, in a time of colored fishes, the Swordtail Characin is not as popular.

T: 72-82° F, **L**: 2¹/₂″, **A**: 27″, **R**: m, t, **D**: 2.
22-28° C, 6-7 cm, 70 cm,

Pseudocorynopoma doriae
Dragon-finned Characin, Dragon-Fin Tetra

PERUGIA, 1891

Syn.: *Bergia altipinnis, Chalcinopelecus argentinus*

Hab.: Southern Brazil and the La Plata region in Argentina, Uruguay, Paraguay.

Fl.: 1905, Oskar Kittler, Hamburg, Germany.

Sex: The dorsal and anal fins of the ♂ are more extended. The photo shows the ♂.

M: A lively swimmer, the fish needs plenty of space. A shallow, roomy tank with lots of water surface to guarantee oxygen, is best. Medium to light vegetation is suggested. The Dragon-Finned Characin is an excellent species for beginners. Water: pH 6.0-7.5 and hardness to 20° dGH.

B: Keep pairs in the breeding tank. During mating the male stands on his head, circling the female in a ritual that may last hours. The dance is worth seeing. Up to 1,000 eggs are released, generally between fine pinnate plants, as with Barbs. The fry hatch quickly, after 12 to 48 hours, and the egg sac is consumed within two or three days. Offer very fine live food and/or finely ground flake food at that time.

F: O; flake.

S: Unlike *Corynopoma*, eggs are not fertilized in the oviduct.

T: 68-75° F, **L**: 3¹/₄″, **A**: 32″, **R**: m, t, **D**: 1.
20-24° C, 8 cm, 80 cm,

Corynopoma riisei ♂

Pseudocorynopoma doriae

Paragoniates alburnus

Syn.: None

Hab.: Central and upper Amazon; Venezuelan streams.

Fl.: Unknown.

Sex: Unknown.

Soc. B.: Peaceful, well suited to community tanks and likes company.

M: Similar to the Danio in behavior and a need for plenty of swimming room, strong water flow (ie - powerful filtration) and a

STEINDACHNER, 1876

bright, well-planted tank. Adapts well to most water conditions. pH 5.6 to 7.8: hardness to 20° dGH.

B: Not currently known but are probably free-spawniing in shallow areas such as those between plants.

F: C, O; omnivorous. Flake, FD foods, fine live food.

S: Although it is not often kept in an aquarium because of its drab coloring, it is a good fish for beginners.

T: 73-81° F,   **L:** 2¹/₂″,   **A:** 28″,   **R:** m,   **D:** 2.
23-27° C,   6 cm,   70 cm,

Xenagoniates bondi

Syn.: None

Hab.: Columbia and eastern Venezuela.

Fl.: ?

Sex: Unknown.

Soc. B.: Details are sketchy and the authors have no personal experience. Our photographer, who tended the fish in our photo for several weeks, offers these details. "Water: pH 7.2; hardness, 20° dGH; temperature 75° F (24° C). Did not damage plants and did not bother tank-

MYERS, 1942

mates. Seemed timid but that reaction is possibly due to the fact that only one specimen was kept."

B: Not thus far.

F: C, O; flakes, FD, *Daphnia* and other small, live food.

S: Similar to the African Glass Fish, *Kryptopterus*, but distinguished by its dorsal and adipose fins and the absence of barbels.

T: 68-79° F,   **L:** 2¹/₂″,   **A:** 24″,   **R:** m,   **D:** 2-3.
20-26° C,   6 cm,   60 cm,

Prionobrama filigera
Glass Bloodfin

Syn.: *Aphyocharax filigerus, Aphyocharax analis, Bleptonema amazoni, Paragoniates muelleri, Aphyocharax analialbis, Prionobrama madeirae*

Hab.: Rio Paraguay, Argentina, Southern Brazil.

Fl.: 1931, "Aquarium Hamburg", Hamburg, West Germany.

Sex: ♂ has a noticably extended anal fin and a black mark behind the frontal white stripe.

Soc. B.: A peaceful fish recommended for all community tanks, even those with African Cichlids.

M: A small school is best since single fish are nervous. The species needs some

(COPE, 1870)

plant protection at the surface such as Giant Vallisneria and Floating Fern. Water: pH 6.0-7.8 and hardness to 30° dGH. An excellent beginner's fish. Enjoys a lazy rest in moving water as that from a filter.

B: Easy to breed at warmer temperatures, 79-86° F (26-30° C). Prefer soft water and floating plants.

F: O; flake foods and live foods such as *Daphnia*.

S: Not always a popular aquarium species because of its glassy look and a lack of color but their blood-red tailfins and vivacity make up for any drabness. The species is hardy, lives a long time and deserves more attention.

T: 72-86° F,   **L:** 2¹/₂″,   **A:** 32″,   **R:** m, t,   **D:** 1-2.
22-30° C,   6 cm,   80 cm,

Paragoniates alburnus

Xenagoniates bondi

Prionobrama filigera

Poptella orbicularis

(VALENCIENNES, 1849)

Syn.: *Ephippicharax orbicularis, Tetragonopterus orbicularis, T. compressus, Fowlerina orbicularis, Gymnocorymbus nemopterus*

Hab.: Northern and central South America.

Fl.: 1934.

Sex: Unknown.

Soc. B.: Peaceful, schooling fish suitable for large community tanks with hardy plants.

M: Needs room for fast swimming and darting movements. Should be kept in a school. Will nibble tender plants so the tank should be decorated with stones, roots, hardy plants such as Java Fern and/or, plastic plants. Water: pH 5.5-7.5 and hardness to 25° dGH.

B: Suggested only in large tanks from 100 gallon capacity or more. Will breed in nearly any water from 72 -86° F (22-30° C). Lays 1,000 to 2,000 eggs and fry swim freely after six days. May be raised on very fine flake food and brine shrimp.

F: H, O; omnivorous.

S: A very pretty fish similar to the Silver Dollar but not such a pronounced plant-eater.

T: 64-75° F, **L:** 5″,   **A:** 56″,   **R:** m, t, **D:** 3 (H).
  18-24° C,   12 cm,   140 cm,

American Characins

Astyanax bimaculatus
Two-Spot Astyanax

(LINNAEUS, 1758)

Syn.: *Salmo bimaculatus, Tetragonopterus maculatus, Astyanax bartlettii, A. jacuhiensis, A. lacustris, A. orientalis, Charax bimaculatus, Poecilurichthys maculatus, Tetragonopterus jacuhiensis, T. orientalis*

Hab.: Eastern South America to Paraguay.

Fl.: 1907 by Vereinigte Zierfischzuechtereien, Conradshoehe, West Germany.

Sex: The anal and caudal fins of the adult ♂ are reddish-yellow in color.

Soc. B.: A peaceful fish recommended for larger tanks. An excellent tank-mate when young, to four inches (10 cm) or so. When older will eat plants if hungry.

M: Grows to a larger size, about 48″ (120 cm) and requires a sizable tank, strong filtration, plenty of food and hardy plants. Water: pH 5.5 to 7.5; hardness to 25° dGH.

B: Considered possible.

F: C, O; large flakes and a variety of live foods.

S: Varied coloring and not recommended for smaller aquariums because of its size as an adult.

T: 68-82° F, **L:** 6″, **A:** 48″, **R:** m, **D:** 2.
20-28° C,   15 cm,   120 cm,

Astyanax fasciatus mexicanus
Blind Cavefish

(CUVIER, 1819)

Syn.: *Anoptichthys jordani, A. hubbsi, A. antrobius*

Hab.: Texas, Mexico and Central America to Panama.

Fl.: 1949, 1951, "Aquarium Hamburg", Hamburg, West Germany.

Sex: ♂ thinner than ♀ .

Soc. B: Peaceful, schooling species recommended for all community tanks.

M: An undemanding fish, the Blind Cavefish can be readily kept in most tanks. Does not require special light levels and will not touch plants. Water: 6.0 to 7.8; hardness to 30° dGH.

B: Relatively easy to breed at 66-68° F (18-20° C). Fry hatch quickly, within two or three days and swim freely from the sixth. Feed on fine food: *Artemia* and very fine flakes. As fry the fish have vision.

F: C, O; omnivorous.

S: The blind form is the cave-dwelling variant of the Characin *Astyanax fasciatus*, widely distributed through Central America. As with their sighted cousins, the Blind Cavefish catch food by scent and accept a similar diet.

T: 68-77° F,   **L:** 3¹/₂″,   **A:** 32″,   **R:** m,   **D:** 1.
   20-25° C,   9 cm,   80 cm,

Axelrodia riesei
Ruby Tetra

GERY, 1966

Syn.: None

Hab.: Rio Meta, southern Colombia.

Fl.: After 1970.

Sex: ♂ thinner, ♀ rounded. (See photo.)

Soc. B: A peaceful, schooling fish.

M: Slightly more difficult to handle than the Cardinal Tetra but as with the latter it loses its color in water harder than 20° dGH. Prefers soft, peaty water to 8° dGH and pH to 7.0. It colors best in subdued lighting, against a darker background with a cover of floating plants.

B: Not successful so far but considered possible. The technique should be similar to that suggested for Neon Tetra. Feed breeding pairs live food, preferably black mosquito larvae.

F: C; flake food and small live foods

S: Rarely imported. Is a bright red in the wild, but pales in an aquarium.

T: 68-79° F,   **L:** 1¹/₂″,   **A:** 20″,   **R:** m,   **D:** 3.
   20-26° C,   4 cm,   50 cm,

Astyanax fasciatus mexicanus

Axelrodia riesei

Boehlkea fredcochui

GERY, 1966

Syn.: *"Microbrycon cochui"*

Hab.: Maranon River, Leticia, Peru.

Fl.: 1956, U.S.; European date unknown.

Sex: Unknown but suggest ♀ stronger.

Soc. B: A lively but peaceful, schooling fish. Can do well in community tanks with appropriate water and proper care. Will not eat plants.

M: Peaty water, dark substrate and low light level will show-off the fish in its best colors. The photo illustrates the species at its most colorful. May pale when crowded or with improper care. Water: pH 5.5 to 7.5 and hardness to 15° dGH.

B: Has been bred, but information is not available.
Presumed to breed like *Hemigrammus* and *Hyphessobrycon*.

F: C, O; small live food, flake and FD foods.

S: Often imported though it is difficult to ship: sensitive to shipping and requires considerable oxygen. An attractive species.

T: 72-79° F,	L: 2″,	A: 24″,	R: m,	D: 2-3.
22-26° C,	5 cm,	60 cm,		

Carlastyanax aurocaudatus
Goldentail Astyanax

(EIGENMANN, 1913)

Syn.: *Astyanax aurocaudatus*

Hab.: Upper Rio Cauca, Columbia (Barranquilla).

Fl.: 1968, Aquarium Rio, Frankfurt, West Germany.

Sex: Unknown.

Soc. B.: A peaceful species, it should be kept with numbers of its own kind.

M: Undemanding but prefers clear, flowing water. Will lack spirit unless kept in a school. Needs lots of oxygen. Peaty water is an advantage though not imperative. The fish can acclimatize to harder water. pH 5.8 to 7.5 and hardness to 20° dGH.

B: Unknown.

F: C, O; omnivorous. Prefers live and flake foods.

S: Beautiful coloring, reminding one of a barb or carp. Rarely imported since its territory, Rio Cauca, makes collecting difficult.

T: 72-77° F,	L: 2″,	A: 24″,	R: b, m,	D: 2-3.
22-25° C,	5 cm,	60 cm,		

Boehlkea fredcochui

Carlastyanax aurocaudatus

Paracheirodon axelrodi
Cardinal Tetra

(SCHULTZ, 1956)

Syn.: *Cheirodon axelrodi, Hyphessobry-con cardinalis*

Hab.: Widely distributed from the Orinoco in Venezuela through Rio Vaupes and north and east tributaries of the Rio Negro in Brazil to western Colombia. Found in slow or standing water. Fish escaped from collectors are often found in streams around Manaus.

Fl.: 1956.

Sex: ♀ somewhat heavier.

Soc. B.: Very peaceful, schooling fish, recommended for most community tanks.

M: *Paracheirodon axelrodi* has until recently been recognized as a blackwater fish. This was proven inaccurate by GEIS-LER & ANNIBAL (1984): Amazonia **9**, 53-86. The fish prefers an open biotope in clear water, positioning itself in tree shaded areas. They in fact have a light phobia,

especially in the fry. The optimal pH value is 5.8 with variances tolerated between 4.6 to 6.2. Water conditions should contain little hardness (4° dGH) with minimal amount of Ca^{2+} - and Mg^{2+} - ions. Hard mineralized water can easily result in damage. As an example, calcium blockages (blockage of the kidney tubulii by calcium salts). The tank should dimly illuminated or provide diffused light. This can be best accomplished with floating plants.

B: Follow suggestions for Neon Tetra (Page 307) but recommend a larger breeding tank. Spawns best in evening, laying up to 500 eggs.

F: C, O; flakes, FD, *Artemia* and other small live food.

S: Highly recommended. One of the finest of all aquarium species and nearly all specimens are imported captured in the wild.

T: 73-81° F, L: 2″, A: 24″, R: b, m, D: 2-3.
   23-27° C, 5 cm, 60 cm,

Cheirodon parahybae

EIGENMANN, 1915

Syn.: None

Hab.: Rio Paraiba Basin, south eastern Brazil; north of Rio de Janeiro.

Fl.: After 1970.

Sex: ♂ clearly more slender, ♀ has rounded stomach (see photo), ♂ has small reverse hooks on the lower tail lobe, which is typical of the genus.

Soc. B: A peaceful, bright schooling fish.

M: As with the Neon Tetra the species prefers a dark gravelled tank bottom, and peaty water with a pH between 6.5 and 7.5 and hardness to 20° dGH. Likes the cover of floating plants and a subdued light level. Needs a full measure of oxygen. Keep only in schools.

B: Not described but probably similar to *Paracheirodon axelrodi.*

F: C, O; flakes, FD and small live foods.

T: 73-81° F, L: 2″, A: 24″, R: m, D: 2.
   23-27° C, 4.5 cm, 60 cm,

Paracheirodon axelrodi

Cheirodon parahybae

Ctenobrycon spilurus hauxwellianus
Silver Tetra

(COPE, 1870)

Syn.: *Tetragonopterus spilurus*

Hab.: Amazon.

Fl.: 1912.

Sex: ♂ rather thinner and more vividly colored.

Soc. B.: Peaceful, schooling fish yet constantly active and not as well suited to a community tank as less active species.

M: Roomy tank with large surface area, robust filtration and hardy vegetation. Needs a few larger plants for hiding places. Can be kept with *Corydoras* and other catfish, hardy cichlids, large Characins and a long list of plant-eating Characins. Water: pH 6.0-8.0 and hardness to 25° dGH.

B: A prolific breeder, the Silver Tetra spawns readily among the plants. Parents should be removed since they will eat the eggs. The fry hatch after one day and can be readily raised on finely ground flakes, egg yolk and *Artemia*.

F: C, O; large flakes and a broad range of live foods. May eat plants.

S: A similar sub-species, *C. spilurus spilurus*, the Sailfin Characin, has a more slender body and is native to areas around Georgetown, Guyana and Venezuela. Not very popular with aquarists.

T: 68-82° F,   L: 3¹/₄″,   A: 40″,   R: m,   D: 2.
20-28° C,   8 cm,   100 cm,

Gymnocorymbus ternetzi
Black Tetra, Black Widow

(BOULENGER, 1895)

Syn.: *Tetragonopterus ternetzi, Moenkhausia ternetzi*

Hab.: Rio Paraguay; Rio Guapore, Bolivia.

Fl.: 1935.

Sex: Frontal portion of anal fin of ♂ noticeably broader than ♀ whose anal fin runs parallel with the stomach line. ♂ dorsal fin is narrower and more pointed.

Soc. B.: Peaceful, schooling fish, ideal for any community tank.

M: In the wild it is found in water whose light is softened by the "green bloom" found in the rivers of south Brazil, but the Black Tetra will do well in tanks with more light. It is hardy and easy to maintain, prefers habitat with a grayish gravel bottom and a few taller plants. Water: pH 5.8-8.5 and hardness to 30° dGH.

B: Similar to the Silver Tetra.

F: O; omnivorous but will not eat plants. Flake food including vegetable flakes.

S: A beginner's fish which will reach maturity within one year. The fine black coloring of puberty changes to grey in adults. Becomes sedentary as it becomes older. A variety known in Europe as the "Long-Fin Black Widow" has been introduced recently.

T: 68-79° F,   L: 2¹/₄″,   A: 24″,   R: m,   D: 1.
20-26° C,   5.5 cm,   60 cm,

Ctenobrycon spilurus hauxwellianus

Gymnocorymbus ternetzi

Gymnocorymbus thayeri
Black Tetra

EIGENMANN, 1908

Syn.: *Moenkhausia bondi, M. profunda, Phenacogaster bondi*

Hab.: Amazon and Orinoco basins.

Fl.: Unknown. Often confused with *G. ternetzi.*

Sex: The male's anal fin is concave while that of ♀ is straight or convex.

Soc. B.: Peaceful, schooling fish, recommended for a community tank.

M: Not as hardy as his cousin, *G. ternetzi* since the species is found in clear water with little hardness and a lower pH. Water: pH 5.5-7.5 and hardness to 20° dGH. Prefers peaty-water but is as tolerant of conditions as the Neon. A darker tank bottom, strong filtration and plants offering hiding places will encourage the brighter colors which come from happy fish.

B: Not yet bred in captivity but the technique is probably similar to that for *Hyphessobrycon* species. (page 276).

F: C, O; flake food, vegetable flakes at times and all types of live foods.

S: Adults have reddish fins but not commonly imported because it has less coloration than its cousin, *G. ternetzi.*

T: 73-81° F, L: 2$^{1}/_{2}$", A: 25", R: m, D: 2.
    23-27° C,   6 cm,   60 cm,

Hasemania nana
Silver-Tipped Tetra

(REINHARDT i. Luetken,1874)

Syn.: *Hasemania melanura, H. marginata, Hemigrammus nanus*

Hab.: Found in white and black water in smaller streams. Rio Sao Francisco Basin, eastern Brazil; Rio Purus tributaries, western Brazil.

Fl.: 1937, Heinrich Roese, Hamburg, West Germany.

Sex: ♂ is slender with brighter colors. The tip of the anal fin is white. On ♀ it is yellow.

Soc. B.: Peaceful, schooling fish, highly recommended for community tanks.

M: An attractive fish with a long life, found in flooded streams with a strong current and plenty of oxygen. It needs a roomy tank and protective vegetation. Peaty water, soft light and dark gravel are suggested.

B: The male displays territorial behavior in larger tanks. Spawns in a manner similar to *Hyphessobrycon flammeus*. The fry are very easy to raise.

F: C, O; flakes, FD and *Artemia.*

S: There have been problems with the name, which, at long last, is correct. The color varies with the origin of the fish. Genus *Hasemania* can be distinguished from *Hemigrammus* and *Hyphessobrycon* by the absence of the adipose fin.

T: 72-82° F, L: 2", A: 25", R: m, D: 1.
    22-28° C,   5 cm,   60 cm,

Gymnocorymbus thayeri

Hasemania nana

Hemigrammus caudovittatus
Buenos Aires Tetra

AHL, 1923

Syn.: *Hyphessobrycon anisitsi* (not EIGENMANN)

Hab.: La Plata Region, Argentina, Paraguay and southeast Brazil.

Fl.: 1922, Martin Becker, Hamburg, West Germany.

Sex: The fins of ♂ are a brighter red or tend toward yellow. ♀ is fuller, rounder.

Soc. B.: Peaceful, schooling fish recommended for any community tank without plants.

M: A hardy, long-lived species which can survive in most waters. pH 5.8-8.5 and hardness to 35° dGH. Requires a larger tank with swimming room and strong filtration. Decoration should be of stone and plastic plants. Java Fern, which will not be eaten, is also suggested.

B: Not difficult at 75° F (24° C). Spawns freely against hardier plants or on green floss. A prolific breeder.

F: H, O; omnivorous.

S: Years ago it was one of the most popular of hobby fishes. It eats many plants, however, and for this reason is not often kept in home aquariums today.

T: 64-82° F, **L:** 2³/₄″, **A:** 32″, **R:** m, **D:** 1.
18-28° C, 7 cm, 80 cm,

Rarely kept *Hemigrammus* species:

Hemigrammus elegans
(STEINDACHNER, 1882)
Amazon

T: 73-81° F, **L:** 1¹/₂″, **A:** 20″, **D:** 2.
23-27° C, 3.5 cm, 50 cm,

Hemigrammus marginatus
ELLIS, 1911
Upper Rio Meta, Columbia; Rio Sao Francisco, Eastern Brazil; Paraguay.

T: 68-82° F, **L:** 3¹/₄″, **A:** 32″, **D:** 1.
20-28° C, 8 cm, 80 cm,

Hemigrammus levis
DURBIN in EIGENMANN, 1908
Central Amazon.

T: 74-82° F, **L:** 2″, **A:** 24″, **D:** 1-2.
24-28° C, 5 cm, 60 cm,

Hemigrammus rodwayi
DURBIN, 1909
See text on page 272.

The rare illustration shows the species in natural coloring.

Hemigrammus caudovittatus

H. elegans

H. levis

H. marginatus

H. rodwayi

Hemigrammus* erythrozonus
Glowlight Tetra

Syn.: *H. gracilis*

Hab.: Native to the Essequibo River, Guyana. Now bred in Germany and Asia.

Fl.: 1933.

Sex: ♀ larger and stronger with round ventral section. ♂ is slenderer.

Soc. B.: Another peaceful, schooling fish recommended for any well-kept community tank.

M: The fish is at its best in schools and in a soft light. Peaty water and floating plant cover is suggested. Water: pH from 5.8-7.5 and hardness to 15° dGH (better 6°).

B: At 82° F (28° C), between pinnate plants in schools as pairs in a breeding tank with soft, peaty water.

F: C, O; flakes, FD and small live food three to four times daily. Feed in small portions.

S: One of the finest of all small Characins. As popular as the Neon.

*According to GERY the species should possibly be assigned to the genus *Cheirodon*.

T: 74-82° F,   L: 1¹/₂″,   A: 24″,   R: m,   D: 2.
   24-28° C,   4 cm,   60 cm,

Hemigrammus hyanuary

Syn.: None

Hab.: Central and Upper Amazon, Lake Hyanuary near Manaus, Brazil. Captive-bred species are primarily from Singapore.

Fl.: Before 1957. Captive-bred fish were, even then, being traded.

Sex: ♂ thinner than the ♀ when spawning. ♂ has a small hook on the anal fin and is therefore more easily caught in a net.

Soc. B.: A peaceful, schooling fish recommended for community tanks, even those with lively fish.

M: Prefers a bright, sunny tank with a some plants and a fine gravel bottom. Water: pH 6.0-7.5 and hardness to 15° dGH. Requires regular water changes with an added water conditioner and/or peat filtration.

B: Water 73-78° F (24-26° C) at a pH of 6.0. Hardness should be less than 4° KH. The larvae emerges after 24 hours and moves to the surface to fill their swim bladders. They swim freely from the sixth day. The best initial nourishment is very fine live food. Freshly hatched *Artemia* can be taken after the egg sac has been consumed, about one week. There is little problem after that. The water in the breeding tank should be changed weekly.

F: C,O; flakes, food tablets.

T: 73-81° F,   L: 1¹/₂″,   A: 20″,   R: m,   D: 1-2.
   23-27° C,   4 cm,   50 cm,

Hemigrammus erythrozonus

Hemigrammus hyanuary

Hemigrammus ocellifer
Head-and-Tail Light

(STEINDACHNER 1882)

Syn.: *Tetragonopterus ocellifer, Holopristis ocellifer*

Hab.: *H. ocellifer ocellifer* in the coastal region of French Guyana; Bolivian Amazon. May be called *H. ocellifer falsus* in Argentina.

Fl.: 1910 by H. Blumenthal, Hamburg *(H. ocellifer falsus.)*

Sex: ♂ swim bladder appears more pointed. The bladder is partially covered in the ♀ so that it appears rounded underneath.

Soc. B.: A peaceful fish recommended for a community tank.

M.: Similar to the genus *Hyphessobrycon.*

B.: Relatively easy, the species is very productive. For details see *Hyphessobrycon.*

F.: C, O; flake food, FD and small live foods.

S.: Two subspecies are known: 1. *H. ocellifer falsus* MEINKEN, 1958 (According to GERY, possibly *H. mattei* EIGENMANN, 1910) and 2. *H. ocellifer ocellifer* (STEINDACHNER, 1882). Introduced in 1960.

T: 1. 72-79° F, L: 2",   A: 24",   R: m,   D: 1-2.
       22-26° C,   4.5 cm,   60 cm,
T: 2. 75-82° F,
       24-28° C,

Hemigrammus pulcher
Pretty Tetra, Black Wedge Tetra

LADIGES, 1938

Syn.: None

Hab.: Such tributaries of the Peruvian Amazon as those near Iquitos, Brazil.

Fl.: 1938, "Aquarium Hamburg", Hamburg, West Germany.

Sex: ♀ fuller and stronger. The swim bladder is rounded beneath. ♂ is noticeably more slender with a pointed swim bladder.

Soc. B.: A peaceful, gentle species recommended for community tanks with soft water.

M.: Similar to other species of the genus.

B.: You may need to exchange individuals until pairing occurs.

F.: C, O; flake foods, FD foods, small live foods.

S.: Two sub-species have been described: 1. *H. pulcher pulcher,* LADIGES, 1938 and 2. *H. pulcher haraldi* GERY, 1961. The latter occurs in the Central Amazon near Manaus. Rarely kept in an aquarium.

T: 73-81° F, L: 2",   A: 24",   R: m,   D: 2.
  23-27° C,   4.5 cm,   60 cm,

Hemigrammus ocellifer

Hemigrammus pulcher

Hemigrammus bleheri
Red-Nose, Rummy-Nose Tetra

GÉRY, 1986

Syn.: None

Hab.: Rio Vaupes, Columbia; Rio Negro, Brazil.

Fl.: 1965 by Heiko Bleher, Kelsterbach (Frankfurt), West Germany.

Sex: ♂ thinner, ♀ more compact with, (during spawning) a larger stomach.

Soc. B.: A peaceful, robust species comfortable with fishes of similar habits.

M.: Not always easy to keep. You must pay attention to the water. Frequent changes are needed along with a good water conditioner. Keep the nitrate content low. It should not exceed 30 mg/l.

B.: In soft water at 77-82° F (25-28° C) with peat filtration and a pH of 6.0-6.5. Water hardness should be less than 4° KH. Spawns on the bottom but in a larger tank may prefer fine pinnate plants. May eat

eggs. The fry hatch after 36 hours and are free-swimming from the fourth day. Feed very small live food since the fry are extremely tiny.

F.: C, O; flakes with FD content, FD tablets, small live foods.

S.: Similar to *Petitella georgiae*, page 308 and *H. rhodostomus*, page 278.
This species so far has been called *H. rhodostomus* AHL, 1924. Yet after thorough examination differences in bone structure of the skull were found, in addition to color distinction.
H. bleheri and *H. rhodostomus* are black-water fish, whereas *Petitella* is a clear water fish.

T: 73-79° F, L: 2″, A: 32″, R: m, D: 2-3.
23-26° C, 4.5 cm, 80 cm,

Hemigrammus rodwayi
Golden Tetra

DURBIN, 1909

Syn.: *H. armstrongi* (a defective golden form.)

Hab.: Guyana.

Fl.: 1930.

Sex: ♀ with fuller stomach area. ♂ anal fin is white the front with more red than ♀. Fish with the most color are nearly always ♂.

Soc. B: A peaceful, attractive fish whose few drawbacks will not affect other species. Natural breeding is difficult.

M.: The species is interesting for its golden coloring. Some writers say it is difficult to maintain while others disagree. The varying views are probably the result of differing habitats. Requires a bright, moderately planted tank.

B.: Fish bred artificially generally lose the golden coloring reverting to a "genuine" form. Breeding temperatures should be around 79° F (26° C). pH value about 6.3 and hardness to 12° dGH is satisfactory.

F.: C, O; flake food, FD foods, small live food.

S.: The species is prone to disease and is affected particularly by Trematodes or skin parasites. The fish protects its skin by secreting guanin which makes it appear as if covered with gold dust. This explains its common name. (*Hemigrammus armstrongi* SCHULTZ & AXELROD, 1955). A photo of the species in natural color can be found on page 267.

T: 75-82° F, L: 2¹/₄″, A: 24″, R: m, D: 2-3.
24-28° C, 5.5 cm, 60 cm,

Hemigrammus bleheri

Hemigrammus rodwayi

Hemigrammus ulreyi
Ulrey's Tetra

(BOULENGER, 1895)

Syn.: *Tetragonopterus ulreyi*

Hab.: Upper Rio Paraguay, South America.

Fl.: 1905, Oskar Kittler, Hamburg, West Germany.

Sex: ♀ larger and fuller than ♂.

Soc. B: Lively, peaceful species recommended for community tanks with smaller fish.

M.: Does best in a larger tank with room for swimming and little vegetation. Current generated by the filter suits this species. pH 5.8 to 7.2 and hardness to 10° dGH.

B.: Not successful to date.

F.: C, O; flake foods, FD foods, small live foods.

S.: At one time was confused with the Flag Tetra *Hyphessobrycon heterorhabdus* (see page 288). Ulrey's Tetra is seldom imported.

T: 73-81° F, **L:** 2″, **A:** 32″, **R:** m, **D:** 1-2.
    23-27° C,   5 cm,   80 cm,

Hemigrammus unilineatus
Featherfin

(GILL, 1858)

Syn.: *Poecilurichthys hemigrammus unilineatus, Tetragonopterus unilineatus*

Hab.: Northern South America, Rio Paraguay, Amazon to Guyana; Trinidad.

Fl.: 1910 by Vereinigte Zierfischzuechtereien, Conradshoehe, West Germany.

Sex: ♂ more slender with a more pointed swim bladder than ♀ .

Soc. B: Active, peaceful fish well suited to a community tank.

M.: Can be kept without problems; likes a sunny, bright tank with plenty of space for swimming. pH 6-7.5 and hardness to 20° dGH.

B.: Usually easy. Use two ♂ and one ♀. After an active courtship 200 to 300 eggs are laid free-spawning, between plants. The larvae hatch after 60 hours then cling to plants and the glass for up to four days. Feed finely powdered food then MikroMin and *Artemia*.

F.: C, O; flake foods, very small live foods.

S.: Seldom imported as the fry are considered unattractive. GERY (1959) described the sub-species *H. u. cayennensis* from Surinam.

T: 73-82° F, **L:** 2″, **A:** 24″, **R:** m, **D:** 1.
    23-28° C,   5 cm,   60 cm,

Hemigrammus ulreyi

Hemigrammus unilineatus

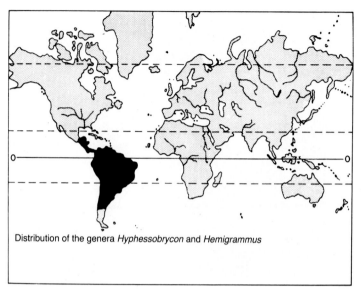

Distribution of the genera *Hyphessobrycon* and *Hemigrammus*

The genus *Hyphessobrycon*

GERY (1977) discovered that the generic name for the more common species was possibly incorrect but since it was in such common useage he refrained from assigning a new one.

"This should be left to a review of all South American *Tetragonopterinae*," he said.

Aquarists have already been forced to deal with many name changes and should be able to accomodate the possible renaming of several species of the more than 60 *Hyphessobrycon*. The genus was established by DURBIN in 1908. The *Hyphessobrycon* (i.e. small *brycon*), is distinguished from the *Hemigrammus* by its scaleless caudal fin and base.

Distribution is restricted to South America with two exceptions which are found in Mexico and Central America.

Maintenance requirements are not necessarily similar for all species so that the proper water conditions must be inferred from the Degree of Difficulty. For example:

D 1 = pH exceeding 6.5-8.0 and hardness to 25° dGH.

D 2 = pH between 5.5 and 7.5 (but preferably below 7.0) and a hardness to 15° dGH.

D 3 = pH between 5.0 and 6.5 with hardness limited to 4° dGH.

276

The species are found in shallow water at depths of 20 inches (50 cm.). In spring-fed streams they stay between plants for protection and in larger rivers, between roots and branches. They venture into open water only in search of food. Temperatures and tank sizes are listed under the individual species. The fish prefer the middle region of an aquarium.

Breeding *Hyphessobrycon* species

In his handbook on the breeding of aquarium fishes, (published by Alfred Kernen, Stuttgart), PINTER gives a table of temperatures and water hardness, indicating the spawning cycle in days. He also describes the differences between the sexes. PINTER's table could not be included within the available space, but anyone who attempts serious breeding should not fail to read the book, if a translation is available.

A low water hardness of 4° KH and a pH value of 5.5-6.5 is recommended for nearly all species. A few species will also spawn in harder water. These values are obtained through complete desalination and filtration with peat although the water can possibly be softened through peat filtration alone. A 10g charge of black peat softens 25 gallons (100 l) of water by approximately one degree KH. On this basis you would need 210g of peat to reduce household water with a hardness of 25° KH to 4° KH. Since it is impossible to utilize this much peat at one time, the water is softened by stages using a new filter pack each time. There are other accepted ways of solving the problem.

It should be noted that the pH value remains constant to approximately 4° KH and only below 4° KH does the buffering effect of the calcium salts stop and the pH value drop. At this point the drop is rapid and must be carefully kept in check since the water will become too acid if the pH value drops below 5.0. This can be harmful to certain species. (See page 62.)

The breeding tank should be carefully cleaned and between 12 and 16 inches (30-40 cm.) in length, about 12 inches (30 cm.) wide and 10 inches (25 cm.) tall. It should be dimly lighted and for of reasons of hygiene, free of a gravel bottom. Green perlon wadding and floating ferns have both proven useful media for spawning. The most common varieties are *Eichhornia* or finely-leaved plants such as *Myriophyllum*. Long-stemmed plants can be anchored with glass rods available from most chemical and laboratory supply centers. Add a small filter, preferably one with a foam cartridge.

We suggest that you keep the aquarium water at temperatures between 75 and 79° F (24-26° C) and in many tanks a 10 to 20W heater will do the trick. For breeding you will need a pair ready to mate.

Differences between the sexes are generally easily recognized. The male tends to be more slender and has a tail fin ending in an extended point. Females are most readily identified by their swim bladder which is sharply rounded at the bottom. In comparison, the male's bladder is pointed. In species with a more transparent body the spawn may even be seen.

Results are best if you can select fish which have already courted and there are a number of publications which describe the courtship of Characins.

Food is an important stimulus. Breeding without the addition of live foods can only be successful in a few species such as *H. heterorhabdus*, *H. bentosi rosaceus*, *H. bifasciatus*, *H. scholzei* and *H. flammeus*. All other species will require live foods, preferably Black Mosquito larvae, to bring the fishes to spawning condition.

Feeding in the breeding tank should be kept to an absolute minimum and to adjust to new osmotic conditions (i.e. in the breeding tank) you must add a good water conditioner. This will protect both the fish and their spawn. After spawning – the species will release 50 to 300 eggs – the parents should be removed.

The fry are raised with very small pond food or with Brine Shrimp (*Artemia*) and, after ten days, very small flake food.If feeding flake foods only, the fry should be fed at least six times a day. Frequent feeding will promote, rapid, healthy growth. A portion of the tank water should be changed weekly.

Hemigrammus rhodostomus, the genuine one was described by AHL in 1924. Until about 1968, it came sporadically to Europe via Belem (Amazon Delta). In 1965 a further Rummy-nose Tetra was imported from the Rio Negro via Manaus. It was also called *Hemigrammus rhodostomus* (sometimes mixed up with *Petitella georgia*), also a Rummy-nose Tetra. See pages 272 and 308.

The Rummy-nose Tetras that were imported via Manaus and partially from Columbia, where only recently found to be *Hemigrammus bleheri* GÉRY, described in 1986. *H. rhodostomus* (Ahls Rummy-nose Tetra) has lately been imported once more. It is not so colorful as *H. bleheri* but easier to keep and breed.

Hemigrammus rhodostomus

Poeciliocharax weitzmani

Hyphessobrycon bentosi bentosi
Bentos Tetra

Syn.: *H. ornatus, H. callistus bentosi*

Hab.: Guyana; lower Amazon. The fish is almost exclusively imported from Asian breeders today.

Fl.: 1933.

Sex: ♂ has an extended, pointed tail fin.

Soc. B.: A peaceful community fish.

M: A tank well planted around the edges with plenty of swimming room in the center. Dark substrate is welcome and a gentle flow from the filter suits the species. Peat filteration is not necessary but can do no harm. pH 5.8-7.5 and a hardness to 20° dGH.

B: The species will willingly spawn in a breeding tank with soft water and finely-leaved plants. The larvae hatch after 24 hours and swim freely from the fifth day. The finest micro-food, including finely pinched flake foods, will be eaten.

F: C, O; flake food, all live foods.

S: One of the finest of Tetra varieties. It may be variously colored from nearly transparent to a striking red, depending on its origin.

T: 75-82° F,   L: 1$^1/_2$″,   A: 24″,   R: m,   D: 1-2.
   24-28° C,   4 cm,   60 cm,

Hyphessobrycon bentosi rosaceus
Rosy Tetra

Syn.: *Hyphessobrycon rosaceus, H. callistus rosaceus*

Hab.: Guyana; the lower Amazon,i.e. Rio Guaporé in Paraguay.

Fl.: 1912, Kropac, Hamburg, West Germany.

Sex: ♂ has larger tail fin, is more slender and more strongly colored.

Soc. B.: A peaceful fish recommended for a community tank.

M: See *H. bentosi bentosi.*

B: See description, page 276.

F: C, O; flake foods, FD, small live foods.

S: The species has no shoulder patch.

T: 75-82° F,   L: 1$^1/_2$″,   A: 24″,   R: m,   D: 1-2.
   24-28° C,   4 cm,   60 cm,

Hyphessobrycon copelandi
Copeland's Tetra

Syn.: None

Hab.: Upper and lower basin of the Amazon.

Fl.: 1934.

Sex: ♂ has sharply extended tail fin.

Soc. B.: A generally peaceful fish that may bite its tank-mates (as *H. callistus*).

M: The species is somewhat timid and, as with others of the genus, needs plenty of oxygen. On the bottom prefers darker gravel and at the surface, floating plants.

B: Unknown.

F: C, O; flake food, FD and live foods.

S: A very attractive species, rarely imported.

T: 75-82° F,   L: 1$^3/_4$″,   A: 28″,   R: m,   D: 2.
   24-28° C,   4.5 cm,   70 cm,

Hyphessobrycon bentosi bentosi

Hyphessobrycon bentosi rosaceus

Hyphessobrycon bifasciatus
Yellow Tetra

ELLIS, 1911

Syn.: None

Hab.: In woodland streams, lakes and estuaries of larger rivers of eastern Brazil such as those around Rio de Janeiro.

Fl : 1925, Ramsperger, Bremen, West Germany.

Sex: ♀ is fuller bodied.

Soc. B.: A peaceful though robust fish highly recommended for a community tank. Should be kept in a school of five to seven.

M: Easy to keep and able to tolerate nearly any water: pH 5.8-8.0 with a recommended value of 7.0. Can tolerate hardness to 30° dGH though ten degrees is recommended. The species is happiest when it has a shaded swimming area bordered by plants. The fish are likely to hide in a densely planted tank with a darker gravelled bottom. Prefers a strong flow of water and plenty of oxygen but can adapt to other situations.

B: See generic desription, page 277.

F: O; omnivorous, but will not consume plants.

S: The guanin or gold color occurs frequently in the wild (see *Hemigrammus rodwayi*, pg. 272). The large photo shows the fish in their gold coloring and the smaller photo, in standard color.

T: 68-77° F, L: 1¹/₂″,   A: 24″,   R: m, t, D: 1.
   20-25° C,   4 cm,   60 cm.

Hyphessobrycon callistus

(BOULENGER, 1900)

Syn.: *Tetragonopterus callistus, Hyphessobrycon melanopterus, Hemigrammus melanopterus*

Hab.: Southern Amazon basin and Paraguay basin. Now imported from Asia and bred in Europe.

Fl.: Possibly 1953.

Sex: ♂ swim bladder points sharply downward while that of ♀ is rounded and concealed. ♀ is rounder and taller.

Soc. B.: Prefers a school but is not as peaceful as others of the genus. Individuals may behave toward each other as do Piranhas – the weaker fish being bitten. An occasional fish may have an eye missing as a result of such predatory behavior, but most often the action can be attributed to insufficient food. Under normal circumstances the species is well suited to a community tank.

M: Similar to others of the genus. pH from 5.8 to 7.5 (6.8) and hardness to 25° dGH (10°).

B: Easily achieved in soft, slightly acid, peaty water.

F: C, O; FD food, flake food, live food such as Mosquito larvae and Brine shrimp.

S: See notes under Soc. B.

T: 72-82° F, L: 1¹/₂″,   A: 24″,   R: m,   D: 2.
   22-28° C,   4 cm,   60 cm,

Hyphessobrycon bifasciatus

Hyphessobrycon callistus

Aphyocharax paraguayensis
Dawn Tetra

EIGENMANN, 1915

Syn.: None

Hab.: Western Guyana.

Fl.: 1933.

Sex: ♂ is more slender; ♀ has a more rounded stomach line.

Soc. B.: A peaceful community fish, it prefers softer water.

M: More sensitive than others of its genus, pH 5.5-7.5 and hardness to 15° dGH. Prefers a shallow tank with planting around the edge. Should be kept with large numbers of its species. Peat filtration is advantageous.

B: Reduce both the water and light levels. Water should have a hardness of 2-4° KH and a pH of 6.0. which will quickly induce breeding. The male swims strongly between plants and over spawning moss.

Eggs and smaller fry are prone to fungus disease. They are smaller than most Tetra. The larvae have a relatively large egg sac and when this has been consumed the fry will eat very small pond food, After twenty days add Brine Shrimp.

F: C,O; small live food, flake food with FD added.

S: A pretty fish as contrasted to Neon Tetras in the community tank.

T: 75-82° F, **L:** 1³/₄″, **A:** 28″, **R:** t, **D:** 2-3.
    24-28° C,   4.5 cm,   70 cm,

Hyphessobrycon erythrostigma
Bleeding Heart Tetra

(FOWLER, 1943)

Syn.: *H. rubrostigma, H. callistus rubrostigma*

Hab.: Upper Amazon Basin, Peru.

Fl.: 1956, "Aquarium Hamburg", Hamburg, West Germany.

Sex: ♂ is readily distinguished by its lengthy, extended dorsal and anal fins. (See photo.)

Soc. B.: A peaceful species and can be kept in larger numbers or in pairs but should be in company of such peaceful species as *Megalamphodus, Corydoras* and *Nannostomus* sp.

M: Similar to *H. bentosi* though you should pay greater attention to water quality. Recommend peat filtration with a pH between 5.6-7.2 and hardness to 12° dGH.

B: Has not been successful in captivity.

F: C,O; flake food, FD and live foods such as Mosquito larvae.

S: In the past the species has been confused with *H. rodwayi* and has a counterpart from Rio Negro, described in 1977 by WEITZMAN as *Hyphessobrycon socolofi*. A picture of the species can be seen on page 213.

T: 73-82° F, **L:** 2¹/₂″, **A:** 24″, **R:** m, **D:** 2.
    23-28° C,   6 cm,   60 cm,

Aphyocharax paraguayensis

Hyphessobrycon erythrostigma

Hyphessobrycon flammeus
Flame Tetra

MYERS, 1924

Syn.: *H. bifasciatus* (not ELLIS, 1911)

Hab.: Eastern Brazil, around Rio de Janeiro.

Fl.: 1920 by C. Bruening, Hamburg, West Germany.

Sex: Anal fin of the ♂ is blood red while ♀ has a lighter color, to yellow. Pectoral fin tips are black on ♀ only.

Soc. B.: A very peaceful fish recommended for all community tanks.

M: The species has no special requirements but, as with all Characins, prefers darker gravel on the tank bottom. The colors of the fish show best under a soft light. pH 5.8 to 7.8 (6.5-7.0) with hardness to 25° dGH (10°). Peat filtration is helpful.

B: As indicated in the generic description.

F: O; omnivorous, flake foods.

S: Not always a popular species, Flame Tetra are easy to keep but many not always show their beautiful colors in a pet store's tank.

T: 72-82° F, **L:** 1¹/₂″, **A:** 20″, **R:** m, **D:** 1.
    22-28° C,   4 cm,   50 cm,

Hyphessobrycon griemi
Griem's Tetra

HOEDEMAN, 1957

Syn.: None

Hab.: Central Brazil (Goias). Fishes currently available are captive bred.

Fl.: 1956 by "Aquarium Hamburg", Hamburg, West Germany.

Sex: Anal fin of ♂ is blood red with a white stripe while ♀ is paler.

Soc. B.: A peaceful fish recommended for all community tanks.

M: The same as *H. flammeus.*

B: Easy to breed. See generic description, page 277.

F: C, O; flake food, FD and small live foods.

S: *H. flammeus* is similar but has two shoulder patches instead of three.

T: 74-82° F, **L:** 1¹/₂″, **A:** 20″, **R:** m, **D:** 1-2.
    23-28° C,   4 cm,   50 cm,

Hyphessobrycon flammeus

Hyphessobrycon griemi

287

Hyphessobrycon herbertaxelrodi
Black Neon

GERY, 1961

Syn.: None

Hab.: Rio Taquari, (a tributary of Rio Paraguay); Mato Grosso, Brazil. Now, generally
captive-bred.

Fl.: 1960, from the U.S.

Sex: ♀ has a more prominent stomach.

Soc. B.: A peaceful fish ideal for combining with other peaceful species.

M: More demanding than the Neon, it
prefers peat filtered water though not the
soft water some Tetras require. pH 5.5-7.5
(6.5) and a hardness of 6° dGH though it
can tolerate water to 15° . The fish likes to
school and frequently will "stand" on the
bottom. Subdued light, a dark gravel bottom and an definite flow of water are
suggested.

B: If well fed with such live food as Black
Mosquito larvae the species will happily
mate in a separate breeding tank with
water filtered through peat. (pH 6.0 and a
hardness about 4° KH.) The larvae will
hatch after 36 hours.

F: C, O; small live food, FD and good flake
food. The species requires a highly varied
diet.

S: While the name "Black Neon" used in
the hobby, the species is distinctly different from the true Neon.

T: 73-81° F, **L:** 1¹/₂″, **A:** 24″, **R:** m, t, **D:** 2-3.
23-27° C, 4 cm, 60 cm,

Hyphessobrycon heterorhabdus
Flag Tetra

(ULREY, 1895)

Syn.: *Tetragonopterus heterorhabdus, Hemigrammus heterorhabdus. Tetragonopterus ulreyi* (not BOULENGER)

Hab.: Southern tributaries of the central
Amazon.

Fl.: 1910, Blumenthal, Hamburg, West
Germany.

Sex: ♀ larger and fuller-bodied.

Soc. B.: A peaceful species, prefering
schools.

M: As for *H. herbertaxelrodi.*

B: Soft, slightly acid water (pH 6.0-6.5)
with hardness to 4° KH is most likely to
induce spawning. The fish is seldom prolific.

F: C, O; FD foods, small live food with
occasional flake food.

S: The species is sometimes confused
with *H. ulreyi.*

T: 73-82° F, **L:** 1³/₄″, **A:** 24″, **R:** m, **D:** 2.
23-28° C, 4.5 cm, 60 cm,

Hyphessobrycon herbertaxelrodi

Hyphessobrycon heterorhabdus

Hyphessobrycon loretoensis
Loreto Tetra

LADIGES, 1938

Syn.: *"H. metae"*

Hab.: Amazon, Peru, Rio Meta (Department of Loreto).

Fl.: 1938, "Aquarium Hamburg", Hamburg, West Germany.

Sex: None in coloring; body of ♀ more distended.

Soc. B.: Peaceful but recommended for an experienced aquarist's community tank.

M: Similar to *H. herbertaxelrodi*.

B: Apparently not successful thus far.

F: C, O; small live food as brine shrimp, FD and a good flake food.

S: Easily confused with *H. peruvianus* (around Iquitos). *H. metae* is also similar but our drawings show the differences. The species can be distinguished by its gill covers. Those of *H. peruvianus* are virtually devoid of pigment; those of *H. metae* are darker with the color extending over much of the body, even to the dark body band itself. *H. peruvianus* is apparently a *Hemigrammus* according to GERY.

T: 72-79° F, L: 1¹/₂″, A: 24″, D: 2-3.
  22-26° C, 4 cm, 60 cm,

Hyphessobrycon inconstans
EIGENMANN and OGLE, 1907
Para, Eastern Brazil

T: 72-82° F, L: 1³/₄″, A: 24″, D: 1.
  22-28° C, 4.5 cm, 60 cm,

Hyphessobrycon minor
DURBIN, 1909
Guyanas.

T: 74-81° F, L: 1¹/₄″, A: 24″, R: , D: 2.
  23-27° C, 3 cm, 60 cm,

Hyphessobrycon robustulus
(COPE, 1870)
Peruvian Amazon.

T: 74-79° F, L: 1³/₄″, A: 20″, D: 2.
  23-26° C, 4.5 cm, 50 cm,

Hyphessobrycon vilmae

GERY, 1966

Syn.: None

Hab.: Mato Grosso, Brazil; spring-fed streams of the Tapajos, Rio Arinos.

Fl.: 1975, Hans Baensch, Melle, West Germany.

Sex: ♀ larger and, along the stomach line, the body is rounder.

Soc. B.: A peaceful, attractive fish recommended for tanks with other gentle species. Lives well with *Hemiancistrus*, *Otocinclus* and most Characins.

M: Only kept in an aquarium for two weeks or less. The fish are found in streams of

pH 5.8 (in September). The hardness was barely measurable (below one degree); the temperature, about 73° F (23° C). The first fish imported tolerated 25° dGH (18° KH) and died only as a result of an accident.

B: Numbers not sufficient for breeding.

F: C, O; small flakes, FD and such live foods as brine shrimp.

S: Found in streams with heavy growth.

T: 72-79° F, L: 1¹/₂″, A: 24″, R: m, t, D: 2-3.
  22-26° C, 4 cm, 60 cm,

Hyphessobrycon loretoensis

H. inconstans

H. minor

H. robustulus

H. vilmae

Hyphessobrycon pulchripinnis
Lemon Tetra

AHL, 1937

Syn.: None

Hab.: In narrow, overgrown streams; Central Brazil; Tocantins tributaries.

Fl.: 1937 by Scholze and Poetzschke, Berlin, Germany.

Sex: The anal fin of the ♂ has a blank edge which dominates.

Soc. B.: Peaceful fish of curious disposition.

M: Needs plenty of room since it enjoys swimming and prefers an edging of dense vegetation, peat filtration and a darkened tank bottom. Recommend subdued light, frequent water changes and soft water. In hard water the fish loses color. pH 5.5 -8.0 (6.0) with hardness to 25° dGH (8°).

B: Little bred since they may not appear attractive unless properly maintained.

F: C, O; flake food, FD and small live food.

S: Their best coloring, a luminous yellow-orange comes only with proper foods. We suggest Tetra Ruby.

T: 73-82° F, L: 1¹/₂″, A: 24″, R: m, t, D: 1-2.
  23-28° C, 4.5 cm, 60 cm,

Hyphessobrycon "robertsi"

not described

Syn.: The species has not been described.

Hab.: Iquitos, Peru.

Fl.: 1962 by Heiko Bleher, West Germany.

Sex: ♂ has a sharply extended dorsal.

Soc. B.: Peaceful fish recommended for a community tank.

M: Similar to *H. bentosi* but, in terms of water, more demanding. pH 5.5-7.5 (6.0) and hardness to 10° dGH. Does best with peat filtration, dense vegetation and a subdued light. In bright light the fish becomes timid and pale.

B: Difficult but chances with subdued light and peat water a pH 5.5 to 6.0. Keep hardness to 3° KH. Chance matings occasionally reported may involve other species.

F: C, O; flake food, FD and live food.

S: One of the finest hobby fishes. The author has seen specimens caught in the wild with markings similar to those found at an exporters in Iquitos. It is probable this is a true species. Crosses with *H. bentosi* (*ornatus*) have proven successful. *"robertsi"* must, therefore, be closer to *Hyphessobrycon* than to *Megalamphodus* as the authors have suspected. In terms of habitat, *"robertsi"* overlaps with *H. erythrostigma*. According to SCHEEL, *H. (ornatus) = bentosi* and *"robertsi"* may be color morphs of *H. bentosi* with different habitat. GERY (in a private letter) feels it is probably an independent species.

T: 73-82° F, L: 2″, A: 28″, R: m, D: 2.
  23-28° C, 5 cm, 70 cm,

Hyphessobrycon pulchripinnis

Hyphessobrycon "robertsi" two ♂

Hyphessobrycon scholzei

Syn.: None

Hab.: Eastern Brazil; Paraguay.

Fl.: 1937 by Scholze and Poetzschke, Berlin, Germany.

Sex: ♀ larger than ♂ which has a deeply forked caudal.

Soc. B.: Eats plants but a peaceful fish, well suited to a community tank with hardy vegetation.

M: An ideal beginner's fish but not popular with hobbyists who own well-planted aquariums but it can form an attractive contrast with other plant-eaters. Suggest an aquarium decorated with stones, roots and such hardy plants as Java Fern. pH 6.8-8.0 (7.0) and hardness to 25° dGH (15°).

B: Since the fish will eat their spawn the tank bottom should be laid with round pebbles or a trap should be used. Place moss, plastic plants or spawning fiber overhead. The fish will lay up to 800 eggs in water 79 to 82° (26-28° C). The larvae will hatch in 24 hours and are free-swimming in two days. Feed infusoria the first two days then brine shrimp and ground flake food.

F: O, H; omnivorous, vegetable diet.

S: Recommended for the tyro though be warned: not every hobbyist will want to trade fry.

T: 72-82° F, L: 2″,   A: 24″,   R: m,   D: 1-2 (H).
    22-28° C,   5 cm,   60 cm,

Paracheirodon simulans

Syn.: *Hyphessobrycon simulans*

Hab.: Brazil; Either Rio Jufaris or Tupari in the region of the Rio Negro rivers.

Fl.: 1962.

Sex: ♀ larger with fuller body.

Soc. B.: A peaceful fish suggested for community tanks.

M: Delicate and sensitive to nitrate levels but similar to *Paracheirodon axelrodi*, page 260. Prone to Oodinium and treatment with proper medications is suggested. Peat filtration and soft, acid water (pH 5.5-6.0 with hardness to 4° KH) are essential. Can tolerate water to 15° KH.

B: Difficult to breed and not prolific. Requires proper feeding conditions and soft water (1-2° KH and pH 5.2-5.8). May spawn best with several of its species. Feed young small pond food.

F: C, O; small flakes, FD and small live food.

S: Similar to the Neon. SCHULTZ believes the species is found in company with the Cardinal Tetra. Not often imported. SCHEEL examined three Neon among others and in *P. simulans* found 25 chromosomes, 16 in *P. innesi* and 26 in *Paracheirodon axelrodi*. The three species are not related but do look much alike. WEITZMAN and FINK combined the three under the genus *Paracheirodon*.

T: 73-81° F, L: 1-1¹/₂″, A: 24″,   R: m,   D: 2-3.
    23-27° C,   2-3.5 cm,   60 cm,

Hyphessobrycon scholzei

Paracheirodon simulans

Iguanodectes spilurus   (GUENTHER, 1864)

Syn.: *Piabucus spilurus, Piabuca spilurus, Iguanodectes tenuis, I. rachovii*

Hab.: Guyana; Madeira River and tributaries of the central Amazon.

Fl.: 1912, Kropac, Hamburg, West Germany.

Sex: Front rays of the anal fin are extended more in the ♂.

Soc. B.: Lively but peaceful, recommended for community tanks.

M: Though unremarkable in appearance it can change color quickly. Coloring of wild populations varies with habitat and the fact that it is found in fast-flowing streams indicates a high oxygen requirement.
The fish adjust rapidly to various water conditions, pH 5.0-7.5 and hardness to 18° dGH. Does not eat plants.

B: The first successful breeding of *Iguanodectes spirulus* was reported by BOEHM (1985) in a short report in TI International No. 69, pages 12-13. For breeding a 20 l aquarium and one pair of fish were used. There was a spawning grill on the bottom of the tank. The water had a pH value of 6.2 and 2° dGH. This species will spawn at intervals. The eggs are relatively large – 2 mm. The fry hatch within 10-14 days and have to be fed finely textured food.

F: C, O; flake and small live food.

S: The fact that the species is difficult to catch, coupled with its apparently "dull" coloring account for it being rarely imported but you should try to keep this one. The experience is rewarding.

T: 73-81° F,   L: 2-2³/₄″,   A: 32″,   R: m, t, D: 2.
   23-27° C,   5-6 cm,   80 cm,

Inpaichthys kerri   GERY and JUNK, 1977

Syn.: None

Hab.: Rio Aripuana in Amazonia. Also bred in Germany.

Fl.: 1977 by Heiko Bleher, West Germany.

Sex: The ♂ is larger, more powerful and more colorful.

Soc. B: A peaceful species recommended for a community tank, especially for tanks with less-active species.

M: A delicate species which is at its best in a tank with a dark bottom and subdued light. Should be kept in a small school and needs plenty of swimming space. Prefers dense vegetation and soft water to 10° dGH. pH around 7.0.

B: Similar to that suggested for Emperor Tetra (page 304).

F: C, O; flake food, FD and small live food.

S: If not maintained properly will lack color. Only adult males exhibit a luminous blue. Differs from *Hyphessobrycon* in its incomplete lateral line, different dentation and scaleless tail fin.

T: 75-81° F,   L: ♂=1¹/₂″, ♀=1¹/₄″, A: 24″,   R: m, D: 2.
   24-27° C,   ♂=4 cm, ♀=3 cm,   60 cm,

Iguanodectes spilurus

Inpaichthys kerri, top ♀, bottom ♂

Megalamphodus megalopterus
Black Phantom Tetra

EIGENMANN, 1915

Syn.: None

Hab.: Headquaters Rio San Francisco; central Brazil.

Fl.: 1956.

Sex: Exception: ♀ is beautifully colored with red adipose, pectoral and anal fins. ♂ smoky glass grey with black fins and a larger dorsal.

Soc. B.: A peaceful fish it can be kept in schools or as pairs. Two ♂♂ will fight in mock battle, which is display behavior, but will not inflict damage.

M: The Black Phantom Tetra is one of the easiest to keep and is not as particular about either water softness nor acidity as its cousin, *M. sweglesi*. pH 6.0-7.5 (6.5) with hardness to 18° dGH (10°). In its natural habitat the stream surface is always covered with such floating plants as *Salvinia, Pistia* and *Eichhornia*.

B: The ♂♂ have an impressive courtship ritual and tank breeding is quite possible following procedures for *Hyphessobrycon* on page 276. Lower pH to 5.5-6.0 with hardness below 4° KH. Subdued lighting recommended.

F: C, O; flake food, FD and such live foods as crustaceans.

S: Every aquarist should keep the Black Phantom at least once.

T: 72-82° F,   L: 1³/₄″,   A: 24″,   R: m,   D: 2.
22-28° C,   4.5 cm,   60 cm,

Megalamphodus sweglesi
Red Phantom Tetra

GERY, 1961

Syn.: None

Hab.: Upper Orinoco basin; Rio Muco, Rio Meta, Colombia.

Fl.: 1961.

Sex: ♀ has multi-colored, red, black and white dorsal. ♂ has an extended red dorsal.

Soc. ᐧB: A gentle fish recommended for community tanks stocked with similar small, peaceful species which can tolerate cooler waters such as Dwarf Cichlids and many Tetras.

M: Requires considerable attention to water conditions and feeding. The common error is a high water temperature. Prefers soft, slightly-acid water with frequent changes, frequent but small feedings and subdued lighting. pH 5.5-7.5 (6.0) and hardness to 20° dGH (4-8°).

B: Soft water at 1-2° dGH, pH 5.5-6.0 with the temperature between 68-72° F (20-22° C). Reduce tank lighting and use Perlon fiber on the bottom. Cleanliness is important. The eggs are reddish-brown. The fry will be free-swimming in five days and can immediately take freshly-hatched brine shrimp.

F: C, O; flake foods, FD and such small live foods as brine shrimp and *Cyclops*.

S: The young resemble *Pristella maxillaris*.

T: 68-73° F,   L: 1¹/₂″,   A: 24″,   R: m,   D: 2-3.
20-23° C,   4 cm,   60 cm,

Megalamphodus megalopterus

Megalamphodus sweglesi

Moenkhausia collettii
Colletti Tetra

(STEINDACHNER, 1882)

Syn.: *Tetragonopterus collettii*

Hab.: Amazon basin; Guyanas.

Fl.: 1970 by Aquarium Rio, Frankfurt, West Germany.

Sex: ♂ has extended anterior anal fin rays.

Soc. B: A peaceful, attractive fish recommended for a community tank stocked with gentle species.

M: Similar to the Indian glassfish, *Chanda ranga*, but is less demanding about food. Prefers subdued lighting, a tank with floating plants, a darker gravel bottom and soft, slightly-acid water. pH 5.6-7.2 with hardness to 15° dGH.

B: A successful breeding was reported in TI International No. 90 (1988).

F: C, O; flake and small live foods.

S: Related to genus *Astyanax* and lacks the scales on the base of the tail fin found on genus *Moenkhausia*.

T: 73-81° F, **L:** 1¹/₄″, **A:** 24″, **R:** m, **D:** 2.
    23-27° C,   3 cm,   60 cm,

Moenkhausia intermedia

EIGENMANN, 1908

Syn.: None

Hab.: Amazon basin; Guyana; Rio Paraguay.

Fl.: Unknown.

Sex: On ♂ the swim bladder is pointed and the anal fin is extended.

Soc. B: A peaceful species recommended for any community tank.

M: Similar to *Moenkhausia pittieri*.

B: Not described, but probably similar to *Hyphessobrycon sp.* See page 277.

F: C, O; flake food, FD and small live foods.

S: Similar to *Moenkhausia dichroura* but differs at the lower premaxillary. Also compare with *Rasbora trilineata*, page 441, and *Hemigrammus marginatus*, page 267.

T: 73-81° F, **L:** 2″, **A:** 24″, **R:** m, **D:** 2-3.
    23-27° C,   5 cm,   60 cm,

Moenkhausia collettii

Moenkhausia intermedia

301

Moenkhausia pittieri
Pittier's Tetra, Diamond Tetra

EIGENMANN, 1920

Syn.: None

Hab.: Venezuela; specifically, Lake Valencia and related environs as Rio Bue and Rio Tiquirito. Bred occasionally in Asia.

Fl.: 1933, Otto Winkelmann, Altona, West Germany.

Sex: Flag-like, pointed dorsal on ♂. (See photo.)

Soc. B.: A peaceful fish which requires swimming room and a tank that is not too heavily planted.

M: Demands little attention but will not do well in a tank with hard water. Prefers peaty water, subdued light, a dark-gravel bottom and floating plants above.

B: Recommend small breeding tanks about 16 inches (40 cm.) long, with soft water filtered through peat and a hardness

to 4° dGH. Use green Perlon fiber as a spawning medium. Initially darken the tank, then gently increase the light. Feed Mosquito larvae to encourage spawning. After an enchanting courtship the spawn is deposited between the fiber, The parents should then be removed. The fry will hatch after two or three days and will consume the egg sac by the fourth to sixth day. Raise as suggested for *M. sanctaefilomenae*.

F: C, O; flake food, FD and live foods.

S: Immature fish can be misleading since the species blossoms to full splendor only when adult.

T: 75-82° F, L: 2$^1/_2$″, A: 24″, R: m, D: 3.
  24-28° C,   6 cm,   60 cm,

Moenkhausia sanctaefilomenae
Yellow-Banded Moenkhausia

(STEINDACHNER, 1907)

Syn.: *Tetragonopterus sanctaefilomenae, Moenkhausia agassizi, M. australis, M. filomenae, Poecilurichthys agassizi*

Hab.: Paraguay; eastern Bolivia; eastern Peru and western Brazil. Imported fish are generally bred in Asia.

Fl.: 1914, C. Kropac, Hamburg, West Germany.

Sex: The adult ♀ has a more rounded stomach.

Soc. B.: Peaceful; recommended for any community tank.

M: Undemanding though the species prefers some plant cover and a darker gravel bottom. pH 5.5-8.5 and hardness to 30° dGH.

B: Free-spawning in schools or pairs, will also lay eggs between the roots of floating plants or on a fiber spawning mat. Suggest a small breeding tank with soft water (below 4° KH) and peat filtration. Since the parents will eat the eggs they should be removed. The fry hatch after one or two days and can be fed small powdered food. After eight days add brine shrimp and flaked baby food.

F: O; omnivorous, will take most flake foods but will not touch plants.

S: A readily-available species found in most community tanks.

T: 72-79° F, L: 2$^3/_4$″, A: 28″, R: m, D: 1.
  22-26° C,   7 cm,   70 cm,

Moenkhausia pittieri

Moenkhausia sanctaefilomenae

Nematobrycon lacortei

WEITZMAN & FINK, 1971

Syn.: *N. amphiloxus*, a variety of *N. palmeri*

Hab.: Rio Atrato, western Colombia.

Fl.: 1967, Heiko Bleher, Germany; after 1970 in the U.S.

Sex: ♂ has an extended dorsal similar to *N. palmeri.*

M: Similar to *N. palmeri* but since the species is rare it requires more attention. pH 5.6-7.2 and hardness to 12° dGH.

B: Not described but since the species is easy to keep the fact that it has not been bred in the hobby may reflect only that it has not been fed the proper foods.

F: C, O; flake and live foods.

S: A third species of *Nematobrycon* has been described: *N. amphiloxus* EIGEN- MANN & WILSON, 1914. According to GERY this is a synonym of *N. palmeri* but the *"amphiloxus"* variant is smokey grey and generally darker than *N. palmeri.*

T: 73-81° F,	**L:** 2",	**A:** 28",	**R:** m,	**D:** 2-3.
23-27° C,	5 cm,	70 cm,		

Nematobrycon palmeri
Emperor Tetra

EIGENMANN, 1911

Syn.: *N. amphiloxus*

Hab.: West coast of Colombia.

Fl.: 1959.

Sex: See the photo: ♂ above, ♀ beneath.

Soc. B.: A quiet, peaceful fish, it should not share a tank with a livelier species. Suggest dense vegetation to reduce light as well as a dark gravel bottom and peat filtration. Water should be changed regularly, adding a good conditioner each time. pH 5.0-7.8 (6.5) and hardness to 25° dGH (10°).

B: Not a prolific species spawning is possible in water at temperatures between 79-82° F (26-28° C). Place the breeding

pair in a small, dark tank with soft water. Eggs are laid one at a time. Since the parents are egg-eaters use a spawning net or water moss on the bottom and remove the pair after several hours of spawning. The fry will hatch in one or two days. Feed very small pond food and, after a few days, brine shrimp.

F: C, O; flake food and such livefoods as *Artemia* (Brine shrimp), *Daphnia* and *Cyclops.*

S: Pretty, popular and peaceful, the Emperor Tetra is an excellent fish for tyro aquarists. It can live as long as six years in a well-maintained tank.

T: 73-81° F,	**L:** 2",	**A:** 28",	**R:** m,	**D:** 2.
23-27° C,	5 cm,	70 cm,		

Nematobrycon lacortei

Nematobrycon palmeri

Paracheirodon innesi

306

American Characins

Paracheirodon axelrodi page 260, *P. simulans* page 294

Paracheirodon innesi   (MYERS, 1936)
Neon Tetra

Syn.: *Hyphessobrycon innesi*

Hab.: Rio Putumayo, eastern Peru. Hobby fish are now virtually all captive-bred, most often in Hong Kong.

Fl.: 1936 by A. Rabaut, Paris, France.

Sex: ♂ more slender with a blue longitudinal line. ♀ has a fuller stomach and the line is bent.

Soc. B.: Peaceful and recommended for most community tanks. Should not be kept with substantially larger fishes – for example, Angels. Monitor water conditions.

M: After acclimation will tolerate water as hard as 30° dGH and a pH to 8.0. Prefers peat-filtered water, subdued lighting and water hardness to 10° dGH. pH 7.0 is ideal. Does best in a school of five to seven tank-mates. Under the proper conditions, such as a darker gravel bottom, regular water changes and vegetation, a Neon can live more than ten years.

B: Suggest very soft water, at 75° F (24° C), 1-2° dGH and pH 5.0-6.0 with subdued lighting. The female may lay as many as 130 eggs on a green Perlon mat. As the female spawns the male embraces her so the ♀ is nearly vertical. Remove the adults after spawning, allowing the eggs to remain in a darkened tank to prevent the growth of fungus. The fry hatch after 24 hours and are free-swimming within five days. Feed small pond foods.

F: C, L; small flake food, FD, tablets, brine shrimp and other small live foods.

S: Easily the most popular of all aquarium fish.

T: 68-79° F,   **L**: 1$^{1}/_{2}$″,   **A**: 24″,   **R**: m, b, **D**: 1-2.
   20-26° C,   4 cm,   60 cm,

Petitella georgiae
False-Red Nose, False-Rummy-Nose Tetra

GERY & BOUTIERE, 1964

Syn.: None

Hab.: In smaller streams near Iquitos, Peru and Rio Branca (state Amazonas) in white water.

Fl.: Before 1960.

Sex: Difficult to distinguish. The contrast between stripes is more pronounced on ♂.

Soc. B.: A peaceful fish.

M: A typical "blackwater" fish, it can be kept in tanks with Discus, Neons, *Corydoras*, Dwarf Cichlids and other peaceful species. pH 5.5-7.0 and hardness to 12° dGH. Suggest peat filtration, dense vegetation (possibly floating plants) and a dark gravel tank bottom. When changing water add a good conditioner.

B: Not described and possibly difficult. Could be triggered by foods and possibly similar to the Cardinal Tetra.

F: C, O; flake foods and small live foods such as brine shrimp and Mosquito larvae.

S: More popular than the Red-Nosed Tetra, *Hemigrammus rhodostomus,* but is more difficult to maintain. *H. rhodostomus* is from Belem in lower Amazon and is rarely imported because of its lack of color. Fish from Manaus, especially the Rio Caures and Rio Jufaris, and from Iquitos are sold under the same name. *Petitella georgiae*, seen in the photo, is imported from Manaus and Colombia.

T: 72-79° F, L: 2″, A: 24″, R: m, t, D: 4.
   22-26° C, 5 cm, 60 cm,

Pristella maxillaris
X-ray Fish

(ULREY, 1895)

Syn.: *Pristella riddlei, Holopristes riddlei, Aphyocharax maxillaris*

Hab.: Venezuela; British Guyana; lower Brazilian Amazon. Hobby fishes now predominantly captive-bred.

Fl.: 1924, W. Eimeke, Hamburg, West Germany.

Sex: ♂ is noticeably slender with a sharply pointed swim bladder. ♀ has a plumper look with a more rounded swim bladder.

Soc. B.: Peaceful and recommended for any community tank.

M: A most undemanding species it does best in soft water. pH 6.0-8.0 (7.0) with hardness to 35° dGH. A dark gravel bottom and subdued light will enhance the colors. The species is also found in brackish water.

B: Easy and very prolific, spawning 300 to 400 eggs. Pairing may be more difficult since not every fish accepts another of the species as a partner.

F: C, O; try flake foods with vegetable flakes as a change of pace.

S: Will not achieve maximum color in hard water or brightly lighted tanks.

T: 74-82° F, L: 1³/₄″, A: 20″, R: m, D: 1-2.
   24-28° C, 4.5 cm, 50 cm,

Petitella georgiae from Manaus

Pristella maxillaris

Tetragonopterus argenteus

CUVIER, 1818

Syn.: *Salmo saua, Tetragonopterus rufipes, T. sawa*

Hab.: Amazon in Brazil and Peru, and possibly Venezuela.

Fl.: Unknown and is frequently confused with *T. chalceus*.

Sex: Not described but probably similar to *T. chalceus*.

Soc. B.: Peaceful.

M: Easier to maintain than many related species and is much like the Black Widow. See page 262.

B: Easy. Is bred in Asia and sometimes, in Florida. Spawns freely on mats. Be sure to remove adults. Raise fry with brine shrimp, fine flake, TetraMin Baby Food and red Liquifry.

F: O; omnivorous but will not eat plants. Suggest flake foods with vegetable mix.

S: Distinguished from genus *Moenkhausia* by a sharp, lateral line which points downward. (See photo on the right.) Differs from *T. chalceus* by less bright coloration and the larger number of scales on the predorsal line (12-16). *T. chalceus* has 8 to 10. The area of the anal fin nearest the body also has more scales on *T. chalceus*. The fish in the photo is typical of the species and is four cm. in length (1$^1/_2''$).

T: 72-81° F,   **L:** possibly 3$^1/_4''$,   **A:** 40″,   **R:** m,   **D:** 1.
    22-27° C,   8 cm,   100 cm,

Tetragonopterus chalceus

AGASSIZ, 1829

Syn.: *Coregonus amboinensis, Tetragonopterus artedii, T. ortonii, T. schomburgki*

Hab.: Guyanas; Rio Sao Francisco and Rio Araguaia, Brazil; Arroyo, Trementina, Paraguay.

Fl.: 1913, Kropac, Hamburg, West Germany.

Sex: ♂ has an extended dorsal and is slighter.

Soc. B: Generally peaceful, an adult may be intolerant of tankmates.

M: Displays best color when fed occasionally with live foods and kept in a tank with good water, a dark bottom and adequate vegetation. (See photo.) pH 5.0-7.5 (6.5) and hardness to 20° dGH.

B: Spawns freely among plants. Keep the breeding tank dark at first, then increase light – possibly even strong sunlight. Will spawn readily if fed well and kept in soft water. Remove the parents and raise the fry as for *G. ternetzi*.

F: C, O; omnivorous, eats plants only if the tank is lacking in other foods. Suggest flakes, including vegetable flakes, FD and most live foods.

S: Some writers have described the species shown as *T. argenteus* as *T. chalceus* and vice versa though the two vary greatly in color. The photo shows a fish 7.5 cm. long (3″).

T: 68-82° F,   **L:** 3$^1/_4$-4$^3/_4''$,   **A:** 48″,   **R:** m,   **D:** 2-3.
    20-28° C,   8-12 cm,   120 cm,

Tetragonopterus argenteus

Tetragonopterus chalceus

Thayeria boehlkei

WEITZMAN, 1957

Syn.: Often confused with *T. obliqua*

Hab.: Rio Araguaia, Brazil; Amazon, Peru.

Fl.: Possibly 1935. Was confused with *T. obliqua* until 1957 or 58.

Sex: When ready to spawn the ♀♀ have a more rounded stomach.

Soc. B.: A peaceful fish recommended for any community tank.

M: Undemanding in terms of food and general water conditons but sensitive to nitrates and nitrites. Suggest a well-planted tank with regular water changes; about one-third twice a month (but less often if there are not many fish in the tank.) pH 5.8-7.5 (6.5) and hardness to 20° dGH. Can tolerate saline conditions.

B: Very prolific; as many as 1000 eggs. Change water after spawning since the large quantity of sperm can cause pollution.

F: C, O; flake food, FD and live foods.

S: The fish swim with their head up, about 30 degrees from the horizontal. Their "see-saw" swimming and strong markings can be diverting.

T: 72-82° F, **L:** 2¹/₂″, **A:** 24″, **R:** m, t, **D:** 2.
22-28° C, 6 cm, 60 cm,

Thayeria obliqua
Penguin Fish

EIGENMANN, 1908

Syn.: None

Hab.: Rio Guapore/Mamore (Madeira River system); Bananal Island in the Araguaia River, Brazil.

Fl.: 1949.

Sex: ♀ has a rounder stomach, noticeable only when ready to spawn.

Soc. B.: A peaceful fish which draws attention in any well-kept community tank. It is similar to *Hemiodus*, with which it is often seen, in its need for fresh water and plenty of oxygen. The writer has found them in dense vegetation in the reedy backwaters of the Rio Mamore. The bottom of the river was thick with algae and the fish lie just beneath the surface, between the reeds, which provide protection. Whether this is the only habitat the writer could not determine. The surface water was very warm, 82-86° F (28-30° C) during the day but cooled to 68° F (20° C) at night, dropping even lower in bad weather. At this time the fish probably sink to lower, warmer water.

B: Not yet, according to GÉRY, 1977.

F: C, O; flake food, FD and live foods such as insects and larvae.

S: The species illustrated up to 1957 or 58 has always been *T. boehlkei!*

T: 72-82° F, **L:** 3¹/₄″, **A:** 32″, **R:** m, t, **D:** 3.
22-28° C, 8 cm, 80 cm,

Thayeria boehlkei

Thayeria obliqua

Characidium fasciatum
Banded Characidium

Syn.: Possibly *Characidium zebra*

Hab.: Found in small, clear streams throughout South America.

Fl.: 1913.

Sex: Dorsal of the ♂ has dots around the base. On ♀ the fin is clear.

Soc. B.: Peaceful, a loner and possibly territorial since in the wild each fish claims a portion of a stream bottom. They are bold, curious and comical with a jerky manner of swimming. Their coloring and markings blend with the habitat. In streams with plants their color is greenish. On a dark bottom they can be a dark olive color with black bands or a chessboard-markings.

M: We do not know if more than one can be kept safely in one aquarium since the species is generally imported singly. Lives in flowing water and requires considerable oxygen. Water should be peat-filtered, soft and slightly acid – pH 5.6-7.5 (6.5 is ideal).

After adaptation can tolerate harder water to 25° dGH.

B: Breeding is not difficult. Free spawning with small eggs which will fall between plants and gravel. The fry will hatch in 30 to 40 hours and need vegetation with hiding places. Suggest removing parents. Feed small live food such as Infusoria and *Artemia* (brine shrimp).

F: C; tablets and FD tablets taken in the wild; also small worms and Mosquito larvae.

S: Species and sub-species can be found in every watercourse and pond in Brazil and are difficult to tell apart because of insufficient details in initial descriptions. Were originally classed in four groups. There are said to be about 50 species; the description for *C. fasciatum* may be regarded as a summary of *fasciatum* as a group.

T: 64-74° F, L: 3$^{1}/_{4}$-4″,   A: 24″,   R: b,   D: 2.
  18-24° C,   8-10 cm,   60 cm,

Characidium rachovii

Syn.: *Jobertina rachovi, Leporinus melanopleura*

Hab.: Southern Brazil.

Fl.: 1912, Karl Kopp.

Sex: ♂ has a dotted dorsal while the dorsal on the ♀ is transparently clear.

Soc. B.: Similar to *C. fasciatum*.

M: Similar to *C. fasciatum*.

B: Probably similar to *C. fasciatum*.

F: C, O; small floating flake particles, FD tablets and small live food.

S: One of many *Characidium* species with a "flash" along the lateral line in place of the more common banding. FOWLER included the *Characidium* genus in the subfamily *Nannostomatinae*. This classification has since been abandoned.

T: 68-74° F, L: 2$^{1}/_{2}$″,   A: 20-24″,   R: b,   D: 2.
  20-24° C,   7 cm,   50-60 cm,

Characidium fasciatum

Characidium rachovii

Boulengerella maculata (VALENCIENNES, 1849)

Syn.: *Xiphostoma maculatum, Hydrocynus maculatus, Xiphostoma taedo*

Hab.: Slower tributaries and bays of the Amazon.

Fl.: 1913.

Sex: Unknown.

Soc. B.: Stay mostly in pairs or in active groups at the surface. Can be kept with other fish of a similar size.

M: Requires space and plenty of oxygen. It is timid and sensitive to bodily injury, especially to its nose. We do not recommend Giant *Vallisneria* as its leaves cover most of the surface, limiting swimming room. pH 6.0-7.5 and hardness to 18° dGH. A short-lived species.

B: Not known.

F: C; the young will accept flake foods; adults prefer small fish and larger insects.

S: A surface predator kept best in a larger tank. The species is caught with lights in the wild.

T: 73-81° F, L: 13″, A: 48″, R: t, D: 3.
23-27° C, 35 cm, 120 cm,

Crenuchus spilurus
Sailfin Characin

GUENTHER, 1863

Syn.: None

Hab.: Guyana.

Fl.: 1912 by Kuntzschmann, Hamburg, West Germany.

Sex: ♂ has a longer, red dorsal which ends in a point. ♀ is smaller, paler.

Soc. B.: A peaceful fish but may be too timid for a commmunity tank. Needs hiding places and is predatory toward smaller species.

M: A small tank with a peat bottom, dense vegetation and hollows are suggested. Soft, slightly acid water will come close to that in nature. pH 5.5-6.5 with hardness to 5° dGH. Can be kept alone or in pairs. ♂ becomes slightly territorial toward his own species and tank-mates.

B: Not known. The species is said to spawn on stones, fanning its eggs. The spawning season is from October to February.

F: C; small to large live foods such as Mosquito larvae and worms. Also small fish.

S: There is an organ on the head which has not been decribed. GÉRY feels it may be heat or light sensitive. The species is similar in appearance to the Killifish. The closely-related *Poecilicharax weitzmani* GÉRY 1965, has become available after a hiatus and should be kept as *spilurus*. A photograph is on page 279.

T: 75-82° F, **L:** 2¹/₂″, **A:** 20″, **R:** b, m, **D:** 3-4.
   24-28° C,   6 cm,   50 cm,

Chilodus punctatus
Spotted Headstander

MUELLER & TROSCHEL, 1845
Sub-Fam.: Chilodinae

Syn.: *Chaenotropus punctatus, Citharinus chilodus*

Hab.: Guyanas; upper Amazon, Rio Tocatins, upper Orinoco.

Fl.: 1912, J.S.Kropac, Hamburg, West Germany.

Sex: Unknown; ♀ recognized only during spawning by a more rounded body.

Soc. B.: A peaceful species found in schools.

M: Maintain suggested water temperatures (as in B), change water frequently and use a good conditioner each time. Can use peatbrown water or clear water with the lighting subdued by floating plants. Need vegetation and wood to hide beneath. They become timid in over-lighted tanks and will not eat.

B: The spotted marking disappear during spawning and are replaced by one or two larger black patches between the eyes and the dorsal. Breeding has been described by GEISLER in the West German maga zine DATZ, In brief: a large tank (one meter) with sandy bottom and ocasional roots and stones with algae. Fill with clear water of a pH between 6 and 7 and a hardness of 10° KH. Peat filtration for a touch of acid is often the key to success. Feed Red Mosquito larvae, *Cyclops* and green algae. Flakes and stewed lettuce may be added.

T: between 77-82° F (25-27° C) with sub-dued light. Pairing occurs immediately below the surface between plants, three to five eggs 1.5 mm in size are shed. The fry headstand like their parents and will accept brine shrimp immediately after hatching. They are not difficult to raise but the parents should be removed. Provide plenty of algae. FRANKE (Aquarian Magazine) provided instructions on ways unhatched larvae (possibly caused by improper water) can be released from the egg sac by means of a dissecting knife.

F: H, L; small live food, algae and vege-tables.

S: A charming species similar to *Anosto-mus* but more peaceful. Every advanced hobbyist should keep at least one. On occasion they are said to make a "grating" noise.

T: 75-82° F, L: 3$^1/_2$″, A: 40″, R: b, m, D: 3.
24-28° C, 9 cm, 100 cm,

Chilodus punctatus

Curimata multilineata

MYERS, 1927
Sub-Fam.: Curimatinae

Syn.: None

Hab.: Rio Negro, Brazil.

Fl.: 1968, Aquarium Rio, Frankfurt, West Germany.

Sex: Unknown.

Soc. B.: A peaceful fish but a plant eater.

M: When establishing the tank use fine sand or mulm on the bottom for burrowing. Java Fern is a suitable plant. In its native habitat the species lives in flood-water regions and has adapted to changing water conditions. pH 5.5-7.5 with hardness to 20° dGH.

B: Unknown.

F: H; all kinds of dry foods including oatmeal; plants and algae.

S: Nearly 90 species of this genus have been described even though specimens rarely found in our aquariums. The genus is unpopular as it eats away the plants in the aquarium.

T: 73-81° F, L: 4³/₄",   A: 32",   R: m,   D: 2.
   23-27° C,   12 cm,   80 cm,

Semaprochilodus taeniurus

(VALENCIENNES, 1817)
Sub-Fam.: Prochilodinae

Syn.: *Curimatus taeniurus, Anodus taeniurus, Prochilodus taeniurus*

Hab.: Brazil and western Colombia.

Fl.: 1912.

Sex: Unknown.

Soc. B.: Peaceful fish which can be kept with any tank of planteaters.

M: Needs a roomy, shallow aquarium with space for swimming. Its burrowing may cloud the water so that a strong filter is important. pH 5.5-7.5 with 6.0 preferred. Hardness to 20° dGH. Decorate the tank with roots and plastic plants.

B: Not successful.

F: H, L; flake food, spinach, lettuce, chickweed and watercress with occasional plankton.

S: A highly colorful fish recommended so called even though it will eat plants. Most specimen will not eat plants; hungry fishes take algae. Frequently confused with *Prochilodus insignis*. Hungry ones eat algae.

T: 72-79° F, L: to 12",   A: 52",   R: m,   D: 3.
   22-26° C,   to 30 cm,   130 cm,

Curimata multilineata

Semaprochilodus taeniurus

Erythrinus erythrinus

(SCHNEIDER, 1801)

Syn.: *Synodus erythrinus, Erythrinus brevicauda, E. kessleri, E. longipinnis, E. microcephalis, E. salmoneus, Cyprinus cylindricus*

Hab.: South America; Brazil.

Fl.: 1910 by the "Linne" Association, Hamburg, West Germany.

Sex: Unknown.

Soc. B.: A predator, not recommended for a community tank.

M: The swim bladder can be used as a respiratory organ and the fish can therefore survive in shallow pools, as those found in fluctuating seasonal streams and flood plains which occasionally dry. Should be maintained in a home aquarium as recommended for the species below. Several writers suggest a shallow tank to 10 inches (25 cm.). Should be kept alone.

B: Unknown.

F: C; small fish, larger live foods.

S: A Characin without the adipose fin. Recommended only for an advanced aquarist and should be maintained alone in larger "display" aquarium.

T: 72-79° F, **L:** 10″, **A:** 40″, **R:** b, **D:** 3.
22-26° C, 25 cm, 100 cm,

Hoplerythrinus unitaeniatus

(AGASSIZ in SPIX, 1829)

Syn.: *Erythrinus unitaeniatus, E. salvus, E. gronovii, E. kessleri, E. vittatus*

Hab.: South America; Venezuela, Trinidad, Paraguay.

Fl.: Unknown.

Sex: Unknown.

Soc. B.: A loner and a predator who, in the wild, preys on small Characins. In turn it becomes food for Electric Eels. LUELING claims that when the fishes rise to the surface to fill their intestines with air they are lured to their death by Electric Eels which lie motionless at the surface. The prey is then stunned by an electric shock. *H. unitaeniatus* can absorb oxygen through its swim bladder as well as through its gills and has a secondary vascular system in the gill covers through which oxygen is absorbed into the blood. The species is thus well adapted for survival in the reduced oxygen levels of shallow, sunbaked pools.

M: Can be kept alone or with larger fish. It is not demanding about water conditions: pH 5.6-7.8 and hardness to 30° dGH. Plants may be kept in the tank and oxygen levels are not critical. A few related species are even suspected of travelling on land at night and the tank cover should be weighted to prevent escape. The species is a food fish in South America.

B: Difficult if not impossible.

F: C; large flake foods, live fish, smaller live foods.

S: Not recommended for an aquarium since it grows larger than a trout. The species has no adipose fin.

T: 73-81° F, **L:** 16″, **A:** 48″, **R:** m, **D:** 4 (Si, C).
23-27° C, 40 cm, 120 cm,

Erythrinus erythrinus

Hoplerythrinus unitaeniatus

323

Carnegiella marthae marthae
Black-Winged Hatchetfish

MYERS, 1927
Sub.Fam.: Gasteropelecinae

Syn.: None

Hab.: Rio Negro territory in small woodland streams; Orinoco, Venezeula.

Fl.: 1935

Sex: Cannot be distinguished.

Soc. B: A peaceful, sensitive fish which is best kept in schools and with gentle tank-mates such as Loreto Tetra, small *Corydoras* and *Crenicara filamentosa*.

M: Similar to *Carnegiella strigata* but with a greater need for soft, slightly acid water: pH 5.5-6.5 and hardness to 4° dGH. A water conditioner must be used with each water change.

B: Unsuccessful to date.

F: C; flake foods, FD, smaller insects such as fruit flies and Black mosquito larvae.

S: Since the fish is extremely sensitive to tank conditions it is recommended only for experts. The sub species *C. marthae schereri* FERNANDEZ-YEPEZ, 1950, has been described and is found in the Peruvian Amazon.

T: 73-81° F, **L:** 1¹/₂″, **A:** 24″, **R:** m, t, **D:** 4 (C).
      23-27° C,   3.5 cm,   60 cm,

Carnegiella myersi

FERNANDEZ-YEPEZ, 1950
Sub Fam.: Gasteropelecinae

Syn.: None

Hab.: Peruvian Amazon, Rio Ucayali; Bolivia.

Fl.: 1957

Sex: Unknown.

Soc. B.: An extremely peaceful, schooling fish, it will not harass fry.

M: Similar to *Carnegiella strigata*.

B: Unsuccessful to date.

F: C; small flake food, FD and Black mosquito larvae.

S: The smallest of all Hatchetfish.

T: 73-79° F, **L:** 1″, **A:** 24″, **R:** m, t, **D:** 3.
      23-26° C,   2.5 cm,   60 cm,

Carnegiella marthae marthae

Carnegiella myersi

a) *Carnegiella strigata strigata*   (GUENTHER, 1864)
Marbled Hatchetfish

b) *Carnegiella strigata fasciata*   (GARMAN, 1890)
                                                  Sub-Fam.: Gasteropelecinae

Syn.: a) *Gasteropelecus strigatus, G. vesca;*
b) *Gasteropelecus fasciatus*

Hab.: a) Iquitos, Peru; b) Guyana.

Fl.: 1910, F. Meyer, Hamburg, West Germany.

Soc. B.: Peaceful shooling fish of which at least five to be kept at a time. Fry in the tank are often chased.

Sex: Can be distinguished by the girth of ♀ . The eggs may be seen when the fish is about to spawn.

M: Fast, darting fishes, they often stand motionless in a powerful filter stream. Since the current may affect plants, we suggest adequate protection. pH 5.5-7.5 (6.0) and hardness to 20° dGH (except during breeding).

B: The fish will spawn frequently with a proper diet (small flying insects such as fruit flies and Black mosquito larvae.) Recommend soft water (to 5° KH) and a pH of 5.5-6.5. Keep the lighting subdued and

you may wish to darken the water with peat extract (2-3 times the normal amount) until it is nearly opaque. The fish will spawn after a lengthy courtship, darting about the surface to deposit their eggs on floating plants or the roots of the Floating Fern. In general the eggs will fall to the bottom and the parents should be removed. The fry will hatch after 30 hours and are free-swimming after the fifth day. They should be fed finely powdered foods as Paramecia and will take Brine Shrimp after the seventh day.

F: Although the fish will eat flake foods they cannot survive on it. Recommend feeding mosquito larvae, bloodworms and other FD foods.

S: Prone to Ichthyo. A quarantine period of two weeks is suggested before the fishes are added to a community tank. The genus *Carnegiella* differs from *Gasteropelecus* in its smaller size and the absence of an adipose fin. The fish from Guyana are less demanding.

T: 75-82° F, **L:** 1¹/₂″,   **A:** 28″,   **R:** m, t, **D:** 3.
      24-28° C,   4 cm,   70 cm,

Gasteropelecus maculatus   STEINDACHNER, 1879
Spotted Hatchetfish   Sub-Fam.: Gasteropelecinae

Syn.: *Thoracocharax magdalenae, T. maculatus*

Hab.: Surinam; Panama; Venezuela; Colombia.

Fl.: 1910.

Sex: Positive identification not available.

Soc. B.: Since the species is a schooling fish five or more should be kept in a tank. May chase fry but can be combined with larger Characins.

M: The fish likes to jump. We suggest a large, shallow tank with plenty of space

between the surface of the water and the cover. Surface plants are suggested but few others. pH 6.0-7.0 and hardness to 15° dGH. Change the water every two or three weeks adding a conditioner when you do. The fish needs a lot of oxygen so use a filter which agitates the surface.

B: Probably similar to that for *C. strigata*.

F: C; flake foods, FD bloodworms and insects such as Black mosquito larvae.

T: 72-82° F, **L:** 3¹/₂″,   **A:** 40″,   **R:** m, t, **D:** 3.
      22-28° C,   9 cm,   100 cm,

Carnegiella strigata strigata below, *C. s. fasciata* above

Gasteropelecus maculatus

Gasteropelecus sternicla
Common Hatchetfish

(LINNAEUS, 1758)
Sub-Fam.:Gasteropelecinae

Syn.: *Clupea sternicla, G. coronatus, Salmo gasteropelecus*

Hab.: Brazil, southern tributaries of the Amazon; Guyana; Surinam. In smaller streams, the species is found in areas of heavier vegetation.

Fl.: 1912, J. S. Kropac, Hamburg, West Germany.

Sex: Not easily distinguished but viewed from above the ♂ is slenderer.

Soc. B.: A peaceful, even timid fish recommended for all community aquariums.

M: Is most comfortable with protective planting over head. Floating plants planted in the tank can be used, but may reduce the space at the surface needed for proper feeding. Hanging plants from outside the aquarium are better. Cover the tank and we suggest water conditions similar to those for *G. maculatus*.

B: Has not been bred in captivity. See *C. strigata*.

F: C; flake food, small insects such as vinegar flies and mosquito larvae.

S: *Gasteropelecus sternicla* can be easily confused with *Thoracocharax securis*.

T: 73-81° F,   **L:** 2¹/₂″,   **A:** 32″,   **R:** t,   **D:** 2.
   23-27° C,   6.5 cm,   80 cm,

Thoracocharax securis
Silver Hatchetfish

(FILIPPI, 1853)
Sub-Fam.: Thoracocharacinae

Syn.: *Gasteropelecus securis, Thoracocharax pectorosus, G. stellatus, Salmo pectoralis, Thoracocharax stellatus*

Hab.: Fast-running streams of central South America: especially in the shallow bends of these waters.

Fl.: 1910, Oskar Kittler, Hamburg, West Germany.

Sex: Unknown.

Soc. B.: A schooling, surface-feeding predator which has been found in streams with *Loricaria, Triporteus albus, Hypostomus* and *Geophagus*.

M: Largest of the species, the Silver Hatchetfish is the "King of Freshwater Flying Fish" and requires plenty of space but apart from a need for space and adequate oxygen it has no other special requirements. Easy to feed, it makes no unusual demands on water quality. pH 6.0-7.5 and hardness to 15° dGH.

B: Unsuccessful.

F: C; will take anything floating from large flake foods to insects.

S: The photo shows the species in its natural habitat, Rio Purus, west Brazil. It is about 3¹/₂ inches in length (8.5 cm.). The fish can fly more than four feet and once in the air the pectoral fins are moved like a bird's wings.

T: 73-86° F,   **L:** 3¹/₂″,   **A:** 48″,   **R:** m, t,   **D:** 3.
   23-30° C,   9 cm,   120 cm,

Gasteropelecus sternicla

Thoracocharax securis

Hemiodopsis quadrimaculatus quadrimaculatus

(PELLEGRIN, 1908)
Sub-Fam.: Hemiodinae

Syn.: *Hemiodus quadrimaculatus*

Hab.: Possibly the Camopi River in French Guyana and the southern portion of Guyana.

Fl.: 1967, Aquarium Rio, Frankfurt, West Germany.

Sex: Unknown.

Soc. B.: An active, peaceful, schooling fish.

M: A very lively species it requires space, oxygen and hardy plants even though the plants are largely ignored. At first the fishes are timid, displaying darting, nervous movements. They can be easily kept with a few bottom dwellers such as *Corydoras*, require plenty of oxygen and cannot survive long out of water. A leak-proof, plastic container should be used to catch and transfer them. pH 6.0-7.5 and hardness to 20° dGH. Frequent water changes are suggested.

B: Unknown.

F: O; an omnivorous, feed flake food, live food and plenty of leafy vegetable foods such as lettuce.

S: Readily confused with *H. sterni* found in the Mato Grosso. The latter has more than 50 scales on its lateral line while the former has only 45. The fish in the photo is 3 inches long (7.5 cm.). STERBA describes a related species, *H. vorderwinkleri*, which differs only in the country of origin and in having one less anal fin ray than *H. q. quadrimaculatus*.

T: 73-81° F, **L**: 4″, **A**: 40″, **R**: m, **D**: 2-3.
    23-27° C,   10 cm,   100 cm,

Parodon pongoense

(ALLEN, 1942)
Sub-Fam.: Parodontinae

Syn.: *Apareiodon pongoense, Apareiodon caquetae*

Hab.: Iquitos, Peru, Ecuador, Colombia.

Fl.: Only other representatives of the genus were probably identified in 1977.

Sex: Unknown.

Soc. B.: A peaceful fish found in small, rocky pools often in company with *Corydoras*.

M: Requires plenty of oxygen. We suggest a filter that creates a current. Can be kept with any fish that is not overly aggressive. The species likes to rest on its pectorals. The tank should have algae-covered roots and stones to provide food (these should be replaced as the algae is eaten). pH 6.0-7.5 and hardness to 15° dGH.

B: Unknown.

F: L; the genus lives on algae but will also take flake and FD foods.

S: Similar to *Crossocheilus siamensis*. It can be distinguished by its adipose fin, the absence of barbels and an additional black stripe the length of its back. There are 20 species in the genus, all of similar appearance.

T: 72-79° F, **L**: 3¹/₄″, **A**: 32″, **R**: b, **D**: 2.
    22-26° C,   8 cm,   80 cm,

Hemiodopsis quadrimaculatus quadrimaculatus

Parodon pongoense

Fam.: Lebiasinidae

Copeina guttata
Red-spotted Charracin

(STEINDACHNER, 1875)
Sub-Fam.: Pyrrhulininae

Syn.: *Pyrrhulina guttata, C. argirops*

Hab.: Amazon basin.

Fl.: 1912, Kropac, Hamburg, West Germany.

Sex: ♀ has weaker colors. The upper portion of the caudal fin on ♂ is extended.

Soc. B.: Peaceful except during spawning, the species is suitable for a community tank with tank-mates from 3¹/₄" (8 cm) or larger.

M: A long tank with a fine gravel bottom and plants. The Red-spotted Charracin does not eat plants but may uproot them during courting or spawning. Water with peat filtration will improve color but since the fish is a little drab, it is frequently overlooked.

B: Water 82-86° F (28-30° C). After a stormy courtship 100 to 2,500 eggs are laid in a hollow on the tank's bottom, a process which requires several passes. These may be broken by periods of rest. The ♂ guards and fans the eggs. The larvae hatch in 30 to 50 hours and should be fed fine Infusoria.

F: C, O; flake food, FD, all live foods, frozen foods such as mosquito larvae.

S: A related species with similar appearance, *C. osgoodi* from Peru, has no teeth in its upper jaw.

T: 73-82° F,　L: 2³/₄ to 6",　　A: 32",　R: b, m, D: 2-3.
23-28° C,　　7 to 15 cm in the wild,　80 cm,

Copella arnoldi
Jumping Characin

(REGAN, 1912)
Sub-Fam.: Pyrrhulininae

Syn.: *Copeina arnoldi, C. callolepis, C. carsevennensis, C. eigenmanni, Pyrrhulina filamentosa, P. rachoviana*

Hab.: Guyana.

Fl.: 1905, Oskar Kittler, Hamburg, West Germany.

Sex: In the photo ♂ is larger and more colorful.

Soc. B.: A gregarious, peaceful fish found in pairs and in schools. Recommended for a community tank.

M: Use a large, bright tank with sun if possible. Use floating plants such as Nymphae for shade. The tank should be well covered since the species may jump in search of food, especially when spawning. Use peat fitration and make regular water changes. pH 6.5-7.5 and a hardness between 2 and 12° dGH.

B: The species will breed readily in smaller breeding tanks, such as those 15 to 16 inches (to 40 cm) in length. The water conditions must be right and live food should be provided. Keep the aquarium covered. The fish will spawn on the underside of the cover or on a plant leaf at the water's level. The pair will jump, their bodies pressed together, their stomachs toward the glass. Ten eggs will be laid in just a few seconds. The process is repeated until 150 to 200 eggs have been deposited. The eggs, which are above water, are kept damp by the male who splashes them with his fins every half minute. Eggs which fall are ignored. The fry hatch in two or three days and will survive on the egg sac for two days. After they should be fed small pond food.

F: C, O; flake food, FD, live food.

S: Recommended if only for its unusual spawning exhibit.

T: 77-84° F,　L: ♂ 3¹/₂", ♀ 2¹/₂",　A: 28",　R: m, t, D: 2.
25-29° C,　　♂ 8 cm,, ♀ 6 cm,　70 cm,

Copeina guttata

Copella arnoldi

Fam.: Lebiasinidae

Copella metae

(EIGENMANN, 1914)
Sub-Fam.: Pyrrhulininae

Syn.: *Copeina metae*; possibly *Pyrrhulina nigrofasciata*

Hab.: In densely vegetated river bends; Peruvian Amazon; Rio Meta, Colombia.

Fl.: Unknown.

Sex: ♂ dorsal more obvious and pointed.

Soc. B.: A peaceful and lively (yet timid) species recommended for community tanks. Keep in small schools since the numbers reduce fighting between males.

M: Prefers a small tank darkened with floating plants such as *Echinodorus* and *Heteranthera.* Do not keep with active, schooling fishes. pH 5.8-7.5 and (after acclimitization) hardness to 25° dGH.

B: Soft water about 79° F (26° C) in a heavily-planted tank. Build a small cave for the ♀ (using plastic tubing or other material) to allow him to hide from an overly active ♂. The fishes will spawn on a broadleaf plant such as *Echinodorus.* 200 to 300 larvae will hatch in 30 hours and are free-swimming in two days. The egg sac is consumed in five days and the fry should then be fed small infusoria. ♂ will guard the brood as long as the eggs remain on the leaf. Add peat extract and a fungicide to the water.

F: C,O; similar to the following species.

T: 73-81° F,   L: 2¹/₂″,   A: 24″,   R: m,   D: 2-3.
    23-27° C,   6 cm,   60 cm,

Copella nattereri
Beautiful Scaled Characin

(STEINDACHNER, 1875)
Sub-Fam.:Pyrrhulininae

Syn.: *Pyrrhulina nattereri, Copeina callolepis*

Hab.: Lower Amazon to Rio Negro.

Fl.: 1908, Haase, Hamburg, West Germany.

Sex: ♂ is brightly colored, slenderer and larger, with a longer dorsal.

Soc. B.: A peaceful species recommended for community tanks with other peaceful fishes.

M: Similar to *C. metae.*

B: Similar to *C. metae.*

F: C, O; flake food with FD added, small live foods and, while breeding, mosquito larvae.

T: 73-81° F,   L: 2″,   A: 24″,   R: m,   D: 2-3.
    23-27° C,   5 cm,   60 cm,

Copella nigrofasciata
Black Banded Pyrrhulina

(MEINKEN, 1952)
Sub-Fam.: Pyrrhulininae

Syn.: *Pyrrhulina nigrofasciata*

Hab.: Rio de Janeiro and environs, Brazil.

Fl.: 1950, "Aquarium Hamburg", Hamburg, West Germany.

Sex: Fins of ♂ are pointed and brightly colored: rounded on ♀. Fins of ♂ more strikingly coloured.

Soc. B.: A very peaceful species which can be kept with other peaceful fishes.

M: Similar to *Copella* sp. Requires careful water quality such as soft water, peat filtration and a water conditioner. pH 6.0-7.0 and hardness to 8° dGH.

B: After an active courtship the male cleans the leaves on which the couple will spawn. The larvae hatch after 25-30 hours and the young will accept food after the fifth day.

F: C, O; small flake food, FD and small live foods.

S: GERY states that the species is probably identical with *C.eigenmanni* (REGAN, 1912). Found in Guyana and Para, eastern Brazil.

T: 70-77° F,   L: 2¹/₂″,   A: 24″,   R: t,   D: 2-3.
    21-25° C,   6 cm,   60 cm,

Copella metae

Copella nattereri

Copella nigrofasciata

Lebiasina astrigata

(REGAN, 1903)
Sub-Fam.: Lebiasininae

Syn.: *Piabucina astrigata*

Hab.: Northern South America; Rio Esmeralda, Rio Vinces, Colombia.

Fl: After 1970.

Sex: ♂ brighter; ♀ has a noticeably rounder stomach.

Soc. B.: Somewhat predatory and should not be kept with smaller fish. Recommended for a community tank only if frequently offered live foods.

M: The species is very adaptable and can tolerate waters with low oxygen levels. As with many predatory Characins, the swim bladder is a respiratory organ. It is timid and interesting to observe. A densely planted tank is best. pH 5.8-7.8 and hardness to 25° dGH.

B: Unsuccessful.

F: C; primarily live foods such as worms and small fish. Can take a little FD after acclimitization.

S: Similar to predatory Characins. Some specimens lack an adipose fin.

T: 72-79° F,   **L**: 3¹/₄″,   **A**: 28″,   **R**: m,   **D**: 2-3.
22-26° C,   8 cm,   70 cm,

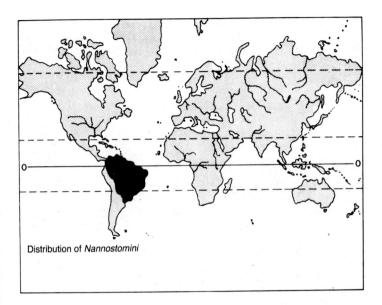

Distribution of *Nannostomini*

The species *Nannostomus* and *Nannobrycon* (Pencilfish).

Nannostomus and *Nannobrycon* (Pencilfish), belong to the family *Lebiasinidae*. WEITZMAN & COBB (1975) placed all species in the genus *Nannostomus* and abandoned the former *Poecilobrycon*. GERY (1977) reintroduced the generic name *Nannobrycon* HOEDEMAN, 1950, for two species, *N. eques* and *N. unifasciatus*. We are following this procedure since no one has studied Characins in as great detail as GERY.

The eight species seen most often are described on the following pages and it should be noted that the popular names *N. anomalus* and *N. aripirangensis* are today regarded as synonyms of *N. beckfordi*.

The other known species, *Nannostomus diagrammus* FOWLER, 1913, *N. erythrurus* (EIGENMANN, 1909), *N. marilynae* WEITZMAN & COBB, 1975, a new species, and *N. minimus* are similar in appearance and should be kept in the same aquarium conditions as we have described. The fishes are not available commercially.

Soc. B.: Pencilfish are a peaceful, timid family which hide by day between roots or plant leaves just beneath the surface. *Nannobrycon*, as an example, lies motionless between twigs floating in the water. Only at dusk do the fishes come alive, searching for food. In their natural habitat they feed on small insects captured at or near the surface. *Nannostomus* and *Nannobrycon* are extremely timid and should not be kept in a tank with lively fish. They may become too frightened to eat.

M: The tank should be at least 20-inches (50 cm) long and all species except *N. beckfordi* require carefully maintained water; soft, slightly acid and free of nitrates. If local water is hard it should be treated by peat filtration.
The pH may fluctuate between 5.5 and 7.0 but should not be subjected to sudden changes (see chapter on Peat Filtration, page 62). Under these conditions the hardness will automatically fall below 4° KH, exactly right for the genera. The tank should have a dark bottom, should be well-planted but not so dense as to loose sight of the fish. The surface may be covered with floating fern or similar plants which help to reduce the light level. Under such conditions only Cryptocorynes will grow on the bottom and we suggest them, despite the fact that they are Asian plants and thus not part of the authentic native habitat. The plant will thrive under these conditions. The water should be changed regularly, adding a conditioner to help the fishes adjust to changes in pH and osmotic pressure. Temperatures are indicated under the individual species.

B: All species illustrated below have been bred in hobby aquariums. *Nannobrycon* will be more difficult to breed than *Nannostomus*, but remember, all species will devour their eggs and the breeding tank should be equipped with a trap (about 3-4 mm mesh). Place a ball of green mat or Java Moss on the top. If a barrier is impractical, the pair should be removed. They can be replaced three days later and will often spawn again. Keep the water soft (to 2° KH) with a pH around 6.0. Use only individual pairs for breeding. The number of eggs deposited will vary with the species. *Nannobrycon*, as an example, will deposit one to three while others may lay several dozen. The eggs may be attached to plants or may fall to the bottom. As with nearly all Characins, the fishes will not guard the brood.
If you try to breed Pencilfish and meet all of the suggested conditions, proper water, a soft, dim light, dark bottom etc, and spawning does not occur, the cause may be food. We recommend Black mosquito larvae which may even be collected locally. Mosquito larvae seem to have a stimulating effect since it contains all

necessary amino acids (see chapter on Food, page 882). *Drosophila* are used by some breeders for the same purpose.

Raising the fry, which hatch in one to three days, is not difficult if you feed infusoria or Rotifers which may be bred at home.

F: The fish are both carnivorous and limnivorous (meat and mud-eaters). If small live foods are not available, FD such as red mosquito larvae, can be offered. Brine shrimp, liver and small flake foods are also recommended. Each of the species listed will accept brine shrimp. Offer generous feedings in the evening, hours the fishes naturally feed. Live foods offered during the day will not be eaten.

S: Some species have an adipose fin while others do not and this difference may be occasionally found in fishes of the same species. The night coloring is appreciably different from that seen during the day. At night, or in weak light, the longitudinal strips virtually disappear and cross-bands, which were difficult to see in daylight, become prominent. *N. espei* is an example.

Fam.: Lebiasinidae

Nannobrycon eques
Three-Striped Pencilfish

(STEINDACHNER, 1876)
Sub-Fam.: Pyrrhulininae

Syn.: *Nannostomus eques, Poecilobrycon auratus*

Hab.: Rio Negro, Brazilian Amazon; Western Colombia; Guyana.

Fl.: 1910, Aquarien Verein Rossmaessler, Hamburg, West Germany.

Sex: ♀ is more compact with a rounder ventral line. It is not as colorful as the male.

Soc. B.: A peaceful, schooling fish.

M: Follow suggestions for *Nannostomus* sp.

B: See page 338.

F: C; small live foods; FD, very fine flakes.

S: Some colorful males have noticeable blue-white tips on their pelvic fins.

T: 73-82° F, **L:** 2″, **A:** 23$^1/_2$″, **R:** t, **D:** 3.
23-28° C, 5 cm, 60 cm,

Nannobrycon unifasciatus
One-Lined Pencilfish

(STEINDACHNER, 1876)
Sub-Fam.: Pyrrhulininae

Syn.: *Nannostomus unifasciatus, N. eques* (not STEINDACHNER),*Poecilobrycon unifasciatus, P. ocellatus*

Hab.: Upper Amazon to Colombia; tributaries of the Rio Madeira; Rio Negro; Guyana.

Fl.: 1910, Jonny Wolmer, Hamburg, West Germany.

Sex: The ♀ has a black anal fin while on the ♂ the fin is black, red and white.

Soc. B.: A peaceful, schooling fish suitable for community tanks stocked with gentle fishes.

M: See page 338.

B: See page 338.

F: C; small, live foods, preferably fed at the surface; if you feed *Artemia* do not feed it continuously; FD.

S: *N. (P.) ocellatus*, described separately by some authorities, is likely to be a questionable color morph from Guyana or the Rio Madeira in Brazil.

T: 77-82° F, **L:** 2$^1/_2$″, **A:** 23$^1/_2$″, **R:** t, **D:** 3.
25-28° C, 6 cm, 60 cm,

Nannobrycon eques

Nannobrycon unifasciatus

Nannostomus beckfordi
Golden Pencilfish

GUENTHER, 1872
Sub-Fam.: Pyrrhulininae

Syn.: *Nannostomus anomalus, N. aripiran-gensis, N. simplex*

Hab.: Guyana; lower Rio Negro; central Amazon.

Fl.: 1911, Carl Siggelkow, Hamburg, West Germany.

Sex: The male has a more slender body with white tips on the fins.

Soc. B.: A peaceful, gentle species, it is the only one of the genus which can be combined with more lively fish. It can be kept in any tank that does not include predators.

M: The species can be kept successfully without the usual set-up, that is dense vegetation, peat filtration, a darker tank bottom and clear water though these are an advantage over the long haul. Suggest a pH of 6.0-7.5 and hardness to 20° dGH.

B: See page 338. When breeding we suggest a water temperature of 86° F (30° C).

F: C, O; flakes; FD; small live foods.

S: The most easily kept of the genus, it is found in various color morphs.

T: 75-79° F, L: $2^1/_2$", A: $23^1/_2$", R: m, t, D: 1-2.
   24-26° C,   6.5 cm,   60 cm,

Nannostomus bifasciatus
Two-Lined Pencilfish

HOEDEMAN, 1954
Sub-Fam.: Pyrrhulininae

Syn.: None

Hab.: Surinam and parts of Guyana.

Fl.: 1953

Sex: ♀ has transparent pelvic fins, those of the ♂ bluish-white.

Soc. B.: A peaceful, schooling fish.

M: See page 338.

B: See page 338.

F: C, O; small live foods; FD; small flakes.

T: 73-81° F, L: $1^1/_2$", A: $23^1/_2$", R: m, t, D: 3.
   23-27° C,   4 cm,   60 cm,

Nannostomus beckfordi

Nannostomus bifasciatus

Nannostomus espei
Espe's Pencilfish

(MEINKEN, 1956)
Sub-Fam.: Pyrrhulininae

Syn.: *Poecilobrycon espei*

Hab.: Southwestern Guyana.

Fl.: 1955, Espe importers and breeders, Bremen, West Germany.

Sex: The golden stripe has less sparkle on the female.

Soc. B.: A peaceful fish, you should keep it in a school of ten or more.

M: See page 338.

B: See page 338.

F: C, O; small live foods; such FD foods as bloodworms and brine shrimp; occasionally flakes. Flying insects are appreciated.

S: In terms of evolution this is one of the least developed species in the genus. The fish can be caught only in autumn when the water is at its lowest level. It is rare in the hobby.

T: 72-79° F, L: $1^1/_3$", A: $23^1/_2$", R: m, t, D: 2-3.
   22-26° C, 3.5 cm, 60 cm,

Nannostomus harrisoni
Harrison's Pencilfish

EIGENMANN, 1909
Sub-Fam.: Pyrrhulininae

Syn.: *Archicheir minutus* (juvenile form), *N. kumini, N. cumuni*

Hab.: Guyana.

Fl.: 1968, Aquarium Rio, Frankfurt, West Germany.

Sex: The anal fin is more brightly colored on the male.

Soc. B.: A peaceful, schooling fish.

M: See page 338.

B: See page 338.

F: C; small live foods; FD; finely powdered flakes.

S: This is the only species in the subgenus *Poecilobrycon*.

T: 75-82° F, L: $2^1/_2$", A: $23^1/_2$", R: m, t, D: 3-4.
   24-28° C, 6 cm, 60 cm,

Nannostomus espei

Nannostomus harrisoni

Nannostomus marginatus
Dwarf Pencilfish

EIGENMANN, 1909
Sub-Fam.: Pyrrhulininae

Syn.: None

Hab.: Surinam; Guyana; possibly the Amazon estuary.

Fl.: 1928, Schulze and Poetzschke, Berlin, Germany.

Sex: ♀ is rounder bodied.

Soc. B.: A peaceful, timid fish which can be successfully combined with other small aquarium fishes.

M: Needs a well planted aquarium with floating plants. Leave room at the surface for swimming. Needs swimming room in the central tank areas as well. Use clear yet peaty-brown water with some noticeable current. pH 5.8-7.5 (average 6.5) and dGH to 15° (average 4°.)

B: See page 338.

F: C, O; such small live foods as brine shrimp and *Cyclops*; FD; small flakes; tablets.

S: The smallest species of the genus. It is joy for any hobbyist who is keen on smaller fishes.

T: 75-79° F, **L:** 1^1/$_3$″, **A:** 15^1/$_2$″, **R:** m, t, **D:** 2-3.
   24-26° C,   3.5 cm,   40 cm,

Nannostomus trifasciatus
Three-lined Pencilfish

STEINDACHNER, 1876
Sub-Fam.: Pyrrhulininae

Syn.: *Poecilobrycon vittatus, P. auratus, P. trifasciatus, N. trilineatus*

Hab.: Brazil; Rio Tocantins; southern Amazon; Belem; Brazil, Guajara-Mirim (Rio Madeira); Mato Grosso.

Fl.: 1912, W. Eimeke, Hamburg, West Germany.

Sex: The ♀ has a rounder body with less obvious coloring.

Soc. B.: A peaceful, schooling fish recommended for some community tanks.

M: See page 338.

B: See page 338.

F: C, O; FD. small live foods; powdered flakes.

S: Many hobbyists consider this the finest of the genus.

T: 75-82° F, **L:** 2″, **A:** 23^1/$_2$″, **R:** m, t, **D:** 2.
   24-28° C,   5.5 cm,   60 cm,

Nannostomus marginatus

Nannostomus trifasciatus

Pyrrhulina filamentosa

VALENCIENNES, 1846
Sub-Fam.: Pyrrhulininae

Syn.: None

Hab.: Guyana; Surinam; Venezuela; Amazon.

Fl.: Unknown,

Sex: The male is larger and slender-bodied. The photo is of three ♀♀.

Soc. B.: Although not predators, the fish are best kept from other species, and, if possible, in a school of seven or more. Quarrelsome males will then be less likely to harass each other.

M: Requires a large, densely-planted tank with a dark bottom of fine gravel or sand. Needs a strong current with places to hide. Suggest water with a pH of 5.8-7.5 and a hardness to 18° dGH.

B: There is no available literature. We suggest following recommendations for *P. vittata*.

F: C, O; live food such as mosquito larvae; flakes mixed with FD.

S: This is the largest and rarest of the genus. Its name, *Pyrrhulina*, means Flame-colored Band.

T: 73-82° F, L: 4^1/$_2$″,   A: 31″,   R: m, b, D: 2-3.
   23-28° C,   12 cm,   80 cm,

Pyrrhulina vittata
Striped Pyrrhulina

REGAN, 1912
Sub-Fam.: Pyrrhulininae

Syn.: None

Hab.: Amazon Basin, Rio Madeira.

Fl.: 1912 by Kropac, Hamburg, West Germany.

Sex: The male's pelvic and anal fins turn red during the breeding season. Males also display in other seasons and will chase weaker tank mates from wanted territory. Females are not as aggressive.

Soc. B.: See "Sex" above. A peaceful species, suitable for community tanks with peaceful fish of finger length size. It is not a true schooling fish though it is often found in groups.

M: Needs a large tank, not too well lighted, with hardy plants and room in the foreground for swimming. Suggest strong filtration, a positive current, and peat; pH 6.0-7.5 and a hardness to 20° dGH. 10° is recommended.

B: Males will tolerate females only during spawning. The male cleans the site selected for spawning, generally on a broad leafed plant or a stone. The female is driven off after spawning while the male aerates the eggs and defends the nest. 200-300 larvae hatch after two days and are free swimming after five. The fry prefer *Cyclops* nauplii first and later, (about the fifth day) brine shrimp. Use aged water for breeding.

F: C: live food; flakes only in emergencies since food is not taken unless it moves.

S: Similar to *P. spilota*, but can be distinguished by a different arrangement of spots as well as a different dorsal position. *Copella arnoldi* is similar in appearance, but differs in behavior.

T: 73-81° F, L: 2^1/$_2$″,   A: 23^1/$_2$″,   R: m, t, D: 3.
   23-27° C,   6 cm,   60 cm,

Pyrrhulina filamentosa

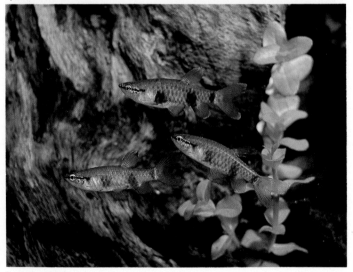

Pyrrhulina vittata

Acnodon normani

GOSLINE, 1951
Sub-Fam.: Myleinae

Syn.: None

Hab.: Rio Xingu, Rio Tocantins, Brazil.

Fl.: 1975 by Hans Baensch, Melle, West Germany.

Sex: Unknown.

Soc. B.: A peaceful but plant-eating species generally found in groups. The German name, Sheep-Pacu, refers the species' habit of browsing on plants like a flock of sheep. Hardy, even in poor water, but prefers a shallow, brightly-lighted tank with some vegetation, roots, plastic plants and a sandy bottom. pH 5.8-7.2 and hardness to 18° dGH.

B: Unknown.

F: H; fruit, plants, seeds, vegetable-based flakes.

S: Not imported since there are no exporters near the source of the fish. Though related to Serrasalmidae it lacks the serrated keel.

T: 72-82° F,   **L:** 4-6″,   **A:** 39″,   **R:** m, b, **D:** 3.
22-28° C,   10-15 cm,   100 cm,

Colossoma macropomum
Black-finned Colossoma, Black-finned Pacu

(COPE, 1871)

Syn.: *Colossoma nigripinnis, C. oculus, Myletes nigripinnis, M. oculus, Piaractus nigripinnis*

Hab.: Amazon.

Fl.: 1912 by A. Rachow and W. Eimeke, Hamburg, West Germany.

Sex: The dorsal has a sharper extension and the anal fin is toothed on the ♂.

Soc. B.: A peaceful species, it likes plants.

M: Requires a roomy tank with plants, roots and other places to hide. The fish become nervous and uneasy in a small tank. They can handle a variety of water conditions such as pH 5.0 to 7.8 and a hardness to 20° dGH.

B: Not successful.

F: H; lettuce, spinach and chickweed.

S: Suggest large display tanks only.

T: 72-82° F,   **L:** over 12″,   **A:** from 47″,   **R:** m,   **D:** 3 (H).
22-28° C,   over 30 cm,   from 120 cm,

Acnodon normani

Colossoma macropomum

Metynnis argenteus
Silver Dollar

AHL, 1923
Sub-Fam.: Myleinae

Syn.: *M. anisurus, M. dungerni, M. eigenmanni, M. heinrothi, M. smethlageae*

Hab.: Guyana, Amazon east of Rio Negro especially in heavily grown smaller tributaries.

Fl.: 1913

Sex: Anal fin of ♂ is longer and has reddish tinge in front.

Soc. B.: Peaceful, schooling species.

M: Roomy, shallow tank with subdued lighting and hiding places among decorations. Plastic plants can be used with dark gravel bottom and peat-filtered water. pH 5.0-7.0 and hardness to 15° dGH.

B: Similar to *M. hypsauchen.*

F: H; a variety of soft plants, lettuce; cress; chickweed, large vegetable flakes.

S: In certain habitats the fish have small dots on their sides. The species is a favorite in the U.S. and looks elegant and exciting in a tank.

T: 75-82° F,   L: 5″,   A: 39″,   R: m,   D: 3 (H).
    24-28° C,   14 cm,   100 cm,

Metynnis hypsauchen

(MUELLER & TROSCHEL, 1844)
Sub-Fam.: Myleinae

Syn.: *M. callichromus, M. erhardti, M. fasciatus, Myletes hypsauchen, M. ocinoccensis, M. schreitmülleri*

Hab.: Guyana, Orinoco, western Amazon and Paraguay basin.

Fl.: 1912

Sex: Anal fin of ♂ is longer, edged in black and a brighter red.

Soc. B.: A peaceful species.

M: Similar to *Metynnis argenteus.*

B: Breeding is relatively simple with suitable pairs. Frequently spawn in a school in water temperatures between 79 and 82° F (26-28° C). Recommend adding soft water. Darken the tank at first, then increase

illumination. pH 6.0-7.0 and hardness to 10° dGH (KH below 4). Try peat filtration. Place several clumps of floating plants on the surface since the fish like to spawn between them. The eggs, up to 2,000 from each female, will drop to the bottom. They are not eaten. The fry will hatch after three days, will be free-swimming within one week and will attach themselves to the tank glass, eating small plankton within that time.

F: H; all vegetable foods; some fish will even consume cornflakes.

S: If one of the school is ill others may attack it.

T: 74-82° F,   L: 6″,   A: 47″,   R: m,   D: 3 (H).
    24-28° C,   15 cm,   120 cm,

Metynnis argenteus

Metynnis hypsauchen

Metynnis lippincottianus

(COPE, 1871)
Sub-Fam.: Myleinae

Syn.: *Myletes lippincottianus, Metynnis roosevelti, M. seitzi, M. goeldii, M. orbicularis, Scalina lippincottianus*

Hab.: Widely distributed through the Amazon basin in fast-moving waters.

Fl.: 1912 by Vereinigte Zierfischzuechtereien, Berlin, Conradshoehe, Germany.

Sex: On ♂ the anal fin is edged in red and longer at the front.

Soc. B.: A peaceful species recommended for any community tank.

M: One of the easiest of all Silver Dollars to maintain. In their natural habitat the fish live in diffused light and will become timid in a bright tank. Java Fern is suggested since the fish like to nibble on them. You can also use root, plastic plants and a dark gravel bottom. Leave room for swimming. Water: pH 5.5-7.5 and hardness to 22° dGH.

B: See *M. hypsauchen.*

F: H; all types of vegetable foods and *Daphnia.*

S: Can be distinguished from the closely related *M. maculatus* by the pre-dorsal spine. This is normally serrated on *M. maculatus* and smoother on *M. lippincottianus*. Can also be identified by the number of serrations on the ventral keep (M.m = 36-41; M.l. = 29-37). The spotted body pattern may vary greatly.

T: 73-81° F, **L**: 4³/₄″, **A**: 39″, **R**: m, **D**: 2 (H).
  23-27° C,   13 cm,   100 cm,

Myleus rubripinnis rubripinnis

(MUELLER & TROSCHEL, 1844)
Sub-Fam.: Myleinae

Syn.: *Myloplus rubripinnis, M. asterias, M. ellipticus*

Hab.: Guyana, Amazon.

Fl.: 1967, Aquarium Rio, Frankfurt, West Germany.

Sex: Unknown.

Soc. B.: A peaceful species.

M: Similar to *Metynnis argenteus*, but needs more oxygen. Sometimes the body is covered with transparent blisters the size of pinhead. These are not air bubbles but the result of an unidentified disease.

B: Has not been bred in captivity.

F: O; vegetable foods and plankton; flakes; *Daphnia.*

S: Adult fish remain silver-colored. Two sub-species have been described: a) *M. rubripinnis rubripinnis* (in the photo) and b) *M. rubripinnis luna*. The generic name *Myloplus* formerly used, is now applied for the sub-genus *Myleus.*

T: 73-81° F, **L**: 4″ in an aquarium, to 10″ in the wild, **A**: 31″, **R**: m, **D**: 3-4.
  23-27° C,   10 cm in an aquarium, to 35 cm in the wild,   80 cm,

Metynnis lippincottianus

Myleus rubripinnis rubripinnis

Mylossoma duriventre
Silver Mylossoma

(CUVIER, 1818)
Sub-Fam.: Myleinae

Syn.: *Myletes duriventris, Mylossoma albicopus, M. ocellatus, M. argenteum, M. unimaculatus* (juvenile form)

Hab.: Southern Amazon to Argentina.

Fl.: 1908 by Oskar Kittler, Aquarium Verein Rossmaessler, Hamburg, West Germany.

Sex: Unknown.

Soc. B.: Peaceful fish. Their native habitat is in shallows. There, as juveniles they live among dense vegetation and feed constantly. As adults they range more to find sufficient vegetation.

M: Not a popular hobby fish because of its size and its consumption of plants. It demands a lot of oxygen and in the wild schools dies by the thousands as the water levels reduce during the dry season. They are then consumed by fish-eating birds. The young survive well in an aquarium. pH 5.0-7.8 and hardness to 20° dGH. Very sensitive to changes in water conditions.

B: Unknown but probably similar to *Metynnis*.

F: H; vegetable food, lettuce, spinach and chickweed.

S: Can be identified by the serrated keel between the pelvic and anal fins. The young are especially attractive with a black marking beneath the dorsal.

T: 72-82° F, **L:** over 8″, **A:** 59″, **R:** m, b, **D:** 4 (H).
     22-28° C,   20 cm,   150 cm,

Serrasalmus nattereri
Red Piranha

(KNER, 1859)
Sub-Fam.: Serrasalminae

Syn.: *Pygocentrus nattereri, P. altus, P. stigmaterythraeus, Rooseveltiella nattereri, Serrasalmo piranha*

Hab.: Guyana to the La Plata region.

Fl.: 1911

Sex: ♂ is silvery gold with a red throat. ♀ has more yellow.

Soc. B.: A dangerous, schooling fish. When hungry they will eat anything living, reducing it to shreds in minutes.

M: Easily kept in a large tank with strong filter flow but must be given a steady supply of food. pH 5.5-7.5 and hardness to 20° dGH.

B: Successfully done in larger tanks. Pairing is induced by adding fresh water. Spawning will occur in subdued light in early morning hours, between four and five a.m. in the wild. The ♂ protects the nest fiercely. The ♀ will defend the nest for 24 hours then is chased away. If the eggs are removed the ♂ will spawn again in two or three days, pairing with another female from the school.

A clutch will comprise 500 to 1,000 transparent golden eggs. They can be safely removed by partitioning them with glass. The young will swim freely from the 8th day. Feed brine shrimp after the egg sac has been consumed, generally in four or five days. The fry must be sorted by size after one month and from the third month should be fed live bloodworms, grated meat and fish filets. Do not feed blood worms too soon since the young may choke.

F: C; all kinds of meat, fish fillets.

S: Handle with care. Even in an aquarium they will bite if they feel threatened. The species cannot be imported to the U.S. because of the risk of escape and local propagation.

The photo on page 359 shows a fish 12 cm (4$^{1}/_{2}$″) in length with typical spotted juvenile markings.

T: 73-81° F, **L:** 11$^{1}/_{4}$″, **A:** 47″, **R:** m, **D:** 4 (C).
     23-27° C,   28 cm,   120 cm,

Mylossoma duriventre

Serrasalmus nattereri, ♂ adult

Serrasalmus rhombeus
Spotted Piranha

(LINNAEUS, 1766)
Sub-Fam.: Serrasalminae

Syn.: *S. paraense, S. niger, Salmo rhombeus, S. albus, S. caribi, S. humeralis, S. immaculatus, S. iridopsis*

Hab.: Guyana and the Amazon basin.

Fl.: 1913 by Wilhelm Eimeke, Hamburg, West Germany.

Sex: The anal fin of ♂ is sharply extended at the front and straight on ♀.

Soc. B.: A predatory fish, it will not attack humans but care should be taken in an aquarium. It may bite a finger from panic and its sharp, razor-like teeth can cause a deep, bleeding wound.

M: Prefers a darkened tank with floating plants. Decorate with rocks and a coarse gravel bottom which can easily be cleaned of uneaten food particles. Recommend soft water, a definite flow, pH 5.8-7.0 and a hardness to 10° dGH. Best kept alone though it will not generally attack larger tank-mates, even of different species unless they are ill.

B: Has been successfully bred at Wilhelma Aquarium in Stuttgart. Probably similar to *S. spilopleura*.

F: C; Large live foods for fry; also large flakes; then fish fillets and beef heart given two or three times weekly.

S: While the fry are attractively marked adult *S. rhombeus* become a monotonous silver-grey. The photo shows a young fish about 9 cm. in length.

T: 73-81° F, **L:** 15″, **A:** 46³/₄″, **R:** m, b, **D:** 4 (S).
23-27° C, 38 cm, 120 cm,

Serrasalmus spilopleura (no picture)
Dark-banded Piranha

KNER, 1860
Sub-Fam.: Serrasalminae

Syn.: *Pygocentrus dulcis, P. melanurus, P. nigricans, Serrasalmus aesopus, S. maculatus*

Hab.: Amazon, La Plata, Orinoco.

Fl.: 1899 by Paul Matte, Berlin-Lankwitz, Germany.

Sex: A deeply indented tailfin on ♀.

Soc. B.: Predatory shooling fish, not suited to the normal aquarium.

M: Adequate filtration is important. The high metabolism of the species requires clean, oxygenated water. pH 5.0 7.0 and hardness to 18° dGH.

B: A *Serrasalmus* sp. has been bred at the Duisburg Aquarium in Germany. The pair spawns between the roots of such plants as *Eichhornia* dropping 4mm eggs from the surface. These hatch after two days. The fry become free-swimming in eight or nine days. Will readily accept brine shimp or *Cyclops* after ten days and then, *Daphnia*. Keep the water at temperatures between 77 and 79° F (25-26° C).

F: C; large earthworms, fish, scraps of fish and meat.

S: Not as predatory as *S. nattereri* or *S. piraya*.

T: 73-82° F, **L:** 10″, **A:** 59″, **R:** m, **D:** 4 (C).
23-28° C, 25 cm, 150 cm,

Serrasalmus rhombeus

Young *Serrasalmus nattereri*

359

Group 3

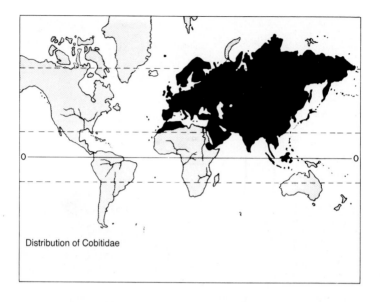

Distribution of Cobitidae

The Family Cobitidae   **Loaches and Thorneyes**

The Loaches and Thorneyes are a small family of freshwater fishes with approximately 100 species distributed over well-defined but self-contained areas of the Old World. Loaches are found through Europe and Asia including the Malaysian Archipelago. Only a few species can be found in Africa, predominantly in Morroco and Ethopia. Cobitidae are widely represented in southern and southeastern Asia but are more difficult to find further north and west. Only three species are native to Germany (*Cobitis taenia, Misgurnus fossilis, Noemacheilus barbatulus*).

Loaches are generally small with only a few, *Misgurnus, Botia* and *Noemacheilus* reaching lengths over 12″ (30 cm.). The Thorneyes are also distinguished by their elongated and generally cylindrical bodies. Some species have a flattened stomach. Their toothless mouths, not a predominant feature, show they are bottom feeders. The body may be covered with small scales or may be partially or without scales.

360

Carassius auratus, see page 410

The fish have acquired their common name, Thorneye, from one or two thorn-like spines generally situated directly between the eyes. (Though they may be lacking on certain *Noemacheilus sp.*) These can be erected at will and in some instances are imbedded in the skin. Thorneye have three to six pairs of short to moderately long barbels on their lips and possess a single row of pharyngeal teeth.

The anterior portion of the swim bladder is surrounded by a bony cover and the intestines of many Loaches, for example the *Misgurnus*, acts as an additional respiratory organ. By absorbing oxygen from the atmosphere through the intestine the species can survive in oxygen-depleted waters.

Thorneyes feed mostly on insect larvae and small worms such as *Tubifex*. The Loach's barbels contain tastebuds and help it find food. In an aquarium certain species will accept dried food and vegetable supplements such as soft algae. Among the prominent features of the species described by SMITH, STERBA and others are:

Acanthopsis: The body is elongated and flattened; the eyes are covered with a transparent layer and there are no scales on the head; the mouth has three pairs of barbels; there is a fully formed lateral line on the body and a single, thorny spine.

Pangio: The body is elongated and worm-like; the eyes are covered with a transparent layer and the head is without scales; it has four pairs of barbels including on the lower jaw; the dorsal begins well back from the pelvic fin; there are two thorny spines.

Botia: The body is compressed and the back arched, often flattened laterally; the eyes are without a transparent cover and the dorsal fin begins above or beyond the root of the pelvic fins; there are three pairs of barbels and two thorny spines.

Cobitis: The head is strongly compressed laterally; the eyes have no transparent covering and the head features three pairs of barbels, one on the lower jaw; the lateral line is incomplete; there may be one or two thorny spines.

Lepidocephalus: The body is elongated and flattish; the eyes are covered by a transparent layer: the head is partially covered with scales and has four pairs of barbels including a pair on the lower jaw; there is a single thorny spine.

Misgurnus: The body is circular at the front but flattens towards the rear; the head has five pairs of barbels including two on the lower jaw; the lateral line is rudimentary and the spine is concealed in the skin.

Noemacheilus: The body may be round or flattish; the head has three pairs of barbels and the lateral line may be complete or broken; the spine may be small or missing; when present it is covered by skin.

The requirements for setting up tanks and establishing the proper water quality, temperature and lighting are described beneath the listings for each species.

Little is known about the reproduction of Loaches and success in breeding has been mostly a matter of chance. Commercial breeding has not yet been achieved despite many attempts and the procedures described in various hobby literature are often contradictory. Reports have even suggested that the Loach builds a "foam" nest though this seems highly unlikely. Such data should not be considered as "gospel" and only proves there is still plenty of opportunity for dedicated hobbyists to provide the kind of accurate scientific observations required to breed the species.

Varieties of *Barbus tetrazona*
Albino above and Moss-banded below.

Pangio kuhlii
Coolie Loach, Prickly Eye

(VALENCIENNES, 1846)
Sub-Fam.: Cobitinae

Syn.: *Cobitis kuhlii, Acanthophthalmus fasciatus, A. kuhlii*

Hab.: Southeast Asia, Thailand, western Malaysia, Singapore, Sumatra, Java and Borneo.

Fl.: 1909 by Vereinigten Zierfischzuechtereien, Berlin Conradshoehe, Germany.

Sex: Unknown.

Soc. B.: A lone, night-feeder, the species becomes active at dusk. It hides during the day.

M: A soft tank bottom covered with sand or gravel with loam or peat. Prefers plenty of vegetation such as pinnate plants and hiding room between roots, stones or tank decorations. Recommend subdued light, either through the use of floating plants or via reduced lighting. Use soft, slightly acid warm water (about a pH of 6.0).

B: Difficult but possible. The bright green eggs are deposited beneath the surface and adhere to the stems and roots of floating plants.

F: C, O; all live foods; FD tablets; feed at night.

S: The species is divided into two subspecies: *Pangio kuhlii kuhlii* (CUV. & VAL., 1846) and, the Sumatra Coolie, *P. kuhlii sumatranus,* (FRASER-BRUNNER, 1940). The latter was first introduced in 1909 and was described as a sub-species in 1940. The two differ only in coloring and markings. According to KLAUSEWITZ, *P. myersi* also belongs to the group and would therefore be called *P. kuhlii myersi.*

T: 75-86° F,   L: 4",   A: 23$^{1}/_{2}$",   R: b,   D: 2.
24-30° C,   12 cm,   60 cm,

Pangio shelfordi
Shelford's Prickly Eye

POPTA, 1901
Sub-Fam,: Cobitinae

Syn.: Acanthophthalmus shelfordii

Hab.: Malaysia Archipelago, Borneo, Sarawak.

Fl.: 1939, perhaps 1933.

Sex: Unknown.

Soc. B.: Similar to *Pangio kuhlii.*

M: See *P. kuhlii.*

B: Not yet captive bred.

F: C, O; live food taken mostly on the bottom;flakes; tablets.

S: *Pangio shelfordi* is assigned to the *Kuhlii* group which includes the larger *Pangio* species such as *P. kuhlii,*

P. semicinctus, P. myersi and *P. shelfordii.* It differs from the *Cuneovirgatus* group *P. cuneovirgatus, P. robiginosus* not only in the size of the fishes but also by the formation of the scales. In the former they are almost round with a wide zone at the edge. In the latter they are elliptical with a narrow edged zone.

According to the photo (compare DATZ 8/86) this could be an *muraeniformis* de BEAUFORT, 1933. This species has 8 barbels, *shelfordii* only 6.

T: 75-86° F,   L: 3$^{1}/_{4}$",   A: 20",   R: b,   D: 2.
24-30° C,   8 cm,   50 cm,

Pangio kuhlii sumatranus

Pangio kuhlii myersi

Pangio shelfordi

Acantopsis dialuzona
Long-nosed Loach

v. HASSELT, 1823
Sub-Fam.: Cobitinae

Syn.: *Acanthopsis choirorhynchus, Acanthopsis choerorhynchus, A. biaculeata, A. diazona, A. dialyzona*

Hab.: Southeast Asia, Thailand, Burma, Malaysian Peninsula, Vietnam, Sumatra, Borneo and Java.

Fl.: 1929 by Edmund Riechers, Hamburg, West Germany.

Sex: Unknown.

Soc. B.: A peaceful loner which becomes active at night. Likes to burrow.

M: Fine sandy bottom (2-3$^1/_2$" = 5-10 cm high). Plants should be grown in containers to protect against destruction from burrowing. Recommend rocks, roots, plastic tubing and other tank decorations as hiding places. pH 6.0 - 6.5 with hardness to 10° dGH. Use floating plants to reduce tank light.

B: Not successful.

F: C, O; will eat nearly anything but prefers such live food as *Tubifex*, white worms and aquatic insect larvae.

S: Found in many color patterns. Often lay buried in a sandy bottom with only their eyes showing and when frightened or disturbed can quickly cover themselves. They are poor swimmers.

T: 75-82° F, L: 8", mature from 2",   A: 31$^1/_2$",   R: b,   D: 2-3.
   25-28° C,   22.5 cm, mature from 6 cm,   80 cm,

Botia berdmorei

(BLYTH, 1860)
Sub-Fam.: Botiinae

Syn.: *Syncrossus berdmorei*

Hab.: Southeast Asia, Burma, Pasalc River (Thailand).

Fl.: Uncertain.

Sex: Unknown.

Soc. B.: Territorial and often quarrelsome with own species though tank-mates are seldom attacked. A powerful, dominant fish, it generally eats first driving smaller fishes away. At such times it may make angry, clicking noises.

M: A roomy tank with fine sand for burrowing and root and rock decorations for hiding. Suggest floating plants overhead. The species is sensitive to nitrate and prefers water with peat filtration, pH 6.5-7.5 and hardness to 12° dGH. As a species *Botia* needs room to burrow and hide.

F: C, O; live foods; tablets; FD; flakes.

S: H. M. SMITH (1945), suggested that *B. berdmorei, B. beauforti* and *B. hymenophysa* might be the same species with variations in color and other features explained by the large area of habitat but they are still regarded as separate species. *Botia* use the two hinged spines beneath the eyes for fighting and when caught can easily become tangled in a net.

T: 72-79° F, L: to 11" in the wild and to 5" in an aquarium,   A: 39",   R: b,   D: 2-3.
   22-26° C,   to 25 cm in the wild and to 15 cm in an aquarium,   100 cm,

Acantopsis dialuzona

Botia berdmorei

Botia morleti
Hora's Loach

TIRANT, 1885
Sub-Fam.: Botiinae

Syn.: *Botia modesta* (not BLEEKER), *B. horae*

Hab.: Northern India, Thailand.

Fl.: 1955 by "Tropicarium Frankfurt", Frankfurt, West Germany.

Sex: Unknown.

Soc. B.: A lively, peaceful fish which becomes active at dusk. Spends days hiding and makes an excellent tank mate for Barbs and Armoured Catfish.

M: Since it burrows it needs a tank bottom of fine gravel. The aquarium should be planted with hardy vegetation with the roots protected against burrowing by containers. Place tank decoration on the glass bottom since burrowing may cause them to fall. Plastic tubes make excellent hiding places. Suggest soft, slightly acid water pH

6.0-6.5 and hardness to 5° dGH. Frequent water changes are important (about 10% weekly) and subdued light (either a low light level or light filtered through floating plants) is recommended. Nearly all *Botia* can be kept in community tanks.

B: Unsuccessful.

F: Will take tablets and frozen foods but prefers live foods. Flakes are not suggested.

S: The fish are poor swimmers and have a characteristic color throughout life (see photo) which distinguishes them from other *Botia* species.

T: 79-86° F, L: 4",   A: 31",   R: b, m, D: 2.
   26-30° C,   9.5 cm,   80 cm,

Botia helodes
Banded-Loach

SAUVAGE, 1876
Sub-Fam.: Botiinae

Syn.: None?

Hab.: Found in streams and rivers throughout southeast Asia, Thailand, Laos and Cambodscha.

Fl.: 1929 by Edmund Riechers, Hamburg, West Germany.

Sex: Unknown.

Soc. B.: A restless, aggressive species which is easily frightened. A night-feeder, it hides during the day.

M: Similar to *Botia morleti*, *B. helodes* should be kept in company only with fish of the same or larger size.

B: Not yet accomplished.

F: C, O; all live foods including small fish.

S: *Botia helodes* does best kept alone. During feeding and when defending their territory the fish makes a clicking sound which may remind an aquarist of cracking glass.
This species is known under the name *Botia hymenophysa* but *B. hymenophysa* has its distribution only at Sumatra, Borneo and South Malaysia.

T: 75-86° F, L: 8",   A: 39",   R: b, (m), D: 2.
   24-30° C,   22 cm,   100 cm,

Botia morleti

Botia helodes

Botia lohachata

CHAUDHURI, 1912
Sub-Fam.: Botiinae

Syn.: None

Hab.: Bihar province, northern and north-eastern India; Bangladesh.

Fl.: 1956, "Tropicarium Frankfurt", West Germany.

Sex: Unknown.

Soc. B.: An aggressive nocturnal fish, best kept alone or with other species.

M: Similar to *Botia morleti*.

B: Has not yet been bred in captivity.

F: O; omnivorous: all types of live foods, dried food and algae.

S: The species takes food at the surface, turning as it feeds. Though the color varies widely, the species can be identified by four pairs of barbels. It may utter audible clicks.

T: 75-86° F,   **L**: $2^3/_4''$,   **A**: 31",   **R**: b, m, **D**: 2.
   24-30° C,   7 cm,   80 cm,

Botia macracanthus
Clown Loach, Tiger Loach

(BLEEKER, 1852)
Sub-Fam.: Botiinae

Syn.: *Cobitis macracanthus, Hymenophysa macracantha*

Hab.: In running and standing waters; Indonesia; Sumatra; Borneo.

Fl.: 1935.

Sex: ♀♀ are thinner.

Active during the day and more visible than many *Botia* sp. *B. macracanthus* is much more nocturnal.

M: Similar to *Botia morleti*.

B: Spawns during the rainy season in foaming, fast-flowing, spring-fed streams, according to information from Dr. LIEM of Djakarta. The fry grow up in slower, lower reaches and estuaries of the same rivers. Now successfully bred in home aquariums.

F: O; omnivorous; live foods; flakes; algae; FD tablets; frozen food.

S: *Botia macracanthus* may make clicking noises. It is a food fish in its native rivers and is said to have a fine flavor. Can be identified by four pairs of barbels. The species is prone to Ich.

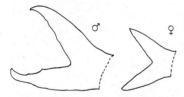

Soc. B.: An active species that can tolerate tank-mates of its own and other species.

T: 77-86° F,   **L**: $11^3/_4''$ (seldom longer than   **A**: 39"   **R**: b, m, **D**: 2-3.
   25-30° C, $6^1/_2''$ in a home aquarium);   100 cm,
                   30 cm (seldom longer than
                   16 cm in a home aquarium),

Botia lohachata

Botia macracanthus

Botia modesta
Orange-Finned Loach

BLEEKER, 1864
Sub-Fam.: Botiinae

Syn.: *Botia rubripinnis*

Hab.: In flowing and standing waters; northeastern India; Thailand; Vietnam; Malaysian penninsula.

Fl.: Possibly in 1935 by "Aquarium Hamburg" and certainly in 1955 by "Tropicarium", Frankfurt, West Germany.

Sex: Unknown but apparently ♂ is smaller than ♀.

Soc. B.: A timid, nocturnal species which becomes quite active at night. It is said the fish will not tolerate other species but will school with its own.

M: Similar to *Botia morleti.*

B: Not yet successful in captivity.

F: C, O; omnivorous; will accept live foods, tablets and flakes; algae.

S: As with other Loaches, this species emits a clicking sound.

T: 79-86° F, L: 9¹/₂″, A: 39″, R: b, (m), D: 2.
  26-30° C, 24 cm, 100 cm,

Botia morleti see page 368

Botia sidthimunki
Dwarf Loach

KLAUSEWITZ, 1959
Sub-Fam.: Botiinae

Syn.: None

Hab.: In small, muddy lakes; northern India; northern Thailand.

Fl.: 1959, A. Werner, Munich, West Germany.

Sex: No discernible features.

Soc. B.: A lively, peaceful, schooling fish, it is an avid swimmer, active by day.

M: Similar to *Botia morleti*. The tank bottom should include a layer of mulm which is appreciated by the species. Should be kept in a school.

B: Not yet bred in an aquarium.

F: C, O; omnivorous; live and flake foods. The species is not choosy about its diet but prefers FD.

S: *Botia sidthimunki* is the smallest of the genus and should be included in every community tank.

T: 79-82° F, L: 2¹/₄″, A: 20″, R: b + m, D: 2.
  26-28° C, 5.5 cm, 50 cm,

Botia modesta

Botia sidthimunki

Cobitis taenia taenia
Spined Loach, Spotted Weather Loach

LINNAEUS, 1758
Sub-Fam.: Cobitinae

Syn.: *Acanthopsis taenia, Botia taenia, Cobitis barbatula, C. elongata*

Hab.: In clear flowing and standing waters in Europe and western Asia, from Portugal to the Lena. The species is not found in Ireland, Scotland, Norway, Corsica, Sardinia and the Peloponnese.

Fl.: A species native to Europe.

Sex: ♂ is smaller than ♀ ; the second ray of the pelvic fin is thicker on ♂♂.

Soc. B.: A sedentary, nocturnal species which prefers the bottom of a tank. Generally peaceful toward its species as well as other fishes. Since it prefers colder water, it should be kept with fishes which prefer a similar temperature and considerable oxygen.

M: Similar to *Barbatula barbatula* but is more sensitive to high temperatures and oxygen-deficient water. The tank should contain plants such as *Vallisneria* and Java Moss.

B: Similar to *B. barbatula* but does not look afer its spawn. The eggs are laid indiscriminately between and on plants. Spawns chiefly from April to July.

F: C; almost exclusively such live foods as small shrimps, mosquito larvae and *tubifex* worms.

S: The species is divided into several subspecies, each with restricted geographical distribution. In their natural habitat the species is an important source of food for trout.

T: 57-64° F (maximum 66° F), **L**: 4³/₄″, **A**: 27″, **R**: b, **D**: 2-3.
   14-18° C (maximum 20° C),   12 cm,   70 cm,

Misgurnus fossilis
Weather Loach

(LINNAEUS, 1758)
Sub-Fam.: Cobitinae

Syn.: *Cobitis fossilis, Acanthopsis fossilis, Cobitis fossilis var. mohoity, C. micropus, Ussuria leptocephala*

Hab.: Throughout much of Europe, from northern France in the west to the Newa in the north and from the Danube to the Wolga and Don. The species is not found in Great Britain, Ireland, Scandinavia, Spain, Portugal, Italy, Greece and the Crimea.

Fl.: A native European species.

Sex: ♂ is smaller and more slender; the second ray on the pectoral fin is thicker; ♀ is fuller-bodied.

Soc. B.: A sedentary, nocturnal, peaceful species which prefers the tank bottom.

M: Should have a muddy or soft bottom and native cold water plants which should be kept in containers (for the species burrows). Needs hiding places among rocks or in plastic pipe. Should have subdued lighting and a good filter system since the water becomes dirty through the digging.

B: Has been bred several times though the successes should be considered accidental. The species spawns with sinuous movements and the eggs are often deposited on plants. The spawning season runs from April through July.

F: C; all types of live foods such as insect larvae, worms and small shrimp. Best fed in the evening.

S: The species was believed to forcast weather, becoming restless on impending storms. They have an excellent intestinal respiratory system which enables them to survive in oxygen depleted waters.

T: 39-77° F, **L**: 11³/₄″, **A**: 31-39″, **R**: b, **D**: 1-2.
   4-25° C,   30 cm,   80-100 cm,

Cobitis taenia taenia

Misgurnus fossilis

Barbatula barbatula for a description, see page 376

375

Barbatula barbatula　　　　　　　　　　　　(LINNAEUS, 1758)
Common Loach　　　　　　　　　　　　Sub-Fam.: Nemacheilinae

Syn.: *Cobitis barbatula, Barbatula toni, B. tonifowleri, B. tonifowleri posteroventralis, Cobitis fuerstenbergii, C. toni, Nemachilus barbatulus, N. compressirostris, N. pechilensis, N. sturanyi, Oreias toni, Orthrias oreas, N. sibiricus, Noemacheilus barbatulus*

Hab.: Europe as far east as Siberia. Found in northeast Spain though not on the Iberian Penninsula. Other exceptions: Scotland, Scandinavia (except for portions of Denmark and southern Sweden), Italy and Greece. Generally accompanies river trout and is found in clear, flowing waters with a firm bottom.

Fl: A native European species.

Sex: ♂ is smaller and more slender, has a longer pectoral fin and a thicker second pectoral ray. Can be placed with fish with similar oxygen and temperature requirements.

Soc. B.: A sedentary, nocturnal bottom fish. Generally a peaceful tank mate.

M: Needs a larger tank with a fine gravel bottom and a few larger, flat stones added. Needs hiding places such as overturned pipe or flower pot shards. Plants are not needed but the water should be well aerated, clear, clean and not too warm. Recommend medium-hard (10-15° dGH) but near-neutral (pH 7.0-7.7) water.

B: Only adults are suitable. The ♀ should show a desire to spawn. The sticky eggs are deposited on stones and in the gravel, generally in the darkest part of the tank. The eggs are often guarded by the ♂. The fry hatch after seven days and should be fed brine shrimp. The spawning season runs from March to May.

F: C; will occasionally accept flake foods but prefers live foods.

T: 58-64° F,　L: 6″,　　A: 31″,　　R: b,　　D: 2-3.
　16-18° C,　　16 cm,　　80 cm,

The Family Cyprinidae　　　　　　　　　　　　　　　Carp

Cyprinidae is the largest family of fishes with more than 1400 documented. Carp can be found in large areas of Europe and Asia as well as throughout Africa and North America. They are not known in South America or Australia and are almost exclusively a freshwater genus. Only a few are able to tolerate brackish water. One, a far-eastern Redfin, can cope with salty ocean water.

Cyprinidae can be characterized by the following features:

1. A small number of teeth which are arranged in one to three rows on the lower pharyngeal bone.

2. A horny plate used to grind food. It is located at the base of the pharyngeal bone. A carp possesses only one set of intermaxillary bones around the mouth and the majority of the genus have the "typical" fish shape. None have an adipose fin.

376

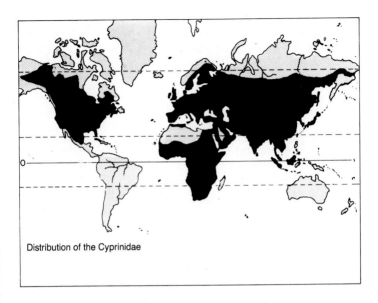

Distribution of the Cyprinidae

Barbels, if found, are limited to two pairs with one exception: the genus *Gobiobotia*. The head is always without scales and body scales, except in the instance of a few naked species, are round. The mouth is usually extended forward and the large swim bladder is divided in two parts. Only in exceptional cases is the front portion of the bladder equipped with a bony cap.

The family includes species of all sizes. The largest is *Barbus tor*, native to India. It reaches a length of more than six feet (2$^1/_2$ meters). Many white fish have a shiny, silvery coat, the result of guanin crystals. Others are strikingly marked with fine, bright coloring. Such visual signs are important to the many schooling fish who use optical markings to recognize the school and to maintain their position in it. The bodies of bottom dwellers are often camouflaged with darker, irregular patches which readily merge with the gravel.

Many Cyprinid males change colors when mating, becoming brighter. Some, such as the Bitterling, may even add new colors to their courtship dress. All regain normal coloration after the spawning season ends.

Carp are quite varied biologically. Some species inhabit fast-flowing rivers and others lakes and ponds. They can be found in waters as cold as that of melting ice (an example is the Minnow, *Phoxinus phoxinus*), as well as in warmer waters, even areas where the oxygen supply is minimal. Two examples are *Carassius carassius and Tinca tinca.*

As omnivores most Cyprinids will accept most foods without special demands but we suggest that if you feed flake foods you add live foods on a regular schedule. When fed flakes exclusively thay have slower growth and less color. Certain species, though, require a vegetable diet – algae, tender shoots of aquatic plants, cooked lettuce, spinach or oatmeal.

The reproductive systems of carp are also varied. Most are free-spawning, that is the eggs and sperm are discharged into the water. Such eggs most often adhere to the substratum, plants, gravel, and decorations. The maturation period is brief and the larvae of these species possess a special organ to promote adhesion as well as larval respiratory organs. In contrast, the larvae of Carp which spawn on stones or gravel have neither the ability to create adhesive nor larval respiratory organs. A few species lay planktonic eggs which simply float in the water. Their larval respiratory organs are poorly developed.

Very few Carp actively protect their brood. Only the male *Pseudogobio rivularis* builds a nest (in the form of groove) and guards the clutch. *Pseudorasbora parva* males and *Pseudogobio* species will guard their spawn and female Bitterlings, *Rhodeus* and *Acanthorhodeus*, lay their eggs between the gill covers of fresh-water Mussels, family *Unionidae*, with the aid of a long ovipositor which grows only during the spawning season. The eggs are reliably protected within the Mussel. When the fry appear the female guards her brood. Details can be found under *Rhodeus sericeus amarus.*

Alburnoides bipunctatus
Chub

(BLOCH, 1782)
Sub-Fam.: Abraminae

Syn.: *Cyprinus bipunctatus, Aspius bipunctatus, Abramis bipunctatus, Alburnus bipunctatus, Leuciscus bipunctatus, Spirlinus bipunctatus*

Hab.: Throughout Europe, from France to the tributaries of the Caspian Sea including the Rhine and Danube. Not found south of the Alps or Pyrenees nor in northern Europe or Denmark.

Fl.: A native European species.

Sex: The ♀♀ are always heavier, larger bodied.

Soc. B.: A schooling fish found most often near the surface.
It is best kept with other coldwater Cyprinids.

M: Requires a tank bottom of fine gravel edged with vegetation, most often fine-leaved plants. Needs plenty of swimming room, good aeration and lots of oxygen (a common requirement of coldwater fishes).

B: Only occasionally in an aquarium. The eggs are laid on the gravel bottom.

F: C, O; such live foods as plankton; flakes.

S: The fishes must be acclimatized to an aquarium and are sensitive to sudden changes in temperature. A characteristic of the species is the lateral line which is framed in black.

T: 50-64° F, **L:** 5¹/₂″, **A:** 31″, **R:** t, **D:** 2.
10-18° C, 14 cm, 80 cm,

Balantiocheilus melanopterus
Silver Shark, Bala Shark

Syn.: *Barbus melanopterus, Puntius melanopterus, Systomus melanopterus*

Hab.: Southeast Asia; Thailand; Borneo; Sumatra; Malayan penninsula.

Fl.: 1955, "Tropicarium", Frankfurt, West Germany.

Sex: No external signs. During the spawning season ♀ is generally fatter.

Soc. B.: A peaceful species which can be kept with smaller fish.

M: Prefers a longer aquarium with good swimming space. Sun is good with soft water (about 5° dGH) and water slightly acid (pH 6.5-7). Keep plants along the tank edges and in the back and use roots for decoration in the center.

T: 72-82° F, **L:** 13", **A:** 39", **R:** all,
22-28° C, 35 cm, 100 cm,
D: 2.

(BLEEKER, 1851)
Sub-Fam.: Cyprininae

B: Not successfully bred in an aquarium and little is known about the species' special breeding habits. Will probably only be successful in a larger tank about 75 gallons (300 liters).

F: O; live foods as *tubifex* worms, *Daphnia* and mosquito larvae; flakes; vegetation.

S: Since the species is a jumper, the tank should be well covered. The fish may make audible sounds.

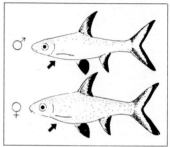

Barbus arulius
Arulius Barb

Syn.: *Puntius arulius*

Hab.: Southeast and southern India.

Fl.: 1954

Sex: Dorsal fins are longer on the ♂, and shorter and more fully edges on ♀. ♂♂ have an eruption indicating by their spawning condition, around the mouth (small white spots). ♀♀ are rounder.

Soc. B.: A hardy, schooling species it is best kept with *Barbus dunckeri, B. everetti* and similar Cyprinids.

M: Keep broad-leaved plants in the tank and decorate the gravel bottom with roots and stones. A layer of mulm is appreciated along with plenty of swimming space. A good community fish. The water should be soft (to 10° dGH) and slightly acid (pH 6-6.5). Replace one quarter of the water weekly.

T: 66-77° F, **L:** 4¹/₄", **A:** 23³/₄", **R:** all, **D:** 2-3.
19-25° C, 12 cm, 60 cm,

(JERDON, 1849)
Sub-Fam.: Cyprininae

B: Not easy, use a large tank with thickets of fine-leaved plants. The fish will spawn near the surface after an active swimming ritual. Usually lays less than 100 eggs.

F: O; live food; flakes; lettuce, spinach and algae.

S: It reaches full color late in life and is often overlooked for this reason.

Balantiocheilus melanopterus

Barbus arulius

Barbus callipterus
Clipper Barb

Syn.: None

Hab.: In running water; west Africa from Cameroon to Niger.

Fl.: 1913, K. Siggelkow, Hamburg, West Germany.

Sex: During the spawning season the ♀ is fatter; cannot be determined otherwise.

Soc. B.: A lively yet peaceful fish not easily disturbed. Not demanding and can survive in most waters at median temperatures.

M: Prefers a dark tank bottom with a few floating plants for shade and others on the tanks edges.

B: Not yet accomplished.

F: O; omnivorous; most live foods; vegetation; flakes.

S: The fish is a jumper. The tank should be well covered.

T: 66-77° F,   L: 3³/₄″,   A: 23¹/₂″,   R: all,   D: 1.
   19-25° C,   9 cm,   60 cm,

Barbus conchonius
Rosy Barb

Syn.: *Cyprinus conchonius, Puntius conchonius, Systomus conchonius*

Hab.: In rivers, ponds and backwater; northern India; Bengal; Assam.

Fl.: 1903, H. Stueve, Hamburg, West Germany.

Sex: Difficult to determine in younger fish but as they mature the color differences become pronounced. ♀ remains smaller while ♂ is more slender.

Soc. B.: A lively, peaceful undemanding species. Does best with tank-mates which require cooler water.

M: Tank should have a soft bottom with mulm. Plant the edges with hardy plants and provide plenty of swimming room. Water should be soft (to 10° dGH) and slightly acid (pH 6.5).

B: Suggest water temperature 73-77° F (23-25° C). Place one ♂ and two ♀♀ in a 5 to 7 gallon (20-30 liter) tank. Use coarse gravel on the bottom or add a plastic divider to let the eggs fall through to protect them. Spawning is preceeded by mock matings and love-play. Several hundred eggs are laid. If there is no divider remove the parents. The fry hatch in 30 hours.

F: O; omnivorous; all live foods; dried food; FD; frozen foods.

S: Will breed only in water a few inches deep. The fry should be fed generously.

T: 64-72° F,   L: 6″, mature from 2¹/₂″,   A: 27″,   R: all,   D: 1.
   18-22° C,   15 cm, mature from 6 cm,   70 cm,

Barbus callipterus

Barbus conchonius (♂ right, ♀ left)

Barbus cumingi
Cuming's Barb

Syn.: *Puntius cumingii, Puntius phutunio* (not HAMILTON)

Hab.: Found in mountain streams in Sri Lanka.

Fl.: 1936, "Aquarium Hamburg", Hamburg, West Germany.

Sex: ♂ is slenderer with a brightly colored tail. ♀ is more rounded at the ventral line and heavier bodied, especially during the spawning season.

Soc. B.: A lively barb it enjoys playing with fish of its own species.

M: Needs a well-planted tank with a layer of mulm and subdued lighting. Floating plants can supply shade. Frequent partial water changes are imporant with water values similar to those recommended for *Barbus filamentosus*. Recommended for a community tank.

T: 72-81° F, L: 2", A: 23¹/₂", R: m, b, D: 2-3.
22-27° C, 5 cm, 60 cm,

(GUENTHER, 1868)
Sub-Fam.: Cyprininae

B: Not easy since they are difficult to pair. Breeding requires care and a "green" tank. Water temperatures 74-79° F (24-26° C) with a hardness to 8° dGH and a pH between 6.2 and 7.4.

F: O; omnivorous; live foods; flakes; vegetation.

S: *Barbus cumingi* is a rare species in Sri Lanka.

Barbus eugrammus
Stripped Barb, Zebra Barb

Syn.: *Barbodes eugrammus, Barbus fasciatus* (not JERDON), *Puntius eugrammus*

Hab.: Malayan penninsula; Johore, southwest Malaysia; Sumatra; Kalimantan, Borneo.

Fl.: 1934, Haertel, Dresden, Germany.

Sex: ♂ has more obvious banding and a more slender body. ♀ is fuller bodied and higher backed with paler banding.

Soc. B.: A peaceful, agile but somewhat timid fish. May be kept with *Danio* or *Brachydanio* sp.

M: Similar to *Rasbora heteromorpha* but needs a larger aquarium.

B: Use about eight inches (20 cm) of water which should be soft (2-3° dGH), acid (pH 5.8-6.3) and at temperatures between 77 and 80° F (25-26° C). Dense vegetation and a dark tank bottom will help. The fish are very prolific and spawning will take

SILAS, 1956
Sub-Fam.: Cyprininae

place after a display of fast, active swimming. Feed the fish white worms during spawning. Remove the parents. The fry will hatch in 24 to 30 hours and are easily raised.

F: O; omnivorous; live foods; vegetable; FD; flakes.

S: DUNCKER, 1904 described a barbelless species, *Barbus lineatus* as coming from the Muar river near Tubing-tinggi in Malaya. The species has not been seen commercially and may be a non-barbelled variety of *B. eugrammus*. JERDON, 1849 was the first to describe the vertically-banded *B. fasciatus*. BLEEKER, 1853, also named the horizontally striped species *B. fasciatus*. (Page 386). Since the name was taken it had to renamed (by SILAS, 1956).

T: 73-77° F, L: 4¹/₄", A: 31-39", R: m, b, D: 2.
23-25° C, 12 cm, 80-100 cm,

Barbus cumingi

Barbus eugrammus

Barbus everetti
Clown Barb

Syn.: *Puntius everetti*

Hab.: Southeast Asia; Singapore; Borneo; Bunguran Islands.

Fl.: 1913, K. Siggelkow, Hamburg, West Germany.

Sex: ♀ noticeably heavier, particularly during the spawning season. ♂ is slender and more brightly colored.

Soc. B.: A lively, peaceful species which should be kept with other species prefering warmer water.

M: Has much in common with *B. conchonius* but needs more heat and a larger tank. Should have room for swimming, with planting around the tank edges and in the background. We recommend hiding places among rocks, roots or in plastic pipe. Suggest soft water (to 10° dGH) that is slightly acid (pH 6-6.5). Make weekly water changes of one fifth to one quarter the total tank volume.

B: Recommend water temperatures between 79 and 82° F (26-28° C). Breeding has been successful only in larger tanks with a low water level. (6-12° dGH, pH about 7). Separate the sexes for two or three weeks prior to breeding and feed them frequently on white mosquito larvae, Enchytraea and lettuce. We keep *Myriophyllum* in our tanks, placing the aquarium where it catches morning sun light.

F: O; omnivorous; live food; flakes; vegetable.

S: When breeding is difficult the cause is usually pairing with a male that is too young. Males mature only after a year and one half or more although the female can be bred after one year. Occasionally when a male is ready to spawn the female is unable to produce.

T: 75-86° F, L: 4″, A: 27″, R: b, m, D: 2-3.
    24-30° C,   10 cm,   70 cm,

Barbus fasciatus
Banded Barb

Syn.: *Barbus melanampyx, Cirrhinus fasciatus*

Hab.: Southeast Asia; Malayan penninsula; and parts of Indonesia.

Fl.: 1960

Sex: ♂ is slenderer and smaller; ♀ has a higher back.

Soc. B.: A lively fish which enjoys swimming. Keep them in schools since they are too timid to be alone.

M: Use darker gravel on the tank bottom with dense vegetation at the tank edges. Allow plenty of space for swimming. Needs hiding places. Water about 5° dGH and pH 6.0-6.5.

B: Difficult to breed. Suggest temperatures between 77 and 79° F (25-26° C) with the water values above.

F: O; all live foods; FD; flakes; lettuce added.

S: *Barbus fasciatus* (JERDON, 1849) is a Cross-banded Barb. The same name has been given a horizontally-striped barb, *Barbus fasciatus* (BLEEKER, 1853). This is the Striped Barb which is now called *B. eugrammus*, see page 385.

T: 72-79° F, L: 5³/₄″, A: 39″, R: b, m, D: 2-3.
    22-26° C,   15 cm,   100 cm,

Barbus everetti

Barbus fasciatus

Barbus filamentosus
Black-Spot Barb

(VALENCIENNES, 1842)
Sub-Fam.: Cyprininae

Syn.: *Leuciscus filamentosus, Barbus mahecola, Puntius filamentosus, Systomus assimilis*

Hab.: Found in mountain streams in southern and southwestern India; Sri Lanka.

Fl.: 1954

Sex: The male is smaller but glossier and more brightly colored with longer rays on the dorsal. Mature ♂♂ display a fine white eruption on the upper lip and gills during spawning season.

Soc. B.: A lively, peaceful species that enjoys swimming.

M: Needs a longer tank with background vegetation and plenty of open swimming space. Needs very little sun. Water hardness to 15° dGH and a pH of 6.0.

B: Water temperature should be 75-79° F (24-26° C), about 10° dGH or less and

slightly acid (pH 6.0). The tank should be fair-sized with a gravel bottom and dense clumps of fine-leaved plants. During spawning the male swims in a nervous, agitated manner and spawning occurs between the plants. The parents should be removed after spawning. The fry hatch in 36 to 48 hours, depending on the water temperature and are easy to raise.

F: O; all types of live foods; meat; lettuce and algae; flakes are taken readily. The fish are hearty eaters.

S: After being introduced *Barbus filamentosus* were called *Barbus mahecola. B. filamentosus* differs from the later in that it has no barbels. *B. mahecola* has a single pair on the upper jaw. The juvenile of *Barbus filamentosus* is shown on the top right of the book's back cover.

T: 68-75° F,   **L:** 5³/₄″,   **A:** 39″,   **R:** m,   **D:** 2.
   20-24° C,   15 cm,   100 cm,

Barbus gelius
Golden Dwarf Barb, Golden Barb

(HAMILTON, 1822)
Sub-Fam.: Cyprininae

Syn.: *Cyprinus gelius, Systomus gelius*

Hab.: In both gently-flowing and standing waters; central India; Bengal; Assam.

Fl.: 1912, Vereinigte Zierfischzuechtereien, Conradshoehe, Berlin, Germany.

Sex: ♂ slenderer and smaller with a more pronounced coppercolored lateral stripe.

Soc. B.: A peaceful, sociable fish which can be combined with other barbs.

M: A dark gravel bottom in an established tank with some mulm. The aquarium should be planted with Cryptocorynes or similar species of plants with plenty of swimming space. Use roots for decoration and soft, slightly acid water to 10° dGH and pH 6.5. Should be keep in schools of six to eight.

B: Water temperature 72-73° F (22-23° C) in a breeding tank 12 inches (30 cm.) long: use about six inches of water at 5° dGH and pH 6.0-6.5. Select only the finest specimens for breeding. Plant the tank with *Ludwigia*, coupling is preceeded by a vigorous courtship. The fish will spawn on the underside of leaves leaving 70 to 100 eggs. The parents will eat their fry and must be removed. The fry hatch in 24 hours and should be fed fine foods.

F: O; all live foods; dried and soft algae;. All foods should be small since the fishes have a small mouth.

S: see page 390.

T: 64-72° F,   **L:** 1¹/₂″,   **A:** 19¹/₂″,   **R:** m,   **D:** 2.
   18-22° C,   4 cm,   50 cm,

Barbus filamentosus

Barbus gelius

S: Water temperature should not exceed 73° F (23° C) during breeding since the eggs may be rendered infertile or fry may not reach adult size. Degeneration may continue until the fish cannot reproduce. This can be countered by (1) using only adult fish for breeding and (2) replacing breeding pairs.

Barbus holotaenia

BOULENGER, 1904
Sub-Fam.: Cyprininae

Syn.: *Barbus camtacanthus* var. *cottesi, B. kessleri* (not STEINDACHNER)

Hab.: Africa; From Cameroon to Zaire and Angola.

Fl.: 1913

Sex: Unknown.

Soc. B.: An active, peaceful, schooling species well suited to a community tank.

M: Prefers a soft bottom with mulm. Use fine-leaved plants such as *Cabomba* and *Myriophyllum* at the edges of the tank,

leaving space in the center for swimming. The fish should be kept in aged water with fresh added from time to time. Suggest soft, slightly acid water to 8° dGH and pH 6.0-6.5.

B: Has not been bred in an aquarium.

F: O; omnivorous; live food; lettuce and algae; FD; flakes.

S: Is similar to the Characin *Nannaethiops unitaeniatus* and is often confused with it.

T: 75-86° F,   L: 4³/₄",   A: 39",   R: all,   D: 2-3.
  24-30° C,   12 cm,   100 cm,

Barbus hulstaerti

POLL, 1945
Sub-Fam.: Cyprininae

Syn.: *Capoeta hulstaerti*

Hab.: Lower reaches of Zaire, esp. Stanley Pool; Angola.

Fl.: 1956

Sex: ♂ is noticeably slender with a round leading lateral patch which may be difficult to see.

Soc. B.: A peaceful, energetic species, it may become timid and lethargic if kept alone. Should be kept in a school and not with larger fishes.

M: Suggest a variegated or multi-colored gravel bottom with plantings along the back and edges of the tank. Use floating plants to filter the light and decorate the bottom with bog-wood roots. Soft, slight acid, aged water 5° dGH and pH 6.0-6.5. Replace about 10% of the water weekly and use light peat filtration.

B: Has not been bred in an aquarium and the available data is inconsistent. Apparently requires very soft, acid water (1-2° dGH and pH 5.0-5.5). Keep the tank dark and the fish will spawn in the darkest part. The fry are said to prefer water temperatures below 72° F (22° C).

F: O; omnivorous; all types of live foods; vegetable; flakes; FD; frozen foods.

S: The species is sensitive to changes in water quality such as pH, hardness and nitrite content.

T: About 74° F,   L: 1¹/₂",   A: 20",   R: m,   D: 3.
  About 24° C,   3.5 cm,   50 cm,

Barbus holotaenia

Barbus hulstaerti

Barbus lateristriga
Spanner Barb

VALENCIENNES, 1842
Sub-Fam.: Cyprininae

Syn.: *Barbus zelleri, Puntius lateristriga, Systomus lateristriga*

Hab.: Found in clear, flowing water and in ponds throughout southeast Asia: Singapore; Thailand; Java; Borneo; Sumatra; other islands of the Malaysian Archipelago.

Fl.: 1914, J. Wolmer, Hamburg, West Germany.

Sex: ♂ thinner and more intensely colored. The red color on the dorsal fin is noticeably brighter. ♀ has a broader ventral area, particularly during spawning.

Soc. B.: A robust, undemanding species which can be kept with other peaceful though not timid fishes. The young will school while the adults tend to be solitary.

M: A gravel bottom with mulm, spotty planting and plenty of swimming space. Needs places to hide behind plants, in plastic pipe or tank decorations. Water quality similar to that for *B. everetti.*

B: Water temperatures 79 to 82° F (26-28° C) with dense plant growth in the breeding tank. ♂ courts ♀ and spawning will occur among the plants. More than 100 eggs are laid which will adhere to the plants. The breeding pair should be removed since they will devour the spawn. The fry hatch after two days. Do not feed them with *Cyclops.*

F: O; omnivorous; live foods even smaller fish; flakes; vegetables. Adults have a voracious appetite.

S: When chased the fish will attempt to bury themselves in the bottom gravel. According to KLAUSEWITZ, *Barbus zelleri* (AHL) is identical with the juvenile form of *B. lateristriga.*

T: 77-82° F,   L: 7″,   A: 35″,   R: b, m, D: 2-3.
   25-28° C,   18 cm,   90 cm,

Barbus nigrofasciatus
Black-Ruby Barb, Purple-Headed Barb

GUENTHER, 1868
Sub-Fam.: Cyprininae

Syn.: *Puntius nigrofasciatus*

Hab.: Slow-flowing mountain streams of Sri Lanka (Ceylon).

Fl.: 1945, Ms. Wagner, Hamburg, West Germany.

Sex: The male is larger and more intensely colored (an example of sexual dichromatism) while ♀ is flatter and does not change color during the spawning season.

Soc. B.: A lively, active but peaceful fish which prefers schools. Can be combined with other barbs with vertical stripes.

M: Likes a layer of mulm on the bottom and a well-planted tank with room for swimming. Lighting should be subdued, diffused by such broad-leaved floating plants as *Eichhornia and Ceratopteris.* The fish become frightened in a brightly-lighted aquarium. The tank should provide hiding places. Water values are similar to those for *Barbus filamentosus.*

B: Water should be 77-82° F (25-28° C) not too hard and slightly acid (to 12° dGH and pH 6.0). The courtship begins when the male swims around ♀, spreading his fins in display and spawning occurs in the morning between the plants. Remove the adults after spawning. The fry hatch in 24 hours and swim freely after a week.

F: O; all types of live foods; flakes with added vegetables.

S: If the eggs are not repeatedly fertilized the problem may lie with the male. Separate the pair and feed the male a plentiful, varied diet for several weeks.

T: 72-79° F summer, 68-72° F winter,   L: 2¹/₂″,   A: 27″,   R: m,   D: 1.
   22-26° C summer, 20-22° C winter,   6.5 cm,   70 cm,

Barbus lateristriga

Barbus nigrofasciatus (♂ in front, ♀ behind)

Barbus oligolepis
Checkered Barb, Island Barb

Syn.: *Capoeta oligolepis, Puntius oligolepis, Systomus oligolepis*

Hab.: In streams, rivers and lakes of Indonesia and Sumatra.

Fl.: 1923, Jonny Wolmer, Hamburg, West Germany.

Sex: The male is larger and more intensely colored. The fins are a bright red-brown with a black edge.

Soc. B.: A peaceful, handsome fish best kept in small schools. The males may seem threatening but will rarely fight.

M: Use fine gravel on the tank bottom with a layer of rich mulm. Planting should be limited to the edges and the rear of the tank with swimming room in the center. Use aged water with fresh added occasionally. The water values are similar to those for *Barbus everetti*.

B: Water temperature 74-79° F (24-26° C). Place only pairs in the breeding tank since extra males will be disturbing to the others. Plant the tank heavily with *Myriophyllum* or *Nitella*. The fish will spawn on the plants near the surface. As many as 300 eggs will be deposited, each laid individually. Remove the breeding pairs since they will eat their spawn. The fry will hatch in 36 to 48 hours.

F: O; omnivorous; prefer flake foods but should be fed fine algae as well to improve their general condition.

S: Grows very fast and, with plenty of food and the right temperature can mature in four to six months. Photo: ♀ top, ♂ beneath.

T: 68-74° F, **L:** 5³/₄″, **A:** 19¹/₂″, **R:** b, m, **D:** 1.
20-24° C, 15 cm, 50 cm,

Barbus orphoides

Syn.: *Barbodes rubripinna, Barbus rubripinnis, Puntius orphoides, P. rubripinna*

Hab.: Found in rivers and standing water in southeast Asia: Thailand; Java; Madura; Borneo.

Fl.: 1951

Sex: Unknown.

Soc. B.: Similar to *Barbus lateristriga*.

M: Needs a soft, mulm bottom. The tank should be decorated with hardy plants, leaving plenty of space in the center for swimming. The water values are similar to those for *Barbus everetti* and ¹/₅th of the total water should be changed weekly.

B: Has not been bred in captivity.

F: O; omnivorous; all types of live foods; vegetable; flakes.

S: While young *B. orphoides* is one of the finest of the *Barbus* species. It is seldom imported because, as an adult it is both large and a plant eater.

B. orphoides, adult

T: 72-77° F, **L:** 10″, mature from 3¹/₄″ **A:** 32″, **R:** b, m, **D:** 2.
22-25° C, 25 cm, mature from 8 cm 80 cm,

Barbus oligolepis

Barbus orphoides, juv.

Barbus pentazona pentazona
Five-Banded Barb

BOULENGER, 1894
Sub-Fam.: Cyprininae

Syn.: *Barbodes pentazona, Puntius pentazona*

Hab.: In calm inland waters of southeast Asia: Singapore; Malayan penninsula; Borneo.

Fl.: 1911, Vereinigte Zierfischzuechtereien, Conradshoehe, Berlin, Germany.

Sex: ♂ smaller, thinner and more brightly colored.

Soc. B.: A peaceful, rather timid species less active than other *Barbus* varieties. Can be combined with other peaceful fishes.

M: Similar to *B. lateristriga* with water values similar to those for *B. everetti*. Needs warmer water than most *Barbus sp.*

B: Difficult to breed. Water temperature 79-86° F (27-30° C), 10° dGH and pH 6-7. It is important that the pairs seem well adjusted. They should not be separated prior to breeding and should be fed Enchy-

traea during spawning,. If not they may consume their spawn. Will deposit as many as 200 eggs which hatch after 30 hours. The fry are free-swimming after five days.

F: C; All types of live foods; the species is more demanding of foods than most *Barbus* and will rarely accept flakes.

S: The fry require very clean water with frequent changes. Polluted water may result in actual losses or in damage to the fins. Several sub-species have been described. *P. pentazona pentazona* is shown here. It is easily confused with the six-banded barb *B. p. hexazona* WEBER & de BEAUFORT, whose first body band is sufficiently wider that it includes the eye. The second band completely surrounds the body while the third does not reach the pelvic fin. On *B. p. pentazona* the third fin does.

T: 72-79° F, **L:** 2″, **A:** 27″, **R:** m, **D:** 2-3.
22-26° C, 5 cm, 70 cm,

Barbus rhomboocellatus

KOUMANS, 1940
Sub-Fam.: Cyprininae

Syn.: *Barbus kahajanio*

Hab.: Perhaps Borneo.

Fl.: Unknown.

Sex: The female is fuller-bodied.

Soc. B.: A peaceful species recommended for community tanks with other peaceful fishes.

M: Subdued lighting with good filtration and flow. Needs nitrate free water (less than 15 mg/l) and peat filtration. pH 6.5-7.5: hardness to 15° dGH. Soft water is recommended.

B: Probably similar to *Barbus p. pentazona* but breeding has not yet been described. Few fish have been imported.

F: O; omnivorous; small live foods; sieved flakes; FD; algae.

T: 73-82° F, **L:** 2″, **A:** 23$^1/_2$″, **R:** all, **D:** 2.
23-28° C, 5 cm, 60 cm,

Barbus pentazona pentazona

Barbus rhomboocellatus

Barbus schwanefeldi
Schwanefeld's Barb, Tinfoil Barb

BLEEKER, 1853
Sub-Fam.: Cyprininae

Syn.: *Puntius schwanefeldi*

Hab.: Southeast Asia: Thailand; Malayan penninsula; Sumatra; Borneo.

Fl.: 1951

Sex: No external signs.

Soc. B.: Though a lively, peaceful, schooling fish, it will feed on smaller fishes. Can be combined with Cichlids.

M: A large, roomy tank is basic. Use fine gravel on the bottom with the densest planting along the edges and back of the tank. Use hardy varieties since the species likes to burrow. Suggest aged water with the same values as for *Barbus gelius*. Not always suitable for a community tank.

B: Not yet bred in an aquarium.

F: O; omnivorous; live food; flakes; vegetable. Grows rapidly.

S: Though it is considered too large for most home aquariums, the adults make a beautiful display.

T: 72-77° F,   L: 13″,   A: 39-47″,   R: b, m, D: 3-4 (H).
    22-25° C,   35 cm,   100-120 cm,

Barbus semifasciolatus
Green Barb, Half-Striped Barb

GUENTHER, 1868
Sub-Fam.: Cyprininae

Syn.: *Capoeta guentheri, Puntius guentheri, P. semifasciolatus, "Barbus schuberti"*

Hab.: Southeast China from Hong Kong to the Island of Hainan.

Fl.: 1909, Vereinigte Zierfischzuechtereien, Conradshoehe, Germany. The specimen came from Hong Kong.

Sex: ♂ is more intensely colored, thiner and smaller.

Soc. B.: A lively, active and undemanding fish best kept in schools.

M: The tank can be kept in a sunny place but the bottom should be of fine gravel with a layer of darker mulm. It should be generously planted yet with room in the center for swimming. Use aged water with regular fresh water changes. The water

values are similar to those for *Barbus gelius* though the species does not require as much oxygen.

B: Use a well-planted tank about 20 inches (50 cm.) in length with water 77° F (25° C). A vigorous courtship usually occurs in the morning hours, each producing ten to 30 eggs. The eggs may adhere to the plants or sink to the bottom and as many as 300 will be laid before the ritual is completed. Remove the parents to protect the eggs. The fry will hatch in 30 to 36 hours and are easy to raise.

F: O; all kinds of live food; dried food; vegetable; The fish are hearty eaters.

S: A yellow morph, called the Golden Barb, is commonly identified as *"Barbus schuberti"*.

T: 64-75° F,   L: 4″,   A: 23¹/₂″,   R: b, m, D: 1.
    18-24° C,   10 cm,   60 cm,

Barbus schwanefeldi

B. semifasciolatus center, *B. "schuberti"* below.

Barbus tetrazona
Tiger Barb

Syn.: *Puntius tetrazona*

Hab.: Indonesia; Sumatra; Borneo; possibly Thailand though this is disputed.

Fl.: 1935

Sex: ♂ is smaller, thinner and more brightly colored.

Soc. B.: A lively, playful, schooling species with an established "pecking order". So active it may even become a nuisance to tankmates. May peck at the fins of Gouramis, Angels and others.

M: Suggest a fine gravel bottom with mulm and an edge of hardy plants. Needs lots of open swimming room though is not demanding in terms of water. Not recommended for a community tank.

T: 68-79° F,   L: 3″,   A: 27″,   R: m,   D: 1-2.
   20-26° C,   7 cm,   70 cm,

(BLEEKER, 1855)
Sub-Fam.: Cyprininae

B: Water temperature 74-79° F (24-26° C) to 10° dGH and slightly acid: pH about 6.5. Breeding pairs selected from the school should have perfect markings and strong color. Technique similar to that suggested for *Barbus p. pentazona*.

F: O; omnivorous; live food; vegetable; flakes.

S: Extremely susceptible to *Ich*. A number of color morphs have been bred and noteworthy is the Green "Moss Barb". Albino variants, which do not always have gill covers, are more a matter of taste and less popular.(See page 363.)

Barbus ticto
Two-Spot Barb, Ticto Barb
(var.: Ödessa Barb, Ruby Barb)

Syn.: *Cyprinus ticto, Barbus stoliczkanus, Puntius ticto, Rothee ticto, Systomus ticto, S. tripunctatus*

Hab.: In rivers, streams and occasionally standing water; from India and Sri Lanka to the Himalayas.

Fl.: 1903, H. Stueve, Hamburg, West Germany.

Sex: Aside from the spawning season it is difficult to determine. Sexually mature ♀ are more powerful and generally have no spots on their dorsal fins. Sexually mature ♂ is thinner and the dorsal normally show black spots toward the fin edge. Their bodies have a reddish-brown tinge.

Soc. B.: An active but peaceful and undemanding species which enjoys tankmates.

M: Similar to *Barbus conchonius* but requires cooler water. Is recommended for community tanks.

T: 57-72° F,   L: 4″,   A: 27″,   R: all,   D: 1.
   14-22° C,   10 cm,   70 cm,

(HAMILTON, 1822)
Sub-Fam.: Cyprininae

B: Water temperatures 74-79° F (24-26° C). Place one ♀ with several ♂♂ and follow suggestions for *Barbus conchonius*.

F: O; omnivorous; all types of live foods; FD; frozen food; flakes.

S: Not a burrower as others of the genus and should have cooler water during the winter: 57-59° F (14-16° C).
A smaller variant is known as the Ruby Barb, a color morph which may have been seen first in Moscow. It quickly conquered the hearts of all aquarists. Unfortunately males acquire full coloring only after six to nine months and before this are an unattractive, pale color. The morph is only 2 $1/2$- 3 inches (6-7 cm.) in length. Its brilliant coloring is achieved by alternate feeding of live foods and Tetra/Ruby.

Barbus tetrazona

Barbus ticto (♂ below, ♀ top)

Barbus titteya
Cherry Barb

(DERANIYAGALA, 1929)
Sub-Fam.: Cyprininae

Syn.: *Puntius titteya, Barbus frenatus*

Hab.: In shaded streams and rivers on the plains of Sri Lanka.

Fl.: 1936, W. Odenwald, Hamburg, West Germany.

Sex: ♂ is fuller-bodied and is a bright, beautiful red color during the spawning season.

Soc. B.: Though generally peaceful, the species is a timid loner and becomes nervous with others of its species as tankmates.

M: A darker tank bottom with mulm, dense vegetation and a cover of floating plants. The fish will seek solitude among the plants. Leave swimming space in the center. Water to 18° dGH and pH 6.5-7.5.

B: Water temperatures from 74 to 79° F (24-26° C) with a hardness to 12° dGH and slightly acid (pH 6.0-6.5). Select breeding pairs and place them in a tank with dense vegetation. One to three eggs are deposited each time until as many as 300 are laid. To prevent the fish from eating their eggs feed them Enchytraea during spawning and remove them when the spawning has been completed. The fry hatch after 24 hours.

F: O; small live foods; vegetable; FD; flakes.

S: The eggs are attached to water plants by a small thread.

T: 73-79° F,   **L:** 2″,   **A:** 20″,   **R:** b+m,   **D:** 1.
     23-26° C,   5 cm,   50 cm,

Barbus viviparus

WEBER, 1897
Sub-Fam.: Cyprininae

Syn.: Probably none

Hab.: Southeast Africa; from the Umtanvuna River through Natal to the Zambesi system.

Fl.: 1955

Sex: Unknown.

Soc. B.: An active, peaceful and undemanding fish, it is best kept in schools.

M: Similar to *Barbus conchonius*.

B: Little data is available.

F: C, O; all kinds of live foods; FD; flakes.

S: The species name, *"viviparus"* (i.e. live-bearing), is inaccurate. As with others of the genus, *B. viviparus* lays eggs (see BARNARD, 1943: Ann. S. Afr. Mus. **36** (2), 101-262).

T: 72-74° F,   **L:** 2¹/₂″,   **A:** 23¹/₂″,   **R:** m,   **D:** 2.
     22-24° C,   6.5 cm,   60 cm,

Barbus titteya

Barbus viviparus

Opsaridium chrystyi

(BOULENGER, 1920)
Sub-Fam.: Cyprininae

Syn.: *Barilius chrystyi*

Hab.: Africa: northern Ghana.

FI.: 1953, A. Werner, Munich, West Germany.

Sex: Details are uncertain; the male is said to be thinner and more brightly colored.

Soc. B.: A nimble, jumping species best kept in schools.

M: A long tank with fine gravel, few plants and plenty of space for swimming. The water should be soft and slightly acid (5-10° dGH and pH 6.5).

B: Not yet accomplished in an aquarium.

F: C; while the species enjoys taking insects at the surface in its natural habitat, it will eat nearly anything in an aquarium. Will accept large flake foods.

S: An arresting species with an eye-catching red-gold patch on its upper jaw. With the exception of *Barilius neglectens*, one finds vertical stripes on these fishes, a marking rarely seen among this type of schooling fish.

T: 72-74° F, **L**: 6″, **A**: 31″, **R**: m, t, **D**: 2-3.
22-24° C, 15 cm, 80 cm,

Brachydanio albolineatus
Pearl Danio

(BLYTH, 1860)
Sub-Fam.: Rasborinae

Syn.: *Nuria albolineata, Danio albolineata*

Hab.: In streams and rivers of southeast Asia; Burma, Thailand. Sumatra and the Malayan penninsula.

FI.: 1911, Scholze & Poetzschke, Berlin, West Germany.

Sex: Adult ♀ are larger and stronger while the ♂ is more brightly colored.

Soc. B.: A pretty, active species. Breeding pairs are very loyal.

M: Need an extra long aquarium though it need not be either wide nor tall. Coarse gravel bottom with moderate planting along the sides and back and open swimming room in the center. Water hardness 5-12° dGH and pH 6.5-7.0).

B: Water temperature 79 to 86° F (26-30° C). Breeding is most successful in fresh water four to six inches (10-15 cm.) deep.

Plant fine-leaved species in groups and begin with two males and one female. Place the female in the tank a day or two prior to introducing the male. The eggs are laid among the plants and the parents should be fed Enchytraea to prevent consuming the spawn. Remove the parents when spawning is over. The fry hatch in 36 to 48 hours.

F: C, O; live foods such as *Tubifex* worms, mosquito larvae and small crabs; vegetable; flakes.

S: A yellow ochre variety is known as the "Yellow Danio". Be sure to cover the tank since the species likes to jump.

T: 68-77° F, **L**: 2¹/₃″, **A**: 31″, **R**: all, **D**: 1.
20-25° C, 6 cm, 80 cm,

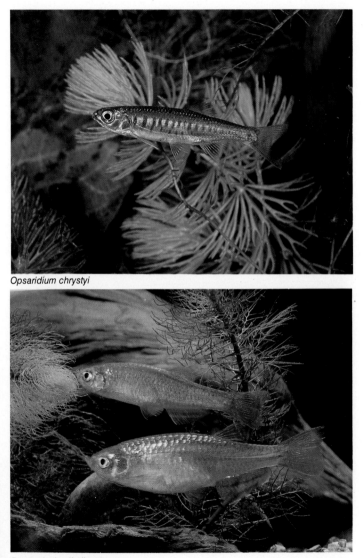

Opsaridium chrystyi

Brachydanio albolineatus

Brachydanio kerri

(SMITH, 1931)
Sub-Fam.: Rasborinae

Syn.: *Danio kerri*

Hab.: Only in the streams and creeks of two islands, Koh Yao Yai and Koh Yao Noi, northwest of the Ligor Isthmus in Thailand.

Fl.: 1956, Erhard Roloff, Karlsruhe, West Germany.

Sex: ♂ is much thinner.

Soc. B.: An active, peaceful fish which can be kept in schools with other *Brachydanio* or *Danio* species.

M: Similar to *B. albolineatus* though plants can be omitted since they are not normally found in the species' natural habitat.

B: Similar to recommendations for other *Brachydanio sp.* except that unlike *B. rerio*, *B. albolineatus* and *B. nigrofasciatus*, the species does not spawn on plants but lays

its eggs freely on the tank bottom. For this reason cover the aquarium with a two-inch layer of coarse gravel. The eggs, falling between them, will then be protected. As many as 400 eggs may be laid. At a water temperature of 74° F (24° C) the fry will hatch in four days.

F: O; omnivorous; all types of live foods; flakes; FD; algae and lettuce.

S: *Brachydanio kerri* can be found in a wide variation of colors and may be crossed with others of the species although the fry will always be infertile.

T: 73-77° F, **L**: 2", **A**: 27", **R**: all, **D**: 1-2.
 23-25° C, 5 cm, 70 cm,

Brachydanio nigrofasciatus
Spotted Danio

(DAY, 1869)
Sub-Fam.: Rasborinae

Syn.: *Barilius nigrofasciatus, Brachydanio analipunctatus, Danio anilipunctatus, D. nigrofasciatus*

Hab.: In the rivers, streams, ponds and paddies of Burma.

Fl.: 1911, Scholze & Poetzschke, Berlin, West Germany.

Sex: ♀ has a rounder, larger body while the ♂ has a light brown edging on the underside of its anal fin. The fin will also have a golden tint seen best as the light catches it. ♀ has only a lighter fin edging without the two-color effect.

Soc. B.: Though lively and faithful to its mate, it is not as active as *Brachydanio rerio.*

M: Similar to *Brachydanio albolineatus* but with a need for warmer water.

B: Water temperatures between 77 and 82° F (25-28° C). Keep the sexes separated for several days prior to breeding then place two males and one female in the tank. The males will perform an active, exciting courting ritual before coupling. The eggs will be deposited in the midst of plants. 10 to 15 eggs are released on each pass with as many as 300 eggs laid. Remove the parents after spawning and raise the fry as recommended for *B. rerio.*

F: C, O; all live foods; FD; flakes.

S: Crosses between *B. albolineatus* males and *B. nigrofasciatus* females are possible. The fry are very attractive though infertile.

T: 74-82° F, **L**: 2", **A**: 23$^{1}/_{2}$", **R**: all, **D**: 1-2.
 24-28° C, 4.5 cm, 60 cm,

Brachydanio kerri

Brachydanio nigrofasciatus

Brachydanio rerio
Zebra Danio, Zebra Fish

(HAMILTON, 1822)
Sub-Fam.: Rasborinae

Syn.: *Cyprinus rerio, Perilampus striatus, Danio rerio*

Hab.: Eastern India from Calcutta to Masulipatam.

Fl.: 1905, P. Matte, Berlin-Lankwitz, Germany.

Sex: Sexually mature ♀ are fuller-bodied and larger with more subdued colors. On the ♂ one can find a golden-yellow background with fine red lines between wider blue longitudinal lines. On ♀ the background is silvery white.

Soc. B.: An active but tempermental species with remarkable loyalty to their mates. Not promiscuous, they normally spawn with just one partner and can barely be persuaded to reproduce with others.

M: Similar to *Branchydanio albolineatus*.

B: Water temperature 74-79° F (24-26° C). During courtship the male will tire rapidly in warmer water. Breeding is most successful in shallow water, about 4^1/$_2$ to six inches deep. The tank should be well planted and exposed to some sun. Place the female in the tank one day before spawning and add the male the same evening. The pair will normally spawn in the early hours of the morning and the eggs will be deposited on the plants. Between 400 and 500 eggs will be laid. Feed the pair well on Enchytraea during spawning then remove them. The fry hatch in two days. Feed with TetraMin baby food and if available, Protogen-Ganulet with fine Enchytraea and/or powdered egg added. The fry will grow rapidly.

F: O; omnivorous; live food; flakes; FD; frozen food and occasionally lettuce, algae and Tetra Conditioning food.

S: *Brachydanio frankei* was described by Hermann MEINKEN in 1963 and since it can be crossed with *B. rerio* the actual existence of *B. frankei* may be in question. Until proven otherwise *B. frankei* should be considered a morph of *B. rerio.*

T: 64-74° F,   **L:** 2^1/$_3$",   **A:** 31",   **R:** all,   **D:** 1.
    18-24° C,   6 cm,   80 cm,

Brachydanio rerio, vieled form

Brachydanio rerio

Brachydanio "frankei", possibly a morph of *B. rerio*

409

Carassius auratus
Goldfish

(LINNAEUS, 1758)
Sub-Fam.: Cyprininae

Syn.: *Cyprinus auratus*

Hab.: Originally from China and now distributed world-wide.

Fl.: Cannot be accurately determined. First bred in Holland in 1728.

Sex: ♂ is thinner and may exhibit breeding spots on the head and flanks during the spawning season. In addition, the anal section is concave on the ♂ and convex in the ♀.

Soc. B.: Similar to the Crucian *Carassius carassius.*

M: Use fine gravel on the bottom and add hardy cold-water plants. Fine-leaved plants are not suggested since goldfish like to dig. The fine particles thrown up may cling to the leaves. Decorate the tank with roots and well-rounded river rocks. Make weekly water changes of about ¹/₄th the tank.

though it is now seldom reported. Use a large tank with clear, neutral water about 72° F (22° C). The spawning is preceeded by a definite courtship ritual resulting in as many as 1,000 eggs. The fry hatch after five or six days and should be fed small live foods. The young require at least eight months to develop color. Before this their drab appearance is less than exciting.

F: O; omnivorous; Will accept every kind of dried and live foods but the diet should not be too rich in protein. Suggest about 30%.

S: Man has developed a broad range of variations among which the more important are the Vieltail, Shubunkin (Calico), Comet, Nymph; Lion-head, Oranda, Tiger, Chinese Telescope, Stargazer, Popeye, Dragon's eye, Curled Gill and Pearly Scale. These are illustrated in many good books including Professor Ladiges'"Cold Water Fish for Home and Garden" available from Tetra.

B: Can be done readily in an aquarium

T: 50-68° F,   **L:** 14″,   **A:** 31-39″,   **R:** m,   **D:** 1.
    10-20° C,   36 cm,   80-100 cm,

Carassius carassius
Crucian, Prussian Carp

(LINNAEUS, 1758)
Sub-Fam.: Cyprininae

Syn.: *Cyprinus carassius, Carassius vulgaris*

Hab.: Large parts of Europe including the Black Sea, Caspian Sea and Siberia. Not found in Ireland, northern Scotland, Wales, Switzerland and the Iberian penninsula.

Fl.: A European species.

Sex: ♀ fatter during spawning season.

Soc. B.: A peaceful, quiet species that is extremely hardy and very adaptable.

M: The tank should have a bottom of fine gravel and be planted with hardy, cold-water plants such as *Egeria* and *Myriophyllum*. Not as demanding of oxygen content or water values as many species but requires regular water changes, about ¹/₅th the tank weekly.

B: Quite possible in larger tanks.

F: O; omnivorous; all types of live foods; flakes; vegetable. The species is a bottom feeder.

S: Spawning season extends from May through June and the fishes are very fertile depositing as many as 300,000 eggs on the plants. May also use spawning mops.

T: 57-72° F,   **L:** 31″ (Generally smaller: 8″),   **A:** 39″,   **R:** b+m,   **D:** 1.
    14-22° C,   80 cm (20 cm)   100 cm,

Carassius auratus

Carassius carassius

Chela laubuca
Indian Glassbarb

(HAMILTON, 1822)
Sub-Fam.: Abraminae

Syn.: *Cyprinus laubuca, Laubuca laubuca, L. siamensis, Leuciscus laubuca, Perilampus guttatus, P. laubuca*

Hab.: Southeast Asia; India; Sri Lanka; Burma; Thailand; Sumatra; Malayan penninsula.

Fl.: 1925 A. Ramsperger, Bremen, West Germany.

Sex: ♀ is fatter.

Soc. B.: An active, peaceful, schooling fish which can be kept with *Brachydanio sp.*

M: The tank should have generous lateral and background planting with plenty of space in the center for swimming. Requires clear water with $^1/_5$ replaced every two weeks. Water values should be similar to those suggested for *Brachydanio albolineatus. Chela laubuca* is recommended for any community tank.

B: Water temperature 79-82° F (26-28° C) with the water soft to medium hard and slightly acid (5-10° dGH). The tank should be planted as recommended for *B. albolineatus.* During spawning the ♂ winds his body around the ♀ and 30 to 40 eggs may be laid. Many pairings occur. The parents will not disturb the spawn and the fry hatch in about 24 hours. They are free-swimming after three or four days.

F: O; omnivorous; undemanding, they will accept live food, flakes, lettuce and algae. Food which falls to the bottom will not be consumed.

S: Do not overfeed since the species tends toward erythropia (i.e. excess concentration of blood in the vessels) which may cause death. The species requires acclimitization and is a jumper so cover the tank.

T: 74-79° F,   **L:** 2$^1/_3$″,   **A:** 27″,   **R:** m+t, **D:** 1-2.
  24-26° C,   6 cm,   70 cm,

Crossocheilus siamensis **see page 418.**

Cyclocheilichthys apogon

(VALENCIENNES, 1842)
Sub-Fam.: Cyprininae

Syn.: *Barbus apogon, Anematichthys apogon, A. apogonides, Cyclocheilichthys rubripinnis, Systomus apogon. S. apogonoides*

Hab.: Northern India; Burma, Thailand, Maylaysia; Sumatra; Borneo, Java: Malaysan penninsula.

Fl.: 1934, E. Koch, Bremerhaven, West Germany.

Sex: Unknown.

Soc. B.: An active yet peaceful fish.

M: Fine gravel bottom decorated with bogwood roots and plenty of open swimming space. Only younger fish are recommended for an aquarium, the species becoming too large as an adult. They have no special water demands.

B: Has not been bred in the hobby.

F: A bottom feeder, the species will accept flakes and live foods.

S: Considered a food fish in its native waters.

T: 74-79° F,   **L:** 6-20″,   **A:** 31″,   **R:** b+m,   **D:** 1.
  24-26° C,   15-50 cm,   80 cm,

Chela laubuca

Cyclocheilichthys apogon

Ctenopharyngodon idella
Silver Orfe

(VALENCIENNES, 1844)
Sub-Fam.: Cyprininae

Syn.: *Leuciscus idella*

Though the species grows too large to be of real interest to an aquarist, it is important to those interested in stocking garden ponds. The fishes eat taller water plants, including reeds (which carp do not) and consequently help thin-out a pond. They are very hardy and can survive cold winters even in European ponds.

T: 50-68° F,   L: to 24",   A: from 48",   R: b, m, D: 4 (H).
   10-20° C,   60 cm,   120 cm,

Cyprinus carpio
European Carp

LINNAEUS. 1758
Sub-Fam.: Cyprininae

Syn.: *Cyprinus acuminatus, C. coriaceus, C. elatus, C. hungaricus, C. macrolepidotus, C. regina, C. rex cyprinorum, C. specularis*

Hab.: Originally from Japan and China, it is now kept in ponds around the world and is feral in many waters.

Fl.: Cannot be determined.

Sex: One can see breeding spots on the male during the spawning season; in the same season ♀ is much fatter.

Soc. B.: The younger fish are schooling, the older ones loners.

M: Prefers fine gravel and dense vegetation with a few roots as decoration. Water hardness 10-15° dGH and neutral to slightly alkaline, pH 7.0-7.5.

B: Not possible in an aquarium. Requires more space.

F: O; prefers live "bottom" foods such as shrimps, molluscs, worms and insect larvae but will accept flakes, FD lettuce, algae, potatoes, oatmeal and soaked corn.

S: There are several artificially-bred varieties in addition to the common carp. Examples include Golden Carp (no scales), King Carp (scales only on the lateral line) and Mirror Carp (a few scales on the back). In their natural habitat feral carp are a food fish and will not be described. They can be kept only in large tanks, those of 250 gallons or more.

The picture shows a mutation, the Colored or Ornamental carp available in a variety of colors. It can be kept in 50 gallon tanks (100 cm lengh) where it will not reach a length of more than eight inches (20 cm.) This form also does well in garden ponds but can accept less cold. It should, like the goldfish, be taken inside during the winter if temperatures fall below 50° F (10° C). The Colored Carp or Koi is kept in ponds in Japan and the U.S. In Japan it is considered a harbinger of good fortune.

T: 50-73° F (cold water fish)   L: 8-48",   A: 39",   R: b, m, D: 1-2.
   10-23° C,   20-120 cm,   100 cm,

Ctenopharyngodon idella

Cyprinus carpio (artificial form)

Danio aequipinnatus
Giant Danio

Syn.: *Perilampus malabaricus, Danio alburnus, D. aurolineatus, D. lineolatus, D. micronema, D. osteographus, Leuciscus lineolatus, Paradanio aurolineatus, Perilampus aurolineatus, P. canarensis, P. mysorius, Danio malabaricus*

Hab.: In standing and flowing waters on the west coast of India and Sri Lanka.

Fl.: 1909

Sex: ♂ is noticeably thinner with a blue stripe running straight over the tailfin; ♀ has less brilliant coloring, a more rounded stomach and a blue stripe that bends upward at the base of the tailfin.

Soc. B.: A lively, active, even restless schooling species which are loyal to their mates. (Though less so than *Brachydanio*.)

M: A fine gravel bottom and a lateral display of hardy plants. Need open swimming room, especially in the upper regions of the aquarium. Recommended for a community tank. Water values similar to those suggested for *Brachydanio albolineatus*.

B: Water temperatures 77-82° F (25-28° C). Needs a larger breeding tank with fresh water and a touch of sun. Feed Enchytraea during spawning and remove parents when the process is finished. Five to 20 eggs are laid after each pairing with as many as 300 in all. The fry hatch in 24 to 48 hours and are easy to raise.

F: O; omnivorous; live food; flakes; FD; vegetable.

S: *Danio aequipinnatus* can be seen in many color variations.

T: 72-75° F,   **L**: 4″,   **A**: 31″,   **R**: all,   **D**: 1.
22-24° C,   10 cm,   80 cm,

Danio devario
Bengal Danio

Syn.: *Cyprinus devario*

Hab.: In flooded areas of the Indus to Assam: Pakistan; northern India; Bangladesh.

Fl.: 1949

Sex: ♂ is thinner and more intensely colored. During the spawning season ♀ is fuller bodied.

Soc. B.: Should be kept in a school since individuals become pale and unusually timid. A very peaceful species, it can be kept with *Brachydanio sp.*

M: Similar to recommendations for *Danio aequipinnatus*. but is more demanding in terms of water temperature.

B: Water temperature 74-77° F (24-25° C) with water values similar to those for *Brachydanio* sp. and *D. aequipinnatus*.

F: O; omnivorous; all types of live foods; vegetable; flakes.

S: Differs from all other *Danio* and *Brachydanio* species in the number of rays in its dorsal fin. With 18 or 19, *Danio devario* has the longer dorsal.

T: 59-79° F,   **L**: 6″, sexually mature from 2³/₄″,   **A**: 31″,   **R**: all,   **D**: 1.
15-26° C,   15 cm, sexually mature from 7 cm,   80 cm,

Danio aequipinnatus

Danio devario

Epalzeorhynchus kallopterus
Flying Fox

(BLEEKER, 1850)
Sub-Fam.: Garrinae

Syn.: *Barbus kallopterus*

Hab.: In flowing waters; northern India; Indonesia; Thailand; Sumatra; Borneo.

Fl.: 1935, Werner Ladiges, Hamburg, West Germany.

Sex: Unknown.

Soc. B.: Though otherwise peaceful it is a territorial species which will defend its space. Aggressiveness increases with age.

M: Fine gravel with hiding places among roots, rocks or plastic tubing. Tank should have dense, broad-leaved vegetation. Suggest soft, slightly-acid water, 5-8° dGH and pH 6.5. Weekly water changes of $^1/_4$ the tank volume will be good for the fishes.

B: Not yet accomplished in an aquarium.

F: O; live food; FD; algae, lettuce and oatmeal. The fish do not eat Thread Algae.

S: The species has an interesting "at rest" position, supporting itself on its pectoral fins. May rest on a broad-leaved plant or on the bottom. Readily accepts Planarian worms.

T: 75-79° F,   **L:** 6″,   **A:** 27″,   **R:** b (m),   **D:** 2.
24-26° C,   15 cm,   70 cm,

Crossocheilus siamensis
Siamese Flying Fox, Siamese Algae Eater

(SMITH, 1931)
Sub-Fam.: Garrinae

Syn.: *Epalzeorhynchus siamensis*

Hab.: Southeast Asia; Thailand; Malayan penninsula.

Fl.: 1962, Andreas Werner, Munich, West Germany.

Sex: Unknown.

Soc. B.: Peaceful toward other species, it sometimes fights with its own. Can be kept in a community tank.

M: Fine gravel and thick, patchy vegetation. Suggest warm, soft, slightly-acid water 5° dGH and pH 6.5 though a hardness to 20° dGH and acidity to pH 8.0 can be tolerated. Requires welloxygenated water.

B: Not yet accomplished in an aquarium.

F: H; all types of live foods – even Planarian Worms; algae – including Thread Algae; lettuce; flakes. Does not eat plants.

S: The fins are transparent, unlike those of *Epalzeorhynchus kallopterus*. Has a single pair of barbels on the upper lip while *E. kallopterus* has two. The species is considered the best algaeeater in an aquarium. It was originally recognized as such by Dr. Baensch and popularized to hobbyists around the world. Despite its relatively unattractive appearance it can now be found in nearly every pet store.

The genus *Crossocheilus* differs from *Epalzeorhynchus* by rhynal lobes (nasal lobes).

T: 75-79° F,   **L:** $5^1/_2$″,   **A:** 31″,   **R:** b (m),   **D:** 1.
24-26° C,   14 cm,   80 cm,

Epalzeorhynchus kallopterus

Crossocheilus siamensis

Tylognathus caudimaculatus

FOWLER, 1934
Sub-Fam.: Cyprininae

Syn.: None

Hab.: Northern Thailand.

Fl.: Possibly 1950.

Sex: Unknown.

Soc. B.: Sometimes a schooling fish and sometimes a loner, it is always a peaceful fish. Recommended for a community tank but water temperature is important. Its natural biotype includes cooler mountain streams.

M: Needs a long tank with good filtration and water rich in oxygen, a neutral pH and a hardness to 12° dGH.

B: Unknown.

F: H, O; flakes, tablets, algae and live foods.

The correct scientific name of this species is *Epalzeorhynchus stigmaeus* SMITH, 1945.

T: 64-72° F, **L:** 5″, **A:** 31″, **R:** b, **D:** 2.
  18-22° C, 12.5 cm, 80 cm,

Gobio gobio
Gudgeon

(LINNAEUS, 1758)
Sub-Fam.: Gobioninae

Syn.: *Cyprinus gobio, Gobio fluviatilis, G. venatus*

Hab.: Throughout much of Europe to the Urals. It is not found in Spain, Italy (except for the north), Greece, Norway, northern Sweden, Finland or Scotland.

Fl.: A native European species.

Sex: With the exception of breeding spots found on ♂ during the spawning season, the sexes are difficult to distinguish.

Soc. B.: A peaceful, agile, schooling species, the Gudgeon will readily mix with the Minnow (*Phoxinus phoxinus*) and Loaches (*Noemacheilus barbatulus* and *Cobitis taenia*).

M: Gravel bottom with hiding places such as rocks or sections of plastic pipe. Use a filter which produces definite currents.

The water should be clean and clear since this is a cold-water species. Use slightly alkaline water of minimum hardness, pH 7.0-7.5 and 10-20° dGH.

B: Though the species has been occasionally bred in an aquarium, success seems mostly a matter of luck. Details are lacking.

F: C, O; all types of live foods – *Tubifex* worms, sand and water fleas and mosquito larvae; FD; flakes; tablets.

S: It is a food fish in many countries and considered a delicacy in France.

T: 50-64° F, (coldwater fish) **L:** 8″, **A:** 31″, **R:** b, **D:** 2.
  10-18° C, 20 cm, 80 cm,

Tylognathus caudimaculatus

Gobio gobio

Epalzeorhynchus bicolor
Red-Tailed Black Shark, Red-Tailed Labeo

(SMITH, 1931)
Sub-Fam.: Garrinae

Syn.: *Labeo bicolor*

Hab.: Thailand; esp. central Thailand – Menam Chao Phya basin and the Paknampo region.

Fl.: 1952, "Aquarium Hamburg", Hamburg, West Germany.

Sex: The shape of the dorsal is said to be an unmistakable feature; it runs to a point on the ♂ while the rear edge forms a right angle on the ♀. ♀ is also less brightly colored and more powerful.

Soc. B.: A loner, the species is territorial and intolerant of its own species though sometimes more accepting of unrelated tankmates. Larger fish may terrorize a tank, even to the point of becoming tyrants and thus recieve a reserved recommendation as a choice for any community tank.

M: Requires a large tank with a fine gravel bottom. Needs hiding places among roots and rocks. Though there should be swimming room the tank should be planted so the fish can stake-out territories without visual contact with neighbors. Use soft to medium hard neutral water (to 15° dGH and pH 7.0).

B: Because of an aggressive attitude toward its own species it is difficult to breed. Success is infrequent.

F: C, O; all types of live foods; flakes; FD; algae, spinach and lettuce.

S: DEAKIN & MORRILL report success in breeding. Soft water was acidified with peat and kept at temperatures between 79-82° F (27-28° C). Spawning took place in a rocky hollow and the fry hatched after two days. They were free-swimming after two more. Their coloring proceeds from a silvery brown to brown to black. The tail fin becomes red after the seventh week.

T: 72-79° F, L: 4³/₄″, A: 31″, R: b+m, D: 2.
    22-26° C, 12 cm, 80 cm,

Epalzeorhynchus frenatus
Ruby Shark, Red-Fin Shark

(FOWLER, 1934)
Sub-Fam.: Garrinae

Syn.: *Labeo erythrurus* (FOWLER, 1937), *L. frenatus*

Hab.: Northern Thailand.

Fl.: 1953

Sex: ♂ is thinner with a distinctive black-lined anal fin.

Soc. B.: Similar to *E. bicolor.*

M: Similar to *E. bicolor.*

B: Though the species has been bred in an aquarium, success is rare.

F: live foods; FD; flakes; algae and lettuce.

T: 72-79° F, L: 6″, A: 31″, R: b+m, D: 2.
    22-26° C, 15 cm, 80 cm,

Epalzeorhynchus bicolor

Epalzeorhynchus frenatus

Leucaspius delineatus

(HECKEL, 1843)
Sub-Fam.: Abraminae

Syn.: *Squalius delineatus, Aspius owsianka, Leucaspius abruptus, L. relictus*

Hab.: Much of Europe and western Asia; from the Rhine to the Caspian Sea though it is not found in Ireland, England, Scandinavia (except southern Sweden), France, Italy and parts of Yugoslavia and Greece. The fish is found in the Danube.

Fl.: A native European species.

Sex: ♂ is thinner-bodied.

Soc. B: Active, peaceful species; ♂ protects the brood.

M: Should be kept in schools in a long tank with a bottom of fine gravel. Plant hardy, cold-water vegetation in clumps on the sides and back, leaving swimming room in the center. Medium-hard, neutral

water (about 15° dGH and pH 7.0) should be especially well aerated at higher temperatures.

B: Water temperature 64-68° F (18-20° C). Place three or four pairs in a tank with reeds. The eggs will be laid in rings around the stalks. ♂ covers the eggs with an antibacterial secretion, looks after the spawn, guarding the eggs, oxygenating them with fresh water by knocking his body against the stalk.

F: O; live foods and flakes.

S: Artificial Mother of Pearl was formerly made from the scales of *Leucaspius delineatus*. Coating the inside of glass balls, the result was very close to the real thing.

T: 50-68° F (not over 72° F),   **L:** 3¹/₂″,   **A:** 24″,   **R:** m+t, **D:** 1-2.
  10-20° C (22° C),   9 cm,   60 cm,

Leuciscus idus
Orfe

(LINNAEUS, 1758)
Sub-Fam.: Leuciscinae

Syn.: *Cyprinus idus, Idus idus, I. melanotus*

Hab.: Throughout most of Europe from the Rhine to the Urals. Is not found in Britain, Ireland, Norway, France, the Danube or Switzerland south of the Alps.

Fl.: A native European species.

Sex: ♂ has breeding spots and during the spawning season ♀ is heavier-bodied.

M: Needs a long aquarium with a fine gravel bottom. Water values similar to those for *Cyprinus carpio*. Needs weekly water changes. Grows very slowly in an aquarium.

B: Difficult in a normal aquarium since the sexually mature fish are very large. In natural habitat the spawning season is from April through July.

F: C, O; all types of live foods; FD; flakes. Larger fish are predators.

S: A golden-white, red-finned variety, the Golden Orfe, is hardy and better suited to garden ponds than goldfish.

T: 39-68° F,   **L:** 31″,   **A:** 39″,   **R:** m+t, **D:** 1-2.
  4-20° C,   80 cm,   100 cm,

Leucaspius delineatus

Leuciscus idus (Golden Orfe)

Luciosoma trinema

Syn.: *Leuciscus trinema, Trinematichthys trinema*

Hab.: Southeast Asia.

Fl.: 1969

Sex: ♂ is generally larger with extended pelvic fin rays. Several writers doubt the long, thread-like pelvics are a distinguishing feature.

Soc. B.: A lively, attractive, schooling species.

M: Since the fish are jumpers they need a long tank, not too deep, but with a good cover. Planting should be limited to the back and sides with water values similar to those for *Epalzeorhynchus kallopterus.*

B: Details of aquarium breedings are sketchy.

F: O; omnivorous; lettuce; beef heart; liver; squid; mealworms; *Tubifex* worms; fish; flakes; tablets.

S: The name *Luciosoma* means "pike body" and refers to the pikelike shape of the species.

T: 75-81° F, **L**: 12″, **A**: 39″, **R**: m+t, **D**: 2.
  24-27° C, 30 cm, 100 cm,

Labeo chrysophekadion*
Black Labeo, Black Shark

Syn.: *Rohita chrysophekadion, Morulius chrysophekadion, Morulius dinema, M. erythrostictus, M. pectoralis*

Hab.: Southeast Asia; Thailand; Cambodia; Laos; Java; Borneo; Sumatra.

Fl.: 1932

Sex: Unknown.

Soc. B.: A loner, it is very intolerant of its species but less aggressive toward others. More peaceful than *Epalzeorhynchus bicolor.*

M: Similar to *E. bicolor* and not recommended for a community tank because of its size and aggressiveness.

B: Not successful.

F: O; omnivorous; live food; algae, lettuce and spinach; flakes; tablets.

S: It is an important food fish and is regarded as a delicacy in its home countries.

* This species now belongs to the genus *Labeo.*

T: 75-81° F, **L**: 23$^1/_2$″, **A**: 31-48″, **R**: b+m, **D**: 2.
  24-27° C, 60 cm, 100-120 cm,

Luciosoma trinema

Labeo chrysophekadion

Notropis lutrensis
Shiner

Syn.: *Leuciscus lutrensis, Cliola billing-siana, C. forbesi, C. gibbosa, C. iris, C. jugalis, C. lutrensis, C. montiregis, C. suavis, Cyprinella bubelina, C. billingsiana, C. complanata, C. forbesi, C. suavis, Hylsi-lepis iris, Moniana couchi, M. gibbosa, M. jugalis, M. leonina, M. laetabilis, M. pul-chella, M. rutila*

Hab.: North America: the midwestern United States from Illinois and Kansas and the Rio Grande.

Fl.: 1935, W. Schreitmueller, Frankfurt, West Germany.

Sex: ♂ is more brightly colored. will have breeding spots and has a black tip on the dorsal. During the spawning season ♀ is fatter and less brightly colored.

Soc. B.: An active but undemanding schooling species.

(BAIRD & GIRARD, 1853)
Sub-Fam.: Leuciscinae

M: Needs a long tank with swimming room and clear, fresh water. Requires frequent water changes and good aeration. Hardy, coldwater plants should be grouped around the edges of the tank. Water should have a hardness value from me-dium to hard (10-20° dGH) and a pH neutral to slightly alkaline (7.0-7.5).

B: There are no reports of successful breeding in an aquarium.

F: O; omnivorous; all types of live foods; vegetable; FD; frozen foods; flakes; ta-blets.

S: The species may have been imported to Germany in 1908 by Paul Matte. In its natural habitat the fish spawns in May. The water should be cooler in winter to keep their resistence high.

T: 60-77° F, (Cold water fish) **L:** 3$^1/_4$", **A:** 23$^1/_2$", **R:** m+t, **D:** 1.
      15-25° C,   8 cm,   60 cm,

Osteochilus hasselti

Syn.: *Rohita hasselti*

Hab.: Southeast Asia: Thailand; Malayan penninsula; Java; Borneo: Sumatra; and many of the Sunda islands.

Fl.: 1931

Sex: Unknown. ♀ is probably fatter.

Soc. B.: An active, peaceful, schooling fish. Only the young are recommended for a home aquarium.

M: Suggest a dark, fine, clean gravel which will not cloud the water since the fish is a bottom feeder and likes to burrow, espe-cially when searching for food. Plants should be dense around the edges and back with hiding places among roots, rocks and other decorations. Water values should be similar to those suggested for *Epalzeorhynchus kallopterus.*

(VALENCIENNES, 1842)
Sub-Fam.: Cyprininae

B: Nothing is known about breeding in a home aquarium since sexually mature fis-hes are probably too large for a normal tank.

F: O; omnivorous; mostly flakes and live foods but will also accept lettuce and spinach.

S: Adults are too large for home aquariums and are mostly seen in public aquariums.

T: 72-77° F, **L:** 12", **A:** 39", **R:** b+m, **D:** 2.
      22-25° C,   32 cm,   100 cm,

Notropis lutrensis

Osteochilus hasselti

Phoxinus phoxinus
Minnow

(LINNAEUS, 1758)
Sub-Fam.: Leuciscinae

Syn.: *Cyprinus phoxinus, Leuciscus phoxinus, Phoxinus aphya, Phoxinus laevis*

Hab.: At altitudes of 6500 ft. (2000 m) in clear, oxygen-rich, fast-flowing waters throughout Europe and Asia; from northern Spain and northern Italy to the Amur though not in the other areas of Spain, Portugal, Scotland, central and south Italy and the Peloponnesus.

Fl.: A native European species.

Sex: Sometimes difficult to determine. ♂ is brightly colored during the spawning season while, at the same time, ♀ are fatter.

Soc. B.: A lively and peaceful fish which prefers the surface and likes to school. Can be combined with other cold water fish such as *Gobio gobio, Noemacheilus barbatulus* and *Cobitis taenia.* Is not a burrower.

M: Keep in a long aquarium with coarse, medium-colored gravel with a few stones and roots. Keep planting to the back and sides, allowing lots of swimming room in the center. Use fresh water with good aeration and values suggested for *Gobio gobio.*

B: Not difficult to breed. Water should be 61-68° F (16-20° C), crystal clear with a fine gravel bottom and a few stones added. The water should be shallow, about 6 inches (15 cm.). Use several breeding pairs. The fish will spawn on the stones and should be removed after spawning. The fry will hatch in about six days and should be fed powdered foods. They grow slowly and become sexually mature in three or four years.

F: C; live foods such as *Tubifex,* small crustaceans, Enchytraea and, only after acclimitzation, flake foods.

S: Breeding spots may be seen on both sexes. Minnows have excellent senses of smell and hearing and are able to distinguish differences in sounds as readily as humans. In many areas they are a food fish and may be processed salted, canned or pickled.

T: 54-68° F (Cold water fish),   **L:** 5″,   **A:** 27″,   **R:** m+t, **D:** 2.
   12-20° C,   14 cm,   70 cm,

Rasbora borapetensis
Red-Tailed Rasbora

SMITH, 1934
Sub-Fam.: Rasborinae

Syn.: None

Hab.: Southeast Asia; Thailand; western Malaysia near Kuala Trengganu.

Fl.: 1954

Sex: Few differences except that ♂ is thinner.

Soc. B.: A peaceful, schooling fish which should be kept with other *Rasbora* species or with *Brachydanio* and small *Barbus* sp.

M: The tank should have dense vegetation with an open swimming area. Avoid strong sunlight and use floating plants to diffuse the overhead light. Add roots for decoration. Water should be slightly acid with a hardness soft to medium: pH 6.5 and to 12° dGH.

B: 77-79° F (25-26° C); keep water level in breeding tank low (15 cm) and add floating plants to diffuse the light. Water not too hard (up to 10° dGH) and slightly acid to neutral (pH 6.5-7.0); add fresh water. The

fishes begin spawning a few days after showing an interest in pairing. The act is preceded by a vigorous courtship. The ♂ winds himself around the female and half a dozen eggs are laid. The species is not very productive so that there will be no more than 30 to 40 in all. Both sexes, though particularly the male, are avid spawn-eaters. They should be well fed during spawning then promptly removed. The fry hatch after 36 hours.

F: C, O; live foods such as small crustaceans, mosquito larvae and *Tubifex* worms; flakes.

S: *Rasbora borapetensis* is one of the few horizontally-striped fishes of the genus with an incomplete lateral line.

T: 72-79° F, **L:** 2″, **A:** 20″, **R:** m+t, **D:** 2.
  22-26° C, 5 cm, 50 cm,

Rasbora dorsiocellata dorsiocellata
Hi-Spot Rasbora

DUNCKER, 1904
Sub-Fam.: Rasborinae

Syn.: None

Hab.: In standing and running waters of southeast Asia; Malayan penninsula and Sumatra.

Fl.: 1935, W. Schreitmueller over Paris, France.

Sex: ♂ has a reddish caudal fin and a straight ventral line; ♀ has a yellow-tinted caudal and a curved ventral line.

Soc. B.: An active, peaceful, undemanding fish. Prefers to live in schools.

M: Conditions similar to those for *Rasbora heteromorpha*; needs a tank with lots of swimming room.

B: Low water level at temperatures between 72 and 74° F (22-24° C). Decorate the tank as suggested for *Barbus conchonius* or *Brachydanio* sp. Allow ♀ to spend one or two days alone in the breeding tank then introduce the male the evening prior to spawning. A vigorous courtship will take place followed by spawning in a thicket of plants. The parents are spawn-eaters and should be promptly removed. The fry will hatch in 24 hours.

F: O; omnivorous.

S: Two sub-species are known: *R. dorsiocellata dorsiocellata*, DUNCKER, 1904, which is identical with the fish described above, and *R. dorsiocellata macrophthalma*, MEINKEN, 1951. The latter grows only to 1 $1/2''$ (3.5 cm.).

T: 68-77° F,   **L:** $2^1/_2''$,   **A:** 27'',   **R:** m,   **D:** 1-2.
    20-25° C,   6.5 cm,   70 cm,

Rasbora elegans elegans
Elegant Rasbora, Two-Spot Rasbora

VOLZ, 1903
Sub-Fam.: Rasborinae

Syn.: *Rasbora lateristriata* var. *elegans*

Hab.: In standing and running waters of southeast Asia; western Malaysia; Singapore; Sumatra; Borneo.

Fl.: 1909, Vereinigte Zierfischzuechtereien, Conradshoehe, West Germany.

Sex: During spawning ♀ has paler coloring and a larger body.

Soc. B.: A peaceful, school species which can be kept with other *Rasbora sp.*

M: Needs a well-established, densely-planted tank with a dark gravel bottom and room for swimming. Decorate with roots. Water hardness to 10° dGH and pH between 6.0- 6.5. Change $1/_4$ of the water twice a month.

B: A highly productive species. Similar to recommendations for *Rasbora dorsiocellata* but do not use young fish for breeding.

F: O; omnivorous; live food; flakes with vegetable added. A voracious eater

S: There are four sub-species: *R. elegans elegans*, VOLZ 1903; *R. elegans nematotaenia*, HUBBS & BRITTAN, 1954 (Moesi River, southeastern Sumatra); *R. elegans bunguranensis*, BRITTAN, 1951 (Bunguran Island); and, *R. elegans spilotaenia*, HUBBS & BRITTAN, 1954 (Sumatra).

T: 72-77° F,   **L:** $7^3/_4''$,   **A:** 31-39'',   **R:** m,   **D:** 2.
    22-25° C,   20 cm,   80-100 cm,

Rasbora dorsiocellata dorsiocellata

Rasbora elegans elegans

Rasbora espei
Espes Rasbora

Syn.: *Rasbora heteromorpha espei*

Hab.: Thailand.

FI.: 1967, Heinrich Espe, Bremen, West Germany.

Sex: ♂ thinner and more intensely colored; ♀ has a higher body and fuller stomach.

Soc. B.: A peaceful, agile species, it schools by day and sleeps alone, lightly supported by a leaf. Suggest keeping it with *Rasbora maculata*.

M: Dark gravel bottom with dense vegetation along the edges of the tank. Use floating plants to reduce the light and decorate with bogwood roots. Water hardness to 12° dGH and pH 6.0-6.5. The species is sensitive to water conditions.

B: Similar to conditions suggested for *Rasbora heteromorpha* though less productive.

F: C, O; omnivorous; flakes and small live foods. *Daphnia* are too large for the small mouthes of this species.

S: MEINKEN describes an interesting schooling behavior he calls "sentry posting". When the school pauses some fish look outward to keep an eye on the surroundings. If they turn to flee the entire school follows.

This species is often mixed up with *R. hengeli* but that species is smaller and originates from Sumutra.

T: 73-82° F, **L:** 1³/₄″, **A:** 20″, **R:** m+t, **D:** 2.
23-28° C, 4.5 cm, 50 cm,

Rasbora heteromorpha
Harlequin, Red Rasbora

Syn.: None

Hab.: Southeast Asia; western Malaysia; Singapore; parts of Sumatra; southeast Thailand.

FI; 1906, Julius Reichelt, Berlin, West Germany.

Sex: The fish can be distinguished by the shape of their markings; The leading edge is straight in ♀ and slightly rounded at the bottom with the tip extended on ♂. ♂ is also thinner.

Soc. B.: A lively, peaceful fish which can be combined with *Rasbora espei, R. maculata* and *R. vaterifloris*.

M: Needs a densely planted tank with a dark gravel bottom and plenty of hiding places. Use floating plants to reduce the light. Keep the fish in a school of not less than eight.
Water values are similar to those suggested for *Rasbora espei*.

B: Difficult. Use very soft, acid water (about 2° dGH and pH 5.3-5.7) at temperatures between 77 and 80° F (25-28° C). Keep the water low (6-8″ = 15-20 cm) and use peat filtration. Prepare the breeding water one month prior to breeding. Add several broadleaved plants such as Cryptocorynes and choose a sunny place for the tank. Place one young female and one two-year old male in the tank. ♂ dances prior to spawning which takes place on the underside of leaves, the partners swimming upside down. Remove the parents and darken the tank with paper. The fry hatch after 24 hours and can be fed such small live foods as Rotatoria.

F: O; all types of live foods; flakes; FD. The fish are demanding eaters.

S: Breeding failures are generally due to the use of an older female. Older females are not recommended.

T: 72-77° F, **L:** 1³/₄″, **A:** 20″, **R:** m (t), **D:** 2-3.
22-25° C, 4.5 cm, 50 cm,

Rasbora espei

Rasbora heteromorpha

Rasbora kalochroma
Clown Rasbora

(BLEEKER, 1850)
Sub-Fam.: Rasborinae

Syn.: *Leuciscus kalochroma*

Hab.: Southeast Asia; western Malaysia; Sumatra; Borneo; Bangku.

Fl.: 1965, Heinrich Espe, Bremen, West Germany.

Sex: ♂ is slender, more intensely colored and has a darker anal fin.

Soc. B.: A lively, peaceful fish not interested in schooling. According to MEINKEN each fish claims a small territory, ten to 12 inches (25-30 cm) square, which it defends against others.

M: A long tank with a dark gravel bottom, fine-leaved plants and plenty of open swimming space. Water to 10° dGH; add one teaspone tablesalt per 10 liters. Use subdued lighting with a few floating plants overhead.

B: Has probably not been bred in an aquarium.

F: O; omnivorous; all types of live food; FD; frozen food.

S: See *Rasbora maculata*.

T: 77-82° F, L: 4″,   A: 31$^1/_2$″, R: m,   D: 2.
   25-28° C,   10 cm,   80 cm,

Rasbora maculata
Dwarf Rasbora, Pygmy Rasbora, Spotted Rasbora

DUNCKER, 1904
Sub-Fam.: Rasborinae

Syn.: None

Hab.: In the slow moving waters, ponds, bogs and ditches of Southeast Asia; western Malaysia; Singapore; western Sumatra.

Fl.: 1905, Julius Reichelt, Berlin, West Germany.

Sex: ♂ slender, intensely colored with a smaller, straight ventral line. ♀ has a rounded ventral line.

Soc. B.: A peaceful, agile, schooling fish which may be kept with such *Rasbora* species as *Heteromorpha* group (*R. espei* and *R. heteromorpha*).

M: Similar to recommendations for *R. espei* and *R. heteromorpha* but because of its small size it is suggested only for certain community tanks.

B: Can be bred in even the smallest tank. Water temperatures from 75 to 82° F (24-28° C). Add a spawning grid on the bottom since the parents will eat their own eggs. Use soft water (2-3° dGH) slightly acid (pH 5.8 to 6.3) of shallow depth, about six inches (15 cm). Use dense vegetation. ♂ has a strong ritual display and spawning takes place among the plants. The species is not very productive, laying no more than 50 eggs. Breeding pairs should be well fed during spawning, then removed. The fry hatch after 24-36 hours and should be carefully raised. They are extremely small and need food commensurate with their size.

F: O; all types of small live food; flakes; FD.

S: *Rasbora maculata* is the smallest known Cyprinid or carp and one of the smallest known vertebrates (ranking about 10th). Has long been regarded as a juvenile form of *Rasbora kalochroma*.

T: 75-79° F, L: 1″,   A: 16″,   R: m,   D: 2-3.
   24-26° C,   2.5 cm,   40 cm,

Rasbora kalochroma

Rasbora maculata

437

Rasbora myersi
Silver Rasbora

Syn.: *Rasbora argyrotaenoides*

Hab.: Southeast Asia; Thailand; Malayan penninsula; southwestern and northern Borneo; Moesi river, Sumatra.

Fl.: Probably after 1970.

Sex: ♀ fuller bodied with a noticeably rounded ventral line.

Soc. B.: A peaceful, schooling species.

M: Similar to recommendations for *R. heteromorpha.*

B: Little is known of the process.

F: All kinds of live food; flakes; tablets.

S: The *Argyrotaenia* group includes five additional species: *R. argyrotaenia* (two sub-species), *R. dusonensis* (two sub-species), *R. philippina, R. tawarensis* and *R. leptosoma.*

T: 73-79° F, **L**: 4″, **A**: 31″, **R**: m+t, **D**: 1-2.
    23-26° C,   10 cm,   80 cm,

Rasbora pauciperforata
Red-Striped Rasbora

Syn.: *Rasbora leptosoma*

Hab.: Southeast Asia; western Malaysia; Sumatra; Belitung.

Fl.: 1928, Scholze & Poetzschke, Berlin, West Germany.

Sex: ♂ slender with a relatively straight ventral line. ♀ is heavier bodied with a sharply curved ventral line.

Soc. B.: A timid yet lively species, it may be combined with other active fishes.

M: Use a dark gravel bottom with vegetation and open swimming areas. Water should be soft and slightly acid, to 10° dGH and a pH of 5.8 to 6.5. Frequent partial water changes are important. The addition of peat is a plus.

B: Not easy since the fish are very selective about their partners. Try keeping a large school so that fishes desiring pairing can find each other. Use very soft water (2-3° dGH) slightly acid (pH about 6.0). Dense vegations is a help since the fish spawn between fine-leaved plants. Remove the parents after the eggs have been laid. The fry will hatch after 24-30 hours and can be fed very fine food.

F: O; all kinds of live foods – *Tubifex,* Enchytraea, mosquito larvae and small crustaceans; will accept flakes, soft algae, lettuce and spinach.

S: *Rasbora pauciperforata* is a typical *Rasbora* possessing a reduced lateral line and a dark flash along its side. The group includes *R. taeniata, R. chrysotaenia, R. borapetensis, R. urophthalma, R. beauforti* and *R. vegae* and apparently, *R. palustris* and *R. semilineata.*

T: 73-77° F, **L**: 3″, **A**: 27″, **R**: m+t, **D**: 2-3.
    23-25° C,   7 cm,   70 cm,

Rasbora myersi

Rasbora pauciperforata

Rasbora trilineata
Scissors-Tail, Scissor-Tailed Rasbora, Three-Lined Rasbora

STEINDACHNER, 1870
Sub-Fam.: Rasborinae

Syn.: *Rasbora calliura, R. stigmatura*

Hab.: In rivers and lakes of southeast Asia: western Malaysia; Sumatra; Borneo.

Fl.: 1932, "Aquarium Hamburg", West Germany.

Sex: With the exception of the fact that ♂ is smaller and slenderer but otherwise the sexes cannot be distinguished.

Soc. B.: A lively, peaceful, schooling fish less restless than many *Rasbora*.

M: Suggest a long tank with a dark bottom of fine gravel. Dense vegetation should be limited to the tank's edges with the center open for swimming. Water conditions as suggested for *Rasbora heteromorpha*.

B: Breeding is difficult. Keep the water between 77 and 82° F (25-28° C). Long

tanks have proven most effective with soft, slightly acid water (5-8° dGH and pH 6.0-6.5) six to eight inches deep (15-20 cm). Recommend plenty of vegetation with a dark gravel bottom. Spawning is preceded by an active courtship. The eggs are laid against the plants and the parents should be removed when spawning is completed. The fry hatch in 24 hours and after consuming the egg sac should be fed *Artemia* (brine shrimp) nauplii.

F: O; omnivorous; all kinds of live food; flakes; FD.

S: Eggs and fry are sensitive to attack from infusoria.

T: 73-77° F, **L**: 6″, **A**: 35″, **R**: m+t, **D**: 2.
    23-25° C, 15 cm, 90 cm,

Rasbora urophthalma brigittae

VOGT, 1978
Sub-Fam.: Rasborinae

Syn.: None

Hab.: Indonesia, Sumatra.

Fl.: 1913, Scholze & Poetzschke, Berlin, West Germany.

Sex: ♂ is smaller, thinner and intensly colored with a white patch at the base of the dorsal. Above it is a noticable black band. This and the patch are missing on the ♀.

Soc. B.: A very peaceful, lively fish which can be kept with others of a similar size. May become timid if kept with larger fish.

M: Use a fine gravel bottom with mulm and plenty of fine-leaved plants. Bogwood roots make excellent decoration. The water can have a hardness to 10° dGH except when spawning. Suggest peat filtration. Change 10 to 15% of the water weekly.

B: Use water at a temperature betwen 78 and 82° F (26-28° C). A 12 inch (30 cm) tank is adequate but it should be planted with *Ludwigia*, Cryptocorynes and similar plants. The spawning act is neither dramatic nor prolific. About 50 eggs are laid and these generally adhere to the underside of leaves. Be sure to remove the parents. The fry hatch in 48 hours. Water values are similar to those for *Rasbora maculata*. Feed the fry tiny micro foods, Tetra Baby Food and equivilent.

F: C, O; very small live food; flakes; algae.

S: The species is probably native to that part of Vietnam near Saigon.

T: 73-77° F, **L**: 1¹/₂″, **A**: 16″, **R**: m, **D**: 2-3.
    23-25° C, 3.5 cm, 40 cm,

Rasbora trilineata

Rasbora urophthalma brigittae

Rhodeus sericeus amarus
Bitterling

(BLOCH, 1782)
Sub-Fam.: Rhodeinae

Syn.: *Cyprinus amarus, Rhodeus amarus, R. sericeus*

Hab.: Europe and Western Asia; from northern and eastern France as well as from the Rhone to the Neva and the Black and Caspian Seas. It is not found south of the Alps and the Pyrenees nor in Scandinavia or the British Isles.

Fl.: A native species.

Sex: Clear sexual dichromatism; during the spawning season ♂ wears a beautifully colored wedding dress. ♀ is plain with less color, clearly recognized by its long ovipositor which is seen before the eggs are laid.

Soc. B.: A cheerful, peaceful fish ideal for a community tank. The species protects its spawn.

M: Tank should be well-planted with cold-water plants, should have a bottom of fine gravel and a layer of mulm. Keep the center open for swimming. The water is best medium-hard (10-15° dGH) and neutral or mildly alkaline (pH 7.0-7.5).

B: Keep the water at 69-70° F (20° C) with a bottom of clean, fine gravel. Place potted plants in the tank along with several Freshwater or Swan Mussels. The Mussels have a stimulating effect on the fish and are used during spawning. During the season ♀ grows an 1 1/2-inch ovipositor which is inserted into the breathing opening of the Mussel where it quickly lays an egg. ♂'s sperm is also passed through the Mussel's respiratory system to fertilize the egg which develops in the Mussel's gill cavity. The fry have a thickened area about the head which keeps them from being expelled with respiratory water but the thickening subsides in four weeks and the young fry are released.

F: O; live food; vegetable; flakes.

S: Bitterlings are easily identified by a bluish-green iridescent longitudinal band along the tail. The fish exhibits concerned brood-care.

T: 64-70° F,   **L:** 4",   **A:** 23",   **R:** b+m,   **D:** 2.
  18-21° C,   10 cm,   60 cm,

Rhodeus sericeus amarus ♀

Rhodeus sericeus amarus ♂

Rutilus rutilus
Roach

(LINNAEUS, 1758)
Sub-Fam.: Leuciscinae

Syn.: *Leuciscus rutilus, Gardonus rutilus*

Hab.: Europe and parts of Asia, from the Pyrenees eastward to the Urals and Siberia. The species is not found in Spain, south of the Alps, central and northern Norway, southern Sweden, Brittany nor in Scotland.

Fl.: A native species.

Sex: In the spawning season ♂ sports a rash. ♀ more powerful.

Soc. B.: A lively, peaceful species which can be kept with other cold water Cyprinids: *Leuciscus idus, Gobio gobio, Cyprinus carpio* or *Carassius carassius.*

M: The aquarium should be kept cool, even in summer. Use fine gravel on the bottom with cold-water plants and decorations of stones and reeds. The tank needs excellent filtration and aeration and one quarter of the water should be changed weekly. Recommended water values as for other European white fish.

B: Not recommended: the species needs a larger tank than is generally available. Breeding is easiest in garden ponds. The spawning period is in April and May.

F: O; omnivorous; live food; flakes; plants; detritus. Larger specimens will even eat smaller fishes.

S: Frequently confused with the Pearl Roach (*Scardinius erythrophthalmus)* but the two differ in the position of their pelvic fins. Those of the Roach are found at the beginning of the dorsal while those of the Pearl Roach begin before the dorsal.

T: 50-68° F, **L**: 16", **A**: 31-39", **R**: b+m, **D**: 1-2.
10-20° C, 40 cm, 80-100 cm,

Scardinius erythrophthalmus
Pearl Roach

(LINNAEUS, 1758)
Sub-Fam.: Leuciscinae

Syn.: *Cyprinus erythrophthalmus, Leuciscus erythrophthalmus, L. scardafa*

Hab.: In streams and standing waters of Europe and Asia to Lake Aral. The species is not found in Spain, Sicily, the Peloponnesus, large areas of Norway, northern and central Sweden, Scotland or the Crimea.

Fl.: A native species.

Sex: ♂ has noticeable breeding spots during the spawning season but otherwise the sexes are difficult to distinguish.

Soc. B.: A peaceful, schooling species which should be kept with fishes of similar habits. (Examples: *Rutilus rutilus* and *Leuciscus idus.*)

M: Similar to *Rutilus rutilus.*

B: Can be bred in a large tank but not in ordinary aquariums. The fish spawn from April to June and lay 100,000 or more eggs.

F: O; an omnivorous but prefers a vegetable diet.

S: Has a sharp-edged keel on its stomach, between the pelvic and anal fins.

T: 50-68° F (Cold water fish), **L**: 16", **A**: 31", **R**: b+m, **D**: 1-2.
10-20° C, 40 cm, 80 cm,

Rutilus rutilus

Scardinius erythrophthalmus

Tanichthys albonubes
White Cloud Mountain Minnow

LIN SHU-YEN, 1932
Sub-Fam.: Rasborinae

Syn.: None

Hab.: In streams of the White Cloud Mountain in south China near Canton.

Fl.: 1938, "Aquarium Hamburg", Hamburg, West Germany.

Sex: ♂ is thinner and more intensely colored.

Soc. B.: An undemanding, agile, peaceful fish.

M: Use plenty of vegetation with a dark, fine-gravel bottom. The center should be open for swimming. Keep the fish in schools since it becomes timid and pale when alone. It is undemanding about water quality but cannot tolerate much heat.

B: Can be bred if you pay close attention to water temperatures between 68 and 72° F (20-22° C). A 10″ x 8″ x 6″ (25 x 20 x 15 cm) tank with plenty of vegetation is adequate for breeding. Introduce only a single pair. The male has a vigorous courtship ritual and the couple will spawn on the plants. The parents should be removed. The fry hatch after 36 hours and grow rapidly. They should be fed fine micro-food.

F: O; omnivorous; flakes and most other foods.

S: You may see spectacular differences in breeding habits of the females. Some rarely spawn but lay up to 300 eggs when they do while others are more often interested but unproductive. Aquarium-bred species may exhibit differences in fin colors.

T: 64-72° F,   **L:** 1¹/₂″,   **A:** 16″,   **R:** all, but prefers the top,   **D:** 1.
18-22° C,   4 cm,   40 cm,

The photo at the top right and the smaller photo beside it show different colors of *T. albonubes*. The photo at the bottom shows the spectacular veiled breed.

Tanichthys albonubes

Tanichthys albonubes, veiled breed

Gyrinocheilus aymonieri
Indian Algae-Eater, Sucking Loach

(TIRANT, 1883)
Sub-Fam.: Gyrinocheilinae

Syn.: *Psilorhynchus aymonieri, Gyrinocheilus kaznakovi, G. kaznakoi, Gyrinocheilops kaznakoi*

Hab.: Northern India; central Thailand.

Fl.: 1956, A. Werner, Munich, West Germany.

Sex: Little is known. Sexually mature fish have multiple "thorns" around the mouth. The thorns are more numerous and more pronounced on the male.

Soc. B.: A territorial fish, it defends its space. The young can be kept with other species, but adults will harass their tankmates and should be kept alone.

M: Generally kept only for their ability to clean a tank, the fish can handle a variety of water conditions. The species prefers hiding places and are suited to smaller community tanks.

B: Has not yet been bred in an aquarium and the courting ritual has not been observed in the wild.

F: H; prefers an algae diet but will eat flake and live foods occasionally.

S: The fish will stop eating algae if the temperature drops below 69° F (20° C).

T: 77-82° F,   **L:** 11″ (Capable of reproduction from 4³/₄″),   **A:** 24-31″,   **R:** all but mainly b.,   **D:** 2.
    25-28° C,   27 cm (12 cm),   60-80 cm,

Homaloptera zollingeri

BLEEKER, 1853
Sub-Fam.: Homalopterinae

Syn.: *Homaloptera maxinae*

Hab.: In fast-flowing, rocky mountain streams of southeast Asia; Java; Sumatra; one specimen was reported from Thailand.

Fl.: Unknown.

Sex: Unknown.

Soc. B.: A very peaceful, restful, bottom-loving species that is possibly territorial.

M: Similar to recommendations for *Noemacheilus* sp. Does best with a definite "current" in the tank.

B: Has not been accomplished in an aquarium and there are no reports of observations in the wild.

F: L; H; prefers algae and live foods; accepts flakes and FD reluctantly.

S: The species are seldom available from pet stores and when found are classified as Algae-eaters. The underside of the body is either flat or slightly concave and when coupled with the pectoral and pelvic fins, which grow into each other, an effective suction is created which can help the fish stay in place in the strong currents of their home waters. The fish often eat blue algae and if these have absorbed medications they may kill the fish. It is suggested that you remove all algae before treating a tank.

T: 72-75° F, **L:** 4″, **A:** 31″, **R:** b, **D:** 3-4.
22-24° C, 10 cm, 80 cm,

Group 4

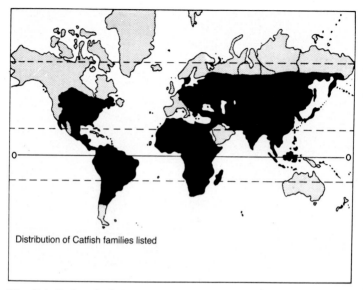

Distribution of Catfish families listed

The Sub-Order: Catfishes and allied species (Siluroidei)

There are almost as many catfish and related fishes as there are Characins, quite probably more than one thousand. Over 400 belong to the genus Loricariidae or armoured catfishes.

Representatves can be found around the world though we have listed and illustrated only those of interest to hobbyists. You'll find all of the well known species here.

Catfish belong to a large family of Carp-like fishes and can be readily recognized by one or more pairs of barbels. Common with Characins and Carp-like fish these have a "Weber's apparatus" (see page 212). They differ from most other fishes in that they lack scales. Callichthyidae and Loricariidae are normally either scaleless or protected by armour or bony-plates. Some *Synodontis* have only armoured heads.

Just as their bony structures differ, so families of catfishes differ in the manner in which they accept food and like Characins they occupy nearly every ecological niche imaginable. You can find plant-eating catfish, omnivores and predators. There are even some who, according to legend, eat children!

Mystus vittatus.:See page 456 for description.

The gigantic *Manguruyu (Paulicea lutkeni)*, from the Amazon basin, is more than three meters long and has been held responsible for the disappearance of small children bathing in such rivers as the Rio Branco. In comparison, *Pangasianodon gigas* from Thailand, which reaches a similar size, is a serene and safe vegetarian. One of the smallest Catfishes is the Dwarf Corydoras which is less than an inch long (2.5 cm).

Catfish live predominantly in freshwater. Only a few saltwater species can be found and even those are believed to spawn in the brackish water of several estuaries.

Most catfish are surprisingly adaptable and many can tolerate oxygen-starved water. In addition to breathing through their gills, many can supply oxygen to their blood through an accessory respiratory system, expelling used air at the water's surface and compressing fresh into the swim bladder. If Catfish frequently surface to gasp air, it may be a sign the aquarium water is deficient. To confirm this, study the gill movements of their tank mates. It may be a signal the filter is blocked, unplugged or not working. Check the tank.

Most Catfish are highly specialized both in their habits and in the manner in which they take food. Some are nocturnal, spending the daylight hours hidden. During the day these fish find hidden hollows sized to fit them and their particular requirements are indicated in the individual descriptions. Nocturnal Catfishes must be fed in the evening. If not, they will fail to realize they are are being fed and may go hungry. The situation can be difficult to detect, especially with armoured fishes, since it is difficult to see a weight loss in these fishes. Generally you can only detect starvation by removing the fish and examining its softer under-belly. The fish are bottom feeders and devour all food which falls to the bottom. Some are industrious algae eaters.

To make it easier for you to choose from among the many possibilities, the table which follows contains all the important details needed to make a decision.

Family		Origin	Behaviour				Food		
			Peaceful	Predaceous	Active by day	Active at night	H	O	C
Aspredinidae	Banjo catfishes	SA	×			×			×
Bagridae	Naked Catfishes	Af/As		×		×		×	×
Callichthyidae	Armoured Catfish	SA	×		×			×	
Chacidae		As	O			×			×
Clariidae		Af/As		×		×		×	×
Doradidae	Thorny Catfishes	SA	×			×		×	×
Ictaluridae	Horned Pouts	CA/NA		×	×				×
Loricariidae	Armour-plated Catfish	SA	×			×	×	×	
Malapteruridae	Electric Catfishes	Af		×		×			×
Mochocidae	Naked Catfishes	Af	×			×		×	×
Pangasiidae		As		×	×			×	×
Pimelodidae	Flat-hosed Catfishes	SA		×		×		×	×
Schilbeidae	Glass Catfishes	Af/As	×		×			×	×
Siluridae	Old World Catfishes	Eu/As	×	O		×		×	×
Trichomycteridae		SA	O		×	×			×

Explanation of Symbols
O   = Special features, see species description
Af   = Africa
As   = Asia
Eu   = Europe
Ca   = Central America
NA = North America
SA = South America
H   = Herbivore
O   = Omnivore
C   = Carnivore

Dysichthys coracoideus

(COPE, 1878)
Sub-Fam.: Bunocephalinae

Syn.: *Bunocephalus bicolor, Bunocephalus coracoideus*

Hab.: Amazon, as far inland as the area around La Plata.

Fl.: 1907

Sex: Unknown.

Soc. B.: A peaceful species.

M: Needs a tank with a dark, preferably sandy, bottom and light vegetation. Good filtration is important. The fish is a burrower and makes few demands in terms of water quality. We suggest a pH 5.8-7.8 and a hardness between 2 and 20° dGH. The recommended water temperature varies with the region from which the fish comes.

B: It is possible the species spawns in groups. It is mature when it is 4¹/₂ inches (12 cm.) long. 4000-5000 eggs are laid on the sandy bottom, usually in more than one spawning. Plants may be inadvertently uprooted during spawning. Water in the aquarium can be as much as 12 inches (30 cm.) deep. The fry should be fed small live food such as Rotifers then, as they grow, *tubifex* worms. They will not accept flakes although moistened FD tablets are taken. They do not feed on *Daphnia*.

F: C: live food; FD tablets.

S: This is a fish for a connoisseur looking for something unusual.

T: 68-81° F, **L**: 5³/₄″,   **A**: 31″,   **R**: b, m, **D**: 3.
    20-27° C,   15 cm,   80 cm,

Leiocassis micropogon

BLEEKER, 1858
Sub-Fam.: Mystinae

Syn.: None

Hab.: Sumatra, Borneo.

Fl.: Unknown.

Sex: Unknown.

Soc. B.: Very territorial, it should be kept alone. The species is predatory and should not be kept with smaller fishes, those less than two inches (5 cm) long.

M: Needs a tank with several hiding places. It will not eat plants but since *L. micropogon* is a burrowing species, it may uproot some while digging hollows. Similar to the Upside-Down Catfish, this one rests on its back during the day.

B: Unknown.

F: C, O: all kinds of live foods; earthworms; FD after acclimitization.

S: When removed from the tank, or when defending its territory, the fish makes a grunting noise.

T: 64-82° F, L: 8″,   A: 39″,   R: b,   D: 2-3.
    18-28° C,   20 cm,   100 cm,

Mystus micracanthus

(BLEEKER, 1846)
Sub-Fam.: Bagrinae

Syn.: *Bagrus micracanthus, Hypselobagrus micracanthus*

Hab.: In rivers through out Sumatra.

Fl.: Unknown.

Sex: Not described.

Soc. B.: A gregarious fish well suited for a community tank. Do not place with fishes of too small a size.

M: An energetic bottom feeder, the fish consumes most detritus. Does best in a roomy tank with good filtration. Suggest water with a pH of 6.5-7.8 and a hardness to 20° dGH.

F: C, O: omnivorous; prefers live foods including fish.

S: Rarely imported.

T: 68-79° F, L: $5^3/_4"$, A: 39", R: b, D: 1.
20-26° C, 15 cm, 100 cm,

Mystus vittatus
Striped Catfish

(BLOCH, 1794)
Sub-Fam.: Bagrinae

Syn.: *Silurus vittatus, Mystus atrifasciatus*

Hab.: In flowing and standing waters of lower India; Burma.

Fl.: 1903, H. Stueve, Hamburg, West Germany.

Sex: Unknown.

Soc. B.: A peaceful catfish active during the day. It will chase younger fish but is suitable for a community tank with fish larger than three inches long. (8 cm.)

M: Does best in a large, shallow tank with plenty of plants and lots of places to hide. The bottom should be coarse, dark gravel with clear, sandy feeding places. Add

rocks and stones. A flowerpot or overturned shard serves as hiding place. Recommend water with a pH 6.0-7.5 and hardness 4-25° dGH.

B: The fish spawn at the bottom between roots and on plants. They have been bred successfully in an aquarium. The female sheds large, yellowish-white eggs after a lively courtship. "Tweeting" noises can be heard during the courting ritual.

F: C; live foods; all kinds of flakes; tablets.

S: A hardy, almost rough catfish which attracts friends through its cheerful, active attitudes. It is active during the day.

T: 72-82° F, L: 8", A: 39", R: b, D: 1-2.
22-28° C, 20 cm, 100 cm,

Parauchenoglanis macrostoma

(PELLEGRIN, 1909)
Sub-Fam.: Bagrinae

Syn.: *Auchenoglanis macrostoma*

Hab.: In the shallows and banks of the Niger Delta; Upper Volta.

Fl.: 1934

Sex: Unknown.

Soc. B.: A loner, the species is territorial. Not suited to a standard community tank, it can be kept with fishes to 3 inches (8 cm) in length.

M: Needs a large tank with fine sand and roots to provide hiding places. It is a burrower and we suggest using only Java Fern. The roots should be well secured.

The fish will not eat plants and you should use a cover of floating plants to reduce light in the tank.

B: Unknown.

F: C, O: live foods such as worms; flakes; FD; tablets. Food is best when taken from the bottom. The fish will burrow if food is found in the sand.

S: The fish is large and recommended only for large tanks. The hard rays of the pectorals and dorsal can be made rigid through special bones and for this reason the fish should be caught only with glass and transported so it cannot harm itself.

T: 73-81° F, L: 9", A: 39", R: b, D: 2.
23-27° C, 24 cm, 100 cm,

Mystus micracanthus

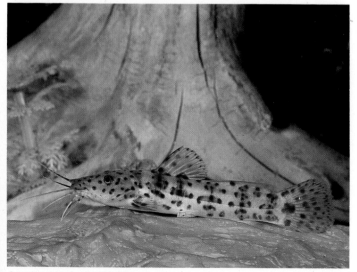

Parauchenoglanis macrostoma

Brochis splendens

Syn.: *Brochis coeruleus, Brochis dipterus, Callichthys splendens, Chaenothorax bicarinatus, C. semiscutatus*

Hab.: Upper Amazon near Iquitos; Brazil, Rio Tocantin; Peru, Rio Ambyiacu; Ecuador, Rio Napo.

Fl.: 1938, Muenchener Tierpark AG, Hellabrunn, West Germany.

Sex: Unknown

Soc. B.: A peaceful, schooling fish, this one can be combined with nearly everything.

M: The species is choosy about its water. Prefers a pH 5.8-8.0 and a hardness from 2-30° dGH. Prefers a dark bottom of gently rounded pea gravel. Sharp rocks will injure the barbels. Include places to hide, dense vegetation and alternating sandy, open places for burrowing. As with many catfishes, the species surfaces to breathe and for this reason the air temperature above the tank should not differ from that of the water.

(CASTELNAU, 1855)
Sub-Fam.: Corydoradinae

B: Breeding is difficult though the procedure is similar to other species in this subfamily. Suggest a pH 6.0-6.5 and a hardness to 4° dGH.

F: O; an enthusiatic bottom feeder. Suggest tablets; FD; live or freshly-killed foods.

S: The genus differs from *Brochis* by the number of rays on the dorsal. *Corydoras* has 6 to 8; *Brochis multiradiatus* has 17: *B. splendens* has 10 to 12. The genus *Brochis* has but three species. These do not have a different number of barbels as some writers have stated since both *Corydoras* and *Brochis* have six barbels each. Some *Corydoras* not imported may differ.

T: 72-82° F,   L: 2¹/₂″,   A: 27″,   R: b,   D: 1.
    22-28° C,   7 cm,   70 cm,

Callichthys callichthys
Armoured Catfish

Syn.: *Callichthys asper, C. coelatus, C. hemiphractus, C. laeviceps, C. loricatus, C. tamoata, Cataphractus callichthys, C. depressus, Silurus callichthys*

Hab.: Eastern Brazil; Peru; Bolivia; Paraguay; Guyana; Venezuela.

Fl.: 1897, Paul Matte, Berlin-Lankwitz, Germany.

Sex: Males have longer, more powerful pectoral rays and more color.

Soc. B.: A peaceful, schooling fish, it may consume smaller tank mates, those to one inch for example.

M: Needs a densely planted tank with hiding places behind roots and stones or in over-turned shards. The fish will hide during the day, coming alive only at night. It is hardy and adaptable. Suggest water with a pH 5.8-8.3 and a hardness of 0-30° dGH.

(LINNAEUS, 1758)
Sub-Fam.: Callichthyinae

B: The male builds a foam nest beneath the floating plants and defends it against all intruders. Up to 120 eggs are laid. The young should be fed hard boiled egg yolk, then brine shrimp and crushed flake foods.

F: O; omnivorous; Feed tablets in the evening just before switching the lights off. We suggest a small tablet, or one-half a larger one, for each fish. Live food is taken from the bottom.

S: A nocturnal species, it grows slowly. When protecting its brood it may make grunting noises. In nature, when the streams dry, the fish crawls across dry land on its strong ventrals. The genus is monotypical, consisting of only this secies.

T: 64-82° F,   L: to 6¹/₂″,   A: 31″,   R: b,   D: 1.
    18-28° C,   to 18 cm,   80 cm,

Brochis splendens

Callichthys callichthys

Corydoras acutus
COPE, 1872
Syn.: *C. stenocephalus*
Peru, Ampiyacu River.
L: to 2″, to 5.5 cm.

Corydoras aeneus
(GILL, 1858)
Bronze Corydoras
Syn.: *Hoplosternum aeneum, Callichthys aeneus, Corydoras macrosteus*
Trinidad; Venezuela to La Plata.
L: to 3″, to 7 cm.

Corydoras agassizii
(photo on page 469)
STEINDACHNER, 1877
Agassiz's Corydoras
Peru, near Iquitos.
L: to 3¹/₂″, to 6.5 cm.

Corydoras arcuatus
ELWIN, 1939
Arched Corydoras
Central Amazon, near Tefe.
L: to 2″, to 5 cm.

Corydoras armatus
(GUENTHER, 1868)
Syn.: *Callichthys armatus, Gastrodermus armatus*
Eastern Bolivia
L: 2″, 6 cm.

Corydoras axelrodi
ROESSEL, 1962
Columbia, Rio Meta.
L: to 2″, to 5 cm.

Corydoras barbatus
(QUOY & GAIMARD, 1824)
Banded Corydoras - Barbatus Catfish
Syn.: *Callichthys barbatus, Scleromystax barbatus, S. kronei, Corydoras eigenmanni, C. kronei*
Brazil, Rio de Janeiro to Sao Paulo.
L: about 4 1/2″, about 12 cm.

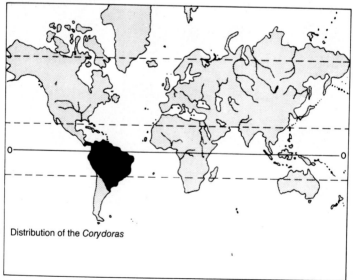

Distribution of the *Corydoras*

C. acutus

C. aeneus, also photo top page 463

C. blochi vittatus

C. arcuatus

C. armatus

C. axelrodi

C. barbatus ♀, photo ♂ see page 474

Corydoras blochi blochi
NIJSSEN, 1971

Guyana
L: to 2″, to 6 cm.

Corydoras blochi vittatus
(See photo on page 461)
NIJSSEN, 1971

Amazon, Rio Itapecuru
L: to 2″, to 6 cm.

Corydoras concolor
WEITZMAN, 1961

Western Venezuela
L: to 2″, to 6 cm.

Corydoras bondi bondi
GOSLINE, 1940

Surinam, Guyana
L: to 2″, to 5.5 cm.

Corydoras loxozonus
NIJSSEN & ISBRUECKER, 1983
Rio Ariari, Western Columbia
L: $1^{1}/_{4}$″ or 4 cm
In New York it is often marketed as *Corydoras "deckeri"*.

The Genus *Corydoras*

Dwarf Catfishes

While nearly 180 species are known to ichthyologists, only fifty are commercially available and more than ten are captive bred. Virtually every river in South America has its own species or sub-species of *Corydoras*. On a recent trip to the south along the Transamazonica, the author crossed more than 50 streams and rivers and caught many fish. On nearly every occasion nets included different species of *Corydoras*. Often two or three species were caught together and, on occasion, more. When observed by artificial light, the Catfishes were found just a few inches above the bottom, in calm, shallow waters. They were easily captured by casting a net over them. By day they could be seen swimming in the strongest current, in the very center of the stream. When fleeing capture they were as nimble as other, apparently more agile fishes. They always fled up-stream but quickly returned, sometimes in a few minutes, often in only seconds.

Corydoras aeneus

C. blochi blochi

C. bondi bondi

C. concolor

Corydoras loxozonus

Corydoras elegans
STEINDACHNER, 1877

Syn.: *Gastrodermus elegans*
Central Amazon
L: to 2″, to 6 cm.

Corydoras eques
STEINDACHNER, 1877
Syn.: *Osteogaster eques*
Central Amazon, Tefe
L: to 2″, to 5.5 cm.

Corydoras evelynae
ROESSEL, 1963

Tributaries of the Puru River.
L: 1¹/₂″, 4 cm.

Corydoras ellisae
GOSLINE, 1940

Paraguay: Sapucay, Arrayo Pona
L: to 2″, to 5.5 cm.

Corydoras garbei
v. IHERING, 1910

Brazil, Rio Xingu
L: to 1¹/₂″, to 4 cm.

These catfish always swim in schools, most often with several dozen of their species. Often they can be found in company with other species, depending on the depth of the water and the time of year. Generally three to six species may be found together, all searching for food in a closely-defined territory. The author was able to entice them with tablets and they came from some distance devouring the tablets directly beneath the net. They must have a great resistence to changing conditions. Once, during the expedition several thousand young *C. garbei* were caught in our net. Such catches are rewarding, especially for local exporters, since to catch a dozen rare catfish is normally a long and laborous project.

C. elegans

C. ellisae

C. eques

C. evelynae

C. garbei

Corydoras gracilis
NIJSSEN and ISBRUECKER, 1975

Transamazonica, tributary of Rio Madeira, near Itaituba.
L: to ³/₄″, to 2.5 cm.
S: A free floating catfish!

Corydoras griseus
HOLLY, 1940

Amazon: southern tributaries
L: to 1″, to 3 cm.

Corydoras habrosus
WEITZMAN, 1960

Venezuela, Rio Salinas
L: to 1″, to 3.5 cm.

Corydoras hastatus
EIGENMANN & EIGENMANN, 1888

Dwarf Corydoras, Pygmy Corydoras
Syn.: *Microcorydoras hastatus*
Brazil; Rio Guapore
L: to 1″, to 3 cm.
see also *C. pygmaeus*, page 472

Corydoras trilineatus
Three line armoured catfish

COPE, 1872

Hab.: South America: Peru, Rio Ampiyacu, Rio Ucayali and the Yarina Cocha.

Fl.: since 1950.

Sex: The ♀♀ grow larger and fatter. Their body pattern is usually paler and the spot on the dorsal fin smaller.

Soc. B.: A peaceful species, keep only in a small school. *Corydoras trilineatus* mix easily with small soft water species.

M: Densely planted tank with a clear sandy area for burrowing, preferrably in the foreground. Water: pH 5.8 to 7.2; 18° dGH up to maximum 10° dKH.

B: After frequent water changes with softest possible water (according to FRANKE catfish spawn also at 15° dGH

and pH 7), the ♂♂ float for several days before spawning in groups. Often only several single ♂♂ pair with several single ♀♀ while the rest of the group does not participate. The fry hatch at 23 to 24° C after four to five days. Unfortunately, many eggs die from fungus. It is however easy to raise newly hatched fry on rotifers, *Artemia nauplii* and the contents of fresh peas, and with frequent partial water changes. Prudence is recommended with micro food.

F: O; omnivorous: live foods such as mosquito larvae and Tubifex preferred.

S: Often mistaken for *C. Julii*, even though the two are easily distinguished (compare picture 2, page 466).

T: 12-26° C, **L:** 5 cm, **BL:** 60 cm, **WR:** u, **SG:** 2.

Species of *Corydoras* can be found throughout South America from Trinidad to Argentine. The greatest concentrations are found in the Amazon basin. The preferred conditions for all species is similar:
T: 72-79° F (22-26° C); **A:** 23″ (60 cm.); **R:** b, some also t+m; , **D:** 1-2.
We suggest water with a pH 6.0-8.0 and a hardness 2-25° dGH. Use a tank with a dark bottom of fine gravel or sand to protect their barbels. Armoured Catfish are ideal for every aquarist. They are active during the day, cheerfully keep the tank bottom clean and have unusual, articulated eyes.

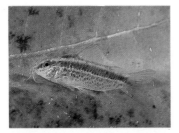

C. gracilis

C. griseus

C. habrosus

C. hastatus

C. trilineatus

photo page 472
Corydoras melanistius melanistius
REGAN, 1912

Black-Spotted Corydoras, Melanistus Catfish
Guyana
L: to 2", to 6 cm.

Corydoras melini
LOENNBERG and RENDAHL, 1930

Colombia
L: to 2", to 6 cm.

Corydoras metae
EIGENMANN, 1914

Colombia; in the Rio Meta and tributaries around Villa Vicente.
L: to 2", to 5.5 cm.

Corydoras rabauti
LA MONTE, 1941
See page 472 for text

The photo on the bottom left illustrates *C. "myersi"*. It can be distinguished from *C. rabauti* only by a diagonal black band which crosses the body and extends on to the head. This is insufficient evidence to create a separate species and the variant is listed here.

Breeding Dwarf Catfishes

Spawning methods vary with the species.
(a) *C. aeneus* lays eggs in small clusters on leaves while
(b) most species attach only two to four eggs per leaf, repeating the process for an hour or two until 100 or more eggs (up to 380 for some species) are deposited. In contrast, *C. hastatus* attaches a single egg to the aquarium glass.

With most species (b) the female holds two to four eggs between her pelvic fins while the male fertilizes them. The two fish are pressed stomach to stomach for 30 seconds, then the female swims to a selected leaf to attach the eggs to the underside. The fish normally spawn in the winter months which corresponds to the rainy season in their native country. Fish which have paired in a tank should be carefully transferred to a prepared breeding tank and fed mosquito larvae, other live foods and FD tablets.

C. agassizii, for text see page 460

C. melini

C. metae

C. rabauti (,,myersi'')

C. rabauti

Corydoras nattereri
(STEINDACHNER, 1877)

Eastern Brazil from Rio de Janeiro to Rio Doce, Rio Jaquia (Sao Paulo).
L: to 2¹/₂″ (6.5 cm)

Corydoras ornatus
NIJSSEN and ISBRUECKER, 1975

Tapajos tributary east of Jacareacanga, Brazil. Discovered by the author and H. Bleher in 1975 on the Transamazonica expedition.
L: to 2″ (5 cm)

Corydoras paleatus
(JENYNS, 1842)

Peppered Corydoras
Syn.: *Callichthys paleatus, Corydoras marmoratus*
La Plata, southeast Brazil.
L: 2³/₄ ″ (7 cm)
The pseudo-albino breed of this species is frequently found in the trade. (Photo bottom left.)

Corydoras punctatus
(BLOCH, 1794)

Syn.: *Cataphractus punctatus, Corydoras geoffroy*
Surinam, southern tributarties of the lower Amazon.
The first *Corydoras* described.
L: 2¹/₃″ (6 cm)

After spawning, the breeding pair should be removed or the eggs transferred to a glass tank. The water quality should be high, well aerated and treated to prevent fungus on the spawn.

Water values are not decisive since many species spawn in hard water. These, however, prefer values of 6.0-7.0 pH and 6° dGH. The best water temperature is around 75-79° F (24-26° C). Species which have been bred so far include: *C. aeneus, C. barbatus, C. hastatus, C. metae, C. nattereri, C. paleatus* and *C. rabauti*, and others.

C. nattereri

C. ornatus

C. paleatus

C. paleatus, Albino variety

C. punctatus

Corydoras pygmaeus
KNAAK, 1966

Pygmy Corydoras
Brazil: Rio Madeira and tributaries.
L: 1″ (2.5 cm)

Corydoras rabauti (Photo page 468)
LA MONTE, 1941

Rabaut's Corydoras, Dwarf Corydoras
Tabatinga, Brazil. Exported via Leticia and
Bogota, Colombia.
L: to 2 ¹/₂″ (6 cm)

Corydoras reticulatus
FRASER-BRUNNER, 1947

Iquitos, Peru.
L: to 2³/₄″ (7 cm)

Free swimming catfish of the central and
upper strata.
Flake food and finely textured live food
are preferred to tablet food.

Corydoras melanistius melanistius

Corydoras pygmaeus

Corydoras reticulatus

473

Corydoras schwartzi
ROESSEL, 1963

Eastern Brazil: tributary of Rio Purus.
L: to 2¹/₂″ (6.5 cm)

Corydoras sychri
WEITZMAN, 1960

South America
L: 1¹/₂″ (4.5 cm)

Corydoras nanus
NIJSSEN & ISBRUECKER, 1967

Surinam
L: to 2″ (5 cm)

Corydoras trilineatus
COPE, 1872
See page 467.

Iquitos, Peru; and such Amazon territories
as Ambiacu.
L: to 2³/₄″ (7 cm)

Corydoras septentrionalis
GOSLINE, 1940

Venezuela
L: to 2¹/₃″ (6 cm)

Corydoras barbatus ♂

C. schwartzi

C. sychri

C. nanus

C. reticulatus

C. septentrionalis

Dianema longibarbis

COPE, 1871
Sub-Fam.: Callichthyinae

Syn.: *Callichthys adspersus, Decapogon adspersus*

Hab.: Peru: Rio Ambyiac, Rio Pacaya.

Fl.: T. Dunker, date unknown.

Sex: ♀ is heavier-bodied before spawning.

Soc. B: A peaceful, schooling fish which may be kept as a species. Will not attack smaller fish except, perhaps, Vivipars fry.

M: A lively species, it needs plenty of daytime hiding areas beneath stones and roots or in thick bottom vegetation. Water values: pH 5.5-7.5 and can tolerate a hardness range of 2-20° dGH.

B: Has been bred very little. Builds a bubble nest as does *C. callichthys*. Reduce the water level, removing salt if necessary. Increasing temperatures to 82° F (28° C) should initiate breeding.

F: O; omnivorous; will not eat plants; offer food tablets in the evening before turning off the lights.

S: The species can be distinguished from the genus *Haplosternum* by its scales and the habit of swimming at the bottom of open water. The fish can "tread water", vibrating its pectoral, dorsal and anal fins.

T: 72-79° F,   **L**: 3¹/₂″,   **A**: 27″,   **R**: b, m, **D**: 1-2.
    22-26° C,   9 cm,   70 cm,

Dianema urostriata

RIBEIRO, 1912
Sub-Fam.: Callichthyinae

Syn.: *Decapogon urostriatum*

Hab.: Brazil: Rio Negro near Manaus.

Fl.: To the US in 1963; to Holland in 1972.

Sex: ♂ is clearly smaller and thinner.

Soc. B: A peaceful, schooling fish.

M: Dark, peat-brown water with few plants and plenty of roots and rocky hollows. pH 4.8-7.0 and hardness 2-10° dGH.

B: Successfully accomplished though not published.

F: C, O; omnivorous; prefers an animal diet; live foods; FD tablets in the evening.

S: Becomes active at dusk. Surfaces occasionally to gulp air.

T: 72-79° F,   **L**: 4¹/₂″,   **A**: 31″,   **R**: b, m, **D**: 2.
    22-26° C,   12 cm,   80 cm,

Dianema longibarbis

Dianema urostriata ♂

Hoplosternum thoracatum

(VALENCIENNES, 1840)
Sub-Fam.: Callichthyinae

Syn.: *Callichthys thoracatus, C. longifilis, C. personatus, C. exaratus, Hoplosternum thorae, H. longifilis, H. magdalenae*

Hab.: In shallow, muddy waters dense with vegetation. Schools of as many as one thousand may be found in waters close to habitation, especially in areas where waste water is deposited. Trinidad; Guyana; Martinique; Venezuela; Brazil; Peru; Paraguay.

Fl.: 1911, Vereinigte Zierfischzuechtereien, Conradshoehe, near Berlin, Germany.

Sex: During the spawning season ♂ has a touch of blue-violet on the belly. The first pectoral fin red-brown and broad. The under-side of ♀ remains white.

Soc. B: Peaceful except during the spawning season. The fish will guard their spawn.

M: Undemanding, but prefers a dark tank with hiding places. Hardy enough to survive even under poor conditions. pH 5.5-8.3 and hardness to 30° dGH.

B: ♂ is very aggressive during spawning. ♀ should be removed after spawning.

F: O; omnivorous; tablets, especially in the evening. Feed fry Tetra Baby Food and small live food.

S: The eggs are deposited in a bubble nest. The parents, especially the ♂, will devour eggs and fry.

T: 64-82° F,   **L:** 7″,   **A:** 27″,   **R:** b,   **D:** 1.
    18-28° C,   18 cm,   70 cm,

Chaca chaca   (HAMILTON, 1822)

Syn.: *Platystacus chaca*

Hab.: Borneo; Burma; India; Sumatra.

Fl.: 1938

Sex: Unknown.

Soc. B.: May become a predator and is not recommended for a community tank.

M: A nocturnal species, it becomes active only when eating. May attack sleeping fishes to 2″ (6 cm.). Undemanding in terms of water quality: pH 6.0-8.0 and hardness range 4-25° dGH. Best hiding places are behind large, flat stones. Will not eat plants.

B: Unknown.

F: C; after it is acclimatized the fish will take FD tablets. The large mouth is that of a predator and it is regarded as a predator though MEINKEN claims the species dines on plankton.

S: Recommended only for an aquarist seeking novelties.

Chaca had been considered as monotypical; in 1983, however, another species of *Chaca bankanensis* was described.

T: 72-75° F,   **L**: 7³/₄″,   **A**: 39″,   **R**: b,   **D**: 3.
    22-24° C,   20 cm,   100 cm,

Clarias batrachus
Clarias Catfish

(LINNAEUS, 1758)

Syn.: *Silurus batrachus, Clarias magur, C. marpus, C. punctatus, Macropteronotus batrachus, M. magur*

Hab.: Sri Lanka; Eastern India to Malaysia.

Fl.: 1899, H. Stueve, Hamburg, West Germany.

Sex: There are dots on the dorsal fin of ♂ and no special markings on ♀.

Soc. B.: The species is greedy and this should be taken into account when placing in a community tank.

M: Adjusts to most water conditions but needs a well-covered tank with a few fast-rooted, luxuriant plants, a dark bottom and goodsized hiding places.

B: Has been bred professionally in Florida.

F: O; omnivorous.

S: Recommended for larger display tanks which can even be unheated in some areas. It is not imported into the U.S. because it may survive in native waters and is considered a "walker". To cross land areas it locks its gills to prevent drying. The fish devours everything edible including fauna and other fishes. The U.S. Fish & Wildlife Service claims it has become a pest in Florida though abnormally cold winters have reduced its numbers. A pseudo-albino form is available.

T: 68-77° F,   **L**: 19¹/₂″,   **A**: 47″,   **R**: b,   **D**: 2-3.
    20-25° C,   50 cm,   120 cm,

Acanthodoras cataphractus

(LINNAEUS, 1758)

Syn.: *Cataphractus americanus, Doras blochii, D. cataphractus, D. polygramma, Silurus cataphractus*

Hab.: Mouth of the Amazon river.

Fl.: Unknown.

Sex: Unknown.

Soc. B.: Peaceful, it may be combined with all species.

M: An undemanding species which will consume detritus or foods left by other fishes. Hides during the day. Prefers peat-brown water with roots and other hiding areas. It likes to burrow in a soft mulm-like bottom. pH 6.0-7.5 and hardness 4-25° dGH.

B: Unknown.

F: O; omnivorous; algae; tablets in the evening.

S: It is not proven that the species is symbiotic with *A. hancockii*. The confusion may result from the fact that the same habitats are mentioned by several authorities.

T: 72-79° F,   **L**: 4″,   **A**: 27″,   **R**: b,   **D**: 1.
   22-26° C,   10 cm,   70 cm,

Agamyxis pectinifrons
Talking Catfish

(COPE, 1870)
Sub-Fam.: Doradinae

Syn.: *Doras pectinifrons*

Hab.: Pebas, Ecuador; eastern Peru.

Fl.: 1933

Sex: Unknown.

Soc. B: A peaceful species.

M: Does not like light but once acclimatized it often leaves its hiding place during the day. Prefers peat-filtered, slightly acid water (pH 5.8-7.5) and with low hardness (0-20° dGH). It likes to burrow so give it a corner without plants. The fish will not eat plants.

B: Unknown.

F: O; omnivorous; small worms; tablets.

S: Can tolerate temperatures to 60° F (15° C) for short periods. The shallow flood waters of its homeland can cool off drastically at night.

T: 68-79° F,   L: 6″,   A: 39″,   R: b,   D: 1-2.
   20-26° C,   16 cm,   100 cm,

Amblydoras hancockii

(VALENCIENNES, 1840)
Sub-Fam.: Doradinae

Syn.: *Amblyodoras affinis, Doras affinis, D. costatus* (not LINNAEUS), *D. hancockii, D. truncatus*

Hab.: In algae-laden waters from Guyana to Colombia; Rio Branco; Rio Guapore.

Fl.: 1950

Sex: Underside of ♀ dirty white, that of ♂ freckled in brown.

Soc. B.: A peaceful, amusing species well suited to a community tank.

M: Use a large, shallow tank with plenty of algae if you can. If not, provide hiding places beneath broad-leaved plants, roots and decorations. Sun will not hurt the tank. The water level should be 4 to 8 inches deep (10-20 cm). Suggest a hardness to 20° dGH and a pH 5.8 to 7.5. We once caught approximately 2,000 fishes 2 to 4 $^1/_2$ inches long (5-12 cm.) in a single cast of our net

B: Only recorded in the wild. According to HANCOCK, the species builds a bubble nest in plants near the surface. The ♂ guards the nest.

F: O; raise fry with algae; detritus; and tablets.

S: The fish make an audible, growling sound and, because of it, are sometimes called "growling" catfish.

T: 73-82° F,   L: to 6″,   A: 31″,   R: b,   D: 1.
   23-28° C,   to 15 cm,   80 cm,

Agamyxis pectinifrons

Amblydoras hancockii

Platydoras costatus

(LINNAEUS, 1766)
Sub-Fam.: Doradinae

Syn.: *Silurus costatus, Cataphractus costatus, Doras costatus*

Hab.: Peru: Amazonas.

Fl.: 1964

Sex: Not certain.

Soc. B.: Peaceful and amusing, the fish is well suited to a large community tank.

M: Often burrows and needs a clean corner with fine gravel. Will not damage plants though fine-leaved vegetation may suffer from the silt. Prefers a cover of floating plants with such hiding places as hollows of roots. Suggest peat filtration, pH 5.8-7.5 and a hardness range 2-20° dGH.

B: Unsuccessful thus far.

F: O; omnivorous; algae; tablets.

S: It is the nicest of the Thorny Catfishes. Do not use a net to catch. Use a glass.

T: 74-86° F,   L: 8¹/₂″,   A: 39″,   R: b,   D: 1-2.
   24-30° C,   22 cm,   100 cm,

Ictalurus punctatus
Graceful Catfish, Stinging Catfish

(RAFINESQUE, 1818)

Syn.: *Silurus punctatus, Amerurus punctatus, Pimelodus caerulescens, P. caudafurcatus, P. argentinus, P. argystus, P. furcifer, P. gracilis, P. graciosus, P. hammondi, P. houghi, P. maculatus; P. megalops, P. nolatus, P. pallidus, P. vulpes, Ictalurus robustus, I. simpsoni, Silurus punctatus, Synechoglanis beadlei*

Hab.: Southern and western U.S.; Rio Grande.

Fl.: 1888

Sex: Unknown.

Soc. B.: A predator; not suited to a community tank.

M: A very hardy, robust species, we suggest a large, dark aquarium with a fine gravel bottom and hardy live or plastic plants. pH 6.0-8.0 and a hardness range 4-30° dGH.

B: Can be accomplished only in ponds. The pair digs a hollow in the bottom and the eggs are laid in clumps, guarded by the ♂.

F: O; omnivorous; a voracious eater.

S: A food fish, only the juvenile is recommended for an aquarium. The albino is popular in the US (large photo). A related species, *I. nebulosus*, has been introduced in European waters where it is doing well. The species grows to 15¹/₂″ (40 cm) and the small photo shows the fish in its normal coloring.

T: room temperature L: to 27″,   **A:** 39″,   **R:** b, **D:** 2-3.
also below,   to 70 cm,   100 cm,

Ancistrus dolichopterus

KNER, 1854
Sub-Fam.: Ancistrinae

Syn.: *Ancistrus cirrhosus* (not VALEN-CIENNES), *A. temminckii* (not VALEN-CIENNES), *Chaetostomus dolichopterus*, *Xenocara dolichoptera*

Hab.: Fast-flowing, clear tributaries of the Amazon.

Fl.: 1911, by two Hamburg importers, West Germany.

Sex: ♂ has an antler-like bump on its forehead. ♀ has a row of short, thin tentacles.

Soc. B.: A peaceful species recommended for larger community tanks.

M: Prefers large tanks and clear water with plenty of oxygen. Add large roots and similar places to hide during the daylight hours. Use a strong filter or aerator to create both a current and the needed oxygen. pH 5.8-7.8 with a hardness 2-30° dGH.

B: Lays eggs in clusters like mustard seed in the hollows of roots. ♂ guards the nest and fans or aerates the water above the brood. Raise with water values of pH 6.5-7.0 and hardness 4-10° dGH. The fry hatch after five days and attach themselves to the tank sides. The yolk sac disappears in 14 days at which time they should be fed very fine green flakes or Tetra-Min Baby Food.

F: H; mainly algae; add a few flakes; vegetable food and lettuce leaves soaked four or five days.

S: A curious fish useful as an algae-eater.

T: 73-81° F,   **L:** 4³/₄″,   **A:** 31″,   **R:** b,   **D:** 2.
    23-27° C,   13 cm,   80 cm,

Ancistrus hoplogenys?

(GUENTHER, 1864)
Sub-Fam.: Ancistrinae

Syn.: *Chaetostomus hoplogenys*, *Chaetostomus leucostictus*, *Chaetostomus alga*, *Chaetostomus malacops*, *Chaetostomus tectirostris*, *Ancistrus leucostictus*, *Xenocara hoplogenys*

Hab.: Spring-fed tributaries of the Amazon.

Fl.: Unknown. It is seldom imported and then, generally under an incorrect name.

Sex: ♂ larger, with barbs. ♀ smaller, without barbs.

Soc. B.: A peaceful species.

M: A nocturnal fish, it becomes active at dusk. The species requires lots of oxygen and prefers a hollow root as a hiding place. Will not damage plants. pH 5.5-7.5 with hardness 2-20° dGH.

B: Successful breeding in an aquarium was accomplished several times, however, not so easily as with other *Ancistrus*. The eggs are preferably laid into a hollow piece of wood, or under a piece of bogwood. The ♂ watches the eggs. 10 days after spawning the fry have eaten up the yolk sac are to be fed blanched, chopped up lettuce.

F: H; vegetable tablets, algae.

S: The fish have very pretty markings.

T: 72-79° F,   **L:** 3″,   **A:** 23¹/₂″,   **R:** b,   **D:** 2-3.
    22-26° C,   8 cm,   60 cm,

Ancistrus dolichopterus

Ancistrus hoplogenys?

487

Farlowella acus

(KNER, 1853)
Sub-Fam.: Loricariinae

Syn.: *Acestra acus*
Hab.: La Plata; southern tributaries of the Amazon.
Fl.: 1933
Sex: Males and females are easily recognized by their beaklike protuberance. That of the ♂ is wider and covered with lots of small bristles, that of the ♀ is narrower and without bristles. Moreover, half a day to one day before spawning the ♀ will have a clearly visible ovipositor.
Soc. B.: Peaceful and shy, these fish are not suggested for a community tank where more active fish may frighten it.
M: Not very adaptable to fluctuating water values. pH 6.0-7.0 and hardness 3-8° dGH. Finding the proper food is difficult. Unlike related species, it does not live in fast-flowing water but in the flood plains and bogs. Its apparently short aquarium life may be due to a seasonal nature. Only adult fish are seen in the trade. We wonder what happens to the fry.

B: Hatching and breeding of *Farlowella acus* are rather simple, at least for an aquarist who has gathered experience with other catfishes. Mr J. ABRAHAM of Pottendorf/Austria noticed that his fishes spawned in the very same spot (front plate) all the time. Spawning was done during the night or early morning. Each time there were about 40-60 eggs with a low yoke content. At 26° C the fry hatch after appr. 240 hours. The ♂ watches and cares for the eggs, delivering the fry from the egg casings. The best hatching is done in oxygen-rich "old water" and under diffused light. The pH value should be neutral, the hardness between 5-10° dGH. It is possible to put some smaller and quiet fishes into the breeding tank.
F: Micro algae foods.
S: Not recommended for a beginner. The fish barely moves and would be considered "boring" by many. *Farlowella* differ from other *Loricaria* by the position of the dorsal which is normally opposite the anal fin. It is found behind it on this *Loricaria*.

T: 75-79° F, L: 5³/₄″,   A: 31″,   R: b, m, D: 3-4.
   24-26° C,   15 cm,   80 cm,

Farlowella gracilis

(REGAN, 1904)
Sub-Fam.: Loricariinae

Syn.: *Acestra gracilis*
Hab.: Rio Caqueta, Cauca, Colombia;
Fl.: 1954
Sex: Unknown.
Soc. B.: A peaceful bottom fish often found in large numbers though not known for schooling.
M: Requires water with a high oxygen content and needs time to acclimate. Prefers a dark bottom of fine gravel and dense vegetatation. The tank should possibly be darkened with a cover of floating plants. Peat filtration is an advantage. Make water changes only with a good conditioner.
B: Unsuccessful.
F: H, L; growth food; tablets.
S: An interesting but very sensitive species suggested only for an experienced hobbyist.

T: 72-79° F, L: to 7¹/₂″,   A: 31″,   R: b, m, D: 3-4.
   22-26° C,   to 19 cm,   80 cm,

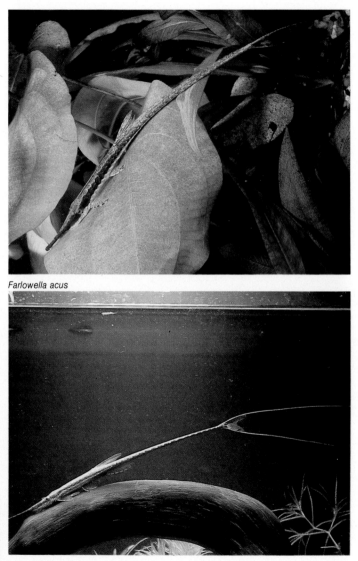

Farlowella acus

Farlowella gracilis

Hypoptopoma thoracatum

GUENTHER, 1868
Sub-Fam.: Hypoptopomatinae

Syn.: *Hypoptopoma bilobatum*

Hab.: The Amazon; mouth of the Rio Negro and, according to authorities, the Rio Xebero in the Mato Grosso.

Fl.: Unknown.

Sex: Unknown.

Soc. B.: A peaceful loner found only in small groups, it is easily combined with other fishes. Will not harm tank mates, even fry.

M: Does not require much "current" and is naturally found in larger bodies of water than *Otocinclus*. Dislikes light and prefers a tank with shaded hiding areas such as roots, rocks and broken pots. When small will venture out only at night but as it grows may become braver. pH 6.0-7.5 and hardness 4-15° dGH.

B: Unknown but may be similar to *Otocinclus*.

F: H; algae; tablets.

S: The species is often sold commercially as *Otocinclus* and is rare. Because of its size it could replace *Hypostomus* as an algae-eater in smaller tanks.

T: 73-81° F, **L:** 3″, **A:** 27″, **R:** b, m, **D:** 2-3.
23-27° C,   8 cm,   70 cm,

Hypostomus punctatus
Suckermouth Catfish

(VALENCIENNES, 1840)
Sub-Fam.: Hypostominae

Syn.: *Plecostomus punctatus, Hypostomus subcarinatus, Plecostomus affinis, P. commersoni, P. commersoni affinis, P. commersoni scabriceps*

Hab.: South and southeastern Brazil.

Fl.: 1928.

Sex: Unknown.

Soc. B.: Harmless loner, well suited to the community tank.

M: A nocturnal species, it needs a large tank with moderately dense vegetation and hollows in which to hide during the day. When young, the fish live in fast-flowing waters, on flood-plains and in deeper side-arms of rivers. Most prefer clear water though some can be found in the coffee-colored waters of rivers after heavy rains. Although adaptable to range of conditions (pH 5.0-8.0 and hardness 0.5-25° dGH) the species prefers slightly acid, soft water.

B: Unsuccessful.

F: H; algae; softened spinach and lettuce; vegetable flakes; tablets in the evening.

S: Since the fish are inveterate burrowers place all plants in pots. In their native country the larger species fish are a food fish.

T: 72-82° F, **L:** to 11³/₄″, **A:** 46¹/₂″, **R:** b, **D:** 1.
22-28° C,   to 30 cm,   120 cm,

Hypoptopoma thoracatum

Hypostomus punctatus

Otocinclus affinis
Dwarf Otocinclus. Golden Otocinclus
Syn.: None

Hab.: Southeastern Brazil near Rio de Janeiro; fast-flowing streams with algae-covered rocks or dense vegetation.

Fl.: 1920

Sex: ♀ is larger and rounder-bodied.

Soc. B: Recommended for community tanks with "tender" species. Do not combine with more active Cichlids.

M: Needs a tank with dense vegetaion, clear water, good filtration and, possibly, added peat extract. (After it is acclimated: pH 5.0-7.5 and hardness 2-15° dGH.)

T: 68-79° F,   L: 1¹/₂″,   A: 19¹/₂″,   R: b, m, D: 2.
   20-26° C,   4 cm,   50 cm,

STEINDACHNER, 1877
Sub-Fam.: Hypoptopomatinae

B: Similar to recommendations for *Corydoras*. The eggs adhere to leaves and the fry hatch in three days. Feed very fine live and dried micro-food. Not a prolific breeder.

F: L, H; algae; tablets.

S: The smallest and most common of the species. All members are good algae-eaters. Some 20 *Otocinclus* sp. have been described though less than six are available commercially.

Panaque nigrolineatus

Syn.: *Cochliodon nigrolineatus, Chaetostomus nigrolineatus*

Hab.: Southern Colombia.

Fl.: Possibly 1974(?), Heiko Bleher, Frankfurt, West Germany.

Sex: Unknown.

Soc. B.: A peaceful species which should only be combined with other placid fishes.

M: Needs a large tank with clear water, large stones, plenty of light and a strong current. Likes hiding places beneath roots but dark hiding places are not as imperative as for other catfishes.
Will not eat plants. pH 6.5-7.5 and hardness 2-15° dGH.

B: Unknown.

F: H; algae is basic but will also accept tablets and vegetable flakes.

T: 72-79° F,   L: in an aquarium 9.75″,   A: 47″,   R: b,   D: 3.
   22-26° C,   25 cm,   120 cm,

(PETERS, 1877)
Sub-Fam.: Ancistrinae

S: An unusual, even comical fish recommended for the connoisseur. Its red-eyes are prominent against a zebra-striped background. The species is standard for the genus. Do not keep these fish in Plexiglas-tanks.

Otocinclus affinis

Panaque nigrolineatus

Peckoltia pulcher

(STEINDACHNER, 1917)
Sub-Fam.: Ancistrinae

Syn.: *Ancistrus pulcher, Hemiancistrus pulcher*

Hab.: Rio Negro, near Moura.

Fl.: About 1960.

Sex: Unknown.

Soc. B: Peaceful toward its own species and most fry.

M: Can introduce several fish, depending on the tank size. We suggest 20 gallons (80 l) of water per fish since crowding would reduce the amount of algae available. Do not combine with other algae eaters since none would be sufficently fed. Provide hiding places in small hollows, half pots or behind stones. There are many plants it will not eat. Avoid treating the water with algae inhibitors. pH 5.5-7.8 (average 7.0) and hardness 2-30° dGH (average 10° dGH.)

The water value averages given are best for the growth of algae.

B: Procedures are not known but it is worth attempting. Probably successful only in tanks heavy with algae and with plenty of food for fry.

F: L,H; lives only on algae; may possibly accept tablets in the evening, just before turning out the lights.

S: Though generally unimposing, the species has attractive markings. It will not do well without algae. Preferable to *Hypostomus* sp. because of its smaller size.

T: 75-82° F, **L**: 2¹/₄″, **A**: 23″, **R**: b, **D**: 1-2.
24-28° C, 6 cm, 60 cm,

Peckoltia vittata

(STEINDACHNER, 1882)
Sub-Fam.: Ancistrinae

Syn.: *Chaetostomus vittatus, Ancistrus vittatus, A. vittatus var. vermiculata, Hemiancistrus vittatus*

Hab.: Amazon; Tajapouru, Rio Xingu near Porto do Moz; Rio Madeira.

Fl.: About 1960.

Sex: Unknown.

Soc. B.: A peaceful fish.

M: A relatively undemanding species, its furious evening activities can deliver a lot of amusement for those watching. The fish rests beneath flat stones during the day. It does not burrow and will attack neither tankmates nor plants. The only requisite for a long life is plenty of algae. pH 5.0-7.5 and hardness 2-20° dGH.

B: Unknown.

F: H; plenty of algae; vegetable tablets may be ignored; FD-tablets.

S: A nocturnal fish.

T: 73-79° F, **L**: 5³/₄″, in an aquarium to 4″, **A**: 23″, **R**: b, **D**: 2.
23-26° C, 14 cm, in an aquarium to 10 cm, 60 cm,

Peckoltia pulcher

Peckoltia vittata

Pterygoplichthys gibbiceps   (KNER, 1854)
                                                 Sub-Fam.: Hypostominae

Syn.: *Ancistrus gibbiceps, Chaetostomus gibbiceps, Hemiancistrus gibbiceps, Liposarcus altipinnis, L. scrophus*

Hab.: Rio Pacaya, Peru.

Fl.: 1961, K. H. Lueling, Bonn, West Germany.

Sex: Unknown.

Soc. B.: In the wild it is a schooling fish, peaceful even toward smaller fishes. Recommended for a larger community tank.

M: Needs a large tank (50 gallons [1,40 m] or more) with large hiding places or dense vegetation. The fish becomes active at dusk and though it inspects the tank thoroughly for algae it will not damage plants. pH 6.5-7.8 and hardness 4-20° dGH.

B: Unknown.

F: Feed at night; Algae; tablets; detritus. Larger fish, from 11 inches (30 cm.) need six to eight Tetra Tip tablets daily or a large quantity of algae. Will accept cooked lettuce only as a last resort.

S: Since the fish excretes heavily, it needs a strong, large volume filter. If the tank is small the fish will grow reluctantly if at all.

T: 73-81° F, **L**: 19$^1/_2$″, **A**: 54$^1/_2$″, **R**: b,   **D**: 1 (despite its size).
    23-27° C,   50 cm,   140 cm,

Pterygoplichthys multiradiatus   (HANCOCK, 1828)
                                                   Sub-Fam.: Hypostominae

Syn.: *Ancistrus multiradiatus, Hypostomus multiradiatus, H. pardalis, Liposarcus jeanesianus, L. multiradiatus, L. pardalis, L. varius, Plecostomus pardalis, Pterygoplichthys jeanesianus, P. pardalis*

Hab.: White-water rivers in Peru; Amazonia; Bolivia; Paraguay.

Fl.: 1970, Aquarium Rio, Kelsterbach (Frankfurt) (as *"Pardalis sp."*).

Sex: Unknown.

Soc. B.: According to LUELING, the fish is not found in large groups as is *Pt. gibbiceps.*

M: Similar to the species above.

B: Unknown.

F: Algae and tablets, given in the evening.

S: Rarely imported because its size is a deterrent for hobbyists. It differs from *Hypostomus* sp. mainly in the number of rays in the dorsal, an easily distinguishable feature: *Hypostomus* has I.7 while *Pterygoplichthys* has I.10-13.

T: 73-81° F, **L**: over 19$^1/_2$″, **A**: 54$^1/_2$″, **R**: b,   **D**: 1.
    23-27° C,   over 50 cm,   140 cm,

Pterygoplichthys gibbiceps

Pterygoplichthys multiradiatus

Rineloricaria microlepidogaster

REGAN, 1904
Sub-Fam.: Loricariinae

Syn.: *Loricaria microlepidogaster*

Hab.: Fast-flowing, spring-fed streams and rivers of central and southeast Brazil.

Fl.: 1928

Sex: ♂ has a "brush" on its mouth.

Soc. B.: A very peaceful species recommended for community tanks. Water quality is important.

M: Needs clear, oxygen-rich water and a tank with hiding places. If the fish attaches itself to the glass just below the surfae, it is an indication there is not sufficient oxygen. Though the fish is vegetarian, it will not damage plants. Feed at night, otherwise the fish may easily go hungry. The species likes to burrow in soft gravel. pH 5.8-7.8 (suggested average, 6.8) and, after it is acclimated, hardness to 20° dGH. Lower dGH levels are preferred.

B: Follow our recommendations for *R. fallax*.

F: H; algae; vegetable diet; tablets at night.

S: The smallest of the *Loricaria* species, the accuracy of the name has not been established. After a review by ISBRUECKER in 1978, the genus was divided and some of the best known aquarium species had their generic descriptions changed.

T: 72-79° F,   **L:** 4¹/₂″,   **A:** 23¹/₂″,   **R:** b,   **D:** 2-3.
     22-26° C,   20 cm,   60 cm,

Rineloricaria fallax
Whiptailed Loricaria

STEINDACHNER, 1915
Sub-Fam.: Loricariinae

Syn.: *Loricaria parva*

Hab.: Fast-flowing streams of the La Plata area of Paraguay. Found in streams with a gravelly bottom and water 4 to 12 inches deep (10-30 cm.)

Fl.: 1908, Vereinigte Zierfischzuechtereien, Conradshoehe, West Germany.

Sex: As in other *Rineloricaria* sp. the ♂ has a thick "brush' on the sides of the mouth. Seen from above, the head of the ♀ comes to a triangular point. According to STEINDACHNER, the head of the ♂ is broader toward the front.

M: Similar to the species above.

B: In addition to favorable water conditions and a good vegetable diet, it requires spawning hollows, 1 to 1¹/₄ inches in diameter (3-4 cm.) and 8 inches long (20 cm.). The ♀ lays 100 to 200 eggs the size of mustard seed which are immediately fertilized by ♂. Several ♀♀ may use the same hollow. The ♀ holds to the pectoral fin of the male by suction of its mouth. The fry hatch after 9 to 12 days and are guarded by the ♂. The ♂ frees the fry from their egg sac by suction with its mouth. In the wild ♂♂ have been caught still holding an entire brood in the mouth sac. The young take *Artemia* or brine shrimp and then *Cyclops* and *Daphnia*. Offer vegetable foods from the second week. Fine flakes and tablets may be accepted. The tank must be scrupulously clean.

F: H; algae; flakes; tablets.

S: Not as hardy as *Hypostomus (Plecostomus).*

T: 59-77° F,   **L:** 4¹/₂″,   **A:** 31″,   **R:** b,   **D:** 2.
     15-25° C,   12 cm,   80 cm,

Rineloricaria microlepidogaster

Rineloricaria fallax

Malapterurus electricus
Electric Catfish

(GMELIN, 1789)

Syn.: *Silurus electricus*

Hab.: Central Africa north of the Zambesi River: Nile, Niger, Volta, Lake Chad; Zaire.

Fl.: 1904

Sex: Unknown.

Soc. B.: A nocturnal loner, it is best suited for a species tank.

M: Needs a large display tank with large hollows of rocks or roots. For protection plant vegetation in pots and use strong filtration. pH 7.0-8.0 and hardness to 20° dGH.

B: Unknown. The ♀ spawn on the bottom in special hollows.

F: C; live fish; large worms; cut meat.

S: Suggested for a display aquarium only. The electric organs run along the entire body and produce enough current to disable prey.

T: 73-86° F, **L**: 39″, **A**: 46$^1/_2$″, **R**: b, **D**: 4.
    23-30° C,   100 cm,   120 cm,

Synodontis decorus

BOULENGER, 1899
Sub-Fam.: Mochocinae

Syn.: None

Hab.: Upper Zaire; Cameroons.

Fl.: About 1960.

Sex: Unknown.

Soc. B.: Very peaceful.

M: Similar to the species below. When transferring use a small net to protect the spines on the pectoral fins. These have serrated teeth and may be difficult to untangle. Rough handling may cause injury.

B: Unknown.

F: O; omnivorous; flakes; tablets; all types of live food.

S: Only the young are recommended for an aquarium. The upper photo shows the juvenile, the smaller picture, the semi-adult.

T: 73-81° F, L: to 9³/₄″,   A: 39″,   R: b,   D: 2-3.
23-27° C,   to 24 cm,   100 cm,

Synodontis alberti

SCHILTHUIS, 1891
Sub-Fam.: Mochocinae

Syn.: None

Hab.: Zaire around Stanley Pool; Kinshasa; Ubunghi-Banziville; Lukulu river, Katanga.

Fl.: 1954, East Germany; 1957 Espe, Bremen, West Germany.

Sex: Unknown.

Soc. B.: Though a peaceful fish, it is generally a loner with restless habits which may disturb tankmates. Its continuous use of tentacles for exploration and sensing may also upset other fish.

M: It is best combined with surface-schooling species or kept on its own in a darkened tank with hiding places. Vertical roots are appreciated. The substrate should be fine gravel with vegetation. pH 6.0-8.0 with a hardness 4-25° dGH.

B: Unsuccessful.

F: Tablets; algae; live worms.

S: Hinged teeth in the lower jaw are used as rasps to remove algae.

T: 73-81° F,   L: 6″,   A: 31″,   R: b,   D: 2.
    23-27° C,   16 cm,   80 cm,

Synodontis angelicus
Angel Catfish

SCHILTHUIS, 1891
Sub-Fam.: Mochocinae

Syn.: None

Hab.: Zaire around Stanley Pool; Mousembe, upper Zaire; Cameroons.

Fl.: 1954

Sex: Unknown.

Soc. B.: A peaceful species. Use as a schooling fish or in a tank with others of the genus. Will co-exist happily with Congo Tetra and other African Tetras.

M: The fish like to dig so place fine gravel on the bottom and add large roots for hiding places. A nocturnal fish, it occasionally swims on its back and will take food by day after it is acclimated. It will not burrow but needs a current. Clean, clear water is healthful and the $^1/_3$ of the water should be changed every three weeks. Add a good water conditioner. Do not plant fine-leaved plants since the species digs and fine

particles swirl upward to collect on leaves. Algae is essential and should be allowed to grow on the back and sides of the tank as well on roots and rocks. Avoid blue algae. The species is sensitive to nitrates. pH 6.5-7.5 and hardness 4-15° dGH.

B: The fish are a protected species and must be bred in captivity. Excluding S. nigriventris and S. nigrita no species of Synodontis has been captive-bred.

F: Fine live food; algae and flakes; tablets. Feed at night.

S: This rare species can no longer be exported. Specimens are rarely seen and then at high prices. A sub-species has also been described, Synodontis angelicus zonatus POLL, 1933. It is found in the Lukulu river in Kantanga.

T: 75-82° F,   L: 6$^1/_2$″,   A: 31″,   R: b, m, D: 2.
    24-28° C,   18 cm,   80 cm,

Synodontis alberti

Synodontis angelicus

Synodontis decorus (see page 501)
Synodontis eupterus (see page 508)
Synodontis flavitaeniatus

BOULENGER, 1919
Sub-Fam.: Mochocinae

Syn.: None

Hab.: Zaire around Stanley Pool; Chiloango river.

Fl.: Possibly 1970.

Sex: Unknown.

Soc. B.: A peaceful fish which can be combined with many other species.

M: Prefers a tank with a mulm or fine gravel bottom and roots for hiding places. It is not as demanding of shade as other *Mochocidae* and can be seen during the day. Burrows less than many of its relatives and plants can be added to the tank. Regular water changes are advisable. pH 6.5-8.0 and hardness 4-25° dGH.

B: Unknown.

F: O; omnivorous; small live food; tablets; some algae.

S: Though one of the prettiest of the genus.It is very rare and expensive. Only a dozen or so are caught annually.

T: 73-82° F,   **L**: 8″,   **A**: 31″,   **R**: b,   **D**: 1.
    23-28° C,   20 cm,   80 cm,

Synodontis schoutedeni

DAVID, 1936
Sub-Fam.: Mochocinae

Syn.: None

Hab.: Central Congo.

Fl.: 1951

Sex: Unknown.

Soc. B.: A peaceful loner which may disturb some tankmates with its barbels and restless swimming habits. As soon as several fish are added the larger specimens will chase the smaller.

M: Needs a large tank with a fine gravel bottom. It may eat softer plants if the food supply is inadequate. The fish enjoys resting on the vertical walls of a root or rock during the day but makes no special demands as to water quality. It will react quickly to untreated, chlorinated water. pH 6.0-7.5 and a hardness 4-15° dGH. Add a strong filter to remove the turbidity caused by the fish.

B: Unknown.

F: O; omnivorous; small to large live food and a vegetable diet; flakes; tablets.

S: One of the most attractively marked of the species, it is seldom imported.

T: 72-79° F, **L**: 5³/₄″,   **A**: 39″,   **R**: b,   **D**: 2-3.
    22-26° C,   14 cm,   100 cm,

Synodontis flavitaeniatus

Synodontis schoutedeni

Synodontis nigriventris
Upside-down Catfish

DAVID, 1936
Sub-Fam.: Mochocinae

Syn.: *Synodontis ornatipinnis* (not BOU-LENGER)

Hab.: Zaire basin from Kinshasa to Basonga.

Fl.: 1950, Belgium.

Sex: ♀ has a more rounded body and pale coloring.

Soc. B.: Peaceful, even with own species. Recommended for community tanks.

M: The tank should be planted with such broad-leaved plants as *Echinodorus* and decorated with roots and stones for hiding. The fish enjoys browsing the underside of leaves for insect larvae.

B: *S. nigriventris* is one of the few *Synodontis* sp. to have been bred in an aquarium. The eggs are laid in a depression on the bottom. The ♀♀ are round-bodied, particularly at spawning and the parents look after the brood. The fry carry a yolk sac to the fourth day and will accept freshly hatched brine shrimp after. From the 7th or 8th week they change to the up-side down swimming position standard for their species and tend to form schools at sizes between one and two inches (2 to 5 cm.). They will later lose this habit.

F: C, O; insect larvae; tablets; do not feed algae. The unique swimming position is especially suited to this fish's life-style. It takes the larvae of the Stinging Mosquito from the water's surface. When conditions are equal this food often initiates breeding.

S: Its name indicates the manner in which it swims.

T: 72-79° F, **L:** ♂ 3″, ♀ 4″,　　**A:** 23¹/₂″,　**R:** t, m, b,　**D:** 1.
　　22-26° C,　　♂ 8 cm, ♀ 10 cm,　　60 cm,

Synodontis notatus

VAILLANT, 1893
Sub-Fam.: Mochocinae

Syn.: *Synodontis maculatus* (not RUEPPEL)

Hab.: Zaire, from Stanley Pool to Mousembe.

Fl.: 1952

Sex: Unknown.

Soc. B: A peaceful species.

M: It enjoys burrowing as do many larger *Synodontis.*

B: Unknown.

F: O; omnivorous.

S: This is the most often imported of more than 80 species though it is not particularly easy to keep. The sub-species *S. notatus ocellatus* is much more robust.

Synodontis schoutedendi, see page 504.

T: 72-79° F, **L:** 5¹/₂″,　**A:** 39″,　**R:** b,　　**D:** 2-3.
　　22-26° C,　　14 cm,　　100 cm,

Synodontis nigriventris

Synodontis notatus

top juv., bottom adult.

Synodontis eupterus

BOULENGER, 1901
Sub-Fam.: Mochocinae

Syn.: None

Hab.: Africa; White Nile; Chad basin; Niger.

Fl.: Unknown.

Sex: Unknown.

Soc. B.: A peaceful species suggested for many community tanks. The size of tankmates is not important.

M: Needs a dark tank with such places to hide as roots or curved flower pot shards. Fine gravel for digging is important since it helps to condition the feelers. Peat extract or peat filtration is a good idea. Add plenty of plants but leave the center open for swimming. pH 6.2-7.5 and hardness to 15° dGH.

B: Has not been bred in captivity.

F: O; tablets; all live foods.

S: Previously sold commercially as *S. ornatus* though this is a synonym of *S. nigrita*.

T: 72-79° F,   **L:** about 6",   **A:** 31",   **R:** b,   **D:** 2.
22-26° C,   about 15 cm,   80 cm,

Pangasius sutchi(?)

FOWLER, 1937
Sub-Fam.: Pangasiinae

Syn.: None

Hab.: Near Bangkok, Thailand.

Fl.: 1964, "Tropicarium", Frankfurt, West Germany.

Sex: Unknown.

Soc. B.: Shoals when young but becomes a loner later.

M: Needs a large aquarium with swimming space. While they occasionally surface to breathe, the species are bottom dwellers. Their eyesight is bad and they are very nervous so be cautious: neither knock on the glass nor switch on tank lights at night. Hiding places are not essential. Does best with a pH around 7.0 and hardness 2-20° dGH.

B: Is bred in ponds in its native land and raised in wooden containers. It is possibly spawned by stroking its sides. Cannot be raised in an aquarium.

F: O; omnivorous; live food is essential especially when young; older fish lose their teeth and become vegetarians.

S: Not an aquarium fish. It is introduced in paddies as a food fish and occasionally imported as finger-length fry. Its German name, "Shark Catfish" has persuaded some aquarists to try keeping one or two in its rubust, juvenile state. The closely-related species, *P. pleurotaenia* has only one longitudinal band and, according to ELIAS, remains smaller.

T: 72-79° F, **L:** to 39″ to 8″ in an aquarium, **A:** 47″, **R:** b, **D:** 3.
 22-26° C, to 100 cm to 20 cm. in an aquarium, 120 cm,

Pimelodus blochii

VALENCIENNES, 1840
Sub-Fam.: Pimelodinae

Syn.: *Ariodes clarias, Fagrus clarias, My-stus ascita, Pimelodus arekaima, P. blochii, P. maculatus, P. macronema, P. schom-burgki, Piramutana macrospila, Pseudario-des clarias, P. albicans, P. pantherinus, Pseudorhamdia uscita, P. piscatrix, Silurus callarias, S. clarias*

Hab.: South America: most larger rivers from Panama to Brazil.

Fl.: 1895, P. Nitsche, Berlin, Germany.

Sex: Unknown.

Soc. B.: Will nip at its own species but can be combined with *Plecostomus, Loricaria, Corydoras, Acanthodoras* and even larger Cichlids.

M: A bottom dweller, kept best in opaque, coffee-colored water. It catches its prey by smell and by probing with its antenna, locating food from some distance. The aquarium should be darkend and provided with hiding places by day. The fish is

nocturnal and, in the evening, becomes very lively. It can be observed. pH 6.0-7.5 and hardness 4-10° dGH.

B: Unknown.

F: C, O; omnivore; prefers worms, espe-cially earthworms; insect larvae; *Tubifex.*

S: The spine on the dorsal is said to be poisonous, causing an allergic reaction if it penetrates the skin. The author cannot confirm this. On a collecting trip he twice got on the wrong side of a *Pimelodus* and, apart from a painful injury, saw no symp-toms of poisoning. The spine is armed with saw-edged teeth which act like bar-bed hooks. When oxygen levels are low, the species may change to surface breat-hing, absorbing oxygen through an intesti-nal respiratory system. When there is plenty of oxygen in the water the fish will surface only occasionally.

T: 68-79° F,   **L**: 8″ (11³/₄″),   **A**: 39″,   **R**: b,   **D**: 1-2.
20-26° C,   20 cm (30 cm),   100 cm,

Pseudoplatystoma fasciatum

(LINNAEUS, 1766)
Sub-Fam.: Sorubiminae

Syn.: *Platystoma fasciatum, P. punctifer, P. truncatum, Pseudoplatystoma punctifer, Si-lurus fasciatus*

Hab.: Paraguay. Venezuela - Rio Lebrijo near Santander; Peru -Rio Negro.

Fl.: Unknown.

Sex: Unknown.

Soc. B.: A predator which should be combined only with much larger fish. It may ignore very small fish.

M: A nocturnal species, it needs a large tank with some hiding places. Makes few demands on water quality. pH 6.0-8.0 and hardness 4-30° dGH.

B: Unknown.

F: C; accepts all live foods it can conquer; after it acclimates the fish will also take cut fish and meat.

S: Not an aquarium fish. Sometimes called the "Tiger Catfish" which also describes its appetite. Five sub-species are known: *P. fasciatum brevifile* EIGENMANN & EIGENMANN, 1882; *P. fasciatum fascia-tum*, LINNAEUS, 1766; *P. fasciatum inter-medium*, EIGENMANN & EIGENMANN, 1888; *P. fasciatum nigricans.* EIGENMANN & EIGENMANN, 1889 and *P. fasciatum reticulatum*, EIGENMANN & EIGENMANN, 1889.

T: 75-82° F,   **L**: 9³/₄-12″ (to 39″!),   **A**: 47″,   **R**: m, b, **D**: 3.
24-28° C,   25-30 cm (to 100 cm!),   120 cm,

Pimelodus blochii

Pseudoplatystoma fasciatum

Sorubim lima
Shovel-Nosed Catfish

(BLOCH & SCHNEIDER, 1806)
Sub-Fam.: Pimelodinae

Syn.: *Platystoma lima, P. luceri, Silurus gerupensis, S. lima, Sorubim infraocularis, S. luceri*

Hab.: Amazon regions; Venezuela; Paraguay.

Fl.: 1929, Scholze and Poetzschke Berlin, Germany.

Sex: Unknown.

Soc. B.: A predatory species, it lies in wait for smaller fishes. Should be combined only with larger tankmates.

M: Needs a large, shallow tank with plenty of roots and other hiding and hunting places. The species is rarely imported and will not harm plants. A nocturnal fish, when feeding it seeks a vantage point behind roots and plants and siezes its dinner. It will also scour the area for anything edible. pH 6.5-7.8 and hardness to 20° dGH.

B: Not successful in an aquarium.

F: C; live fish; tablets; and, after it acclimates, large earthworms.

S: Keep only if you have a reliable source of live food. According to FOWLER (1951) this fish was already described in 1801.

T: 73-86° F, **L:** 8″ (23¹/₂″),   **A:** 39″,   **R:** b,   **D:** 4 (C).
    23-30° C,   20 cm (60 cm),   100 cm,

Eutropiellus buffei
African Glass Catfish

GRAS, 1960
Sub-Fam.: Schilbeinae

Syn.: *Eutropius buffei, Eutropiellus vandeweyeri*

Hab.: Africa; Nigerdelta, Nigeria.

Fl.: 1954

Sex: ♀ has a larger, more rounded stomach.

Soc. B.: A peaceful, schooling fish it is lively and active by day. Needs tankmates of its species since single specimens feel insecure. Recommended for a community tank.

M: Reduce lighting with floating plants and provide lots of swimming room. Use a strong filter to create a current but otherwise the species makes few demands on water condition. Will not eat plants so choose them according to the water conditions in your tank. Use dark gravel on the bottom. Peat filtration is helpful because it darkens the water. pH 6.0-7.5 and hardness 1-25° dGH.

B: Unknown.

F: C; O; flakes; small live foods.

S: The fish swim and rest with the caudal fin canted downward and waggling.

T: 75-81° F,   **L:** 3″,   **A:** 31″,   **R:** m, t,   **D:** 2.
    24-27° C,   8 cm,   80 cm,

513

Schilbe mystus

Syn.: *Silurus mystus*

Hab.: Nile; Lake Victoria; Lake Chad; West Africa - Niger Delta.

Fl.: 1934

Sex: Unknown.

Soc. B.: A schooling species. Larger specimens may attack smaller inmates of the tank.

M: Lively schooling fish which need a large tank with plenty of swimming space as from 120 cm in length. The bottom should be soft since a number of these species prefer loamy mud. They feel at home only against a dark bottom and when kept alone will not eat.

B: Only occasionally successful in aquariums.

F: O; omnivore; larger live foods; large flakes.

(LINNAEUS, 1762)
Sub-Fam.: Schilbeinae

S: A demanding fish which may grow large. Imported mostly to Europe where they are of special interest to catfish lovers because of their swimming habits.

T: 73-81° F,   **L:** to 13$^1/_2$",   **A:** 47",   **R:** m,   **D:** 2.
     23-27° C,   to 35 cm,   120 cm,

Kryptopterus bicirrhis
Ghostfish, Ghost Catfish

Syn.: *Cryptopterichthys bicirrhis, Cryptopterus amboinensis, Kryptopterichthys palembangensis, Silurus bicirrhis, S. palembangensis*

Hab.: Eastern India; Thailand; Malaysia; Indonesia; Sumatra; Java; Borneo.

Fl.: 1934, Winkelmann, Hamburg-Altona, West Germany.

Sex: Unknown.

Soc. B.: A peaceful, schooling fish suggested for community tanks with small, peaceful fishes $1^1/_2$-$2^1/_2$" (4-6 cm). Will chase fry.

M: Prefers light and open water but needs an individual territory that includes plants. Suggest a dark tank bottom. Floating plant cover is good idea but not mandatory. Needs lots of swimming room and the obvious current a strong filter can provide.

(VALENCIENNES, 1839)
Sub-Fam.: Silurinae

B: Only occasionally successful and data is incomplete.

F: C, O; small live food; flakes floated in the current; FD.

S: A sensitive but interesting species.

T: 70-79° F,   **L:** 6",   **A:** 31",   **R:** m,   **D:** 3.
  21-26° C,   15 cm,   80 cm,

Ompok bimaculatus
Glass Catfish

(BLOCH, 1794)
Sub-Fam.: Silurinae

Syn.: *Silurus bimaculatus, Callichrous bimaculatus*

Hab.: Coast of Malabar; Nepal; Thailand; Sumatra; Java; Borneo; Vietnam; India; Sri Lanka.

Fl.: 1934

Sex: Unknown.

Soc. B.: A peaceful, schooling fish which could be combined with larger fish,. Will not survive alone.

M: One of the few catfish active by day. The tank should be placed in a well lighted area. The fish is happiest in a noticeable current and a school of at least five of its species. All of this adds up to a larger tank and plenty of available food since Ompok are greedy, hardy eaters. Does not dig: add broad leaved plants. pH 6.0-8.0 and a hardness 4-28° dGH.

B: Though bred successfully in ponds, it has not been bred in aquariums, due mostly to the lack of space.

F: O; omnivore; prefers meat; large flakes; fragmented tablets.

S: Very transparent when young, it may be confused with the Ghostfish but *Ompok bimaculatus* has four dorsal spines while *Kryptopterus bicirrhis* has only one – which is generally withdrawn. The species is widely distributed and considered a food fish.

T: 68-79° F,   **L:** 4¹/₂-8″ in an aquarium, to 17″ in the wild,   **A:** 39″,   **R:** m,   **D:** 2.
    20-26° C,   12-20 cm in an aquarium, to 45 cm in the wild,   100 cm,

Tridensimilis brevis

Syn.: *Tridens brevis*

Hab.: Regions of the Amazon.

Fl.: 1967, Heiko Bleher, Frankfurt (Kelsterbach), West Germany.

Sex: Unknown.

Soc. B.: A loner though several fish can live in a larger tank if there is sufficient territory.

M: The fish are found in the sandy shallows of rivers and streams in the wild. They are seldom kept in an aquarium because they are plain-appearing and prefer to hide. Need a bottom of fine gravel or mulm. pH 5.5-7.0 and hardness 2-10° dGH.

T: 68-86° F, **L:** 1″, **A:** 16″, **R:** b, **D:** 2.
    20-30° C, 3 cm, 40 cm,

(EIGENMANN & EIGENMANN, 1889)

B: Unknown.

F: C, L; *Daphnia*; mosquito larvae.

S: The group to which this species belongs is noted for its unusual habit of living symbiotically in the gill hollows of larger fish – generally larger catfish. It occasionally finds its way into the urethra of mammals which urinate underwater.

Group 5

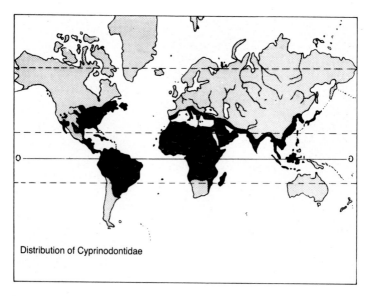

Distribution of Cyprinodontidae

The families Cyprinodontidae
(Egg-Laying Toothcarps and Killifishes

Egg-Laying Toothcarp comprise a large family with more than 450 species, found in every continent except Australia. The largest number live in the tropics. Certain sub-families, Fundulinae and Aphaniinae for example, have penetrated far into the temperate zones and are found in North America, Europe and Asia.

As one might deduce from their slender, pike-shaped bodies, many Killifishes are excellent swimmers. Others have a more cylindrical body with short, rounded fins. Certain South American bottom spawners, *Cynolebias, Pterolebias* and *Rachovia*, have a taller, stockier body. Their fins are remarkably long and broad. The unpaired fins are particularly well developed as the ♂ uses them, like arms, to embrace the ♀ during spawning.

Egg-Laying Toothcarps are generally small fishes, 2 to 4 inches (5-10 cm.) long. Only a few species exceed this size. The largest Killifish is *Orestias cuvieri* which can reach a length of 12″ (30 cm.). At 8 inches (20 cm.) *Fundulus catenatus* is the largest Cyprinodontid in North America and at 5 inches (13.5 cm.) *Lamprichthys tanganicanus* is the largest African species – though it may seem small in comparison.

Nothobranchius melanospilus

However there are also true dwarf Killifish. *Oryzias minutillus* and *Aplocheilichthys myersi* are examples. Each is less than one inch (2 cm.) long.

The heads of most Egg-Laying Toothcarp are flattened on the upper side. Their mouths are situated either at the end of the head or in a slightly up-turned position. Killifish have no barbels but have long, pointed teeth which are usually curved. Most subfamily representatives have tricuspid or three-pointed teeth. The bodies of nearly all Cyprinodontids are covered with round scales and, on many, the lateral line is restricted to the area around the head. Killifish may be characterized as having scales and lateral line organs on the head.

The large majority of Egg-Laying Toothcarp are found neither in shallow water nor schools. Exceptions are representatives of three sub-families of which only the Oryziatinae are of interest to aquarists. Some Cyprinodontids and Aphaniids will temporarily form schools.

The reproduction and egg-development of Egg-laying Toothcarps are of particular interest and will be explained in detail in the appropriate descriptions. In Killifish a distinction can be made between "egg-hangers", which attach their eggs to plants and those which lay or bury their eggs on the bottom. The two differ not only in their choice of a tank bottom but also in their biology. Fishes which attach their eggs to plants live in waters which remain relatively high, even during dry periods. The fish generally survive more than one season and thus, have little need to adjust their embryonic development to yearly cycles. Bottom layers, on the other hand, inhabit waters which become completely dry during rainless periods. They survive — as fish — only until the stream beds are dry. Beyond this, generations survive as embryos wrapped in their egg-sacs, buried in the damp muddy bottom. The development of bottom-layers is interrupted by diapauses or arrested development. Two diapauses are typical of most Killifishes though one sub-family, Rivulinae must endure three. When such conditions are considered, a distinction must be be made between the non-annual species of Egg-Laying Toothcarp — the "egg-hangers" — and the annual life-cycle of the bottomlayers and an aquarist should consider these differences when breeding them. Other special considerations are indicated under each species. Sub-families are the Aphaniinae, Cyprinodontinae, Fundulinae, Procato-podinae and Rivulinae.

Killifishes, Egg-Laying Toothcarps

Adinia multifasciata

GIRARD, 1859
Sub-Fam.: Fundulinae

Syn.: *Fundulus xenicus, Adinia xenica*

Hab.: In brackish and fresh waters of the southern US; from Texas to western Florida.

Fl.: Uncertain though probably from 1975.

Sex: ♂ has 10 to 14 narrow, pearl-colored bands between darker cross-stripes. These are not found on the ♀.

Soc. B.: If given sufficient space and hiding places they are a peaceful species and can be combined with such other brackishwater species as *Cyprinodon variegatus, Monodactylus* sp., and certain species of *Fundulus*.

M: Requires a soft, dark bottom and sufficient hiding places among roots, stones and such. The tank should be planted with vegetation tolerant of brackish water. One example: *Vallisneria americana.*. To make brackish water add $1/4$ to $1/2$ seawater to fresh.

B: Does best in brackish water about 72° F (22° C). Place several clumps of fine-leaved plants in the aquarium. The fish will spawn on these, or on the bottom. Feed the fry *Artemia* nauplii.

F: O; omnivorous; mosquito larvae, small crustaceans and other types of live food; spinach and lettuce, dried or moist. The fish are not choosey.

S: The species has a much paler coloring in fresh water than in water with added salt. In some areas it is used as a natural form of mosquito control.

T: 68-73° F, **L:** 2″, **A:** 23″, **R:** b+m, **D:** 2.
20-23° C, 5 cm, 60 cm,

Fam.: Cyprinodontidae

Aphanius iberus
Spanish Toothcarp

(VALENCIENNES, 1846)
Sub-Fam.: Aphaniinae

Syn.: *Cyprinodon iberus, Lebias ibericus*

Hab.: Found only in fresh water in parts of Spain: Catalonia, Valencia and Murcia; and Morocco, Algeria.

Fl.: 1911

Sex: Evidence of sexual dichromatism; ♂ blue-green to aquamarine. Dorsal and anal fins are dark with lighter spots. The caudal fin is dark blue with lighter markings. ♀ is olive-green or bluegreen with a colorless tail.

Soc. B.: A peaceful, undemanding fish. It may be combined with fish of a similar disposition.

M: A fine gravel bottom with plenty of plants and roots for decoration. Leave open spaces for swimming. Use medium-hard, neutral water (8-10° dGH and pH 7.0).

B: The temperature should be about 86° F (30° C) with fine-leaved plants in the bottom and floating plants above for shade. The fish will spawn on the plants and must be well fed. If not, they will devour their eggs. To be safe you should remove the parents after spawning. The young hatch after one week and can be fed very fine micro-food after the egg-sac is absorbed.

F: C; live foods; mosquito larvae is suggested.

S: When breeding, the best results come when the fish are held in cooler water (12-16° C) during the winter. The species was used to control mosquitos before *Gambusia affinis*.

A. iberus ♀

T: 50-90° F, **L:** 2″, **A:** 19¹/₂″, **R:** m, **D:** 1-2.
10-32° C, 5 cm, 50 cm,

Aphanius fasciatus

(HUMBOLDT & VALENCIENNES, 1821)
Sub-Fam.: Aphaniinae

Syn.: *Lebias fasciatus, Aphanius calaritanus, Cyprinodon calaritanus, C. fasciatus, C. marmoratus, Lebias calaritanus*

Hab.: Much of Europe and Asia; Mediterranean; Maritime Alps; Sardinia; Sicily; Italian coasts to Venice; Istria and Dalmatia, Yugoslavia; Cyprus; Turkey; Syria; Israel; north coast of Africa from Egypt to Algeria.

Fl.: 1913

Sex: ♂ is olive-brown with a whitish belly and 10 to 14 bright, whitish-yellow cross stripes broadening as they descend. The fins are yellow to orange-yellow. ♀ is grey-brown, lighter beneath, with a row of round, dark patches on each side. The fins are almost without color.

Soc. B.: A peaceful, undemanding killifish which may be combined with other peaceful species.

M: Similar to suggestions for *Aphanius iberus*. The addition of sea salt is recommended though you should use less – one to two teaspoons of salt to every three gallons of water (10 l).

B: Similar to recommendations for *A. iberus*. Detailed information is simply not available.

F: C; such live foods as mosquito larvae.

S: *Aphanius fasciatus* is closely related to *A. iberus* and *A. dispar* RUEPPELL, 1829. It differs from these in its reproductive system.

T: 50-75° F, **L:** 2³/₄″, **A:** 23¹/₂″, **R:** m, **D:** 1-2.
10-24° C, 7 cm, 60 cm,

Aphanius iberus ♂

Aphanius fasciatus

Fam.: Cyprinodontidae

Aphyosemion australe
Lyretail, Cape Lopez Lyretail

(RACHOW, 1921)
Sub-Fam.: Rivulinae

Syn.: *Haplochilus calliurus var. australis, H. calliurus, Panchax polychromus, P. australe*

Hab.: Western Africa.

Fl.: 1913, J. Wolmer, Hamburg, West Germany.

Sex: ♂ is brightly colored, the caudal fin has three points, the rays of the upper and lower dorsal and anal fins are extended. ♀ has less coloring, a rounded caudal and is smaller.

Soc. B.: A peaceful fish which is best combined with surface dwellers and other *Aphyosemion* sp.

M: Excellent for a community tank when tank and water conditions are right. The tank should have a dark bottom with peat or loam, dense vegetation, soft lighting and hiding places among roots and plants. Floating plants insure shade. The water should be soft, to 10° dGH, and moderately acid, pH 5.5-6.5. Add salt, about one teaspoon for every $2^{1}/_{2}$ gallons (10 l) of water. Use peat filtration.

B: Breeding is possible in small tanks with soft, slightly acid water (5° dGH and pH 6.5) about 74° F (23° C). Add a perlon mop or finely-leaved plants. To initiate breeding add one female and two or three males. Feed well and remove 10 to 20 eggs from the spawning substrate daily. Transfer the eggs to a small breeding tank which contains water from the spawning tank. The eggs will develop in two weeks. Though this species is an "egg hanger" the eggs can be treated as you would those which are buried. See *Cynolebias* sp.

F: C, O; all types of live foods. Will also take frozen and flake foods.

S: In terms of the life-span of killifish, these will live a long time in an aquarium, up to three years. The ♂ will develop an impressive display behavior toward tankmates, their fins wide spread and intensely colored.

T: 70-75° F, **L**: $2^{1}/_{3}$″, **A**: $19^{1}/_{2}$″, **R**: b+m, **D**: 2.
21-24° C,   6 cm,   50 cm,

Aphyosemion bivittatum
Red Aphyosemion

(LOENNBERG, 1895)
Sub-Fam.: Rivulinae

Syn.: *Fundulus bivittatus, Fundulopanchax bivittatum*

Hab.: West Africa; southeastern Nigeria; southwestern Cameroons.

Fl.: 1908, Carl Siggelkow, Hamburg, West Germany.

Sex: ♂ is brightly colored with the caudal fins extended to points at the top and bottom; ♀ is paler.

Soc. B.: An active yet peaceful fish. The ♂ puts on a remarkable display and will rarely harm the ♀.

M: Follow recommendations for *Aphyosemion mirabile*. Use clear water, free of infusoria and bacteria. Shade the tank and keep away from direct light.

B: Water temperature should be 75 to 79° F (24-26° C). Follow recommendations for *A. mirabile*.

F: C; will accept only live foods (*Daphnia, Cyclops*, insect larvae, Enchytraea) and small earthworms.

S: There are several varieties. All have the typical *bivittatum* shape but differ widely in colors and markings.

T: 72-75° F, **L**: 2″, **A**: $23^{1}/_{2}$″, **R**: m+b, **D**: 2.
22-24° C,   5 cm,   60 cm,

Aphyosemion australe

Aphyosemion bivittatum, large photo. The small photo shows *A. bitaeniatum* (Syn.: *A. multicolor*) which is often misrepresented as *A. bivittatum*.

Fam.: Cyprinodontidae

Aphyosemion bualanum

(AHL, 1924)
Sub-Fam.: Rivulinae

Syn.: *Haplochilus bualanus, Aphyosemion elberti, A. rubrifascium, A. tessmanni*

Hab.: Found in the African savannah; eastern Cameroons; Central Africa.

Fl.: 1938

Sex: ♂ is brightly colored with a blue or bluish-violet metallic shimmer on the sides. Fins are uneven with pointed extensions. ♀ is greenish-brown and lacks the pointed fin extensions.

Soc. B.: A relatively lively fish tolerant of most tankmates.

M: Similar to recommendations for *Aphyosemion australe* or *A. mirabile*. Water should be soft to medium hard and slightly to moderately acid (5-15° dGH and pH 5.5-6.5).

B: Similar to suggestions for *A. australe*. Use soft, slightly acid water (2-5° dGH and pH 6.0-6.5). The fish will spawn on finely-leaved plants and the eggs require 21 days to hatch. Though the fry are slow to grow, there should be no problems in raising them.

F: O; omnivorous.

S: The fish are sensitive to a pH above 7.0.

T: 70-77° F,   L: 2″,   A: 19¹/₂″,   R: m+b,   D: 1-2.
21-25° C,   5 cm,   50 cm,

Aphyosemion cognatum

MEINKEN, 1951
Sub-Fam.: Rivulinae

Syn.: None

Hab.: Africa: Zaire - the region around Stanley Pool.

Fl.: 1950, "Aquarium Hamburg", Hamburg, West Germany.

Sex: ♂ is brighter and more colorful. The dorsal and anal fins have red seams and blue edges. ♀ is grey to yellow.

Soc. B.: An active, peaceful fish which can be combined with other *Aphyosemion* or kept in a species tank.

M: Similar to suggestions for *Aphyosemion striatum*: relatively dense vegetation with such hiding places as roots and decorations. Needs soft, slightly acid water (5-8° dGH, pH 6.0-6.5). Partial regular water changes are recommended.

B: Similar to suggestions for *A. striatum*. An "egg-hanger", the fish lays 200-250 eggs and breeding is initiated by adding one ♂ and two ♀♀. The eggs develop continuously without diapause and hatch in two weeks.

F: C; live foods.

S: Closely related to *A. elegans* BOULENGER, 1899.

T: 72-75° F,   L: 2¹/₄″,   A: 27″,   R: m+b,   D: 2.
22-24° C,   5.5 cm,   70 cm,

Aphyosemion bualanum, top, Western Cameroons. Below, Eastern Cameroons.

Aphyosemion cognatum

527

Fam.: Cyprinodontidae

Aphyosemion deltaense

RADDA, 1976
Sub-Fam.: Rivulinae

Syn.: None

Hab.: West Africa; Nigeria and western Niger delta.

Fl.: 1974, Dr. A. Radda, Vienna. Austria – a few specimens were imported, but died. 1975, E. Puerzl, Vienna, Austria.

Sex: ♂ is larger and more intricately colored.

Soc. B.: An active, tolerant species though the males tend to bite each other. The solution: keep only a large number of males. Where there are many of the same sex, aggression is divided or diluted, and thus reduced.

M: Similar to recommendations for *Aphyosemion sjoestedti*. Needs room for swimming.

B: A water temperature between 72-75° F (22-24° C) is best. The fish buries its eggs which take about three months to develop. Breed as you would for *A. sjoestedti*. The ♀ must be ready when you initiate breeding. The ♂ become anxious and angry toward nonspawning ♀ and the female needs hiding places. If there are none the ♀ may die.

F: All kinds of large live foods – mosquito larve, adult insects, *Tubifex* worms, Enchytraea; also flakes.

S: none.

T: 72-79° F, **L:** 4″, **A:** 31″, **R:** m+b, **D:** 2.
22-26° C, 10 cm, 80 cm,

Aphyosemion exigoideum

RADDA & HUBER, 1977
Sub-Fam.: Rivulinae

Syn.: None

Hab.: Gaboon, Africa; in small rain forest streams near Mandilou.

Fl.: 1977

Sex: ♂ is rusty brown with a whitish belly with red patches. The fins are brightly colored. ♀ is brownish-grey and a light beige underneath. The fins are without color.

Soc. B.: Unknown.

M: The only a few details are in a piece by RADDA & HUBER, 1977; Aquaria 24, pp 138-143. Soft to medium hard, slightly alkaline water (1-12° dGH and pH 7.5).

B: Successful though no data is available. The embryos require 10-20 days to develop.

F: C; live food.

T: 72-75° F, **L:** 1″, **A:** 19$^1/_2$″, **R:** b+m, **D:** 2-3.
22-24° C, 3.5 cm, 50 cm,

Aphyosemion deltaense

Aphyosemion exigoideum

Fam.: Cyprinodontidae

Aphyosemion exiguum

(BOULENGER, 1911)
Sub-Fam.: Rivulinae

Syn.: *Haplochilus exiguus, Aphyosemion jaundense, A. loboanum, Panchax loboanus, P. jaundensis*

Hab.: West Africa; In the waters of rain forests in eastern Cameroons and northern Gaboon.

Fl.: 1966

Sex: ♂ is substantially brighter and more intensely colored. The dorsal fin is frequently pointed.

Soc. B.: An active, elegant Killifish. Very peaceful and well behaved.

M: See recommendations for *A. australe* or *A. mirabile*.

B: A perennial species: follow recommendations suggested for *A. australe*. Water should be soft and slightly acid (about 5° dGH and pH 6.0-6.5). The parents spawn on plants, and pause between passes. The eggs hatch after 21 days and the fry grow slowly.

F: C; all types of live foods.

S: The fish can also be bred in hard, alkaline and are closely related to *A. bualanum*.

T: 70-75° F,   **L:** 1¹/₂″,   **A:** 15¹/₂″ to 19¹/₂″,   **R:** m+b,   **D:** 2.
   21-24° C,   4 cm,   40 to 50 cm,

Aphyosemion filamentosum
Plumed Lyretail

(MEINKEN, 1933)
Sub-Fam.: Rivulinae

Syn.: *Fundulopanchax filamentosus, "Aphyosemion ruwenzori"*

Hab.: In ponds in West Africa; western Nigeria; Togo.

Fl.: 1913

Sex: ♂ are larger and brighter in color. The rays on their tails and anal fins are more obviously extended.

Soc. B.: An active, predominantly peaceful annual species. They react aggressively when disturbed during courtship and are best kept in a species tank. If kept in a community tank limit fish to other *Aphyosemion* species and/or surface-dwellers.

M: Needs a dark, soft, loamy bottom with shade or subdued lighting. Likes plenty of plants and lots of hiding places but makes no special demands in terms of water quality. Soft water to 10° dGH is suggested.

B: Slightly acid, soft water (pH 5.5-6.0 and hardness to 8° dGH) at temperatures between 72 and 77° F (22-25° C) is best. Recommend a low water level, about 8 inches (20 cm.) with dense, finely leaved vegetation and subdued lighting. The tank should be darkened with a peat bottom (the species buries its eggs). Spawning is initiated with one ♂ and two or three ♀. Remove peat three weeks after spawning and store four to 12 weeks at a moderate temperature. It should not dry out. Then fill with soft water. Feed the fry well after hatching.

F: C, O; predominantly all types of live foods; flakes; FD; frozen food.

S: Found in many morphs with different colorings, markings and fin shapes. A fish decribed as *"A. ruwenzori"* was imported in 1966 and is a morph of *A. filamentosum* with bright reddish colored fins reccuring in later generations.

T: 70-73° F,   **L:** 2″,   **A:** 19¹/₂″,   **R:** m,   **D:** 3.
   21-23° C,   5.5 cm,   50 cm,

Aphyosemion exiguum

Aphyosemion filamentosum

Fam.: Cyprinodontidae

Aphyosemion gardneri
Steel-Blue Aphyosemion

(BOULENGER, 1911)
Sub-Fam.: Rivulinae

Syn.: *Fundulus gardneri, Fundulopanchax gardneri*

Hab.: In waters of the savannahs and forests of west Africa; Nigeria; western Cameroons.

Fl.: 1913, Brandt, Leipzig, East Germany.

Sex: ♂ is brightly colored with 30 to 90 red dots along the body. ♀ is less brightly colored with numerous small brown dots on the sides.

Soc. B.: A relatively aggressive, intolerant annual species. ♂♂ often fight among themselves, nibble at fins and harrass ♀.

M: Similar to suggestions for *A. australe* but sea salt should be omitted. Needs a tank with plenty of hiding places and soft, slightly acid water (5-8° dGH and pH 6.5).

B: Suggest a water temperature between 74 and 79° F (24-26° C). The species spawns on finely-leaved plants and the fry usually hatch in 14 to 21 days. A diapause can be forced by drying the tank though the embryos do not survive longer for it. The water must be returned after 28-30 days.

F: C; live foods; flakes on occasion.

S: In different locations the species is found with different color patterns. A number of sub-species have been described.

T: 72-77° F, **L:** 3″,   **A:** 19$^{1}/_{2}$″, **R:** t+m, **D:** 2.
22-25° C,   6 cm,   50 cm,

Aphyosemion gulare

(BOULENGER, 1901)
Sub-Fam.: Rivulinae

Syn.: *Fundulus gularis, Aphyosemion beauforti, A. fallax, Fundulopanchax gularis*

Hab.: In water holes in west Africa; southern Nigeria.

Fl.: 1907, C. Siggelkow, Hamburg, West Germany.

Sex: ♂ is more intricately and brightly colored. Pectoral fins tend toward yellow with red or blue edging. The pelvic fins are yellow. On the ♀ they are without color.

Soc. B: These Killies will not tolerate each other. Larger specimens are predators and should only be combined with substantially smaller fishes.

M: Similar to recommendations for *A. filamentosum*. Needs plenty of hiding places. pH and hardness are not cricital. We suggest the fish be kept in a species tank.

B: An annual, try water temperatures between 72-74° F (22-24° C). The fish buries its eggs and thus needs a peat bottom. The fry hatch after three months and are easy to raise.

F: C; live foods; flakes.

S: It is now assumed *A. gulare* is a super species.

T: 68-72° F, **L:** 3″,   **A:** 27″,   **R:** m+b, **D:** 2.
20-22° C,   8 cm,   70 cm,

Aphyosemion gardneri nigerianum

Aphyosemion gulare

Aphyosemion marmoratum

RADDA, 1973
Sub-Fam.: Rivulinae

Syn.: None

Hab.: West Africa; Cameroons, the Meme river and in the neighbourhood of the Mbonga.

Fl.: 1972, Dr. Alfred Radda, Vienna, Austria.

Sex: ♂ is more intricately colored.

Soc. B.: A peaceful Killifish, it may be combined with other *Aphyosemion* or kept in a species tank.

M: Similar to suggestions for *A. australe* and *A. striatum*.

B: Easy to breed. Follow suggestions for *A. striatum*

F: C; primarily live foods; frozen food. Will not accept flakes.

S: *A. marmoratum* appears to rank systematically between *A. mirabile*, a representative of *A. gardneri* super-species, and the *A. cameronense* complex.

T: 70-73° F, **L:** 2″, **A:** 19¹/₂″, **R:** b+m, **D:** 1-2.
21-23° C, 5 cm, 50 cm,

Aphyosemion volcanum

RADDA & WILDEKAMP, 1977
Sub-Fam.: Rivulinae

Syn.: *A. bivittatum* (not LOENNBERG, 1895)

Hab.: West Africa; volcanic soils of Mt. Cameroon and around Kumba; in a small area of western Cameroon.

Fl.: Probably 1966 by Clausen and Scheel.

Sex: ♂♂ are brightly colored and have uneven fin extensions, the points generally a sulphur yellow. The body is bronze to copper. ♀ have smaller, rounded fins which are usually transparent.

Soc. B.: Somewhat aggressive towards ♂ of its own and other species of Aphyosemions, but peaceful toward all other fish. Should be accompanied only with smaller fish or kept in species tank. Lamp-eye Panchax are also suitable tankmates.

M: It is at home in the coastal tropical areas of West Africa, found in warm, soft slightly acid waters with temperatures between 25.5-27° C (pH 6.0 and 1° dGH). The fish can cope with temperatures between 23 and 26° C (73-79° F) in an aquarium. The water should not be too hard and should tend toward acidity. If conditions are otherwise good, particularly with lots of vegetation – Java Fern, Java Moss and *Anubias barteri* are examples – the water values are of secondary impor-

tance. The water should be changed often and a dark substrate is suggested to show off the colors. Subdued lighting is best. Use roots as decoration. Check pH often.

B: Place one ♂ and two ♀ in a special breeding tank with Java Moss, perlon wadding or a mop for spawning. Check regularly for eggs and place these in the breeding bowl with a trace of Trypaflavine to prevent mould. The fry will hatch in about 14 days.

Hatching will be more regular if peat fibers are used as the spawning material. It should be removed after one week and stored in a plastic bag to keep it moist for two or three weeks then cooler water (16° C) should be added. When the fry hatch feed them brine shrimp.

F: C; when possible white and black mosquito larvae or other live foods; accepts flakes unwillingly.

S: Belongs to the sub-genus *Chromaphyosemion* together with *A. bivittatum, A. loennbergii, A. riggenbachi* and *A. splendopleure.* All populations of this fish should be identified by their place of origin since frequently they cannot be crossed for several generations.

T: 73-79° F, **L:** 2″, **A:** 23¹/₂″, **R:** all, **D:** 2-3.
23-26° C, 4.5 cm, 60 cm,

Aphyosemion marmoratum

Aphyosemion volcanum

535

Aphyosemion mirabile

RADDA, 1970
Sub-Fam.: Rivulinae

Syn.: None

Hab.: West Africa; Mbio, western Cameroons.

Fl.: 1970, Dr. Alfred Radda, Vienna, Austria.

Sex: ♂ is more brightly colored. ♀ is brown with rows of spots.

Soc. B.: A peaceful, lively Killifish.

M: Prefers a well-planted tank with a dark bottom of peat or mulm decorated with roots and other hiding places. Avoid bright lights. Use soft, slightly acid water 1-6° dGH and pH 6.0-6.5. Occasional water changes are recommended.

B: Can be bred in one gallon (5 liter) tanks. Use Java Moss or perlon for spawning and the water values suggested above. Place one ♂ with two or three ♀. Remove the eggs and place in a bowl with tank water. Disinfect the water with a little Trypaflavine (the color of the water: a pale yellow). The

fry hatch after three weeks and should be fed powdered foods.

F: C; live food, particularly white and black mosquito larvae.

S: Four sub-species have been described: Aphyosemion mirabile mirabile RADDA, 1970 (see photo); A. mirabile moense RADDA, 1970; A. mirabile intermittens RADDA, 1971 and A. mirabile traudeae RADDA, 1972. The use of too much Trypaflavine or similar medications can harden the egg sacs. The fry cannot then hatch.

A. m. traudeae

T: 72-77° F,   L: 3″,   A: 23¹/₂″,   R: b,   D: 2.
  22-25° C,   7 cm,   60 cm,

Aphyosemion puerzli

RADDA & SCHEEL, 1974
Sub-Fam.: Rivulinae

Syn.: None

Hab.: West Africa; western Cameroon.

Fl.: 1973, Drs. Alfred Radda and J. Scheel.

Sex: ♂ is more brightly colored with the brightest markings on the head and gill covers.

Soc. B.: Similar to A. gardneri.

M: Follow suggestions for A. australe or A. gardneri. The choice depends on whether the species is considered an "egg-hanger" or as one which buries its spawn.

B: 22-25° C (72-77° F) water soft around 5° dGH and neutral to slightly alkaline (pH 7-7.5). A. puerzli may be regarded as a semi-annual species. The fish may be

treated as either "egg-hangers" or "egg-buriers". The spawn of this semi-annual species develops continuously in water, but as it receeds typical signs of diapause appear. The aqueous development of A. puerzli is 18 to 21 days. The water should not contain too much oxygen since, if it does, difficulties in hatching may be experienced. If treated as a species which buries its eggs, hatching will require 7 to 8 weeks.

F: C; all kinds of live foods, white and black mosquito larvae is the preferred choice.

T: 70-75° F,   L: 3″,   A: 23¹/₂″,   R: b+m,   D: 2.
  21-24° C,   6 cm,   60 cm,

Aphyosemion mirabile

Aphyosemion puerzli

Aphyosemion riggenbachi

(AHL, 1924)
Sub-Fam.: Rivulinae

Syn.: *Haplochilus riggenbachi*

Hab.: In spring-fed ponds in west Africa; southwestern Cameroons.

Fl.: 1971, Dr. Alfred Radda, Vienna, Austria.

Sex: ♂ is most brightly colored, their fins spotted with carmine. The caudal fins are pointed at top and bottom. The fins of ♀ are shorter, rounded and with less color.

Soc. B.: A relatively active though peaceful species. Keep in a species tank or in company with other peaceful, not too small species of *Aphyosemion*.

M: Use little water, about 4 inches (10 cm.) with added roots or rocks as hiding places with heavy vegetation along the edge and back of the tank. The bottom should be dark with peat or mulm. Recommend very soft, moderately acid water, to 5° dGH and pH 5.5. The fish react quickly to polluted water exhibiting such signs as clamped fins.

B: An easy species to breed and are prolific with proper food. Follow our recommendations for *A. mirabile*.

F: C; all kinds of live food. Use moderation in feeding since the fish will overeat and eventually die.

S: Fish bred in captivity may not reach the size of those in the wild. *A. riggenbachi* belongs to the super-species *A. bivittatum*.

T: 68-73° F, L: 4″, A: 27″, R: b+m, D: 2.
20-23° C, 10 cm, 70 cm,

Aphyosemion sjoestedti
Red Aphyosemion, Golden Pheasant

(LOENNBERG, 1895)
Sub-Fam.: Rivulinae

Syn.: *Fundulus sjoestedti, Fundulopanchax sjoestedti, Nothobranchius sjoestedti, Aphyosemion coeruleum, Fundulus caeruleum*

Hab.: Found in water holes in west Africa; from southern Nigeria and the western Cameroons as far as Ghana.

Fl.: 1909, J. Wolmer, Hamburg, West Germany.

Sex: ♂ more brightly coloured than the ♀. The ♂ also being larger.

Soc. B.: An active, aggressive seasonal species.

M: Needs a roomy tank with 8 to 12 inches of water (20-30 cm.). Add a dark tank bottom and lots of vegetation with plenty of hiding places such as roots and stones. The species is not demanding about water conditions but we suggest soft, slightly acid water, to 12° dGH and pH 6.5.

B: It is possible in a small tank but we suggest at least two gallons (10 liter) of water per pair. We recommend a water temperature of 72 to 74° F (22-24° C) with the values outlined above. Add a tank bottom of thick peat since the fish bury their eggs. After spawning press excess moisture from the peat and keep it in plastic bags for 4 to 6 weeks at temperatures between 18 and 20° C. Do not let the peat dry. Add soft water to hatch the fry. Feed them *Artemia* nauplii.

F: C; will eat only live foods; recommend *Tubifex*, Enchytraea, mosquito larvae, adult insects and small fish.

S: The species was originally described in 1895 and rediscovered in 1981 by a group of German Killifish enthusiasts in the area from which the original species came (mouth of the Ndian river in West Cameroon).

T: 73-79° F, L: 4¹/₂″, A: 31″, R: m, D: 3.
23-26° C, 12 cm, 80 cm,

Aphyosemion riggenbachi

Aphyosemion sjoestedti

Aphyosemion striatum

(BOULENGER, 1911)
Sub-Fam.: Rivulinae

Syn.: *Haplochilus striatus*

Hab.: Africa; northern Gaboon.

Fl.: 1961

Sex: ♂ are very colorful; ♀ is olive-colored.

Soc. B.: Peaceful fish.

M: Needs a tank with a dark bottom, plenty of vegetation and subdued lighting. Suggest a cover of floating plants. Prefers places to hide among plants and roots and clean, soft and slightly acid water (to 12° dGH and pH about 6.0). A touch of salt (one teaspon to two gallons = 10 liters) prevents the growth of parasites.

B: The fish have been bred in shallow $^1/_2$-gallon (2 liter) tanks. Suggest Java Moss or perlon for spawning. The species is easy to raise. Use soft, slightly acid water to 6° dGH and pH 6.5. The spawning period will continue for several weeks and a pair will produce up to 30 eggs in a day. The eggs have tiny adhesive threads which stick to the tank bottom. They will hatch in 10 to 15 days and should be fed *Artemia* nauplii and/or Protogen granulate.

F: C; primarily all types of live foods. Will also enjoy FD but will reject flakes.

S: As with many killifish consistently high water temperatures will shorten the life of *A. striatum*. The tank should be covered since the species is a jumper.

T: about 72° F,   **L**: 2",   **A**: 19$^1/_2$",   **R**: b+m,   **D**: 2-3.
about 22° C,   5 cm,   50 cm,

Roloffia toddi

(CLAUSEN, 1966)
Sub-Fam.: Rivulinae

Syn.: *Aphyosemion occidentale toddi, A. toddi, Roloffia occidentalis toddi*

Hab.: In spring-fed forest ponds of west Africa; Sierra Leone.

Fl.: 1963, Erhard Roloff, Karlsruhe, West Germany.

Sex: ♂ is more intensely colored with a pointed anal fin.

Soc. B.: When sexually mature, the fish do not tolerate each other well and bite. Death may therefore occur in a small tank. The fish are relatively peaceful in large aquariums as they can escape from each other's dangerous attacks.

M: Needs a dark tank with a soft dark bottom of peat or mulm with hiding places among roots and stones. Use floating plants to diffuse the light. Add soft slightly acid water, to 8° dGH and pH 6.0-6.5. Keep in a species tank only.

B: Recommend a water temperature about 73° F (23° C). Cover the bottom of the tank with two inches (5 cm) of peat. Remove the peat every one or two weeks, carefully press out excess moisture and keep the peat moist in a sealed plastic bag in a dark place at temperatures between 72 and 74° F (22-24° C). After five months add water. When the fry hatch remove them with a glass tube then dry the peat. Add water a second time one month later. In most cases a second hatching will occur. The young will take *Artemia* nauplii immediately and Grindal worms after a few days.

F: C; all kinds of live foods; Use *Tubifex* sparingly since a steady diet will produce losses.

S: *Roloffia toddi* was originally considered a sub-species of *A. occidentalis* but attempts at crossing the two produced sterile offspring, indicating the species are unrelated.

T: 72-75° F,   **L**: 3",   **A**: 23$^1/_2$",   **R**: b,   **D**: 3.
22-24° C,   8 cm,   60 cm,

Aphyosemion striatum

Roloffia toddi

Aphyosemion volcanum see page 534

Aphyosemion walkeri

(BOULENGER, 1911)
Sub-Fam.: Rivulinae

Syn.: *Haplochilus walkeri, Aphyosemion spurrelli*

Hab.: In forest waters of west Africa; southern Ghana and southeastern Ivory Coast.

Fl.: 1952, L. Sheljuzhko. (Commissioned by A. Werner, Munich, West Germany).

Sex: ♂ is larger and more brightly colored.

Soc. B.: A lively, aggressive Killifish, it should not be combined with very small fish. These will be eaten.

M: Similar to recommendations for *A. australe* or *A. striatum*. Water values of 5-10° dGH and pH 6.5. Recommend peat filtration.

B: Suggest a water temperature of 73-77° F (23-25° C). Initiate breeding with one ♂ and two ♀. The species may be treated as one which spawns on plants or which buries its eggs. For details see *A. puerzli*. The maturation period for an egg-hanger is 4-5 weeks and 6-weeks for one which buries its eggs.

F: C; all live foods. Will reluctantly accept flakes.

S: As water temperatures rise, the coloring diminishes. Warmer water also invites disease.

T: 68-73° F, **L**: 2¹/₂″, **A**: 23¹/₂″, **R**: m+t, **D**: 2.
    20-23° C,   6.5 cm,   60 cm,

Aplocheilichthys macrophthalmus
Lamp-Eye Panchax

MEINKEN, 1932
Sub-Fam.: Procatopodinae

Syn.: *Fundulopanchax luxophthalmus*

Hab.: In forest waters of west Africa; from southern Dahomey to the Niger delta.

Fl.: 1929, "Aquarium Hamburg", Hamburg, West Germany.

Sex: ♂ is more brightly colored with a noticeable extension at the back of the dorsal and anal fins. ♀ has much less body color with almost colorless, rounded fins.

Soc. B.: A very peaceful yet lively schooling species which is best kept with *Telmatherina ladigesi*.

M: Recommend a tank with a dark bottom and heavy vegetation along the edges and back. Use floating plants to reduce the light and add roots and rocks for hiding places but keep areas open for swimming. Use a filter to create a current. The water should be medium-hard and slightly alkaline, about 10° dGH and pH 7.2 -7.5. The fish show their colors best in direct light.

B: Suggest a water temperature 76-79° F (24-26° C). Follow recommendations for *Aplocheilichthys pumilus* but with water medium hard (around 10° dGH) and neutral to slightly alkaline (pH 7.0-7.5). The small eggs (Ø 1 mm) are suspended from plants by adhesive threads and require 10 to 14 days to develop. Raise fry with small live food.

F: Firs, all kinds of live foods; also flakes; FD.

S: The fry are sensitive to infusoria. Two species are known as Lamp-Eye Panchax to hobbyists: *A. macrophthalmus macrophthalmus* MEINKEN, 1932 and *A. macrophthalmus hannerzi* SCHEEL, 1967. The former sub-species *A. macrophthalmus scheeli* is now considered an independent species.
The fry of *A. macrophthalmus* are sensitive to Infusoria.

T: 72-79° F, **L**: 1¹/₂″, **A**: 19¹/₂″, **R**: m+t, **D**: 3.
    22-26° C,   4 cm,   50 cm,

Aphyosemion walkeri

Aplocheilichthys macrophthalmus

Fam.: Cyprinodontidae

Aplocheilichthys pumilus

(BOULENGER, 1906)
Sub-Fam.: Procatopodinae

Syn.: *Haplochilus pumilus, Haplochilichthys pumilus, Haplochilus dhonti, Aplocheilichthys dhonti*

Hab.: In crater lakes of east Africa; Lake Victoria; Lake Tanganyika; Lake Edward; Lake Kivu.

Fl.: Possibly, 1930.

Sex: On ♂ all fins except the pectorals are orange-brown. On ♀ they are rounded and without color.

Soc. B.: A peaceful, easily frightened, timid schooling fish. The species is best combined with fish which prefer the bottom and middle ranges of water.

M: Prefers a dark tank bottom with background vegetation and hiding places among roots. Also likes open areas for swimming and hard, slightly alkaline water, from 12° dGH and pH 7.5. Aerate the tank

well: the colors are brighter in water with a high oxygen content.

B: Water should be soft and slightly acid (5° dGH and pH 6.5) at temperatures between 77 and 80° F (25-27° C). Use about half the salt suggested in a "normal" tank and add fine-leaved plants. A low water level is best with plenty of aeration. The fish will spawn on plants and the eggs should mature in 15 days. Added light may speed the process. Feed the young soft foods.

F: C; all types of live foods – *Daphnia*, mosquito larvae, *Tubifex*. Enchytraea, etc.; sometimes flakes.

S: Soft, acid water may promote tuberculosis. Keep some light in the tank at night since the fish lose control in darkness and may injure themselves.

T: 75-79° F, **L**: 2″, **A**: 23$\frac{1}{2}$″, **R**: m+t, **D**: 2-3.
    24-26° C,   5.5 cm,   60 cm,

Aplocheilichthys spilauchen

(DUMERIL, 1861)
Sub-Fam.: Procatopodinae

Syn.: *Poecilia spilauchen, Aplocheilichthys typus, Epiplatys spilauchen, Haplochilus spilauchen, Poecilia bensoni*

Hab.: In estuaries, mangrove swamps and brackish water of west Africa; from Senegal to lower Zaire.

Fl.: 1906, H. Stueve, Hamburg, West Germany.

Sex: ♂♂ are taller and larger with silvery cross-stripes at the base of the tail stem and have intensely colored fins.

Soc. B.: A lively, active, schooling fish.

M: Similar to recommendations for *Aplocheilichthys pumilus* but requires more warmth. If possible, the temperature should not drop below 74° F (23° C). The species prefers brackish water so add 2-3 teaspoons of salt for each 2$\frac{1}{2}$ gallons (10 l) of water.

B: Water temperature (79-86° F) 26-30° C with 10-15% seawater added. In other respects follow recommendations for *A. pumilus*. The species is not as prolific.

F: C, O; all types of live foods; flakes.

S: Very sensitive to an accumulation of infusoria.

T: 75-90° F, **L**: 3″, **A**: 27″, **R**: t, m, **D**: 2.
    24-32° C,   7 cm,   70 cm,

Aplocheilichthys pumilus

Aplocheilichthys spilauchen

Aplocheilus blockii
Green Panchax

(ARNOLD, 1911)
Sub-Fam.: Rivulinae

Syn.: *Haplochilus panchax* var. *blockii, Aplocheilus parvus, Panchax parvus, P. panchax* var. *blockii*

Hab.: Madras, southern India; possibly Sri Lanka.

Fl.: 1909, Captain Block.

Sex: ♀ is less intensely colored, smaller and has fewer markings.

Soc. B.: A lively fish recommended for the upper and middle tank strata. They are peaceful towards their own species and other tankmates and may be kept with other fish of similar size.

M: Similar to recommendations for *A. lineatus* in water that is not too hard (to 10° dGH.)

B: Follow recommendations for *A. lineatus.* Success is influenced by the food which should be mostly mosquito larvae and insects.

F: C, O; all types of live food; flakes.

S: This is the smallest known species of *Aplocheilus.*

T: 72-79° F, **L:** 2″, **A:** 15$^1/_2$″, **R:** m+t, **D:** 2.
  22-26° C, 5 cm, 40 cm,

Aplocheilus dayi
Ceylon Killifish

(STEINDACHNER, 1892)
Sub-Fam.: Rivulinae

Syn.: *Haplochilus dayi, Panchax dayi*

Hab.: Southern India; Sri Lanka.

Fl.: 1937, Fritz Mayer.

Sex: ♀ has shorter, more rounded fins. The dorsal has a black patch at the base.

Soc. B.: A timid, hardy surface dweller it often becomes active with its own species. Should be kept with fish of its own size or larger.

M: Follow suggestions for *A. lineatus.* Hiding places are important since the dominant fish are often aggressive and hostile toward subordinate members of their species.

B: Suggest a water temperature of 77° F (25° C). See recommendations for *A. lineatus. A. dayi* lays about ten colorless eggs a day (Ø 2 mm). These require 12 to 14 days to develop. The fry grow quickly.

F: C; all types of live foods; flakes; tablets.

S: Cover the tank since the fish are excellent jumpers.

T: 68-77° F, **L:** 4″, **A:** 31″, **R:** t, **D:** 2.
  20-25° C, 10 cm, 80 cm,

Aplocheilus blockii

Aplocheilus dayi

Fam.: Cyprinodontidae

Aplocheilus lineatus
Sparkling Panchax

Syn.: *Panchax lineatum, Aplocheilus affinis, A. rubrostigma, A. vittatus, Haplochilus lineatus, H. lineolatus, Panchax lineatus*

Hab.: Southern India.

Fl.: 1909, Vereinigte Zierfischzuechtereien, Conradshoehe, West Germany.

Sex: ♂ is brighter and larger with 6-8 narrow, dark cross stripes. On the ♀ the black body markings are larger.

Soc. B.: A surface-dwelling predator often aggressive against its own species. Should be combined only with larger fish.

M: Needs a tank bottom of fine gravel with dense planting at the edges. Add a few floating plants to reduce the light and add roots and stones for hiding places. Cover the tank since the species is a jumper. The fish is not demanding about water quality though it should not be too hard.

(VALENCIENNES, 1846)
Sub-Fam.: Rivulinae

B: Suggest four to 6 gallons (20-30 liters) of soft to medium hard, slightly acid water (to 12° dGH and pH 6.0-6.8) at temperatures between 77-82° F (25-28° C). Add fine-leaved plants and floating plants for cover. Bright light helps. The tank must be covered. The fish will spawn on or in the plants or on perlon wadding. Transfer the eggs to a shallow bowl or tank. The spawning should be interupted after eight days since the fish may exhaust themselves. The fry will hatch after 12-14 days and should be fed powdered foods.

F: All kinds of live foods – insects, *Tubifex*, small crustaceans, earthworms, small fish; flakes; tablets.

S: None.

T: 72-77° F, **L:** 4″,   **A:** 31″,   **R:** t, occasionally m, **D:** 2.
   22-25° C,   10 cm,   80 cm,

Aplocheilus panchax
Blue Panchax

Syn.: *Esox panchax, Aplocheilus chrysostigmus, Haplochilus panchax, Panchax buchanani, P. kuhlii, P. melanopterus, P. panchax*

Hab.: Southern India; Burma; Thailand; Malaysian penninsula; Greater Sunda Islands (Sumatra, Borneo, Java); several smaller islands in the Indo-Australian Archipelago.

Fl.: 1899, Hans Stueve, Hamburg, West Germany.

Sex: Slight differences; ♀ may have orange-colored fins of more intensity.

Soc. B.: A lively, peaceful surface dweller which may be predatory. The ♂♂ consider each other rivals.

M: Similar to recommendations for *A. lineatus.*

(HAMILTON, 1822)
Sub-Fam.: Rivulinae

B: Similar to recommendations for *A. lineatus* with water temperatures between 73-82° F (23-28° C). Lays its eggs on algae, moss or fine-leaved plants. The eggs require 10 to 14 days to hatch. The fry are easy to raise.

F: C; all types of live foods; small fish; flakes.

S: Similar to *A. blockii* in appearance though the two are not related. The species can be distinguished by the number of lateral line scales. *A. panchax* has 30-33. *A. blockii* has only 24-29. Two sub-species are known: *A. panchax panchax* (HAMILTON-BUCHANAN, 1822) and *A. panchax siamensis* SCHEEL, 1968. The latter is found only in Thailand.

T: 68-77° F, **L:** 3″,   **A:** 23$^{1}/_{2}$″, **R:** t,   **D:** 1-2.
   20-25° C,   8 cm,   60 cm,

Aplocheilus lineatus

Aplocheilus panchax

Cynolebias bellottii
Argentine Pearl

STEINDACHNER, 1881
Sub-Fam.: Rivulinae

Syn.: *Cynolebias maculatus, C. gibberosus, C. robustus*

Hab.: South America: headwaters of Rio de la Plata.

Fl.: 1906

Sex: ♂ is larger with a dark or grey-blue body which becomes almost black during spawning. ♀ is yellow-grey to olive.

Soc. B.: A lively, often irritable seasonal species. In the spawning season ♂ is especially hostile toward the ♀.

M: Needs a tank with a soft bottom and a low water level, about 10-12 inches (30 cm.) Plant lightly with *Myriophyllum* and *Elodea* sp. Suggest soft, slightly acid water, 5° dGH and pH 6.5 with frequent water changes. Best kept as a species.

B: Water temperatures between 64 and 77° F are best (18-25° C). Use a small tank. A light layer of boiled peat should be used on the bottom. Spawning is instigated with one ♂ and two ♀♀ and takes place on the peat. The parents should be removed then separated since the ♂ will continue the spawning ritual. Dry the peat and eggs then add water after three or four months. The fry should be raised on *Artemia* nauplii.

F: C, O; all types of live foods; flakes.

S: The fish are short-lived annuals (about ten months) and spawn on the bottom, even on hard sand or bare glass.

T: 64-72° F, but even 39° F, not over 77° F, **L:** 2³/₄", **A:** 23¹/₂", **R:** b+m, **D:** 3.
18-22° C, but even 4° C, not over 25° C, 7 cm, 60 cm,

Cynolebias nigripinnis alexandri

(CASTELLO & LOPEZ, 1974)
Sub-Fam.: Rivulinae

Syn.: *Cynolebias alexandri*

Hab.: South America; Argentina, near Gualeguaychu, Entre Rio Province.

Fl.: 1974

Sex: ♂ is gray-green to blue-green with colored fins and brownish cross bands over its body. ♀ is a lighter brown with nearly colorless fins and many irregular body patches.

Soc. B.: A lively, relatively peaceful annual species. ♂ is much more aggressive toward the ♀ during the spawning season than other species of *Cynolebias*.

M: Follow suggestions for *C. bellottii*. Information regarding water values is not available. VAN DEN NIEUWENHUIZEN indicates medium hardness (about 8° dGH) and slightly acid to neutral water (pH 6.5 to 7.0). (DATZ **30**, 364-369, 1977) Change water frequently.

B: Water temperature between 73 and 76° F (23-24° C). Use a two inch layer of peat on the bottom. Breeding is instigated with one pair. After spawning keep the peat damp in a plastic bag for three weeks. At the end of the time shake the pouch well then reseal and store at temperatures between 72-76° F (22-24° C) for three months. At the end of this time add the contents to a breeding tank with about four inches of water.

F: C; all types of live food such as *Tubifex*, mosquito larvae, small crustaceans, Enchytreae and small water beetles.

S: Adding dry food to the breeding tank can encourage hatching since decomposition reduces oxygen levels. The embryo are suspected of breaking the egg sac as soon as they fail to obtain adequate oxygen.

T: 72-82° F, **L:** 3¹/₂", **A:** 23¹/₂", **R:** b+m, **D:** 3.
22-28° C, 9 cm, 60 cm,

Cynolebias bellottii

Cynolebias nigripinnis alexandri

Cynolebias nigripinnis nigripinnis
Black-Finned Pearl, Dwarf Argentine Pearl

REGAN, 1912
Sub-Fam.: Rivulinae

Syn.: None

Hab.: South America; near Rosario de Santa Fe, Parana.

Fl.: 1908, Wilhelm Eimeke, Hamburg, West Germany.

Sex: Sexually mature ♂ are blue-black to black with iridescent green or blue spots on the body and fins; ♀ may be light grey to ochre.

Soc. B.: A lively, often aggressive Killifish.

M: Keep in a species tank only and follow recommendations for *Cynolebias bellottii*. Use soft, slightly acid water, 4° dGH and pH 6.0. Regular water changes are recommended.

B: See suggestions for *C. bellottii*. The fish bury their eggs and need a bottom layer of peat. Keep eggs moist and add water after a minimum of three months.

F: C; live food; flakes.

S: The eggs of this species may remain viable for three years or more if kept in a closed container, bedded in mud, beneath a layer of water. The fish are prone to *Oodinium*.

T: 68-72° F, L: 2″, A: 19¹/₂″, R: b, D: 3.
20-22° C, 4.5 cm, 50 cm,

Cynolebias whitei

MYERS, 1942
Sub-Fam.: Rivulinae

Syn.: *Pterolebias elegans*

Hab.: Brazil; in small, seasonal waters near Rio de Janeiro.

Fl.: 1958

Sex: ♂ is larger with smaller, rounded fins, less color and a shimmering soft-green tone on the sides.

Soc. B.: A very lively fish with the ♂ displaying color. Tankmates may bite and damage each other's fins though the injuries are rarely serious.

M: Similar to suggestions for *C. bellottii*. Keep in a species tank.

B: See recommendations for *C. bellottii*. The fish are annuals which bury their eggs.

F: C; live foods such as bloodworms and *Daphnia*; accept flakes unwillingly.

S: If water of a temperature above that recommended is added to the eggs a high percentage of "belly sliders" may result. Water of 19° C is best. Adults can accept fluctuating temperatures.

T: 68-72° F, L: ♂ = 3″, ♀ = 2″, A: 23¹/₂″, R: b, D: 3.
20-22° C, ♂ = 8 cm, ♀ = 5.5 cm, 60 cm,

Cynolebias nigripinnis nigripinnis

Cynolebias whitei

Cynopoecilus ladigesi

(FOERSCH, 1958)
Sub-Fam.: Rivulinae

Syn.: *Cynolebias ladigesi*

Hab.: In seasonal pools in Brazil; near Rio de Janeiro.

Fl.: 1955, "Aquarium Hamburg", Hamburg, West Germany.

Sex: ♂ is more intricately colored, emerald green with cross stripes of dark red. ♀ is brown.

Soc. B.: A peaceful, short-lived annual species.

M: Needs a soft, dark tank bottom with dense planting along the edges and back with open swimming space. Add roots and rocks as hiding places. Aeration and filtration are not essentials. Use soft to medium, slightly acid water, to 10° dGH and pH about 6.0.

B: Suggest water about 72° F (22° C) in a small breeding tank. Place a layer of peat on the bottom since the fish bury their eggs. Spawning takes place after a lively courtship. The eggs have many pistil-like projections. Place the peat and eggs in plastic bags where they should be kept damp, not wet. Add water after two or three months. This process may need to be repeated several times (to 8 months) for all the fry to hatch. Raise the fry on very fine micro food.

F: Predominantly live foods; will also accept frozen and sometimes FD foods.

S: The fish are prolific. FOERSCH (1975) reports that an ♀ laid 2140 eggs in five months. Another produced as many as 3346 in 12 months. (Aquarienmagazin **9**, 404-409).

T: 68-72° F, L: 1$^1/_2$", A: 15$^1/_2$-19$^1/_2$", R: b, D: 3.
20-22° C, 4 cm, 40-50 cm,

Cyprinodon macularius

BAIRD & GIRARD, 1853
Sub-Fam.: Cyprinodontinae

Syn.: None

Hab.: Southern U.S. to northern Mexico; from southern Nevada and California as far south as Sonora, Mexico.

Fl.: 1963, Dr. Haas.

Sex: During the spawning season ♂ has luminous coloring; ♀ are spotted and a drab brown.

Soc. B.: A loner, ♂ rests in shallow water in crater-like depressions which he has dug, driving off all intruders.

M: Needs a fine gravel bottom and, as vegetation, algae (*Chara*) and reeds. Prefers hard, moderately alkaline water, over 15° dGH and pH 8.0 Suggest adding 2-3 teaspoons of salt to each two gallons of water. The species needs heat. Keep in a species tank or in a community tank with other Lyretails of the genera *Cyprinodon* and *Empetrichthys*.

B: Easily bred in a small tank. Use water with salt added inserting perlon webbing since it protects the eggs. Keep the sexes separated for two or three days then place them together in the breeding tank. Courtship will begin in an hour or so and spawning follows a vigorous ritual. The fish will eat their spawn if not removed when the courtship is ended. The ♂♂ are aggressive after spawning. Transfer the webbing and eggs to a breeding tank. The fry will hatch in 6 to 10 days and are easy to raise.

F: C; the species lives chiefly on algae, mosquito larvae, small crustaceans, insects, *Tubifex* worms, flakes and frozen foods.

S: Found naturally in hot springs and water holes where temperatures may reach 113° F (45° C) with concentrations of salt six times greater than seawater (to 20%).

T: 77-95° F, L: 2$^1/_2$", A: 19$^1/_2$", R: t+m, D: 3.
25-35° C, 6.5 cm, 50 cm,

Cynopoecilus ladigesi

Cyprinodon macularius

Cyprinodon nevadensis

EIGENMANN, 1889
Sub-Fam.: Cyprinodontinae

Syn.: None

Hab.: US; California.

Fl.: 1963

Sex: During the spawning season the colors of ♂ are iridescent. ♀ is brown.

Soc. B.: Similar to *C. macularius.*

M: See *C. macularius.*

B: See *C. macularius.*

F: O; primarily an algae diet; also eats small crustaceans, mosquito larvae and *Tubifex* worms; flakes.

S: Certain species have been described.

T: 75-89° F, L: $2^1/_2''$, A: $19^1/_2''$, R: t+m, D: 3.
    25-32° C,   6 cm,   50 cm,

Diapteron cyanostictum

(LAMBERT & GERY, 1967)
Sub-Fam.: Rivulinae

Syn.: *Aphyosemion cyanostictum*

Hab.: Africa; Gaboon.

Fl.: 1972, Herzog and Bochtler, Stuttgart, West Germany.

Sex: ♂ is darker and more intensely colored with noticeably dotted patterns.

Soc. B.: A very peaceful species.

M: Follow suggestions for *Aphyosemion striatum.* Frequent water changes and artificial lighting are recommended. Keep in a species tank.

B: There should be no difficulties. The first fry will hatch after six days and can be raised without problems.

F: C; small, live food such as small crustaceans, mosquito larvae and *Tubifex*; FD.

S: *D. cyanostictum* can be distinguished from other *Aphyosemion* sp. by its dorsal which begins forward of the anal fin.

T: 70-75° F, L: 1'', A: $15^1/_2''$, R: b+m, D: 2.
    21-24° C,   3 cm,   40 cm,

Cyprinodon nevadensis mionectes

Diapteron cyanostictum

Pseudepiplatys annulatus
Rocket Panchax

(BOULENGER, 1915)
Sub-Fam.: Rivulinae

Syn.: *Haplochilus annulatus, Epiplatys annulatus*

Hab.: West Africa; from Guinea to Niger.

Fl.: 1955, Belgium; 1965, Miss Kretschmer, Mr. E. Roloff and Mr. Clausen, West Germany.

Sex: ♂ is larger with colored fins; on ♀ the caudal fin alone is colored and the body lacks the red color of the male.

Soc. B.: A very peaceful species which may be kept with other small, peaceful species or in a species tank.

M: Requires a bottom of peat with a cover of floating plants to diffuse the light. Suggest soft, slightly acid water, 5° dGH and pH 6.5. Make frequent water changes.

B: Breeding is difficult. Recommend soft, moderately acid water (1-3° dGH and pH 5.0-5.5) at a temperature about 77-79° F (25-26° C). Since the fish are "egg hangers" use finely-leaved plants or perlon webbing as spawning material. The eggs require 8 to 10 days to develop but, since the parents will not disturb the eggs, the pair can remain in the breeding tank. Feed the fry infusoria. The young grow slowly.

F: C; all types of live food – such as *Cyclops,* small water fleas, Grindal worms and Rotatoria.

S: According to STERBA *P. annulatus* is a throw-back restricted to certain waters in the forest and savannahs of west Africa. Rarely found in the wild.

T: about 74° F, L: 1¹/₂″, A: 15¹/₂-19¹/₂″, R: t, D: 4.
about 24° C, 4 cm, 40-50 cm,

Epiplatys chevalieri
Chevalier's Epiplatys

(PELLEGRIN, 1904)
Sub-Fam.: Rivulinae

Syn.: *Haplochilus chevalieri, Panchax chevalieri*

Hab.: Africa; Zaire, around Stanley Pool.

Fl.: 1950, "Aquarium Hamburg", Hamburg, West Germany.

Sex: ♂ is brightly colored with large red patches and pointed anal fins; ♀ has less coloring, smaller red patches and a rounded anal fin.

Soc. B.: Active fish, relative peaceful. Best accompanied with peaceful, not over-large fish.

M: Follow suggestions for *Epiplatys dageti.* Does best in a densely-planted tank with medium-hard, slightly acid water, 7-10° dGH and pH 6.5. Add salt and make regular water changes.

B: Suggest water temperatures 74 to 79° F (24-26° C) and suggest following recommendations for *E. dageti.* The fish are "egg hangers" and the fry hatch in two weeks. Since the parents will not disturb their spawn they may remain in the tank. Use soft water, 3-5° dGH, for breeding.

F: C; live food such as insect larvae; flakes.

S: The species is sensitive to infusoria.

T: 74-79° F, L: 2¹/₂″, A: 19¹/₂″, R: t+m, D: 2.
24-26° C, 6 cm, 50 cm,

Pseudepiplatys annulatus

Epiplatys chevalieri

Epiplatys dageti

POLL, 1953
Sub-Fam: Rivulinae

Syn.: None

Hab.: West Africa; Sierra Leone; Liberia; southeastern Ivory Coast; southwestern Ghana.

Fl.: 1908, C. Siggelkow, Hamburg, West Germany.

Sex: ♂ is larger with a pointed anal fin and is seen in a variety of colorations; ♀ is brownish red with a rounded anal fin.

Soc. B.: A lively and peaceful predator when young, the species becomes aggressive with age. The ♂♂ fight each other during spawning. Combine with peaceful fish of similar size.

M: Needs a tank with a dark, fine gravel bottom and dense planting on the edges and back. Suggest floating plants for cover and roots and rocks as decoration. Prefers soft, slightly acid water, to 10° dGH and pH 6.0-6.5. Old water is best so make water changes infrequently.

B: Easy to breed. Water temperature between 24-26° C (74-79° F). The tank should be darkened, planted with fine-leaved vegetation and Riccia on the surface. Breeding can be induced with one female and several males. As many as 200-300 eggs are laid on plants which, since the parents will eat the eggs, should be removed after spawning is complete. Replace removed vegetation with new plants since the spawning extends over a period of weeks. The eggs will hatch in 8-10 days and fry should be fed micro food.

F: C, O; such live food as small crustaceans, adult insects, mosquito larvae, Enchytraea and small fish; enjoy flakes.

S: There are two sub species: Epiplatys dageti dageti POLL, 1953 and E. dageti monroviae DAGET & ARNOULT, 1964. Since 1908 the latter species has been known as E. chaperi which remains the name most used in the hobby.

T: 70-73° F, L: 3", A: 23¹/₂", R: m+t, D: 2.
  21-23° C,   7 cm,   60 cm,

Epiplatys lamottei

(DAGET, 1954)
Sub-Fam.: Rivulinae

Syn.: Epiplatys fasciolatus lamottei

Hab.: West Africa; Liberia; Guinea.

Fl.: 1971, Erhard Roloff, Karlsruhe, West Germany.

Sex: ♂ is the most brightly colored with an extended pelvic fin.

Soc. B.: A peaceful though territorial species which may bite if the tank is too small or if others of its species are added.

M: Recommend a subdued bottom with roots added for hiding places and dense background planting. Darken the back and sides of the tank with daylight entering only from the front. Will accept a range of water conditions. Suggest soft, neutral to alkaline water, 3-5° dGH and pH 7.0-7.8. Change half the water every two or three weeks. Do not add peat.

B: Can be successful in a two-gallon tank (10 liters). Add Java Moss for hiding places and spawning. Water should be medium-hard (8° dGH) and slightly alkaline (about pH 7.5) at a temperature of 73° F (23° C). The spawning will continue for a week with parents producing up to 70 eggs. The fry hatch in two weeks and are easy to raise. (Data from BOEHM: DATZ 27, 223-225, 1974.)

F: C; Primarily ants; also flakes.

S: Bright lighting will weaken body colors.

T: 70-73° F, L: 3", A: 23¹/₂", R: m, D: 4 (C).
  21-23° C,   7 cm,   60 cm,

Epiplatys dageti

Epiplatys lamottei

Epiplatys sexfasciatus
Six-barred Epiplatys

(BOULENGER, 1899)
Sub.Fa,: Rivulinae

Syn.: *Aplocheilus sexfasciatus, Lycocyprinus sexfasciatus, Panchax sexfasciatus*

Hab.: West Africa; from Togo to the mouth of the Zaire river.

Fl.: 1905, H. Schroot, Hamburg, West Germany.

Sex: ♂ has a definite metallic shimmer along the sides of its body, a pointed anal fin and extended pelvic fins which are also pointed; ♀ lacks the metallic sheen, has a rounded anal fin and shorter, squat pelvic fins.

Soc. B.: A surface-dwelling predator. Combine only with fish of similar size.

M: Follow recommendations for *E. dageti.*

B: Follow recommendations for *E. dageti.* Suggest about 8 inches (20 cm) of water at temperatures between 74-79° F (24-26° C). The fry are susceptible to bacterial fin rot.

F: Live food; will also accept frozen food and flakes.

S: There are many varieties of *E. sexfasciatus* which may be attributed to the large territory over which the species is distributed. These differ in shape and fin and body coloring.

T: 72-82° F, **L:** 4", **A:** 31", **R:** t, **D:** 2.
22-28° C, 11 cm, 80 cm,

Epiplatys singa
Spotted Epiplatys

(BOULENGER, 1911)
Sub-Fam.: Rivulinae

Syn.: *Haplochilus macrostigma, Epiplatys chinchoxcanus, Haplochilus senegalensis* (not STEINDACHNER), *Panchax macrostigma, Epiplatys macrostigma*

Hab.: Africa: lower Zaire.

Fl.: 1911, Kropac, Hamburg, West Germany.

Sex: ♂ is more intensely colored with a blue metallic shimmer along the sides of the body; dorsal and anal fins have short, whitish points; ♀ is without the metallic sheen and has rounded dorsal and anal fins.

Soc. B.: A timid predator, the species avoids the company of active fish. In tanks with competition it hides and looses color.

M: Follow recommendations for *E. dageti* but with more plants in the tank. The species prefers soft, old water free of

infusoria (5° dGH and pH 6.0). Not recommended for a community tank.

B: Follow suggestions for *E. dageti* with water temperatures between 73-75° F (23-24° C). Use about 8 inches of water in the breeding tank. The fish are not prolific and 80 to 100 eggs are laid on the plants. Do not expose them to sunlight. The fry will will hatch in 10 days. They grow slowly.

F: C; prefers black and white mosquito larvae; live foods. Will reluctantly accept flakes.

S: Is very sensitive to water changes.

T: 73-77° F, **L:** 2$^1/_2$", **A:** 23$^1/_2$", **R:** m+t, **D:** 4 (C).
23-25° C, 5.5 cm, 60 cm,

Epiplatys sexfasciatus

Epiplatys singa

Fam.: Cyprinodontidae

Fundulosoma thierryi

AHL, 1924
Sub-Fam.: Rivulinae

Syn.: Also traded as *Aphyosemion walkeri*, *A. spurrelli* and *Nothobranchius walkeri*

Hab.: West Africa; Guinea; southern Ghana; Upper Volta; northern Togo; southwestern Niger.

Fl.: 1959, Klaus Kluge.

Sex: There is a blue shimmer of the sides of the body of ♂. ♀ is grey with a larger, fuller stomach during the spawning season.

Soc. B.: A lively fish sometimes aggressive towards its species. Suggest a species tank.

M: Needs a darkened tank with low water level and dark tank bottom of mulm or peat. Recommend subdued light and dense planting with an open space for swimming. Use medium-hard, neutral water, 8-10° dGH and pH 7.0. Keep the water clean with frequent water changes.

B: The species is easily bred in a small tank (such as a plastic bowl). Will accept a range of food; feed in quantity. Add well weathered peat as the spawning medium. Use the water values above. The ♂ courts the ♀ before spawning and the eggs are laid on, or fall to, the bottom. Restrict the spawning to four hours so the female is not taxed. Remove most moisture from the peat and eggs and store in the plastic bags for three to four months. When you are ready to hatch add water. The fry may be fed infusoria.

F: C, O; such live foods as mosquito larvae, water fleas, *Cyclops*, *Tubifex* worms; flakes.

S: The genus was established in 1924 by the ichthyologist AHL. It is intended as a link between the genera *Aphyosemion* MYERS, 1924 and *Nothobranchius* PETERS, 1868. *Fundulosoma thierryi* is very susceptible to the parasite *Oodinium pillularis*. The use of Trypaflavine is recommended. (0.6 g to 100 liters).

T: about 72° F,   **L:** 1″,   **A:** 19$^{1}/_{2}$″,   **R:** b+m,   **D:** 1-2.
   about 22° C,   3.5 cm,   50 cm,

Jordanella floridae
American Flagfish

GOODE & BEAN, 1879
Sub-Fam.: Cyprinodontinae

Syn.: *Cyprinodon floridae*

Hab.: North America: in bogs, ponds, lakes and slow-moving water from Florida south to Yucatan, Mexico.

Fl.: 1914, F. Kurich, Berlin, Germany.

Sex: ♀ are larger, fuller bodied and more noticeably yellow with a dark patch in the dorsal fin and above the pectorals; ♂ are olive to brown-grey.

Soc. B.: Often aggressive against their own species, especially ♂ during the spawning season. In another sense they are timid. The parents guard their brood.

M: Needs a tank with a dark, fine-gravel bottom, dense planting on the edges and back with swimming room in the center. Suggest that you place the aquarium in a sunny place. Algae should be left on the tank sides. Add fresh water occasionally. The species demands no other special water values.

B: Water temperature between 73-77° F (23-25° C) with dense plantings of finely-leaved vegetation. Use a fine gravel bottom with a cover of floating plants. The fish spawn after a stormy courtship, generally held between the plants and hollows on the bottom. They lay to 70 eggs over a week or more. ♂ will not consume eggs or fry but ♀ should be removed. The eggs develop in one week and the fry can be fed micro food.

F: O; all types of live foods; algae; detritus; spinach; flakes; frozen foods.

S: An active species, the fish like to dart around the tank.

T: about 68° F,   **L:** 2$^{1}/_{2}$″,   **A:** 15$^{1}/_{2}$″,   **R:** b+m,   **D:** 1-2.
   about 20° C,   6 cm,   40 cm,

Fundulosoma thierryi

Jordanella floridae ♂ top, ♀ bottom

Lamprichthys tanganicanus

(BOULENGER, 1898)
Sub-Fam.: Procatopodinae

Syn.: *Haplochilus tanganicanus, Lamprichthys curtianalis, Mohanga tanganicana*

Hab.: Africa; found only along the rocky shores of Lake Tanganyika. Contrary to previous opinion it is not found in open waters and has never been seen over a sandy bottom (cf. SEEGERS, 1983; DATZ 36, (1): 5-9).

Fl.: 1959

Sex: ♂ is larger with brilliant blue spots on the body; ♀ has silver spots on her body.

Soc. B.: The fish are a timid, schooling species. A tall-finned alpha male claims the larger territory with a large rock or stone in the center. Several subordinate ♂ s may be found in the territory but no one knows whether they claim smaller territories or roam without a base.

M: Need a large tank with a rocky bottom and rock-like structures. Plants are not required. Water should be medium-hard to hard and moderately alkaline, from 12° dGH and pH about 8.5.

B: Has been accomplished at Aquarium Hamburg and under the proper conditions can be done easily at home. A detailed report on feral reproduction was written by SEEGERS (1983 in DATZ 36 (1): 5-9): Courting begins as an alpha male displays to a female passing his territory. The couple spawn on a rock, a process which consumes considerable time. *L. tanganicanus* is bottom spawner and not, as had been suspected, a species that releases eggs freely. In its natural habitat the fry are reduced by such predator Cichlids as *Lamprologus, Telmatochromis* and *Julidochromis* sp.

F: C; such live foods as small shrimps, insects and even fish scales.

S: The largest species of African Killifish.

| T: 73-77° F, | L: ♂ to 6″, | A: 31 to 39″, | R: t+m, | D: 3. |
| 23-25° C, | ♂ to 15 cm, | 80 to 100 cm, | | |

Lucania goodei
Blue-Fintop Minnow

JORDAN, 1879
Sub-Fam.: Fundulinae

Syn.: *Chriopeops goodei, Fundulus goodei*

Hab.: In quiet streams and lakes of southern Georgia and Florida.

Fl.: 1928, Aquarienfisch Import und Export Co., Wandsbek, West Germany.

Sex: ♂ is more slender-bodied and more intricately colored, particularly on the fins; the dorsal is larger and has an orange base with a blue, sickle-shaped area; the anal fin is larger and there is a reddish area on the tail; ♀ has a yellowish dorsal with a whitish color at the base of the tail.

Soc. B.: An undemanding, peaceful, active species which accepts its own as tankmates though it may be aggressive towards others. Best kept with other active fish.

M: Needs a tank with a bottom of mulm, dense vegetation along the edges and back with open swimming space in the center. Add a few roots for hiding places; use old water (15° dGH, pH 6.5-6.8).

B: Water temperature between 68-74° F (20-24° C) with plenty of vegetation and floating plants overhead. The ♂ dances and courts vigorously around the ♀ before spawning. The two spawn in the upper area of the plants in a process which may cover five weeks. The ♀ lays three to five eggs per day until as many as 200 have been laid. The eggs hang by short threads and the parents, which will consume the spawn, should be removed. Feed the adults well during the prolonged spawning period. (Information from BREITFELD, Aquarien Terrarien 24, 344-349, 1977.)

F: All types of live food; particularly mosquito larvae; flakes.

S: Becomes timid if winter temperatures are too warm or if kept in a tank with too warm water. It is also sensitive to water changes and may suffer when transferred to another tank, even under the best of conditions. Added fresh water can increase a readiness to spawn.

| T: 62-72° F (during winter 54-71° F), | L: 2¹/₂″, | A: 23¹/₂″, | R: all, | D: 1-2. |
| 16-22° C (during winter 12-16° C), | 6 cm, | 60 cm, | | |

Lamprichthys tanganicanus

Lucania goodei

Fam.: Cyprinodontidae

Nothobranchius guentheri
Gunther's Notobranch

(PFEFFER, 1893)
Sub-Fam.: Rivulinae

Syn.: *Fundulus guentheri, Adiniops guentheri*

Hab.: Africa; Zanzibar.

Fl.: 1913, C. Siggelkow, Hamburg, West Germany.

Sex: ♂ larger and more intricately colored.

Soc. B.: A relatively aggressive, short-lived annual species.

M: Similar to recommendations for *N*.

rachovii. Suggest water to 10° dGH and neutral to slightly acid (pH 6.5-7.0); keep in a species tank.

B: Follow recommendations for *N. rachovii* with water temperatures between 72-74° F (22-24° C); The fish bury their eggs which require 3-4 months to develop.

F: Such live foods as insect larvae, small crustaceans and *Tubifex*; flakes.

S: The tail fin has a black edge.

T: 72-77° F, **L**: 1³/₄″, **A**: 23¹/₂″, **R**: b+m, **D**: 3.
22-25° C, 4.5 cm, 60 cm,

Nothobranchius kirki
Kirk's Nothobranch

JUBB, 1969
Sub-Fam.: Rivulinae

Syn.: *Nothobranchius schoenbrodti*

Hab.: East Africa; Malawi, the area of Lake Chilwa.

Fl.: Unknown.

Sex: ♂ is more brightly colored.

Soc. B.: A lively, aggressive, annual species.

M: Follow recommendations for *N. rachovii*. Keep in a species tank.

B: Follow recommendations for *N. rachovii* with water temperature between 70-73° F (21-23° C).

F: Live foods such as mosquito larvae; *Tubifex*, Enchytreae, small crustaceans; flakes.

S: Requires the longest diapause of all species of *Nothobranchius*, about seven months.

T: 68-73° F, **L**: 2″, **A**: 19¹/₂″, **R**: b+m, **D**: 3.
20-23° C, 5 cm, 50 cm,

Nothobranchius korthausae
Korthaus' Northobranch

MEINKEN, 1973
Sub-Fam.: Rivulinae

Syn.: None

Hab.: East Africa; in wet bogs on Tanzania's Mafia Island.

Fl.: 1972, Edith Korthaus, Dahl, West Germany.

Sex: ♂ is more brightly colored with fins edged in sky blue; the tail fin has 6-8 irregular cross-stripes; ♀ is grey-olive with a cinnamon gloss on her sides; the fins are colorless.

Soc. B.: An aggressive, lively annual species. ♂ actively courts ♀.

M: Follow recommendations for *N. racho-*

vii. The water should be soft and relatively acid, about 5° dGH and pH 5.8-6.4. At a pH of 6.8 the fish will slowly die. Keep in a species tank.

B: Follow recommendations for other species of *Nothobranchius*. To instigate breeding combine several females with one male. The male courts energetically.

F: C; All kinds of live foods such as small crustaceans, mosquito larvae and *Tubifex*.

S: When courting, ♂ slides its anal fin further back on ♀ than do males of other species of *Nothobranchius*.

T: 73-79° F, **L**: 2¹/₂″, **A**: 23¹/₂″, **R**: b+m, **D**: 3.
23-26° C, 6 cm, 60 cm,

Nothobranchius guentheri

Nothobranchius kirki

Nothobranchius korthausae, Normal form

Nothobranchius palmqvisti
Palmqvist's Nothobranch

(LOENNBERG, 1907)
Sub-Fam.: Rivulinae

Syn.: *Fundulus palmqvisti, Adiniops palmqvisti*

Hab.: East Africa; coastal waters of south Kenya and Tanzania.

Fl.: 1957, Tropicarium Frankfurt on Main, Frankfurt, West Germany

Sex: ♂ is more brilliantly colored, marked in a net-like pattern; the dorsal fin is arched, the ventral is flat; ♀ is grey or brown, smaller and without the net-like pattern; both the ventral and dorsal lines are arched.

Soc. B.: An extremely aggressive, short-lived annual; the ♂♂ are very competitive and court the ♀♀ continuously.

M: Follow recommendations for *N. rachovii*. Water hardness should remain below 10° dGH with a pH 7.0. Keep in a species tank.

B: Should be successful in even the smallest tank. Suggest a water temperature between 72-74° F (22-24° C) and a bottom of peat. The eggs are dropped individually until as many as 200 are laid. Keep them in the moist peat and add water after three months. After the fry hatch change $1/3$ of the water weekly.

F: C; live food, especially insect larvae.

T: 64-68° F, **L:** 2″, **A:** 23$1/2$″, **R:** b+m, **D:** 3.
  18-20° C, 5 cm, 60 cm,

Nothobranchius rachovii
Rachow's Nothobranch

AHL, 1926
Sub-Fam.: Rivulinae

Syn.: *Adiniops rachovii*

Hab.: Africa; in smaller savannah streams which are seasonally dry, Mozambique to South Africa.

Fl.: 1925; reintroduced in 1958 by Erhard Roloff, Karlsruhe, West Germany.

Sex: ♂ is larger and brightly colored; ♀ is grey to brown.

Soc. B.: A generally peaceful, quiet annual that may be belligerent towards its own species. ♂ is often territorial.

M: Recommend a species tank with a dark, soft bottom, loosely planted with open space for swimming; decorate with roots; 8 inches (20 cm) of soft, slightly acid water is suggested (4-6° dGH, pH 6.5); make frequent water changes.

B: The fish bury their eggs and need a bottom of peat or sand; recommend a water temperature between 70-73° F (21-23° C). Remove the peat with the eggs and store in plastic bag. When ready to hatch add soft water (2° dGH) which improves the yield. The fry are easy to raise and are sexually mature in 12 weeks. Newly-hatched fry may be susceptible to *Oodinium*.

F: C; live food, especially insect larvae; also small crustaceans, *Tubifex*; flakes.

S: If the food is not sufficiently nourishing it may affect growth, stunting ♀ for several generations.
The photo shows the red variant. ♂ top, ♀ below.

T: 68-75° F, **L:** 2″, **A:** 23$1/2$″, **R:** b+m, **D:** 3.
  20-24° C, 5 cm, 60 cm,

Nothobranchius palmqvisti

Nothobranchius rachovii

Fam.: Oryziatidae (Ricefish)

Oryzias celebensis
Celebes Medaka

(M. WEBER, 1894)

Syn.: *Haplochilus celebensis, Aplocheilus celebensis*

Hab.: In flowing and standing waters of Indonesia; southern Celebes.

Fl.: 1912

Sex: ♂ is grey-green with pointed dorsal and anal fins; ♀ is larger.

Soc. B.: A peaceful, active schooling fish, it can be combined with other fish of similar size.

M: Follow recommendations for *O. melastigmus*. Can be kept alone or in a community tank.

B: Follow recommendations for *O. melastigmus*.

F: C, O; live food of appropriate size; will also accept flakes.

S: A rarity, it is seldom seen in the hobby.

T: 72-86° F, **L**: 2″, **A**: 15$^1/_2$″, **R**: t+m, **D**: 3.
22-30° C,   5 cm,   40 cm,

Oryzias melastigmus
Java medaka

(MC CLELLAND, 1839)

Syn.: *Aplocheilus melastigmus, Panchax cyanophthalmus, Panchax argenteus, Aplocheilus javanicus, Oryzias javanicus.*

Hab.: Southern Asia: from Ceylon (Sri Lanka) and India eastward to Burma, Thailand, Malaysia, as far as Java.

Fl.: November 1910, SCHOLZE & POETSCHKE, Berlin.

Sex: The ♀♀ have a fuller forebody and eggs occasionally shimmer through. The ♂♂ have a more fringed anal fin, also a larger dorsal fin.

Soc. B.: A peaceful fish which likes to live in groups or schools.

M: A big tank is recommended with heavy vegetation along the edges, but enough swimming space up front. Also with *O. melastigmus* water values are not critical. A slight salt content is tolerated since the species prefers fresh water coastal areas.

B: With this species as well, the eggs link in grapelike clusters and are towed by the ♀♀ until they become attached to a plant.

F: O, C; all types of live foods as well as flakes and frozen food.

S: *O. melastigmus* is widely found in south eastern Asian zones. Depending on the area, they may have different colour patterns, ranging from rather intense black marbling to more yellowish tones with only slight black marbling. In general, however, very little ichthyologic research on *Orzyias* has been carried out. Only a limited few species are well known and categorized. *O. melastigmus* is not one of them.

T: 72-86° F, **L**: 1$^1/_2$″, **A**: 15$^1/_2$″, **R**: generally t, **D**: 3.
22-30° C,   4 cm,   40 cm,

Oryzias celebensis

Oryzias melastigmus

Pachypanchax playfairii
PLayfair's Panchax

(GUENTHER, 1866)
Sub-Fam.: Rivulinae

Syn.: *Haplochilus playfairii, Panchax playfairii*

Hab.: The islands of east Africa; Seychelles, Zanzibar, Madagascar.

Fl.: 1924, August Schlueter, Altona, West Germany.

Sex: ♀ is uniformly colored with a dark patch at the base of the dorsal fin; ♂ have rows of red dots along the body with a black edge on the tail fin.

Soc. B.: An aggressive, territorial predator always ready to bite. Eats smaller fish.

M: Needs a darkened tank with a fine gravel bottom and hiding places; dense vegetation is required and the water should be medium-hard and slightly acid, 8-15° dGH and pH 6.5-7.0. The fish is a jumper and the tank should be well covered.

B: The tank should have 2-2$^1/_2$ gallons of water (10 liter) at a temperature between 74-79° F (24-26° C) with the water values as listed above. Use Hornfern, Java Moss, fine-leaved plants or perlon webbing for spawning. Breeding can be induced by placing a pair in the tank. Spawning will last about one week with 50 to 200 eggs laid. The parents will devour their spawn and should be removed. Dense vegetation reduces the cannibalism some. At a water temperature of 75° F (24° C) the fry hatch in 12 days and should be fed *Artemia* nauplii and similar small food.

F: Such live foods as small crustaceans, insects, insect larvae, *Tubifex* and small fish; flakes.

S: The scales of ♂ will stand from the body during the spawning season and are shed, especially during pairing and courting.

T: 72-75° F, **L:** 4″, **A:** 23$^1/_2$″, **R:** b, **D:** 1.
22-24° C, 10 cm, 60 cm,

Procatopus nototaenia

BOULENGER, 1904
Sub-Fam.: Procatopodinae

Syn.: None

Hab.: West Africa; south Cameroons.

Fl.: 1960

Sex: ♂ is larger with a deep blue though matted shimmer on the sides of the body and a straight tail; ♀ is smaller with a rounded tail fin and a less pronounced blue tone.

Soc. B.: A lively, peaceful schooling species recommended for a community tank. Do not combine with aggressive fish and always keep in a school.

M: Needs a bottom of fine gravel with a loose planting of finely leaved species around the edges. Decorate with roots and use a soft, slightly acid water, 1-3° dGH and pH 6.0. Create a current with strong aeration. The fish will swim against it.

B: Recommend water values above at a temperature between 72-75° F (22-24° C). Add a little Trypaflavine to keep fungus from forming. The fish spawn small, yellowish eggs in hollows among the roots. The fry hatch in three weeks. Adding fresh water can speed the process. Feed the fry infusoria and Rotifers.

F: C; all types of live foods; flakes.

S: *Procatopus nototaenia* is one of the finest representatives of the genus. The genus can be distinguished from *Aplocheilichthys* by a slender, triangular fold of skin extending from the gill cover.

T: 68-77° F, **L:** 2″, **A:** 19$^1/_2$″, **R:** t, **D:** 2-3.
20-25° C, 5 cm, 50 cm,

Pachypanchax playfairii

Procatopus nototaenia

Fam.: Cyprinodontidae

Pseudepiplatys annulatus page 558

Pterolebias longipinnis
Longfin Killifish

GARMAN, 1895
Sub-Fam.: Rivulinae

Syn.: *Rivulus macrurus*

Hab.: South America; Brazil; Amazon; Argentina; central and lower Rio Paraguay; central Rio Parana.

Fl.: 1930

Sex: ♂ is larger and has extended, pointed fins with markings absent from ♀; the fins on ♀ are rounded.

Soc. B.: Both active and aggressive in its youth, the fish slows with age. Never keep two ♂♂ together since they fight continuously though if you keep several males they rarely battle. Keep in a species tank.

M: Follow recommendations for *Cynolebias bellottii*.

B: Follow recommendations for *C. bellottii* with water at temperatures between 68-72° F (20-22° C). The fish buries its eggs.

F: C, O; all types of live foods; frozen food; flakes. The species is a voracious eater.

S: *P. longipinnis* is sensitive to sudden changes in water hardness and similar values.

T: 63-72° F, L: 4″, A: 31″, R: b+m, D: 3.
   17-22° C,   10 cm,   80 cm,

Pterolebias zonatus

MYERS, 1935
Sub-Fam.: Rivulinae

Syn.: None

Hab.: South America: in seasonal streams of Venezuela which occasionally dry.

Fl.: 1963 into the US.

Sex: ♀♀ are smaller with rounded fins; ♂ has extended, pointed fins.

Soc. B.: Similar to *P. longipinnis*.

M: Similar to *Cynolebias bellottii*.

B: Breeding has been difficult and disappointing. Similar to recommendations for *C. bellottii* with water at a temperature between 70-73° F (21-23° C).

F: C; all types of live foods such as mosquito larvae, *Tubifex*, Enchytreae, small crustaceans and adult insects.

S: *Pterolebias zonatus* differs from *P. longipinnis* by the number of lateral line scales. *P. zonatus* has 34 while *P. longipinnis* has only 31-32.

T: 64-73° F, L: 3¹/₂″, A: 27″, R: b+m, D: 3-4.
   18-23° C,   9 cm,   70 cm,

Pterolebias longipinnis

Pterolebias zonatus

Rivulus cylindraceus
Green Rivulus, Brown Rivulus, Cuban Rivulus

POEY, 1861
Sub-Fam.: Rivulinae

Syn.: *Rivulus marmoratus* (not POEY, 1880)

HAB.: In the clear mountain streams of Cuba.

Fl.: 1930, Fritz Mayer, Hamburg, West Germany.

Sex: ♂ is more brilliantly colored with a blue edging to the dorsal and caudal fins; ♀ has rounded fins with a clear, dark patch on the upper base of the tail.

Soc. B.: A lively, tolerant fish which may be combined with peaceful fishes of similar size. The ♂ is the more aggressive.

M: Needs a dark, gravelly tank bottom with dense vegetation and a cover of floating plants; add a few plants for decoration. Can tolerate a range of water conditions but suggest medium-hard, neutral water, around 8° dGH and pH 7.0. Hollows such as upturned coconuts and pots are welcomed in the tank.

B: Can be bred in a small tank with about one gallon of water at temperatures between 73 and 75° F (23-24° C). Separate the sexes for a time to induce spawning and start with one male and two females. Use peat, perlon webbing or fine-leaved plants (*Myriophyllum*) as a spawning surface. Remove the fish after spawning. The fry, which have a characteristic marking (a fine, black stripe from the mouth to the tail) hatch in 12-14 days and can be fed *Artemia* nauplii.

F: C, O; such live foods as mosquito larvae, *Tubifex*, Enchytreae, Drosophila; flakes.

S: Water should be changed every two weeks to promote growth of the fry. The species can be readily recognized by their drumshaped body.

T: 72-75° F,   **L:** 2″,   **A:** 19½″,   **R:** m+b,   **D:** 1-2.
22-24° C,   5.5 cm,   50 cm,

Rivulus xanthonotus
Yellowback Rivulus

AHL, 1926
Sub-Fam.: Rivulinae

Syn.: None

Hab.: Possibly South America; no exact origin is known.

Fl.: 1926, J. Wolmer, Hamburg, West Germany.

Sex: The body of ♂ is dark brown with rows of dots on the sides; ♀ is ochre.

Soc. B.: An active, remarkably peaceful Killifish.

M: Similar to recommendations for *R. cylindraceus*. The fish are superb jumpers and the tank should be well covered. Use soft to medium hard, slightly acid water, 5-9° dGH and pH 6.5.

B: Follow recommendations for *R. .cylindraceus*.

F: C, O; live food; flakes.

S: Some ichthyologists regard the species as a variety of *Rivulus urophthalmus* GUENTHER, 1866.

T: 72-77° F,   **L:** 3″,   **A:** 23½″,   **R:** m+b,   **D:** 2.
22-25° C,   7 cm,   60 cm,

Rivulus cylindraceus

Rivulus xanthonotus

579

Roloffia bertholdi

(ROLOFF, 1965)
Sub-Fam.: Rivulinae

Syn.: *Aphyosemion bertholdi, "Aphyosemion muelleri"*

Hab.: In shady rain forests of west Africa; Sierra Leone; Guinea; Liberia.

Fl.: 1962, Erhard Roloff, Karlsruhe. West Germany.

Sex: ♂ is larger and more brightly decorated with a black throat during the spawning season; ♀ is smaller and light brown to olive green.

Soc. B.: Lively and peaceful, they may be combined with other species of *Roloffia* or similar fishes.

M: Follow recommendations for *R. chaytori*. Needs a tank bottom of boiled peat and does best with frequent water changes.

B: Use a small breeding tank, a low level of soft, slightly acid water (around 4° dGH and pH 6.5) and temperatures between 72

and 75° F (22-24° C). The species lay their eggs on the bottom rather than burying them. After a moderate courtship by the ♂ the pair lay 10 to 30 eggs on the tank bottom. Remove the parents and reduce the water to an inch or so. Fry will hatch in 14 to 18 days and can be fed *Artemia* nauplii. Frequent water changes are needed to influence growth.

F: C; all types of live foods - mosquito larvae, adult insects, small crustaceans, *Tubifex* and more.

S: The species jumps and can escape through the smallest opening. The tank needs to be completely covered. The lifespan can be extended by separating the sexes, joining them only during spawning.

T: 72-75° F,   **L:** 2″,   **A:** 19$^1/_2$″,   **R:** m+b,   **D:** 3.
    22-24° C,   5 cm,   50 cm,

Aphyosemion roloffi

AHL, 1937
Sub-Fam.: Rivulinae

Syn.: *Roloffia brueningi*

Hab.: West Africa; near Giema, Kenema District, Sierra Leone.

Fl.: 1963, Erhard Roloff, Karlsruhe, West Germany.

Sex: ♂ is greenish-blue to dark blue with red pectorals; ♀ is olive-brown to red-brown and lack the touch of red on the fins.

Soc. B.: A lively, generally peaceful fish best kept in a species tank or in company of fish with similar qualities.

M: Follow recommendations for *R. chaytori.*

B: Suggest a water temperature between 22-24° C. Follow recommendations for *R. chaytori.* The fish buries its eggs.

F: All types of live foods – particularly mosquito larvae, small crustaceans, *Tubifex* and Enchytreae.

S: Some researchers regarded *Roloffia brueningi* as an independent species.

T: 72-75° F,   **L:** 2″,   **A:** 19$^1/_2$″,   **R:** b+t,   **D:** 2-3.
    22-24° C,   5 cm,   50 cm,

Roloffia bertholdi

Aphyosemion roloffi

Roloffia chaytori

ROLOFF, 1971
Sub-Fam.: Rivulinae

Syn.: None

Hab.: West Africa; In moving waters near springs in Sierra Leone. Avoids open waters with higher temperatures.

Fl.: 1963, Erhard Roloff, Karlsruhe, West Germany.

Sex: ♂ is the brighter colored; ♀ is olive brown with red spots.

Soc. B.: A lively, mostly peaceful species which can be kept in a species tank or in company with *Epiplatys* of similar size.

M: Needs a tank with a bottom of soft, boiled peat and finely leaved plants around the edges; Add floating plants to reduce the light and decorate with roots; Do not use an overhead light but let it come naturally through the front glass, the sides and back being covered. Too much light reduces the coloring of the fishes. Water should be very soft and slightly acid, 1-6° dGH and pH 6.3-7.0.

B: Use the water values suggested above at temperatures between 73-75° F (23-24° C) with finely-leaved plants. The eggs are laid on plants near the surface and should be collected occasionally. The fry hatch in 12-14 days and may be fed brine shrimp nauplii. The addition of Trypaflavine may cause the fry to hatch prematurely. In that case they quickly die.

F: C; all types of live foods; feed such things as mosquito larvae, insects, small crustaceans, Enchytreae and *Tubifex* for variety.

S: The species are jumpers and the tank must be covered. If you avoid higher temperatures, keep the water soft and the light level low, the fish can live 2- 2 $^1/_2$ years and are capable of reproducing throughout their lives.

T: 72-75° F, **L:** 2″, **A:** 19$^1/_2$″, **R:** m+b, **D:** 2.
22-24° C, 5 cm, 50 cm,

Roloffia liberiensis

(BOULENGER, 1908)
Sub-Fam.: Rivulinae

Syn.: *Haplochilus liberiensis, Aphyosemion calabaricus, A. liberiense, Roloffia calabarica*

Hab.: In water holes in west Africa; western Liberia, possibly Nigeria.

Fl.: 1908, O. Winkelmann, Hamburg, West Germany.

Sex: ♂ has a blue to green metallic shimmer to the body and fins; its head darkens substantially before spawning; ♀ is brown to olive green.

Soc. B.: A lively but essentially peaceful Killifish which is best combined with other species of *Roloffia* and *Aphyosemion*.

M: Follow recommendations for *Aphyosemion australe*. Suggest soft, slightly acid water, around 5° dGH and pH 6.0-6.5.

B: A semi-annual species with suggestions similar to those for *Aphyosemion puerzli*. Breeding is easy. Use soft, slightly acid water, 4-7° dGH and pH 6.2.

F: C, O; live food; flakes.

S: ROLOFF(1970) suggests that *Roloffia liberiensis* and *R. calabaricus* (AHL, 1935) are separate species and deserve independent status. (The Aquarium, 12-1970, 9-12, 46.)

T: 72-75° F, **L:** 2″, **A:** 23$^1/_2$″, **R:** b+m, **D:** 1-2.
22-24° C, 6 cm, 60 cm,

Roloffia chaytori

Roloffia liberiensis

Roloffia occidentalis
Red Aphyosemion

(CLAUSEN, 1965)
Sub-Fam.: Rivulinae

Syn.: *Aphyosemion occidentalis*

Hab.: In the primeval forests and savannahs of Sierra Leone; Western Africa.

Fl.: 1911

Sex: The male is brightly colored with a fringe on the white anal fins. Similar though smaller fringes can be found on the dorsal. The female is brownish-red and, during spawning, has a darker patch at the throat.

Soc. B.: A lively, relatively aggressive seasonal fish.

M: See *R. chaytori*.

B: The species is a bottom spawner and needs a layer of peat in the tank. Keep water temperatures between 23-24° C. The eggs are small and develop after several months. Treat the eggs and peat as you would for other seasonal fishes.

F: C; all types of live foods such as mosquito larvae, small crustaceans, *Tubifex* worms and Drosophila and similar insects. Flakes are rarely accepted.

S: Adults are susceptible to piscine tuberculosis.

T: 68-75° F, **L:** 3¹/₂″, **A:** 27″, **R:** m+b, **D:** 2-3.
20-24° C, 9 cm, 70 cm,

Roloffia toddi see page 540

Terranatos dolichopterus
Sabre Fin

(WEITZMAN & WOURMS, 1967)
Sub-Fam.: Rivulinae

Syn.: *Austrofundulus dolichopterus, Cynolebias dolichopterus*

Hab.: In seasonal ponds in Venezuela.

Fl.: 1967

Sex: The male has long, brightly colored sickle-shaped dorsal and anal fins. Fins on the female are shorter, with less color.

Soc. B.: A peaceful, timid fish.

M: Requires a tank with a dark bottom of fine gravel or sand. Add roots and stones for hiding places and provide open areas for swimming. The lighting should be subdued and the water slightly acid, pH 6.0-6.5, and soft, 4-6° dGH. Add fresh water occasionally. The fish do best in their own tank.

B: Suggest about four gallons (15 l.) of slightly acid (pH 6.0), soft (2-3° dGH), water about 26° C. The fish bury their eggs and we suggest boiled, rinsed peat on the tank bottom. Induce spawning with one male and two females or any larger number of fishes with an excess number of females. When the fish spawn on the peat remove it along with the eggs. You may need to do this every two or three weeks. Keep it dry until the development period ends. After five or six months pour soft water, at 22-23° C, to hatch the eggs.

F: C; all types of live foods; flakes are rarely taken.

S: The fish have a lifespan of one or two years. They are excellent jumpers and the aquarium should be well covered.

T: 68-77° F, **L:** ♂ = 2″, ♀ = 1¹/₄″, **A:** 19¹/₂″, **R:** m+b, **D:** 3.
20-25° C, ♂ = 5 cm, ♀ = 3.5 cm, 50 cm,

Fam.: Oryziatidae, page 572

Roloffia occidentalis

Terranatos dolichopterus

Group 6

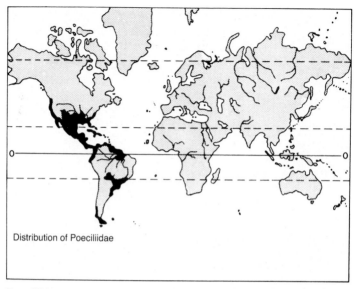

Distribution of Poeciliidae

Poeciliidae   Live-Bearing Toothcarp

Nature has always devised ways to preserve and perpetuate her
many species and in the way egg-laying saurians were replaced by
live-bearing mammals, so the Live-Bearing Toothcarp, which
appeared late in the evolutionary process during the Oligocene and
Miocene periods (44-38 million years ago), superceded egglayers.
Egg-layers are at the mercy of predators until their fry are free-
swimming but the spawn of live-bearers can immediately hide and
escape capture, finding safety in tiny cracks and crevices larger fish
cannot penetrate. Thus, live-bearers are not under pressure to
produce as many young to cover possible predatory losses. Today,
most female live-bearers produce 20-40 young, though a few drop as
many as 150.
In the way that many Characins can be identified by their adipose fin,
Live-Bearing Toothcarps can be identified by their gonopodium.

Poecilia velifera, description on page 604

In many species of Poeciliidae the females are pursued almost incessantly by males whose pelvic fins have been converted to genital organs. The organ releases spermatophores within the female. The eggs mature within her body, the egg sacs bursting shortly before birth. The fry can eat immediately and if sufficiently protected, some species will reproduce in large numbers within a brief period.

Through a process called "superfetation" they are capable of delivering several broods without further impregnation by a male. Many an aquarist has been amazed to find fry appearing even though only one female has been kept in an aquarium.

Livebearers have rendered an invaluable service to mankind in many tropical and sub-tropical countries by combatting the malarial mosquito. Their ease of breeding, their adaptability to a range of water conditions, even that with a high chalk content, and their number of variations and opportunities for crosses have made livebearers popular. Of the world's ten million or more hobbyists all must, at one time or another, have kept Guppies, Swordtails or Platties.

The World Health Organization (WHO) utilizes Mosquito Fish and Guppies in many waters. Even drinking water, reservoirs, wells and many other standing waters are stocked with these fish to help control mosquitos. The adaptability of cerain species to hard, brackish water is so amazing that species such as *Mollienesia* and some *Gambusia*, after adjusting, can survive in salt or brackish water.

The conditions for **maintenance** are the same for most livebearers and are summarized below:

The aquarium size is indicated for each species.

The substrate, when only livebearers are kept, should consist of standard fine river gravel but can include quartz if you wish. Even chalky gravel (marble) can be tolerated in spite of the fact that it increases hardness. Hardness should be avoided if livebearers are kept with other species not able to cope with rising hardness.

Vegetation: we suggest hardy such plants as Java Moss, Java Fern, *Sagittaria* and *Vallisneria*, which can tolerate the increased hardness. The fish make no special demands in terms of oxygen or filtration.

Breeding Live-bearing Toothcarps.

Breeding comes naturally to these fish. Though livebearers reproduce prolifically it is not always easy to successfully raise the fry. The parents and other tankmates may become predators, hunting the fry when they reach the size of mosquito larvae. To succeed, pregnant females must be placed in a separate spawning tank. They can be recognized by their round, tight stomachs (and in some species by the eyes of the fry which can literally be seen glowing through the mother's body). Use a breeding trap which will let the fry fall to the bottom, out of reach of hungry parents.

The fry can be fed *Artemia* or brine shrimp, finely ground flakes and hard boiled eggs. They grow rapidly.

With the selective breeding of Guppies, the males should be separated from females after three weeks so that malformed males cannot fertilize them. Only experts can identify the sexes at this early stage but the fish should be kept separate if possible. Only the finest pairs should be bred.

With the selected breeding of pedigreed Guppies and other Live-Bearing Toothcarp, the food they eat should have variety. Flakes are not enough. Male Swordtails in particular will only develop to full size and color when given live food. Black mosquito larvae are preferred but FD such as liver, bloodworm and adult *Artemia* or brine shrimp are also good. The well-known Tetra-Tips FD adhesive tablets contain these ingredients.

Flake Food should always be added for the vegetables and chalk.

You'll discover it requires considerable effort to breed new varieties of some popular species such as Swordtails, Platies, Black Mollies and Guppies. Most, if not all possible combinations of color and shape have been bred and many fish are no longer capable of reproducing (an example, the excessively long gonopodium of some over-bred males). The standard rules for individual species can be obtained from hobby groups. No attempt has been made to indicate the sub-family since all of the species listed belong to the sub-Family Poeciliinae.

Fam.: Poeciliidae

Belonesox belizanus
Piketop Minnow

KNER, 1860

Syn.: None

Hab.: Eastern Cental America: southern Mexico south to Honduras.

Fl.: 1909, Carl Siggelkow, Hamburg, West Germany.

Sex: ♀ is significantly larger with a yellow or occasionally orange base to the anal fin.

Soc. B.: A predator which should be combined only with large, hardy tankmates. Young fish may be tolerant but older specimens are always aggressive.

M: Needs a large tank with plenty of plants such as the Giant *Vallisneria* (which tolerates hard water), roots and good filtration. Water should have a little salt added, pH 7.5-8.2 and a hardness above 25° dGH.

B: Breeding is easy in larger tanks. Add a tablespoon of salt to every $2^1/_2$ gallons of water. As many as 100 live-born fry, nearly an inch in length, can be spawned by one female. The female will not eat them. The fry grow rapidly with proper filtration and live food. Larger ones will eat live-bearing toothcarps (one guppy a day).

F: C; fish, all types of larger live foods.

S: This is the only species in the genus which lurks behind plants and roots to strike, hit-or-miss, at its prey. In this, it is similar to *Esox lucius*.

T: 79-89° F, **L:** ♂ = $4^1/_2$″, ♀ = 8″, **A:** 39″, **R:** t, **D:** 3.
26-32° C, ♂ = 12 cm, ♀ = 20 cm, 100 cm,

Gambusia affinis holbrooki
Holbrook's Mosquitofish

GIRARD, 1859

Syn.: *Gambusia holbrooki, G. patruelis holbrooki, Haplochilus melanops, Heterandria holbrooki, H. uninotata, Schizophallus holbrooki, Zygonectes atrilatus, Z. melanops*

Hab.: In fresh and brackish water of North America: US from Florida to Texas between the 20th and 35th latitudes; Mexico. Both sub-species becomes naturalize in the Mediteranean sea.

Fl.: 1898, West Germany; Hans Stueve, Hamburg; Paul Nitsche, Berlin.

Sex: ♂ can be recognized by its bright color and gonopodium.

Soc. B.: An occasionally aggressive species suggested only for a community tank with hardy, tough fishes.

M: One of the hardiest of fishes. Is tolerant of many water values but we suggest pH 6.0-8.8 and a hardness to 40° dGH.

B: Although easy to keep, the fish is more difficult to breed. Use only adult ♀ from $2^1/_2$″ (6 cm.). Introduce several ♂ with one or more ♀. Use a low level of water at temperatures between 20 and 24° C with floating plants overhead. The ♀ will chase their fry. Under the best of conditions – as when the parents are fed mosquito larvae –40 to 60 fry will be dropped every 5 to 8 weeks.

F: C, O; insect larvae; algae; all types of flakes.

S: Second only to the guppy, species of *Gambusia* are the primary species stocked in tanks and ponds to destroy insects. The genus is also found in Europe and even in the Klongs of Bangkok. It is difficult now to differentiate between feral and introduced fishes. The sub-species *G. a. affinis* reportedly is found only in Texas.

T: 59-95° F, **L:** ♂ = 1″, ♀ = $3^1/_4$″, **A:** $23^1/_2$″, **R:** m, t, **D:** 1.
15-35° C, ♂ = 3.5 cm, ♀ 8 cm, 60 cm,

590

Belonesox belizanus

Gambusia affinis holbrooki

Girardinus metallicus
Girardinus

POEY, 1854

Syn.: *Girardinus garmani, G. pygmaeus, Heterandria cubensis, H. metallica, Poecillia metallica*

Hab.: Cuba (endemic).

Fl.: 1906, W. Schroot, Hamburg, West Germany.

Sex: ♂ has a black gonopodium, the shining metallic cross stripes typical of the species and are more intensely colored.

Soc. B.: A lively, peaceful species recommended for most community tanks. Older ♀♀ may be quarrelsome as they advance in years.

M: The species prefers clear, gently-moving water and needs good filtration. Suggest pH 6.5-7.5 and a hardness 10-25° dGH. The tank should be well planted and include floating plants for cover.

B: Suggest water at a temperature between 24-26° C. 10 to 100 small fry (about 6-7 mm) are delivered every 20 to 30 days. They should be separated from the mother to prevent her from devouring the new young. If they must be kept in the same tank dense plant cover is needed.

F: C, O; omnivorous; flakes; tablets; algae; all types of small live foods.

S: A beautiful fish, it is not bred often enough. There is a checkered variant.

T: 72-77° F,   L: ♂ = 2″, ♀ = 3$^{1}/_{2}$″,   A: 27″,   R: m, t, D: 1-2.
  22-25° C,   ♂ = 5 cm, ♀ = 9 cm,   70 cm,

Heterandria formosa
Dwarf Livebearer, Dwarf Top Minow
Mosquito Fish

AGASSIZ, 1853

Syn.: *Girardinus formosus, Gambusia formosa, Heterandria ommata, Hydrargyra formosa, Rivulus ommatus, Zygonectes manni*

Hab.: US; South Carolina.

Fl.: 1912, Carl Siggelkow, Hamburg, West Germany.

Sex: ♂ has a gonopodium and is smaller.

Soc. B.: Peaceful but recommended only for a community tank with smaller tankmates.

M: Place in a small tank with dense vegetation.

B: Breeding is easy. The young are generally delivered over a period of two weeks but occasionally to 77 days.

F: Small water fleas; brine shrimp; small FD; flakes.

S: The seventh smallest fish in the world and recommended only for connoisseurs. It is beautifully colored but has a brief lifespan – 1$^{1}/_{2}$ to two years. Despite rumors the literature does not confirm that the ♀ of the species are cannibals.

T: 68-79° F,   L: ♂ = $^{3}/_{4}$″, ♀ = 1$^{3}/_{4}$″,   A: from 12″,   R: t, m, D: 1.
  20-26° C,   ♂ = 2 cm, ♀ = 4.5 cm,   from 30 cm,

Girardinus metallicus top ♀, bottom ♂

Heterandria formosa ♂ top, ♀ bottom

Phallichthys amates amates
Merry Widow

(MILLER, 1907)

Syn.: *Poecilia amates, Poeciliopsis amates*

Hab.: Guatemala; Panama to Honduras.

Fl.: 1937, Fritz Mayer, Hamburg, West Germany.

Sex: ♂ has a gonopodium and is smaller.

Soc. B.: Even though it will chase its young it is a peaceful species. Suggested for a community with tankmates who are not too greedy.

M: Needs to kept in a well-planted tank as do other livebearers. The species is more sensitive to tank conditions than many Guppies, Platies and Mollies. pH 6.5-7.5 and hardness 10-25° dGH.

B: 10 to 80 fry are dropped every 28 days. Separate parents or use a spawning box. A limited number of fry can survive in a tank with good plant cover.

F: O, H; flakes; live foods; FD; algae.

S: The ♂ is sexually mature in six months, the ♀ in one year. There is one sub-species, *P. a. pittieri*, the Orange-Dorsal Livebearer (MEEK, 1912).

T: 72-82° F, L: ♂ = 1″, ♀ = 2″, A: 23¹/₂″, R: m, t, D: 2.
22-28° C, ♂ = 3 cm, ♀ = 6 cm, 60 cm,

Phalloceros caudimaculatus (Goldform)
Spotted Livebearer

(HENSEL, 1868)

Syn.: *Girardinus januarius reticulatus, G. reticulata, G. caudimaculatus, Poecilia caudomaculatus, Glaridichthys caudimaculatus, Phalloceros caudomaculatus*

Hab.: Central Brazil; Paraguay; Uruguay.

Fl.: 1905, Koeppe and Carl Siggelkow, Hamburg, West Germany.

Sex: The gill cover is the key; the gill cover on ♂ has more color and a black edging.

Soc. B.: A peaceful species recommended for a community tank even though it occasionally chases its young.

M: Like all livebearers it does better in harder water and since most community tanks tend in this direction the species will do well. pH 6.8-8.0 and a hardness 15-30° dGH.

B: Recommend a small, well-planted tank. 10 to 40 fry (7 mm.) are dropped in moderately hard water (15-20° dGH). They are free-swimming within the hour. Be sure there is no mulm on the tank bottom.

F: C, O; flakes; FD; all types of small live foods.

S: The fish rarely deliver "normally". In most cases the fry leave the mother's body rolled together and sink to the bottom where they remain for an hour before becoming untangled and freeswimming.

T: 64-75° F, L: ♂ = 1″, ♀ = 1¹/₂″, A: 23¹/₂″, R: m, t, D: 1.
18-24° C, ♂ = 3 cm, ♀ = 4.5 cm, 60 cm,

Phallichthys amates amates

Phalloceros caudimaculatus "auratus"

Limia melanogaster
Black-Bellied Limia

GUENTHER, 1866

Syn.: *Poecilia melanogaster, L. caudo-fasciata tricolor, L. tricolor*

Hab.: Jamaica; Haiti.

Fl.: 1908, Carl Siggelkow, Hamburg, West Germany.

Soc. B.: A peaceful, schooling fish.

Sex: ♂ with gonopodium, ♀ plainly coloured but with pregnancy patch.

M: Needs a medium-sized tank with algae and hard water (20-30° dGH) and a pH between 7.5 and 8.5. Use plants tolerant of harder water such as Java Moss, *Sagittaria* and Java fern. Leave an open space for swimming and decorate the tank as a stream bed. Do not combine with predators.

B: Can be done but it is seldom attempted since the species needs algae and eats plants and is, thus, not popular.

F: H, O; algae; vegetables; small crustacaens; brine shrimp; flakes.

S: The fish is not often kept since it is sensitive to soft water and will not do well without plenty of algae.

T: 72-82° F, **L:** ♂ = 1$^1/_2$″, ♀ = 2$^1/_2$″, **A:** 19$^1/_2$″, **R:** m, **D:** 2.
22-28° C, ♂ = 4 cm, ♀ = 6.5 cm, 50 cm,

Limia nigrofasciata
Black-Barred Limia

REGAN, 1913

Syn.: *Poecilia nigrofasciata, Limia arnoldi*

Hab.: All waters of Haiti.

Fl.: 1912, Carl Siggelkow, Hamburg, West Germany.

Sex: ♂ is identified by an arched back, unique tail section (wedged-shaped on the bottom and bent upwards) and gonopodium; on ♀ the tail is straight.

Soc. B.: Peaceful species which eats its own offspring on occasion. Well suited to the community tank with hard water.

M: Though it is found in both fresh and brackish water, it does not do well in soft water. Suggest a hardness above 10° dGH and pH 7.0-8.5. Add water conditioner with each change and we suggest a teaspoon of salt for each two gallons of water. Plant with *Vallisneria* and other plants tolerant of hard water.

B: Breeding is easy. 20-30 fry are dropped each time the fish spawn. The young must be protected, especially from the ♀.

F: H, O; vegetable diet; algae; *Daphnia*; TabiMin Tablets.

S: The arch, noticeable in the backs of ♂, increases with age.

T: 72-79° F, **L:** ♂ = 2″, ♀ = 2$^3/_4$″, **A:** 23$^1/_2$″, **R:** m, t, **D:** 2-3.
22-26° C, ♂ = 4.5 cm, ♀ = 7 cm, 60 cm,

Limia nigrofasciata

Limia melanogaster

Poecilia reticulata
Guppy, Millions Fish

Syn.: *Lebistes reticulatus, Acanthocephalus guppii, A reticulatus, Girardinus guppii, G. petersi, G. poeciloides, G. reticulatus, Haridichthys reticulatus, Heterandria guppyi, Lebistes poeciloides, Poecilia poecilioides, Poecilioides reticulatus*

Hab.: Central America to Brazil; generally captive-bred in Asia, especially Singapore.

Fl.: 1908, C. Siggelkow, Hamburg, West Germany.

Sex: ♂ is smaller, with brighter color and gonopodium; ♀ has pregnancy patch.

Soc. B.: A livebearer, parents may chase young immediately after spawning, though they are otherwise peaceful. The young are not guarded.

M: The durable Guppy is very tolerant of tank conditions though inbred, pedigreed species may be sensitive. Suggest a hardness 10-30° dGH and pH 7.0-8.5. Can adapt to most well-planted tanks if need be.

B: Suggest a cover of floating ferns and a breeding box to protect the fry. 20 to 40 are dropped during spawning. The ♀ will be sexually mature at three months, the ♂ sooner. Feed fry brine shrimp, micro food and pulverized flakes.

F: O; omnivorous; prefers mosquito larvae; flakes.

S: The fact that it matures quickly, offers a variety of shapes and colors and is hardy has made the Guppy a favorite of beginning hobbyists.

Lately the guppy has been classed with the genus *Lebistes*. Thus the guppy is once again correctly identified as *Lebistes reticulatus*.

Don't put guppies together with Fighting Fish. Both sexes of Fighting Fish nip at the fins of the ♂♂.

T: 64-82° F,   **L:** to 2¹/₂″,   **A:** 15¹/₂″,   **R:** t, m,   **D:** 1.
    18-28° C,   to 6 cm,   40 cm,

Fantail Guppy

Fantail Guppy

The righthand photos, starting at top left, illustrate:

roundtail

pintail

swordtail

Vienna fantail

From right:

feral Guppy

lacetail

(upper) swordtail

(double) swordtail

The pictures on the left illustrate various Guppy hybrids:

roundtail

pintail

lacetail

spadetail

lyretail

(upper) swordtail

(lower) swordtail

(double) swordtail

flagtail

veiltail

fantail

triangletail

Paintings: B. Kahl

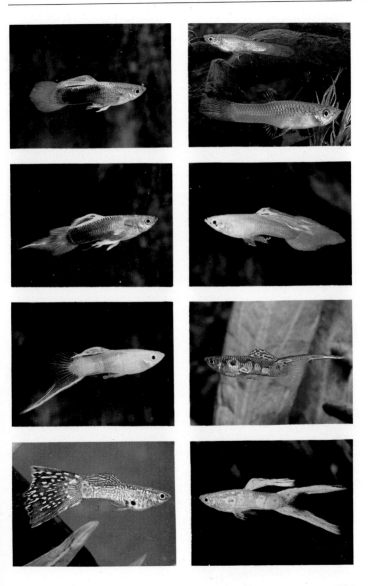

Poecilia sphenops
Pointed-Mouth Molly, Short-Finned Molly

VALENCIENNES, 1846

Syn.: *Mollienesia sphenops, Gambusia modesta, G. plumbea, Girardinus vandepolli, Lembesseia parvianalis, Platypoecilus mentalis, P. spilonotus, P. tropicus* and others

Hab.: Mexico to Colombia.

Fl.: 1899 by Umlauff of Hamburg. The black hybrid (Black Molly) first appeared in 1909.

Sex: ♂ has a slender body and a gonopodium; ♀ is larger and fuller-bodied.

Soc. B.: Very peaceful and a good algaeeater, though not longlived in an aquarium. Hybrids are prone to disease.

M: Hybrid forms (Black Molly) need warmth (26-30° C); the feral variety can tolerate temperatures to 64° F (18° C). Needs a tank with fast-growing plants on the bottom and top. Recommend hiding places. Water values: pH 7.5-8.2, hardness 11-30° dGH. Suggest adding a little salt.

B: Very prolific. Spotted young can be obtained from black parents. Hybrids include Lyretail, Moonfish Molly, Flag Molly.

F: Algae; vegetables; flakes; tablets.

S: Black Mollies are not long-lived. Aquarium-bred varieties may last no more than three years. The broad range of variations has led to a large number of synonyms.

The photos: top, the feral form of the pointed-mouth molly; top right, the standard Black Molly; bottom right, the Black Moonfish Molly.

T: 64-82° F, **L:** 2¹/₂″, **A:** 15¹/₂″, **R:** t, m, **D:** 1-2.
   18-28° C,   6 cm,   40 cm,

P. sphenops (Black Molly)

Poecilia latipinna, black variety

Poecilia velifera
Mexican Sailfin Molly, Green-Sailfin Molly

(REGAN, 1914)

Syn.: *Mollienisia velifera*

Hab.: Yucatan, Mexico.

Fl.: 1913, Josef Kropac, Hamburg, West Germany.

Sex: ♂ has a tall, imposing dorsal fin.

Soc. B.: Peaceful with a remarkable behavioral display by the ♂.

M: Prefers hard water, 25-35° dGH and pH 7.5-8.5. To harden we recommend Dolomite. Add salt, 2-3g for each 1 or 2 quarts (1 l) of water. Can even combine with marine fish after the Sailfin is adapted to your tank. Needs lots of swimming room and algae. The dorsal fin of the ♂♂ will only develop when there is adequate room for swimming.

B: Difficult to breed and tank-bred males seldom have the large dorsal found in pond and wild-caught specimins. Raise with algae, crushed flakes (vegetable) and brine shrimp.

F: **Algae**; boiled and diced spinach; lettuce; insects; larvae; flakes.

S: Combine only with fishes such as the Argus, those that like hard, saline water. The red and black hybrids are hardier than the green. Those sold in the trade are often *P. latipinna* x *P. velifera* crosses. It is only possible to tell the species from wild-caught imports. The dorsals of *P. velifera* have 18-19 rays and those of *P. latipinna* only 14.

T: 75-82° F, L: ♂ = 4-6″, ♀ = to 6¹/₂″,   A: 39″,   R: m, t,   D: 2-3.
   25-28° C,   ♂ = 10-15 cm, ♀ = to 18 cm,   100 cm,

Limia vittata
Cuban Limia

GUICHENOT, 1853

Syn.: *Gambusia vittata, Limia cubensis, Limia pavonina, Poecilia cubensis, Gambusia cubensis, Poecilia pavonina, P. vittata*

Fl.: 1907 by P. Schwarzer of Berlin.

Sex: ♂ has more colourful dorsal and tail-fin and with gonopodium.

Soc. B.: Peaceful, cheerful species. Suited to the community tank with hard water.

M: The fish is regarded as undemanding in hard water exceeding 25° dGH. The pH value should lie between 7.5 and 8.2. The water can be hardened with sea salt to approx. 0.3% (30g to 10 l water). The fish will, however, last quite long in saltfree water.

B: The ♀ drops 20-50 fry every 3-5 weeks at 22-24° C water temperature. The fry are seldom eaten, if at all.

F: H, O; algae, Vegetable Food, Food Tablets, Live Food, F/D Food.

S: A particularly lively fish. Sensitive to fresh water so use a good water conditioner when changing water.

T: 64-74° F, L: 5″,   A: 27″,   R: m, t,   D: 2.
   18-24° C,   12 cm,   70 cm,

Poecilia velifera

Limia vittata

Priapella intermedia

ALVAREZ, 1952

Syn.: None

Hab.: Mexico; in the clear waters of Rio Coatzacoalcos.

Fl.: 1964, by Zoologisches Staatsinstitut, Hamburg, West Germany.

Sex: For approximately five months the male can be identified by a gonopodium.

Soc. B.: Though a peaceful, schooling fish, the species is not recommended for a conventional community tank.

M: The species is quite sensitive to fluctuating temperatures which are not common to its native waters. Needs clear water, frequent water changes and a identifiable current. They like to swim beneath a cover of floating plants and show best against a dark tank bottom. Changes in light can make them nervous. We recommend water with a pH 7.0-7.5 and a hardness 10-20° dGH.

B: Not a productive species, younger females may drop only six fry. Older ones may produce to 20 though never more. Fry can be delivered every four to six weeks and should be fed Brine Shrimp and micro food with algae.

F: C, O; small live foods; flakes; FD.

S: Though some consider the species "unattractive" it appears best in a soft light. The eyes and gill patches have a metallic sheen.

T: 75-79° F, L: ♂ = to 1³/₄″, ♀ = to 2¹/₂″, A: 27″, R: m, t, D: 3.
   24-26° C, ♂ = to 5 cm, ♀ = to 7 cm, 70 cm,

Xiphophorus helleri
Swordtail

HECKEL, 1848

Syn.: *Mollienisia helleri, Xiphophorus jalapae, X. rachovii, X. strigatus, X. brevis, X. helleri helleri, X. h. brevis, X. h. strigatus*

Hab.: Central America: between latitudes 12-26° N.

Fl.: 1909, W. Schroot, Hamburg, West Germany.

Sex: The male has a gonopodium and a "sword" or extension on the lower portion of its tail equal to one-third to one-quarter the length of its body. The female has a rounder body and, during spawning, a noticeable patch.

Soc. B.: Peaceful though occasionally cannibalistic towards fry, including its own. It is well suited to community tanks. ♂♂ are often very quarrelsome amongst each other, only one male will hold its ground.

M: Needs a well-planted tank with plenty of open swimming areas. Water pH 7.0-8.3 and a hardness 12-30° dGH.

B: A live-bearer, the female drops up to 80 fry. We recommend a spawning box or dense floating cover to protect the young. Many color morphs are available: red, green, blue-black, Wagtail (i.e. with a black tail fin), Tuxedo (black-red or black-yellow check), Simpson (with a large dorsal) and the beautiful and popular Lyretail.

F: Flake food with a large amount of freeze-dried meat; brine shrimp; algae.

S: No true sexual transformation can be demonstrated, i.e. functional ♀ to functional ♂. Often late-developing ♂ s or arrhenoid ♀ are involved.(That is, females showing male characteristics.)

T: 64-82° F, L: ♂ = 4″, ♀ = 4¹/₂″, A: 23¹/₂″, R: m, t, D: 1.
   18-28° C, ♂ = 10 cm, ♀ = 12 cm, 60 cm,

Priapella intermedia

Top: Neon Swordtail, bottom: Red Swordtail

Red Simpson Swordtail

Red Lyretail Swordtail

Xiphophorus helleri (spotted)
Spotted Swordtail

HECKEL, 1848

Syn.: *X. brevis, X. guentheri, X. helleri guentheri*

Hab.: In flowing waters, Southern Mexico to Guatemala.

Fl.: 1864 to Great Britain.

Sex: The male has the typical sword-like tail; the female, in season, has a spawning patch.

Soc. B.: A peaceful, lively fish ideal for any community tank.

M: Needs a well-planted tank with clear water, some current and, if you plan to breed, floating plants to protect the fry. If there are predators in the community tank, move pregnant females to a separate tank or use a spawning box. Suggest water with a pH 7.2-8.4 and a hardness 15-30° dGH.

B: Follow recommendations for *X. helleri*.

F: C, O: omnivorous; suggest mosquito larvae first; if not well fed the males become sluggish. Can safely be fed a wide range of live foods and FD tablets.

S: The photo shows an aquarium-bred fish. The wild form has less red on its body and fins.

T: 68-82° F, **L:** ♂ = 2¹/₂″, ♀ = 3¹/₂″, **A:** 31″, **R:** m, t, **D:** 1-2.
20-28° C, ♂ = 7 cm, ♀ = 10 cm, 80 cm,

Coral Platy - Red Platy

Xiphophorus maculatus (GUENTHER, 1866)
Platy, Moonfish: hybrids have many other names.

Syn.: *Platypoecilus maculatus, P. nigra, P. pulchra, P. rubra, Poecilia maculata*

Hab.: Atlantic coast of Mexico and Guatemala; northern waters of Honduras.

Fl.: 1907, Mrs. Bertha Kuhnt, Vereinigte Zierfischzuechtereien, Berlin-Conradshoehe, Germany.

Sex: The male is smaller and more colorful: can be identified by his gonopodium.

Soc. B.: A peaceful fish, even toward its own species. Well suited to any community tank.

M: Can adapt to any size aquarium with peaceful tank mates. Use only hardy plants such as *Vallisneria, Sagittaria*, Java Fern and moss. pH 7.0-8.2 and hardness 10-25° dGH.

B: Can reproduce at three or four months of age and fry often reach maturity in a community tank. Not as productive as *X. helleri.*

F: O; omnivorous; flakes; algae.

S: Platies are an ideal addition to a community tank because of their brilliant red coloring. *X. maculatus* occupies the southernmost range of the genus.

T: 64-77° F, **L:** ♂ = 1″, ♀ = 2¹/₂″,   **A:** from 15¹/₂″,   **R:** m,   **D:** 1.
18-25° C,   ♂ = 3.5 cm, ♀ = 6 cm,   from 40 cm,

Wagtail Platy

Blue Mirror Platy

Golden Moon Platy

Simpson Tuxedo Platy

Simpson Coral Platy

Xiphophorus montezumae
Montezuma Helleri, Mexican Swordtail

Syn.: *Xiphophorus m. montezumae*

Hab.: Eastern central Mexico.

Fl.: 1913, a female specimen; 1933, Fritz Mayer, Hamburg, West Germany.

Sex: The male can be identified by a larger dorsal, shorter sword and gonopodium. Some variants have a longer sword-tail.

Soc. B.: A peaceful species.

M: A more sensitive species than *X. helleri*, it needs a large tank with lots of swimming room and places to hide. It can be recommended for some community tanks but is sensitive to nitrate. Regular water changes are important. pH 7.0-8.0 and hardness 10-20° dGH.

B: May be crossed with *X. helleri*. The hybrids are hardy, covered with irregular black spots.

F: O; omnivorous; prefers insect foods; FD; brine shrimp.

S: Unfortunately the fish is rarely imported. Captive-bred fishes are not as prolific.

T: 68-79° F, **L:** ♂ = 2″, ♀ = 2¹/₂″, **A:** 19¹/₂″, **R:** m, t, **D:** 2.
20-26° C, ♂ = 5.5 cm, ♀ = 6.5 cm, 50 cm,

Xiphophorus pygmaeus
Dwarf Helleri, Dwarf Swordtail

Syn.: *Xiphophorus p. pygmaeus*

Hab.: Mexico; Rio Axtla.

Fl.: 1959

Sex: The male has a gonopodium; the female is larger and rounder bodied. (See also "S").

Soc. B.: A peaceful species, well suited for a community tank with the proper water conditions and gentle tank mates.

M: Needs clear, oxygen-rich water with a strong current. Does best with hiding places among rocks and roots.

B: Not very productive, we suggest a spawning box since the parents will sometimes harass the fry. Plant cover in the breeding tank also assures protection. Raise the fry with brine shrimp.

F: C, O: small live foods such as black mosquito larvae, brine shrimp and *Cyclops*; FD; TetraTips.

S: Two sub-species have been described: *X. pygmaeus pygmaeus* (the male lacks a sword) and *X. pygmaeus nigrensis* (the male has a short to medium-length sword, 1/5th to 1/3rd the body length.) Today both are considered individual species.

T: 74-82° F, **L:** 1¹/₂″, **A:** 19¹/₂″, **R:** all, **D:** 2.
24-28° C, 4 cm, 50 cm,

Xiphophorus montezumae

Xiphophorus pygmaeus

Xiphophorus variatus
Variegated or Variatus Platy

(MEEK, 1904)

Syn.: *Platypoecilus variatus, P. maculatus dorsalis, P. variegatus, Xiphophorus variegata* (a trade name only)

Hab.: Southern Mexico.

Fl.: 1931, Seeman Conrad, Hamburg, West Germany.

Sex: The male has a gonopodium; in season the female has a spawning patch.

Soc. B.: A peaceful fish, recommended for all community tanks.

M: Needs a densely-planted tank with algae, on the back glass if possible. pH 7.0-8.3 and hardness 15-30° dGH.

B: Separate pregnant females, placing them in a spawning box. Raise the fry with fine flakes and brine shrimp.

F: H, O: algae; all types of live foods; vegetables.

S: Can be kept in an unheated aquarium, to 55° F (12° C) after acclimatization. Colder water will make the fish more colorful. They can survive on algae for months. Found in various color morphs. The breeding tanks should be kept at a temperature between 68-82° F (20-28° C).

T: 59-77° F, **L**: ♂ = 2″, ♀ = 2¹/₂″, **A**: 15¹/₂″, **R**: t, m, **D**: 1.
15-25° C, ♂ = 5.5 cm, ♀ = 7 cm, 40 cm,

Xiphophorus xiphidium
Swordtail Platy

Syn.: *Platypoecilus xiphidium*

Hab.: Mexico.

Fl.: 1933, Fritz Mayer, Hamburg, West German.

Sex: The male has a short sword.

Soc. B.: A peaceful species best kept separately in larger numbers.

M: Can occasionally be kept in a community tank. In summer the fish may also be kept in a garden pond. The nitrate level must be low, below 20 mg/l. Needs lots of light to insure the growth of algae. pH 7.2-8.2 and hardness 15-25° dGH.

(HUBBS & GORDON, 1932)

B: Not a productive species, rarely more than 24 fry are born at a time. Feed algae and live foods such as mosquito larvae.

F: C, O: mosquito larvae; brine shrimp; FD; flakes; algae.

S: A sensitive, rare species.

T: 64-77° F,   **L:** ♂ = 1¹/₂″, ♀ = 2″,   **A:** 19¹/₂″,   **R:** m,   **D:** 2-3.
18-25° C,   ♂ = 4 cm, ♀ = 5 cm,   50 cm,

Group 7

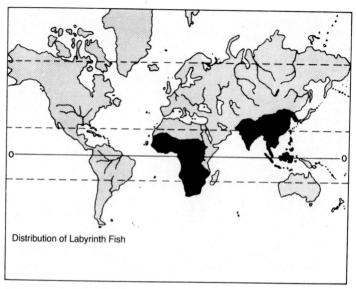

Distribution of Labyrinth Fish

Sub-order Anabantoidei   Labyrinth Fish

Anabantids probably developed 50-60 million years ago during the Tertiary period and belong to the order of Bass fishes. Fossil Gouramis have been found in Sumatra though we do not know whether or not they also occur in Africa. Pliocene layers in Java, 7.5 to 28 million years old, contain fossilized *Ophicephalus* or Snakeheads.

In terms of evolution Labyrinth fishes are relatively new and possesses an additional respiratory organ which distinguishes them from other fishes. The organ allows them to survive in shallow, oxygen-short water and dried ponds and even allows them to search for new water since they can "walk" on their pectoral fins. The labyrinth also enables them to settle in areas otherwise biologically hostile. If kept humid the fish can survive for hours out of water. One species, *Anabas testudineus,* is said to be able to climb trees and the entire sub-order is sometimes known as "Climbing Bass" after them.

Ctenopoma acutirostre, see page 619 for description

Fam.: Anabantidae
Sub-Fam.: Anabantinae

Some Labyrinth Fish are excellent fish for beginners. They are hardy enough to tolerate a range of "abuses" in terms of differing water values, temperatures and foods but the tank must be kept in a warm area. The maintenance and breeding conditions of each species appears beneath the description.

The suborder of Labyrinth Fishes comprises four families:

Anabantidae
Belontiidae
Helostomatidae
Osphronemidae

Family and sub-family affiliations are indicated in the descriptions.

Anabas testudineus

Anabas testudineus
The Climbing Bass, Climbing Perch

Syn.: *Amphirion scansor, A. testudineus, Anabas elongatus, A. macrocephalus, A. microcephalus, A. scandens, A. spinosus, A. trifoliatus, A. variegatus, Antias testudineus, Cojus cobujius, Lutjanus scandens, L. testudo, Perca scandens, Sparus scandens, S. testudineus*

Hab.: In brackish and clear waters throughout many parts of the world: India; southern China; Indonesia; Malayan Archipelago.

Fl.: 1891, Dr. Schad-Treptow.

Sex: The anal fin of ♂ is longer.

Soc. B.: Timid yet aggressive behaviour prevents this species from being kept in a community tank — except with large, hardy specimens.

M: An extremely hardy species, proven by the fact that, when they were first imported at the turn of the century, many survived a gruelling, long journey by sea from Asia. The first Climbing Perch were displayed at

the London Zoo's aquarium about 1870. The fish needs a large, shallow tank with 8 to 12 inches (20-30 cm) of water, floating plants, hiding places and, since the fish jumps, a good aquarium cover.

B: Can be bred in tanks from 45″ in length (1.20 m). If fed live food the fish will be mature from 4″ (12 cm). The eggs float after spawning and at higher temperatures hatch after 24 hours. Use infusoria as the initial food.

F: O; vegetables; live foods; even grains of rice.

S: They were among the first species kept in an aquarium. Since they travel across land on their pectoral fins and may even climb trees, the fish have given their name to an entire family. In damp weather they can survive two days out of water. In drier times they dig into the mud to survive. The fish are prized as a delicacy in some areas.

T: 72-86° F,	L: 4-8″,	A: 31″,	R: all,	D: 1.
22-30° C,	10-23 cm,	80 cm,		

Photo page 617

Ctenopoma acutirostre
Spotted Climbing Perch

Syn.: None

Hab.: In tributaries and deeper streams of Zaire, from Lisala to Kinshasa.

Fl.: 1955

Sex: ♂ has patches of spines on the body; ♀ may have fewer spots on the fins.

Soc. B.: A large, peaceful, bottom-dwelling fish, specimens should be selected carefully. Not particularly suited to a community tank.

M: May hide in a small tank but in the right environment and company it is a bright, friendly tankmate. Needs swimming space with hiding places such as roots or shards. Prefers a dark tank bottom and subdued lighting.

B: Builds a bubble nest. The fry should be raised as our suggestions for *Macropodus operculari*. Water should have a hardness between 2-4° dGH, a pH between 6.5-7.0 and a temperature between 26-29° C.

F: C; live food; mosquito larvae; small earthworms; *Tubifex*; FD.

S: The behaviour is similar to *Nandus*.

T: 73-82° F,	L: 4-6″,	A: 31″,	R: m, b,	D: 3.
23-28° C,	10-15 cm,	80 cm,		

Ctenopoma ansorgii
Ornate Ctenopoma

(BOULENGER, 1912)

Syn.: *Anabas ansorgii*

Hab.: Tropical west Africa; Kinshasa, Zaire.

Fl.: 1955

Sex: ♂ has brighter colors.

Soc. B.: Though not aggressive the species may become predatory toward smaller tankmates.

M: Needs soft water, 3-20° dGH hardness and pH 6.5-7.5. When making changes use peat extract and conditioner. Add plants but leave open room for swimming.

T: 79-82° F,   L: 3¹/₂″,   A: 23¹/₂″,   R: m, b,
26-28° C,   8 cm,   60 cm,

May be combined with such gentle, bottom dwellers as *Corydoras.*

B: Little is known of its habits. The species uses a loose, surface bubble nest, about 4 inches deep (12 cm.). Recommend soft water. Raise the fry with such micro food as Slipper animacules, then, after 8 days, brine shrimp.

F: Live food; flakes occasionally; FD occasionally. Feed sparingly.

S: The coloring varies from turquoise to orange. It is difficult to import from the Congo and has become rare.

D: 2-3.

Ctenopoma argentoventer

Syn.: *Anabas africanus, A. argentoventer, A. peterici, Ctenopoma peterici*

Hab.: West Africa; Niger.

Fl.: 1912, Kuntzschmann, Hamburg, West Germany.

Sex: The ♂♂ bear two yellow bands when almost full-sized.

Soc. B.: Can be used in a community tank, but only with large, robust tankmates.

(SCHREITMUELLER & AHL, 1922)

M: Needs a large, well-planted tank with subdued lighting and roots or other hiding places.

B: Follow recommendations for other *Ctenopomas*. The nest is not guarded. The larvae hatch in 48 hours and grow rapidly.

F: C; live food; large flakes after acclimization.

S: A rare species recommended only for experts.

T: 72-81° F, **L:** to 6″,   **A:** 39″,   **R:** m,   **D:** 3.
 22-27° C, to 15 cm, 100 cm,

Ctenopoma fasciolatum
Banded Ctenopoma

(BOULENGER, 1899)

Syn.: *Anabas fasciolatus, A. fasciatus*

Hab.: Zaire; Stanley Pool, near Kinshasa.

Fl.: 1912 by Siggelkow, Hamburg, West Germany.

Sex: The dorsal and anal fins on ♂ are greatly extended similar to those of the Paradise Fish. ♀ has less color.

Soc. B.: A generally peaceful species.

M: Easy and pleasant to keep, the fish are at their best in a roomy tank. Need both planting and space for swimming. Suggest water with a hardness 4-20° dGH and pH 6.5-7.5 with frequent changes advised.

B: No data is available; water values probably include hardness 2-4° dGH, pH about 6.5 and a temperature around 82° F (28° C).

F: O; omnivorous; flakes; vegetables; FD; live food.

S: Coloring is excellent though variable. The photograph shows a young ♂.

T: 75-82° F, **L:** 3¼″,   **A:** 31″,   **R:** m, b,   **D:** 2.
 24-28° C, 8 cm, 80 cm,

Ctenopoma kingsleyae
Kingsley's Ctenopoma

GUENTHER, 1896

Syn.: See S

Hab.: In flowing waters of west Africa; from Zaire to Gambia.

Fl.: 1933

Sex: Distinguishable only because ♂♂ have more obvious spiny patches behind the eye and at the base of the tail.

Soc. B.: A generally timid species which should not be kept with either over-active or substantially smaller tankmates. We suggest keeping them in a species tank.

M: Requires a roomy tank with a darkened surface and a heavy planting of hardy plants. Needs hiding places, a root or tunnel, for each fish. Strong water filtration is essential. Recommend water with a hardness to 15° dGH and pH 6.5-7.5.

B: Breeding is possible in a large tank. Up to 20,000 eggs can be laid. These float and must be removed. Placed in water with a temperature of 29° C, the larvae will hatch after 24 hours. They become free swimming after an additional 48 hours and will take brine shrimp.

F: C, O; omnivorous; feed mostly small fish and active live foods such as earthworms and water insect larvae; large flakes; tablets.

S: The species name is not firmly established. According to DAGET the fish may be a color morph of *Ctenopoma petherici. C. kingsleyae* would then be a synonym.

T: 77-82° F, L: 7¹/₂″, A: 39″, R: m, b, D: 3.
     25-28° C,   19 cm,   100 cm,

Ctenopoma maculatum

THOMINOT, 1886

Syn.: *Anabas pleurostigena, A. maculatus, Ctenopoma weeksii, C. multifasciata*

Hab.: South Cameroons; Upper Zaire.

Fl.: 1954

Sex: The ♂ has scales with armoured spikes. See *C. kingsleyae.*

Soc. B.: Relatively tolerant toward larger tankmates.

M: Follow recommendations for *C. kingsleyae.*

Labyrinth Fishes

B: Does not guard the nest.

F: C, O; live food; large flakes; tablets.

S: The young, with two dark brown stripes behind the eyes, have a different color pattern than adults. Initially the pelvic fins are black.

T: 72-82° F, L: 8″, A: 47″, R: m, D: 3.
22-28° C, 20 cm, 120 cm,

Ctenopoma muriei

Syn.: *Anabas muriei, A. houyi*

Hab.: In bogs and slow-moving waters; Nile; Lake Albert; Lake Edward; Chad Basin.

Fl.: Unknown.

Sex: Similar to *C. kingsleyae*, ♂ has spined scales.

Soc. B.: A cheerful, active species, it can be combined with robust fish from 2¹/₂″ (6 cm.).

M: Easier to keep than larger Ctenopomas, it is more lively and tolerant and needs more space for swimming. Suggest water with a hardness to 20° dGH and pH 6.0-7.5. Add some floating plants to control the light.

B: After an active, nocturnal courtship ♂ embraces ♀ for several seconds as she lays 10 to 30 eggs. At a water temperature of 27° C the larvae hatch within 24 hours. The brood is not guarded. Feed infusoria first and after one week, brine shrimp.

(BOULENGER, 1906)

F: C, O; live food; flakes.

S: A sub-species from the swamps of the Sudan Nile, *Ctenopoma muriei ocellifer*, has been described.

T: 74-82° F, L: 3¹/₂″, A: 31″, R: m, D: 2.
23-28° C, 8.5 cm, 80 cm,

Ctenopoma nanum
Dwarf Climbing Perch

Syn.: *Anabas maculatus, A. nanus*

Hab.: Africa; Cameroons to Zaire.

Fl.: 1933

Sex: The anal and dorsal fins are longer on ♂. ♀ is less brightly colored.

(GUENTHER, 1896)

B: ♂ builds a bubble nest beneath floating plants. When spawning the fish drop beneath the nest and let the eggs float upward. ♂ guards the nest. The larvae hatch after 24 hours and are free-swimming from the third day. Give them infusoria first and after a few days, brine shrimp.

Soc. B.: The ♂♂ are territorial and aggressive fighters, especially at the time of spawning.

M: Of all Ctenopomas, this species is the easiest to combine with other fishes. They appreciate a well-planted tank with floating plants, an open swimming area and water that is clear, has a hardness to 15° dGH and a pH 6.0-7.2.

F: C; fine live food; flakes later.

S: The smallest of all Ctenopomas.

T: 73-79° F, **L:** 3″, **A:** 23¹/₂″, **R:** m, **D:** 2-3.
    23-26° C, 7.5 cm, 60 cm,

Ctenopoma ocellatum   PELLEGRIN, 1899

Syn.: *Anabas ocellatus, A. weeksii, Ctenopoma acutirostre, C. denticulatum, C. petherici* (not GUENTHER)

Hab.: Zaire; Stanley Pool and Stanley Falls; Kasai Province.

Fl.: About 1957.

Sex: ♂ has an eyepatch and the base of the tail is darker. ♀ has an arched back.

Soc. B.: Fish of similar size do best and the species are timid if kept alone. The fry may be regarded as prey.

M: Cannot handle a strong flow of water, which makes them nervous. Prefers a slightly acid water (a peat bottom or in filtration). pH 6.2-7.2 and hardness 4-15° dGH. Make frequent water changes.

B: Unknown.

F: O; omnivorous; mosquito larvae; flakes.

T: 74-82° F, **L:** 4″, **A:** 31″, **R:** m, b, **D:** 2.
    24-28° C, 10 cm, 80 cm,

Ctenopoma oxyrhynchum   (BOULENGER, 1902)
Mottled Ctenopoma

Syn.: *Anabas oxyrhynchus*

Hab.: Zaire; Stanley Pool.

Fl.: 1952

Sex: The dorsal and anal fins on ♂ are more sharply pointed.

Soc. B.: Though generally peaceful, the fish may become predatory toward smaller fish. Not recommended for a community tank.

M: Needs a well planted tank with open areas for swimming. Recommend hiding places, subdued lighting and peat filtration. Water hardness 4-15° dGH and pH 6.2-7.2.

B: The small, oleaginous eggs float. The fry hatch in three or four days and should be raised as you would other Labyrinth Fishes.

F: C; live food; FD; flakes.

S: Markings on the young are different. According to LADIGES the rear body section is nearly black.

T: 74-82° F, **L:** 4″, **A:** 31″, **R:** m, b, **D:** 2-3.
    24-28° C, 10 cm, 80 cm,

Ctenopoma ocellatum

Ctenopoma oxyrhynchum

Fam.: Belontiidae
Sub-Fam.: Belontiinae

Belontia hasselti

Syn.: *Polyacanthus einthovenii, P. hasseltii, P. helfrichii, P. kuhli, P. olivaceus*

Hab.: Java; Sumatra; Borneo; Singapore; Malacca.

Fl.: 1968; first captive bred in 1970 by Verfuerth.

Sex: The ♂ has fatter fins. During the spawning season ♀ lacks a mesh-like pattern on its fins.

Soc. B.: A peaceful species though ♂ becomes aggressive after spawning and the ♀ should be removed. At that time ♂ will even attack a finger inserted in the tank.

M: Needs a densely-planted tank and bright lighting. Lacking that, the tank can be placed in a sunny window. Water should have a hardness to 35° dGH and pH 6.5-8.0.

T: 77-86° F, **L:** 8″, **A:** 31″, **R:** m, t, **D:** 2.
25-30° C, 19 cm, 80 cm,

(CUVIER & VALENCIENNES, 1831)

B: Spawns in shallow water, 4 to 6 inches (12-15 cm.) at temperatures between 28-30° C. While many ♂ s build a bubble nest, not all do. Though the fish are prolific, laying 500-700 eggs, they will not spawn in the company of other fishes. The fry hatch after 24-48 hours and are free-swimming after the third day. Feed infusoria initially, then brine shrimp after one week. The temperature of the air and the water should be similar, otherwise the fish will "catch cold".

F: C. O; flakes with vegetable supplement; all types of live foods.

S: While the fish is rarely bred or imported, it is worthwhile and should be kept.

Belontia signata
Combtail, Comb-Tailed Paradise Fish

Syn.: *Polyacanthus signatus*

Hab.: Sri Lanka, in standing waters.

Fl.: 1933

Sex: Not easily distinguished. Dorsal fin of ♂ more greatly extended.

Soc. B.: Often boisterous so keep together with larger fish only. May bite; often timid. Young are tame.

M: Densely planted-up tank with swimming space; light; hiding places amid roots. Flourishing plants. May be combined with *H. temminckii* and Cichlids.

B: As for Paradise Fish. Eggs are laid in clumps beneath a plant leaf. No bubble nest, usually one large air bubble. The fry swim freely only after 6 days and then immediately eat *Artemia* and very fine Flake Food.

T: 74-82° F, **L:** 5″, **A:** 31″, **R:** m, b, **D:** 2.
24-28° C, 13 cm, 80 cm,

(GUENTHER, 1861)

F: O; omnivorous, live food, flake food, vegetable diet.

S: Only young fish are to be recommended for the community tank. The sub-species *B. signata jonklaasi* has recently been described.

Belontia hasselti

Belontia signata

Betta coccina

VIERKE, 1979

Syn.: *Betta tussyae*

Hab.: Possibly central Sumatra, Malayan Peninsula.

Fl.: Unknown.

Sex: ♂ has larger and longer dorsal and anal fins. During spawning very much like *B. splendens*. ♀ has diagonal stripes.

Soc. B.: A timid fish which is short-lived and uncomfortable in a community tank. No one knows whether or not the fish is aggressive though several dozen were kept in a retailer's tank without incident.

M: Does best in a small tank with places to hide and peaceful tankmates. The tank needs planting with some tall enough to reach the surface. Suggest minimal filtration, subdued light and soft water, to 4° dGH and pH 6.0-7.5. Can tolerate water to 18° dGH.

B: They are bubble nest builders.

F: C; such small live foods as brine shrimp and *Cyclops*; crushed flakes.

S: The species *B. tussyae* – described only in 1985 – is identical to *Betta coccina*.

T: 75-81° F, L: 2",   A: 20",   R: m, t,   D: 2.
    24-27° C,   4.5 cm,   50 cm,

Betta bellica
Striped Fighting Fish

REGAN, 1909

Syn.: *Betta fasciata*

Hab.: Sumatra.

Fl.: 1906

Sex: ♂ is brightly colored with longer pelvic and anal fins.

Soc. B.: Not as bellicose as *B. splendens*. Though several pairs can be kept in a single tank, they should be separated at spawning time.

M: Follow suggestions for other species of *Betta*. Water hardness to 15° dGH and pH 6.5-7.5.

B: Though there are no reports, the species is a nest builder and can probably be bred like *B. splendens*.

F: C; live foods; FD; a few flakes.

S: Stripes seem to appear only in captive-bred specimens.

T: 74-86° F, L: 4",   A: 31",   R: m,   D: 2.
    24-30° C,   10 cm,   80 cm,

Betta coccina

Betta bellica

Fam.: Belontiidae
Sub-Fam.: Macropodinae

Betta imbellis

Syn.: *"Betta splendens"*

Hab.: Indonesia (Kuala Lumpur).

Fl.: 1970, D. Schaller.

Sex: ♂ is more brightly colored and has larger fins.

Soc. B.: Unlike *B. splendens* males, these do not battle to the death. Mock fights and related display behavior does not inflict injury and only adds to the charm of the species.

M: Follow recommendations for *B. splendens*. Hardness 6-8° dGH and pH 7.0.

B: The species is less prolific than *B. splendens* but is similar in other ways.

F: C, O; live foods; flakes; FD.

S: The species deserves a wider audience and should be bred more. ROLOFF bred six generations in five years.

T: 75-77° F,   L: 2″,   A: 8″,   R: t, m, D: 2.
   24-25° C,   4.8 cm,   20 cm,

Betta pugnax
Penang Mouth-Brooding Fighting Fish

Syn.: *Macropodus pugnax*

Hab.: Malaysia.

Fl.: 1905, Reichelt, Berlin, West Germany.

Sex: ♂ is more brightly colored and has longer fins.

Soc. B.: A pair can be kept in a quiet community tank. During spawning the males can become very aggressive. It is recommended to keep more males than females in a tank.

M: Needs clear water with a good flow pattern (from a powerful external filter). Do not keep the tank in sunlight. Soft water, to 12° dGH and pH 6.0-7.2 contribute to their well-being.

B: A mouth-brooder, the ♂ keeps the eggs. More than 100 eggs are laid, first caught in batches of 10 to 20 with ♂ 's anal fin. They are then "spat" by the ♀ into the ♂ 's mouth. The fry grow rapidly on infusoria and can be fed brine shrimp after the first week.

F: C; all types of live foods.

S: The species has been largely ignored because its coloring is less variable than that of *B. splendens*. The photo shows the non-typical variety from Penang island with a red-brown coloration of the body.

T: 72-82° F,   L: 4″,   A: 31″,   R: m, t, D: 2-3.
   22-28° C,   10 cm,   80 cm,

Betta imbellis

Betta pugnax, Penang

Fam.: Belontiidae
Sub-Fam.: Macropodinae

Betta smaragdina

Syn.: None

Hab.: Northeast Thailand.

Fl.: 1970 by Dietrich Schaller.

Sex: ♂ has longer pelvic fins; during pairing ♀ has several noticeable stripes which, at other times, are darker and less noticeable with only a trace of a lighter color.

Soc. B: Considered more peaceful than B. splendens and may be combined with other peaceful, quiet fishes. LINKE says in its native country the species is placed in small jars for fighting matches.

M: Follow recommendations for B. splendens. If several young fish are kept together, they are more likely to tolerate each other as they age.

LADIGES, 1972

B: Bubble nest builders. Suggest fresh water at a temperature of 82° F (28° C). Breeding can be initiated by placing a pair in a tank about 20" long (50 cm.). It should be well planted on one side with a cover of floating plants. Pairs may spawn only in hollows.

F: C; small live food; FD natural food; occasional flakes.

S: A beautifully colored, different fish which deserves more attention.

T: 75-81° F, L: 3", A: 27", R: m, t, D: 2-3.
24-27° C, 7 cm, 70 cm,

Betta splendens
Siamese Fighting Fish

Syn.: Betta trifasciata (not BLEEKER), B. pugnax, B. rubra (not PERUGIA)

Hab.: Thailand; Cambodia; possibly Laos.

Fl.: 1892 to France; 1896, Paul Matte, Berlin, Germany (from Moscow).

Sex: ♂ has larger fins and is more colorful.

Soc. B.: ♂♂ cannot be kept together. They spread gills, attack and tear each other's fins. Several ♀ can be kept in an aquarium.

M: Keeping ♂♂ individually in small glass containers holding less than one quart of water must be regarded as cruel. With smaller containers the surface must be kept free of dirt and the water must be changed frequently. Bettas need plenty of heat and a single ♂ can be kept in a community tank. Water hardness to 25° dGH and pH 6.0-8.0.

REGAN, 1910

B: ♂ builds a bubble nest in shallow water (no more than 6" deep). Disconnect the filter and aerator as a current may destroy the nest. The fry hatch after 24 hours and may be fed micro food, crushed flakes and hard-boiled egg yolk.

F: All types of live foods; flakes; FD.

S: The fish are sensitive to temperature changes. Feral specimens are difficult, if not impossible, to find. A variety known as "Fighting Veiltail" can be found in many colors: red, blue, turquoise, green, white, black and in many combinations.

T: 75-86° F, L: 2¹/₂-3", A: 10", R: t, D: 2.
24-30° C, 6-7 cm, 25 cm,

Betta smaragdina

Betta splendens

Colisa sota
Honey Gourami

(HAMILTON, 1822)

Syn.: *Trichopodus chuna, Trichogaster chuna, T. sota, Colisa chuna*

Hab.: Northeastern India; Assam; Bangladesh.

Fl.: 1962

Sex: The sexes are similar appearing except during spawning. At that time ♂ runs from shades of honey to ochre, has a blue throat and a touch of black on the front section of the anal fin; ♀ is brown.

Soc. B.: Though peaceful and timid, the species are territorial, especially during spawning.

M: Needs a heavily-planted tank with a cover of floating plants. Recommend water hardness to 15° dGH and pH 6.0-7.5. Combine only with smaller, peaceful, gentle fish.

B: During the spawning season a pair will defend their territory, about 80 sq. in. (500 cm^2). ♂ builds a bubble nest though it may spawn before. The larvae hatch in 24-36 hours, depending on temperature, and are free-swimming after one day. Feed infusoria first and later, brine shrimp and finely-ground flakes. FD tablets are also suitable.

F: C, O; small live foods; flakes; vegetables; tablets.

S: This Labyrinth Fish is harder to keep than some, is only occasionally suitable for a community tank, and is susceptible to *Oodinium pillularis*. In the photo ♂ is above, ♀ is below.

T: 72-82° F,   **L:** 2″,   **A:** 15^1/$_2$″,   **R:** t, m,   **D:** 2-3.
     22-28° C,   5 cm,   40 cm,

Colisa fasciata
Banded Gourami

(BLOCH & SCHNEIDER, 1801)

Syn.: *Trichogaster fasciatus, Trichopodus colisa, T. bejeus, T. cotra, Colisa vulgaris, Polyacanthus fasciatus, Colisa bejeus, C. ponticeriana*

Hab.: India; Bengal; Assam; Burma.

Fl.: 1897, Paul Matte, Berlin, Germany. (40 specimens were imported from Calcutta.)

Sex: The dorsal fin on ♂ ends in a point and the body is darker, becoming nearly black during spawning.

M: Prefers a darker tank bottom with heavy vegetation along the edges of the aquarium. Leave room in the center for swimming. Water hardness 4-15° dGH and pH 6.0-7.5.

B: The water in the tank should be soft, pH 6.5, shallow, about 8″ deep (20 cm.) and at a temperature of 82° F (28° C). A large bubble nest is built. ♂ fully embraces ♀ during the act of spawning, turning his stomach toward the surface. 20 to 50 eggs are laid each time – 500 to 600 in all – which float to the surface. These hatch within 24 hours. ♂ will jealously guard the nest and ♀ should be removed.

F: O; flakes; vegetables; tablets.

S: The species is a food fish in parts of India, where it is dried and eaten.

T: 72-82° F,   **L:** 4″,   **A:** 23^1/$_2$″,   **R:** t, m,   **D:** 2.
     22-28° C,   10 cm,   60 cm,

Colisa sota

Colisa fasciata

Fam.: Belontiidae
Sub-Fam.: Trichogasterinae

Colisa labiosa
Thick-lipped Gourami

(DAY, 1878)

Syn.: *Trichogaster labiosus*

Hab.: Burma; northern India.

Fl.: One specimen was imported in 1904. In 1911 several fish were imported by Scholze and Poetzschke, Berlin, West Germany. These appear to have been *C. fasciata*.

Sex: The sex of adults can be readily determined. ♂♂ are more colorful with a noticeably pointed dorsal.

Soc. B.: A peaceful, quiet fish recommended for a community tank. When breeding we suggest that the fish be kept in a separate tank 23 inches (60 cm) or more in length.

M: Similar to other Labyrinth Fish; the tank should not be too deep (about 15″ (40 cm), with plenty of vegetation and a dark bottom. The water, at a hardness between 4-10° dGH, should be slightly acid, pH 6.0-7.5.

B: Builds a bubble nest similar to *C. lalia* but does not use bits of vegetation and the fragile nest is easily destroyed. It is extremely large, covering as much as half the surface of the aquarium. *C. labiosa* is perservering in both the construction of the nest and guarding of the brood. While on her back and in the course of many embraces by the ♂, the ♀ lays 500-600 eggs. The eggs float upward to the nest and hatch after 24 hours. The fry leave the nest two days later.

F: O; omnivorous; flakes; vegetables; tablets.

S: The species is frequently confused with *C. fasciata* and crosses make them even more difficult to distinguish.

T: 72-82° F, L: 4″,   A: 19¹/₂″, R: t, m, D: 1.
   22-28° C,   9 cm,   50 cm,

Colisa lalia
Dwarf Gourami

(HAMILTON, 1822)

Syn.: *Colisa unicolor, Trichogaster lalius, Trichopodus lalius, Trichopsis lalius, Trichogaster unicolor, Colisa cotra*

Hab.: Wetlands of the Ganges; Jumna; Bramaputra. According to POPTA, the species is also found in the Baram river in Borneo.

Fl.: 1903, H. Stueve, Hamburg, West Germany.

Sex: ♂ is much more colorful. See photo.

Soc. B.: A peaceful, timid species. Pairs generally swim together.

M: Does well in a small to medium-sized aquarium. The tank should be heavily planted with a cover of floating plants. A darker bottom emphasizes the fish's colors. Peat filtration is recommended and, since the fish are susceptible to disease, regular water changes are important. Combine only with other quiet, peaceful fishes.

B: The fish builds a tall, sturdy bubble nest of bits of plant and algae. Keep the water depth at 8″ (20 cm) during spawning. ♂ guards the eggs which hatch after 24 hours. Raise the fry as you would *C. sota*. After spawning remove the ♀ and also the ♂ after 2-3 days, because they will eat the fry (to 600).

F: O; omnivorous; vegetables; algae; tablets.

S: One of the most lovely colored of all aquarium fishes. No aquarist beyond the beginning stages should be without them. The species will not tolerate poor water conditions.

T: 72-82° F, L: 2″,   A: 15¹/₂″, R: t, m, D: 2.
   22-28° C,   5 cm,   40 cm,

Colisa labiosa

Colisa lalia

Fam.: Belontiidae
Sub-Fam.: Macropodinae

Macropodus concolor AHL, 1937

Syn.: *"Macropodus opercularis concolor"*, *Macropodus opercularis var. spechti*

Hab.: Southern China; Vietnam.

Fl.: 1935

Sex: The dorsal and anal fins of ♂ end in a point; on ♀ they are shorter.

Soc. B.: A generally peaceful species, it is better suited to a community tank than *M. opercularis*. During spawning ♂ becomes aggressive.

M: Follow recommendations for such other Labyrinth Fish as *Trichogaster leeri*. The fish is tolerant of varying water values but suggest a hardness to 20° dGH and pH 6.5-7.8.

B: The fish spawn willingly in soft water to 4° KH at temperatures between 26-30° C.

F: C, O; flakes; small live foods. Adult ♂♂ will also accept mosquito larvae and small worms.

S: The species is considerably more peaceful than Paradise Fish and deserves more attention from connoisseurs.

T: 68-79° F, L: ♂ = 4", ♀ = 3¹/₄", A: 27", R: m, t, D: 1.
   20-26° C,   ♂ = 12 cm, ♀ = 8 cm,   70 cm,

Macropodus opercularis
Paradise Fish

(LINNAEUS, 1758)

Syn.: *Labrus opercularis, Macropodus viridi-auratus, Polyacanthus opercularis, Macropodus concolor, Platypodus gurca, Macropodus filamentosus, M. venustus, M. opercularis var. viridi-auratus*

Hab.: In shallow waters (such as rice paddies) of eastern Asia; China; Korea; Taiwan; Ryukyu Islands: Malacca.

Fl.: The second tropical fish brought to France (the Goldfish was first), it was imported in 1869 and was brought to Berlin by Sasse in 1876.

Sex: ♂ has substantially longer fins and is more brightly colored.

Soc. B.: Young fishes can be easily kept together but adult ♂♂ battle as fiercely as fighting fish.

M: Needs a larger aquarium with lots of swimming space and some places for ♀ to hide. The fish will not eat plants but only hardy vegetation is suggested because of

the fish's active courtship and the mock battles between tankmates. Water hardness to 30° dGH and pH 6.0-8.0.

B: Easy to breed, the fish prefers to build a bubble nest beneath a large leaf. To induce breeding reduce the water level and increase the temperature. Up to 500 fry result. Feed them infusoria first then brine shrimp.

F: O; omnivorous; active live foods; large flakes; tablets.

S: There are black and albino forms (which are pink with red stripes). The fish virtually eradicates planaria (discworms) if short of other food. The fish is a jumper so cover the tank.

T: 61-79° F, L: 4", A: 27", R: m, b, D: 1.
   16-26° C,   10 cm,   70 cm,

Macropodus concolor

Macropodus opercularis

Malpulutta kretseri   DERANIYAGALA, 1937

Syn.: None

Hab.: Sri Lanka.

Fl.: Into Germany by Geissler and Bader, 1966.

Sex: ♂ is larger with longer caudal and dorsal fins.

Soc. B.: A peaceful, timid and sluggish species which should be kept only with a few gentle tankmates, preferably small Labyrinth Fish.

M: The fish are jumpers and the tank must be well covered. They need such hiding places as rocks, roots or half-buried pots. The tank should have a dark bottom, Cryptocoryne plants and, if possible, floating plants above. Water hardness to 20° dGH and pH 5.5-7.5.

B: If given live foods the fish will breed in soft water. They spawn in small caves near the bottom and rarely eat their larvae. The fry swim to the surface and, when free-swimming, can be fed brine shrimp.

F: C; most live foods; flakes are accepted unwillingly.

S: The species is rare in its natural habitat and is seldom sold. It is recommended only for experienced hobbyists.

T: 74-82° F,   **L**: ♂ = 3^1/$_2$″, ♀ = 1^1/$_2$″,   **A**: 23^1/$_2$″,   **R**: m,   **D**: 2-3.
24-28° C,   ♂ = 9 cm, ♀ = 4 cm,   60 cm,

Parosphromenus deissneri   (BLEEKER, 1859)

Syn.: *Osphronemus deissneri*

Hab.: In moderately-flowing waters; Malaysia; Singapore.

Fl.: Before 1914.

Sex: ♂ is more brightly colored, especially during courtship.

Soc. B.: Though a peaceful, gentle fish it is not recommended for a community tank.

M: Does best in a small, well-planted species tank with soft, slightly acid water and good filtration. It can be kept it in a community tank if it will not be bred. Water hardness to 10° dGH and pH 5.6-7.2.

B: A cave breeder, ♂ will drive away ♀ and assume care of the nest. In water temperatures of 25° C the larvae hatch after 72 hours and are free-swimming in 6 days. The fry grow slowly and require very clear, pure water. Feed infusoria and brine shrimp.

F: C; small live foods; flakes after they overcome their timidity.

S: One of the smallest and most beautifully colored of all Labyrinth Fish, it is a jewel for an accomplished hobbyist. Since the species can breathe through their gills they rarely surface for air.

T: 74-82° F,   **L**: 1^1/$_2$″,   **A**: 23^1/$_2$″,   **R**: b,   **D**: 4.
24-28° C,   3.5 cm,   40 cm,

Malpulutta kretseri

Parosphromenus deissneri

Pseudosphromenus cupanus
Spike-Tailed Paradise Fish

(CUVIER & VALENCIENNES, 1813)

Syn.: *Polyacanthus cupanus, Macropodus cupanus*

Hab.: Southern India; Sri Lanka.

Fl.: 1903 by Stueve, Hamburg, West Germany.

Sex: Though difficult to sex, species can be distinguished during pairing; ♂ is a colorful red, with a more pointed dorsal; the female is almost black.

Soc. B.: A peaceful species best kept in pairs, it can be kept in a community tank with smaller, peaceful fishes or in a species tank.

M: Does well in a shallow, well lighted, well-planted tank with a dark bottom of fine gravel and caves made of coconut shells or over-turned pots. Water hardness to 15° dGH and pH 6.5-7.8.

B: Builds a bubble nest of wood or stones near the surface. Suggest a water temperature of 82° F (28° C). The tank should have a growth of green algae. ♂ guards the nest. The larvae hatch in 48 hours (27° C) and are free-swimming two days later. The parents can remain in the tank.

F: C, O; small live foods; flakes; with added FD.

S: The exciting color traditional of the species is brightest under good tank conditions.

T: 74-81° F, **L:** 2¹/₂″, **A:** 23¹/₂″, **R:** m, t, **D:** 1-2.
24-27° C, 6 cm, 60 cm,

Pseudosphromenus dayi
Brown Spike-Tailed Paradise Fish

(KOEHLER, 1909)

Syn.: *Polyacanthus cupanus var. dayi, Macropodus dayi, Polyacanthus dayi*

Hab.: In ditches and bogs of western India.

Fl.: 1908, Scholze and Poetzschke, Berlin, West Germany.

Sex: The tailfin rays of ♂ are sharply extended.

Soc. B.: A peaceful species, both parents look after the nest but the pair should not be combined with aggressive or active species.

M: Does well in a tank with a dark bottom, subdued lighting and enough planting to do justice to its beautiful color. Needs peat filtration and regular water changes. Water hardness 4-15° dGH and pH 6.5-7.5.

B: Reduce the water level to 4″ (10 cm.) and keep at a temperature of 82° F (28° C). A bubble-nest builder, the fish is a prolific spawner which occasionally chooses hollows. Both parents guard the nest, returning the eggs and fry if they fall out. The fry hatch in 30 hours. Feed infusoria, brine shrimp and small flakes.

F: O; omnivorous; flakes; live foods; brine shrimp.

S: A charming fish, it is not often imported.

T: 77-82° F, **L:** 3″, **A:** 23¹/₂″, **R:** m, t, **D:** 2.
25-28° C, 7.5 cm, 60 cm,

Pseudosphromenus cupanus

Pseudosphromenus dayi

Fam.: Belontiidae
Sub-Fam.: Trichogasterinae

Sphaerichthys osphromenoides osphromenoides
Chocolate Gourami

CANESTRINI, 1860

Syn.: *Osphromenus malayanus, O. notatus*

Hab.: Malacca; Malaysian Penninsula; near Djambi, Sumatra; Borneo.

Fl.: 1905, J. Reichelt. (The specimens did not survive.) The species was reintroduced in 1934 and regularly imported from 1950.

Sex: ♂ has a yellow border along the edge of the anal and caudal fins.

Soc. B.: A peaceful, even timid fish best kept in pairs, it should not be combined with active species.

M: The fish is delicate, prone to bacteria and skin parasites, and water quality is important: hardness 2-4° dGH, pH 6.0-7.0 with peat extract. The tank should be well planted and the water changed frequently.

B: A mouth brooder or nest builder, it is a frugal spawner (20 to 40 fry). Spawns on the bottom and the ♀ keeps the eggs in her mouth for 14 days.

F: Such live food as black mosquito larvae, bloodworms and brine shrimp; flakes, possibly with FD.

S: If you are an advanced hobbyist, this species is worth your attention. Try breeding pairs.

1979 VIERKE described the subspecies *S. osphromenoides selatanensis*.

T: 75-86° F, **L:** 1³/₄″, **A:** 31″, **R:** m, b, **D:** 3-4.
   25-30° C,   5 cm,   80 cm,

Trichogaster leeri
Pearl Gourami, Leeri Gourami

(BLEEKER, 1852)

Syn.: *Trichopodus leeri, Osphromenus trichopterus, Trichopus leeri*

Hab.: In rivers heavy with plants; Malaysia; Borneo; Sumatra.

Fl.: 1933

Sex: ♂ has an extended, pointed dorsal and anal fins and more red in the body color.

Soc. B.: A very peaceful fish though ♂♂ may fight occasionally.

M: Water should be about 12″ deep (30 cm) with a cover of floating ferns for hiding places. Do not combine with such aggressive species as Cichlids. If you do the fish will hide in a corner, loose color and may even refuse to eat. The room temperature should be above 20-22° C, otherwise the tank will become chilled, affecting the fish. Water hardness 5-30° dGH and pH 6.5-8.5.

B: When breeding reduce the water level to 4-5 inches (12 cm.). Builds a large bubble nest between water plants which, after spawning, is guarded by the ♂. ♂ is not as aggressive with the female as many Labyrinth Fish.

F: Flakes; vegetables; live foods; FD.

S: Very hardy; with the exception of the Blue Gourami, the hardiest of all Labyrinth Fishes. Will live about 8 years.

T: 74-82° F, **L:** 4″, **A:** 23¹/₂″, **R:** t, m, **D:** 1.
   24-28° C,   12 cm,   60 cm,

Spaerichthys osphromenoides osphromenoides

Trichogaster leeri

Fam.: Belontiidae
Sub-Fam.: Trichogasterinae

Trichogaster microlepis
Moonlight Gourami

(GUENTHER, 1861)

Syn.: *Osphromenus microlepis, Trichopsis microlepis, Trichopodus microlepis, Trichopus microlepis, T. parvipinnis, Deschauenseeia chryseus*

Hab.: In standing and slow-moving waters; Thailand; Cambodia.

Fl.: 1952

Sex: The pelvic fins of ♂ are orange to red; yellow on ♀. Healthy adults have a red iris.

Soc. B.: A peaceful, rather timid species, as for *T. leeri*.

M: Needs a roomy tank to 16″ deep (40 cm). It should be heavily planted with Giant *Vallisneria* and Java Fern. Fine-leaved plants may be damaged and used for nest building. Water hardness 2-25° dGH and pH 6.0-7.0.

B: Since it is a bubble best builder, you should reduce the water level. Lays 500 to 1000 eggs. Raise with an infusoria of lettuce leaves and banana skins.

F: O; omnivorous; flakes; vegetables; FD.

S: In their native countries the fishes are prized for food.

T: 79-86° F, L: 6″,   A: 31″,   R: m, t, D: 2.
   26-30° C,   15 cm,   80 cm,

Trichogaster pectoralis
Snake-Skinned Gourami

(REGAN, 1910)

Syn.: *Trichopodus pectoralis, Osphromenus trichopterus var. catoris*

Hab.: In shallow waters and rice paddies; Thailand; Cambodia; Malaysian Penninsula.

Fl.: 1896, J.F. G. Umlauff, Hamburg, West Germany.

Sex: The dorsal fins of ♂ are pointed and there is a fringe on the orange-red pelvic fins; on the ♀ the fins are yellow.

Soc. B.: A very peaceful species, even during spawning.

M: Does well in a shallow tank with the water to 12″ (30 cm.). It can be planted or not, depending on your choice of water quality. The species needs places to hide. Water hardness 2-30° dGH and pH 6.0-8.3.

B: A bubble nest builder, you should reduce the water level. Follow suggestions for *T. leeri*.

F: O; omnivorous.

S: A rather unappealing species, it is rarely imported.

T: 73-82° F, L: 8″,   A: 23¹/₂″, R: m, b, D: 1.
   23-28° C,   20 cm,   60 cm,

Trichogaster microlepis

Trichogaster pectoralis

Trichogaster trichopterus
Three-Spot Gourami, Blue Gourami

(PALLAS, 1777)

Syn.: *Trichopodus trichopterus, Osphromenus trichopterus var. koelreuteri, Labrus trichopterus, Trichopus trichopterus, T. sepat, T. cantoris, T. siamensis, Osphromenus saigonensis, O. siamensis, O. trichopterus*

Hab.: Southeast Asia; Malaysia; Thailand; Burma; Vietnam; Islands of the Indo-Australian Archipelago.

Fl.: 1896, J.F.G. Umlauff, Hamburg, West Germany.

Sex: The dorsal fins of ♂ is pointed.

Soc. B.: A peaceful fish its lack of movement becomes almost boring with age. Younger specimens are comical. Do not keep more than one ♂ in a tank.

M: A very hardy fish, it reacts to its environment. Kept with active, aggressive tankmates, it will retire to a corner. If, as an adult, it is transferred to a new tank it may become very timid. Water hardness 5-35° dGH and pH 6.0-8.8.

B: A nest builder, you should reduce the water level to 6″ (15 cm.). Remove ♀ after spawning since ♂ may become aggressive.

F: O; omnivorous; since it will accept a variety of foods from oatmeal to dried water flies, the amazing ease of feeding keeps it the number 1 hobby species in many underdeveloped nations.

S: One of the hardiest of hobby fishes, it eats planarians or disc worms. The photo on the right shows the hybrid *T. trichopterus "cosby"* with a traditionally-colored fish below. A yellow-pink pseudo-albino morph (shown in the lower photo) is appearing more frequently in the trade.

T: 72-82° F,   **L:** 4″,   **A:** 19$^1/_2$″,   **R:** t, m,   **D:** 1.
    22-28° C,   10 cm,   50 cm,

648

T. trichopterus "cosby", above. A normally colored specimen is below

T. trichopterus, pseudo-albino morph

Trichopsis pumila
Dwarf Croacking Gourami

(ARNOLD, 1936)

Syn.: *Ctenops pumilus*

Hab.: Vietnam; Thailand; Sumatra.

Fl.: 1913

Sex: The yellowish spawn can be seen through the body of the ♀. ♂ has a pointed dorsal.

Soc. B.: A peaceful, gentle species, it becomes aggressive when spawning.

M: Does well with peaceful tankmates. Suggest a peat bottom, acid water, hardness 2-10° dGH and pH 5.8-7.0. The tank can be planted with Cryptocorynes and fine-leaved plants.

B: Builds a "half-hearted" bubble-nest without the use of plants. The nest, generally built near the surface and beneath larger plant leaves, is often so incomplete it goes unseen. The species seldom spawns in hollows and the ♂ does not change color. Croaking noises are heard during the brief courtship when ♂ embraces ♀ at the throat. 1-10 eggs are laid at each embrace (VIERKE) for a total of 100-170 in all. ♂ expectorates the eggs into the nest and guards it. The larvae hatch within two days at 80° F (27° C). They are free swimming two additional days and grow well if fed small live foods.

F: C, O; flakes; small live foods; FD.

S: During courtship, or when excited, the fish make an audible croaking sound.

T: 77-82° F, **L**: 1", **A**: 15¹/₂", **R**: m, **D**: 2.
25-28° C, 3.5 cm, 40 cm,

Trichopsis vittata
Croaking Gourami

(CUVIER & VALENCIENNES, 1831)

Syn.: *Osphromenus vittatus, Trichopus striatus, Ctenops nobilis* (not McCLELLAND), *Ctenops vittatus, Osphromenus striatus, Trichopsis harrisi, Trichopsis striata*

Hab.: Eastern India; Thailand; Vietnam; Malaysia; Indonesia.

Fl.: 1899, H. Stueve, Hamburg, West Germany. First bred in 1903.

Sex: ♂ has more color with a red edge to its longer anal fin.

Soc. B.: A peaceful, happy species, with some tankmates it may need hiding places.

M: May be successfully combined with gentle Characins, Barbs and other small Labyrinth Fish. Water hardness 3-15° dGH and pH 6.5-7.5.

B: A bubble nest builder, it is difficult to breed and not prolific. Reduce the water to 4" (10 cm). Keep temperatures at 86° F (30° C). Soft water treated with a conditioner induces courtship.

F: O; omnivorous; small live food; small, sifted flakes; FD.

S: Both sexes make croaking noises, hence the name. The smaller photo shows *T. schalleri.*

T: 72-82° F, **L**: 2¹/₂", **A**: 19¹/₂", **R**: m, **D**: 2-3.
22-28° C, 6.5 cm, 50 cm,

T. pumila

T. vittata

Fam.: Helostomatidae

Helostoma temminckii
Kissing Gourami

CUVIER & VALENCIENNES, 1831

Syn.: *Helostoma oligacanthum, Helostoma rudolfi, H. servus, H. tambakkan*

Hab.: Thailand and Java.

Fl.: About 1950, from commercial breeders in Florida.

Sex: Difficult to distinguish, ♀ fatter.

Soc. B.: A tolerant species though ♂♂ will occasionally fight by pressing their mouths together (i.e. kissing). The weaker fish eventually gives in.

M: Needs a roomy tank with stones, Java Fern, and possibly Java Moss. Plastic plants can be used since virtually all vegetation is regarded as food. Do not clean the back aquarium glass since the fish will browse on the algae grown there. Use a large gravel bottom to prevent digging. Water hardness 5-30° dGH and pH 6.8-8.5.

B: Prefers soft water. Does not build a nest and you should use lettuce leaves on the surface as the spawning material. The eggs float and the lettuce offers nourishment for bacteria and infusoria which will be consumed by the fry. The ♂ is induced to spawn by the ♀.

F: O; omnivorous; vegetables; cooked lettuce; all types of live foods.

S: The fish filter plankton through their gills for added nourishment.

T: 72-82° F,   **L:** 6 to 12″,   **A:** from 27″,   **R:** m, t,   **D:** 3.
22-28° C,   15 to 30 cm,   from 70 cm,

Fam.: Osphronemidae

Osphronemus gorami
Common Gourami

(LACEPEDE, 1802)

Syn.: *Osphronemus olfax, O. notatus, O. satyrus, O. gourami*

Hab.: China; Java; Malaysia; eastern India. It is imported and sometimes grown as a food fish.

Fl.: 1895

Sex: The dorsal and anal fins are pointed on ♂.

Soc. B.: A loner, small specimens may be combined with larger fish in a community tank. Young fish may fight between themselves but older fishes are peaceful.

M: The fish can easily reach four inches (10 cm.) in length, though as they increase in size you must be certain tankmates do not disappear. The tank should be well planted with floating plants. Water hardness to 25° dGH and pH 6.5-8.0 Needs good filtration.

B: Because of their size, breeding in an aquarium is difficult though possible ... possible because many fish are ready to reproduce at six months. The fish builds a ball-shaped nest of bits of plants, just below the surface, and large eggs are guided into the nest. The fry are guarded until they are ready to leave the nest – in about 2$\frac{1}{2}$ weeks.

F: O; will accept any food from oatmeal to live foods – and smaller tankmates.

S: Recommended for an aquarium only when young. When young it may be confused with the Chocolate Gourami since the markings are similar. Prized as food in its native countries.

T: 68-86° F,   **L:** Possibly to 27″,   **A:** 56″,   **R:** m, t,   **D:** 4 (SI).
20-30° C,   Possibly to 70 cm,   150 cm,

Helostoma temminckii

Osphronemus gorami

Group 8

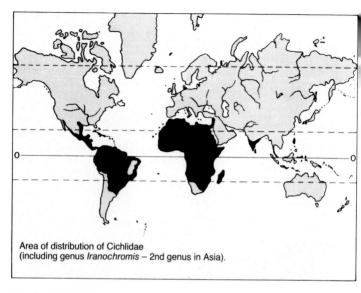

Area of distribution of Cichlidae
(including genus *Iranochromis* – 2nd genus in Asia).

The family Cichlidae   Cichlids

With about 160 genera and more than 900 described species, Cichlids comprise one of our largest families of fishes. Nearly half belong to the gigantic genus *Haplochromis* and according to recent research from GREENWOOD (1979, 1980), the genus could be divided into several genera. In addition to the three largest genera, *Haplochromis, Cichlasoma* and *Tilapia (Sarotherodon)*, there are several others which have but a single species (i.e. monotypic genera).

Cichlids are found in Central and South America, Africa and in parts of Asia. In Africa they are distributed across the continent except in the extreme northwest and south. Several species are found on Madagascar. On the American continent the distribution of Cichlids stretches from southern Texas through Central America, Cuba and Haiti as far south as Argentina. They are absent from Tierra del Fuego, southern Chile and the Argentine. In Asia they are found only in southern India and Sri Lanka. The number of species varies widely across the three continents. In Africa there are close to 700 species and in America more than 200 yet in Asia there is only one genus *Etroplus* with three species.

,,Haplochromis" spec.

Cichlids are found in three widely separated areas (see map), a phenomenon which remained a mystery for some time. The explanation was found recently in geo-physicist Alfred Wegener's theory of continental drift and plate tectonics.

200 million years ago there were but two gigantic continents, one in the northern hemisphere, the other in the south. The northern continent included present-day North America, Europe and Asia while the southern continent included Africa, South America, Australia and the Antarctic. Present-day India, which then formed part of Africa, was included. This large country was called Gondwanaland. When the continent broke apart India was torn from Africa and Africa and South America were separated and created in their present form, though in fact, they were literally drifting apart for nearly 60 million years. The ancestors of Cichlids were already established in Gondwanaland and their currently separated distribution can be explained by the original break-up of continents.

The family Cichlidae includes small to medium-sized fish, most with a perch-like body, though the shape varies. Some Cichlids have elongated bodies and others are tall with slender sides. Examples of the former are found in the genera *Cichla*, *Crenicichla*, *Julidochromis* and *Teleogramma* while *Symphysodon* and *Pterophyllum* represent the latter. Cichlids differ from related families such as Nandus (Nandidae), true perches (Percidae) and Sunfish (Centrarchidae) in several ways: by having a single nostril on each side of the head and by generally unified pharyngial bones.

Cichlids have a single dorsal consisting of a hard-rayed segment in front followed by a soft-rayed section. The lateral line is generally in two parts and the head is large, a recognizable fatty projection normally appearing on the foreheads of older males. We can draw some conclusions about the fishes' life style from its body though it is beyond our perview to discuss the many adaptations Cichlids have made in the environment. Cichlids can be found in dramatically varied habitats and there is scarcely another family of fishes which has adjusted to as many environmental changes and circumstances. Details can be found in readily available literature in the U.S. and abroad.

Cichlids

Cichlids have been particularly successful in fitting into the large rift-valley lakes of Africa, Tanganyika and Lake Malawi are examples. Here they occupy the most unusual ecological niches and hold their own against very competitive pressures. A number of Cichlids even live under such unfavorable conditions as salt water, warm water, water with low oxygen content, in caves and in hard-running rapids. *Etroplus suratensis, E. maculatus, Hemichromis bimaculatus, H. fasciatus, Chromidotilapia guentheri* and several *Tilapia, (Sarotherodon)* are among the examples. *Sarotherodon alcalicus grahami* and *S. alcalicus alcalicus* survive in so-called soda lakes, waters with high sodium carbonate content, where the pH is 10.5, surprisingly alkaline for any fish! *S. a. grahami* can be found in the thermal waters of Lake Magadi where water temperatures top 104° F (40° C). Others visit, if not inhabit, water with little oxygen. *S. aureus* seems to prefer the warm, shallow waters of Lake Victoria and scientists have discovered these fishes can survive in water with almost no measurable oxygen. *Cichlasoma urophthalmus* is the only known cave-dwelling Cichlid and can be found in caves through out the Yucatan Peninsula. Finally, fish in several genera, *Steatocranus, Teleogramma* and at least two *Lamprologus (L. congoensis, L. werneri)* live in the fastest flowing rapids of certain rivers.

Because of their wide range of environments, Cichlids will accept a variety of foods but in general terms, excluding the herbivorous *Tilapia* and *Geophagus*, all cichlids are predaceous. In the wild they prefer insect larvae, worms and fishes. *Cichla ocellaris, Boulengero-chromis microlepis* and some *Crenicichla* prefer fish over all other choices.

Most Cichlids are sized between two and 12 inches (5-30 cm). The largest, *Boulengerochromis microlepis*, reaches a length of 31 inches (80 cm.) and weighs six pounds. Other large Cichlids include *Cichlasoma managuense* (to 27 inches or 70 cm.), *Cichla ocellaris* (to 23 inches or 60 cm), *C. dovii* (to 20 inches or 50 cm) and *Sarotherodon esculentum* which reaches a length of 19 inches or 50 cm.

The larger fishes above, as well as others, are popular food fishes in their native lands and form an important source of nutrition. *S. esculentum* are even being raised commercially in many parts of the world including Asia.

Many aspects of Cichlid behavior are of special interest and a number of species have become the subject of scientific papers. Details concerning learning procedures, hereditory behaviour, intra-species rivalry, "pecking" orders, communication and other rituals, territorial behaviour, display behaviour and pairing have been described in specialty literature. We will not detail much of this but will cover the factors important to hobbyists, reproductive behaviour and brood-care among them.

Nearly all Cichlids lay their eggs on some substrate such as rocks, leaves, wood and sand. A few release their eggs at random and the free-spawners include fish in the genus *Tropheus*. It is now customary to catagorize cichlids as "open" and "shelter" breeders according to the way they raise and protect their broods. Both mouth and cave brooders are listed as "shelter" species. (WICKLER, 1966: Zool. Jb. Syst. 93, 127-138). A further division is made of mouthbrooders, categorizing ovophile types – which take the eggs into their mouths when laid (e.g. *Haplochromis* and *Pseudotropheus*) and larvophiles – which lay eggs on stones and take the brood into their mouths only after or just before the larvae hatch (e. g. *Geophagus* and *Gymnogeophagus*). In outline form it would be thus:

I. Openbreeders
II. Shelter breeders
   1. Cave breeders
   2. Mouth breeders
      a. Ovophile mouth-brooders
      b. Larvophile mouth-brooders

As we shall see, open and shelter breeders differ in many ways.

Open Breeders

The eggs of open breeders are generally small and plainly colored, oval shaped and designed to stick together on their longer sides. A clutch can comprise as many as 10,000. In general there are substantial differences between the sexes and in only a few cases are the differences minor. Examples include *Symphysodon*, *Pterophyllum* and *Cichlasoma managuense*.

Shelter Breeders

The eggs of cave-breeders are normally medium-sized, have large yolks and stick together at the ends. The species lay fewer eggs, about 200, and there is clear sexual dimorphism and dichromatism between males and females. The males are larger, brighter and more brilliantly colored. Eggs of ovophile mouth-brooders are large and often brightly colored. The number of eggs spawned varies from fewer than 15 in the case of *Tropheus sp.* to as many as 100 for others. It is easy to distinguish the sexes since the males have bright, exciting colors while the females are much plainer.

To classify Cichlids as open or shelter breeders according to the manner in which they care for their eggs seems logical at first blush but in truth, it does not catagorize all of the individual characteristics found among the many species. To be able to include the surprising variety in natural breeding techniques one must also consider the distribution of roles between males and females. On this basis there are five forms of families. (PETERS, 1948, Basic Questions of Animal Psychology):

1. Nuclear Family:

Duties are shared by the male and female though defence of the brood falls to the male. When the fry are free-swimming parents share responsibilities equally. Many Cichlids classified as monogamous open breeders appear polygamous when an opportunity arises. *Cichlasoma maculicauda* have been seen maintaining pairbonding only as long as offspring are present. When the duties are done, the male may pair with another female in a period as short as three days. There is little, if any, sexual dimorphism.

Examples: Open breeders – *Symphysodon* and *Pterophyllum*; cave breeders – *Julidochromis*; mouth-brooders – *Chromidotilapia, Geophagus, Sarotherodon.*

2. Matriarch/Patriarch Family:

This form differs from the nuclear family only in the care of the spawn and larvae. The mother is exclusively concerned with brood care while the male defends the territory. After the fry are free-swimming, both parents share the duties equally. The parents are monogamous throughout the brood period though not for life. Sexual dimorphism and dichromatism occur.

Examples: *Pelvicachromis* sp.; *Cichlasoma nigrofasciatum.*

3. Patriarch/Matriarch Family:

The male dominates, laying claim to a large territory which includes the smaller breeding territories of several females. The male accepts responsibility for defence of all the breeding territories, but is not involved in the care of individual broods. The male is polygamous. Clear sexual dimorphism occurs, the males are larger and often exhibit entirely different colors and patterns.

Examples: *Apistogramma* and *Nannacara* sp.

Apistogramma agassizii

Cichla ocellaris

4. Matriarchal Family:

The female dominates, looking after her nest, which is not located in a male's territory. There is no bond between sexual partners, the male and female being agamous, spawning with various partners. Sexual dimorphism and dichromatism is strong. Maternal families occur exclusivly among mouth-brooders.

Examples: *Haplochromis* and *Pseudotropheus* sp.

5. Patriarchal Family:

A truly paternal family is only found in one mouth-brooder, *Sarotherodon melanotherow*. The male carries the eggs and larvae in his mouth while the female rarely does (in observations, only 10% of the time.) When the fish pair they remain monogamous for at least one spawning period and males and females are barely distinguishable with neither sexual dimorphism or dichromatism occurring. In some cases males of the *Crenicichla* sp. look after the brood but authorities such as STAECK (1974) consider the genus as members of the patriarch/matriarch group.

The attraction of dummy eggs:

Many Cichlids have unusual color markings, often yellowish patches on the anal fin, which serve a specific purpose in terms of signals, triggering instinctive responses. They can be used to identify one fish to another and often facilitate reproduction. The color patches are very similar to eggs in size, shape and color and are known to hobbyists as "dummy eggs". They are used to guarantee fertilization of the real eggs and work this way: many mouth-brooding females take the eggs into their mouths as soon as they are laid, which makes insemination or fertilization difficult. The dummy eggs are real enough to confuse the female. The male spreads his anal fin in front of the female and sheds his milt at the same time. When the female attempts to take the false eggs into her mouth she gathers the milt, fertilizing eggs currently in her mouth. Obviously, this is an ingenious, important part of courtship.

Acarichthys geayi, page 666

Aequidens curviceps (AHL, 1924)
Flag Cichlid

Syn.: *Acara curviceps*

Hab.: In protected places in quiet streams through the Amazon basin. Captive-bred fishes are most common though wild-caught fishes are available occasionally.

Fl.: 1909, C. Siggelkow, Hamburg, West Germany.

Sex: The male is larger with extended dorsal and anal fins.

Soc. B.: Keep the fish in pairs since they are peaceful except during spawning when they become intolerant. A nuclear family, they will not attack plants. Keep in a community tank, but separate during spawning.

M: The tank should include stones, roots and plants with places to hide and open areas for swimming. Use fine gravel on the bottom. pH about 7.0 with a hardness to 20° dGH.

B: Recommend soft to medium-hard, slightly acid water, 2-14° dGH (best choice: 2-6° dGH) and pH 6.0-6.8. Replace a portion of the water regularly since the fish become prone to such diseases as Exophthalmia (bulging of the eyes) with old water. Open breeders, they lay as many as 300 eggs, spawning on flat stones or on roots. Feed the fry *Artemia* nauplii once they are free-swimming.

F: C, O: all types of live foods; FD; flakes.

S: While the fish may eat the first spawn, they will care for eggs laid after. Occasionally two females will act like a pair though the eggs remain infertile. The coloring is variable.

T: 72-79° F, **L:** 3-3½″, **A:** 23½″, **R:** m, b, **D:** 2.
22-26° C, 8-10 cm, 60 cm,

Aequidens dorsiger (HECKEL, 1840)

Syn.: *Acara dorsigera, Aequidens dorsigerus*

Hab.: Boliva; Rio Paraguay, Villa Maria and Puerto Suarez.

Fl.: Unknown.

Sex: The male is larger, has a higher back and more developed fins. A dark patch may be found on the dorsal of both sexes.

Soc. B.: Related to *A. curviceps,* the species has the character of a dwarf cichlid. It will not attack plants, is peaceful and even timid.

M: Add rocks, roots and plants to the tank to provide hiding places. Leave open room for swimming. The bottom should be of fine gravel, even a mix of sand and gravel. Suggest water with a pH around 7.0 and a hardness to 20° dGH.

B: Recommend soft to medium hard water at a temperature between 25-30° C. The fish will spawn on horizontal rocks or plants and the eggs are small. The fry are delicate and are sensitive to differences in water chemistry. Do not make severe water changes. The parents may exchange larvae before it is free-swimming.

F: Small live food; all types of flakes.

S: Science has not determined the roles each sex handles in brood care. Some reports indicate the female dominates or at least shares equally. Others claim the male is the most active while the female defends the territory. Either way, the species is most attractive, noted for its sudden color change to a complete red-black.

T: 73-79° F, **L:** 2-3″, **A:** 23½″, **R:** b+m, **D:** 3-4.
23-26° C, 6-8 cm, 60 cm,

Aequidens curviceps, ♀ with eggs

Aequidens dorsiger, ♀ with eggs

Aequidens pallidus

Syn.: *Aequidens duopunctatus*

Hab.: Amazon, near Manaus.

Fl.: 1968, Heiko Bleher, Frankfurt, West Germany.

Sex: It is difficult to distinguish the sexes by the genital papillae alone though that of the male is pointed and that of the female is blunt.

Soc. B.: The fish is territorial, forms pairs and creates a nuclear family and though a mouth-brooder, it exhibits some behaviour of open breeders. *A. pallidus* may be combined with several peaceful *Cichlasoma*.

M: Follow recommendations for other *Aequidens* sp. as well as *Cichlasoma meeki*. Suggest neutral water, about pH 7.0 with a hardness of 10° dGH.

B: Follow water values listed above at temperatures about 77° F (25° C). The fish lay as many as 300 eggs on a freshly cleaned rock. Two days later the larvae are taken into the mouth and during maturation the brood is exchanged once between the pair. The fry are free-swimming in eight days and are then returned to the mouth only in the face of danger. The fish are patient and good parents.

F: C, O: all types of live foods; FD; flakes.

T: 72-75° F, **L**: 6″, **A**: 31″, **R**: b, m, **D**: 1-2.
22-24° C, 15 cm, 80 cm,

Laetacara thayeri

Syn.: *Acara thayeri, Aequidens thayeri*

Hab.: Upper Peruvian Amazon.

Fl.: 1981, Sven Kullander, Stockholm, Sweden.

Sex: Identification is difficult since the coloring is similar for both sexes. On the ♂ the soft-rayed portion of the dorsal has a short point while on the ♀ it is rounded.

Soc. B.: The fish is territorial. Some authorities say the species is peaceful, others feel it is aggressive. It forms pairs, creates a nuclear family and cares for broods.

M: See recommendations for *A. curviceps*.

B: Keep water at temperatures around 77° F (25° C) and follow recommendations for *A. tetramerus* (Open Breeders).

F: C; hardy live foods; FD; frozen foods; beef.

S: Fishes imported to 1980 as *Laetacara flavilabris* were *L. thayeri*.

T: 72-79° F, **L**: 6″, **A**: 31″, **R**: m+b, **D**: 2.
22-26° C, 15 cm, 80 cm,

Aequidens pallidus

Laetacara thayeri

Fam.: Cichlidae

Acarichthys geayi

(PELLEGRIN, 1902)

Syn.: *Acara geayi, Aequidens geayi*

Hab.: Guyana; northern Brazil. It is not captive-bred and is rarely imported.

Sex: The male is larger with a higher, sharply-angled forehead. The female often has more contrasting colors. As an example, her black markings will be more obvious against a lighter background. Positive identification can normally be made by the shape of the genital papilla which is pointed, sloping to the rear on the male and blunt and directed forward on the female.

Soc. B.: Territorial and peaceful, the fish form pairs and are intolerant only during spawning when they burrow. They form a patriarch/matriarch family.

M: Be sure to place plants around the edges of the tank and use over-turned pots, shards or rocks as hiding places. Requires a bottom of fine gravel or sand.

B: While pH and hardness can vary, keep the temperature between 25 and 27° C. A cave-breeder, as many as 500 eggs are normally laid on a vertical wall. After spawning the male is driven from the cave. Then, the female guards the brood and the male protects the territory. The pair carefully protect and feed the brood for a month.

F: C, O: all types of live foods such as *Daphnia, Cyclops*, mosquito larvae and *Tubifex* worms; flakes.

S: Though it differs from the nuclear family common to many open and mouth-brooding *Aequidens,* it is similar to *Pelvicachromis* sp. in its patriarch/matriarch family. The family philosophy and a different body structure indicate the fish belongs to the genus *Acarichthys* and not to *Aequidens* as previously thought.

T: 72-77° F, L: ♂ = 6", ♀ = 5",   A: 31",   R: b,   D: 2.
  22-25° C,   ♂ = 15 cm, ♀ = 13 cm,   80 cm,

Aequidens guianensis

REGAN, 1905

Syn.: *Aequidens itanyi*

Hab.: Tributaries of Rio Itanyi, French Guyana. Captive-bred specimens are rare.

Fl.: 1963

Sex: ♂ is larger and more brilliantly colored with longer dorsal and anal fins. The male's pelvic fins extend to the softrayed portion of the anal fin while those of the female are shorter.

Soc. B.: Territorial and often aggressive, particularly when spawning, the fish do not burrow and will leave plants alone. Forms a nuclear family.

M: Needs a bottom of fine gravel with rocks and roots to create places to hide. Suggest hardy plants and an open swimming area.

B: Recommend slightly acid, soft to medium hard water (pH 6.0-7.0 and 5-14° dGH) at temperatures between 75-77° F (25-26° C). Frequent water changes ($\frac{1}{3}$ weekly) are important since the water should be pure and oxygen-rich. The fish are open breeders and lay to 500 eggs on freshly-cleaned rocks. Both parents care for the brood.

F: C, O: live foods such as *Tubifex* worms, earthworms and mosquito larvae; FD.

S: The upper lobe of the tail fin is longer and pointed while the lower lobe is rounded.

T: 73-77° F, L: 6",   A: 31",   R: m, b,   D: 3.
  23-25° C,   15 cm,   80 cm,

Acarichthys geayi

Aequidens guianensis

Fam.: Cichlidae

Aequidens mariae
Mary's Cichlid

EIGENMANN, 1922

Syn.: *Geophagus vittatus*

Hab.: Colombia: western and northern Brazil.

Fl.: 1973

Sex: ♂ can be as much as one-third larger than the ♀ with pointed fins. The female develops a short ovipositor during the spawning season.

Soc. B.: Territorial and remarkably gentle for Cichlids, the fish form a nuclear family. They are larvophile mouth-brooders.

M: See recommendations for *A. maronii* or *A. geayi*.

B: Suggest slightly acid, soft to medium water, pH 6.5 and hardness 5-12° dGH, at temperatures between 77-82° F (25-28° C). The fish will drop 100 to 400 eggs on leaves or rocks as open breeders might. After two days these are taken into the mouth.

Released when the fish become free-swimming, the fry return to her mouth in case of danger and at night. The parents protect and feed the brood for four to eight weeks.

F: C, O: all types of live foods such as insects, insect larvae, earthworms, small crustaceans and *Tubifex* worms; frozen and FD.

S: The species can be identified by a black diagonal stripe which stretches from the final dorsal ray to the upper gill cover where it turns upward, crosses the neck and joins an identical stripe on the other side.

T: 74-79° F, L: 6″,   A: 46¹/₂″, R: m+b, D: 2.
   24-26° C,   15 cm,   120 cm,

Aequidens maronii
Keyhole Cichlid

(STEINDACHNER, 1882)

Syn.: *Acara maronii*

Hab.: Guyana. Specimens sold currently are captive-bred and often dwarfed through in-breeding.

Fl.: 1936

Sex: It is difficult to distinguish sexes. The male's anal fin is normally longer and the female is often smaller in size. ♀♀ may also be identified by the genital papillae.

Soc. B.: One of the most peaceful of Cichlids, the species seldom burrows and rarely damages plants. They form a nuclear family and carefully care for their fry which may remain with the family unit for as long as six months.

M: Needs a bottom of fine gravel or sand with hiding places among rocks and roots. Suggest an open area for swimming and water with a pH 6.0-8.0 and hardness to 20° dGH.

B: Recommend slightly acid, soft to medium-hard water, pH 6.5 and hardness 4-12° dGH, at temperatures between 73-79° F (23-26° C). An open breeder, the fish lays as many as 300 eggs on carefully cleaned rocks. The eggs are protected and fanned by the parent's fins to keep the water circulating.

F: C, O: all types of live foods; FD; flakes; tablets.

S: The fish are nervous and easily frightened at which time they turn an irregular brown.

T: 72-77° F, L: 3¹/₂ to 6″,   A: 23¹/₂″, R: m, b, D: 1-2.
   22-25° C,   10 to 15 cm,   60 cm,

Aequidens mariae

Aequidens maronii

Aequidens portalegrensis
Black Acara, Port Acara

(HENSEL, 1870)

Syn.: *Acara minuta, A. portalegrensis*

Hab.: In shallow, peaceful streams of southern Brazil; Bolivia; Paraguay. Wild-caught fish are rare today and most specimens are captive-bred.

Fl.: 1913, C. Siggelkow, Hamburg, West Germany.

Sex: It is difficult to distinguish sexes though during spawning identification can be made by the genital papillae. The male is often noticably green-colored while the female tends more to browns and reds.

Soc. B.: Territorial and peaceful, the fish pair and burrow. Sexually mature fish are intolerent of others of their species. They form nuclear families and both parents care for the fry.

M: Need rocks and roots in the tank for hiding and an open area for swimming is important. Recommend hardy plants or,

better, a cover of floating plants. Needs a bottom of gravel.

B: Suggest neutral to slightly acid, soft to medium-hard water, pH 6.5-7.0 and hardness 3-10° dGH, at a temperature between 23-26° C. Change $1/3$ of the water weekly. The fish are open breeders and will lay up to 500 eggs on carefully-cleaned rocks.

F: C: all types of live foods; FD; occasional flakes; tablets.

S: The fish will readily accept a wide range of foods; the young may be combative and during spawning both adult sexes are black. The mouths are often damaged by combat, the weaker fishes adopting a submissive posture.

T: 61-74° F,　L: 6″,　　A: 39″,　　R: b,　　D: 2.
　16-24° C,　15 cm,　100 cm,

Aequidens pulcher
Blue Acara

(GILL, 1858)

Syn.: *Aequidens latifrons, Cychlasoma pulchrum*

Hab.: Trinidad: Panama; northern Venezuela; Colombia. Until recently fish in the hobby were captive-bred. Recently, wild-caught specimens have been imported.

Fl.: 1906, Hans Stueve, Hamburg, West Germany.

Sex: It is difficult to distinguish between sexes. The fins on ♂♂ are longer and the extended rays of the dorsal and anal fins often arch around the caudal fin.

Soc. B.: Territorial, peaceful even toward its own species, the fish form pairs. They burrow but do not destroy plants. Pairs form a nuclear family and make excellent parents.

M: Need a bottom of sand or fine gravel with rocks and roots for hiding. Use hardy

plants such as Giant *Vallisneria* and *Sagittaria*. Water should have a pH 6.5-8.0 and a hardness to 25° dGH.

B: Follow water values suggested for *A. portalegrensis* at temperatures between 26-28° C. Open breeders, the fish will spawn on rocks. The larvae and fry are well guarded and are easy to raise. Well adjusted pairs may spawn several times a year. Fish are sexually mature from two and one-half inches (7 cm).

F: C: all types of live foods; FD; flakes rarely.

S: Frequent water changes, $1/3$ to $1/2$ weekly) are suggested because excretion can cloud the water. Dirty water can promote diseases.

T: 64-73° F,　L: to 8″,　　A: 31″,　　R: b, m,　　D: 1.
　18-23° C,　to 20 cm,　80 cm,

Aequidens portalegrensis

Aequidens pulcher

671

Aequidens rivulatus
Green Terror

(GUENTHER, 1859)

Syn.: *Chromis rivulatus, Acara aequinoc-tialis, A. rivulata*

Hab.: Western Ecuador; central Peru.

Fl.: 1971; earlier it was identified as "*Aequidens pulcher*".

Sex: The female is darker, with less contrast between colors while the ♂♂ are larger and, with age, generally develop a bump on their head.

Soc. B.: Territorial, pairs form nuclear families and while they may be a bit lax with their first spawn, they become excellent parents thereafter. The fish are aggressive and intolerant and should be kept only with tank mates hardy enough to fend for themselves.

M: Follow recommendations for *A. maronii* or *A. pulcher*. A tank needs plenty of hiding places.

B: Follow recommendations for *A. maronii* and *A. tetramerus* with water temperatures between 25-26° C. The fry hatch in three or four days and are free-swimming by the 11th. Make frequent water changes and feed brine shrimp. The fry are slow growing to $^1/_2$-$^3/_4$" (2 cm) then grow faster.

F: C: feed a variety of live foods if possible: flakes; FD; frozen foods; beef heart.

S: The fish has been known for some time as *A. pulcher*, which is incorrect. It is an independent species.

T: 68-74° F, L: 8", A: 39", R: m+b, D: 2-3.
  20-24° C, 20 cm, 100 cm,

Aequidens tetramerus
Saddle Cichlid

(HECKEL, 1840)

Syn.: *Acara dimerus, A. tetramerus, A. viridis, Chromis punctata, C. uniocellatus, Pomotis bono*

Hab.: In peaceful rivers and standing water throughout central and north-eastern South America. Nearly all fish currently available are captive-bred since fish are rarely caught in the wild. New imports would be desirable.

Fl.: 1910, C. Siggelkow, Hamburg, West Germany.

Sex: It is difficult to distinguish between the sexes even though the dorsal and anal fins on the ♂ are more pointed and the male is more brilliantly colored.

Soc. B.: Territorial, they pair and form nuclear families. The species is intolerant and will bite, particularly as adults age. They will not harm plants. The fry are more peaceful than their parents.

M: Follow recommendations for *A. curviceps.*

B: Recommend slightly acid, soft to medium-hard water, pH 6.5 and hardness 5-12° dGH. Needs frequent water changes. Open breeders, the female will lay as many as 1,000 eggs on a rock or root. Both parents tirelessly share responsibilities of the fry.

F: C: all types of live foods; FD.

S: An important food fish in its range.

T: 74-79° F, L: 6-10", A: 39", R: m, b, D: 2-3.
  24-26° C, 15-25 cm, 100 cm,

Aequidens rivulatus

Aequidens tetramerus

Apistogramma agassizii
Agassiz' Dwarf Cichlid

(STEINDACHNER, 1875)

Syn.: *Biotodoma agassizii, Geophagus agassizii, Mesops agassizii*

Hab.: Amazon; southern tributaries in Brazil.

Fl.: 1909, C. Siggelkow, Hamburg, West Germany.

Sex: Marked sexual dimorphism: the ♂♂ are larger and more brightly colored with longer dorsal, anal and caudal fins; the tail is pointed. The female's tail is rounder.

Soc. B.: Territorial and peaceful, the fish is not a burrower. A male lays claim to several females, forming a patriarch/matriarch family. Couples share work in caring for the brood. The female protects the brood, the male defends the territory. Within that boundry, the male may spawn with several females, each defending her smaller territory, though not from the dominant male.

M: Needs a tank with dense vegetation and places to hide among rocks and roots.

Recommend a dark tank bottom, possibly lavalit, with clear, nitrate-free water. Frequent water changes are suggested, with a good water conditioner added.

B: Recommend slightly acid, soft to medium-hard water, pH 6.0-6.5 and hardness 5-10° dGH. Add fresh water frequently. A shelter breeder, the female lays to 150 eggs on the roof of a cave where she fans the eggs. When the fry hatch they are generally moved into shallower water, if available. The female is seen at the head of the school and signals young by her movements.

F: C, O; needs a variety of hardy live foods; flakes; FD Menu; tablets.

S: A delicate fish, it is susceptible to medication, toxins such as nitrate and a lack of oxygen. Be careful when using medication, especially against *Hydra*. The eggs can mould quickly. The sex ratio of offspring is often based in favour of ♂♂.

T: 72-75° F, L: 3″, A: 23$\frac{1}{2}$″, R: m, b, D: 3.
22-24° C, 8 cm, 60 cm,

Apistogramma bitaeniata
Banded Dwarf Cichlid

PELLEGRIN, 1936

Syn.: *Apistogramma klausewitzi, A. kleei, A. pertense var. bitaeniata*. The species is seldom found commercially since it is rarely imported or captive-bred.

Hab.: Amazon; Peru and Brazil.

Fl.: 1961

Sex: Sexual dimorphism; the ♂ is larger with the dorsal fin more brightly colored.

Soc. B.: Territorial and tolerant with its own species it is polygamous, forming "harems". Allow at least three females for each male. The females will select smaller territories with the male dominant over all. Patriarch/matriarch arrangement.

M: Needs at least a 20-inch (50 cm) long tank, large enough to hold several females and one male. Recommend dense vegetation with places to hide among rocks and roots. An open area for swimming is important. A dark bottom is basic.

B: Needs acid, soft to medium-hard water, pH 5.0-6.0 and hardness 2-6° dGH at temperatures between 25-27° C. Do not allow a hardness above 10° dGH. Add peat and regular changes of fresh water. The fish are cave breeders and generally spawn 40-60 eggs, attached to the roof. The ♀ guards the eggs, the male the territory. The female leads her fry in schools.

F: C; all types of live food such as *Daphnia*, *Tubifex* worms and mosquito larvae; we do not know whether or not they accept flakes.

S: Red spots at the rear of the gills on males is typical although their number, size and brilliance may vary.

T: 73-77° F, L: ♂ = 2″, ♀ = 1$\frac{3}{4}$″, A: 20″, R: b, D: 3.
23-25° C, ♂ = 6 cm, ♀ = 4 cm, 50 cm,

Apistogramma agassizii

Apistogramma bitaeniata

Apistogramma borellii
Borelli's Dwarf Cichlid

(REGAN, 1906)

Syn.: *Heterogramma borellii, Apistogramma ritense, A. reitzigi, A. aequipinnis, A. rondoni.*

Hab.: South America: Matto Grosso and rivers near Rio Paraguay. Imported and captive-bred specimens are available in nearly equal numbers.

Fl.: 1936

Sex: Clear sexual dimorphism; ♂ is larger and more brilliantly colored with sharply pointed dorsal and anal fins.

Soc. B.: A territorial, peaceful cichlid, it rarely burrows. It is polygamous so one should keep several females with a single male. The male claims the upper tank areas while the females utilize the lower. Forms a patriarch/matriarch family.

M: Follow recommendations for *A. agassizii.*

B: Suggest moderately acid, soft to medium-hard water, pH 6.0-6.5 and hardness 2-15° dGH at a temperature between 25-28° C. A cave breeder, the female will lay 50-70 eggs against the roof of her cave. A ♀ may not labor over the eggs, but she will carefully guard the fry, leading them around the tank.

F: C; all types of live foods; rarely accepts flakes.

S: The species is sensitive to water conditions and medication.
According to VIERKE, there are often barren females in a group. In some cases young males will adopt the female coloring and are not, thereafer, regarded as rivals for territory. When buying fish include several females to be certain you do not get many "pseudo-females".

T: 75-77° F,   **L:** ♂ = 3″, ♀ = 2″,   **A:** 19¹/₂″,   **R:** b,   **D:** 3-4.
   24-25° C,   ♂ = 8 cm, ♀ = 4-5 cm,   50 cm,

Apistogramma cacatuoides
Cockatoo Dwarf Cichlid, Crested Dwarf Cichlid

HOEDEMAN, 1951

Syn.: *Apistogramma U²*

Hab.: Between 69th and 71st parallels W. in the Amazon basin. H. Meinken mistakenly identified the fish as *A. borellii* in 1961 (REGAN, 1906) and they were sold to hobbyists under this name.

Fl.: 1950

Sex: Clear sexual dimorphism; the ♂ is substantially larger, has longer fins and lacks a forked caudal fin. While caring for the brood, the ♀ may be bright yellow.

Soc. B.: Territorial and polygamous, you should allow five or six ♀ for each male. ♂ will claim the upper area of the tank while the females select smaller breeding territories near the bottom.

M: Need a tank with fine, dark sand. Build a breeding cave of rocks or a pot, near the center of each female's territory.

B: Recommend neutral, soft to medium-hard water, pH about 7.0, hardness to 10° dGH at a temperature between 25-27° C. Cave breeders, the females lay as many as 80 eggs against the roof. The female guards the eggs and brood, the male guards the entire territory. Fry will often change mothers as they grow.

F: C; all types of live foods such as water fleas, *Cyclops*, mosquito larvae and *Tubifex* worms.

S: The species is sensitive to water and medication. Do not treat eggs for fungus. Various color morphs can be found.

T: 75-77° F,   **L:** ♂ = 3¹/₂″, ♀ = 2″,   **A:** 31″,   **R:** b,   **D:** 3.
   24-25° C,   ♂ = 9 cm, ♀ = 5 cm,   80 cm,

Apistogramma borellii

Apistogramma cacatuoides

Fam.: Cichlidae

Apistogramma macmasteri
Macmaster's Dwarf Cichlid

KULLANDER, 1979

Syn.: None

Hab.: South America; Orinoco Basin, esp. Rio Meta near Villavicencio.

Fl.: Possibly in the early 1970's when it was known as *A. ornatipinnis*.

Sex: Marked sexual dimorphism and dichromatism; ♂♂ are larger, have slightly longer dorsal membranes with a rounded tail edged in red. Some ♂♂ may exhibit a forked tail. The female's tail is always rounded.

Soc. B.: A territorial, peaceful Dwarf Cichlid, it seldom burrows. Males are polygamous but will pair in smaller tanks. The species should be kept with peaceful surface-dwelling Characins just so ♂ can display his territorial defence. It can be seen after the ♀ has spawned and is well worth viewing. The pair forms a patriarch/matriarch family.

M: Needs a tank with dense vegetation and cave-like hiding places among rocks and roots. Pots and shard are acceptable

with a bottom of fine gravel. Recommend soft, slightly acid water, 2-4° dGH and pH 6.0-6.5. The fry may do well in harder, slightly alkaline water.

B: Suggest soft, slightly acid water at temperatures between 23-30° C. Shelter breeders, the female will lay 60-120 eggs on the roof of a cave. The female guards the eggs while the male guards the territory though the male may also help with care of the fry. The fry are free-swimming after one week and the male may take charge of the school after two weeks if the female is ready to spawn again.

F: Hardy live foods; difficult to convert to dried foods.

S: In hobby literature the species has been identified as *A. ornatipinnis* though the name is a synonym of *A. steindachneri*. Other names commonly used include *A. taeniatum* and *A. pleurotaenia*.

T: 73-86° F,   **L:** to 3",   **A:** 19^1/$_2$",   **R:** b,   **D:** 3.
    23-30° C,   to 8 cm,   50 cm,

Apistogramma steindachneri
Steindachner's Dwarf Cichlid

(REGAN, 1908)

Syn.: *Heterogramma steindachneri, Apistogramma wickleri, A. ornatipinnis*

Hab.: Guyana. Captive-bred specimens are rare.

Fl.: Unknown.

Sex: Clear sexual dimorphism; ♂♂ are larger with the tail fin longer and with two points (on top it is the second ray, on the bottom it is the third.) ♀♀ tail is shorter and rounded.

Soc. B.: Territorial and peaceful, it becomes aggressive only during spawning. It will not burrow and several ♀♀ should be kept with one ♂ since the male is polygamous. They form a patriarch/matriarch family and are excellent parents.

M: Needs a tank with a dark bottom, dense vegetation and hiding places among rocks and roots. Leave some open space for swimming.

B: Does best in slightly acid, soft water, pH 6.2-6.8 and hardness 3-5° dGH and never above 10° dGH, at a temperature between 24-27° C. Make frequent changes of fresh water, Shelter breeders, they spawn in caves, each female claiming her own territory. The lone male happily guards his harem.

F: C; almost exclusively live foods; rarely flakes.

S: ♂ will claim an entire tank, even a large aquarium. In it he will mate with several ♀♀. The fry remain in the cave for some time.

T: 73-77° F, **L:** ♂ = 3^1/$_2$", ♀ = 2^1/$_2$",   **A:** 19^1/$_2$", **R:** b,   **D:** 3.
   23-25° C,   ♂ = 10 cm, ♀ = 7 cm,   50 cm,

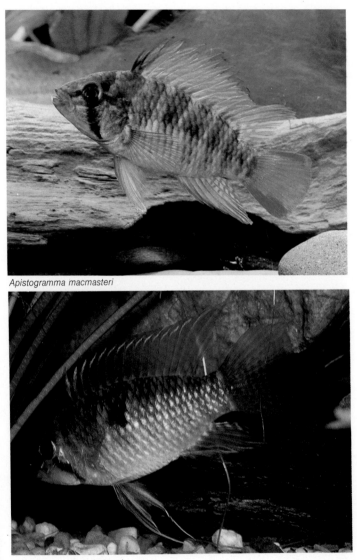

Apistogramma macmasteri

Apistogramma steindachneri

Fam.: Cichlidae

Apistogramma trifasciata
Three-Stripe Dwarf Cichlid, Blue Apistogramma

(EIGENMANN & KENNEDY, 1903)

Syn.: *Biotodoma trifasciatum, Heterogramma trifasciatum*

Hab.: South America: in the thickets and lagoons of northern Rio Paraguay and Rio Guapore. Imported feral specimens are rare.

Fl.: 1959

Sex: Pronounced sexual dimorphism and dichromatism; the third to fifth rays of the male dorsal are pointed and long.

Soc. B.: Territorial and polygamous, you should always keep several ♀♀ with one ♂. The ♂ chooses upper tank areas while the ♀♀ use the lower. Peaceful, the fish will burrow some, especially during spawning. Patriarch/matriarch family.

M: Needs as large a tank as possible to allow you observe the interesting family structure. Recommend a tank 30-inches long or more with three or four ♀♀ and one male. Territorial females need an area about 8-inches square. Keep the tank well planted with natural boundaries of rock or roots. Put a breeding cave in the center of each territory and use a sandy bottom.

B: Does best in soft, slightly acid water, 2-5° dGH and pH about 6.5 at temperatures between 28-30° C. A cave breeder, a ♀ will lay to 100 eggs. The mother cares for the fry intensively, often for weeks.

F: C; such live foods as *Daphnia, Cyclops* and mosquito larvae exclusively.

This species is very susceptible to water changes. The ♀ like to kidnap each other's fry. Sometimes the ♀ are so intent on care that they even care for water fleas or *Tubifex*.

T: 79-84° F,　**L:** ♂ = 2″, ♀ = 1¹/₂″,　**A:** 31″,　**R:** b,　**D:** 3.
　　26-29° C,　　♂ = 6 cm, ♀ = 4.5 cm,　80 cm,

Astatotilapia burtoni
Burton's Mouth-brooder

(GUENTHER, 1893)

Syn.: *Chromis burtoni, Haplochromis burtoni*

Hab.: Eastern and central Africa: Lake Tanganyika, Lake Kivu. Most fish available to the hobby are captive-bred.

Fl.: Unknown.

Sex: Clear sexual dimorphism; ♂ is larger and more intensely colored with dummy egg shapes on the anal fin. The male's dorsal is also edged in red.

Soc. B.: Territorial and often aggressive against its species, it is peaceful toward other tank mates. ♂ is polygamous and should be kept with several ♀♀. Forms a matriarchal family.

M: Needs a tank with dense planting around the edges and hiding places beneath rocks. Allow some open space for swimming. Use a bottom of gravel with patches of sand.

B: Use alkaline, medium-hard water, pH 8.5-9.0 and hardness 12-16° dGH at a temperature between 26-28° C. Mouth-brooders, the eggs are laid in pits and then taken into the female's mouth. Up to 35 eggs are laid and fertilized by the dummy-egg method. The fry may return to the mother's mouth at night or in times of danger up to a week after leaving it.

F: C, O; all types of live foods; lettuce and algae supplement; captive-bred fishes also accept flakes.

S: Regular water changes, ¹/₃ a month, are recommended. Recent research indicates *A. burtoni, A. desfontainesii* and *Thoracochromis wingatii* are independent species.

T: 68-77° F,　**L:** ♂ = 4¹/₂″, ♀ = 2¹/₂″,　**A:** 31″,　**R:** m, b,　**D:** 2.
　　20-25° C,　　♂ = 12 cm, ♀ = 7 cm,　80 cm,

Apistogramma trifasciata

Astatotilapia burtoni

Astronotus ocellatus
Oscar

(CUVIER , 1829)

Syn.: *Acara ocellatus, A. crassipinnis, Cychla rubroocellata, Hygrogonus ocellatus, Lobotes ocellatus*

Hab.: South America; Amazon; Parana; Rio Paraguay; Rio Negro. While most fish available to the hobbyist are captive-bred, limited numbers of wild-caught specimens are again imported.

Fl.: 1929, Scholze & Poetzschke, Berlin, Germany.

Sex: It is difficult to distinguish between the sexes though during spawning the female has noticeable genital papilla.

Soc. B.: Pairs form a nuclear family and despite their size, are generally peaceful. They are boisterous during spawning and are burrowers when courting and rearing fry.

M: Needs a tank bottom of deep sand with a few large rocks. Plants should be potted, their root surfaces covered with rocks. Floating plants are a good solution.

B: While they can accept a range of water values, temperatures should be kept between 26-30° C. The fish can be kept in soft or hard water as long as it is clear and clean and are sexually mature from 4¹/₂″ (12 cm). Open breeders, ♀♀ drop 1,000 to 2,000 eggs on carefully cleaned rocks. The brood is carefully guarded and cared for. Fry are kept in pits and are sometimes covered. When free-swimming they will accept *Cyclops*. Use a large tank, as much as 100 gallons if possible.

F: C; all types of live foods, particularly fish and earthworms. The fish are predaceous and hearty eaters.

S: The fry sometimes cling to their parents. The eggs are opaque when first dropped and become transparent after 24 hours.

T: 72-77° F, **L:** 12″, **A:** 78″, **R:** b, m, **D:** 4 (C).
22-25° C, 33 cm, 200 cm,

Aulonocara hansbaenschi
African Peacock

MEYER, RIEHL & ZETZSCHE, 1987

Syn.: None

Hab.: Africa: endemic in Lake Malawi to a transitional region between rock and sand. Rare even in Lake Malawi, the fish is seldom caught and less often available to the hobby.

Fl.: 1973, Bibau, Hamburg, West Germany.

Sex: Clear example of sexual dimorphism and dichromatism; ♀ is plain while ♂ is considered one of the finest of Cichlids. He has a wide white or light blue border on the dorsal; the head and body are an inky blue.

Soc. B.: Territorial and peaceful, the fish exhibit an aggressive but ritualized display behaviour. They may or may not burrow. Forms matriarchial family.

M: Create rocky hollows for hiding.

B: Does best in a moderately alkaline, medium-hard water, pH around 8.0 and hardness 10-15° dGH, at a temperature between 26-28° C. Mouth-brooders, the female spawns on the rocky bottom, taking up to 60 eggs eggs immediately into her mouth. The eggs are fertilized by the false-egg method.

F: C; live foods such as insects, insect larvae and small crustaceans; frozen and FD; flakes.

S: A number of furrows across the head are typical of the genus.

A. hansbaenschi ♀

T: 77-79° F, **L:** 6″, **A:** 39″, **R:** m, b, **D:** 2-3.
25-26° C, 18 cm, 100 cm,

Astronotus ocellatus

Aulonocara hansbaenschi ♂

Fam.: Cichlidae

Biotodoma cupido

(HECKEL, 1840)

Syn.: Geophagus cupido, Acara subocularis, Mesops cupido

Hab.: Central Amazon; western Guyana. Wild-caught fishes are rare and the fish are difficult to keep.

Fl.: 1935, Haertel, Dresden, East Germany.

Sex: Complete identification is unavailable; the dorsal and anal fins of the ♂ are pointed.

Soc. B.: Territorial, aggressive and intolerent, the fish form monogamous pairs and a nuclear family. A burrower.

M: Place rocky formations against the rear glass of the tank, creating caves and other hiding places. Add hardy plants and in the foreground place sand and a few rocks.

B: Follow water recommendations for Geophagus surinamensis with water temperatures between 24-27° C. The values of the water are the same as for

Geophagus surinamensis. KUHLMANN published the first exact breeding report on a kind of Biotodoma (1984): DATZ 37, 14-17. His observations show that the fish are open breeders. The ♀ makes a hollow with its mouth; the ♂ does not help. The spawn goes into this hollow. The eggs are approximately 2 mm long, grayish-white and either stick to the ground or clump together. The ♀ cares for the eggs, sometimes numbering over 100. KUHLMANN noticed, moreover, that the parents swam about with the fry (3 mm) ten days after spawning. Feeding of fry was with smallest crab nauplii. Intensive care of the fry by parents.

F: C; all types of live foods such as water fleas, Tubifex worms, mosquito larvae and earthworms; flakes.

S: There appears to be three species of Biotodoma including B. wavrini (GOSSE, 1963).

T: 73-77° F, **L:** 4¹/₂″, **A:** 31″, **R:** m, b, **D:** 3.
23-25° C, 13 cm, 80 cm,

Chromidotilapia finleyi

TREWAVAS, 1974

Syn.: None

Hab.: West Africa; western Cameroons; areas of the Lobe River near Rio Muni and in the rain forest around Campo Reservation.

Fl.: Possibly 1972.

Sex: Clearly marked sexual dimorphism; the males are larger with a red-edged dorsal; the female has a red stomach.

Soc. B.: See comments for Chromidotilapia guentheri C. finleyi is also a mouthbrooder but represents a special type of nuclear family.

M: Follow recommendations for C. guentheri. Use the water values listed below.

B: See suggestions for C. guentheri. The fish have a different behaviour pattern. Prefer a moderately acid, soft water, pH 4.8-7.0 and hardness 1-7° dGH.

F: All types of live foods; FD; frozen foods; flakes.

S: C. finleyi is a special kind of mouthbrooder with traits not observed in other Cichlids. Sexually mature fish pair and claim a territory which is energetically defended against all intruders. The fish will pair sometime before spawning and may spawn many places in the tank, the choice depending on the design of the aquarium. The eggs are laid in clutches and when finished the female will take them into her mouth. Unlike many African mouthbrooders the pair remain together to care for the brood. At first the female keeps the eggs, the male defends the territory and after a day or two the roles are exchanged. The fish not incubating the eggs will accept food and the exchange of roles is repeated several times. When the fish are free-swimming both parents protect them.

T: 73-77° F, **L:** 4¹/₂″, **A:** 31″, **R:** b, **D:** 2.
23-25° C, 12 cm, 80 cm,

Biotodoma cupido

Chromidotilapia finleyi

Chromidotilapia guentheri
Gunther's Cichlid

(SAUVAGE, 1882)

Syn.: *Hemichromis guentheri, H. tersquamatus, H. voltae, Pelmatochromis guentheri, P. pellegrini*

Hab.: Western Africa; in coastal rivers and lagoons from Sierra Leone to the Cameroons; recently discovered in Gaboon. Captive bred specimens now available.

Fl.: 1913, Christian Bruening, Hamburg, West Germany.

Sex: Sexual dimorphism; the ♂ is larger; the ♀ has a broad, shiny silver or mother-of-pearl crest on the dorsal; ♀♀ are more brightly colored.

Soc. B.: Territorial, aggressive toward their species, the fish have a pronounced pecking order in a tank. Pairs form nuclear or patriarch-matriarch families. They are burrowers. Although mouthbrooders, they are monogamous, make excellent parents and form permanent pairs.

M: Need a tank with a fine sandy bottom and hiding places among roots and rocks. Plants should be placed in pots and protected. The fish should be kept in a specimen tank.

B: Does well in neutral, medium-hard water, pH 7.0, hardness to 10° dGH, at temperatures between 25-28° C. ♀ spawns openly, dropping up to 150 eggs which are then taken by ♂. When free-swimming the fry are cared-for by both parents. At this time ♀ will accept the fry at night or in times of danger.

F: C, O; all types of live foods; FD; frozen foods. The fish are surprisingly greedy.

S: The species can change colors quickly and will exhibit many different combinations, possibly according to mood. There are two sub-species: *Ch. guentheri guentheri* SAUVAGE, 1882 and *Ch. guentheri loennbergi* TREWAVAS, 1962.

T: 73-77° F, **L:** 5¹/₂-8″, **A:** 31″, **R:** b, **D:** 2-3.
  23-25° C, 16-20 cm, 80 cm,

Cichlasoma cyanoguttatum page 724

Hypselecara temporalis

(GUENTHER, 1862)

Syn.: *Heros temporalis, Acara crassa, Astronotus crassa, Cichlasoma crassa, C. hellabrunni, C. temporale, Heros crassa, H. goeldii*

Hab.: Brazil; upper central Amazon between Tefe and Obidos; Lago Hyanuary, Lago Saraca, Rio Hyutay.

Sex: Older ♂♂ are larger, often with a fatty lump on their head; the lump is absent from ♀♀. Otherwise the fish are sexually monomorphic and pointed fins are not a certain sign of sex.

Soc. B.: Territorial and peaceful, the Cichlids are surprisingly docile in view of their size. Their movements are majestic and somewhat elegant. Use only hardy plants.

M: Needs a tall tank with a simple decoration of roots and rocks. Vertical hiding places are indispensable. Use water with a pH 7.0 and hardness to 20° dGH at temperatures between 25-28° C.

B: Open breeders, the fish spawn exclusively on vertical plants or rocks. The larvae are protected in hollows. Some pairs may remain together after the spawning season. Initially, they may seem inept at caring for their brood, but become better as days pass.

F: In nature the fish are surface-feeders specializing in catching moving food such as flies, moths and grasshoppers. All are caught in flight. In a tank the fish will accept a range of frozen and commercial foods.

T: 77-82° F, **L:** 12″, **A:** 47″, **R:** b+m+t, **D:** 2-3.
  25-28° C, 30 cm, 120 cm,

Chromidotilapia guentheri

Hypselecara temporalis

Fam.: Cichlidae

"Cichlasoma" facetum
Chanchito, Chameleon Cichlid

(JENYNS, 1842)

Syn.: *Acara faceta, Chromis facetus, Heros acaroides, H. facetus, H. jenynsii*

Hab.: In standing and slow waters of Southern Brazil; northern Argentina; Paraguay; Uruguay; also found in brackish water. The fish is rare and though imports have begun again. Most specimens are captive-bred.

Fl.: 1894, P. Nitsche, Berlin, Germany. The fish was first bred by Mattesche Zuchtanstalt, Lankwitz, Germany in 1894.

Sex: Difficult to distinguish between the sexes; the ♂ sometimes has heavier fins, though not often enough for identification. The fish can be identified best during spawning and then by the shape of the genital papillae; on the ♂ it is pointed and sloped to the rear, on ♀ it is pointed and straight.

Soc. B.: Territorial and intolerant toward tank mates, they readily pair and may bite, particulary during spawning. They are powerful burrowers, form nuclear families and make excellent parents.

M: Needs a gravel bottom with larger rocks stacked to form hiding places. Place the rocks on the bottom, not on the gravel, since the fish burrow. Uses hardy plants or better, a floating cover.

B: Prefers neutral to slightly acid, soft to medium-hard water, pH 6.5-7.0 and hardness 5-12° dGH, at a temperature between 25-27° C. An open breeder, the ♀ drops 300 to 1,000 eggs on carefully cleaned rocks. The fry are suspended on the roots of floating plants and both parents guard both the eggs and fry. They will lead the young about the tank for six to eight weeks.

F: C, O; such live foods as *Tubifex* worms, mosquito larvae, earthworms, fishes and meat; dry food; flakes; tablets.

S: The fish are extremely intelligent, soon know their keeper, and will often accept food from the hand of one they know. They prefer warmth but are resistent to cooler temperatures.

T: 79-86° F, 27-30° C,   **L:** 27″, 70 cm (25 cm), in an aquarium barely larger than 8-9″,   **A:** 47-59″, 120-150 cm,   **R:** b, m,   **D:** 2.

"Cichlasoma" managuense
Managua Cichlid

(GUENTHER, 1866)

Syn.: *Heros managuense, Cichlosoma managuense, Parapetenia managuense*

Hab.: Eastern Honduras; Lake Managua, Lake Nicaragua – Nicaragua; Costa Rica.

Fl.: 1971

Sex: It is difficult to distinguish sexes though the ♂ is generally larger with pointed dorsal and anal fins. ♂♂ are also more brightly colored.

Soc. B: The fish are territorial, intolerant of their own species and will bite. They also burrow, but on the bright side they form nuclear families and are excellent parents.

M: Need a roomy tank with plenty of open swimming room and places to hide among rocks and roots. The rocks should be placed on the bottom since the fish burrow. They prefer a bottom of coarse gravel but do not add plants since these will be torn apart. Use neutral to moderately alkaline, medium-hard water, pH 7.0-8.7 and hardness 10-15° dGH.

B: Breeding is difficult and only a few successes have been reported. The species is quite productive, spawning as many as 5,000 yellow eggs. The ♀ does much of the work of caring for the larvae and fry. (DI PIRRO, 1975; Tropical Fish Hobbyist 23, 227: pp. 58-62.)

F: C, O; chiefly such large live foods as insects, earthworms, fishes and tadpoles. Fish are the main food. They will accept FD and dry foods.

"Cichlasoma" facetum

"Cichlasoma" managuense

S: Among the largest of Cichlids they rank with *Boulengerochromis microlepis* (to 31″ or 80 cm) and *Cichlasoma dovii* (to 23¹/₂″ or 60 cm). In native waters it is an important freshwater food fish.

T: 73-77° F, **L:** 3¹/₂-11″,   **A:** 37″,   **R:** b,   **D:** 2.
    23-25° C,   10-30 cm,   90 cm,

Thorichthys meeki
Firemouth Cichlid

(BRIND, 1918)

Syn.: *Cichlasoma meeki, Thorichthys helleri meeki*

Hab.: Guatemala; Yucatan. Some fine feral specimens have been imported in the past decade but captive-bred fish are most common.

Fl.: 1937, H. Roese, Hamburg, West Germany.

Sex: ♂ has smartly pointed dorsal and anal fins and is more intensely colored. The genital papilla of ♂ is pointed; on ♀ it is blunt.

Soc. B.: Territorial, the species pairs and burrows but will not damage plants except during spawning. Peaceful to tank mates except during spawning, then pairs are aggressive to smaller tank mates of their species. During spawning many fish are extremely pugnacious.They form nuclear families and make superb parents.

M: Requires a tank with a bottom of fine sand and hiding places among rocks and roots. Use such hardy plants as *Sagittaria*. Plants should be potted with root surfaces protected. An open swimming area is important.

B: The water should be neutral, pH 7.0, no more than medium hard, 10° dGH, and at temperatures between 24-26° C. The female spawns on carefully cleaned rocks, dropping 100 to 500 eggs. Fry are protected in pits, The parents may raise several broods in a year.

F: C, O; all types of live foods; FD; tablets; flakes.

S: As an aggressive stance, the fish will threaten others of their species by inflating a throat sac and extending their gill covers.

T: 70-75° F, **L:** 6″, **A:** 31″, **R:** b, **D:** 2.
21-24° C, 15 cm, 80 cm,

"Cichlasoma" nigrofasciatum
Zebra Cichlid, Convict Cichlid

(GUENTHER , 1866)

Syn.: *Heros nigrofasciatus, Astronotus nigrofasciatum*

Hab.: Guatemala; El Salvador; northwest Honduras; Nicaragua; Costa Rica; Panama. Mostly captive-bred specimens are available now, many showing symptoms of in-breeding: i.e. a lack of green on their fins, smaller size and a trend toward poor parenting.

Fl.: 1934, J. P. Arnold, Hamburg, West Germany.

Sex: ♂ is larger, less colorful, has a steeper forehead and longer fins. With age ♂♂s acquire a vestigal fatty lump on the forehead. ♀♀s have orange scales on their lower bodies and dorsal fin.

Soc. B.: The fish pair readily, are intolerent and bite. They eat plants. Couples form a patriarch/matriarch family and both care for the young. Not recommended for a community tank.

M: Needs a tank with a gravel bottom and hiding places in rocks or inverted pots. Suggest a cover of floating plants.

B: Can accept a range of water conditions and will spawn at temperatures 24-26° C. A cave-breeder or a transitional breeder (between cave and open). Cares well for the eggs and fry; the fry respond to signals from both parents.

F: O; live food; FD; flakes; tablets. Supplemental vegetables are important: lettuce, algae, Tetra conditioning foods.

S: A pseudo-albino variety has been bred recently. ♂♂ are monotone, the ♀♀ have an orange patch on the stomach.

T: 68-73° F, **L:** 6″, **A:** 23$^1/_2$″, **R:** m, b, **D:** 3.
20-23° C, 15 cm, 60 cm,

Thorichthys meeki

"Cichlasoma" nigrofasciatum

"Cichlasoma" octofasciatum
Jack Dempsy

(REGAN, 1903)

Syn.: *Heros octofasciatus, Cichlasoma hedricki, "C. biocellatum"*

Hab.: In bogs and slow-moving water; Guatemala; Yucatan; Honduras.

Fl.: 1904, Umlauff Pet Stores, Hamburg, West Germany.

Sex: The ♂ has pointed dorsal and anal fins; the upper edge of his dorsal is dark red; on the ♀ the same edge is less brilliantly colored. Sexes can also be identified by the shape of the genital papilla; on the ♂ it is pointed and on the ♀ it is rounded.

Soc. B.: Territorial, intolerant and a biter, the fish burrow and eat plants. They pair readily, form nuclear families and are good parents.

M: Needs a thick bottom layer of fine sand and caves among rocks and roots to hide in. Recommend a cover of floating plants.

B: Does well in slightly acid to neutral, medium-hard water (pH 6.5-7.0, hardness 8-12° C at a temperature between 26-28° C. An open breeder, the ♀ lays a clutch of 500-800 eggs on carefully cleaned rocks. The fry are kept in pits, carefully guarded and attended by both parents.

F: O; all types of hardy live foods; such vegetable supplements as algae, pondweed, waterweed, lettuce.

S: The species has been kept for many years in European aquariums under the name *C. biocellatum*. This error was discovered in 1975 by KULLANDER (Akvariet, p 379).

| T: 72-77° F, | L: to 8", | A: 35", | R: m, b, | D: 3. |
| 22-25° C, | to 20 cm, | 90 cm, | | |

"Cichlasoma" salvini

(GUENTHER, 1862)

Syn.: *Heros salvini, H. triagramma*

Hab.: In lakes and rivers of southern Mexico; Guatemala; Honduras. Captive-bred specimens are commercially available.

Fl.: 1913, C. Siggelkow, Hamburg, West Germany.

Sex: The sexes are readily distinguished; the ♂ has pointed fins and brighter colors with noticeable contrast between patches of black and whites; The ♀ has a patch in the center of her dorsal and a dark spot on the lower edge of her gill cover.

Soc. B.: Territorial, intolerant and a biter yet the fish does not burrow nor damage plants. It is a predator. Forms a nuclear family and is a good parent.

M: Needs a tank with a bottom of fine gravel or sand with hiding places created from rocks or roots. Leave an open area for swimming.

B: Follow water value recommendations for *C. meeki*. The fish are open breeders, laying clutches with as many as 500 eggs on carefully cleaned rocks. Both parents care for the fry, which are carefully guarded.

F: C, O; live food; FD; frozen food; also flakes.

S: MILLER, (1907), reported specimens caught in the Sulphur River. They were found near a hot spring in water with temperatures exceeding 32° C.

| T: 72-79° F, | L: 6", | A: 35", | R: m, b, | D: 2. |
| 22-26° C, | 15 cm, | 90 cm, | | |

"Cichlasoma" octofasciatum

"Cichlasoma" salvini

Fam.: Cichlidae

Heros severus
Banded Cichlid, Severum

HECKEL, 1840

Syn.: *Acara spuria, Astronotus severus, Heros coryphaeus, H. efasciatus, H. modestus, Cichlasoma severum, H. spurius*

Hab.: In rivers and lakes rich in plant life from northern South America to the Amazon basin, though not in Rio Magdalena. Captive-bred specimens are common now.

Fl.: 1909, C. Siggelkow, Hamburg, West Germany.

Sex: Sexes can only be positively determined by examination of the genital papillae; the fins of the ♂ are pointed and there are reddish-brown spots and "worm-like" markings on the head; These are lacking on the ♀ who has a dark patch on her dorsal.

Soc. B.: A territorial, gentle, peaceful species which does not burrow. It pairs, forms a nuclear family and can be aggressive when spawning. Both parents attend the brood.

M: See suggestions for *Symphysodon* sp.

B: Recommend moderately acid, soft water with a pH 6.0-6.5, a hardness around 5° dGH and temperatures between 25-28° C. An open breeder, the ♀ will spawn as many as 1,000 eggs on rocks. The fry are carefully cared-for.

F: C; live food of all kinds. Frozen Food is sometimes taken, but Flake Food only by fishes used to it.

S: The fish do not pair as readily as some, carefully choosing their partner. Pairing may require time – and a choice of females. The fish are trusting and often take food from their keeper's hand.

H. severus juvenile.

T: 73-77° F,   **L:** to 8",   **A:** 39",   **R:** b,   **D:** 2.
   23-25° C,   to 20 cm,   100 cm,

"Cichlasoma" spilurum

(GUENTHER, 1862)

Syn.: *Heros spilurus*

Hab.: Guatemala. Supplies are predominantly wild-caught though some captive-bred specimens are now offered in the hobby.

Fl.: Probably 1964.

Sex: Readily distinguished; the ♂ has pointed dorsal and anal fins and adult ♂♂ have a bump on the forehead; the forehead is steeper. ♀♀ are larger and, when sexually mature, fullerbodied.

Soc. B.: Territorial and peaceful, they neither burrow nor harm plants, except during spawning. Pairs form nuclear families.

M: Needs rocks erected to form caves and hiding places otherwise the alpha male will claim all of the territory. Use a gravel

bottom with such hardy plants as *Sagittaria* and *Vallisneria*. Floating plants are a good choice.

B: The species can accept a range of water values if temperatures are kept between 26-27° C. Cave breeders, the ♀ lays to 300 eggs. After hatching the fry are carried to protective pits by the ♀. Both parents stand guard and care for the brood.

F: C, O; all types of live foods; meat; FD; frozen foods; flakes. The fry need vegetable supplements.

S: Like *"C."* *nigrofasciatum*, the species is a "transitional" breeder, described as someplace between a cave and an open breeder.

T: 72-77° F,   **L:** ♂ = 4¹/₂", ♀ = 3",   **A:** 23",   **R:** m, b,   **D:** 2.
   22-25° C,   ♂ = 12 cm, ♀ = 8 cm,   60 cm,

Heros severus

"Cichlasoma" spilurum

Crenicara filamentosa
Chessboard Cichlid

LADIGES, 1958

Syn.: None

Hab.: South America: Rio Negro; Orinoco basin. Rarely seen in the hobby, the few available fish are wild-caught.

Fl.: 1951

Sex: Clear sexual dimorphism; the ♂ is substantially larger with a longer, forked caudal fin; all fins are red, blue and black. The female's fins are transparent.

Soc. B.: Territorial and peaceful though somewhat aggressive during the spawning season. The species will not burrow or harm plants. Since you are dealing with a patriarch/matriarch family, one ♂ should be kept with several ♀♀. Its social habits are similar to those of *Apistogramma* though the species controls a smaller territory.

M: Needs a heavily planted tank with a bottom of fine sand. Add flat stones and places to hide. The fish is timid when kept alone and should be combined with several live-bearers or Characins.

B: Recommend acid, soft water with a pH around 5.5 and 0.1-2° dGH hardness at a temperature between 26-27° C. Suggest the addition of peat. Open breeders, the fish spawn 60-120 eggs on plants or rocks. The ♀ guards the larvae and fry.

F: C; only live foods; Keep well supplied with brine shrimp. Feed flakes rarely.

S: A delicate species, it requires cautious care. The fish is very susceptible to deteriorating water conditions. Fungus will develop on the eggs if the water is not sufficiently soft.

T: 73-77° F, L: ♂ = 3$^{1}/_{2}$", ♀ = 2", A: 23$^{1}/_{2}$", R: b, D: 2-3.
23-25° C, ♂ = 9 cm, ♀ = 6 cm, 60 cm,

Crenicara punctulata

(GUENTHER, 1863)

Syn.: *Acara punctulata, Aequidens hercules, A. madeirae, Crenicara elegans*

Hab.: Guyana; northern Brazil; Ecuador; Peru.

Fl.: 1975

Sex: The ♂ is more intensely colored with blue pelvic and caudal fins; The caudal fins of the ♀ are reddish.

Soc. B.: Territorial and peaceful, the species becomes aggressive during spawning; The social habits are similar to those of *Apistogramma*. Forms a patriarch/matriarch family.

M: See suggestions for *C. filamentosa*.

B: The species is an open breeder and though it is not often bred in captivity, follow suggestions for *C. filamentosa*.

F: C; the species eats most types of live foods and rarely accepts flakes.

S: The fish was first sold commercially as *"Aequidens hercules"*. Later this was discovered to be an early synonym.

Sex changes occur in the development of individual *C. punctulata*. For details see OHM (1980): DCG-Information 11 (9): 161-170.

T: 73-77° F, L: 4$^{1}/_{2}$", A: 31", R: b, D: 3.
23-25° C, 12 cm, 80 cm,

Crenicara filamentosa

Crenicara punctulata

697

Crenicichla notophthalmus
Two-Spot Pike Cichlid

REGAN, 1913

Syn.: *C. dorsocellatus*

Hab.: Amazon; Manaus, Santarem.

Fl.: Unknown.

Sex: A sexually dimorphic species, it is of special interest for its evident polychromatism. The ♀♀ have white edges on black patches at the end of the hard-rayed portion of their dorsal. A red halo may be included. The ventral region is rounded and cream colored. The ♂♂ are more slender without dorsal markings at least on the first rays. Markings are similar to those on *Papiliochromis ramirezi*. The dorsal is long.

Soc. B.: The fish belong to a genus of small, graceful *Crenicichla*. They are territorial but will not harm other medium sized Cichlids.

M: They will not attack plants and prefer a tank with plenty of hiding places. Suggest a pH around 7.0 and hardness to 20° dGH.

B: The ♀♀ have a distinctive courtship similar to that of the *Pelvicachromis* of west Africa, twisting their bodies to show their red stomachs. Swimming ahead they attempt to entice the ♂ into their breeding cave. We suspect the ♀ cares for the brood while the male guards the territory.

F: All types of live foods such as mosquito larvae. earthworms, and small fishes; beefheart.

S: The species is closely related to *C. wallacii* and *C. nanus*. Complete identification is currently uncertain.

T: 75-79° F, L: to 6″, A: 31″, R: b+m, D: 3-4 (C).
24-27° C, to 16 cm, 80 cm,

Crenicichla strigata

(GUENTHER, 1862)

Syn.: *C. johanna* var.*strigata*, *C. johanna* var. *vittata*, *C. brasiliensis* var. *strigata*, *C. brasiliensis* var. *vittata*

Hab.: Amazon; Guyana; northern Brazil.

Fl.: Unknown.

Sex: Sexes can be distinguished by color when the fish reach maturity (from 10″ or 30 cm.). The ♀ has a violet-red stomach.

Soc. B.: Territorial, the fish prefer a roomy aquarium with hiding places. They are tolerant of each other and form schools. It is common for hobbyists to raise several juveniles to maturity in the same tank.

M: Needs as large a tank as possible with roomy caves, made of rugged rocks. Adds hardy vegetation and subdued lighting. Recommend water with a pH around 7.0 and a hardness to 20° dGH.

B: Not yet bred in captivity but the fish are cave breeders and suspend their eggs by adhesive threads. Both parents share in the caring of the brood.

F: Since the fish is a predator it should be given hardy live food occasionally – fishes, earthworms and such; it will also accept chopped fish, beef heart and tablets.

S: The Striped Cichlid recieved its name from its juvenile coloring when it has narrow longitudinal bands and rows of spots on the front and sides of the head. The same species has been described as *C. lenticulata* and/or *C. johanna*.

T: 73-79° F, L: over 15¹/₂″, A: from 59″, R: b+m, D: 4 (C, Si).
23-27° C, over 40 cm, from 150 cm,

Crenicichla notophthalmus

Crenicichla strigata

Cyphotilapia frontosa
Frontosa Cichlid

(BOULENGER, 1906)

Syn.: *Paratilapia frontosa, Pelmatochromis frontosus*

Hab.: Africa: endemic to the sloping lake bottom off shore in Lake Tanganyika. Generally found at a depth of 65-100 feet (20-30 m). Feral specimens are rarely seen in the hobby.

Fl.: 1958

Sex: It is difficult to distinguish between the sexes; the best method is through behaviour. The common forehead bump is more pronounced on the ♂ and the ♀ is commonly larger.

Soc. B.: Territorial, the fish is gentle and tolerant. It rarely burrows and will not harm plants. Forms a matriarchal family.

M: Likes rocky structures with fissures and caves for hiding. Can accept a bottom of fine sand. Plants are not essential.

B: Prefers moderately alkaline, medium-hard water with a pH around 8.0 and a hardness about 10° dGH. Keep temperatures between 25-28° C. A mouth-brooder, as many as 50 eggs are deposited in a cave then taken into the female's mouth. ♀♀ care for fry for up to six weeks and after will take them back into her mouth at night or in times of danger.

F: C; live food, preferably molluscs, crustaceans and fishes.

S: The fish are considered a delicacy in their native land. The frontal bump is not a secondary sexual feature and is present on both males and females.

T: 75-79° F,   L: 15″,   A: 47″,   R: b,   D: 4.
24-26° C,   35 cm,   120 cm,

Cyprichromis leptosoma

(BOULENGER, 1898)

Syn.: *Paratilapia leptosoma, Limnochromis leptosoma*

Hab.: Endemic to Lake Tanganyika, especially areas around Kigoma and the southern part of the lake.

Fl.: 1975

Sex: Clear sexual dimorphism and dichromatism; the ♂♂ are generally brown colored. Their pelvic fins have sulphur-yellow tips and the dorsal and anal fins are blue, either a dark to inky blue or much lighter. ♀♀ are plainer, grey, with a touch of silver on the sides of their head.

Soc. B.: A peaceful, schooling fish, it is not territorial. It forms a matriarchial family and is a mouth-brooder.

M: You need a large aquarium to keep this fish since it needs lots of swimming space. Since they prefer the upper strata they can be kept with other Cichlids. Keep the fishes only in a sizeable school and cover the tank; the ♂♂ often jump during

courtship. Use water values suggested for other Lake Tanganyika Cichlids.

B: Has been bred in the hobby. Courtship and spawning take place just beneath the surface. The fish are free-spawners and after each egg has been laid the female turns quickly, following it as it sinks. She then takes it into her mouth where it is fertilized. The eggs hatch in three weeks and development can be followed through the female's nearly transparent laryngeal sac. After the fry leave the mother's mouth they remain close to the surface, unlike many Cichlids which hide in the bottom. The mother then ignores the brood neither caring for them nor hunting them.

F: C, O; such live foods as *Cyclops* and *Daphnia*; flakes.

S: The species is found in two color morphs, one with a bright yellow caudal fin, the other with the same fin violet-blue to bluish-black.

T: 73-77° F,   L: 5¹/₂″,   A: from 39″,   R: t,   D: 2-3.
23-25° C,   14 cm,   from 100 cm,

Cyrtocara moorii, page 718

Cyphotilapia frontosa

Cyprichromis leptosoma

Eretmodus cyanostictus
Striped Goby Cichlid

BOULENGER, 1898

Syn.: None

Hab.: Africa: endemic to the rocky shallows of Lake Tanganyika. Imports are generally wild-caught specimens. Captive-breeding has rarely been successful.

Fl.: 1958

Sex: It is difficult to determine sex; the predominant distinguishing feature is the longer pelvic fins of the ♂.

Soc. B.: Territorial, intolerant toward its species, the fish is monogamous. Pairs make lasting bonds and form nuclear families, something rare among mouth-brooders. Both parents take the spawn and embryo in their mouths. The ♂ has false or dummy eggs on his anal fin.

M: The tank needs an assortment of rocks with caves and hiding places built in. Roots should not be used since they may acidify the water.

B: The species is difficult to breed. Recommend alkaline (pH about 9.0), medium-hard to hard water (15-20° dGH) at a temperature between 26-28° C. Since the fish are mouth-brooders the ♀ spawns 20-25 eggs on a previously cleaned rock. These are then fertilized by the male and are taken into the female's mouth. Both parents care for the brood.

F: All types of live foods.

S: One of the most difficult of Lake Tanganyika Cichlids, the fish demand pure water. They require freqeuent water changes, ($^1/_3$ weekly) as well as good aeration and filtration. Their mouth is inset.

T: 74-79° F, L: 3", A: 31", R: b, D: 3.
   24-26° C, 8 cm, 80 cm,

Etroplus maculatus
Orange Chromide

(BLOCH, 1795)

Syn.: Chaetodon maculatus, Etroplus coruchi, Glyphisodon kakaitsel

Hab.: In fresh and brackish water in Western India; Sri Lanka.

Fl.: 1905, Reichelt, Berlin, Germany.

Sex: Difficult to identify the sexes though the ♀♀ are generally paler, lacking a red edge to their fins.

Soc. B.: Peaceful, the species does not burrow. The pairs form a nuclear family with the brood well cared-for by both parents.

M: Needs a tank with a sandy bottom and heavy planting, providing hiding places among the roots and rocks. The fish are open breeders and need an open area with rocks for spawning.

B: Recommend the addition of 5% seawater to the tank since the fry may suffer from a fungal disease. Temperatures between 25-28° C are best. The fish spawn on rocks and roots, dropping 200 to 300 distinctly "stemmed" eggs. The fry are protected in pits or depressions and both adults care for the brood for some time.

F: C, O; live food; FD; algae; flakes and tablets occasionally.

S: The species is sensitive to changing water conditions and the addition of one or two spoons of sea-salt makes them more resistant. The fry often follow their parents closely, possibly ingesting a mucous secretion as a supplementary food.

T: 68-77° F, L: 3", A: 19$^1/_2$", R: m, b, D: 2-3.
   20-25° C, 8 cm, 50 cm,

Eretmodus cyanostictus

Etroplus maculatus

Geophagus brasiliensis
Pearl Cichlid

(QUOY & GAIMARD, 1824)

Syn.: Acara brasiliensis, Chromis brasiliensis, Geophagus bucephalus, G. labiatus, G. obscura, G. pygmaeus, G. rhabdotus, G. scymnophilus

Hab.: In coastal rivers, standing and brackish water of eastern Brazil; prefers steep, rocky banks with caves and hiding places. The species is becoming popular after a temporary lack of interest and wild-caught specimens are again imported.

Fl.: 1899, P. Matte from Argentine.

Sex: Difficult to indentify sexes though there is a difference in the genital papillae. It is pointed on the ♂ and round and blunt on the ♀. The male's dorsal is often longer and there are sometimes traces of a bump on the forehead of older ♂♂.

Soc. B.: Territorial, the species is a burrower. It is more tolerant of tank mates than most Geophagus sp. and is territorial.

It forms a nuclear family, the female guarding the eggs, the male the territory.

M: Needs a bottom of coarse gravel with fine sand in areas. Add hiding places among rocks and roots. Plants should be hardy, planted in pots, the surface protected. Temperature drops of 10°.C can be tolerated.

B: Recommend water neutral to slightly acid and soft to medium-hard, pH 6.5-7.0 and 5-10° dGH, at a temperature between 24-27° C. Open breeders, the ♀ spawns 600-800 eggs on such cleaned surfaces as rocks, in darker, hidden places. The fry are well cared-for.

F: C, O; all types of live foods; FD; flakes; also accepts tablets, beef-heart and chopped fish-meat.

S: It is sometimes difficult to find a pair suitable for breeding. If the fish do not harmonize, the parents may devour the eggs.

T: 68-73° F, **L:** 3¹/₂-10", **A:** 39", **R:** b, **D:** 3.
  20-23° C, 10-28 cm, 100 cm,

Satanoperca jurupari
Earth-Eater, Demon Fish

(HECKEL, 1840)

Syn.: Geophagus jurupari, G. leucostictus, G. pappaterra, Satanoperca leucosticta, S. macrolepis

Hab.: Brazil, Guyana. Most fish commercially available are captive-bred though wild caught specimens have been imported recently.

Fl.: 1909, C. Siggelkow, Hamburg, West Germany. First breeding reported by H. Haertel, Dresden, Germany in 1936.

Sex: It is difficult to distinguish between the sexes. They are similarly colored. The ♂ has a more slender body and the most obvious differences are in the genital papillae. These are pointed for the ♂ and short and blunt in the ♀.

Soc. B.: A territorial but peaceful and non-aggressive Cichlid, it has been called the most tolerant of the genus. Its name means "earth eater" and the species frequently burrows. Pairs form nuclear families and carefully attend their brood.

M: The tank needs a bottom of fine sand

since the fish burrow. Coarser gravel could damage their mouths. Use only well-rooted, hardy plants and rocks with hiding places. These will be used for spawning.

B: Does best in water neutral to slightly acid, soft to medium hard, pH 6.3-7.0 and 5-10° dGH. Temperatures between 27-29° C are best. A mouth-brooder, the ♀ lays 150-400 eggs on carefully cleaned rocks, taking them into her mouth after 24 hours. Both parents share the care, each keeping the eggs for a time. They carefully look after the eggs and after the fry are free-swimming the small fishes return to the safety of the mouth at night and in times of danger.

F: C, O; live food; FD; frozen food; flakes; tablets.

S: While some fish keep their eggs in a throat-sac, these fish keep them in the front of the mouth, near their gums. The fish must be kept warm and will die if temperatures drop.

T: 74-79° F, **L:** 3¹/₂-10", **A:** 39", **R:** b, m, **D:** 2-3.
  24-26° C, 10-25 cm, 100 cm,

Geophagus brasiliensis

Satanoperca jurupari

Geophagus steindachneri

EIGENMANN & HILDEBRANDT,1910

Syn.: *G. hondae, G. magdalenae*

Hab.: Columbia; upper reaches of the Rio Magdalena and tributaries.

Fl.: 1972

Sex: ♂♂ have a pronounced cranial bump. ♂ genitalia appears ten days before spawning while those of the ♀ are visible for only few hours prior.

Soc. B.: Barely territorial, the fish are peaceful towards their own species and other tank mates. They become aggressive only during spawning. They are inveterate burrowers, mouth-brooders and form a matriarchal family.

M: Needs a tank with a bottom of thick sand, 2 to 3 inches (5-8 cm.) deep. Create hiding places among rocks and roots and add neutral to slightly acid water, pH 6.5-7.0, at a hardness 5-15° dGH.

B: Use the water values above at temperatures between 26-28° C. Open breeders, the fish will spawn yellow eggs on selected rocks. The eggs are immediately taken into the female's mouth. After gathering in the eggs the pair split up. As with most mouthbreeders, you should not offer food at this time since the eggs may be accidently swallowed. The fry are released after 20 days.

F: C, O; live food; flakes; tablets; FD; frozen foods.

S: *G. steindachneri* is the only South American mouth brooder to retrieve its eggs immediately after spawning and for this fact must be considered a highly specialized species. Interestingly, the ♂ has an orange-colored patch at each corner of its mouth. These are used just as the dummy eggs on the anal fin of certain *Haplochromis* mouth-brooders — to guarantee fertilization.

| T: | 75-79° F, | L: | 10", sexually mature from 3", | A: | 39", | R: b, | D: 2. |
| | 24-26° C, | | 25 cm, sexually mature from 7.5 cm, | | 100 cm, | | |

Geophagus surinamensis

(BLOCH, 1791)

Syn.: *Sparus surinamensis, Chromis proxima, Geophagus altifrons, G. megasema, Satanoperca proxima*

Hab.: In standing and slow-moving waters of South America; Guyana south to the Amazon. Commercially available fishes are mostly captive-bred though some wild-caught specimens have been offered since 1970.

Fl.: 1914, Mazatis, Berlin, Germany.

Sex: Difficult to distinguish the sexes; the ♀♀ are said to noticeably silver with longer fins though this is not a certain point of identification by the ♂.

Soc. B.: Territorial, aggressive and intolerant, the fish are confirmed burrowers. A larvophile mouth-brooder, they form nuclear families and are good and careful parents. They can be kept in tanks with larger Catfishes.

M: Create caves in the rear of the tank using rocks and roots. Decorate the edges with such hardy plants as *Sagittaria, Vallisneria* and larger Cryptocorynes. The plant should be potted. Use sand on the tank bottom with a few flat rocks added.

B: Suggest neutral, medium hard water, pH 7.0 and 10° dGH at a temperature between 25-28° C. Partial mouth-brooders, the ♀ lays to 250 eggs on a rock. These are taken into the mouth of both parents shortly before or while the larvae hatch and are protected at night and in times in danger.

F: C, O; all types of live foods; also flakes and FD.

S: As with *Satanoperca jurupari*, some other *Geophagus* sp. are incorrectly sold under this name.

| T: | 72-77° F, | L: | 12", | A: | 39", | R: b, | D: 3. |
| | 22-25° C, | | 30 cm, | | 100 cm, | | |

Geophagus steindachneri

Geophagus surinamensis

Fam.: Cichlidae

Gymnogeophagus australis

(EIGENMANN, 1907)

Syn.: *Geophagus australe, G. australis*

Hab.: Argentina; in an area near La Plata.

Fl.: 1936

Sex: A monomorph with no sexual dimorphism; the sexes can be distinguished during spawning by the shape of their genital papillae. On the ♂ it is pointed and directed to the rear; in the ♀ it is rounded and smaller.

Soc. B.: Territorial, the species can defend itself against most tank mates. It does not burrow as much as some earth-eaters. They do not disturb plants, are open breeders and form nuclear families.

M: Needs a bottom of fine sand with hiding places among the roots and rocks. Add flat rocks for spawning. The species is tolerant of a range of water chemistry but should not be kept in water that is too warm. In the winter we suggest temperatures 18-20° C. Use only hardy plants and keep these in

pots. Keep with fish preferring similar tank conditions. Avoid demanding Cichlids.

B: They are not difficult to breed, form true pairs and spawning is preceeded by a boistrous courtship. A water temperature around 24° C is best. Both partners clean the spawning area and will dig one or more pit for the fry. The female is particularly concerned for her brood but the male takes over from time to time. Several hundred eggs are laid and the fry kept in protective pits. They are free-swimming by the sixth day. (WERNER, 1978: Das Aquarium **12**; 475-479). Feed the fry brine shrimp. Both parents can be seen leading their fry.

F: O; all types of live foods; frozen foods; flakes; tablets.

S: Because it is able to handle cooler waters (according to STERBA, 12-15° C can be tolerated) the fish can be kept in garden ponds during the summer.

T: 72-75° F,   **L:** to 6½″, approx. 5″ in an aquarium,   **A:** 39″,   **R:** b, m,   **D:** 2.
22-24° C,   to 18 cm, approx. 12 cm in an aquarium,   100 cm,

Gymnogeophagus balzanii

(PERUGIA, 1891)

Syn.: *Geophagus balzanii, G. duodecimspinosus*

Hab.: Paraguay; Rio Parana. The fish are captive-bred and wildcaught specimens are rare.

Fl.: 1972, Heiko Bleher, Frankfurt, West Germany and Thomas Horeman, London, England.

Sex: Pronounced sexual dimorphism; the dorsal and anal fins of older ♂♂ are longer. Older ♂♂ also have a noticeable cranial bump; the rear of their gill covers have bright green spots. The lower section of the gill cover on a ♀ is orangered.

Soc. B.: Territorial and peaceful, the fish is an inveterate burrower. It will not attack plants and forms a matriarchal family.

M: Needs a bottom of fine sand with hiding places among rocky caves. Use hardy plants and keep them potted.

B: Recommend neutral, medium-hard water, pH around 7.0, 8-13° dGH at a temperature between 25-28° C. A mouth-brooder, the ♀ spawns up to 500 eggs on rocks, taking them into her mouth after 24 to 36 hours. The ♂ departs and the ♀ is left with the care of her fry. Free-swimming fry retreat into her mouth at a sign of danger; usually a flap of her fins signals retreat.

F: C, O; all types of live foods; FD; frozen foods; dried food; flakes; tablets.

S: The head has a distinctive steep rise to it.

T: 72-79° F,   **L:** 8″,   **A:** 39″,   **R:** b,   **D:** 3.
22-26° C,   20 cm,   100 cm,

Gymnogeophagus australis

Gymnogeophagus balzanii

Fam.: Cichlidae

Cyrtocara chrysonota*

(BOULENGER, 1908)

Syn.: *Paratilapia chrysonota, Haplochromis chrysonotus*

Hab.: Endemic to Lake Malawi, especially in Nkata and Monkey Bays. They are found in the upper stratas close to shore.

Fl.: 1975

Sex: Clear dimorphism; the ♂ is larger, with brighter colors and dummy egg shapes on the anal fins.

Soc. B.: A quiet, peaceful species, several ♂♂ can be combined in a tank without problems. They will attack plants, and a ♂ may try to spawn with several ♀♀. The ♂ select miniterritories, though only during spawning. Mouth brooders, they form a matriarchial family.

M: Similar to suggestions for *Cyrtocara polystigma* with water values as for other Lake Malawi Cichlids (10-15° dGH and a pH 8.0-8.5).

B: Not difficult; follow recommendations for other Lake Malawi species of *Cyrtocara*. In the lake, the ♂♂ seek sandybottomed areas near shore where they form "courtship colonies", each staking out a territory a short distance from each other. They dig shallow spawning pits inside these boundries.

F: C, O; live food; FD; flakes.

S: The species belongs to the so-called Utaka group which includes about 15 species of *Cyrtocara*. Most live pelagically, in open water, feeding off plankton and small vegetable matter.

* *Copadichromis chrysonotus*

T: 73-79° F,   L: 6″,   A: 39″,   R: m, t,   D: 2-3.
    23-26° C,   15 cm,   100 cm,

Cyrtocara compressiceps*
Malawi Eye-Biter

(BOULENGER, 1908)

Syn.: *Paratilapia compressiceps, Haplochromis compressiceps*

Hab.: Endemic to Lake Malawi, above sandy bottoms with patches of *Vallisneria*. In these transitional zones between a sandy bottom and rocky shores, the water is calm, virtually without waves. Wild-caught fishes are often available.

Fl.: 1964, Walter Griem, Hamburg, West Germany.

Sex: The anal fin of the ♂ has dummy egg shapes and the head of a sexually mature ♂ is a shinny blue-green. The head of a ♀ is golden.

Soc. B.: Little is known about the social behaviour of the species. The fish is a predator and forms a matriarchal family. The female is a mouth-brooder.

M: Needs as large a tank as possible with a deep, sandy bottom and piles of rocks placed to create caves. Plant the edges heavily with *Vallisneria* or reedy aquatic plants.

B: Follow recommendations for water values and temperatures for other Lake Malawi *Cyrtocara*. Breeding has been successful.

S: The species is similar to the pike, a darting predator, and is the only predator known which devours its prey tail first. Native fishermen have noticed the species bites the eyes of other fishes, possibly to blind them prior to capture. A prognathous-toothed lower jaw is important in this respect.

* *Dimidiochromis compressiceps*

T: 72-82° F,   L: 6-10″,   A: 39″,   R: m, b,   D: 3.
    22-28° C,   15-25 cm,   100 cm,

Cyrtocara chrysonota

Cyrtocara compressiceps

Fam.: Cichlidae

Cyrtocara epichorialis*

Syn.: *Haplochromis epichorialis*

Hab.: Endemic to Lake Malawi, Africa.

Fl.: 1978

Sex: The ♂ is more brilliantly colored, with false egg decorations on the anal fin.

Soc. B.: Unknown.

M: Follow recommendations for *Cyrtocara euchila*.

B: There are no reports of successful breeding in an aquarium but procedures are presumably similar to those for other Lake Malawi species of *Cyrtocara*.

F: All types of live foods; vegetable supplements; flakes; FD.

S: The lower pharyngeal bone is large, bearing a few blunt teeth. These are not molars.

T: 74-79° F, **L**: 8″, **A**: 39″, **R**: m, b, **D**: 2.
24-26° C, 20 cm, 100 cm,

(TREWAVAS, 1935)

In the fall of 1989 the book "Malawian Cichlid Fishes – the classification of some Haplochromine genera" by D. H. ECCLES and E. TREWAVAS was published, in which both authors revise the genera *Cyrtocara* (previously *Haplochromis*) and *Lethrinops*. Representative species of these genera are thereby reclassified into 20 new groups. Since this systemization has so far not been debated scientifically, we will wait to apply it to the aquarium atlas until such classification has been accepted by other scientists. Nevertheless, we do not want to withhold this taxa from our readers. You will find this information usually at the end of a text on *Cyrtocara* genera.

* *Maravichromis epichorialis*

C. epichorialis ♀

Cyrtocara euchila*
Big-Lipped Cichlid

Syn.: *Haplochromis euchilus*

Hab.: Endemic to the rocky coasts of Lake Malawi. Most fish available commercially are wild-caught. Captive-bred specimens are uncommon.

Fl.: Possibly 1964.

Sex: Clear sexual dimorphism; the ♂ is larger and more brilliantly colored.

Soc. B.: Slightly territorial, peaceful and often found in schools. The ♂ may spawn with several ♀♀. Forms a matriarchal family.

M: Needs a tank with piles of rocks creating caves and hiding places. Plants can be used but are not required.

B: Recommend slightly alkaline, medium-hard water, pH 8.0-8.5 and 10-15° dGH, at a temperature between 26-27° C. Place one

T: 75-79° F, **L**: to 12″, **A**: 39″, **R**: m, b, **D**: 3.
24-26° C, to 35 cm, 100 cm,

(TREWAVAS, 1935)

♂ with at least three ♀♀. A mouth-brooder, the ♀ spawns 150 eggs on a rock then places them in her mouth. Fertilization is by the false-egg method. Unlike others of the genus, *C. euchila* does not dig a spawning pit. The ♀ cares for the larvae and eggs, and when they become fry, takes them back to the safety of her mouth at night or in the face of danger.

F: L, O; live foods; algae; FD; frozen foods; flakes; tablets.

S: A specialized feeder, the fish consumes animal matter found on rocks; also eats algae rich in such micro-fauna as mosquito larvae and Rotatoria.

* *Cheilochromis euchilus*

Cyrtocara epichorialis ♂

Cyrtocara euchila

Fam.: Cichlidae

Labidochromis lividus

Syn.: none.

Hab.: Africa, Lake Malawi, endemic to rocky coastlines. So far this species has been found only along the northern and western coast of Likoma Island where it settled on rock formations in water depths down to 6 m; mostly found at 3 m, seldom below 6 m.

Fl.: 1978.

Sex: Body colouring of courting ♂ is bluish black with 5–6 delicate vertical bands under the dorsals; lower body half dark olive to bluish black; dark eye band and 2 blue interorbital stripes; dorsal fin black with white or light blue fringe, occasional orange brown spots. ♀ plain olive brown colouring.

Soc. B.: Agamous, ovophil mouth breeder (matriarchal), the ♂ in spawning season is agressive against his own kind and other tank inhabitants (territorial).

M: Rock groupings and formations to

T: 24-26° C, **L:** 7 cm, **BL:** 80 cm, **WR:** m, u, **SG:** 2.

LEVIS, 1982

provide sufficient hiding places. Make sure water is oxygen rich and clean (regular water changes). Water values: pH 7.7–8.3, dGH 7–20°. Combination with other *Mbuna* cichlids recommended.

B: Easy; matriarchal mouth breeders. If raising whole brood is desired, separating the pregnant female is recommended. On average, young fry are released from the mouth after 3 weeks incubation. No problem raising the approx. 1 cm long baby fish on small live foods such as *Artemia* and fine flake food.

F: L, O; in the wild, the species feed on loose growth. In tank, omnivorous, especially mosquito larvae, small crab-like and flake foods. FD food tablets.

S: The male *Labidochromis lividus* features a dark eye band and 2 interorbital stripes. This colour pattern is also prevalent in some other *Mbuna* genera, such as *Melanochromis* and *Pseudotropheus* species (colour convergence).

Melanochromis labrosus

Syn.: *Cyrtocara labrosa, Haplochromis labrosus*

Hab.: Endemic to Lake Malawi.

Fl.: Possibly 1973.

Sex: The ♂ is more brilliantly colored and has false egg patterns on the anal fin.

Soc. B.: Unknown, though evidently similar to other Lake Malawi *Cyrtocara* sp.

M: Follow recommendations for *C. euchila*.

B: A typical mouth-brooder.

F: O; large live foods; animal flesh; flakes; tablets.

S: The fish has unusual fleshy lips whose purpose have not been determined. Possibly they act as sensory organs to detect food.

T: 73-79° F, **L:** 5", **A:** 35", **R:** m+b, **D:** 2.
23-26° C, 13 cm, 90 cm,

TREWAVAS, 1935

Labidochromis lividus

Melanochromis labrosus, black morph

Fam. Cichlidae

Cyrtocara linni*
Elephant-Nose Cichlid

(BURGESS & AXELROD, 1975)

Syn.: *Haplochromis linni*

* *Nimbochromis linni*

Hab.: Endemic to Lake Malawi.

Fl.: 1973

Sex: The dorsal of the ♂ has a red-yellow-white edge while the ♀ lacks the red. There is a false egg pattern on the male's anal fin. ♂ is more brightly colored.

Soc. B.: Follow recommendations for *C. polystigma*. The fish are predaceous and should be kept only with tank mates of similar or larger size.

B: See suggestions for *C. polystigma*.

F: C, O; all types of hardy live foods, chiefly fish or chopped fish: beef heart; liver; tablets; frozen foods.

S: This may not be a separate species since the description by BURGESS and AXELROD was based on one single specimen. *C. linni* and *C. polystigma* are closely related and this may be a morph of the latter.

♀

T: 73-77° F, L: 10″, A: 39″, R: m, b, D: 2.
23-25° C, 25 cm, 100 cm,

Cyrtocara livingstonii*

(GUENTHER, 1893)

Syn.: *Hemichromis livingstonii, Haplochromis livingstonii*

Hab.: Endemic to the sandy-bottomed, inshore areas of Lake Malawi. Found in regions with *Vallisneria.*

Fl.: Possibly 1972.

Sex: ♂ has egg-shaped patterns on his anal and is more brilliantly colored.

Soc. B.: Territorial, the fish are predators though relatively peaceful among themselves. ♂ is polygamous and should be placed with several ♀♀. A mouth-brooder, the pairs form a matriarchal family.

M: Needs a tank with a bottom of fine sand, densely planted with *Vallisneria.* Leave some space for swimming and create hiding places among the rocks and roots. Be sure to place rocks on the aquarium bottom, not on the sand. Use water values suggested for related Lake Malawi species.

B: Follow water recommendations for related species such as *C. euchila* or *C. polystigma* at temperatures 26-27° C. The female lays as many as 100 small eggs.

F: C, O; such live foods as fish; water fleas; mosquito larvae; earthworms; beef heart; mussel; large flakes; spinach; lettuce.

S: The species can be distinguished by its unusual behavior. It has a habit of lying on its side on the bottom for long periods of time, seemingly dead. When smaller fish approach as if to eat the carcass, they are captured with a lightening-quick lunge. The behaviour has been observed in the wild as well as in home aquariums, which provides the origin of the German name for the fish, "sleeper".

* *Nimbochromis livingstonii*

T: 74-79° F, L: 8″, A: 39″, R: b, D: 2.
24-26° C, 20 cm, 100 cm,

Cyrtocara linni

Cyrtocara livingstonii

Cyrtocara moorii

BOULENGER, 1902

Syn.: *Haplochromis moorii*

Hab.: Endemic to Lake Malawi; found in the sandy coastal areas. Captive-bred specimens are rare and most fish available are wild caught.

Fl.: 1968

Sex: It is difficult to distinguish between the sexes. The cranial bump is not a certain sign since it occurs on ♂ and ♀. ♂ is sometimes larger and more brightly colored.

Soc. B.: Territorial and peaceful, the fish will school in a large enough tank. The ♂ is polygamous and should be kept with at least three ♀♀. Forms a matriarchal family. The fish burrow but will not harm plants.

M: The tank should have rocky formations with caves in the back and sand in front. The species needs lots of open space for swimming.

B: Needs slightly to moderately alkaline, medium-hard to hard water, pH 7.2-8.8 and 10-18° dGH. A temperature range of 25-26° C is best. Frequent water changes are essential, $^1/_3$ to $^1/_2$ one or two times weekly. A mouth-brooder, the ♀ lays 20-90 eggs on a selected rock, then takes them into her mouth. They are fertilized as are others of the genus though the mother is a more dedicated parent than many.

F: Live foods; beef heart; tablets.

S: Growth of the fry is determined by frequent water changes.
This species remains in the genus **Cyrtocara**.

T: 74-79° F,	L: 10″,	A: 39″,	R: m, b,	D: 3.
24-26° C,	25 cm,	100 cm,		

Cyrtocara polystigma*
Polystigma

(REGAN, 1921)

Syn.: *Haplochromis polystigma*

Hab.: Endemic to the rocky coast of Lake Malawi. Wild-caught and captive-bred fish are available.

Fl.: Unknown.

Sex: ♂ has a noticeable egg pattern on his anal fin. The ♂ is more brilliantly colored.

Soc. B.: Territorial, the ♂ is peaceful toward tank mates though aggressive toward ♀♀ of his species. Consequently, the species should be kept with fish of similar or larger size. It will not burrow or harm plants. ♂ is polygamous and should be kept with several ♀♀. It is a mouth-brooder and forms a matriarchal family.

M: The species needs hiding places among roots and rocks. We suggest heavy planting along the edges and open swimming space in the center. The latter is important.

B: We recommend moderately alkaline, medium hard to hard water, pH 7.5-8.5 and 10-18° dGH. The fish are mouth-brooders. The ♀ lays to 20 eggs which are fertilized via the false-egg method. The mother cares for her fry carefully the first week. They spend nights in her mouth.

F: C; such live foods as *Tubifex* and earthworms; beef heart; chopped fish; flakes.

S: A confirmed predator, the fish is a hearty, greedy eater. It should never be kept with smaller fish.

* *Nimbochromis polystigma*

T: 73-77° F,	L: to 9″,	A: 39″,	R: m, b,	D: 2-3.
23-25° C,	to 23 cm,	100 cm,		

Cyrtocara moorii

Cyrtocara polystigma ♀ above, ♂ below

Fam.: Cichlidae

Cyrtocara rostrata*

(BOULENGER, 1899)

Syn.: *Tilapia rostrata, Haplochromis macrorhynchus, H. rostratus*

Hab.: Endemic to the sandy shores of Lake Malawi.

Fl.: Possibly 1968.

Sex: Clear sexual dimorphism and dichromatism; ♂ has a different and more brilliant coloring.

Soc. B.: Territorial, the species is often aggressive and intolerant of its kind. A mouth-brooder, it forms a matriarchal family.

B: Follow recommendations for *C. venusta.*

B: There are no reports of successful breeding in an aquarium but procedures would follow those for related Lake Malawi species.

F: All types of live foods; FD; frozen; vegetable supplement; beef heart; dried food. Food is generally taken from the bottom.

S: When in danger the fish quickly buries itself in the sand and for this reason it is seldom caught in nets. There is a symbiotic feeding between *C. rostrata* and *C. moorii.* While *C. rostrata* burrows in search of food, *C. moorii* remains close to search through the resulting debris.

* *Tossochromis rostratus*

T: 75-82° F, **L:** 10″, **A:** 39″, **R:** b, m, **D:** 2-3.
24-28° C, 25 cm, 100 cm,

Cyrtocara venusta*
Venustus

(BOULENGER, 1908)

Syn.: *Haplochromis simulans, H. venustus*

Hab.: Endemic to the sandy shores of Lake Malawi. Wild-caught fish are rarely available.

Fl.: 1970

Sex: Clear sexual dichromatism between adults; the ♂ is larger and more brilliantly colored.

Soc. B.: Territorial, the fish are aggressive and intolerant of their species; they burrow but generally will not harm plants; one ♂ spawns with several ♀♀ and forms a matriarchal family.

M: Needs a tank with at least 50 gallons of water (200 l). Add rocky formations with caves and other hiding places along the back. Place a sandy bottom in the front with plants along the sides.

B: Follow water value recommendations for *C. moorii* at a temperature between 26-29° C. A mouth-brooder, the ♀ drops as many as 120 eggs. The mother is one of the most dedicated of her genus, looking after the fry for ten days. They spend nights in her mouth.

F: C, O; all types of live foods; beef heart; lettuce; spinach; flakes.

S: Avoid frightening ♀♀ with eggs. They may expectorate the larvae. Recommend a weekly change of $^1/_3$rd the water. The species is predatory.

* *Nimbochromis venustus*

T: 77-79° F, **L:** to 10″, **A:** 47″, **R:** b, m, **D:** 3.
25-27° C, to 25 cm, 120 cm,

Cyrtocara rostrata ♂

Cyrtocara venusta ♂

Hemichromis bimaculatus
Jewel Cichlid

GILL, 1862

Syn.: *Hemichromis fugax*

Hab.: In rivers and tributaries along the coastal basins of Africa from southern Guinea to central Liberia. PAYNE and TREWAVAS have demonstrated the species is found in forested areas.

Fl.: 1907, Vereinigte Zierfischzuechtereien, Conradshoehe, West Germany.

Sex: It is difficult to distinguish the sexes except by their genital papillae. A spot on the base of the dorsal and anal fins is less noticeable on ♀♀. The male's caudal fin is reticulated near the center.

Soc. B.: Territorial and peaceful except during spawning, then the species is aggressive and intolerant. It is a burrower, especially during the spawning season. Pairs form nuclear families and are excellent parents.

M: Needs a well planted tank with such hardy varieties as *Vallisneria* and *Sagittaria*. Add a few large rocks. The fish will dig spawning pits behind these. Clutches of 200-500 eggs are laid on carefully-cleaned rocks, then moved to the protective pits. Fry may be moved several times to new pits as they grow. The parents guide the schools of fry.

F: C, O; all types of live foods; FD; flakes; tablets.

S: The species is selective and slow to pair; incompatibility can end in the death of one of the partners. Parents identify the fry by visual and chemical characteristics.

T: 70-73° F,   **L:** 2¹/₂-6",   **A:** 27",   **R:** b,   **D:** 3.
21-23° C,   7-15 cm,   70 cm,

Hemichromis lifalili
Lifalili Cichlid

LOISELLE, 1979

Syn.: None

Hab.: Zaire basin; Zaire River, Ruki River, Lake Tumba, Lake Yandja and upper reaches of the Ubanghi River. It is not found in waters low in oxygen.

Fl.: In the late 1960's.

Sex: Sexually inactive ♂♂ are colored similar to ♀♀ though they have a brighter orange-red hue on the sides of their stomach. See photo for both sexes in spawning colors.

Soc. B.: Similar to *H. bimaculatus.*

M: See recommendations for *H. bimaculatus.* Needs plenty of oxygen.

B: Follow recommendations for *H. bimaculatus.* Needs neutral, soft to medium-hard water, pH about 7.0, 2-12° dGH. Open breeders, the fish are good parents.

F: C, O; such live foods as insects, worms and brine shrimp; frozen food; FD. Will also accept flakes and tablets.

S: The species differs from *H. bimaculatus* in three ways – by the length of its nose (3.6 to 4.6 times the length of the head for *H. lifalili* and 3 to 3.7 times for *H. bimaculatus*), by the shape of it lower pharyngeal bone and by its color.

T: 72-75° F,   **L:** to 4",   **A:** 27",   **R:** b,   **D:** 3.
22-24° C,   to 10 cm,   70 cm,

Hemichromis

Hemichromis lifalili, ♂ front, ♀ background

Cichlasoma cyanoguttatum
Rio Grande Perch, Texas Cichlid

(BAIRD & GIRARD, 1854)

Syn.: Herichthys cyanoguttatum, Heros cyanoguttatus, H. temporalis. Neetroplus carpintis

Hab.: In rivers and lakes of Texas and north-eastern Mexico. The northern-most of all neo-tropical cichlids, captive-bred specimens are readily available.

Fl.: 1902, C. von dem Borne-Berneuchen.

Sex: It is difficult to distinguish between the sexes; the ♀ is less brilliantly colored and smaller. Older ♂♂ have a typical cranial bump.

Soc. B.: Territorial, intolerant and waspish, the fish burrow and attack plants. Pairs form a nuclear family.

M: Needs places among roots and rocks to hide. You should divide the tank into territories, using small hardy plants if possible and floating cover as well. Suggest a bottom of fine sand. Can winter in temperatures to 15-18° C.

B: Suggest neutral, soft to medium hard water, pH around 7.0, 5-12° dGH, at temperatures between 25-28° C. Open breeders, the fish need well oxygenated water. They will spawn on cleaned rocks, dropping to 500 eggs. The fry are suspended from stones and are guarded by both parents who are less dilligent about child rearing than some others in the genus.

F: C, O; such live foods as mosquito larvae and Tubifex and earthworms; lettuce; spinach; oatmeal; large flakes.

S: The species is sensitive to old water and needs frequent changes, $^1/_4$th to $^1/_2$nds weekly. Parents may eat their spawn.

Juvenile

T: 68-75° F,	L: 4-12″,	A: 39″,	R: b, D: 3.
20-24° C,	10-30 cm,	100 cm,	

Herotilapia multispinosa

(GUENTHER, 1866)

Syn.: Heros multispinosus

Hab.: Panama to Lake Managua, Nicaragua. Though it has been captive-bred in Canada, commercial fish are wild-caught.

Fl.: 1969, W. Foersch, Munich, West Germany.

Sex: It is difficult to distinguish between the sexes; ♂♂ tend to be longer and larger with pointed dorsal and anal fins; a more certain sign is the short ovipositor of the ♀.

Soc. B.: Territorial, peaceful and rarely aggressive except during spawning. It does not often burrow. Pairs form lasting relationships and a nuclear family. While the brood is generally well cared-for, the parents may cannabalize some of the fry.

M: Needs a tank with fine gravel with rocks and roots providing hiding places. Over-turned pots and shards work well too. Recommend hardy, well-rooted plants.

B: Recommend neutral, soft to medium-hard water, pH around 7.0, 5-10° dGH at a temperature of 26-27° C. Open breeders, the fish drop 600-1,000 eggs on roots and rocks. They are carefully guarded by the ♀ who circulates water by fanning the eggs with her fins. The fry are protected in pits.

F: C, O; all types of live foods; stewed lettuce; spinach; large flakes.

S: The fish can quickly change colors according to mood. The genus is monotypic, embracing but this single species. It is closely related to the genus Cichlasoma differing only by its three-pointed teeth

T: 72-77° F,	L: 2$^1/_2$-5″,	A: 27″,	R: m, b,	D: 2.
22-25° C,	7-13 cm,	70 cm,		

Cichlasoma cyanoguttatum

Herotilapia multispinosa

Julidochromis dickfeldi
Brown Julie

STAECK, 1975

Syn.: None

Hab.: Endemic to the transitional rocky areas of Lake Tanganyika. Found on the southwest side of the lake, on the Zambian shoreline.

Fl.: 1975, Dr. Wolfgang Staeck, Berlin, West Germany.

Sex: Uncertain. The ♀♀ are probably larger.

T: 72-77° F, **L:** 3″, **A:** 23¹/₂″, **R:** m, b, **D:** 2.
22-25° C, 8 cm, 60 cm,

Soc. B.: See *J. ornatus.*

M: See *J. regani.*

B: Follow recommendations for *J. regani.* The fry hatch after 60 hours in water about 28° C.

F: C, O; all types of live foods; FD; frozen food; flakes.

S: Differs from others of the genus by its light brown coloring.

Julidochromis marlieri

POLL, 1956

Syn.: None

Hab.: Endemic to the rocky shores of Lake Tanganyika. Wild caught fishes are available but captive-bred specimens are becoming increasingly common.

Fl.: 1958

Sex: It is difficult to distinguish between the sexes; during spawning season the ♀♀ can be recognized by their genital papillae; adult ♂♂ have a lump-like swelling on the neck and are normally smaller.

Soc. B.: Intolerant towards their own spe-

T: 72-77° F, **L:** 4-6″, **A:** 27″, **R:** m, b, **D:** 2.
22-25° C, 10-15 cm, 70 cm,

cies, they do not attack plants; pairs form nuclear families and both guard the brood.

M: Needs rock formations in which to hide. Plants are not essential.

B: Recommend moderately alkaline, medium-hard water, pH 7.5-9.0, 12° dGH, at a temperature between 24-26° C. Shelter breeders, the ♀ generally lays 70-100 eggs, never more than 360.

F: C, O; live food; frozen food; flakes and tablets.

S: Can be crossed with *J. ornatus* though the off-spring are sterile.

Julidochromis ornatus
Yellow Julie

BOULENGER, 1898

Syn.: None

Hab.: Endemic to the rocky coast of Lake Tanganyika.

Fl.: 1958

Sex: The ♀♀ can be distinguished by their genital papilla; the ♂ is usually smaller. Fish commercially available are difficult to sex.

Soc. B.: Intolerant toward its own species, it forms a nuclear family. The parents do not directly care for their fry though their protectioin of the territory is an important peripheral benefit. The young spend several weeks in the protection of a breeding pit.

Julidochromis dickfeldi

Julidochromis marlieri

M: Needs a tank with rocky formations which provide areas in which to hide. Add a few hardy plants such as *Vallisneria*.

B: Suggest moderately alkaline, medium-hard to hard water. pH 8.0-9.0, 11-20° dGH, at a temperature between 24-26° C. Shelter breeders, the ♀ drops 20-50 eggs in caves. Never more than 100 are laid.

F: C, O; live foods; FD; flakes; tablets.

S: Eggs are deposited on the roof of the cave. The fry are free-swimming but still remain near the area in which they were hatched, their stomachs against the roof or wall of the cave.

T: 72-75° F, L: 3″, A: 19″, R: m, b, D: 2.
   22-24° C, 8 cm, 50 cm,

Julidochromis regani

POLL, 1942

Syn.: None

Hab.: Endemic to the rocky shores of Lake Tanganyika. Wild-caught fishes are frequently available.

Fl.: 1958

Sex: It is difficult to distinguish between the sexes; ♀♀ are generally larger and, in spawning season, have rounded stomachs. One obvious identification factor: the genitalia of the ♂.

Soc. B.: Territorial, these are the most tolerant of the genus, aggressive only during spawning; the fish then may burrow. Forms a nuclear family.

M: Suggest a tank with rocky formations and caves and hiding places. If these

reach to the surface you will discover all levels of the tank are occupied. Add a few hardy plants such as *Sagittaria* and *Vallisneria*. The fish likes a bottom of fine sand.

B: Suggest moderately alkaline, medium-hard water, pH 8.5-9.2, 8-14° dGH, at a temperature between 25-27° C. Cave breeders, the ♀ lays as many as 300 eggs on the roof of a chosen cave. Both parents care for the fry and energetically defend the territory.

F: C, O; all types of live foods; FD; frozen foods; vegetable supplements; flakes.

S: The fish are extremely sensitive to sulphur. ♀♀ have been observed taking over the territorial defence duties of the ♂.

T: 72-77° F, L: to 12″, A: 31″, R: all, D: 2.
   22-25° C, to 30 cm, 80 cm,

Julidochromis transcriptus
Black -and-White Julie

MATTHES, 1959

Syn.: None

Hab.: Endemic to the rocky shores of Lake Tanganyika.

Fl.: Possibly 1964

Soc. B.: Identification is most certain via the genital papilla which is longer on the ♀. ♀♀ are also larger with a more rounded stomach.

Soc. B.: See *J. marlieri*.

M: See *J. regani*.

B: Although less productive, follow recommendations for *J. regani*. May only lay 30 eggs.

F: C, O; all types of live foods; FD; frozen foods; flakes.

S: The head of *J. transcriptus* is flat and, unlike *J. marlieri*, does not have a bump. It is the smallest species in the genus and can be distinguished from *J. marlieri* by two rows of white spots. *J. marlieri* has three.

T: 72-77° F, L: 2¹/₂″, A: 23¹/₂″, R: m, b, D: 2.
   22-25° C, 7 cm, 60 cm,

Julidochromis ornatus

Julidochromis regani

Julidochromis transcriptus

Fam.: Cichlidae

Labeotropheus fuelleborni
Fuelleborn's Cichlid

AHL, 1927

Syn.: *Labeotropheus curvirostris*

Hab.: Endemic to Lake Malawi.

Fl.: 1964

Sex: Clear sexual dimorphism; the ♀ is polychromatic; the ♂ has yellow egg-shapes on his anal fins.

Soc. B.: Territorial and aggressive, the species forms pairs only while spawning. The ♀ is a mouth-brooder; keep several ♀♀ with each male.

M: Needs a tank with rocky formations with plenty of caves and other hiding places. Use hardy plants. The tank should be well lighted to promote the growth of algae. The species eats microfoods.

B: Suggest moderatly alkaline, medium-hard water, pH 7.5-8.5, 12° dGH at a temperature between 24-28° C. Eggs are deposited on carefully cleaned rocks and taken into the female's mouth immediately. Oral fertilization is via the false-egg method.

T: 72-77° F, **L:** 6″, **A:** 27″, **R:** m, b, **D:** 2.
22-25° C, 15 cm, 70 cm,

F: L, O; all types of live foods; algae; flakes; tablets.

S: The ♀ is found in several color morphs. Most ♀ variations are sexually specific. Apart from the standard color, which is similar to that of the ♂, a checkered morph can be found occasionally. (See small photo.)

Labeotropheus trewavasae
Trewavas' Cichlid

FRYER, 1956

Syn.: None

Hab.: Endemic to the rocky shores of Lake Malawi. Wild-caught and captive-bred fishes are available commercially.

Fl.: 1964

Sex: Clear sexual dimorphism and dichromatism; the ♂ has more obvious false-egg patterns on his anal fin. These are faint or missing on ♀♀.

Soc. B.: Territorial, the fishes are extremely aggressive and intolerant. The ♂ is polygamous and should be kept with several ♀♀. Forms a matriarchal family.

B: Needs neutral to slightly alkaline, medium-hard to hard water, pH 7.0-8.0, 10-15° dGH, at a temperature between 24-27° C. As many as 40 eggs are laid and fertilized orally. Remove the ♂ after spawning.

T: 70-75° F, **L:** 4¹/₂″, **A:** 27″, **R:** m, b, **D:** 2.
21-24° C, 12 cm, 70 cm,

F: L, O; live food; algae; frozen food; FD.

S: As with *L. fuelleborni*, the species is sub-divided geographically, each clearly distinguishable by its color. There are even pure white specimens. The ♂ has been observed in ♀ colors, carrying eggs in his throat sac.

Labeotropheus fuelleborni

Labeotropheus trewavasae

Neolamprologus brichardi
Fairy Cichlid, Lyretail Lamprologus

(POLL, 1974)

Syn.: *Lamprologus savoryi elongatus, L. brichardi*

Hab.: Endemic to the rocky shoreline of Lake Tanganyika.

Fl.: 1958

Sex: It is difficult to distinguish between the sexes. The dorsal fin and tip of the caudal fin are longer on the ♂. The female's dorsal is blunt.

Soc. B.: The species pairs only during spawning, otherwise it is a schooling fish. Forms a nuclear family and provides only cursory care for the fry.

M: Needs a tank with rocky formations and many caves as hiding places. Plants are not necessary.

B: Suggest moderately alkaline, medium-hard to hard water, pH 7.5-8.5 and 10-20° dGH, at a temperature between 25-30° C. A shelter breeder, the ♀ spawns in caves. The site is carefully cleaned and up to 200 eggs laid there. The ♀ guards the family.

F: C, O; all types of live foods; flakes; FD.

S: The parents leave older fry to fend for themselves if they spawn again. Younger fishes of several ages can be found in the same tank, an example of what is called "stepped breeding". The older fry defend younger siblings and help with their care.

T: 72-77° F, **L:** 4″, **A:** 23^1/$_2$″, **R:** m, b, **D:** 2.
22-25° C, 10 cm, 60 cm,

Altolamprologus compressiceps
Compressed Cichlid

(BOULENGER, 1898)

Syn.: *Lamprologus compressiceps*

Hab.: Endemic to rocky bottoms of Lake Tanganyika. Commercial fishes are almost exclusively wild-caught.

Fl.: 1958

Sex: Unknown.

Soc. B.: Territorial, peaceful towards tank mates of similar size, it will not attack plants or burrow. Possibly forms a patriarch/matriarch family.

M: Needs a roomy tank with rocky formations full of caves as hiding places.

B: Suggest neutral, medium-hard water, pH about 7.0, 10° dGH, at a temperature between 24-26° C. A shelter breeder, the ♀ lays as many as 300 eggs in caves. She cares for the brood while the ♂ probably guards the territory.

F: C; live food – enjoys small fresh fish best.

S: The unusually high-backed, laterally-compressed body is an adaptation to the fish's way of feeding. Its shape allows it to catch such small prey as crustaceans and fry, even in narrow cracks in the rocks.

T: 73-77° F, **L:** 6″, **A:** 31″, **R:** m, b, **D:** 3.
23-25° C, 15 cm, 80 cm,

Neolamprologus brichardi

Altolamprologus compressiceps

Neolamprologus leleupi
Lemon Cichlid

(POLL , 1956)

Syn.: Lamprologus leleupi

Hab.: Endemic to the rocky shores of Lake Tanganyika. Readily available in the hobby.

Fl.: 1958

Sex: It is difficult to distinguish between the sexes; ♂ has a thicker head, is larger, and often has the typical cranial bump. His pelvic fin is also longer. The forehead of the ♀ has a steeper rise.

Soc. B.: A relatively peaceful species though the ♂ becomes aggressive toward superfluous or undesirable ♀♀. The fish do not burrow and form monogamous pairs and a nuclear family but only while tending the fry. They are cave breeders. The ♀ guards the clutch, the male defends the territory.

M: Needs a tank with a fine, sandy bottom. Add rocky formations with plenty of hiding places.

B: Recommend slightly alkaline, medium-hard to hard water, pH 7.5-8.0, 12-15° dGH, at a temperature between 25-30° C. A shelter breeder, the female lays 50-150 eggs on the roof of a cave.

F: C; live foods only.

S: The fry are sensitive to bacterial build-up. There are three sub-species: L. leleupi leleupi POLL, 1956 (yellow morph), L. l. melas (MATTHES, 1959 – dark morph) and L. l. longior STAECK, 1980.

T: 74-79° F, **L:** 4″, **A:** 23$^{1}/_{2}$″, **R:** m, b, **D:** 3-4.
24-26° C, 10 cm, 60 cm,

Neolamprologus tetracanthus

(BOULENGER, 1899)

Syn.: Lamprologus brevianalis, L. marginatus, L. tetracanthus

Hab.: Endemic to Lake Tanganyika. It is the most common Cichlid in the coastal zone.

Fl.: 1972

Sex: The ♂ is larger and, with age, displays the typical cranial bump.

Soc. B.: Territorial, the fish are generally peaceful though predaceous toward smaller tank mates. Cave breeders, they form monogamous pairs and a nuclear family during spawning. Both parents defend the fry.

B: See L. leleupi. Suggest a water temperature between 25-28° C. The eggs, spawned in caves, are energetically defended.

F: L; predominantly such live foods as small crustaceans, insect larvae, fry and molluscs.

S: This one of a few Cichlids inhabiting the transitional zone between a rocky bottom and the sandy shore. Its favorite foods are snails found the top layer of the sand.

T: 73-77° F, **L:** 7$^{1}/_{2}$″, **A:** 31″, **R:** m, b, **D:** 2-3.
23-25° C, 19 cm, 80 cm,

Neolamprologus leleupi

Neolamprologus tetracanthus

Neolamprologus tretocephalus

(BOULENGER, 1899)

Syn.: *Lamprologus tretocephalus*

Hab.: Endemic to the rocky shore areas of Lake Tanganyika.

Fl.: 1974

Sex: It is difficult to distinguish between the sexes; the ♂♂ may be larger with darker fins. Certainly they are more active during courting and their dorsal and anal fins are longer.

Soc. B.: Territorial, the pairs form a nuclear family. The male guards a large territory.

M: See suggestions for *L. brichardi*. Suggest a slightly alkaline, medium-hard water, pH 7.6-8.0, 10° dGH.

B: See recommendations for *L. brichardi*. Breeding is difficult and has rarely been successful. Water temperatures should be between 25-28° C. Relatively productive, the ♀ drops to 400 eggs in a prepared cave. The eggs hatch in 48 hours.

F: L, O; omnivorous; live foods, primarily insect larvae; FD; frozen foods; flakes; vegetable supplement.

S: The species is occasionally confused with *L. sexfasciatus* and *Cyphotilapia frontosa*. It differs from both by having only five cross bands. The species above have six.

T: 74-79° F, **L:** 6″, **A:** from 39″, **R:** m, b, **D:** 2-3.
24-26° C, 15 cm, from 100 cm,

Lamprologus werneri

POLL, 1959

Syn.: None

Hab.: The Zaire rapids near Kinshasa; Stanley Pool.

Fl.: 1957

Sex: Unknown.

Soc. B.: Territorial, aggressive towards its species and other tank mates, the ♂ is polygamous. It is best to keep several ♀♀ in a tank with one ♂. Possibly forms a patriarch/matriarch family.

M: Needs a tank with a gravel bottom. Add a rocky formation with hiding places. May be kept with larger surface-feeders. Suggest a current produced by a strong filter; does best in a shallow tank with a large surface area.

B: The species is a cave breeder.

F: Mosquito larvae, *Tubifex* worms, water fleas and earthworms. Will take flakes.

S: The species is adapted to life in such fast-moving water as rapids and waterfalls.

T: 72-77° F, **L:** 4$^{1}/_{2}$″, **A:** 31″, **R:** b, **D:** 2-3.
22-25° C, 12 cm, 80 cm,

Neolamprologus tretocephalus

Lamprologus werneri

Lobochilotes labiatus

(BOULENGER, 1898)

Syn.: *Tilapia labiata*

Hab.: Endemic to Lake Tanganyika.

Fl.: Possibly 1970.

Sex: The ♀ has the more pronounced body stripes; the male's anal fin has dark-edged false egg-shapes on it.

Soc. B.: Territorial, very aggressive and predaceous fish. They occasionally burrow. The species are probably mouth-brooders as the anal fin bears egg dummies (matriarchal family?).

M: Needs a roomy tank with lots of places to hide; Suggest rocky formations at the back of the tank with plenty of caves. Prefers a sandy bottom. Plants can be omitted. Likes moderately alkaline medium-hard water, pH around 8.0, hardness around 15° dGH.

B: There is no literature concerning successful breeding.

F: C; all types of live foods; vegetable supplement; FD; frozen foods; flakes.

S: Adults have well-developed, pronounced lips similar to those of *Cyrtocara labrosa* and *C. euchila*. These act as sensors to help find food.

T: 75-79° F, **L:** 13½″, **A:** 39″, **R:** m, b, **D:** 2-3.
    24-27° C,   37 cm,   100 cm,

Melanochromis auratus
Malawi Golden Cichlid, Auratus

(BOULENGER, 1897)

Syn.: *Tilapia aurata, Pseudotropheus auratus*

Hab.: Endemic to the rocky shore line of Lake Malawi.

Fl.: 1958

Sex: Pronounced sexual dimorphism and dichromatism; the ♂ sports a different color pattern than the ♀, has yellow false-egg shapes on his anal fin and a deep, black ventral.

Soc. B.: A territorial and intolerant species. The ♂ is polygamous and should be kept with several ♀♀. A mouthbrooder, the species forms a matriarchal family and will neither burrow nor harm plants.

M: Needs a tank with rocky formations with plenty of opportunity for hiding.

B: Suggest neutral to slightly alkaline, medium-hard water, pH 7.0-8.5, hardness 10-15° dGH, at a temperature between 25-28° C. Place at least four ♀♀ in a breeding tank with a single ♂. The ♀♀ are mouthbrooders and lay 20-30 eggs which are fertilized orally. The female is a casual parent, caring for her fry for one week after they leave her mouth.

F: L, O; live food; occasionally FD. Tank-bred specimens will also accept flakes. The fish like Blue Algae.

S: Belongs to that group called Mbuna Cichlids. A pale blue variety has been imported from water near the Likoma Islands in eastern Lake Malawi. It is similar in shape but has a different coloring.

T: 72-79° F, **L:** ♂ = 4¼″, ♀ = 3½″, **A:** 31″, **R:** all, **D:** 2-3.
    22-26° C,   ♂ = 11 cm, ♀ = 9 cm,   80 cm,

Lobochilotes labiatus

Melanochromis auratus

Melanochromis joanjohnsonae

(JOHNSON, 1974)

Syn.: *"Labidochromis caeruleus likomae"*, *Labidochromis joanjohnsonae, Pseudotropheus joanjohnsonae, Melanochromis exasperatus*

Hab.: Endemic to the rocky shores around the Likoma Islands, Lake Malawi.

Fl.: 1972

Sex: Clear sexual dimorphism and dichromatism; the ♂♂ have yellow false egg-shapes on the anal fin and a broad, black submarginal stripe along the dorsal.

Soc. B.: See *M. auratus* and *M. johannii*.

B: Follow suggestions for *M. auratus*.

F: L, O; all types of live foods; flakes; FD; lettuce, spinach; algae.

S: As with others of the genus, this species feeds on microfoods. The ♀ continues care of the fry after they leave her mouth. They return to it in times of danger. This behaviour differs from most Mbuna Cichlids.

♂

T: 75-79° F, **L**: 4", **A**: 31", **R**: all: if rocky formations reach the surface, **D**: 2.
 24-26° C, 10 cm, 80 cm,

Melanochromis johannii

(ECCLES, 1973)

Syn.: *Pseudotropheus johannii, "Pseudotropheus daviesi"*

Hab.: Endemic to the rocky coastline of Lake Malawi.

Fl.: 1972

Sex: Clear sexual dimorphism and dichromatism; the ♂♂ have false egg-shapes on the anal fin and are larger; ♀♀ are orange colored. The photo shows a male.

Soc. B.: Territorial and intolerant, the fish neither burrow nor disturb plants. ♂♂ are polygamous and should be kept with several ♀♀. They form a matriarchal family.

M: Needs a tank with rocky formations and many hiding places.

B: Recommend moderately alkaline, medium-hard water, pH around 8.5 and hardness 12-18° dGH at a temperature between 26-27° C. Keep at least three females for each male in the breeding tank. As many as 35 eggs are laid and fertilized orally. The ♀ casually cares for the brood for one week after the fry leave her mouth.

F: L, O; prefers live foods. Captive-bred fish will accept FD and flakes.

S: Counted among the Mbuna Cichlids, the fry have ♀ coloring. The ♂♂ change color after they are 2" (5 cm.) long. In poor water conditions all colors are pale.

T: 72-77° F, **L**: 4¹/₂", **A**: 31", **R**: all, **D**: 2.
 22-25° C, 12 cm, 80 cm,

Melanochromis joanjohnsonae ♀

Melanochromis johannii

Fam.: Cichlidae

Melanochromis vermivorus
Syn.: None

Hab.: Endemic to the rocky coastline of Lake Malawi. Wild-caught fish are the only stock offered to hobbyist and are rarely available.

Fl.: Possibly 1958.

Sex: Clear sexual dimorphism and dichromatism; false egg patterns on the male's anal fin.

Soc. B.: Territorial, intolerant and aggressive during spawning, the male is agamous; keep several females with one male. They are catagorized as Mbuna Cichlids. Mouth-brooders, they form a matriarchal family.

TREWAVAS, 1935

M: Needs a tank at least 35 inches (90 cm) long for each male and three or four females. Add rocky formations with caves and a bottom of fine sand. Add an open space for swimming.

B: See *M. auratus*.

F: Live foods such as *Daphnia*, *Tubifex* worms and mosquito larvae; algae; lettuce; flakes; FD.

S: The species is easily confused with *M. auratus* though the head is significantly longer and pointed and the mouth is larger and deeper. The females are also differently colored.

T: 72-79° F, L: 6″, A: 35″, R: m, b, D: 2.
22-26° C, 15 cm, 90 cm,

Mesonauta festiva
Festivum

(HECKEL, 1840)

Syn.: *Acara festiva, Chromys acora, Cichlasoma insigne, C. insignis, Heros festivus, H. insignis, Mesonauta insignis, Cichlasoma festivum*

Hab.: Near the bank in quiet, protected streams with enough vegetation for concealment; in western Guyana and the Amazon basin. Most fish available in the hobby are captive-bred and many display signs of inbreeding – smaller size and stunted fins.

Fl.: 1908, E. Reichelt, Berlin, Germany. First captive bred in 1911 by the Weinhausen Aquarium, Brunswick, West Germany.

Sex: Not readily identifiable except during spawning when the ♂ has longer fins. The genital papilla is a certain factor. It is pointed on the ♂, blunt on the ♀.

Soc. B.: Territorial, peaceful, it will not damage plants. The fish are timid and easily frightened. Pairs form nuclear families.

M: Needs a tank with dense vegetation

and hardy plants such as *Sagittaria, Vallisneria* and *Cryptocorynes*. Create places to hide among rocks, roots and bog-wood. Needs a few flat rocks for spawning.

B: The species is more difficult to breed than most *Cichlasoma*. Recommend slightly acid, soft water, pH 6.5 and 5° dGH. Keep temperatures between 25-28° C. Open breeders, the ♀ spawns on leaves or flat rocks. After cleaning the site she drops 200-500 eggs. The fry are suspended (cf. SCHMETTKAMP 1979: DCG-Info. 10 (1): 10). Both parents carefully guard the brood.

F: C, O; such live foods as *Tubifex* worms, water fleas and mosquito larvae; dried food; supplements of lettuce or oatmeal are important.

S: One of the most common Cichlids in the central Amazon, the species is sensitive to chemicals and nitrates. They should not be kept with Neons as they are a preferred food and will be eaten. They are best combined with *Pterophyllum scalare*.

T: 73-77° F, L: 6″, A: 39″, R: m, b, D: 2-3.
23-25° C, 15 cm, 100 cm,

Melanochromis vermivorus

Mesonauta festiva

Nannacara anomala
Golden Dwarf Acara

REGAN, 1905

Syn.: *Acara punctulata, Nanacara taenia*

Hab.: Western Guyana. Captive-bred specimens now dominate the hobby.

Fl.: 1934, Fritz Mayer, Hamburg, West Germany.

Sex: Clear sexual dimorphism; the ♂ is larger and more brilliantly colored. The ♂ is up to 3-12″ (9 cm.) long; the ♀ is to 2″ (5 cm.).

Soc. B.: The fish pair during spawning and, excepting spawning, are tolerant. The ♂ should be removed after spawning; if not it will harass the ♀. In larger tanks the ♂ will take charge of a large territory, guarding it while the ♀ cares for the brood. The fish will not burrow.

M: Needs a well-planted tank with rocks and roots for hiding.

B: Suggest slightly acid, medium-hard water, pH 6.2-6.5, 10° dGH, at a temperature between 26-28° C. Shelter breeders, the ♀ lays 50-300 eggs in caves. The ♀ has a special spawning color.

F: C; all types of live foods exclusively. Rarely accepts flakes.

S: Experiments with dummy fish have proven that the mother's jerky manner of swimming is a message to her fry to follow.

T: 72-77° F, **L:** ♂ = 3¹/₂″, ♀ = 2″,   **A:** 23¹/₂″, **R:** b,   **D:** 2.
22-25° C,   ♂ = 9 cm, ♀ = 5 cm,   60 cm,

Nanochromis dimidiatus
Dimidiatus Cichlid

(PELLEGRIN, 1900)

Syn.: *Pelmatochromis dimidiatus*

Hab.: Africa; Ubanghi River, a tributary of the Zaire.

Fl.: 1952.

Sex: The ♂ is generally larger with a shiny silver scale over the anal orfice and a dark net pattern on the dorsal, anal and caudal fins. These are lacking on the ♀. The female is a more intense violet color and has a black patch along ²/₃rds of her dorsal.

Soc. B.: Territorial, relatively aggressive, the species is a burrower though it will not harm plants. Forms a nuclear family.

M: Needs a tank with rocky formations, hiding places and dense plantings around the edges. An over-turned pot makes a good spawning cave. The bottom should be of gravel.

B: Breeding has been successful only in soft water; slightly acid, pH 6.5 with a hardness 5-8° dGH. A temperature between 25-28° C is best. Occasional changes of freshwater are suggested. The ♀ spawns to 60 eggs in a cave and, after they are freeswimming, the fry are cared-for by both parents.

F: C, O; all types of live foods; FD; flakes.

S: The genital papilla appear only a few hours prior to spawning. The species can surprise you with rapid color changes.

T: 73-77° F, **L:** ♂ = 3″, ♀ = 2″,   **A:** 19¹/₂″, **R:** b, m, **D:** 3.
23-25° C,   ♂ = 8 cm, ♀ = 6 cm,   50 cm,

Nannacara anomala

Nanochromis dimidiatus

Nanochromis parilus

Syn.: *Nanochromis nudiceps*

Hab.: Zaire basin, particularly Stanley Pool. Captive-bred specimens are rare.

Fl.: 1952

Sex: The ♂ is generally larger with longer, pointed dorsal and anal fins; when ♀♀ are about to spawn their bodies are distended; the genital papilla of sexually mature ♀♀ is visible outside the spawning season.

Soc. B.: Territorial and generally tolerant though ♂♂ may bite each other. The fish burrow but do not disturb plants. They forms a patriarch/matriarch or nuclear family.

M: Needs a well-planted tank with many places to hide. Suggest a bottom of coarse gravel.

ROBERTS & STEWART, 1976

B: Slightly acid, soft, peaty water, pH 6.5 and 5-8° dGH, at a temperature between 25-28° C. A shelter breeder, the ♀ lays 80-120 eggs in a cave; never more than 250. ♀ cares for the brood while the ♂ defends the territory. The fry may be led by either parent as they leave the breeding cave.

F: C; all types of live foods.

S: The eggs are stemmed and the genus is closely related to *Pelvicachromis*. The name is the proper one for Cichlids long known as *N. nudiceps*, which is possibly a color morph of *N. parilus*.

T: 72-77° F, L: ♂ = 3″, ♀ = 2³/₄″,   A: 19¹/₂″,   R: b,   D: 2-3.
 22-25° C,   ♂ = 8 cm, ♀ = 7 cm,   50 cm,

Ophthalmotilapia ventralis

Syn.: *Paratilapia ventralis, Ophthalmochromis ventralis*

Hab.: Endemic to the transitional zone between the sandy bottom and rocky shore in Lake Tanganyika; found where small patches of sand can be seen between larger blocks of rock. Wild-caught specimens have been regularly available for half a decade.

Fl.: Possibly 1958.

Sex: Clear sexual dimorphism; ♂ is larger with brighter coloring and longer pelvic fins; his dorsal and anal fins are also pointed. ♀ is grey.

Soc. B.: Territorial only during spawning when they are intolerant of their species and all tank mates; otherwise they live in a loose-knit community; they often burrow while spawning. They form a matriarchal family: keep one ♂ with several ♀♀.

(BOULENGER, 1898)

M: Needs a tank with a sandy bottom and a taller arrangement of rocks near the back glass with an open swimming area in front.

B: Recommend moderately alkaline, medium-hard water, pH over 7.5 and 10° dGH, at a temperature between 25-27° C. A mouth-brooder, the ♀ lays to 60 eggs which are fertilized orally by a modified false-egg method. The yellow, thickened ends of the male's pelvic fins are used as false egg-lures instead of patches on the fins as with others. The fish spawn in shallow, sandy pits.

F: C, O; all types of live foods; algae.

S: There are two sub-species: *O. ventralis ventralis* (BOULENGER, 1898) and *O. ventralis heterodontus* (POLL & MATTHES, 1962.) The sub-species differ in dentition.

T: 73-77° F, L: to 6″,   A: 35″,   R: m, b,   D: 2-3.
 23-25° C,   to 15 cm,   90 cm,

Nanochromis parilus ♂

Ophthalmotilapia ventralis

Papiliochromis ramirezi
Butterfly Cichlid, Ram

(MYERS & HARRY, 1948)

Syn.: *Apistogramma ramirezi, Microgeophagus ramirezi*

Hab.: Western Venezuela; Columbia. Bred frequently in captivity and so inbred small size and weaker colors often result. Wild caught fishes have been imported in recent years.

Fl.: 1948

Sex: Sexes can be readily distinguished. ♀ is smaller, has a shortened second ray on the dorsal, and a reddish stomach; just prior to spawning a short ovipositor can also be seen. The dorsal fin on ♂ is much longer.

Soc. B: A very tolerant family, apt to form pairs but without a clear-cut division of roles.

M: Likes a tank with several densely-planted groups, areas for hiding and open spaces for swimming. When changing water add a good conditioner.

B: Suggest soft water to 10° dGH (optimum 3° dGH) and pH about 7.0. Add peat occasionally. The fish breed clutches of 150-200 eggs on stones or in pits.

F: C, O; live food; FD; flakes; tablets.

S: Very sensitive to chemicals, changes of environment and piscine tuberculosis. Has a short life, 2-3 years. Tank-bred species often lose their fins.

T: 72-79° F, **L:** 3″, **A:** 19¹/₂″, **R:** m, b, **D:** 3.
22-26° C, 7 cm, 50 cm,

Anomalochromis thomasi
African Butterfly Cichlid

(BOULENGER, 1915)

Syn.: *Paratilapia thomasi, Hemichromis thomasi, Pelmatochromis thomasi*

Hab.: Africa; Sierra Leone; southeast Guinea; western Liberia. Wild-caught fish are common; captive-bred specimens are rare.

Fl.: 1966

Sex: It is difficult to distinguish between the sexes. Adult ♀ generally have more intense black markings and more rounded-bodies, especially when ready to spawn.

Soc. B.: A peaceful species which form pairs and are territorial. They do not burrow and form tight family groups. Both parents will guard the eggs and fry.

M: Needs a heavily-planted tank with hiding places of rocks, roots and upturned pots. They use flat stones for spawning and enjoy open swimming areas. Recommended for a community tank.

B: Needs soft, slightly acid water 7-9° dGH and pH 6.5 at a temperature between 26-27° C. After a site is cleaned they spawn in the open on flat stones or plants depositing up to 500 eggs. The fry are kept in shallows on the bottom or paraded around the tank, guarded by both parents. The parents will only eat the eggs or larvae if the tank is too small.

F: C, O; live food; occasional vegetable supplement; FD; flakes.

S: Thanks to the work to GREENWOOD (1985): Bull. Br. Mus. Nat. Hist. (Zool.) **49**, 257-272, the genus of this fish has finally been established. GREENWOOD has created the mono-typical genus *Anomalochromis* for it.

T: 73-81° F, **L:** ♂ = 4″, ♀ = 2³/₄″, **A:** 27″, **R:** b, **D:** 1.
23-27° C, ♂ = 10 cm, ♀ = 7 cm, 70 cm,

Papiliochromis ramirezi

Anomalochromis thomasi

Pelvicachromis pulcher
Purple Cichlid, Kribensis

(BOULENGER, 1901)

Syn.: *Pelmatochromis pulcher*

Hab.: Africa; found in brackish water in southern Nigeria. Specimens seen are nearly all captive-bred. In the last decade wild-caught fish have been imported only occasionally.

Fl.: 1913, Christian Bruening, Hamburg, West Germany.

Sex: ♂ is larger with pointed anal fins and extended central rays on the caudal fins; ♀ has rounded anal fins and is brightly colored.

Soc. B.: Forms pairs and close-knit family groups, is relatively peaceful and tolerant and is territorial. Likes to burrow but does not touch plants.

M: Likes a heavily-planted tank with such hiding places as rocks, caves, roots and rocks. Needs an open area for swimming.

B: Needs medium-hard, slightly acid water, 8-12° dGH and pH 6.5 at a temperature between 26-27° C. Generally spawns 200-300 eggs on the roof of a cave, over-turned pot or similar shelter. ♀ guards the eggs and fry while ♂ defends the territory. When schooling both parents lead.

F: C, O; flakes; such live food as *Daphnia*, *Cyclops* and mosquito larvae.

S: In a school of younger fish the ♂ s become territorial first. The ♀ are more active in courtship. The fry should be left with the parents, if possible, until the adults are ready to spawn again. If the fry are removed too soon the adult male, willing to spawn while the female is not, becomes aggressive.

T: 75-77° F,   **L:** 3-4″,   **A:** 23¹/₂″,   **R:** b,   **D:** 1.
24-25° C,   8-10 cm,   60 cm,

Pelvicachromis subocellatus
Eye-spot Cichlid

(GUENTHER, 1871)

Syn.: *Hemichromis subocellatus, Pelmatochromis subocellatus*

Hab.: A wide range of western Africa extending into the brackish water of some estuaries; from Gaboon to the mouth of the Congo river in Zaire.

Fl.: 1907, W. Schroot, Hamburg, West Germany.

Sex: ♂ has pointed dorsal and anal fins and longer pelvic fins; ♀ is more active in courtship, has rounded dorsal and anal fins and, before spawning, is the brighter colored.

Soc. B.: Territorial, the fishes form pairs and close-knit families; they are peaceful toward tankmates though they may become aggressive at spawning time. A burrower, the fish will not bother plants.

M: The best tank is 9 to 20″ tall (20 to 50 cm) decorated with caves of rock, roots and over-turned pots. Needs open swim-

ming areas and a bottom of fine gravel. Recommended for a community tank.

B: Try the water values suggested for *Pelvicachromis pulcher* at temperatures between 25-28° C. The tank should be well aerated and salt may be helpful for newly-imported fishes (1 teaspoon to one to 5 quarts [1-5 liters]). The fish deposits 60-200 eggs in caves and the young are kept in depressions on the bottom. The ♀ guards the fry while her male protects the territory. Schools of younger fishes are led by both parents.

F: C, O; mostly live foods; will also accept FD, frozen foods and flakes.

S: The eggs hang from fine threads. According to THUMM the fish makes croaking noises at night.

T: 72-79° F,   **L:** 4″,   **A:** 31″,   **R:** b,   **D:** 2.
22-26° C,   10 cm,   80 cm,

Pelvicachromis pulcher

Pelvicachromis subocellatus

Pelvicachromis taeniatus
Striped Dwarf Cichlid

(BOULENGER, 1901)

Syn.: *Pelmatochromis taeniatus, P. klugei, P. kribensis, P. kribensis klugei*

Hab.: In rivers and brackish waters of Africa; southern Nigeria; Cameroons. Rarely available and then generally via individual wild-caught catches.

Fl.: 1911, Christian Bruening, Hamburg, West Germany.

Sex: ♂ is larger with an angular caudal fin and longer anal and dorsal fins; ♀ is more brilliantly colored with a rounded caudal fin.

Soc. B.: A peaceful species that pairs, forms close-knit families and is territorial. Burrows but will not bother plants. May be aggressive during the spawning season.

M: Likes a heavily-planted tank with cave-like hiding places among roots, rocks and over-turned pots. Needs an open area for swimming and a bottom of fine gravel.

B: Suggest soft to medium hard and slightly acid water (5-10° dGH and pH 6.2-6.8) at a temperature between 25-28° C. Needs good aeration and a cave-like shelter to breed in. Will lay a clutch of 40-150 eggs which are guarded by the ♀. ♂ protects the territory and both parents lead the fry as they leave the breeding cave.

F: C, O; flakes; all types of live foods.

S: The young are often difficult to raise since they are sensitive to infusoria. ♀ is the majority sex in a brood. The fish will be of varying colors depending on their origin. LINKE provides some excellent color photos in Tl 43.

T: 72-77° F, **L**: ♂ = 4″, ♀ = 2³/₄″, **A**: 23¹/₂″, **R**: b, **D**: 1.
22-25° C, ♂ = 9 cm, ♀ = 7 cm, 60 cm,

Petrotilapia tridentiger

TREWAVAS, 1935

Syn.: None

Hab.: Africa; endemic to the rocky regions of Lake Malawi.

Fl.: Unknown.

Sex: There is marked sexual dimorphism and dichromatism in the species. Stylized egg designs are seen more strongly on the anal fin of ♂.

Soc. B.: The species is very territorial, has a matriarchal society and is intolerant toward tankmates whether of its species or others. May bite. Will not burrow.

M: Likes a bottom of fine gravel and some sand with rock structures and caves for hiding. Suggest a well lighted tank with algae.

B: We recommend medium-hard, moderately alkaline water, 10-15° dGH and pH 8.5 rich in oxygen and at a temperature of 26-27° C. A mouth breeder, the ♀ lays as many as 35 eggs which are fertilized by the "egg dummy" method. ♀ will guard the brood for a short time.

F: L, O; all types of live foods; algae; well cooked lettuce.

S: The genus *Petrotilapia* is monotypic, i.e. it includes only the species *P. tridentiger*. It belongs to the Mbuna Cichlids and, at 10″ (25 cm) is their largest representative. It is found in several breeds differing according to color and geographical area.

T: 75-79° F, **L**: 10″, **A**: 39″, **R**: m, b, **D**: 3.
24-26° C, 25 cm, 100 cm,

Pelvicachromis taeniatus

Petrotilapia tridentiger

Pseudocrenilabrus multicolor
Dwarf Egyptian Mouth-Brooder

(SCHOELLER, 1903)

Syn.: *Paratilapia multicolor, Haplochromis multicolor, Hemihaplochromis multicolor*

Hab.: Northeast Africa from the lower Nile to Uganda and Tanzania; today virtually only tank-bred specimens for sale.

Fl.: 1902 by Dr. C. H. Schoeller.

Sex: The ♂ wears courtship dress during the spawning period, the ♀ being much paler. No red patches on the ♀'s anal fin.

Soc. B.: Pair-forming, (at least during the spawning season); often intolerant, matriarchal family.

M: Well planted up tank with opportunities for concealment, open swimming space, fine sandy bottom.

B: 25–26° C; water medium-hard (12° dGH) and neutral (pH value around 7). Mouth-brooder, ♀ laying eggs in spawning pit which she takes into her mouth after they have been fertlized by the ♂. The fry hatch after approx. 10 days; 30–90 eggs laid.

F: C, O; live food of all kinds, F/D food, flake food, tablets.

S: ♀ offers the fry shelter in her mouth for a week or so in case of danger and at night. The young retreat to the mother's gaping mouth on being given a very specific signal. The ♂ has no true egg dummies on its anal fin. The ♂ should be removed from the tank after spawning as the ♀ is otherwise harassed.

T: 68-75° F, **L:** 3″, **A:** 16″, **R:** b, m, **D:** 2.
    20-24° C,   8 cm,   40 cm,

Pseudocrenilabrus philander dispersus
Dwarf Copper Mouth-Brooder

(TREWAVAS, 1936)

Syn.: *Haplochromis philander dispersus, Hemihaplochromis philander dispersus, Tilapia philander*

Hab.: Africa, South Africa, Namibia, Zambia, Mozambique, Zimbabwe, Angola and Southern Zaire. Tank-bred specimens and feral catches, the species only occasionally being offered for sale.

Fl.: 1911 by Vereinigte Zierfischzuechtereien of Conradshoehe near Berlin. Reintroduced in 1969 under the name "*Haplochromis kirawira*".

Sex: Clear sexual dichromatism, the ♂ being much more finely colored, the ♀ appearing plain; the ♂ has a bright red patch on his anal fin and a golden sheen along his body.

Soc. B.: Territorial; the fishes are very aggressive and pugnacious; they burrow strongly during the spawning period; they are agamous; matriarchal family.

M: Hard plants which are best placed in pots, a few large stones, rocky caves or flower pots as hiding places, bottom of fine sand, open swimming space.

B: 24–27° C; water values as for *Pseudocrenilabrus multicolor*; mouth-brooder, the eggs being laid in pits dug out of the ♂, the ♀ taking them into her mouth when they are fertilized; up to 100 eggs laid; ♀ offers the fry protection by taking them back into her mouth in case of danger and at night.

F: C, O; live food of all kinds, F/D food, flake food.

S: This fish occurs in several morphs distinguished as to size, coloring and origin – a large morph from Beira (Mozambique), up to 11 cm (4¹/₄″); small morph from Beira, up to 8 cm (3″); small morph from Lake Otjikoto (Namibia), up to 8 cm (3″).

T: 68-76° F, **L:** 4¹/₄″, **A:** 23¹/₂″, **R:** b, **D:** 2-3.
    20-24° C,   11 cm,   60 cm,

Pseudocrenilabrus multicolor

Pseudocrenilabrus philander dispersus

Pseudotropheus aurora

BURGESS, 1976

Syn.: *Pseudotropheus lucerna*

Hab.: Africa, lake Malawi, shores of the Likoma Islands (endemic). The habitat of this fish is the transitional zone between Sandy and rocky Shore.

Fl.: 1964 (?) as *Pseudotropheus lucerna*.

Sex: Clear sexual dimorphism and dichromatism. The ♂ far more finely colored and with eye-catching egg dummies on the anal fin.

Soc. B.: Territorial; the fishes are intolerant and rough towards their own kind and other species. ♂s are agamous, keep several ♀s for each ♂. Mouth-brooder, matriarchal family.

M: As for *Pseudotropheus tropheops*. Water values: hardness 12-30° dGH, pH 7.5-8.5.

B: 26-28° C, water values as indicated above. At least 3 ♀s for each ♂; mouth-brooder, the ♀ taking the eggs into her mouth immediately they are laid. 40-70 eggs, fertilized by the "egg dummy" method. The eggs take about 18-21 days to hatch. The fry

when swimming freely can easily be fed on Small Food (*Artemia* nauplii).

F: C, O; makes no great demands as to food. Live food, finely chopped beef hearts, Flake Food (large).

S: *Pseudotropheus aurora* was long confused with *Pseudotropheus lucerna* TREWAVAS, 1935. *P. aurora* differs from all other *Pseudotropheus* species by its large eyes. The "eye-diameter to head-lenth" ratio is 2.6–3.2x and is the smallest so far encountered in Cichlids.

♀

T: 75-79° F, L: 4¹/₄″, A: 46¹/₂″, R: m, b, D: 1-2.
    24-26° C,   11 cm,   120 cm,

Pseudotropheus elongatus

FRYER, 1956

Syn.: None

Hab.: Africa, Lake Malawi (endemic), in the Rocky Zone. Feral catches, tank-bred specimens occasionally available for sale.

Fl.: 1964

Sex: Sexual dimorphism and dichromatism between ♂ and ♀; egg patches on the ♂'s anal fin generally more intensely coloured; the ♂ is usually larger than the ♀.

Soc. B.: Territorial; is one of the most aggressive members of the genus and is intolerant towards its own kind and other fishes; ♂ polygamous, on account of its aggressiveness keep as many ♀s as possible with one ♂ (not less than 5 ♀s); matriarchal family.

M: Stony structures with plenty of caves required, otherwise hardy plants only to delimit territories.

B: 26–27° C; water medium-hard to hard (10–18° dGH) and moderately alkaline (pH value 8.5); mouth-brooder, the ♀ taking the eggs into her mouth. Up to 37 but usually 20 eggs laid and fertilized by the "egg-dummy" method. The fry are looked after for two days after they have left the mouth at the most; they then remain within the mother's territory and so still enjoy indirect protection.

F: L, O; live food of all kinds, Vegetable Supplement (algae, boiled lettuce, spinach).

S: The species occurs in various colour morphs. *Pseudotropheus elongatus* is one of the Mbuna Cichlids.

T: 72-77° F, L: 5¹/₂″,   A: 39″,   R: b,   D: 2-3.
    22-25° C,   13 cm,   100 cm,

Pseudotropheus aurora ♂

Pseudotropheus elongatus

Pseudotropheus fainzilberi

STAECK, 1976

Syn.: None

Hab.: Africa, Lake Malawi (endemic), NE Coast close to the township of Makonde.

Fl.: 1976 by Dr. Wolfgang Staeck of Berlin, West Germany.

Sex: Clear sexual dimorphism and dichromatism, the ♂ being much more intensely and finely colored, the egg patches on his anal fin being particularly marked.

Soc. B.: ♂ territorial and very intolerant towards its own kind and other species. The fishes are very lively; the ♂ polygamous, always keep several ♀s for one ♂; mouth-brooder, matriarchal family.

M: As for *Pseudotropheus zebra*.

B: See *P. zebra*

F: C, O; live food, algae; flake food, F/D food.

S: *Pseudotropheus fainzilberi* differs from all other *Pseudotropheus* species by its tooth pattern, having 5-7 rows of teeth, i.e. one or two additional rows on each jaw. A special feature is that the bicuspid teeth are not limited to the outer rows of teeth. It is most closely related to *Pseudotropheus zebra*.

T: 72-79° F,   L: 5¹/₂″,   A: 31″,   R: b, m,   D: 2.
   22-26° C,   13 cm,   80 cm,

Pseudotropheus lanisticola

BURGESS, 1976

Syn.: None

Hab.: Africa, Lake Malawi (endemic). The fishes live over Sandy Bottoms.

Fl.: 1964 (?)

Sex: Clear sexual dimorphism and dichromatism; ♂ with clearly visible egg-dummies on his anal fin.

Soc. B.: As for *Pseudotropheus macro-phthalmus*, which see for details.

M: Background with stony structures offering plenty of hiding places; a 5–7 cm layer of fine sand in the foreground. Leave room for swimming. Hardy species planted around the edges; a few larger, empty snail shells. Water moderately alkaline (pH 8-8.5) and medium-hard to hard (12–20° dGH).

B: As for *Pseudotropheus zebra*.

F: O; omnivorous; live food of all kinds, plants (lettuce, spinach, algae) F/D and frozen food, flake food and tablets.

S: *Pseudotropheus lanisticola* is one of the smallest Cichlids from Lake Malawi. They use the large empty houses of snails of the genus *Lanistes* as hiding places. *P. lanisticola* differs from *Pseudotropheus livingstonii*, which occupies the same ecological niche, by the divergent shape of its teeth and its goldenyellow anal fin.

T: 73-77° F,   L: 2¹/₂″,   A: 27″,   R: m, b,   D: 2.
   23-25° C,   7 cm,   70 cm,

Pseudotropheus fainzilberi

Pseudotropheus lanisticola

Pseudotropheus macrophthalmus

AHL, 1927

Syn.: None

Hab.: Africa, lake Malawi (endemic), along the Rocky Shore. Wild-caught imports regularly available for sale.

Fl.: 1964

Sex: Clear sexual dimorphism and dichromatism; ♂ with intensely marked egg-dummies on his anal fin.

Soc. B.: Territorial; ♂ agamous, 1 ♂ to several ♀s; the species appears to be one of the most peaceable of Mbuna Cichlids as most ♂'s show little aggression towards their own kind or other species; matriarchal family.

M: Rocky structures with plenty of nooks and crannies as hideaways. Bottom of gravel or sand.

B: 25–28° C; water medium-hard (12–18° dGH) and moderately alkaline (pH around 8.5); one ♂ to at least 3–4 ♀s; mouthbrooder, the ♀ taking the eggs into her mouth; 40–70 eggs laid and fertilized by the "egg-dummy" method; the ♀ continues to look after the fry for several days after they have left her mouth.

F: L, O; live food, F/D and frozen food, vegetable supplement (algae, boiled lettuce and spinach), flake food, Tetra Tips.

S: FRYER doubts the individual classification of *Pseudotropheus macrophthalmus* and the closely related species *Pseudotropheus microstoma* TREWAVAS, 1935. He regards both *P. macrophthalmus* and *P. microstoma* as subspecies of *Pseudotropheus tropheops* REGAN, 1921.

T: 73-77° F,   **L:** 6″,   **A:** 39″,   **R:** m, b,   **D:** 2.
    23-25° C,   15 cm,   100 cm,

Pseudotropheus tropheops
Golden Tropheops

REGAN, 1921

Syn.: None

Hab.: Along the rock shoreline of Lake Malawi. Both wild-caught and captive-bred fishes are available.

Fl.: 1964

Sex: There are signs of pronounced sexual dimorphism and dichromatism in the species. ♂ is larger and has stylized egg symbols on its anal fin.

Soc. B.: An aggressive, territorial species, ♂ does not pair but spawns with several ♀ and is aggressive toward its own species and others. The family is matriarchal.

M: Needs a tank that simulates Lake Malawi – with stony and rocky outcroppings, hiding places and a few plants to create territorial boundries.

B: Suggest medium to hard and slightly alkaline water, 10-20° dGH and pH 8.0-8.5. Place one ♂ with at least three or four ♀♀. A mouth breeder, the fish lay to 40 eggs which the ♀ shelters in her mouth. The eggs are fertilized by the "egg dummy" method and the female guards the fry for a short time.

F: C, O; all types of live foods; algae; lettuce, spinach; beef heart; flakes.

S: The species is polymorphous and its versatility extends not only to color variations but to anatomical and morphological differences as well. There are two sub-species: *Ps. tropheops tropheops* REGAN, 1921 and *Ps. tropheops gracilior* TREWAVAS, 1935. These are now regarded only as morphs of the polyvalent species above.

T: 75-79° F,   **L:** to 8″,   **A:** 39″,   **R:** m, b,   **D:** 2-3.
    24-26° C,   to 20 cm,   100 cm,

Pseudotropheus macrophthalmus

Pseudotropheus tropheops

Pseudotropheus zebra
Nyassa Blue Cichlid, Zebra Cichlid

(BOULENGER, 1899)

Syn.: *Tilapia zebra*

Hab.: Along the rocky shoreline of Lake Malawi. Adequate supplies of captive-bred fishes are now available.

Fl.: 1964

Sex: Shows marked signs of sexual dimorphism and dichromatism. ♂ has well-developed stylized egg replicas on the anal fin. These are weaker or missing on the ♀.

Soc. B.: The species is territorial, aggressive toward their own and other species, matriarchal and very lively. ♂ is polygamous and needs several ♀ in the tank. The ♀♀ often swim in groups.

M: The tank should be at least 31″ long (80 cm.) to house one ♂ and several females. Needs pyramids of rocks with nooks for hiding and you should add hardy plants to help define territories.

B: Needs medium hard to hard, moderately alkaline to alkaline water (10-18° dGH and pH 8.0-9.0) at a temperature between 25 and 28° C. Lays up to 60 eggs which the female protects in her mouth. Fertilization is by the "egg-dummy" method. The mother watches over the brood for 8 days after they leave her mouth.

F: L, O; flakes; all types of live food; algae; lettuce; spinach; even duckweed.

S: The species is found in a number of color morphs and belongs to the Mbuna Cichlids. It is often called the "Red Zebra" in the hobby, but is not a separate species. The fishes were introduced in 1974 as "Dwarf Zebras" or *Microchromis zebroides* by JOHNSON.

T: 72-82° F,   **L:** 5¹/₂″,   **A:** 31″,   **R:** m, b,   **D:** 1-2.
22-28° C,   12 cm,   80 cm,

Pseudotropheus spec. aff. zebra
The Orange-blue Mouth-breeder is frequently regarded as a variety
of *P. zebra* but is an undescribed, independent species. The ♂♂ are
generally blue and the ♀♀, orange to red. Checkered morphs are
also known. Another species is called the "Bright Blue."

Pseudotropheus spec. ♂

Pseudotropheus spec. ♀

Pterophyllum altum

Pterophyllum altum
Deep Angelfish - Altum Angel

PELLEGRIN, 1903

Syn.: None

Hab.: South America; The Orinoco and its tributaries. It is available only as a wild-caught fish and is rare.

Fl.: 1950, "Aquarium Hamburg", Hamburg, West Germany. Reintroduced in 1972 by Heiko Bleher at Aquarium Rio, Frankfurt, West Germany.

Sex: Aside from the spawning season there are no discernible identifying features. The ♀ is often fatter during the spawning season. According to MEIER-BOEKE the ♀ have a thicker dorsal line.

Soc. B.: A territorial, peaceful species with close-knit family groups.

M: Arrange the tank as you would for *Pterophyllum scalare*.

B: Tank breeding is possible though not recorded. Use soft, acid water, 1-5° dGH and pH 5.8-6.2 at temperatures between 30 and 31° C. Raise according to suggestions for *P. scalare*. The cross *P. altum* x *P. scalare* has produced fish resistent to fin rot and with especially tall, pointed fins. The parents should be conditioned with live food and TetraRuby.

F: Live foods; lettuce; spinach; oatmeal; flakes.

S: The species differs from *P. scalare* by its steeply rising head, dorsal line and a dipping saddle across the nose. Do not place in a tank with Neon Tetras since these will be eaten. The species is sensitive to *Ichthyosporidium* and should be kept at higher water temperatures to prevent it.

T: 82-86° F, **L:** 7¹/₂", **A:** 31", **R:** m, **D:** 3.
28-30° C, 18 cm, 80 cm,

Pterophyllum scalare, golden morph.

Pterophyllum scalare

Marbled Angelfish

Pterophyllum scalare
Angelfish

(LICHTENSTEIN, 1823)

Syn.: *Platax scalaris, Zeus scalaris, Ptero-phyllum eimekei*

Hab.: Central Amazon and tributaries to Peru and eastern Ecuador. The species is found in company with *Mesonauta festivus*. Currently, only captive-bred fish are offered in the hobby. Some may display such symptoms of inbreeding as stunted growth, pale colors and poor parenting.

Fl.: 1909, C. Siggelkow, Hamburg, West Germany.

Sex: There are no external differences distinguishable except in the breeding season; positive identification can be made by the shape of the genital papillae; on the ♂ it is pointed, on the ♀ it is rounded.

Soc. B.: Territorial, the fish school when young then form pairs. They are peaceful, do not burrow and are faithful to their mates. They form nuclear families.

M: Needs a well-planted tank with hardy

plants around the edges. Suggest *Sagitta-ria* and *Vallisneria*. Add rocks and roots and leave an open area for swimming.

B: Pairs can be selected from a school of younger fishes. Follow recommendations for *Mesonauta festivus* with temperatures between 26-28° C. Open breeders, the ♀ spawns on previously-cleaned plant leaves, laying as many as 1,000 eggs. The larvae and fry are carefully guarded. Schools of fry are lead by their parents.

F: C, O; all types of live foods; supplement with lettuce and spinach; FD; flakes.

S: Feed mosquito larvae, only in careful amounts since the fish will readily over-eat. Over-eating may kill them. The fish need to be kept warm.
There are many artificial morphs. The males may emit a loud, grating sound with their jaws while courting.

T: 75-82° F,   **L:** 6″,   **A:** 31″,   **R:** m,   **D:** 2.
    24-28° C,   15 cm,   80 cm,

Veiltail Angelfish

Half-Black Angelfish

Oreochromis mossambicus
Mozambique Mouth-Breeder

(PETERS, 1852)

Syn.: *Chromis mossambicus, C. dumerili, Tilapia dumerili, T. mossambica, T. natalensis, Sarotherodon mossambicus*

Hab.: In running, standing and brackish waters of east Africa. The species is not often kept and is rare in the trade. Because it is large, it is suited only for a display tank.

Fl.: 1925, A. Dietz, Hamburg, West Germany.

Sex: During spawning clear sexual dichromatism is seen; the ♂ is brightly colored, the ♀ is a monotone grey-green.

Soc. B.: Territorial only during the spawning season, it remains an aggressive, schooling species intolerant towards its species but peaceful with others. The fish burrows, especially when spawning, and is plant-eater. ♂ is agamous, forming a matriarchal family.

M: Needs a bottom of deep sand with large stones bedded on the bottom. Do not add plants.

B: The species can tolerate a range of water conditions but temperatures should be kept between 24-26° C. ♂ digs a pit in which up to 300 eggs are placed. ♀ carefully guards them and cares for the fry after they are free-swimming. They retreat to the mother's mouth at night in times of danger.

F: Such hardy live foods as mosquito larvae, dragonfly larvae, earth and *Tubifex* worms; algae; lettuce; spinach; oatmeal; beef heart; flakes.

S: The species is an important food fish at home. Sexually mature ♂♂ form colonies. As many as eight, each 5″ (10 cm) long, may dig their spawning pits close together.

T: 68-75° F, **L**: 4-15¹/₂″, **A**: 39″, **R**: m, **D**: 3-4.
20-24° C, 10-40 cm, 100 cm,

Steatocranus casuarius
African Blockhead

POLL, 1939

Syn.: *Steatocranus elongatus*

Hab.: In the quieter areas of rapid-flowing water in lower and central Zaire. Captive-bred fish are most common in the hobby.

Fl.: 1956

Sex: ♂ has a pronounced fatty lump on his forehead; ♀ is smaller with a less conspicuous lump.

Soc. B.: The fish often pair for life, going without a partner if one of the pair dies; they are intolerant and pugnacious, particularly during spawning; wild-caught ♂♂ are impressive for their size and unusual cranial decoration.

M: Needs a tank with rocky formations with many hiding places; an over-turned pot makes a good spawning cave. Use only hardy plants individually potted.

B: Recommend neutral to slightly acid, medium-hard water, pH 6.5-7.0 and 15-17° dGH, at a temperature between 26-29° C. A cave breeder, the brood is carefully watched. The female generally lays between 20 and 60 eggs, never more than 150. Forms a patriarchal/matriarchal family.

F: O; omnivorous; live foods; FD; tablets; flakes.

S: The fry are fed by the mother. Their swim bladder is smaller to adjust to life in the highly-oxygenated waters of the rapids in which they are found. The fish do not hover, but move foward in jerks.

T: 75-82° F, **L**: ♂ = 4¹/₂″, ♀ = 3″, **A**: 23¹/₂″, **R**: b, **D**: 2.
24-28° C, ♂ = 11 cm, ♀ = 8 cm, 60 cm,

Oreochromis mossambicus

Steatocranus casuarius

Symphysodon aequifasciatus aequifasciatus
Green Discus

PELLEGRIN, 1903

Syn.: None

Hab.: Amazon, near Santarem and Tefé. Fishes sold in the hobby are generally wild-caught.

Fl.: 1921

Sex: It is difficult to distinguish the sexes outside the spawning season; during the breeding season the shape of the genital papillae is the best identification; it is pointed on ♂ and round on the ♀.

Soc. B.: Territorial only during spawning; otherwise the fish are a schooling species. They are peaceful, do not burrow and form a nuclear family.

M: See recommendations for *S. discus.*

B: Recommend slightly acid, soft water, pH about 6.5 and 2-3° dGH at temperatures

between 28-31° C. Water changes are important, one quarter of the tank should be changed every three weeks. Open breeders, ♀ spawns on carefully-cleaned rocks and leaves; she lays several hundred eggs. After the fry are free-swimming they feed on a secretion produced on the parent's skin. Both parents care-for and guard the fry.

F: C; such live foods as mosquito larvae, waterfleas, water insects, brine shrimp and *Tubifex* worms.

S: There are two sub-species: *S. a. axelrodi* SCHULTZ, 1960, the Brown Discus, and *S. a. haraldi*, the Blue Discus. The fish differ only in color.

T: 79-86° F,　**L:** to 6″,　　**A:** 39″,　**R:** m, b,　**D:** 4.
　26-30° C,　　to 15 cm,　100 cm,

Symphysodon aequifasciatus axelrodi

Symphysodon aequifasciatus haraldi ,,Royal Blue''

Symphysodon discus
Discus, Heckel Discus

HECKEL, 1840

Syn.: None

Hab.: South America: only in the quiet, heavily-planted waters of the Rio Negro. Though wild-caught fishes are available, captive bred supplies are both adequate and common.

Fl.: 1921, W. Eimeke, Hamburg, West Germany.

Sex: It is often difficult to distinguish the sexes; certain identification comes only during spawning from the shape of the genital papillae; ♂ organ is pointed, ♀ is rounded and blunt.

Soc. B.: Territorial only during spawning, otherwise a peaceful, schooling species. It does not burrow; forms a nuclear family.

M: Needs a tank as large and tall as possible, not less than 40 or 50 inches long (100-120 cm) and 20 inches (50 cm) tall. The species prefers a lightly-planted aquarium with a soft bottom and a few rooted plants. Add a couple of larger rocks

which will not affect the water and provide an open area for swimming. The lighting should be subdued. Water temperatures should range between 26-28° C; in winter 23° is better. The fish need heat and prefer the middle and lower stratas of water.

B: Prefers slightly acid, soft water, pH 6.0-6.5, 1-3° dGH, at a temperature between 28-31° C. Regular water changes are important. An open breeder, the female spawns on rocks and plants, laying several hundred eggs. Both parents care for the fry and after the first few days they feed on a secretion produced on the parent's skin. The species is more difficult to breed than *S. aequifasciatus.*

F: C; all types of live foods; flakes are rarely accepted. Young Discus will accept TetraTips (FD tablets) after acclimatization.

S: The unusual secretion comes from special cells on the parent's back and may include a single-celled algae and protozoa.

The fish can be crossed with *S. discus willischwartzi*. All Discus probably belong to a single species (cf. ALLGAYER & TETON (1981); Aquarama **15** (57): 17-21, 58-59; (57): 21-24). The sub-species above was described by BURGESS in 1981.

T: 79-86° F,   L: 8″,   A: 39″,   R: m, b,   D: 4.
    26-30° C,   20 cm,   100 cm,

Symphysodon aequifasciatus haraldi with young

Fam.: Cichlidae

Teleogramma brichardi

POLL, 1959

Syn.: None

Hab.: In rapids in the lower reaches of the Zaire river between Kinshasa and Matadi. Fish available in the hobby are all wild-caught.

Fl.: 1957

Sex: ♀ has a broad, white edge to the dorsal and upper portion of the caudal fin. The edging is narrower on the ♀ who has a broad red band during spawning. At that time it begins at the rear of the pectorals and extends to the anal fin.

Soc. B.: Territorial and intolerant towards its species, the fish claim large territories. They form patriarch/matriarch families, and neither burrow nor harm plants.

M: Needs a long, roomy tank since the fish claim large territories. Height is not important: 10 inches is sufficient. Add rocky formations with plenty of hiding places. Plants can be used to help define territories.

B: Suggest slightly acid, medium-hard water, pH 6.5, 7-10° dGH, at a temperature between 23-25° C. A cave breeder, the ♀ drives the ♂ away once the eggs have been laid and fertilized. She lays 10-30 eggs and guards her brood in the cave. ♂ guards the territory. Once the fry are free-swimming neither parent cares much about the fry and they quickly become aggressive towards each other, fighting for territories.

F: C, O; such live foods as mosquito larvae and *Tubifex* worms; flakes; tablets.

S: Their rounded, long body shows how well the fish are adjusted to life in the rapids. Pelvic fins are close to the chest, the eyes near the top of head. There is no visible swim bladder. The lateral line continues undivided to the caudal fin.

T: 68-73° F, **L:** ♂ = 4^1/$_2$″, ♀ = 3^1/$_2$″, **A:** 31″, **R:** b, **D:** 2-3.
20-23° C, ♂ = 12 cm, ♀ = 9 cm, 80 cm,

Telmatochromis bifrenatus
Two Banded Cichlid

MYERS, 1936

Syn.: None

Hab.: Endemic to the rocky shoreline of Lake Tanganyika near Kigoma.

Fl.: Possibly 1972.

Sex: ♂♂ are larger, with longer fins, especially the pelvic fin. ♀♀ are fuller-bodied.

Soc. B.: Territorial, the fish are peaceful and normally pair for life. ♂ may occasionally have two ♀♀, A shelter breeder, they form a patriarch/matriarch family.

M: Needs a tank with rocky formations with caves and other room for hiding. Plants are not required. The water should be moderately alkaline, medium-hard, pH around 9 and hardness 10-15° dGH.

B: An over-turned pot makes a good spawning cave. The ♀ will lay her small, yellow-to-orange eggs there after a vigorous courtship. They hatch in 10 days and the fry are free-swimming eight days later. ♂ guards the territory and the ♀ is less interested in her fry once they are free-swimming. Try a water temperature between 26-28° C.

F: C, O; live food; flakes; tablets; FD; frozen food.

S: Barely reaching two inches (6 cm.) this is one of the smallest Cichlids known.

T: 75-79° F, **L:** 2″, **A:** 23^1/$_2$″, **R:** b, **D:** 2-3.
24-26° C, 6 cm, 60 cm,

Teleogramma brichardi ♀

Telmatochromis bifrenatus

Telmatochromis caninus
Caninus Cichlid

POLL, 1942

Syn.: *Lamprologus dhonti*

Hab.: Endemic to the shorelines of Lake Tanganyika.

Fl.: Possibly 1958.

Sex: ♂♂ are larger, have a highly-arched forehead and longer pelvic fins.

Soc. B.: Territorial, often aggressive towards ♂♂ of its own and other species, it is particularly intolerant of others when caring for its brood. A cave breeder, it forms a patriarch/matriarch family.

M: See recommendations for *T. bifrenatus*. Suggest moderately alkaline, medium-hard water, pH 8.5-9.0 and 10-15° dGH.

B: Follow water values above at a temperature between 26-28° C. Inverted pots make excellent spawning caves. Use one ♂ and several ♀♀. As many as 500 eggs may be laid and these hatch in four to seven days. The ♀ guards the eggs and fry but abandons them once they become free-swimming.

F: C, O; the fish prefer live foods but will accept FD and flakes.

S: This is the largest species in the genus. The photo shows a ♂.

T: 75-79° F,	L: 4¹/₂″,	A: 35″,	R: b,	D: 2-3.
24-26° C,	12 cm,	90 cm,		

Telmatochromis vittatus

BOULENGER, 1898

Syn.: None

Hab.: Endemic to Lake Tanganyika near Mbity Rocks.

Fl.: 1973

Sex: The ♂♂ are larger and slender-bodied.

Soc. B.: Territorial and not as peaceful as some in the genus, it pairs for life. A cave breeder, the species forms a patriarch/matriarch family.

M: Follow recommendations for *T. bifrenatus*. Needs moderately alkaline, moderately-hard water, pH 8.5-9.0 and 10-20° dGH.

B: See recommendations for *T. bifrenatus*.

F: Live food; frozen food; flakes.

S: A steeply-rising, curved forehead is a distinguishing feature of the species.

T: 75-79° F,	L: 1³/₄″,	A: 35″,	R: m, b,	D: 2-3.
24-26° C,	4 cm,	90 cm,		

Telmatochromis caninus

Telmatochromis vittatus

Tilapia mariae

BOULENGER, 1899

Syn.: *Tilapia dubia, T. mariae dubia, T. meeki*

Hab.: In basin areas of the Niger along the African Ivory Coast as far as the Cameroons. Wild-caught fishes are available now; captive-bred specimens are rare.

Fl.: 1962

Sex: There is some sexual dimorphism; the dorsal and caudal fins of the ♂ are longer, decorated with shimmering white spots; the spots are missing on the female. The ♂ is larger with a steeper rise to his forhead.

Soc. B.: Territorial, often intolerant and pugnacious toward its species, the fish is a burrower, particularly during spawning. Pairs form a patriarch/matriarch family.

M: Needs a tank with a bottom of fine sand and a few flat stones; since the species eats plants, do not use them.

B: Suggest neutral to slightly acid, soft to medium-hard water, pH 6.5-7.0, 6-10° dGH, at a temperature between 25-27° C. An open breeder, the species is conside-

red transitional since the ♂ prepares a spawning site by digging shelter beneath a rock. Up to 2,000 eggs are laid and transferred to the pit on the second day. Both parents carefully guard the site and, after hatching, the fry.

F: L, O; herbivore; algae; aquatic plants; lettuce, spinach; oatmeal. Will also accept live and dried foods.

S: The intestines of wild-caught fishes contain $^1/_5$th to $^1/_4$th sand which is used in digestion. It helps grind the food.

T. mariae, juv.

T: 68-77° F,	L: to 12$^1/_2$",	A: 78",	R: b,	D: 3-4.
20-25° C,	to 35 cm,	200 cm,		

Tilapia zillii
Zilli's Cichlid

(GERVAIS, 1848)

Syn.: *Acerina zillii, Chromis andreae, C. busumanus, C. tristrami, C. zillii, Glyphisodon zillii, Haligenes tristrami, Coptodon zillii, Tilapia tristrami, T. menzalensis*

Hab.: Throughout northern Africa (i.e. above the equator); in the Jordan river and tributaries, Jordan; Syria; Lake Tiberias. The species will enter brackish water. The fish is rare in the hobby and those few available are wild-caught.

Fl.: 1903, Dr. Schoeller, Alexandria, Egypt.

Sex: It is difficult to distinguish between the sexes. ♀♀ are generally paler in color with two white spots at the base of the dorsal. The ♂ has a "peacock" eye patch on the first rays of his broad dorsal. The most certain identification comes from the shape of the genital papillae which is pointed on the ♂ and rounded on the ♀.

Soc. B.: Territorial and pugnacious, the species is a burrower and plant eater. It forms a nuclear family.

M: Needs a tank with a bottom of deep sand, large rocks and no plants.

B: The species can accept a range of water values but temperatures should be kept between 25-28° C. An open breeder, the female drops 1,000 eggs on a cleaned rock. When hatched they are carefully tended by both parents.

F: O; hardy live foods; vegetable supplements are essential – *Elodea*, pondweed, algea and lettuce are examples; rarely accepts flakes.

S: The fish is a jumper; the tank must be covered.

T: 68-74° F,	L: 6-12",	A: 39",	R: b,	D: 4 (Si).
20-24° C,	15-30 cm,	100 cm,		

Tilapia mariae ♂

Tilapia zillii

Aulonocara jacobfreibergi

(JOHNSON, 1974)

Syn.: *"Trematocranus trevori"*, *Tremato-cranus jacobfreibergi*

Hab.: Endemic to caves along the rocky shores of Lake Malawi.

Fl.: 1973

Sex: Clearly marked sexual dimorphism and dichromatism; the ♂ is larger with longer pelvic fins and pointed dorsal and anal fins; ♀♀ have a red stripe on the dorsal.

Soc. B.: The fish live in groups as large as 100. Each includes only one fully-colored ♂. They are mouth-brooders and form a matriarchal family.

M: See suggestions for *Aulonocara nyassae*. Recommend moderately alkaline, medium-hard water, pH 7.5-8.2, 10-20° dGH. See page 682.

B: Use water values above at temperatures between 25-27° C. The ♀ is a mouth-brooder, taking the eggs into her mouth as they are laid. They are orally fertilized – even though the ♂♂ have no egg-shaped markings on their fins. The fry are easy to raise.

F: C; live food: insects, insect larvae, small crustaceans, *Tubifex*; dried food, FD food, beef hearts.

S: Most species in the genus can be identified by tiny wrinkles around the head. These are sensory pits forming a part of the lateral line. They are also found in *Aulonocara*. This species recently had been placed into the genus *Aulonocara*.

T: 74-79° F, **L:** 6″, **A:** 31″, **R:** m+b, **D:** 2.
    24-26° C, 15 cm, 80 cm,

Triglachromis otostigma

(REGAN, 1920)

Syn.: *Limnochromis otostigma*

Hab.: Endemic to Lake Tanganyika, in a muddy and sandy bottom at depths of 20-60 m.

Fl.: Possibly 1973.

Sex: Unknown.

Soc. B.: A relatively peaceful and territorial species, they do not defend their space as rigorously as some Cichlids. Interestingly, they make a threatening display by opening their giant mouths as wide as possible.

M: Needs a tank with rocky formations (or lava) laid against the back glass. They should reach to the surface and include many hiding places. Allow a sandy area in front for swimming. Use moderately alkaline, medium-hard water, pH 8.5-9.0, 10-15° dGH. Make regular water changes, at least $^1/_3$rd every three weeks.

B: Rarely successful in an aquarium. The fish are mouth-brooders but little is known about the species.

F: C, O; such live foods as *Gammarus*, mosquito larvae and maggots; beef heart; flakes.

S: The generic name was adopted by THYS van den AUDENAERDE. There appear to be parallels between this species and the marine dwelling Fam.: Triglidae, especially in the pectoral fins and some aspects of behaviour.

T: 74-79° F, **L:** 4$^1/_2$″, **A:** 31″, **R:** b, m, **D:** 2.
    24-26° C, 12 cm, 80 cm,

Aulonocara jacobfreibergi

Triglachromis otostigma

Tropheus duboisi
White-Spotted Cichlid

MARLIER, 1959

Syn.: None

Hab.: Endemic to Lake Tanganyika; above a rocky bottom at depths between 3 an 15 meters. Captive-bred and wild-caught fishes are readily available.

Fl.: 1958

Sex: It is difficult to distinguish between the sexes; though there are no major differences in color, the ♂ is larger and has longer pelvic fins; adult ♀♀ have white patches on their backs.

Soc. B.: Territorial, peaceful toward other species, they are sometimes aggressive toward each other; unlike *T. moorii*, it does not school but prefers to swim alone or in pairs. Forms a matriarchal family.

M: See recommendations for *T. moorii*.

B: Recommend moderately alkaline, medium-hard to hard water, pH 8.5-9.0, 10-12° dGH, at a temperature between 26-27° C. A mouthbrooder, ♀ drops 5-15 eggs in openings in the rocks and then takes the eggs into her mouth. The fry are carefully cared for a week after they are free-swimming.

T: 74-79° F, **L:** 4¹/₂″, **A:** 31″, **R:** m, b, **D:** 3.
24-26° C, 12 cm, 80 cm,

F: L, O; all types of live foods. The fish is a highly specialized feeder, preffering micro-life. Feed only small amounts of *Tubifex* worms. They must have such vegetable supplements as algae, lettuce, spinach and oatmeal.

S: The species is closely related to *T. moorii* but is found at a greater depth implying a different ecological niche. It has different social behaviour as well. The fry sport many blue-grey spots on a blue-black background. (See small photo.)

T. duboisi juv.

Tropheus moorii

BOULENGER, 1898

Syn.: *T. annectens*

Hab.: Endemic to the rocky shores of Lake Tanganyika. Captive bred and wild-caught specimens are commonly available.

Fl.: 1958, Walter Griem.

Sex: It is difficult to distinguish between the sexes since, as mouth-brooders, they display no sexual dimorphism; ♀♀ may be more brightly colored and smaller; the pelvic fin on ♂ is longer. The fish do not have false-egg patterns on the anal fin.

Soc. B.: Territorial, the fish are often intolerant toward others of their species though not toward other tank mates. The sexes often live together in groups. They tend to form nuclear families, but not the prolonged pairs often associated with openbreeders.

M: Needs a tank with rocky formations and hiding places; use strong overhead lighting to encourage algae. Leave open space for swimming.

B: Suggest neutral to alkaline, medium-hard water, pH 7.0-9.0, 10-15° dGH, at a temperature between 27-28° C. The fish are mouth-brooders and spawn freely, laying 5-17 eggs in the open water. These are taken into the female's mouth before they reach bottom but even so, ♀ goes through a careful spawning ritual, cleaning a rock and digging a pit. The mother cares for the fry for a week or more after they are free-swimming.

F: O; all types of live foods; algae and other vegetable supplements are important – cooked lettuce, spinach and oatmeal are examples. Try Tetra Conditioning food.

S: The species is found in a range of color morphs including fish with yellow stomachs, striped tails, rainbow markings, crossstripes, bright yellows, blacks and reds. All are typical of geographical differences.

T: 74-79° F, **L:** 6″, **A:** 39″, **R:** m, b, **D:** 4.
24-26° C, 15 cm, 100 cm,

Tropheus duboisi ♂

Tropheus moorii

Fam.: Cichlidae

Tropheus polli

G. AXELROD, 1977

Syn.: None

Hab.: Endemic to Lake Tanganyika, found exclusively along the southern coast, near the Bulu Islands and at Bulu Point in the Kigoma district. Found above a rocky bottom.

Fl.: 1976

Sex: It is difficult to distinguish between the sexes; ♂ has a noticeable forked tail.

Soc. B.: Territorial, intolerant and aggressive toward each other, the fish are peaceful toward other tank mates. Their behaviour is still the subject of study.

M: See recommendations for *T. moorii*.

B: See suggestions for *T. moorii* and *T. duboisi* with water temperatures between 26-28° C.

F: O; all types of live foods; such vegetable supplements as algae, lettuce, spinach and oatmeal.

S: The species is easily distinguished from others of the genus by its deeply-forked caudal fin.

T: 74-79° F, **L:** 6″, **A:** 47″, **R:** m, b, **D:** 3-4.
24-26° C, 16 cm, 120 cm,

Uaru amphiacanthoides
Waroo, Triangle Cichlid

HECKEL, 1840

Syn.: *Acara amphiacanthoides, Pomotis fasciatus, Uaru imperialis, U. obscurus*

Hab.: Amazon and Guyana. Captive-bred specimens are rare; wildcaught fishes are available occasionally.

Fl.: 1913, C. Siggelkow, Hamburg, West Germany.

Sex: The one certain feature is the shape of the genital papillae; it is pointed on the ♂ and blunt on the ♀.

Soc. B.: A schooling species, the fish are peaceful and pair only during spawning season. At that time ♂♂ are intolerant; forms a nuclear family.

M: Needs a tank with a gravelly bottom and rocks with caves and hiding places; lighting should be subdued so the tank will need a few hardy plants rather than a lot. Use peat filtration and soft water, pH 5.8-7.5.

B: Excluding *Symphysodon* sp. this is one of the most demanding of Cichlids and breeding is difficult. During the first days of their lives, the fry – like discus – feed on a secretion exuded from the skin of their parents. Breeding without parents is almost impossible. Recommend moderately acid, soft water, pH 6.0 and hardness 2-5° dGH at a temperature between 27-30° C. The addition of peat is suggested. An open breeder, ♀ prefers spawning in darker places on rocks or plants, dropping 300 eggs. The fry are very delicate at first and should be fed copious amounts of micro-food.

F: C; all types of live foods.

S: The species is closely related to *Cichlasoma psittacus* but differs in its teeth and coloring. A fully grown specimen develops a heavy cushion of fat about the neck. In its native waters it can be found with *Pterophyllum* and *Symphysodon*.

T: 79-82° F, **L:** to 12″, **A:** 47″, **R:** m, b, **D:** 3-4.
26-28° C, to 30 cm, 120 cm,

Tropheus polli

Uaru amphiacanthoides

Group 9

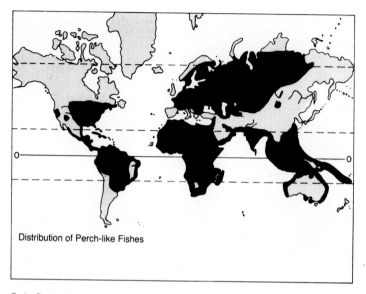

Distribution of Perch-like Fishes

Sub-Order Percoidei (Perches)

In our book Perches have been separated from the various True Bony Fishes to emphasize their relationship. Cichlids, Group 8, and Labyrinth Fishes, Group 7, should properly be listed here, but this has been omitted to provide a better insight for hobbyists.

Fam. Badidae (Badis)

The family is a new one, established only recently and includes a single genus with one species, *Badis badis*. The genus differs from Nandus by its remarkably small mouth and unusually colorful markings. There are also differences in the morphometrical values and in behaviour. The fish has no labyrinth organ. Together, these differences justify a separate classification.

Fam. Centrarchidae (Sunfishes)

Most Sunfishes have an egg-shaped form with flat sides though some are elongated. The dorsal and anal fins are long, composed of a hard-rayed section in the front and a soft-rayed section behind. Younger fishes are usually more brilliantly colored and may pale with age. All species in the genus care for their broods, the male being primarily concerned with the eggs. Thus the family is patriarchal though in certain species, as the genus *Micropterus*, the brood is cared for by both parents, that is, forming a nuclear family.

Scatophagus argus, adult, s. page 810.

Fam. Chandidae (Glassfishes)

True to their name, the fish in this genus have transparent bodies. The backbone and swim bladder are easily seen and the dorsal fin is divided. The scales are predominantly cycloid though those of a few species are odontoid. The lateral line extends to the caudal fin and most species are found in salt or brackish water.

Fam.: Lobotidae (Flashers)

There are few species in the genus and most live in the brackish waters of larger estuaries. They also enter fresh water and are found mostly in south-east Asia. Their bodies are tall and flat, covered with ctenoid scales and the lateral line curves upward. Their dorsal fins include a hard-rayed segment in front and a soft-rayed portion behind. Their jaws are toothed while the vomar and palatine are toothless.

Fam. Monodactylidae (Fingerfishes)

Included are fish with disc-shaped bodies. The head and mouth are small, the dorsal and anal fins are similar in shape and both are continuous. The initial spikes of the dorsal fin are small and often erect. The bodies are covered with small ctenoid scales. The fish generally school and live in brackish water in Africa, southern Asia and Australia. They can periodically be found in fresh water as well.

Fam. Nandidae (Nandus)

The Nandus is found in South America and Africa as well as in south-east Asia. They are generally small fish with a large head and mouth. The spiny rays of the dorsal are well developed. The mouth will usually open wide and the body is covered with ctenoid scales. The lateral line may be incomplete or missing. All Nandus are predaceous and apart from one species, all form matriarchal families, caring carefully for their brood.

Fam. Percidae (True Perches)

The family can usually be identified by two broad, often divided dorsal fins. The front one consists of spiny rays, the back one of soft rays. The pelvic fins project from the stomach and the head is large. The mouth, too, is large and the genus has two nostrils on each side. Their scales are ctenoid and the lateral line is normally incomplete.

Fam. Scatophagidae (Argusfishes)

Argusfish are a coastal genus found in southeast Asia and Australia, in both sea and brackish water. They may enter fresh water occasionally. Their bodies are disc-shaped with flat sides. Their heads, bodies and the soft-rayed section of the dorsal and anal fins are covered with small ctenoid scales. The lateral line is incomplete and the anal fin is preceded by four spines. The fry may pass through a larval or "Tholichthys" stage.

Fam. Toxotidae (Archerfishes)

Archerfishes are found in the brackish coastal waters of Asia and northern Australia. They can be distinguished by their straight lateral line, pointed heads, large eyes and wide mouths as well as by dorsal and anal fins which begin well back towards the tail. The genus has acquired its popular name from its ability to down insects by accurately expectorating drops of water above the surface. Luminous, reflective patches of irridescent yellow are found on their bodies and the fishes signal each other with these. In some cases the patches may disappear with age. The family includes five species, all surface dwellers.

Badis badis
Badis

(HAMILTON, 1822)

Syn.: *Labrus badis, Badis buchanani.*

Hab.: In standing water in India.

Fl.: 1904, H. Stueve, Hamburg, West Germany.

Sex: ♂ is more brilliantly colored with a concave ventral line. The ventral line on the ♀ is convex.

Soc. B.: A peaceful fish in the wild, it may become territorial in a species tank though not in a community aquarium. They form a patriarchal family.

M: Prefers a densely-planted tank with a sandy bottom. Add an inverted pot for hiding and spawning. The species can accept a range of water values however, a periodical change of water is recommended.

B: Breeding is easiest in a small aquarium. Suggest a water temperature of 26-30° C with an inverted pot or other place to hide. When spawning ♂ embraces the ♀ and 30-100 eggs are laid, generally in a cave. ♂ guards them and the fry hatch in three days. They are cared for until the egg sac is consumed. The parents should be removed when the fry are free-swimming. Feed the fry with small live food.

F: All types of live foods; also finely-cut or grated meats including liver.

S: There are two Sub-species, *B. b. badis,* described, and *B. b. burmanicus* AHL, 1936, a reddish-brown morph. The latter is found in Burma. This species is susceptible to fish tuberculosis.

T: 73-79° F,   L: 3″,   A: 27″,   R: m, b,   D: 4 (C).
23-26° C,   8 cm,   70 cm,

Centrarchus macropterus
Flier, Round Sunfish, Peacock Sunfish

(LACEPEDE, 1802)

Syn.: *Labrus macropterus, L. irideus, Centrarchus irideus, C. sparoides*

Hab.: Eastern US from Illinois to North Carolina to Florida; limited on the west by the Mississippi river.

Fl.: 1906, Otto Preusse, Fischzuchtanstalt Thalmuehle, Frankfurt/Oder, Germany.

Sex: The anal fin of the ♂ is edged in black and the swim bladder can be distinguished when the fish is held against the light. On a ♂ it is pointed in the rear and rounded on the ♀. An eyepatch associated with the species disappears on the ♂ at spawning season and becomes more obvious on the ♀. The female's anal fin is edged in white.

Soc. B.: Generally tolerant and playful, though only with their own species. They ignore tank mates.

M: Prefers a tank with a bottom of fine sand. Add such plants as *Cabomba, Myriophyllum* and *Egeria* along the edges. Leave space in front for swimming. Needs hiding places among rocks and roots.

B: Water should not be more than 6 inches (15 cm.) deep, medium hard to hard, from 10° dGH, at temperatures between 20-22° C. Prior to spawning the male digs a pit and initiates a shadow courtship. About 200 eggs are laid and placed in the pit. The ♀ should be removed after spawning; the ♂ will care for the brood.

F: C, O; all types of live foods; tablets; flakes; FD.

S: Once acclimated to their tank the fish will recognize their keeper. They are very sensitive to changing water conditions and fluctuations in pH and can be subject to a body fungus which is generally terminal.

T: 54-72° F,   L: 6″,   A: 23¹/₂″,   R: m to b,   D: 2.
  12-22° C,   16 cm,   60 cm,

Chaenobryttus gulosus
Warmouth

(CUVIER & VALENCIENNES, 1829)

Syn.: *Pomotis gulosus, Centrarchus viridis, Calliurus floridensis, C. melanops, C. punctulatus, Chaenobryttus antistius, Ch. coronarius, Lepomis charybdis, L. gillii*

Hab.: Eastern U.S. from the Great Lakes to the Carolinas and Texas. They are found as far west as Iowa and Kansas.

Fl.: 1896

Sex: ♂ is more brightly colored and slender-bodied, particularly during spawning.

Soc. B.: Similar to *Lepomis* species though it does not school.

M: See suggestions for *Lepomis gibbosus.*

B: See *L. gibbosus.*

F: C, O; all types of live foods; flakes; frozen food; FD.

S: The species differs from *Lepomis* sp. in that there are many tiny teeth on its tongue. These are lacking on *Lepomis.*

T: 50-68° F,	L: 8″,	A: 31″,	R: b, m,	D: 2.
10-20° C,	20 cm,	80 cm,		

Elassoma evergladei
Everglades Pigmy Sunfish, Florida Pigmy Sunfish

JORDAN, 1884

Syn.: None

Hab.: U.S.; from North Carolina to Florida.

Fl.: 1925, Arthur Rachow, Hamburg, West Germany.

Sex: The male's fins blacken as spawning approaches while the ♀♀ are colorless.

Soc. B.: A peaceful, often timid fish, it is territorial and should be combined only with small cold water fishes.

M: The fish should be kept in a species tank with a fine sandy bottom, heavily planted with cold-water plants. Add several rocks to limit territories and leave lots of open swimming space. Algae is an advantage. The fish do best in "old" water, neutral to slightly alkaline and medium-hard, pH 7.0-7.5, about 10° dGH.

B: Breeding is possible in a species tank if temperatures are kept between 15-25° C. The mating ritual, which takes place among the plants, is beautiful to watch. ♀ lays 40-60 eggs which hatch in 2-3 days. The parents can remain; they will not harm their fry. Feed the fry fine micro-food.

F: C, O; all types of live foods including *Daphnia, Cyclops,* brine shrimp and *Tubifex* worms. They will also accept algae and flakes.

S: To help the fish breed, winter them in a cool tank at 8-12° C. The species is resistent to temperature fluctuations. They move strangely across the bottom, appearing to walk on their pectoral fins.

T: 50-86° F,	L: 1″,	A: 15¹/₂″,	R: b, m,	D: 2.
10-30° C,	3.5 cm,	40 cm,		

Chaenobryttus gulosus

Elassoma evergladei

Enneacanthus chaetodon
Black-banded Sunfish
(BAIRD, 1854)

Syn.: *Pomotis chaetodon. Bryttus chaetodon, Apomotis chaetodon, Mesogonistus chaetodon*

Hab.: In lakes and slow-moving waters along the eastern U.S. seaboard; New York; New Jersey; Maryland.

Fl.: 1897, W. Geyer, Regensburg, West Germany.

Sex: It is difficult to distinguish between the sexes; ♀♀ are generally heavier-bodied and more brightly colored. With practice you can also distinguish sexes by their behaviour.

Soc. B.: A peaceful, friendly fish which forms a patriarchal family and carefully cares for their fry. They should not be combined with restless tank mates.

M: Needs a tank with a bottom of fine sand planted along the edges with such plants as *Egeria* and *Myriophyllum*. Needs open room for swimming. Suggest neutral,

medium-hard to hard water, pH 7.0, 10-20° dGH. The fish need lot of oxygen and the tank should be well aerated.

B: Follow water values above at temperatures between 15-25° C. ♂ will dig a spawning pit in the shade of plants and defend it against all comers. Spawning is preceded by a loveplay ritual and the eggs, which are sticky, are laid in the pit. The ♀ should then be removed since the ♂ will guard the nest. ♂ can be removed once the fry are free-swimming.

F: C; all types of live foods such as *Tubifex* worms, mosquito larvae, *Cyclops, Daphnia* and brine shrimp.

S: The fish are sensitive to temperature fluctuations, water changes and chemicals. If the water quality drops, they suffer. The fry grow very fast and are colored after just six weeks.

T: 39-72° F,   L: 4", sexually mature from 2",   A: 31",   R: m, b,   D: 3.
4-22° C,   10 cm, sexually mature from 5 cm,   80 cm,

Enneacanthus gloriosus
Blue-spotted Sunfish
(HOLBROCK, 1855)

Syn.: *Bryttus gloriosus, Enneacanthus margarotis, E. pinniger, Hemioplites simulans*

Hab.: Eastern U.S. seaboard; from New York to Florida.

Fl.: Unknown; possibly early 1900's.

Sex: It is difficult to distinguish between the sexes; mature ♂♂ are higher-backed with longer fins.

Soc. B.: A schooling fish except during spawning. The ♂♂ choose territories then and defend them against all comers. Forms a patriarchal family.

M: See recommendations for *E. obesus.*

B: See recommendations for *E. obesus.*

F: See recommendations for *E. obesus.*

S: Unlike *E. obesus,* this species has a small black patch on its gill cover. Like *E. obesus,* it loses its cross-banding as it ages.

T: 50-72° F,   L: 3",   A: 27",   R: m, b,   D: 2.
10-22° C,   8 cm,   70 cm,

Enneacanthus chaetodon

Enneacanthus gloriosus

795

Enneacanthus obesus
Diamond Sunfish, Little Sunfish

(GIRARD, 1854)

Syn.: *Pomotis obesus, Apomotis obesus, Bryttus fasciatus, B. obesus, Copelandia eriarcha, Enneacanthus eriarchus, E. margarotis, E. pinniger, E. simulans, E. guttatus, Hemioplites simulans, Pomotis guttatus*

Hab.: Eastern U.S. seabord; from New England to Florida.

Fl.: 1895

Sex: It is difficult to identify the sexes except during spawning. Then, ♂ is more brightly colored with luminous spots. The soft-rayed part of his dorsal and anal fins is taller. The swim bladder, visible when the fish are held to the light, is pointed in the rear of the ♂ and rounded in the ♀.

Soc. B.: A timid, schooling species, the ♂♂'s choose territories. Forms a patriarchal family.

M: Needs a bottom of coarse sand or fine gravel with dense vegetation. Use such plants as *Eleodea, Myriophyllum* and *Cabomba*. The fish need hiding places among rocks and roots.

Suggest a neutral to slightly alkaline, medium-hard water, pH 7.0-7.5 and around 10° dGH.

B: Follow water values above with temperatures between 18-22° C. Reduce the water level to 6" (15 cm) while breeding is in progress. Pairs chosen for breeding should be wintered in cooler water. Spawning is preceeded by a vigorous ritual. The ♂ constructs a pit near plants and the ♀ will lay to 500 eggs. ♂ will create a current which forces the eggs toward the plants where they adhere. He watches over the eggs and the fry as long as they have their egg sacs.

F: C, O; primarily a variety of live foods; flakes and oatmeal are also accepted.

S: The fish are sensitive to fluctuations in pH and one must be careful when making water changes. When transferred from acid to slightly alkaline water (pH 7.5 or higher), even healthy fish become susceptible to fungus and may die. The fish often dig themselves into the bottom so that only their eyes show.

T: 50-72° F,	L: 4",	A: 27",	R: m, b,	D: 2.
10-22° C,	10 cm,	70 cm,		

Lepomis cyanellus
Green Sunfish

RAFINESQUE, 1819

Syn.: *Apomotis cyanellus, Bryttus longulus, B. melanops, B. mineopas, B. murinus, B. signifer, Calliurus diaphanus, C. melanops, Icthelis cyanella, I. melanops, Chaenobryttus cyanellus, Lepidomus cyanellus, Lepomis lirus, L. melanops, L. microps, L. mineopas, L. murinus, Pomotis longulus, P. pallidus, Telipomis cyanellus*

Hab.: North America; east of the Rockies, from Canada to Mexico.

Fl.: 1906, H. Stueve, Hamburg, West Germany.

Sex: It is difficult to distinguish between the sexes; ♀♀ are generally fatter as spawning approaches.

Soc. B.: See recommendations for *L. gibbosus.*

M: See recommendations for *L. gibbosus.*

B: See recommendations for *L. gibbosus.* Suggest a water temperature between 20-22° C.

F: C, O; live food; flakes; FD; frozen foods.

S: Needs more heat than others of the genus. Though the fish can be wintered at 10-12° C, the temperature should not fall below 4° C.

T: 64-72° F (cold water fish),	L: 8",	A: 39",	R: m, b,	D: 2.
18-22° C,	20 cm,	100 cm,		

Enneacanthus obesus

Lepomis cyanellus

Lepomis gibbosus
Pumpkinseed, Kiver

(LINNAEUS, 1758)

Syn.: *Perca gibbosa, Eupomotis aureus, E. gibbosus, Pomotis gibbosus, P. ravenelli, P. vulgaris, Sparus aureus*

Hab.: U.S.; from New England west to the Great Lakes and south to Florida and Texas. Since the turn of the century the species has been established in many places in Europe, particularly Germany.

Fl.: 1877, M. Beck, Paris, France.

Sex: It is difficult to determine the sexes; ♂ are more brightly colored while ♀♀ are generally fuller-bodied. A typical red "ear" patch, a rounded projection on the rear of the gill cover, is less brilliant on the ♀.

Soc. B.: A normally peaceful species, they become territorial during spawning and may become intolerant. They do best with other gentle surface fishes, forming a patriarchal family.

M: Needs a tank with a bottom of fine gravel, planted with finely leaved plants which have been potted. The species prefers lots of open swimming room. Good aeration is important and should be used to create a current as well. Recommend neutral to slightly alkaline, medium-hard water, pH 7.0-7.5 and 10-15° dGH.

B: Recommend medium-hard water never below 10° dGH at a temperature between 18-20° C. ♂ will dig a nesting pit nearly one-foot in diameter with his tail, defending it against all comers. Spawning is preceded by a courtship ritual and the ♀ will lay as many as 1,000 eggs in several spawnings. ♀ should be removed otherwise ♂ will kill her. ♂ carefully cares for the brood.

F: C; all types of live foods; FD; flakes.

S: If the fish winter in too-warm water they will be difficult to breed. Winter temperatures should be around 12° C though the fish can tolerate water to freezing. In some areas it can be kept in a garden pond.

T: 39-72° F, **L:** 8″, **A:** 31″, **R:** m, b, **D:** 1-2.
    4-22° C,   20 cm,   80 cm,

Lepomis macrochirus
Bluegill

RAFINESQUE, 1819

Syn.: *Eupomotis macrochirus, Lepomotis nephelus*

Hab.: U.S.; a rare species found in the Ohio valley south as far as Arkansas and Kentucky.

Fl.: Unknown; possibly after 1975.

Sex: Difficult to determine.

Soc. B.: Similar to *L. gibbosus.*

M: See recommendations for *L. gibbosus.*

B: Little is known about breeding the species in an aquarium.

F: C; all types of live foods such as mosquito larvae, small crustaceans, *Tubifex* and earthworms and insects. The species rarely accepts flakes.

S: Its name comes from its luminous, steely-blue color.

T: 39-72° F (cold water fish), **L:** 5″, **A:** 27″, **R:** m, b, **D:** 2.
    4-22° C,   13 cm,   70 cm,

Lepomis gibbosus

Lepomis macrochirus

Chanda ranga

Syn.: *Ambassis lala, A. ranga, Chanda lala, Pseudambassis lala*

Hab.: In fresh and brackish water in India; Burma; Thailand.

Fl.: 1905, Paul Matte, Lankwitz.

Sex: ♀♀ are a paler yellow with a swim bladder rounded in the front. ♂♂ have a blue edge to their dorsal and anal fins. Their swim bladder is pointed at the rear.

Soc. B.: A peaceful, schooling fish, they are timid and easily frightened. Keep them with gentle tank mates. They are territorial.

M: Prefers a heavily-planted tank with a dark bottom of lavalit or basalt chips. Needs hiding places among rocks and roots. Old water is best and the tank should be placed where it can catch some sun. The addition of one or two spoons of salt for each $2^1/_2$ gallons of water (10 l) improves the health of the fish.

B: Breeding is easy. Water temperatures between 24-28° C are best since pairs are induced to spawn by an increase in temperature as well as by the addition of fresh water and increased morning sunlight. 150 eggs are laid between the plants and adhere to the stalks. They hatch in 24 hours and fry are free-swimming the following day. They are difficult to raise.

F: All types of live foods. They will accept flakes but cannot subsist on this alone.

S: Their eggs are small and susceptible to fungus. Trypaflavine should be added in a concentration of 1:100,000 (i.e. 1 g to 25 gallons water [1 g to 100 l])

T: 68-86° F, **L**: 3″, **A**: 27″, **R**: m, **D**: 3.
  20-30° C,   8 cm,   70 cm,

Chanda wolffii

Syn.: *Ambassis wolffii, Acanthoperca wolffii*

Hab.: Thailand; Sumatra; Borneo.

Fl.: 1955

Sex: Unknown.

Soc. B.: A peaceful, schooling species, it is territorial. It may be combined with other peaceful fishes.

M: See recommendatons for *C. ranga*.

B: Not yet successful in an aquarium.

F: C; all types of live foods. The species cannot survive on flakes, and will need supplementation.

S: In an aquarium the fish will not reach a length greater than $2^1/_2$″ (7 cm). Well adjusted fish have a reddish sheen around the mouth.

T: 64-77° F, **L**: 8″, **A**: 31″, **R**: m, **D**: 3-4.
  18-25° C,   20 cm,   80 cm,

Chanda ranga ♀

Chanda wolffii

Datnioides microlepis

Syn.: None

Hab.: In the brackish waters of Thailand; Cambodia; Borneo; Sumatra.

Fl.: Probably 1969.

Sex: Unknown.

Soc. B.: Tolerant of each other but defensive when attacked by other species.

M: Prefers a tank with lush vegetation. Use plants which can tolerate brackish water. Needs places to hide among rocks, roots and up-turned pots. The fish prefer shady places; use subdued lighting. Add 2-3 tablespoons of sea salt to each $2^1/_2$ gallons (10 l) of water.

B: Unknown.

F: C; predators, they prefer such live foods as fish and *Tubifex* worms; raw liver; meat. Rarely accepts flakes.

S: Differs from *D. quadrifasciatus* in several ways: they lack a black patch on the gill; the first body stripe reaches to the throat; the third body stripe, excluding an angled band which crosses the eye, ends at the center of the anal fin. In contrast *D. quadrifasciatus* has an eye patch, the first body stripe does not reach to the throat and the third body stripe ends before the anal fin.

T: 72-79° F, **L:** $15^1/_2$" in the wild, smaller in an aquarium, **A:** 35",   **R:** b,   **D:** 3-4.
  22-26° C,   40 cm,   90 cm,

Datnioides quadrifasciatus

Syn.: *Chaetodon quadrifasciatus, Datnioides polote*

Hab.: In brackish waters, rivers, estuaries and coastal lakes of Asia: from the Ganges in India to Burma; Thailand; Malayan Peninsula; Indo-Australian Archipelago.

Fl.: 1955

Sex: Unknown.

Soc. B.: Similar to *D. mīcrolepis.*

M: See suggestions for *D. microlepis.*

B: Not yet successful in an aquarium.

F: C; a greedy predator, it should be primarily fed fishes and other live foods; meat; liver.

S: Fry can be recognized by a black patch on the gill cover and by three stripes radiating from the eye.

T: 72-79° F, **L:** 12",   **A:** from 31",   **R:** b,   **D:** 3-4 (C).
  22-26° C,   30 cm,   from 80 cm,

Datnioides microlepis

Datnioides quadrifasciatus

Monodactylus argenteus
Fingerfish, Mono

(LINNAEUS, 1758)

Syn.: *Chaetodon argenteus, Acanthopodus argenteus, Centogaster rhombeus, Centropodus rhombeus, Monodactylus rhombeus, Psettus argenteus, P. rhombeus, Scomber rhombeus*

Hab.: In brackish and fresh water through out Africa; Asia; from the eastern coast of Africa to Indonesia. The fish will even venture into seawater briefly.

Fl.: 1908

Sex: Unknown.

Soc. B.: A peaceful, lively, schooling fish in captivity they are timid and easily frightened. They will eat smaller fishes.

M: Prefers a tank with a bottom of coral sand and salt water plants. Add rocks and roots resistant to salt water. The fish should be kept only in brackish water with plenty of aeration. Use a protein skimmer.

B: Not yet successful in an aquarium.

F: Omnivorous; all types of live foods; flakes; lettuce; spinach. The fish are very greedy.

S: The coloring, black and yellow, pales with age.

T: 75-82° F, **L:** 10″, **A:** 39″, **R:** all, **D:** 3-4.
    24-28° C, 25 cm, 100 cm,

Monocirrhus polyacanthus
South-American Leaf-Fish

HECKEL, 1840

Syn.: *Monocirrhus mimophyllus*

Hab.: In slow-moving streams and standing waters of the Peruvian Amazon.

Fl.: 1912, Vereinigte Zierfischzuechtereien and from Kuntschmann, Hamburg, West Germany.

Sex: Little is known; ♀♀ are often larger-bodied.

Soc. B.: A predator, it should be combined only with larger tank mates.

M: Needs a heavily-planted tank with roots to hide behind. Once acclimated do not add new elements to a tank. The fish will become nervous.

B: Recommend slightly acid, soft water, pH 6.0-6.5, hardness 2-4° dGH at a temperature between 25-28° C. Add plants with large leaves, rocks and/or plates of glass. These will be cleaned prior to spawning.

The ritual itself is simple and the ♀ will deposit to 300 eggs on the chosen surface. A patriarchal family, the ♂ will guard the larvae and ♀ should be removed. The eggs hatch in four days at a temperature of 25° C.

F: C; these are greedy predators; fry will consume their weight in food daily. Feed such live foods as fishes and mosquito larvae.

S: Leaf fishes can be seen floating diagonally among the plants, their heads down. With their brownish coloring they resemble dead leaves and thus camaflouged, they drift close to smaller, unsuspecting fishes. When in range, open their giant mouths. Often the prey is siphoned in by the vacuum.

T: 72-77° F, **L:** to 4",   **A:** from 31",
  22-25° C,   to 10 cm,   from 80 cm,

R: m,   **D:** 3-4.

Nandus nandus
Nandus

(HAMILTON, 1822)

Syn.: *Coius nandus, Bedula hamiltonii, Nandus marmoratus*

Hab.: In fresh and brackish waters of India; Burma; Thailand.

Fl.: 1904, H. Stueve, Hamburg, West Germany.

Sex: Identification is difficult; the ♂ has a darker coloring with larger fins.

Soc. B.: A predaceous nocturnal fish, they are generally loners. Do not keep with smaller tank mates.

M: Needs a tank with a gravel or sand bottom, densely planted on the sides and back with a cover of floating plants. Create hiding places among the roots and rocks. Likes a clear, hard water, over 10° dGH. Suggest the addition of 1-2 teaspoons of salt for each $2^1/_2$ gallons (10 l) water. Try subdued lighting.

B: Has been occasionally bred in a tank. RUCKS describes a successful attempt (DATZ 26, 158-160, 1973); neutral, soft to medium-hard water, pH about 7.0, 6-8° dGH at 25° C. RUCKS considers the addition of sea salt harmful. The fish spawn after a short courting ritual, scattering to 300 eggs across the bottom. The eggs are small, the size of a pinhead, and clear. They hatch in 48 hours. Fry should be fed small live food. The male does not care for the brood and neither parent attends to the eggs once they are laid.

F: C; such live foods as mosquito larvae, earthworms, dragonfly larvae, tadpoles and fishes.

S: The fish have a large, extendable mouth which allows them to swallow prey half as large as themselves. This is the only species in the genus which does not care for its brood.

T: 72-79° F, 22-26° C, **L:** 8″, 20 cm, **A:** 31″, 80 cm, **R:** m, b, **D:** 2-3.

Polycentrus schomburgki
Schomburgk's Leaf-Fish

MUELLER & TROSCHEL, 1848

Syn.: *Polycentrus tricolor*

Hab.: Guyana; Venezuela; Trinidad.

Fl.: 1907, Captain Vipan, England; 1909, G. P. Arnold, Germany.

Sex: The ♂ is darker colored, generally brown but becoming black while spawning; ♀ is brown but lighter-colored and heavier bodied during spawning.

Soc. B.: Loners, the fish spend much of their time hiding. Combine only with gentle tank mates of a similar size. Smaller tank mates will be eaten. Forms a patriarch family.

M: Needs a bottom of fine sand with plants along the back and sides; create hiding places with rocks, roots and over-turned pots. The fish are nocturnal and the aquarium should be dimly lit.

B: Suggest neutral to slightly acid, hard water, pH 6.0-7.0 and hardness 18-20° dGH at a temperature between 28-30° C. Predominantly cave breeders, the females will also deposit up to 600 eggs on the underside of leaves. When the spawning is over the ♀ is driven off and should be removed. The ♂ guards the eggs and the fry hatch in three days (at 27° C). They are free- swimming by the 7th or 8th day.

F: C; takes live food only (Fishes, Mosquito Larvae, *Tubifex, Daphnia* and chopped-up Earthworms). The species are greedy predators.

S: The fish may change color for no apparent reason.

T: 72-79° F, 22-26° C, **L:** 4″, 10 cm, **A:** $19^1/_2$″, 50 cm, **R:** m, **D:** 2.

Nandus nandus

Polycentrus schomburgki

Gymnocephalus cernua
Ruffe, Blacktail

(LINNAEUS, 1758)

Syn.: *Perca cernua, Acerina cernua, A. czekanowskii, A. fischeri, A. vulgaris*

Hab.: Europe and Asia; from England and northeastern France to tributaries of the White Sea and Kolyma, Siberia. It is not found in Ireland; Scotland; parts of Norway; the Pyrenees; Balkans - except for the Danube; Italy; the Crimea.

Fl.: Native to Europe.

Sex: There are no visible clues apart from a noticeable fatness of ♀ body during spawning.

Soc. B.: A gregarious, bottom-dwelling fish, peaceful toward tank mates of a similar size. It will eat smaller fishes.

M: See suggestions for *Perca fluviatilis*. The species need a lot of oxygen and is but conditionally recommended for a cold-water tank.

B: Has not been bred in an aquarium. In the wild it spawns from March to May. The eggs are laid individually on plants and rocks near the bank and will hatch in 12-14 days.

F: C; all types of live foods such as *Tubifex*, fresh water shrimp, insect larvae and fish meat. Will rarely accept flakes.

S: Four species are known. Anglers dislike the Ruffe since it likes to dine on fish eggs.

T: 50-68° F (cold water fish),   L: 10″,   A: 31″,   R: b,   D: 2-3.
  10-20° C,   25 cm,   80 cm,

Perca fluviatilis
River Perch

LINNAEUS, 1758

Syn.: None

Hab.: Throughout Europe as far east as Kolyma in eastern Siberia. The species is not found in: Scotland; Norway north of the 68th parallel; Spain; central and southern Italy; western Balkans; the Peloponesus; the Crimea.

Fl.: Native to Europe.

Sex: ♂♂ are more brightly colored; ♀♀ are more fullerbodied during spawning.

Soc. B.: A schooling species when young and a loner when older, it is a predator. The species should be kept with fishes of similar size.

M: Prefers a tank with a fine, sandy bottom, dense vegetation (cold-water varieties such as *Elodea* and *Myriophyllum*). Add rocks and an inverted pot for shelter. Suggest a clear water that is not too warm: neutral to slightly alkaline, medium hard, pH 7.0-7.5 and 10° dGH.

B: A conventional aquarium is not large enough for breeding. In the wild it breeds from March to June. The eggs are attached to rocks and plants in strings. The fry hatch in 18-20 days.

F: C; all types of live foods; predominantly invertebrates.

S: The growth of the species is controlled by the available space. In a small tank it will grow very little and will rarely reach feral size in captivity.

T: 50-72° F,   L: 17″,   A: 31-39″,   R: all,   D: 4 (C).
  10-22° C,   45 cm,   80-100 cm,
(cold water fish) sexually mature from 6″ sexually mature from 17 cm.

Gymnocephalus cernua

Perca fluviatilis

Scatophagus argus argus
Argusfish, Scat

(LINNAEUS, 1766)

Syn.: *Chaetodon argus, Ch. atromaculatus, Ch. pairatalis, Cacodoxus argus, Ephippus argus, Sargus maculatus, Scatophagus macronotus S. ornatus*

Hab.: In tropical fresh, salt and brackish waters of the Indian and Pacific Oceans; esp. Indonesia; Philippines. Tahiti forms an eastern boundry to their range.

Fl.: 1906

Sex: Unknown.

Soc. B.: Peaceful toward tank mates, it is a lively schooling species with but one fault: it eats plants.

M: Add plants resistent to sea water around the edges of the tank with rocks for hiding. Allow plenty of open space. Add 3-4 teaspoons of salt for each $2^1/_2$ gallon (10 l) of water.

B: Has not been bred in an aquarium. Little is known of its requirements or habits.

F: O; omnivorous; all types of live foods; fine-leaved plants; algae; lettuce; oatmeal; flakes.

S: The fish are extremely sensitive to nitrites. Younger specimens can be kept in brackish water but older fish prefer sea water. The fish undergo metamorphosis; the larvae are characterized in the tholichthys stage by their large heads and sturdy bony plates. At this point they are similar to the marine butterfly fish, Chaetodontidae. They mature by changing their armour plating. *A. argus atromaculatus* (BENNET, 1828), must be regarded as a sub-species. It is sometimes sold as *S. "rubrifrons"* (See the small photo). The sub-species is found only in Sri Lanka, New Guinea and Australia.

T: 68-82° F,   **L:** 12″,   **A:** 39″,   **R:** m,   **D:** 4 (C).
   20-28° C,   30 cm,   100 cm,

S. a. atromaculatus, adult

Important: Java fern, which is often put into aquariums for herbivorous fishes, seems to be poisonous. It has been observed that scats died after eating this plant, whereas others, which did not touch the fern, survived.

Scatophagus tetracanthus
African Scat

(LACEPEDE, 1880)

Syn.: *Chaetodon tetracanthus, C. striatus, Ephippus multifasciatus, Scatophagus fasciatus, S. multifasciatus*

Hab.: In brackish and fresh waters of the coastal regions of east Africa.

Fl.: 1932, Scholze & Poetzschke, Berlin, Germany.

Sex: Unknown.

Soc. B.: A peaceful, schooling species, it will attack plants.

M: See recommendations for *S. argus*.

B: Has not been bred in captivity;

F: O; omnivorous; live foods; aquatic plants; algae; lettuce; oatmeal; flakes.

S: Like others of the genus it goes through a metamorphosis. This is the most rare of all Argusfishes.

T: 72-86° F,   **L:** $15^1/_2$″,   **A:** 39″,   **R:** m,   **D:** 3.
   22-30° C,   40 cm,   100 cm,

Scatophagus argus argus, juv.; adults see page 787

Scatophagus tetracanthus

Toxotes chatareus

(HAMILTON, 1822)

Syn.: *Coius chatareus*

Hab.: Mostly in the brackish waters of estuaries in Asia; eastern India; Thailand; Malaysian Peninsula; Malayan Archipelago; Vietnam; Philippines; central and western Australia.

Fl.: 1949

Sex: Unknown.

Soc. B.: Generally tolerant with its own species but may become nervous around larger tankmates. Can be combined with fishes of similar size and the species generally live together in small groups.

M: Follow suggestions for *T. jaculatrix.*

B: Not yet successful. Little is known about the species reproductive behaviour.

F: C; exclusively live foods, particularly flies, crickets, cockroaches and daddy-long-legs. The fish is a surface feeder.

S: *T. chatareus* differs from *T. jaculatrix* in several ways: it has 29-30 lateral line scales while *T. jaculatrix* has 33-35 (33) and if counting the vertical black stripes as one through six from the eye, a black patch will be found between stripes 3 and 4 on *T. chatareus*. Similar patches may occur between 2 and 3, 4 and 5 and 5 and 6. These are lacking on *T. jaculatrix.*

T: 77-86° F,   **L:** 11″,   **A:** from 39″,   **R:** t,   **D:** 3-4.
    25-30° C,   27 cm,   from 100 cm,

Toxotes jaculatrix

(PALLAS, 1766)

Syn.: *Sciaena jaculatrix, Labrus jaculatrix, Toxotes jaculator*

Hab.: Asia: Gulf of Aden along the coastline of India and Southeast Asia to North Australia. This species is supposed to live in some parts of the southern coastline of Australia as well. These fish are found in salt, brackish and fresh water.

Fl.: 1899 by P. Nitsche

Sex: Unknown

Soc. B.: Placid shoal fish. Fishes of the same size usually get along, whereas larger ones are often aggressive towards smaller ones.

M: Large aquarium with moderate plant growth, lots of space for swimming; depth of water 20-30 cm. Water must not be too fresh nor hard (add sea salt: 2-3 tsp./10 l of water). This species needs a lot of warmth.

B: Not yet successful in captivity.

F: C; live food, possibly insects (flies, grass hoppers, cockroaches, etc.) The food is mainly taken from the surface of the water.

S: *Toxotes jaculatrix* are able to shoot insects that are on plants outside the water by means of a forceful stream of water. the maximum distance of such shot is about 150 cm.

T: 77-86° F,   **L:** 10″,   **A:** from 39″,   **R:** t,   **D:** 3-4.
    25-30° C,   24 cm,   from 100 cm,

Toxotes chatareus

Toxotes jaculatrix

Group 10

Group 10 includes all species and families which cannot be assigned to any of the previous groups. Their classification has been systematized on page 148.

Fam. Anablepidae (Four-Eyes)
The family consists of one genus and three species all characterized by large protruding eyes which are divided by a strip of tissue. (See the description under *Anableps anableps*. Each is a live-bearer with a gonopodium ($\male$) modified from the anal fin.

Fam.: Apteronotidae (Speckled Knifefishes)
Every fish in this family has a small swordtail and a noticeably small dorsal fin. Their body cavities are toward the front and the anal opening is located at the underside of the head. The fish are very flat-sided.

Fam.: Atherinidae (Silversides)
The family generally inhabits the flat coastal areas of moderate and tropical seas. Only a few species have become acclimated to freshwater. They are distinguished by two widely-separated dorsal fins. The pectoral fins are high on the body and well to the front and the eggs of many are suspended by adhesive threads or by thread-like appendages.

Fam.: Belonidae (Needlefishes)
The family includes very elongated fishes with little if any flattening on the sides. The lower jaw is longer than the upper and is pointed. Both jaws are heavily toothed. The fins have only soft rays and the dorsal and anal fins oppose, swept well back. The lateral line is located low on the ventral side and the bones are often light green in color. Needlefishes are predominantly deep-sea and coastal dwellers.

Fam.: Blenniidae (Blennies)
Their elongated body, either naked or covered with small scales, possesses a large number of skin glands. The fish have no swim bladder but many have tentacles on their heads. They are brightly colored and are generally found in coastal waters. Some inhabit freshwater and a few can leave water for short periods.

Fam.: Channidae (Snake-heads)
The body is elongated, rounded at the front with flattened sides near the rear. The mouth can be opened wide and has the deep cleft associated with predators. The anterior nostril has a tube-like extension.

Three-Spined Stickelback spawning

The dorsal and anal fins are long, composed only of soft rays. Snake heads can breath air and many are popular as food fish.

Fam.: Electrophoridae (Electric Eels)
There is but one species in the family, a typically eel-shaped species with long anal fins. It lacks dorsal and pelvic fins and has a small tail fin which merges with the anal fin to form a continuous line.

Fam.: Eleotridae (Sleeper Gobies)
The fish are characterized by an elongated body which is round at the front and becomes flattened further back. The pelvic and dorsal fins are separate and the body is covered with tenoid scales. Normally there is no lateral line. Most Sleepers are found in brackish tropical waters though a few are at home in fresh water.

Fam.: Gasterosteidae (Stickelbacks)
A family of small fishes, Stickelbacks live in fresh, brackish and sea water in northern temperate zones. The body is streamlined, the caudal fin is slender and the mouth is large. The jaws are toothed though there are no teeth on either the vomer or maxillary. The skin may be without scales or covered with bony plates. Many species build nests and are patriarchal in that the males guard the brood.

Fam.: Gobiidae (Gobies)
The family can be identified by its united pelvic fins. Only a few smaller species since the pelvics generally form a suction device which is used to anchor the fish to a solid base. They have two dorsal fins and a rounded caudal. A number of species display sexual dimorphism and dichromatism. Most are patriarchal in that the male guards the eggs and the brood. Most Goby are at home in saltwater.

Fam.: Gymnotidae (Knifefishes)
From Central and South America, these freshwater fishes have a pointed tail, are either scaleless or with small scales and have small heads, eyes and mouths. The jaws are toothed, the anal fin is large and the dorsal is small or thread-like. The body cavity is forward and the anal opening is located at the underside of the head.

Fam.: Hemirhamphidae (Half-Beaks)
Hemirhamphidae are found around the world in salt, brackish and freshwater. Most members of the species have an elongated body and an extended lower jaw. The jaws, which are combined and can be moved in conjunction with the skull, are a feature unique to the species. Their bodies identify them as predators, with dorsal and anal fins swept well back towards the tail. Most of the fishes lay eggs with unusual, lengthly projections though a few are livebearers. In the case of livebearers the milt is transferred by a modified anal fin called an andropodium.

Fam.: Kneriidae
A complete description of the family can be found on page 844.

Fam.: Luciocephalidae (Pikeheads)
There is but one genus in the family, *Luciocephalus pulcher,* and it has the elongated, pike-like shape associated with fast swimming predators. The swim bladder has been replaced with a labyrinth organ which is used for supplemental breathing. The anal fin is so deeply divided as to appear to be in two parts.

Fam.: Mastacembelidae (Spiny Eels)
True to their name the family, found in the fresh and brackish waters in southeast Asia and tropical Africa, are eel-shaped. Their noses, a prehensile projection, has the nostrils in extended tubes on on either side. Excluding the genus *Macrognathus,* the dorsal, caudal and anal fins are combined into a single continuous fin. There is a small gill opening at the throat.

Fam.: Melanotaeniidae (Rainbow Fishes)
Found in eastern Australia, the Arn Islands, Waigeu and New Guinea, the family was only recently separated from Atherinidae by ROSEN. The fishes have long, oval, laterally compressed bodies and become high-backed with age. They have two narrowly divided dorsal fins which distinguish them from Atherinidae. Rainbow fish are often used to control mosquitos.

Fam.: Mormyridae (Mormyrids)
A freshwater species, their shape differs from that of many fishes. On some the mouth is extended and more like a nose and on others there is an extension on the chin which is used as a sensory organ.

Their skin is normally thick and wrinkled and on some there is a weak electrical organ near the caudal peduncle. It is used to defend territory. The dorsal and anal fins are positioned well back and the caudal fin is deeply forked.

Fam.: Notopteridae (Featherbacks)
Members of this family of freshwater fishes are larger with elongated, laterally compressed bodies. They are found throughout west and southeast Africa as well as in southeast Asia. The anus is positioned well forward and the long anal fin and smaller caudal fin merge into a single appendage. Fins other than the anal and pectoral are either missing or quite small.

Fam.: Osteoglossidae (Bony-Tongued Fishes)
A number of large freshwater fishes, in four genera and six species, comprise this family. One, the Arapaima (*Arapaima gigas*), is among the largest of all freshwater fishes. Another, the Bandfish, found in northern sections of South America and in west Africa, is noted for several interesting, primitive features. It has remarkably large eyes, a head protected by bony plates and large, powerful scales. There is an accessory respiratory organ located near the fourth gill. Certain species are mouth-breeders.

Fam.: Pantodontidae (Butterfly Fishes)
A single species, *Pantodon buchholzi* complete the family and while there is a relationship with Osteoglossidae these fishes are different. The anal fin of the male has been transformed into a genital organ and Butterfly Fishes are fertilized internally. Their ventral fins are at the breast while those of Osteoglossidae are ventral. The fishes are found in freshwater in many parts of tropical Africa.

Fam.: Phractolaemidae
A family of primitive fishes with but a single species, *Phractolaemus ansorgei* are found in a very limited area of the Niger Delta and Ethiope river in upper Zaire. Their toothless mouth can be extended like a nose and the upper jaw is lined with thin bones. The fish have an accessory respiratory organ and are considered relatives of Kneriidae and Chanidae.

818

Various True Bony Fishes

Fam.: Rhamphichthyidae (American Knifefishes)

A native of northern and Central America, the fish differ from Apterno-notidae and Gymnotidae. In comparison with the first, American Knifefishes lack caudal fins and when compared with the second, the species either lacks teeth or posseses only small ones.

Fam.: Syngnathidae (Pipefishes)

The family has a number of unusual, identifying features: its fishes are covered with a bony armour, have a tube-like snout, lack pelvic fins, have different "prehensile" eyes, bunched gills and, in some, a breeding pouch. The female lays her eggs in the male's pouch beneath his tail where they are instantly fertilized. When a breeding pouch, or marsupium, is not featured the eggs are protected by folds of skin in the stomach area. Care of the fry is patriarchal and is unique in the kingdom of fishes. The family is large and lives mostly in the sea. Only a few species are found in freshwater.

Fam.: Tetraodontidae (Pufferfish)

The fish, with club-shaped, unarmoroured bodies, are well known. Their protection is a sac which can be inflated with air and water like a balloon, billowing them to a size too large to be consumed. They have large heads and widely-spaced eyes which are often very mobile. Their bodies are often covered with spines or small plates. The fish lack pelvic fins and the existing fins do not have rays. The teeth are joined in a sharp frame commonly called a "parrot beak". They are found in salt, brackish and fresh water and their flesh carries a toxin.

Fam.: Umbridae (Mudminnows)

The family is comprised of small fishes found in two widely separated places, the Danube river and in parts of western North America. There are two genera, *Umbra and Novumbra*, closely related to the Pike. Both families originated from a common ancestor during the middle geological period. When frightened or in danger Umbrids dig into the bottom. They have rounded bodies which are flattened at the sides with the head and body covered by large, round scales. The fish can breath air with the aid of a swim bladder and by digging into the mud, *Umbra limi* can survive when the waters in which they live run dry. The family is matriarchal.

Anableps anableps
Four-Eyes

(LINNAEUS, 1756)

Syn.: *Anableps anonymus, A. gronovii, A. lineatus, A. surinamensis, A. tetrophthalmus, Cobitis anableps*

Hab.: In brackish and fresh waters of Central America and northern section of South America.

Fl.: 1938, "Aquarium Hamburg", Hamburg, West Germany.

Sex: On ♂ the anal fin has been transformed into a gonopodium.

Soc. B.: A surface-loving, schooling, livebearer.

M: Does best in a shallow tank (8 to 11" [20-30 cm.]) , with warm, brackish water. Needs a fine gravel bottom with brackish-water plants as background and adequate open swimming space.

B: About 4 to 6" of water at temperatures between 26-30° C. The fry are about one inch at birth.

F: C; such live foods as insects; will accept flakes.

S: Since the male gonopodium is rather inflexible, moving only to one side, conception occurs from that side. *A. anableps* is easily distinguished from *A. dovii* and *A. microlepis* by the central lateral line scales. *A. anableps*, 11; *A. dovii*, 14-15; *A. microlepis*, 17-18).

Since Four Eyes are excellent jumpers, the tank must be covered. The cornea, pupil and retina are divided by a horizontal strip, a constriction of the conjunctiva. The eyes project forward and there are distinctive upper and lower eye parts, hence the common name. The two upper portions project from the water and are used chiefly to locate enemies. The lower segments provides vision beneath the surface.

T: 74-82° F,   **L:** 12", sexually mature from 6",   **A:** 39",   **R:** t,   **D:** 3.
     24-28° C,   30 cm, sexually mature from 15 cm,   100 cm,

Apteronotus albifrons

Syn.: *Sternarchus albifrons, S. maximiliani*

Hab.: Amazon; Rio Paraguay; Brazil; Peru; Ecuador; Venezuela; Guyana.

Fl.: 1934

Sex: Unknown.

Soc. B.: May be aggressive.

M: The fish are generally timid and should be kept in a dark aquarium with numerous hiding places such as roots and rocks. If properly cared for they can become quite trusting and can be kept with larger peaceful species. Needs a fine gravel bottom with many plants.

B: Unsuccessful and little is known about their reproductive behavior.

F: C, O; all types of live foods; cut meat; chopped earthworms; occassionally, oatmeal.

T: 73-82° F, L: to 19¹/₂″, A: 39″, R: m, D: 3.
23-28° C, to 50 cm, 100 cm,

LINNAEUS, 1758

S: The fish will soon become too large for a home tank though they are often maintained in public aquariums. They are very sensitive to water conditions. One fish, fed BioMin, lived for more than 16 years and grew from six inches (15 cm) to a length of more than 16″ (40 cm.). The fish possesses a weak electrical organ at the caudal peduncles. It is used to search for food.

Bedotia geayi
Madagascar Rainbow Fish

PELLEGRIN, 1907

Syn.: None

Hab.: In mountain waters; Madagascar.

Fl.: 1958, Aquarium Westhandel, Amsterdam, Netherlands.

Sex: ♂ has bright, contrasting colors, uneven fins and a pointed front dorsal fin. ♀ is yellow with a rounded dorsal.

Soc. B.: A peaceful, sensitive, schooling species, it can be combined with other peaceful fishes.

M: Needs a long tank with open room for swimming and plants set along the edges and back. Suggest medium hard to hard, neutral water, from 10° dGH and pH 7.0. Needs frequent water changes, $^1/_4$ to $^1/_3$, weekly. Keep only in schools.

B: You need at least a 15 gallon (50 liter) tank with clear, not too soft water (over 10° dGH) at a temperature between 22-24° C. It should be planted with fine-leaved plants. The eggs are deposited on plants and hang by a thread similar to those of *Melanotaenia*. The parents will neither eat their spawn nor fry. The young are difficult to raise and are very sensitive to the turbidity caused by infusoria.

F: C, O; all types of live foods; flakes. Will not accept food on the bottom.

S: When first hatched the fry are free swimming though they move with their heads angled upward. They quickly adapt a normal swimming position.

T: 68-75° F,   L: 6″,   A: 31-39″,   R: m, t,   D: 2.
    20-24° C,   15 cm,   80-100 cm,

Pseudomugil signifer
Australian Blue-Eye

KNER, 1864

Syn.: *Atherina signata, Pseudomugil signatus.*

Hab.: Australia; northern and eastern Queensland.

Fl.: 1936, Fritz Mayer, Hamburg, West Germany.

Sex: During spawning ♂ has a red anal fin and year around is larger and more brilliantly colored.

Soc. B.: A peaceful, active, schooling fish.

M: Follow recommendations for *Telmatherina ladigesi* utilizing these water values: a hardness of 12-15° dGH and a pH 7.0.

B: Easy to breed, follow suggestions for other Rainbow Fishes. The water should not be too soft. The eggs are large and develop in 12 to 18 days, depending on the water temperature. The parents may be kept in the tank since they will not bother the eggs or the fry.

F: C, O; all types of live foods; flakes – though not too often.

S: The species is sensitive to the turbidity of infusoria.

T: 73-82° F,   L: 1$^3/_4$″,   A: 23$^1/_2$″,   R: m, t,   D: 2.
    23-28° C,   4.5 cm,   60 cm,

Bedotia geayi

Pseudomugil signifer, from Cairns

Telmatherina ladigesi
Celebes Rainbowfish

AHL, 1936

Syn.: None

Hab.: In remote areas of the Celebes.

Fl.: 1933, Otto Winkelmann, Altona, West Germany.

Sex: ♂ is brilliantly colored and has extended rays on the second anal and dorsal fins.

Soc. B.: A lively, peaceful, schooling species, it can be combined with *Aplocheilichthys macrophthalmus* or kept in a community tank.

M: Needs a fine gravel bottom, a moderate amount of planting and open swimming areas. Position the tank so it can catch the morning sun. Use hard, neutral water, above 12° dGH at a pH 7.0 Add one tablespoon of salt to each 2 gallons of water and change ¹/₄ of the tank weekly.

B: Needs a relatively roomy tank with the water values above at temperatures between 22-24° C. Add fine-leaved plants with floating plants above. The fish have a vigorous courting ritual and will spawn among the plants. Spawning can be continued for a period of months and the parents, who will consume the eggs, should be removed. The eggs will develop in 8 to 11 days. The fry can be fed Baby Food.

F: C, O; all types of live foods; flakes.

S: The fish is sensitive to water conditions and may react adversely if transferred to another tank with different water. They will tolerate a shift from soft to hard water better than the reverse.

T: 72-82° F,   L: 3″,   A: 31″,   R: m, t,   D: 2-3.
22-28° C,   7.5 cm,   80 cm,

Salaria fluviatilis

(ASSO, 1801)

Syn.: *Blennius fluviatilis, B. alpestris, B. anticolus, B. frater, B. lupulus, Salaria varus*

Hab.: In fresh water through the the Mediterranean; southeastern Spain; south-western and southeastern France; Corsica; Sardinia; Sicily; Italy, north of the Po; Lake Garda; Lake Vrana, Jugoslavia; Cyprus; Asia Minor; Marocco; Algeria.

Fl.: Unknown.

Sex: ♂ has a more fully developed comb atop the head.

Soc. B.: A territorial, burrowing fish. Since it is polygamous you will need three or four ♀ for each ♂. A patriarchal species, the ♂ guards the brood.

M: Does best in a wide, squat tank with about 12 inches of water and a bottom of fine gravel with roots, rocks, and over-turned pots and inert pipe as hiding places. Suggest clear medium-hard, neutral water around 10° dGH and pH 7.0. The water should be well aerated since the fish require plenty of oxygen. Best kept in a species tank.

B: Requires medium hard, neutral water (10° dGH at pH 7.0), 64° F (18° C) or warmer. ♂ will select a cave and defend it against all comers. When spawning ♀ will visit ♂ , spawning several times at intervals of 10 to 15 days. The eggs adhere to the wall and roof of the cave. A brood consists of 200 to 300 eggs. ♀ leaves the cave while ♂ guards the eggs until they hatch.

F: C; live food; water fleas; fresh-water shrimp; aquatic insect larvae; *Tubifex* worms; flakes; tablets.

S: The first clutch is larger than the last (200 eggs as compared with 10 to 100). Since one male will mate with several ♀ the eggs are often in many different stages of development.

T: 64-75° F, **L**: 6″, **A**: 35″, **R**: b, **D**: 2-3.
18-24° C,   15 cm, 90 cm,

Xenentodon cancila   (HAMILTON, 1822)
Silver Needlefish

Syn.: *Esox cancila, Belone cancila, Mastemcembalus cancila*

Hab.: Found in freshwater: Asia; India; Sri Lanka; Thailand; Burma; Malayan Peninsula.

Fl.: 1910

Sex: The dorsal and anal fins on ♂ often have a black edge.

Soc. B.: A relatively timid, schooling fish which should be combined only with such fishes of similar size as catfishes. Be cautious. The fish is a predator.

M: Keep alone. Requires a wide, broad, low tank with about 12 inches (30 cm) of water. Suggest a fine gravel bottom with vegetation along the edges and back. Do not use floating plants and allow much open space for swimming. A lower water level inhibits the fish's tendency to jump. Suggest hard, neutral water, from 20° dGH and about pH 7.0. The fish can tolerate added salt, 1 g to one quart (1 l) of water.

B: Not successful in an aquarium

F: C; live foods. The species, which eats mostly fishes and frogs, is not particular about diet.

S: The fish are jumpers and the tank must be covered. They react to sudden changes in light, become agitated and may repeatedly hurtle themselves against the aquarium cover resulting in injury.

A detailed report on breeding *Xenentodon cancila* was given by SCHMIED (1986) in the "Aquarienmagazin" **20** (7): 280-283. The fishes had already been bred for the

first time in the Biological Station Wilhelminenberg/Austria in 1963. Large tanks are suitable (140 x 45 x 40 cm), with bogwood to which Java fern has been attached. The water showed the following values: pH 6.4, 13° dGH, 25° C. Spawning was done before noon and resulted in 7-15 eggs daily. The eggs are clear as glass, colorless, with a diameter of 3.5 mm and hang from the leaves on threads appr. 20 mm in length. The development of the eggs takes about ten days at 25° C, when the fry hatch, they are almost 12 mm long. The best food was deemed to be week-old labyrinth fishes. (*Macropodus opercularis, Betta splendens,* etc.) The young *Xenentodon* could well cope with them. Later, larger fishes can be fed.

T: 72-82° F,   **L:** 12",   **A:** from 39",   **R:** t,   **D:** 4 (C).
  22-28° C,   32 cm,   from 100 cm,

Channna micropeltes
Red Snakehead

(CUVIER & VALENCIENNES, 1831)

Syn.: *Ophiocephalus micropeltes, O. serpentinus, Ophicephalus micropeltes, O. stevensi*

Hab.: India; Thailand; Burma; Vietnam; western Malaysia.

Fl.: Possibly 1969.

Sex: Little information is available. ♀ may become fatter during the spawning period.

Soc. B.: Similar to data for *Channa obscura*.

M: Similar to data for *C. obscura*.

B: Possible only in larger tanks. Suggest water temperature between 27-32° C. For more details see *C. obscura*.

F: C; live food, chiefly fish.

S: A popular table fish in its native land, it is the largest of all Snakeheads. The illustration shows a young specimen.

T: 77-82° F,   L: 39″,   A: from 47″,   R: all,   D: 4 (C).
    25-28° C,   100 cm,   from 120 cm,

Parachanna obscura (GUENTHER, 1861)
For description see the following page.

Parachanna obscura, juv.

Syn.: *Channa obscura, Ophiocephalus obscurus, Parophiocephalus obscurus*

Hab.: West Africa; Senegal, to the White Nile; central Africa.

Fl.: 1908

Sex: ♀ may have a fatter stomach during spawning.

Soc. B.: A predatory loner, the fish should be kept on its own. A patriarchal species, ♂ looks after the brood.

M: Needs a heavily planted tank with a bottom of fine sand and a few hiding places among rocks or roots. Can tolerate a range of water conditions but needs a reasonable amount of heat.

B: Details are given by ARMBRUST, 1963: DATZ **16**, 298-301. The species lays 2,000 to 3,000 eggs which are guarded by the ♂. Once hatched, the male guards the fry for four to five days. The fry are very cannibalistic.

F: All types of live foods. Larger fish feed almost exclusively on each other. The species will seldom adapt to meat.

S: ARMBRUST observed the fry banding together to defend against a larger Snakehead. The form of their mass resembled an even larger Snakehead. (Aquarien-Terrarien **18**, 229, 1971.)

T: 79-82° F,	L: 13",	A: 39",	R: all,	D: 4 (C).
26-28° C,	35 cm,	100 cm,		

Channa orientalis   BLOCH & SCHNEIDER, 1801

Syn.: *Ophiocephalus kelaartii, Channa gachua*

Hab.: Sri Lanka; Afghanistan through China to the Sundra Isl.

Fl.: 1929

Sex: ♀ is stronger than ♂.

Soc. B.: Individual specimens can be easily kept in a species tank and may soon become tame enough to take food from your hand. In their habitat they live in small ponds and jump across land when these dry.

M: Needs a heavily planted, darkened tank and since the fish are jumpers, it should be covered. Suggest water with a hardness to 20° dGH and a pH 6.4 to 7.5.

B: Sexually mature from 4 inches. Though little is known about breeding procedures in an aquarium, breeding should be possible. The difficulty may come in finding a suitable pair since the fish are loners.

F: C; all types of live foods; worms, fishes, etc.

S: Can be found with and without pelvic fins in Sri Lanka.

The first, excellently written report on successful breeding in an aquarium was made by ETTRICH (1986) in the DATZ **39** (7): 289-293. The fishes are mouth brooders. When coupling, the partners embrace in the way of the labyrinth fishes. The eggs are expelled all at once. After fertilization they rise slowly to the surface, on account of their oil content, and then the ♂ takes them into its mouth. The duration of mouth brooding differs: the variant with ventral fins carries the eggs 3-4 days in its mouth, the one without ventral fins about 9-10 days. The former hatches up to 200 offspring, the latter hardly more than 40 fry. The fry of both variants differ in their behavior as well (see details in the report by G. ETTRICH). ETTRICH noticed that the ♀ of the variant without the ventral fins swam rapidly in a circle, expelling a cloud of eggs. These were heavier than water, sank quickly to the bottom, and were devoured voraciously by the fry!!

T: 73-79° F,	L: to 12", generally 4-8",	A: 27",	R: b,	D: 4.
23-26° C,	30 cm, generally 10-20 cm,	70 cm,		

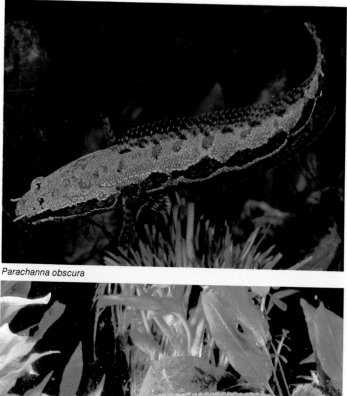

Parachanna obscura

Channa orientalis

Channna striata
Striped Snakehead

(BLOCH, 1797)

Syn.: *Ophicephalus striatus; Ophiocephalus striatus, O. vagus*

Hab.: Sri Lanka; China; Thailand through the Philippines to the Moluccas. Has been established in Hawaii.

Fl.: Unknown.

Sex: Unknown.

Soc. B.: A predator, the fish will quickly empty a community tank.

M: Needs a heavily planted tank with a soft bottom and good filtration. It is a large fish with a high metabolic rate and a large excretory output. Water hardness to 20° dGH and pH 7.0-8.0.

B: In the wild the parents clear all plants from the spawning site. ♂ guards the eggs which float and also watches the fry for four to six weeks. The eggs hatch in 1 to 3 days and will become 17-20 mm long in nine weeks. The fry may fall prey to their parents.

F: C: all types of live foods.

S: The most important food fish in southeast Asia, the species is not recommended for an aquarium. Young specimens are very curious and trusting. The ♂♂ will not rise to bait during the spawning season. Providing their skin remains damp, Snakeheads can survive for months in holes dug into bogs. This may explain their wide distribution.

T: 73-81° F, **L:** 35″, **A:** 47″, **R:** b, m, **D:** 4.
23-27° C, 90 cm, 120 cm,

Electrophorus electricus
Electric Eel

(LINNAEUS, 1766)

Syn.: *Electrophorus multivalvulus, Gymnotus electricus, Gymnotus regius*

Hab.: Amazon; Brazil; Peru; Venezuela; Guyana.

Fl.: 1913, Siggelkow, Hamburg, West Germany.

Sex: Unknown.

Soc. B.: Larger specimens are peaceful but younger fishes will snap at their own kind. The fish are nocturnal.

M: Needs a darker aquarium with a bottom of medium-sized gravel and hiding places among rocks and roots. The fish do best in a species tank.

B: Have not been bred in captivity.

F: C; larger specimens need fishes; younger ones, worms and insect larvae.

S: A large organ, consisting of thousands of elements and capable of producing electrical current, comprises 80% of the sides of an Electric Eel. The fishes transmit direction-finding pulses at a frequency of 50Hz and are capable of shocks reaching one amp and 600 volts. Fishes and mammal as large as horses may be paralyzed by it.

T: 73-82° F, **L:** to 7$^1/_2$ feet, **A:** 47″,   **R:** b, m,   **D:** 3.
    23-28° C,   to 230 cm,   120 cm,

Dormitator maculatus
Spotted Goby, Striped Sleeper

Syn.: *Sciaena maculata, Eleotris mugi-loides, E. grandisquama, E. sima, E. som-nolentus, E. omocyansus, E. gundlachi, Dormitator lineatus.*
Eleotris latifrons is a species by itself = *Dormitator latifrons.* Syn: *Dormitator microphthalmus*

Hab.: Mainly in brackish water of upper regions of estuaries and lagoons; also in fresh and salt water.

Soc. B.: During spawning season ♂ is territorial.

M: Brackish water, temporarily also fresh water.

F: Herbivore: in the wild, mainly feed on live, higher plants (for ex. roots of water hyacinths) and algae as well as plant detritus. They also feed on insect larvae

and small shrimp (compare Nordlie, 1981, J. Fish, Biol. 18: 99–101). When kept in tank, accept all current types of dry, live and frozen foods, *Tubifex, Mysis* etc.). Also like soft vegetables and fruit (tomatoes, bananas) as well as noodles. Will eat soft water plants. However, growing Java fern and hornwort in the tank is possible.

B: Addition of fresh water facilitates spawning; breeding possible since try grow quickly, but not easy in aquarium conditions!

S: none.

Sex: ♂ has prolonged back rays in D_2 and A and sometimes hump on top of head; Genital papilla of ♂ very long and flattened, in ♀ shorter and blunt.

T: 72-75° F, **L:** 10″, sexually mature from 4″, 22-24° C, 25 cm, sexually mature from 10 cm, **A:** 31″, 80 cm, **R:** b, **D:** 3-4.

Oxyeleotris marmoratus
Marbled Sleeper

Syn.: *Eleotris marmorata, Callieleotris pla-tycephalus*

Hab.: A freshwater species found in the calm and slow-moving waters of Southeast Asia; Indonesia; Borneo; Sumatra; Malayan Peninsula; Thailand.

Fl.: 1905, J. Reichelt, Berlin, West Germany.

Sex: Though the coloring is not uniform, the second dorsal is higher, the anal fin longer and the genital papillae conical on the ♂ ; the ♀ is more uniformly colored with a cylindrical genital papillae.

Soc. B.: A nocturnal, predatory, burrowing fish, it needs hiding places among rocks, caves and pots. Suggest a heavily planted tank though the plants should be potted. Keep the lighting dim. Suggest medium-hard, neutral water, 10-15° dGH and pH

7.0. Slightly saline water may help acclimate the fish – 1-2 teaspoons to $2^1/_2$ gallons (10 l).

B: Not successful.

F: C, O; omnivorous with a preference for live foods; worms; bloodworms. The fish are extremely greedy and will daily consume their own weight.

S: One of the largest Sleepers; one of the largest Gobies.

T: 72-82° F, **L:** 19$^1/_2$″, **A:** 39″, **R:** b, **D:** 4 (Si).
22-28° C, 50 cm, 100 cm,

Dormitator maculatus

Oxyeleotris marmoratus

Gasterosteus aculeatus
Three-Spined Stickelback

LINNAEUS, 1758

Syn.: *Gasterosteus argyropomus, G. biaculeatus, G. brachycentrus, G. bispinosus, G. cataphractus, G. cuvieri, G. gymnurus, G. leiurus, G. niger, G. noveboracensis, G. obolarius, G. ponticus, G. semiarmatus. G. semiloricatus, G. spinulosus, G. teraculeatus, G. tetracanthus, G. trachurus, Leiurus aculeatus*

Hab.: Excepting the Danube it is found in fresh and brackish waters throughout Europe: Greenland; Iceland; Algeria; northern Asia; North America.

Fl.: A native species.

Sex: Clear sexual dichromatism is seen during breeding; ♂ are then intensely colored in red and blue while ♀ is a greenish grey; other times the ♂ are more slender and lively.

Soc. B.: A schooling species, ♂♂ are territorial during the spawning season and will defend an area against all comers. Polygamous, the tank should contain three or four ♀♀ for each ♂. The male cares for the brood.

M: Plant the tank with local plants, decorate with rocks and pots for hiding and place the tank in a sunny area. The water should be well aerated. Use a fine gravel bottom.

B: Use soft, chalk-free water at temperatures between 10-20° C. ♂ will mark his territory and build a nest from plant materials. Cement is made from a substance taken from the adrenal cortex. ♂ will then lure a nubile ♀ to the nest and after spawning ♀ leaves while ♂ fertilizes the eggs. After spawning with several ♀ there will be 20 to 50 eggs in the nest. ♂ will care for the eggs and the brood, watching the fry for some time.

F: C; live foods; *Tubifex*; *Daphnia*; *Cyclops*; insect larvae. Will rarely accept flakes.

S: The fish must be kept cool during the winter to spawn the following spring. Stickelbacks are very sensitive to *Ichthyophthirius* and *Calcareum glugea.* Stickelbacks cannot live long in chalky water.

T: 39-68° F (Coldwater fish), **L:** 4$^1/_2$", **A:** 27", **R:** m-b, **D:** 2.
   4-20° C,   12 cm,   70 cm,

Pungitius pungitius
Ten-Spined Stickelback

(LINNAEUS, 1758)

Syn.: *Gasterosteus pungitius, Gasterostea pungitius, Gasterosteus bussei, G. occidentalis, Pygosteus occidentalis, P. pungitius*

Hab.: Found in the same areas as *Gasterosteus aculeatus*, though not as far south. It is not found in the Mediterranean and little is known of its distribution.

Fl.: A native species.

Sex: During spawning ♂ has a black throat and breast with orange pectoral fins.

Soc. B.: Similar to *Gasterosteus aculeatus* though the young prefer smaller schools.

M: Follow recommendations for *G. aculeatus.*

B: Conditions are similar to *G. aculeatus* though the nest is built above the tank bottom.

F: C; all types of live foods. Generally will not accept flakes.

S: Not as apt to eat spawn and larvae as *G. aculeatus*. There are two sub-species: *Pungitius pungitius pungitius* (LINNAEUS, 1758), which has similar distibrution, and *P. pungitius sinensis* (GUICHENOT, 1869), found only in eastern Asia.

T: 50-68° F, **L:** 2$^3/_4$", **A:** 19$^1/_2$", **R:** b, m, **D:** 2.
   10-20° C,   7 cm,   50 cm,

Gasterosteus aculeatus

Pungitius pungitius

Brachygobius doriae
Golden-Banded Goby

(GUENTHER, 1868)

Syn.: *Gobius doriae*

Hab.: In both fresh and brackish water; eastern India; Thailand; Malayan Peninsula; Borneo; Sumatra; Java.

Fl.: 1905

Sex: The ♂ are generally more brightly colored; during spawning ♀ is fatter-bodied and, two days or so befor spawning, can be identified by the appearance of an ovipositor.

Soc. B.: A peaceful, restful fish though very territorial. Will not tolerate the intrusion of tankmates into its area.

M: Best kept in a species tank which should include lots of hiding places such as rocks, roots and inverted pots. Suggest a hardness of 20-30° dGH and a pH 7.5-8.5.

B: Recommend hard water, from 15° dGH at a temperature between 26-29° C. Though you need some sea water to approximate brackishness, the addition of freshwater often induces spawning. The spawn is laid beneath rocks or inside pots. The clutch contains 150-200 eggs which hatch in four days. The ♂ guards the brood.

F: C; small live foods; *Tubifex*; whiteworms; mosquito larvae; *Daphnia*; *Cyclops*.

S: The species is sensitive to freshwater and we advise the addition of 1-2 tablespoons of salt for each $2^1/_2$ gallons (10 l) of water. At first the fry are free swimming in the lower areas of the tank and later become bottom dwellers.

B. doriae normal color.

T: 72-84° F, **L:** $1^3/_4$″, **A:** $23^1/_2$″, **R:** bottom, **D:** 3.
22-29° C,   4.2 cm,   60 cm,

Brachygobius xanthozona
Bumblebee Fish

(BLEEKER, 1849)

Syn.: *Gobius xanthozona, Thaigobiella sua*

Hab.: In fresh and brackish waters of southeast Asia: Thailand; south Vietnam.

Fl.: 1905, J. Reichelt, Berlin, West Germany.

Sex: ♀ has a fatter body and during the spawning season is less colorful with a visible ovipositor.

Soc. B.: Gentle and peaceful though territorial. A patriarchal species, the ♂ guards the brood. Tankmates are not tolerated within the marked territory.

M: Follow recommendations for *B. nunus* with the addition of 1-2 tablespoons of salt for each $2^1/_2$ gallons (10 l) of water.

B: See recommendations for *B. doriae.*

F: C; all types of live foods; whiteworms; *Tubifex*; small crustaceans; mosquito larvae. Will not accept flakes.

S: As with the fry of *B. doriae*, these swim freely at first then decend to the bottom as they grow.

T: 77-86° F, **L:** $1^3/_4$″, **A:** $23^1/_2$″, **R:** b, **D:** 3.
25-30° C,   4.5 cm,   60 cm,

Brachygobius doriae in spawning colors

Brachygobius xanthozona

Periophthalmus barbarus
Mudskipper

Syn.: *Gobius barbarus, Euchosistopus koelreuteri, Gobiomarus koelreuteri, Periophthalmus argentilineatus, P. dipus, P. juscatus, P. kalolo, P. koelreuteri, P. modestus*

Hab.: In the brackish waters of African estuaries: from the Red Sea to Madagascar; southeast Asia; Australia; the South Sea.

Fl.: 1896

Sex: Unknown.

Soc. B.: Territorial and partially amphibious.

M: The fish are hard to keep because their habitat is difficult to imitate in an aquarium. If kept we suggest a species tank with a large bottom area with a "bank" of fine sand which is kept in position with sticks and stones. Fill the aquatic portion of the

aquarium with well filtered brackish water, then cover the tank well to create high humidity. The air temperature needs to be as high as that of the water. Suggest a pH 8.0-8.5 with the addition of 1-2% sea salt.

B: Not successful.

F: C; chiefly live foods; all types of worms; crickets; flakes.

S: The fish are typical tide-water residents living on the border beween shore and water. Mangrove swamps are a favorite. As the water level falls the fish dig pits in the sand. They can become very trusting around humans.

T: 77-86° F, **L:** 6″, **A:** 31-39″, **R:** t, dry land, **D:** 4.
25-30° C, 15 cm, 80-100 cm,

Stigmatogobius sadanundio

Syn.: *Gobius sadanundio, Gobius apogonius, Vaimosa spilopleura*

Hab.: Chiefly in freshwater; southeast Asia; Borneo; Sumatra; Java.

Fl.: 1905

Sex: ♂ has larger fins; ♀ are smaller and light yellow in color.

Soc. B.: Though territorial, they are a peaceful species and can be combined with fishes which prefer the middle region of a tank.

M: Suggest a squat species tank with a large, sandy bottom area with such hiding places as rocks and inverted pots. You could add a few plants which can tolerate brackish water.

B: Recommend hard water with added salt at a temperature between 24-28° C. The fish generally spawn on the roof of caves or pots after an extended courtship. Clut-

ches with as many as 1,000 eggs are guarded by the ♂.

F: C, H; all types of live foods; worms; mosquito larvae, etc.; frequently algae (grown in the tank).

S: The fish will be healthier if 1-2 tablespoons of salt is added per $2^1/_2$ gallons (10 l) of water. Do not try to acclimate the fish to soft water. The temperature should be allowed to fluctuate a few degrees each day – higher during the day, lower at night.

T: 68-79° F, **L:** $3^1/_2$″, **A:** 27″, **R:** b, **D:** 3.
20-26° C, 8.5 cm, 70 cm,

Periophthalmus barbarus

Stigmatogobius sadanundio

839

Gymnotus carapo
Banded Knifefish

LINNAEUS, 1758

Syn.: *Carapus inaequilabiatus, Carapus fasciatus, Giton fasciatus, Gymnotus brachiurus, G. carapus, G. fasciatus, G. putaol, Sternopygus carapo, S. carapus*

Hab.: Central and South America, from Guatemala to the Amazon; Ecuador; Peru; Guyana; Paraguay to Rio de la Plata in the south and the Andes in the west.

Fl.: 1910, Vereinigte Zierfischzuechtereien, Conradshoehe, West Germany.

Sex: Unknown.

Soc. B.: Generally ill-tempered toward their species but peaceful toward larger tankmates.

T: 72-82° F, **L:** 23¹/₂″, **A:** from 39″,
22-28° C, 60 cm, from 100 cm,

M: An undemanding fish, the tank should provide plenty of hiding places among roots and rocks. The fish are nocturnal and a well planted tank is preferred. Suggest water with hardness to 15° dGH and pH 6.0-7.5.

B: Unknown.

F: C; all types of live foods; chopped earthworms; will rarely accept flakes.

S: When first imported the fish may "headstand", an action probably caused by damage to the swim bladder.

R: m, b, **D:** 2-3.

Dermogenys pusillus

Syn.: *Hemirhamphus fluviatilis*

Hab.: In fresh and brackish waters of southeast Asia; Thailand; Malayan Peninsula; Singapore; Great Sunda Islands, Indonesia.

Fl.: 1905, J. Reichelt, Dresden, Germany.

Sex: ♂ is smaller, has a red patch on the dorsal and an andropodium or genital organ modified from an anal fin.

Soc. B.: Though often timid during the first days in a tank, Halfbeaks are lively, often bellicose surface-dwellers. ♂♂ often fight, their battles sometimes ending in injury.

M: Recommend keeping the fish in a species tank with a large bottom area of fine gravel and 8 inches (20 cm) of water. The edges should be lightly planted with floating plants overhead and lots of open swimming space between. Let algae grow on all glass areas except the front since this helps to calm the fish. They can tolerate temperatures below 64° F (18° C) but are more active in warmer water. The addition

VAN HASSELT, 1823

of a little salt is welcome (2-3 teaspoons for each $2^1/_2$ gallons). After acclimitization the fish can be kept in water to 10° dGH and pH 7.0.

B: A live bearer, Halfbeaks are not easy to breed. Pairs have an interesting courtship ritual and conception is via the ♂ s andropodium. Pregnancy lasts 20 to 60 days and though females may successfully produce one or two generations they often deliver dead fry. Vitaminized food – especially with vitamin D – will improve the condition. Between 10 and 30 fry are born and should be raised on very small live food. Recommend water at a temperature between 24-28° C.

F: C; chiefly live food; *Drosophila*; other flies; mosquito larvae; small crustaceans; *Tubifex*; flakes.

S: When startled the fish may dart about the tank, striking the glass, possibly injuring their beaks. Death often results. The tank should be covered since Halfbeaks jump. Subsequent breeds will lose this nervousness.

T: 64-86° F,   **L**: 3″,   **A**: 27″,   **R**: t,   **D**: 3.
     18-30° C,   7 cm,   70 cm,

Nomorhamphus liemi liemi
Celebes Halfbeak

VOGT, 1978

Syn.: None known

Hab.: South-Celebes.

Fl.: Unknown.

Sex: The anal fin of ♂ is an andropodium or modified genital organ. ♂ is smaller with deep black fleshy lobes on the lower jaw. The fleshy lobes of ♀ are smaller and red or without color.

Soc. B.: A lively surface-dweller, it lives in loosely-formed schools and may be combined with other peaceful fishes.

M: Needs a roomy tank with a large bottom area and about 8 inches (20 cm) of water. Strong filtration is recommended and the tank should be lightly planted with hiding places provided by rocks or pots. The water is best medium-hard to soft, 5-12° dGH and slightly acid to slightly alkaline, pH 6.9 - 7.5.

B: Breeding is most often accomplished in soft water and we recommend water with a hardness of 5° dGH, pH 6.5 at a temperature of 76° F (25° C) though breeding cannot often be successfully repeated. The males court continually and since they are liverbearers ♀♀ are fertilized internally. The eggs develop in a sac-like extension of the ovary and gestation requires 6-8 weeks. The fry are 18 mm at birth and litters are small, from 9 to 11. The fry must be isolated immediately since the ♀ will devour them.

F: C; live foods; predominantly such passing insects as flies and flying ants; mosquito larvae; *Tubifex*; flakes.

S: The species differs from *Dermogenys* in that their lower jaws do not form a beak. Only the fleshy lobes on the lower jaw reach beyond the upper jaw. The genus is endemic to Sulawesi, formerly the Celebes. The fish jump and the tank should be covered.

T: 75-79° F, **L:** ♂ = 2³/₄", ♀ = 3¹/₂", **A:** 27", **R:** t, **D:** 3.
24-26° C, ♂ = 6 cm, ♀ = 9 cm, 70 cm,

Nomorhamphus liemi snijdersi

VOGT, 1978

Syn.: None

Hab.: Indonesia; central Sulawesi (Celebes); east of Maros.

Fl.: 1977, Dieter Vogt, Stuttgart, West Germany.

Sex: The anal fin of ♂ is an andropodium.

Soc. B.: Similar to *N. liemi liemi.*

M: Follow recommendations for *N. liemi liemi.*

B: See *N. liemi liemi.*

F: C; all types of live foods; readily accepts passing insects; flakes.

T: 72-79° F, **L:** 3¹/₂", **A:** 27", **R:** t, **D:** 3.
23-26° C, 9 cm, 70 cm,

Nomorhamphus liemi liemi

Nomorhamphus liemi snijdersi

Kneria sp.

Hab.: Ten species have been described from Angola to East Africa.

Fl.: 1963, "Aquarium Hamburg", Hamburg, West Germany.

Sex: See "S".

Soc. B.: A peaceful even gregarious fish which can be kept with any species with similar requirements, i.e. cooler water and algae foods.

M: The fish are found in clear flowing stream commonly associated with such cold-water fishes as trout which points to a need for good filtration and lots of oxygen. Suggest very soft water to 3° dGH, though in an aquarium hardness to 18° dGH can be tolerated.

B: Not difficult. After a brief courtship the eggs are shed throughout the aquarium and fall to the bottom. They hatch in four days. The parents ignore the fry.

F: O; omnivorous; live foods. In their native streams the fish live on such microfoods as algae.

S: ♂♂ have a plated, bean-shaped adhesive organ on the gill and behind it an occipital organ or ear which is used for reproduction. To experts it represents the preliminary stage of a "Weber's aparatus" (see page 212). For this and other reasons Kneriidae are considered the precursors of Carp-like fishes.

T: 64-72° F,   **L:** 3",   **A:** 23¹/₂",   **R:** b,   **D:** 1-2.
    18-22° C,   7 cm,   60 cm,

Luciocephalus pulcher
Pikehead

(GRAY, 1830)

Syn.: *Diplopterus pulcher*

Hab.: Southeast Asia: Malayan Peninsula, Singapore, Sumatra, Borneo, Bangka, Belitung: standing waters and calm areas of flowing waters.

Fl.: 1905, J. Reichelt, Berlin.

Sex: ♀ fuller. In domineering and courting ♂ the stripe pattern changes to spotty rows.

Soc. B.: Predator of medium water regions, yet peaceful towards fish of same size. Pikehead can be kept in small groups and are very sociable with one another.

M: Well planted and spacious species tank. Contrary to previous assumptions regarding water conditions this species is not especially difficult. Tolerates medium hardness and pH of up to 7.5. However, since these fishes' natural habitat is very soft acid water which is relatively bacteria free, they often fall victim to infection from the live fish upon which they feed.

B: Successful in 1987 (KOKOSCHKA 1988, DATZ: 34–35, 80–81). ♂ courts by billowing throat and contrarotating the pelvic fins. Male mouth-breeders.

After a minimum 28 days gestation in the mouth, up to ninety 12–13 mm long fry are released. Especially suitable for initial feeding are black mosquito larvae passed through a sieve and the larvae of bubble nest building labyrinth fish. Bubble nest should be scooped up and transferred to breeding tank.

F: Only live food: mainly fish, but also shrimp and insect larvae that are captured from the water by sudden darting attack. Just as the South American leaf-fish (*monocirrhus*) they turn their mouths inside out and suck the food in. Food intake from the ground causes problems, because gravel gets in the mouth. No feeding from water surface.

S: Pikeheads possess an additional respiratory organ (labyrinth). Because of similarities in the shape of the air-bladder and their particular kind of hearing organ (tympanic membrane covered *Foramen exoccipitale*), it is highly probable that *Luciocephalus pulcher* are related to the labyrinth fish family. The anal fin is deeply divided, giving the impression of two separate fins (therefore *Diplopterus* in the syn.).

T: 72-79° F,   **L:** 7",   **A:** 47",   **R:** m,   **D:** 4.
22-26° C,   18 cm,   120 cm,

Mastacembelus armatus
Spiny Eel

GUENTHER, 1861

Syn.: *Macrognathus armatus*

Hab.: Southeast Asia; India; Sri Lanka; Thailand; south China; Sumatra.

Fl: 1922

Sex: During the spawning season ♀ is noticeably fatter.

Soc. B.: Similar to recommendations for *M. erythrotaenia.*

M: Follow suggestions for *M. erythrotaenia. M. armatus* appreciates the addition of sea salt, 2-3 teaspoons to each $2^1/_2$ gallons (10 l). The fish needs hiding places.

B: Not successful in an aquarium.

F: C; live food; small crustaceans; worms; mosquito larvae; tablets; flakes only with difficulty.

S: As with others of its species, *M. armatus* is a burrower. In its native lands it is a food fish.

T: 72-82° F,   L: 28″,   A: 39″,   R: b,   D: 3.
22-28° C,   75 cm,   100 cm,

Mastacembelus circumcinctus

HORA, 1924

Syn.: None

Hab.: Southeast Thailand.

Fl.: Unknown.

Sex: Unknown.

Soc. B.: Though it is aggressive toward its own species and genus and attacks smaller fish, it can be combined with larger fishes of other genera.

M: A soft bottom of sand and peat is important since the Eel burrows when threatened. Needs a heavily planted tank with a cover of floating plants to soften the light. The fish prefers hiding and may disappear for days. Sometimes only the head can be seen. Suggest water conditions as for the species above.

B: Unsuccessful in an aquarium.

F: C; foods as for the previous species; nocturnal, it feeds only at night. Food should be offered then.

S: If you can attach a dimmer control, the fish can be induced to leave their hiding places to be seen.

T: 75-81° F,   L: 6″,   A: 31″,   R: b,   D: 3.
24-27° C,   16 cm,   80 cm,

Mastacembelus armatus

Mastacembelus circumcinctus

Macrognathus aculeatus

Syn.: *Macrognathus maculatus*

Hab.: Found in fresh and brackish waters of southeast Asia; Thailand; Sumatra; Moluccas; Borneo; Java.

Fl: Unknown.

Sex: Unknown.

Soc. B.: See *M. erythrotaenia*.

M: See *M. erythrotaenia*.

B: Little is known about attempts to breed in an aquarium. R. STAUDE (1985) was the first one who published a report on the successful breeding in an aquarium, in "Aquarien Terrarien" 32: 262-264. The fish were fed a diversified diet, and one-third of the water was changed weekly. The larger fish (19 cm) showed the tip of an ovipositor and could thus be identified as female. The

smaller fish (11 cm) was the male. Before spawning the female had a noticeable anal papilla. After vehement mating, over 1000 eggs, clear as glass, 1.2 mm in diameter were laid. The larvae hatched after three days, after another 3 days the 6 mm long larvae were swimming freely. They were fed radiolarians and *Cyclops* nauplii. The value of the water for spawning and breeding were the same: 24-26° C, pH 7.2 and 39° dGH.

F: Live foods; mosquito larvae; white worms; *Tubifex*; small crustaceans; earthworms; fish.

S: The true Spiny Eel can be easily identified by the characteristic markings of *Mastacembelus*. Among the ways *Macrognathus* differs is a ruffled area on the lower portion of the snout.

T: 73-82° F,   L: 13^1/$_2$″,   A: 31″,   R: b,   D: 3.
    23-28° C,   35 cm,   80 cm,

Mastacembelus erythrotaenia
Fire Eel

Syn.: Macrognathus erythrotaenia

Hab.: Southeast Asia; Thailand; Burma; Sumatra; Borneo.

Fl.: Unknown; probably after 1970.

Sex: Identification possible only with sexually mature fishes. ♀ are fatter than ♂♂.

Soc. B.: Should be kept alone or with other fishes of similar or larger size , since they will not tolerate tankmates of their species. A nocturnal predator.

M: Needs a bottom of soft sand with hardy

plants and such hiding places as stones, inverted pots or caves. Use floating plants to reduce the light. Suggest soft to medium, neutral water to 15° dGH and pH 7.0. Add a little salt (1-2 teaspoon to 2^1/$_2$ gallons). The water should be well aerated.

B: Not successful.

F: C; all types of live foods; *Tubifex*; *Daphnia*; *Cyclops*; brine shrimp; mosquito larvae. Larger specimens are predators.

S: *M. erythrotaenia*, the most sensitive of the genus, is prone to attack by parasitic ciliates and injuries.

T: 74-82° F,   L: 39″,   A: from 39″,   R: b,   D: 3.
    24-28° C,   100 cm,   drom 100 cm,

Mastacembelus zebrinus
Short-Finned Spiny Eel

Syn.: None

Hab.: Found in an area of Eastern India around Trang; in streams with waterfalls.

Fl.: See *M. erythrotaenia*.

Sex: Unknown.

Soc. B.: See *M. erythrotaenia*.

M: Follow suggestions for *M. erythrotaenia*.

B: Has not been bred in captivity.

F: C; all types of live foods; mosquito larvae; small crustaceans; *Tubifex* worms; small earthworms.

S: Differs from other species of *Mastacembelus* by a lower number of spiny rays on its dorsal fin (16).

T: 75-82° F,   L: 3^1/$_2$″,   A: 19^1/$_2$″,   R: b,   D: 3.
    24-28° C,   9 cm,   50 cm,

Macrognathus aculeatus

Mastacembelus erythrotaenia

Mastacembelus zebrinus

Glossolepis incisus

WEBER, 1908

Syn.: None

Hab.: Northern New Guinea; in Lake Sentani and surrounding areas.

Fl.: 1973, A. Werner and Frech.

Sex: An example of clear sexual dimorphism and dichromatism. ♂ has a higher back and fins and a luminous pink body. ♀ has a more elongated, yellow-olive body with gleaming golden-yellow scales and transparent yellow fins.

Soc. B.: A peaceful, timid, active, schooling fish.

M: Recommend hard water neutral to slightly alkaline: 18-25° dGH and pH 7.0-7.5.

B: Breeding is easy. Recommend water 24-26° C with courtship and pairing as

suggested for others of the genus. Use Java Moss as a bottom spawning medium. The eggs, which require 7-8 days to hatch, are tacky and initially as clear as glass. The slow growing fry are immediately free-swimming and seek food directly below the surface. Feed them Rotifers and pulverized egg yolk.

F: C; all kinds of live foods; finely chopped beef.

S: Do not feed *Cyclops* nauplii since these, after ecdysis, will attack the fry. The ♂♂ begin to change to brighter color after reaching a length of 2 inches (5-7 cm).

| T: 72-75° F, | L: 6", | A: 31", | R: m+t, | D: 2. |
| 22-24° C, | 15 cm, | 80 cm, | | |

Melanotaenia fluviatilis
Australian Rainbowfish

(CASTELNAU, 1878)

Syn.: *Aristeus fluviatilis*, *Melanotaenia splendida fluviatilis*, *Nematocentris fluviatilis*

Hab.: Australia: New South Wales and Queensland in the Murray-Darling-System.

Fl.: 1961, "Tropicarium", Frankfurt, West Germany.

Sex: ♂ is more intensely colored with redlines on the caudal peduncle; ♀ lacks both the brilliant coloring and the red lines.

Soc. B.: See *M. maccullochi*.

M: Similar to recommendations for others of the genus: mediumhard water – to 10° dGH – rich in oxygen.

B: Similar to *M. maccullochi*. The breeding is easy.

F: C, O; all kinds of live foods; flakes.

S: This is not an independent species but is probably identical to *M. nigrans*. Some experts feel it may be a cross between *M. nigrans* and *M. maccullochi*.

| T: 72-77° F, | L: 4", | A: 31", | R: m, | D: 2. |
| 22-25° C, | 10 cm, | 80 cm, | | |

Glossolepis incisus ♂

Melanotaenia fluviatilis

Melanotaenia maccullochi   OGILBY, 1915
Dwarf Rainbowfish, Black-Lined Rainbowfish

Syn.: *Nematocentris maccullochi*

Hab.: Fresh waters of northern Australia to Sydney.

Fl.: 1934, "Aquarium Hamburg", Hamburg, West Germany.

Sex: ♂♂ are more brightly colored with sharply extended dorsal and anal fins.

Soc. B.: A lively, peaceful, schooling fish.

M: Recommend a tank moderately planted along the edges and back with fine-leaved varieties and plenty of open swimming space in the front. Use a fine gravel bottom and place the tank where it can catch the morning sun.

B: Use medium to hard water, from 10° dGH at a temperature between 24-26° C. The fish will spawn among the plants in the morning leaving behind 150 to 200 eggs, all suspended by short threads. These will hatch in seven days at 25° C. If fed well the parents will not touch the eggs.

F: C; All types of live foods. Will also take such flakes foods as Tetra Menu.

S: Needs frequent partial water changes. The eggs are sensitive to light.

T: 68-77° F, **L:** 3", **A:** 27", **R:** m to t, **D:** 1.
      20-25° C,   7 cm,   70 cm,

Melanotaenia splendida splendida   PETERS, 1866
Cape York Rainbowfish

Syn.: *Nematocentris splendida, Aristeus fitzroyensis, A. rufescens, Strabo nigrofasciatus*

Hab.: Australia; eastern Queensland, Cape York Penninsula.

Fl.: Possibly 1968 in Europe; 1970 from the US.

Sex: ♂ has a higher back and brighter colors with pointed anal and dorsal fins.

Soc. B.: Similar to data for *M. maccullochi.*

M: Similar to *M. maccullochi.*

B: Follow recommendations for others of the genus. The fish are sexually mature from 2" (5 cm.). The ♂ are very lively during courtship and spawning.

F: C; all types of live foods; *Tubifex; Daphnia; Cyclops;* brine shrimp; mosquito larvae; flakes.

S: While young the fish are slender but as they age they become high-backed, particularly the males. The eggs can be handled if they are kept damp.

T: 68-77° F, **L:** 6", **A:** 35", **R:** b (particularly older specimens), **D:** 2.
      20-25° C,   15 cm,   90 cm,

Melanotaenia maccullochi

Melanotaenia splendida splendida

Gnathonemus petersii
Peter's Elephantnose

(GUENTHER, 1862)

Syn.: *Mormyrus petersii, Gnathonemus pictus*

Hab.: West and central Africa; Nigeria; Cameroons; Zaire.

Fl.: 1950

Sex: Unknown.

Soc. B.: Though peaceful toward tankmates it will harass the weaker of its own species. It is territorial.

M: The fish are nocturnal and need a heavily planted tank with areas of darkness plus caves or other hiding places. The fish burrow and need a soft, sandy bottom. Occasional water changes are suggested along with a good conditioner.

F: Not yet successful.

F: C, O; live foods; *Tubifex*; whiteworms; *Cyclops*; *Daphnia*; mosquito larvae. Will also accept flakes and FD.

S: The fish possess an electrical organ. Their ratio of brain to body weight is larger than with man but unlike man, the cerebellum and not the front brain, is larger.

The fish has been introduced in a German water supply to monitor water quality. The fish normally emit 800 electrical pulses per minute. If the purity of the water drops the fishes become nervous and pulsations increase.

T: 72-82° F, **L:** 9″, **A:** 31″, **R:** b, **D:** 3.
22-28° C, 23 cm, 80 cm,

Gnathonemus tamandua

(GUENTHER, 1862)

Syn.: *Mormyrus tamandua, Gnathonemus elephas* (not BOULENGER) *Campylomormyrus tamandua*

Hab.: Africa; Niger; Volta; Zaire.

Fl.: Unknown. It is often caught along with *G. petersii* and thus overlooked.

Sex: See drawing.

Soc. B.: A relatively peaceful loner, it can be kept with other fishes of similar size. It is suitable for a community tank with large, gentle fishes. Larger fishes will chase smaller ones, preventing the weaker ones from eating.

M: Suggest a large, shallow tank with a sandy bottom, peat filtration and a good water conditioner. Likes a heavily-planted tank (along the edges) and the current supplied by a strong filter. Recommend water with a hardness to 20° dGH and pH 6.0-7.8.

B: Unknown.

F: C; live foods, particularly worms.

S: Is seldom imported and is considered a fish for a specialist.

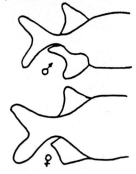

T: 73-81° F, **L:** 16″, **A:** 47″, **R:** b, **D:** 4 (Si).
23-27° C, 43 cm, 120 cm,

Gnathonemus petersii

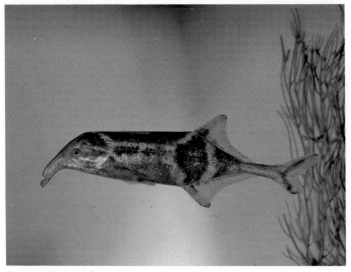

Gnathonemus tamandua

Notopterus notopterus
Asiatic Knifefish

(PALLAS, 1769)

Syn.: *Gymnotus notopterus, Notopterus kapirat*

Hab.: Southeast Asia; India; Burma; Thailand; Malaysia; Sumatra; Java.

Fl.: 1933

Sex: Unknown.

Soc. B.: An intolerant, nocturnal fish, it lives a solitary life and is best kept alone. Patriarchal during spawning.

M: Follow recommendations for *Xenomystus nigri.*

B: VAN PINXTEREN (1974) reports on a successful breeding: DATZ 27, 364-369. The fish spawned at night, dropping eggs on the bottom and on rocks. They were guarded by the ♂ who fans fresh water over the eggs with his pectoral fins, chasing off all other fishes. The eggs required two weeks to develop and the newly hatched young were sensitive to handling. Feed brine shrimp nauplii.

F: C; exclusively live foods; small crustaceans; aquatic insect larvae; snails; worms; fishes.

S: The family consists of the genera *Notopterus* LACEPEDE, 1800 and *Xenomystus* GUENTHER, 1868. The two can be distinguished by the dorsals, which are lacking on *Xenomystus.*

T: 75-82° F,   L: 13¹/₂″,   A: 39″,   R: b,   D: 3.
    24-28° C,   35 cm,   100 cm,

Xenomystus nigri
African Knifefish

(GUENTHER, 1868)

Syn.: *Notopterus nigri*

Hab.: Africa; upper reaches of the Nile; Zaire; Gaboon; Niger. Liberia.

Fl.: 1909, K. Siggelkow, Hamburg, West Germany.

Sex: No external differences have been noted.

Soc. B.: When young the fish school but as adults they are loners; frequently intolerant of their genera though peaceful toward other tankmates.

M: Suggest dense vegetation along the edges with open swimming space in the center (important) with hiding places among roots and rocks. The tank should be slightly darkened. Since the fish are nocturnal, they are best kept alone. Recommend soft, acid water, about 5° dGH at a pH of 6.0-6.5.

B: Little is known about aquarium breeding. In the wild the fish lays 150-200 eggs each about 2mm in diameter.

F: C; avid predators the fish eat all types of live foods; *Tubifex*; whiteworms; insects; insect larvae; molluscs; fishes; earthworms. They can be fed pieces of meat.

S: The fish will emit bell-like sounds, produced by ejecting air from the swim bladder. The fish can be distinguished from other Knifefishes by an absence of the dorsal fin.

T: 72-82° F,   L: 12″,   A: 35″,   R: m,   D: 2-3.
    22-28° C,   30 cm,   90 cm,

Notopterus notopterus

Xenomystus nigri

Osteoglossum bicirrhosum
Arowana

Syn.: *Ischnosoma bicirrhosum, Osteoglossum vandelli*

Hab.: Amazon flood plains.

Fl.: 1912, Arthur Rachow.

Sex: Mature ♀♀ are fatter and adult ♂♂ identifiable by their prognathous jaws and longer anal fin.

Soc. B.: Predators, ready to snap at each other, they should be kept only with larger fishes.

M: Prefers a tank with a fine gravel bottom, loosely planted with hardy plants and with soft, peaty water. Create open areas above for swimming.

B: The fish become large and are too much for most aquarists. Breeding is possible. Spawning is preceded by a simple loveplay. The eggs are very large (to $^1/_2''$ i.e. 1.6 cm). ♂ broods them in his mouth and the eggs develop in 50-60 days. The fry leave after the egg sac is gone and are 3 to 4" in length (8-10 cm.).

F: C; larger specimens eat mostly fishes; otherwise - waterfleas, mosquito larvae etc. Will occasionally accept flakes and tablets.

S: The fish are excellent jumpers and the tank must be covered. Arowana can breath air via their swim bladders.

T: 75-86° F,   **L:** to 47",   **A:** from 39",   **R:** upper, **D:** 4 (C).
24-30° C,   to 120 cm,   from 100 cm,

Osteoglossum ferreirai
Black Arowana

Syn.: None

Hab.: South America; Rio Negro.

Fl.: 1968

Sex: Unknown.

Soc. B.: Similar to *O. bicirrhosum.*

M: Follow recommendations for *O. bicirrhosum.* Suggest slightly acid water to 10° dGH and pH 6.5. Add peat.

B: Successful only in large tanks. A normal hobbyist will lack the necessary space. The fish are mouth-brooders, the ♂ taking the cherry-sized eggs into his mouth. The eggs require 6-8 weeks to develop and on leaving the male the fry are nearly 4" long (9 cm.).

F: C; live food, most commonly fishes; also, tadpoles, large insects and insect larvae.

S: The fish are excellent jumpers and the tank must be well covered.

T: 74-86° F,   **L:** 39",   **A:** from 39",   **R:** t,   **D:** 4 (C).
24-30° C,   100 cm,   from 100 cm,

Osteoglossum bicirrhosum

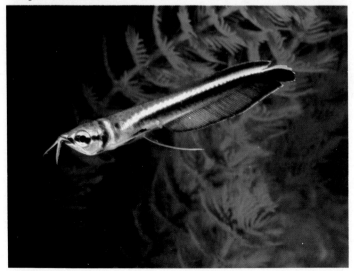

Osteoglossum ferreirai

Pantodon buchholzi
Butterflyfish   PETERS, 1876

Syn.: None

Hab.: West Africa; Nigeria; Cameroons; Zaire.

Fl.: 1905, W. Schroot, Hamburg, West Germany.

Sex: The trailing edge of ♂♂ anal fin features a convex curve and the central rays form a tube. The trailing edge of ♀♀ anal fin is straight.

Soc. B.: Often intolerant of surface fishes, these should be kept with fishes who prefer an aquarium's middle and bottom areas. Smaller fishes may be eaten.

M: Does well in a shallow tank with a large bottom area. Suggest a water level of 6 to 8" (15-20 cm.). The fish will accept any kind of plant though a cover of floating plants is important. Follow the water values given for breeding.

B: Suggest soft to medium hard, slightly acid water, 10° dGH and pH about 6.5 at tempera-

tures between 25 and 28° C. Add peat and instigate breeding with a pairing of one fish of each sex. Successful breeding depends on the parents being fed a variety of foods as well as pupae to induce spawning. 3 to 7 eggs are deposited at each pairing. The eggs are lighter than water and surface quickly. The fish will spawn for a lengthy period each day, dropping 80 to 220 eggs. These are lighter than water, surface quickly and can be scooped from the surface with a large spoon. They can be transfered to a special breeding aquarium. In 25° C water the fry hatch in 36 hours. The young are difficult to raise.

F: C; all types of live foods; flies; mosquito larvae; Daddylong-legs; meal worms; fishes; large flakes.

S: When first laid the eggs are transparent but turn dark brown to black in 8 to 10 hours. The fish are jumpers and the tank must be well covered.

T: 73-86° F,   **L:** 4",   **A:** 31",   **R:** t,   **D:** 3.
23-30° C,   10 cm,   80 cm,

Various True Bony Fishes

Phractolaemus ansorgei   BOULENGER, 1901

Syn.: None

Hab.: In muddy, overgrown areas of freshwater in West Africa; Niger delta; Ethiope River; upper Zaire.

Fl.: 1906, K. Siggelkow, Hamburg, West Germany.

Sex: Mature ♂ have a white bump on their heads and two rows of pointed growths on the caudal peduncle.

Soc. B.: A peaceful, active bottom dweller: borrows.

M: Needs a soft, muddy bottom with dense vegetation and hiding places among the roots. Water quality is not as important as heat. Suggest a hardness to 25° dGH and pH 6.0-8.0.

B: Not successful.

F: C; all types of live foods; chopped meat; flakes, tablets.

S: The fish have a small mouth, barely discernible. It is extended like a nose when feeding. They also have an accessory respiratory system.

T: 77-86° F,   **L:** 6″,   **A:** 31″,   **R:** b,   **D:** 2.
    25-30° C,   15 cm,   80 cm,

Eigenmannia virescens (VALENCIENNES, 1849)

Syn.: *Sternarchus virescens, Cryptops humboldtii, C. lienatus, C. virescens, Eigenmannia humboldtii, Sternopygus humboldtii, S. limbatus, S. lineatus, S. microstomus, S. tumifrons, Cryptops virenscens*

Hab.: Found in fresh-water flood plains of Tropical South America; from Rio Magdalena to Rio de la Plata.

Fl.: 1909

Sex: Illustrates a clear sexual dimorphism of size; the ♂♂ are substantially larger.

Soc. B.: A nocturnal, timid yet gregarious fish. A group will form a rigid social structure with dominant and submissive members. The fish recognize each other and will not inflict injury. They are best kept in a species tank.

M: Use moderately fine gravel. Plants are not essential though a floating cover will create welcome shade. Add hiding places among rocks and pots. The species prefers "old" water with good filtration and subdued lighting. Suggest water with a hardness between 2-15° dGH and a pH 6.0-7.0. In the wild the fish are found in strong-flowing streams laced with occasional dense vegetation.

B: Only recently successful. Data can be found in a paper by KIRSCHBAUM (1982) – Aquarien Magazin, **16** (12) 738-742. According to the author four environmental factors influence maturing of the sex organs: 1 - a continuously low electrical conductivity; 2-a drop in pH; 3 - An increase in the water level; 4 - an imitation of rain. The fishes spawn in the early morning hours. The dominant ♂, nearly always the larger, spawns with the rutting ♀ s. The eggs are tacky, a few being laid at each pairing. They are laid on floating plants if they are available. Depending on the size of the female, 100 to 200 eggs are laid per session. A pairing lasts for several hours.

F: C; all types of live foods; *Tubifex*; mosquito larvae; small crustaceans; snails; small fishes.

S: *E. virescens* have neither dorsal nor caudal fins. The anal fin has about 240 rays. The fish are sensitive to fresh water and you should always use a good water conditioner when making water changes.

T: 72-82° F,   **L**: ♂ = 13$\frac{1}{2}$″, ♀ = 8″,   **A**: 39″,   **R**: m, b,   **D**: 2-3.
     22-28° C,   ♂ = 35 cm, ♀ = 20 cm,   100 cm,

Steatogenes elegans (STEINDACHNER, 1880)

Syn.: *Rhamphichthys elegans, R. mirabilis, Brachyramphichthys elegans*

Hab.: In fresh waters of northeastern South America; Peru; Guyana; Brazilian Amazonia.

Fl.: 1912, Mr. Zeller.

Sex: Unknown.

Soc. B.: A gentle species avoided by tankmates. Can be kept with peaceful fishes of similar or larger size.

M: Suggest a darkened aquarium with plenty of hiding places among roots and rocks. Plant densely. Use old water, soft to medium hard and slightly acid, to 12° dGH and pH 6.0-6.5.

B: Has not succeeded.

F: C; small live foods; *Daphnia; Cyclops*; mosquito larvae. *Tubifex*.

S: Unlike other Knifefishes, *S. elegans* is toothless. The fish is also sensitized to water changes.

T: 72-79° F,   **L**: 8″,   **A**: 31″,   **R**: m, b,   **D**: 3.
     22-26° C,   20 cm,   80 cm,

Eigenmannia virescens

Steatogenes elegans

Enneacampus ansorgii
African Freshwater Pipefish

(BOULENGER, 1910)

Syn.: *Syngnathus ansorgii, S. pulchellus*

Hab.: In fresh and brackish waters of west Africa; from Cameroons to Gaboon in Zaire and Ogowe rivers.

Fl.: 1973

Sex: ♂ has a noticeable stomach ridge which becomes a breeding pouch during the spawning season.

Soc. B.: A harmless, peaceful fish which looks after its brood, it should be combined only with other peaceful species or kept in a species tank.

M: Needs a tank with a fine, sandy bottom and such loose vegetation as *Vallisneria*. We suggest keeping the tank in a sunny area. Use light filtration, aeration and medium hard, neutral water, 10-18° dGH and pH 7.0. Add salt or sea water, 1-2 teaspoon of salt to 2¹/₂ gallons (10 l) of water. The fish will die in soft, acid water.

B: Successful breeding in an aquarium was reported by PEKAR and ZUKAL in Tropical Fish Hobbyist **30** (11): 28-333 (1985). The ♀ spawns above the male's brooding pouch. The eggs adhere to the back of the ♂ s anal opening and are covered by two lateral folds which form the sac.

F: C; exclusively live foods; small crustaceans; *Daphnia*; *Bosmina*; *Cyclops*; diaptomus; brine shrimp; white mosquito larvae. Small fry such as Guppies.

S: The prey is not attacked but simply sucked in. The hyoid bone is imbedded in a flexible membrane attached beneath the oral tube, at eye level. When prey is taken the bone is depressed, stretching the membrane. The gill covers and mouth are closed simultaneously. This produces a vacuum in the mouth which is filled by a sharp intake of water when the mouth is opened. The prey is literally flushed into the oral cavity.

T: 74-82° F, **L:** 6″, **A:** 31″, **R:** m, b, **D:** 4.
24-28° C, 15 cm, 80 cm,

864

Microphis smithi   DUMERIL, 1870

Syn.: None

Hab.: Africa: Found close to banks in areas of dense plant growth in Nigeria and Zaire.

Fl.: 1954.

Sex: ♂ has two ridges along its ventral which form a V-shaped groove. The stomach of ♀ is rounded and, after spawning, the eggs adhere to the stomach of ♂.

Soc. B.: A very peaceful species which attends it brood as a patriarchal family. Be sure to keep it in a species tank.

M: Needs a tank bottom of fine gravel with a sparse planting of such species as *Vallisneria*. Allow open room in the center for swimming. The fish prefer hard water, over 10° dGH with salt added – 2 to 3 teaspoons for each $2^1/_2$ gallons (10 l) of water.

B: Unsuccessful.

F: C; live foods; crustaceans; *Daphnia; Bosmina; Cyclops; Diaptomus;* brine shrimp.

S: The eggs adhere to the male's stomach within the protected shaped area.

T: 72-79° F,   **L:** 8″,   **A:** 39″,   **R:** m,   **D:** 4.
    22-26° C,   20 cm,   100 cm,

Tetraodon lorteti

TIRANT, 1885

Syn.: *Tetraodon somphongsi, Carinotetraodon chlupatyi, C. somphongsi*

Hab.: In fresh waters of eastern India; Thailand; the flood plains of Tachin (Nakornchaisri).

Fl.: 1957, "Tropicarium", Frankfurt, West Germany.

Sex: ♂ has a reddish stomach and a rust-red dorsal fin with greyish-blue at the top and white lines at the rear; the stomach of the ♀ is a light grey with dark spots and stripes.

Soc. B.: A territorial fish, it it is intolerant and aggressive against most tankmates. Though it likes to hide, it will defend the territory vigorously against its own species and occasionally, against other tankmates. According to HOLLY the ♂ adopts a hostile display attitude: a ridge appears along its stomach while a comb is simultaneously erected on its back.

M: Similar to suggestions for *T. palem-*

bangensis. Do not add sea water. The hardness should not be more than 10° dGH with a pH 6.5. A hardness of 5° dGH is preferable.

B: Has been accomplished. Suggest a soft, slightly acid water, 5° dGH and pH 6.5 at a temperature of 26° C. Add Java Moss. Spawning is preceded by marked, almost temperamental love-play, the male holding the female in his jaws. Up to 350 eggs are laid in the moss and will hatch in 30 hours. Remove the parents after spawning. The fry are difficult to raise since many perish through a lack of suitable food.

F: C; live foods; snails; shellfish; earthworms; occasionally such tablets at TetraTips.

S: The pufferfish can often change color. The back may become pale or turn very dark, the choice depending on the surroundings. In lighter areas the fish displays has a light color, in darker surroundings, the fish becomes darker.

T: 75-82° F, 24-28° C, **L:** 2¹/₂″, 6.5 cm, **A:** 23¹/₂″, 60 cm, **R:** m, b, **D:** 3.

Tetraodon fluviatilis
Green Pufferfish

(HAMILTON, 1822)

Syn.: *Tetrodon fluviatilis, Arothron dorsovittatus, A. simulans, Crayracion fluviatilis, Dichotomycter fluviatilis, Tetraodon potamophilus, Tetrodon nigroviridis, T. simulans*

Hab.: In fresh and brackish waters of southeast Asia; India; Sri Lanka; Burma; Thailand; Malayan Penninsula; Indonesia; Philippines.

Fl.: 1905, Julius Reichelt, Berlin, West Germany.

Sex: Unknown.

Soc. B.: A lively, intolerant, aggressive fish though the young are generally peaceful. At all ages they are aggressive toward their own species. Best kept alone and if kept in a community tank, combine only with fish of similar size. ♂ looks after the brood. The fish will attack plants.

M: Needs a bottom of fine gravel, planted densely around the edges and rear. Leave open swimming space in the center and add hiding places among rocks and inverted pots. Suggest hard, neutral water from 10° dGH and pH 7.0. The fish can tolerate fresh water but is at its best in brackish water. They cannot survive in sea water.

B: Has been bred in an aquarium, but only in brackish water. They are substrate spawners and the male guards the fry.

F: C, O; snails; shellfish; earthworms; *Tubifex*; waterfleas; mosquito larvae; lettuce; such tablets as TetraTips.

S: The flesh is poisonous to humans and domestic animals, retaining its toxic effect even after cooking.

T: 74-82° F, 24-28° C, **L:** 6¹/₂″, 17 cm, **A:** 31″, 80 cm, **R:** all, **D:** 3.

Tetraodon lorteti ♀ above, ♂ below.

Tetraodon fluviatilis

867

Tetraodon steindachneri

DECKERS, 1975

Syn.: *Crayracion palembangensis, Tetraodon palembangensis, Tetrodon palembangensis*

Hab.: In fresh waters of Southeast Asia; Thailand; Malaysian Penninsula; Borneo; Sumatra.

Fl.: 1953, Muehlhaeuser, Schopfheim, West Germany.

Sex: Identification is difficult and only possible with adults. ♀ becomes larger and more compressed.

Soc. B.: Intolerant and aggressive, they often attack plants (as they go after snails), leaving holes in the leaves. (See photo, page 895).

M: Needs a bottom of sand with plants along the edges and back. Leave room in the center for swimming. The fish needs hiding places among rocks, roots or inverted pots. The water should be fresh, not brackish, soft to medium hard and neutral, 5-12° dGH and pH 7.0. The fishes should be kept alone.

B: Little is known about breeding methods.

F: C; live foods, predominantly such soft animals as snails and shellfish. Will also eat lettuce and liver.

S: Can be easily identified by the fine network of black lines covering its body and head.

T: 72-79° F, **L:** 2¹/₂″, **A:** 27″, **R:** m, b, **D:** 2-3.
22-26° C,   6 cm,   70 cm,

Tetraodon schoutedeni

PELLEGRIN, 1926

Syn.: *Arthrodon schoutedeni*

Hab.: In fresh waters of central Africa; Stanley Pool, lower Zaire.

Fl.: 1953, A. Werner, Munich, West Germany.

Sex: The ♀ is substantially larger.

Soc. B.: One of the most peaceful of puffers, the fish are tolerant of tankmates though rivals may fight on sight. At that time the fins spread and the contestants nudge each other. The ♂ guards the brood. The fish may attack plants but will not eat them.

M: Similar to recommendations for *T. fluviatilis.*

B: Suggest medium to hard, neutral water, 10-20° dGH and pH 7.0.

The breeding tank should be heavily planted. The fish often lays its eggs at random.

The ♂ holds on to the larger ♀ 's stomach with its mouth and immediately fertilizes the eggs as they are deposited. The eggs may be laid on leaves and are guarded by the ♂. The fry are difficult to raise since the proper food is often lacking.

F: C; live foods exclusively: *Tubifex*; whiteworms; thin-shelled snails and shellfish; earthworms.

S: Much of their skin is covered with tiny spikes, though not around the mouth and tail.

T: 72-79° F, **L:** 4″, **A:** 27″, **R:** all, **D:** 3.
22-26° C,   10 cm,   70 cm,

Tetraodon steindachneri

Tetraodon schoutedeni

Umbra limi
Central Mudminnow

(KIRTLAND, 1840)

Syn.: *Hydrargyra limi, H. fusca, Hydragira atricauda*

Hab.: North America; From Quebec, Canada to portions of the U. S.; i.e. the Ohio River and the Great Lakes.

Fl.: 1901

Sex: ♂ is smaller, lemon yellow to red in color during the spawning season.

Soc. B.: A peaceful, gentle fish, it is territorial only during spawning. At that time it becomes aggressive and intolerant. Matriarchal, the ♀ guards the brood.

M: Needs a bottom of fine, soft sand with dense planting along the edges and back of the tank. Use cold water plants and provide space in the center for swimming. Do not place the tank in direct sunlight. The fish prefer peaty, soft, slightly acid water, about 5° dGH and pH 6.0-6.5. Aeration is not important.

B: The fish spawns in the spring and the eggs require 12 days to develop. Follow recommendations for *U. pygmaea.*

F: All types of live foods; mosquito larvae; freshwater shrimps; most crustaceans; *Tubifex.* The fish will also eat spawn.

S.: Like all mudminnows, the fish can breathe air through its swim bladder. For this reason a space at the top of the tank is required. If the fish cannot gulp air from the surface they will die even though the water is heavily oxygenated. The Hungarian Mudminnow, *Umbra krameri,* most frequently cited in literature, is not available commercially. The species may be extinct.

T: 63-72° F, **L:** ♂ = 4$^{1}/_{2}$″, ♀ = 6″, **A:** 31″, **R:** b, **D:** 2.
   17-22° C,   ♂ = 11.5 cm, ♀ = 15 cm,   80 cm,

Umbra pygmaea
Eastern Mudminnow

(DE KAY, 1842)

Syn.: *Leuciscus pygmaeus, Fundulus fuscus, Melanura annulata, Umbra limi pygmaea*

Hab.: Found in the shallow rivers and marshes of the U.S.: from Long Island to the Neuse river.

Fl.: Possibly 1901.

Sex: ♂ is smaller.

Soc. B.: A peaceful, undemanding, schooling fish, it is territorial only during spawning. It also matriarchal, ♀ guarding the brood.

M: Follow recommendations for *U. limi.* The fish is well suited to a cold water community tank.

B: Suggest water with a temperature of 19-23° C. The fry will hatch in six days at a temperature of 73° F (23° C). The ♀ digs a nesting pit which is aggressively defended against all comers. The ♀ is less aggressive while spawning. 200-300 eggs are laid and are guarded and cleaned by the ♀. She loses interest when the fry hatch. The fry are easy to raise but are quite cannibalistic.

F: C; all types of live foods; flakes.

S: The species differs from *U. krameri* in the number of spiny rays on the dorsal. *U. pygmaea* has three, *U. krameri* has but one. The fishes tame easily, learning their keeper and becoming quite trusting. They can breath through their swim bladders and, in this manner, can meet their oxygen requirements despite adverse water conditions.

T: 63-73° F (Coldwater fish), **L:** ♂ = 4$^{1}/_{2}$″, ♀ = 6″, **A:** 23$^{1}/_{2}$″, **R:** b, **D:** 2.
   17-23° C,   ♂ = 12 cm, ♀ = 15 cm, 60 cm,

Umbra limi

Umbra pygmaea

Aquarium Fish Foods

The Importance of Flakes

80% of today's hobbyists feed their fish flake and tablet foods exclusively. 15% supplement the diet with such live foods as *Tubifex* worms, mosquito larvae and Daphnia at least once a week. Some catch or raise their food while others buy it at a pet store. Only 5% of the world's hobbyists feed foods seasonally, live foods from spring to autumn and flakes in the winter when little else is available. Even in the "off season" some breed Vinegarflies, Fruitflies, Whiteworms, and Grindal worms to feed species choosey about their food and to bring others into breeding condition. Surprisingly, most of the aquarium books written for hobbyists take a negative view of dried and artificial foods.* Modern flake foods are too often ignored or dismissed as offering less than a complete diet, which is far from the truth.

Today's aquarist would face serious feeding problems without the range of staple flakes available from the world's pet stores. In Germany alone, more than one million aquarists keep more than 36 million fish – a staggering number of hungry mouths ready to consume 3,000 tons of live food annually. Where will it come from? Most hobbyists would turn in their tanks and fish if they had to feed live foods exclusively and we can prove the point with just a few figures: an aquarium fish consumes an average of 0.038 grams a day (compared with the Neon's need for 0.014 gram.) That adds up to half an ounce of food per fish per year and with 36 million in Germany alone, it converts to 500 tons of flake food a year.

Feeding Flakes

Within seconds after they are dropped into a tank, flakes absorb water, swelling to three or four times their original volume. The flakes should reach their full size before the fish reach them, and not later in the stomach, and in most cases they will. Only a few fish, such as the Sumatra Barb feed so quickly they reach dry flakes. You can quickly tell if a fish eats dry flakes. It will hang diagonally, its head downward, its stomach swollen.

---

* Neither of the terms "dried food" nor "artificial food" will be used in this book. Both once referred to such replacement foods as wheat flakes, dried Daphnia, dried skimmed milk, yeast flakes and similar items. These were artificial foods in the most basic sense and cannot be equated with today's scientifically-developed foods. Todays foods are truly complete diets.

If you have a tank full of such hasty eaters hold the flakes between your fingers and dip them into the water for ten seconds before releasing them, but in most cases it is sufficient to simply broadcast the flakes across the surface. We do not recommend a feeding ring since the flakes will not have sufficient time to asborb water. In addition, timid fish will not get their share since the food is not dispersed.

Feeding Frequency

Two to four feedings per day is enough in a community tank and at night be sure to feed flakes more than half an hour before the lights go out. Such nocturnal species as catfish will feed after the lights go out. We suggest using one half to one Staple Tablet Food , one half a Tetra Tip or similar tablet food for every two inches (5 cm) of catfish in your tank. Fry to $3/4$ of an inch long (2 cm.) should be fed four to six times a day and breeders may need more, perhaps as many as 8 feedings a day.

An Analysis of Food

In many countries there is no requirement to indicate analytically, the contents of a package of fish food and often, on smaller packs, there is not even room, but a manufacture should provide this information – if not on a package, then in readily available brochures and leaflets.

Fats

The amount of fat in a food plays an important role in determining its quality. The amount should be as low as possible. For carnivores or meat-eaters 3-6% is ideal. For herbivores the content should not exceed 3%. A higher concentration can be harmful, affecting the liver, even damaging reproductive organs.

Fiber Content

The fiber content should be substantially higher than the fat. The minimum is 2% and good foods will have considerably more. Fibers stimulate intestinal activity.

Albumen or Protein Content

The desirable amount of albumen depends on the species of fish being fed. Fish considered as carnivores (C) under the "F" category in the species description, should be fed food with an albumen content of 45% or more. Herbivores (H) in the same description, require a protein content between 15 and 30%.

Carbohydrate Content

Carbohydrates are organic compounds consisting of carbon, hydrogen and oxygen. They can be found in potatoes, cereals and such pulses as beans, peas and lentils. Some authorities feel carbohydrates in fish foods can be harmful to many species. For example, they are said to cause infertility in Labyrinth Fish and Characins through a degeneration of the liver and reproductive organs. Such fatty degeneration considered as a pathological change and attributed to certain types of flake foods may not be caused by carbohydrates. The experts may be wrong. Labyrinth Fish can be fed flake foods for years without the problem developing and we feel it is more likely to result from the wrong composition of albumen and too much fat (i.e. the wrong albumen and fat combination). Such herbivores as Carp-like fishes are able to form carbohydrates from their own body fat. On the other hand, predators or carnivores cannot. Consequently, the latter generally excrete carbohydrates undigested.

Water Content

In most flakes this ranges between 6 and 12%. Add more and the food may deteriorate quickly. Since a flake is designed to be hygroscopic, that is water absorbent, the containers should be kept tightly covered and food should be used within one year. As the food absorbs humidity the bacterial action increases, breaking down the food, eventually turning it into a brownish dust. In the end it gives off an unpleasant ammonia-like smell. Keeping the container tightly covered keeps oxygen out, avoiding the premature oxidation of important vitamins.

The Vitamin Content

The quality of the various foods and the nutrients in them is decisively determined by the number of vitamins included and their ratios. Unfortunately you can learn little of this from information supplied on most packages. There is not a lot of information on many foods and you cannot discover how much, or, how little, to feed. Nor can you learn how rich in vitamins the food is. Experts raising food fishes know exactly how much to feed Carp or Trout but the hobbyist has little data to help him feed Neons and other aquarium fishes.

Meeting the Vitamins

There are a number of recognized vitamins. Among them: A, D_3, E and K are liposoluble, that is can be dissolved in fat. Vitamins B_1 (Thiamin), B_2 (Riboflavin), B_3 (Nicotin acid), B_5 (Pantothene acid), B_6 (Pyridoxin), B_{12} (Cyanocobalamin), and C (Ascorbic acid) and folic acid are all water soluable.

Vitamins And What They Do

Vitamin A is important for cellular growth, particularly in younger fish. The extent of its influence in the development of eyes remains uncertain.
Symptoms of deficiency: poor growth and distortions of the back and fins. Since Vitamin A is liposoluble it cannot be added to water, only to food. It is unstable and sensitive to air and light.

Vitamin D_3 plays an important role in developing a fish's boney structure. Most fish foods contain a large amount of fishmeal and since fishmeal is generally derived from the liver it has a high proportion of Vitamin D_3 and there are rarely problems. No symptoms of a deficiency are known.

Vitamin E has been called the fertility vitamin. It is particularly important in the development of sexual organs in breeding pairs. Vitamins E and A must always be present in the proper portions since one cannot be effective without the other.

Vitamin K is important in the formation and coagulation of blood. If deficient, a fish may become aneamic, bleeding to death if scratched or cut.

Vitamin B_1 helps to break down carbohydrates and is needed to maintain the normal functions of the nervous system. It also promotes growth and fertility and plays an important role in digestion.
If deficient a fish becomes listless, refusing to eat, showing poor growth and becoming timid.

Vitamin B_2 is needed to regulate the body's various enzymes, digestive and otherwise, and it important for utilizing protein.
Signs of deficiency include poor growth and a loss of appetite and may lead to a clouding of the eyes.

Vitamin B_3 the body needs to extract the various amino acid components for forming its own albumen from the food consumed. It is therefore especially important in breaking-down food. Signs of a deficiency include weakness, poor digestion, listlessness and, at a later stage, open sores.

Vitamin B$_5$ controls both metabolism and the production of hormones in the suprarenal glands. A deficiency may produce atrophied cells, sticking gills and a general debility.

Vitamin B$_6$ is important to the enzyme system and is essential for the metabolism of proteins. A deficiency may lead to rapid breathing, loss of appetite, stunted growth and timidity.

Vitamin B$_{12}$ is also important for metabolism.

Vitamin C is essential for the formation of teeth and bones. It helps heal wounds, is essential to the enzyme system for purposes of digestion and promotes the formation of cartilage. A deficiency produces marked changes in the skin, liver, kidneys and muscle tissue. The full importance of vitamin C to the health of fish remains largely unresearched.

Vitamin H (= Biotin) promotes cell growth. A deficiency hinders the formation of blood, particularly the red corpuscles.

Cholin is needed for good growth and to help break down nutrients, particularly fats. It regulates the blood's glucose or sugar content and a deficiency may produce enlargment of the kidney and liver.

Vitamin M or folic acid, plays a part in metabolism and in the formation of blood. A deficiency is seen in dark pigmentation on the skin, weakness and changes in the kidney and related organs.

Inositol plays an important role in the permeability of cell membranes and, if there is a deficiency, may be seen as a difficulty in processing food, a loss of appetite, poor growth and, quite often, ulcerations.

p-Aminobenzoid Acid stimulates growth but science has not yet proven whether or not the vitamin is essential.

Live and frozen foods do not necessarily contain more vitamins than flakes. A staple diet must contain an adequate quantity of all vitamins plus the other substances fish need and a good flake food does. You can choose a prepared food with confidence if it is an advertised brand from a major manufacturer with a date showing its optimum shelf life. You can then be certain of its freshness and freshness is an important guarantee of an active, balanced vitamin content.

Minerals and Trace Elements

Calcium and Phosphorous are particularly important for the development of a fish's boney skeleton. In most commercial fish foods the two components are found naturally in fishmeal processed from fish bones. There should be few problems. It should be noted that, unlike vitamins, minerals and trace elements have a long shelf life. They are not adversely affected by prolonged storage.

Since the natural ingredients used to manufacture fish foods include vegetable matter the major products offered in pet shops supply all of the important trace elements in sufficient quantity. Deficiencies are more likely to occur when you try to feed live and dried animals foods and any dietary problem that develops can be corrected by the regular addition of a good flake food.

The following percentages can be considered as comprising a good fish food:

Fish Group	Protein (albumen)	Fat	Raw Fiber
C*	over 45%	min. 3%, max. 6%	min. 2%, max. 4%
H	15-30%	min. 1%, max. 3%	min. 5%, max. 10%
L	30-40%	min. 2%, max. 5%	min. 2%, max. 6%
O	35-42%	min. 2%, max. 5%	min. 3%, max. 8%

These guidelines apply most to manufacturers. In actual brands of food sold in pet stores the fluctuations should be much less.

* Explanation see page 200.

Live Food

Live food caught in local waters and fed to hobby fishes introduces a risk of disease, which greatly increases in the warmer waters of a tropical aquarium. Examples include the dreaded *Ichthyophthirius multifiliis* or Whitespot disease.

In addition *Hydra* or freshwater polyps, fish lice, leeches and other ectoparasites can be introduced to an otherwise clean tank. The danger is substantially reduced if food is caught in a small pond that does not contain fish and the ideal solution is to keep the necessary food in your own – fishless – garden pond, in a discarded bathtub, large cans such as milk cans and similar containers. This kind of isolation gives you a margin of safety.

Examples of Live Foods:

1. Crab-like Foods

a) Waterfleas *(Daphnia pulex, Daphnia magna, Cyclops,* etc.)

Waterfleas such as these, given once a week for variety, are a good suplementary food. Their chitin external skeleton and intestinal tract (filled with single-celled algae) form a valuable balance for many species of fish (C,L and O in our Feed Plan). They provide a healthy stimulant for the digestive tract though many fishes, if fed these frequently, will spit out the flea or its empty shell or merely toy with it. Few fish can be fed waterfleas exclusively and, placed on a prolonged diet will soon show signs of dietetic deficiencies. Fed with care however, no aquarist need deny himself the pleasure of feeding waterfleas to fishes whose predatory instincts, barely seen when fed flakes, is restored in seconds as you add waterfleas and all fishes in a tank zero in on the live food.

b) Cyclops, particularly those a bright red, are an excellent source of nourishment for younger fishes. But remember, *Cyclops* can be harmful to fry since *Cyclops* is a small crab and can dig its claws into the small fry's body, literally eating into its flesh.

c) Freshwater Shrimps (*Gammarus* sp.) are a welcome food for most the larger Cichlids. They are found in small, clean streams between the roots of plants, most often on the decaying portions. Most fish reject the hard shell and *Gammarus* die quickly in most aquariums because of high temperatures and a lack of oxygen. Particular care must be taken when offering them as food.

Gammarus is the primary food of most wild Trout and is of undisputed, high nutritive value but, all things considered, are hardly suitable for a tropical aquarium. Among other problems they are difficult to catch.

d) *Artemia* or Brine Shrimps (*Artemia salina*), have become the main source of animal food for most of the world's aquatic breeders, hobby or commercial. It is found in a number of brackish waters around the world, from the salt lakes of Utah to parts of San Francisco Bay and since no fish can live in such salty water there is no danger of disease. The eggs are collected in the fall by the ton as a by-product of salt-making and are dried, cleaned or hatched, then sold in many forms – from fresh, living brine shrimp to freezedried and vacuum packed brine shrimp and eggs. Special production processes guarantee a high yield in years with good harvests and hobbyists who hatch their own eggs find a satisfying percentage of the eggs readily. But during bad years many infertile eggs are produced. The shells are empty or the nauplii or larvae are dead in their cases. It is wise to buy only from a well-known, major supplier who can guarantee a fair yield. The eggs can be kept for more than ten years when they are vacuum-packed and stored in a cool place.

The nauplii are an excellent starter food for most fry, both livebearers and for many larger egg layers. The nauplii of brine shrimp from San Francisco Bay are somewhat smaller than those from Utah and are preferred by most breeders. Young fish can be safely fed this food and it is easy to hatch at home.

How to Cultivate *Artemia*

Place the eggs in a weak salt solution, 1-2% iodine-free table salt, about one heaping teaspoon to a quart of water. Aerate and the nauplii will hatch after 24-36 hours at a water temperature around 24° C.

When properly set-up with a good air supply both the *Artemia* culture and the aquarium filter can be operated from one diaphragm pump.

To collect *Artemia* nauplii the air hoses on the culture bottle are changed round. The pressure hose is placed on the shorter pipes on the bottle. The nauplii are then caught with an *Artemia* sieve.

Brine shrimp can grow to adulthood in a 3% concentration of salt water and can be fed single-celled algae. They reach a length of 8-10 mm and while this may seem like a lot of work, marine aquarists take it in their stride. They breed brine shrimp in order to continually have live food on hand. However even small fish cannot survive on a diet of brine shrimp alone. Eventually signs of a dietetic deficiency become obvious. Experienced aquarists therefore add supplemental feedings of either live pond foods or a flake food rich in vitamins.

2. Worms

a) *Tubifex* (River Worms)

Considering that these worms are found in muddy river bottoms, heavy with ofal and detritus, in water so polluted no fish could live in it, the worms can hardly be recommended as a perfect food though they do make and excellent emergency fill-in for species which will not touch food which does not move. *Tubifex* worms are also low on the list of recommended foods because of their high albumen content, which produces a slimy excretion in the fish which eat them, and because of the risk of absorbing toxins found in the waters from which the worms are collected. If you feed *Tubifex* worms they should be soaked in water for several days to remove the accumulated poisons. They should be rinsed several times or washed in a bucket which has a sieved bottom.

Feed the worms sparingly and in small quantities. The fish should immediately swallow the worm, which is one milimeter wide and 3-5 cm long ($1-\frac{1}{2}''$). If not, a portion of the worm may fall to the bottom and dig into the gravel where it will die and rot.

Tubifex

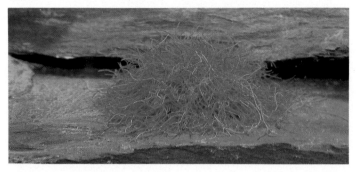

b) Enchytraea

The favorite haunt of these 10-30 mm long white worms is beneath damp leaves, in compost and between seaweed at the seashore. While fish love them they should be never be considered more than an occasional supplement. They are rich, fatty and if given in excess will cause constipation and degeneration of the liver. They can be cultured at home in a cool cellar, at temperatures around 15° C.

To raise, combine equal amounts of loose garden soil, sand and granulated, unfertilized peat in a plastic flower pot or container. Keep it slightly damp. Breeding stock can be obtained from pet shops or from sources listed in hobby magazines. The worms can be fed with Tetra Conditioning Food and a little oatmeal which has been boiled with $^1/_3$ milk and $^2/_3$rds water, then cooled. Feed one heaping teaspoon of oatmeal gruel for each one thousand worms. The surplus should be removed as it curdles.

Place a sheet of glass over the bucket to prevent the soil from drying since the worms naturally prefer moist areas. On a beach they spend high tide under water.

Mites will find their way into the culture and inhibit its growth and the soil mix should, from time to to time, be removed and replaced. The culture should be kept dark.

c) Grindal Worms

These can be conveniently cultivated on a layer of foam in almost any bowl, which neatly avoids the necessity of mixing soil —and generally prevents an infestation of mites. The worms are cultured as you would Enchytraea. Grindals are a good substitute food for fry to a size just under one inch in length (2 cm). Feed five to 10 worms per fish but remember, most fry will overeat. They love the food.

d) Earthworms

Large Cichlids and other predators enjoy earthworms, which should be cleaned and free of dirt, their natural mucuous covering removed. Worms can be cleaned by allowing them to crawl through damp grass. The so-called "red dew" worms, found in many fishing stores, are a favorite bait and can be recommended. The browngray chestnut worm, not common in the U.S., is less popular.

Earthworms are rich in albumen and since its composition is clearly acceptable to fish, the food is heartily recommended. Continual feeding will neither create a dietetic deficiency nor fatty degeneration. Culturing the worms, however, is laborious, requiring considerable space. Hobbyists with gardens should grow worms in compost piles. The worms prefer a rich but friable soil and you can mix sawdust with earth to keep it soft and moist. Vegetable matter, such as clippings, grass cuttings and weeds are suitable foods.

3) Mosquito Larvae

a) **Bloodworms** *(Chironomus).* These larvae are relished by most fish. Their red coloring is remarkably similar to the blood's own hemoglobin, which accounts for their name. The worms are difficult to catch since, like the caddis fly, they build small cocoons of earth, mud or plant particles, hiding on the bottom of clean ponds. Bloodworms hatch from autumn to spring and form swarms of several hundred to several million insects, a black cloud sweeping across the landscape. Fertilization takes place during swarming, the eggs are laid immediately and the cycle is repeated on the bottom of the pond. *Chironomus* mosquitos do not sting.

b) **Black Mosquito Larvae** belong to a variety of mosquito species. The males have bushy feelers and the females a stinging proboscis which punctures the skin. They must ingest the blood of mammals to reproduce and always keep their hind legs off ground. For identification purposes, the midge stands on all six.
Black mosquito larvae are an excellent food for aquarium fish. They contain a number of important elements such as vitamins and an albumen which seems to encourage many fish to spawn. The larvae are much simpler to catch than bloodworms since they live on the water's surface. They use a special breathing tube which looks much like their proboscis or "stinger". It is located at the rear. Pupated larvae have two breathing tubes at the front.

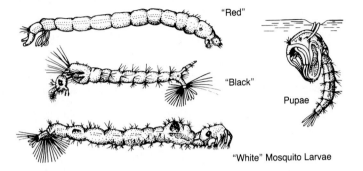

"Red"

"Black"

Pupae

"White" Mosquito Larvae

If the surface of the water is disturbed the larvae and pupae head toward the bottom in jerky movements and if you try to catch some, you must act very quickly. If not, you will miss them. If you use the larvae for feeding, keep the aquarium covered so that those not consumed will not hatch and escape. You can slow down the process, for two or three days at least, by adding 1/2% table salt to the water in which you keep them. Decreasing the water temperature also slows the hatch. If you are lucky enough to catch a large number, you can preserve the excess by freezing.

c) **White Mosquito Larvae,** also known as Glassworms, are found only in clean water. They are both scarce and an unimportant aquarium food. The larvae belong to the genus *Corethra* or *Chaoborus,* the gnats. They do not sting, stay in open water, generally swim horizontally, and feed on a variety of small organisms. Some breeders insist the larvae will attack fry but they are a popular pond food for fish from $1^1/_2$ inches (5 cm).

d) Drosophila

A culture of the stump-winged fruit flies can be bought from breeders. There are ads in aquarium magazines. Insects that can already fly can be caught from acid fruit or in an open red wine bottle. However, these flies can hardly be used as fish food. They disappear from the aquarium at once.

It is important that no normal-winged fruit flies are used for breeding, because this cross breeding would result in great masses of winged flies. These are inappropriate as fish food or would at least become a complete nuisance in the room.

The stump-winged flies rest on the surface of the water and can thus be used as food for different species of fish like Hatchetfish, *Nannostomus* (Pencilfish) of for fish which are ready for spawning (especially when no live pond food is available in winter).

The fruit flies to be bred are fed with an acidic mush or rotten food like bananas and peaches. This mush can also be made from canned plums, pears and peaches. The fruit is thickened with wheat bran and boiled, the addition of a piece of bakers' yeast (the size of a filbert) will start fermentation. After cooling, pour into a mason jar, cover with very fine gauze or pantyhose, to prevent the fruit flies from flying off. It is necessary to start several jars in order to have another jar after the contents of the first one have been fed. The temperature of this culture should be between 20° and 24° C. Such fly breeding is very cumbersome, yet it can be rather rewarding to succeed in breeding a rare species of fish.

e) Microscopic food

Good microscopic food from ponds cannot be bought. One has to catch it. The mesh size of the net should be less than 0.1 mm for the forenet and 0.01mm for the main net. Such netting material is sold under the name of miller's gauze and has to be ordered from a specialized dealer. Micro food consists of plankton (although not all can be used. e.g. paramecium, as these sting and are scorned by fry), bosmides, radiolarians, etc. Whoever is interested in microfood should get special books. Every trip to a pond becomes an event when you take a microscope or 10× magnifying glass along. The breeding of certain fry is impossible without micro food from ponds. You can breed your own micro food. There are several recipes. Some swear by steeping hay, some by protogene granulate, others try dried banana peel. Sponge filter pads or cartridges usually contain lots of microscopic food!

4. Frozen Food

Bloodworms, Black Mosquito Larvae and various species of small shrimp and brine shrimp are available from most pet shops, frozen and packed in a variety of sizes including individual feedings. These are more readily available in the U.S. and Canada than in Europe and are said to account for 50% of all fish food sales reported there in the last decade. While frozen foods are still popular, flakes are cutting into their sales.

An increased interest in freeze dried foods has also reduced interest in frozen foods since freeze dried foods are easier to handle, package and store.

Freeze Dried Foods

The list of available foods includes *Tubifex*, Bloodworms, brine shrimp and various small shrimps, shellfish, plankton and more. Our comments about live food also applies to freeze dried foods. The advantage of these is that they can stored, almost without limitation, provided they are kept cool and dry. When food is freeze dried all of the nutrients available when the food was alive is preserved.

Even so, you are advised not to feed freeze dried foods exclusively, particularly in the case of *Tubifex* worms, brine shrimp and plankton since these may cause dietic deficiencies. *Calanus*, especially, demands caution since it is quite heavy in fats. In nature it is a food for Hering and similar plankton eaters and when given to fish for prolonged periods the imbalance may affect internal organs, particularly the liver and kidneys (in a process called fatty degeneration). Brine shrimp can be too salty and if the intake exceeds 1-2%, the build-up of salt may prove to be toxic over a period of time. Most recommended of all freeze dried foods are blood worms which are commercially available.

When food is freeze dried it is first frozen then the moisture is evaporated at a temperature low enough to preserve the food elements. The process does not disturb vitamins, minerals and other important nutritonal elements. In short, the moisture evaporates, the nutrition remains.

Freeze dried foods have the same nutritional value as live food but are preferred over it because disease cannot be transmitted. If there is a draw back it is that the food does not have the same active appeal live foods have. In our opinion, it has no advantage over flakes. The food is appreciably more expensive and not nearly as versatile as a good flake though we'll admit some fish prefer freeze dried bloodworms to flakes everytime.

Routine Aquarium Care

Once your aquarium has been established, once the plants are growing, the fish eating and the biological system working, you can relax. Let the tank settle and adjust. The plants should not be changed for several months but after a week or so the tank will need to be cleaned, removing such detritus as dead leaves, algae and the excrement from fish. Algae can be controlled indirectly by the water conditions and more directly by algae eating fish.

Your aquarium should be cleaned regularly every two to six weeks and we suggest this plan:

1. Turn off the electrical equipment, heating, lighting and such, by unplugging it. If you use a bottom heating mat or a cable, these can remain connected during cleaning.

2. Remove and throughly clean the aquarium hood and glass cover. Deposits of chalk can be removed with vinegar and water, household decalcifiers or an application of hydrochloric acid gently diluted with water. But remember, what ever the solution, rinse the parts thoroughly.

3.Clean the inside front glass, removing all signs of algae. The easy way is to use a magnet or long-handled scraper. Algae on the side panes can remain if you

keep algae-eaters in the tank. Remove algae from the rear glass only if it interferes with the backdrop.

If there is any sign of blue algae on the glass or brownish algae on the gravel, it should be removed completely. If you've used medication all algae should also be removed. It will absorb and store toxins which are dangerous to your fish.

4. Next, clean vegetation, removing dead leaves, pruning faster-growing and taller plants and add gravel around the roots if burrowing fish have disturbed it. The leaves can be nipped with your finger nails and the gravel can be moved by hand.

5. Detritus and other debris can be removed from the gravel with a hose or suction-type bottom cleaner. You must be thorough since decaying material consumes a lot of oxygen. Do not over look the filter strainer, removing any vegetation which has collected on it. As you do this you'll remove water, sometimes as much as one third of the tank. (More if the water is especially dirty.)

Whether you use a hose or a suction-type bottom cleaner, be careful. Do not accidently remove any of the smaller fish. Black Mollies are particularly thick-skinned and curious. As a precaution do not insert the open end of the drain hose directly in the drain, but place a net in front of it. It will safely catch any fish which might be accidently drawn in. A suction cleaner is safer. When siphoning water, aquarists generally place one end of the hose in a bucket, moving the other end over the bottom of the tank. If you are not careful you can remove gravel as well as debris and to prevent this, we suggest inserting a small funnel into the end of the hose or in the input basket of an external filter.

6. You should also disconnect power to the filter, stopping the air supply in the tank. Do not touch either the wall socket or the filter switch, if it has one, with wet hands. Dry your hands or use a dry towel.

It is not easy to clean an external power filter so that sometimes the job may be put off for months on end – which is not good for the tank. The process of decomposition consumes valuable oxygen and is not good for your fish. In time the water develops a distinctive odor and the fish are stressed and weakened.

Once you learn, it is easy to clean a filter. Here is one easy way:

a) Remove the input pipe. The pump will continue to drain surplus water for a few moments.

b) As soon as the water stops flowing remove the discharge pipe as well. Drain any remaining moisture into a bucket until the hose, above the top end of the filter, is dry.

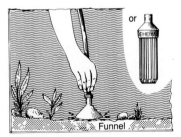

or

Funnel

If you are not careful the bucket could overflow before you can stop the flow of water. We suggest placing it in a sink or larger bucket to prevent spills.

c) Place the input end of the filter in the bucket, holding it at a point lower than the filter itself, removing any water which may remain. If you would rather, remove the filter and drain it into a tub or bucket.

d) Now, remove the filter's lid. If it is a screw-on type it may be difficult but here is a trick which makes it easy. Hold your thumb over one of the hose openings, then blow on the other. This increases pressure inside the filter and the lid can be removed.

7: Remove the filter material and, depending on the design, either replace it or rinse it thoroughly. Do not use hot water since heat will destroy the carefully cultivated bacteria which comprises the biological filter. The foam cartridges used in smaller external models can be cleaned by squeezing them under running water and other filter mediums should be cleaned in accordance with the manufacturer's instructions. Remember, activated charcoal cannot be used a second time. It will have absorbed toxic materials and it is safest to replace it with new carbon. Likewise, peat should not be cleaned and reused. If you use peat to soften water, the old should be replaced with new, clean material.

8. Reassemble the cleaned filter and connect it to the tank. Plug in the power and restart the motor. Here is an easy way to restore the siphoning action:
Refill the tank with clean water, adding a good water conditioner in whatever ratio the manufacturer requires for the amount of water you've added. The filter's discharge outlet should now be under water. Hold the outlet hose a few inches above the tank's water level and the filter should automatically fill. Once the water in the filter is level with that in the tank you can plug in the power supply and the filter will automatically start. If the pump makes any noise it is generally caused by residual air bubbles which will be quickly expelled. The process can be speeded up by shaking the filter several times.

Once a constant flow of water comes from the hose, the unit is working properly. It may take an experienced hobbyist less than ten minutes to clean an external unit, though a new hobbyist may need an hour. The job can be made easier by using valves and quickrelease couplings on the important lines. The more you plan ahead and, in a sense, the more you spend on valves and accessories, the easier the job will be. Don't forget to use washers on all hose connections. If you don't, the connections may leak – quite often directly on a carpet. If there's no safety vent on your external filter it is worth the time it takes to drill one. Make an opening 2-3 mm in size, an inch or two below the water level. Then, if a hose bursts, only a little water can escape instead of the entire contents of the tank.

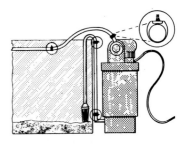

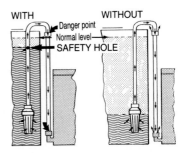

WITH   WITHOUT

Danger point
Normal level
SAFETY HOLE

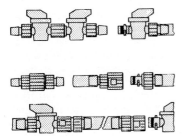

9. Reconnect the heater.

10. Replace the glass and the aquarium hood. Plug it in and turn on the light. As a final step, clean the outside of the glass.

We recommend a good commercial window cleaner on the outside, but use it with care. Be sure none of the cleaner sprays into the tank – it could be poisonous.

An additional word on water changing. Old time hobbyists feel the water in an aquarium can never be "too old", however there is little scientific data to support such a theory. Toxins and other harmful substances, particularly waste albumen from food and excrement, must be removed regularly. The way to do that is with a water change. The frequency depends on plant growth and the number of fish in your tank. The more plants you have, the less often the water needs to be changed. On the other hand, the more fish you keep, the more frequently water needs changing. The term, however does not imply replacing the entire contents of the tank. As a rule, one quarter to one third of the water is siphoned off during the cleaning process. The lost water should be replaced with fresh tap water. Tap water, however, often contains such chemicals as chlorine and chloramines, especially in the U.S. You may need to control these with special chlorine and chloramine conditioners. Sodium Thiosulfate, a photographic chemical known as a "fixer", makes a good dechlorinating agent, but commercial products have the added advantage of stabilizing the pH. Water which is too hard can be treated by passing it through a softener (see the chapter on Chemistry, page 37). Boiling water helps to reduce its chalk content.

Many hobbyists feel tap water should be heated to the tank temperature before it is added, but this can be difficult if there is no easy way to heat it in quantity. Experience indicates that there is no objection to adding cold water provided it is done slowly and not more than one third of the water is changed. As an example let us assume that the temperature of tap water is 12° C while the water in the tank is 26° C. The temperature of the water in the tank, after mixing, would be 21° C, acceptable for most fish and harmful only for such delicate species as Discus. We feel you should fill a tank in stages, waiting after each, until the aquarium heater has raised the water to the proper temperature. If you don't want to go through this process, then the tank must be filled with properly heated water. If the aquarium water is particularly dirty, it may be necessary to remove more than one third. In that case too, you may need to heat the replacement water.

If the water is this dirty change two thirds, rather than one half, and remember if the water is high in ammonium (which would normally be converted to ammonia) it is potentially poisonous. With the recommended two-thirds water change, enough is removed to substantially reduce that problem.

If, for any reason, you must make a complete water change, remove the fish to a bucket or plastic bowl and aerate the emergency quarters with a pump and airstone. If the fish must remain there for some time add a heater to keep the water at the proper temperature. Do not place the bucket on any surface which may alter the temperature, for example on a cold, concrete floor or against a heater vent.

As soon as the tank has been cleaned and refilled, you must check the water to be certain it is adjusted to values familiar to the fish. This means temperature, hardness and pH must be similar to the water you removed, though there is room for fluctuation. A drop in pH from 8.0 to 7.0 is not harmful nor is a difference of 10° dGH in hardness. On the other hand, transferring fish from water with a pH of 6.5 to one with a pH of 8.0 can induce serious shock in many species. Stress of this kind (called osmosis change) can be reduced by adding a product like AquaSafe.

Aquarium Pests

1. Algae
2. Duckweed
3. Hydra, leeches, diskworms
4. Snails

1. Algae
a) Green Algae

Green algae generally develops as a result of uneaten food and too much light. To nip the problem in the bud, add algae-eating fish. Possibilities include various types of catfish, *Hypostomus, Ancistrus, Hemiancistrus,* and *Pterygoplichthys*, the Siamese Flying Fox, *Crossocheilus siamensis*. *Poecilia* (formerly *Limia*) such as *Poecilia melanogaster* are also good algae eaters. Since many are nocturnal they gain little from the daily feedings and will starve if there is no algae. To be certain they get enough to eat, feed them food tablets just before dimming the lights for the night.

If you try to control or reduce algae chemically you will probably inhibit or eliminate growing plants at the same time. As explained in our chapter on tank cleaning, green algae should be left on the sides of the aquarium as well as on rocks and decorative items for your algae-eaters.

The family of green algae includes varieties of thread, which, as the name implies, form long threads. It can be removed easily with a plastic scraper. The group also includes a single-celled green algae which can cause a condition called "water bloom". It may occur with explosive suddenesss in the spring, when the water turns an opaque green in a few days — the result of too much light and uneaten food. The solution is to reduce the size of the feeding, limit the amount of light in the tank and make an immediate water change. If you do not reduce the light, the algae will simply bloom again in the fresh, new water. Another possibility is to use very strong filtration or add *Daphnia* or water-fleas. If you try filtration, change the material daily.

Fur Algae (green algae)

Bear Algae (red algae)

Free-floating thread algae (green algae)

893

b) Blue Algae

These generally form in water of poor quality, the result of a high nitrite and nitrate level. Green algae cannot grow in polluted water, but blue algae can – in nitrate levels near 200 mg/liter. Green algae will die above levels of 30 mg/liter. Nitrate can be removed with a water change and by filtration through an apporpriate exchanger. In practice, a regular water change offers you the best protection since it removes detritus and mulm as well. If the tap water contains more than 30 mg/liter of nitrate (and it can) green algae will not grow and common aquatic plants will never fully develop. The reason: the higher the nitrate content, the more light plants and algae need. Vegetation aborbs only a small amount of nitrate as a nutrient and denitrification is strongly recommended. Fish do not eat blue-green algae and in the ocean, only a few crustaceans find it palatable.

Infestations of blue-green algae can be controlled chemically, but removing the causes and changing water is the preferred treatment.

c) Algae on gravel

The algae found on the bottom of an aquarium is often incorrectly called "brown algae". The true brown algae are seaweeds such as kelp, found only in the ocean.

The "brown algae" found on the sides of an aquarium indicates a shortage of light. The glass appears brownish and seems covered with a thin layer of chalk. The algae can be easily removed with a sharp-bladed scraper. When similar algae is seen on the bottom gravel it generally indicates extra-hard water. Plants seldom do well in a tank with super hard water and the water values should be checked immediately. Replace part of the contents with soft, desalinated water. The quantity of light should be increased, doubled or more. You may need to add an additional tube or a more powerful bulb.

Blue-green algae

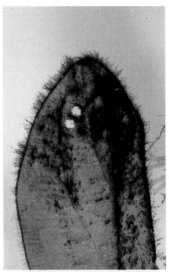

Brush algae (red algae)

Gravel algae

d) Beard Algae

Though similar to green algae, this variety produces a larger shoot, sometimes as thick as a ribbon and, though deep green in color, it belongs to the same family as red algae.

Fish do not eat it and chemical controls are not always effective. The only way to remove it is to remove the plants and decorations which are affected. Wind the threads around a thin, rough stick and pull them free. If the algae returns, repeat the treatment.

You'll often spot it first in the filter and on decorations such as roots and rocks. Remove these items, place them in boiling water to remove the algae, then replace them.

e) Brush Algae

These belong to the same family as red algae and are considered the most difficult of all to deal with. Unfortunatly, they are often found in an aquarium. You'll rarely see it on younger plants since it is generally introduced on older plants recently added to a tank. It varies from dark green to black in color and is difficult to remove. Pulling it out by hand, as you might thread algae, is impossible since the hairs are minute, 2-10 mm. in length and cannot be scraped or wound on a stick. If you spot it, strike instantly. Break off all leaves which harbor the algae with a

clippers or your finger nails. Chemical controls are possible only in tanks without fishes. Cichlids are especially vulnerable.

Another problem algae, both rare and difficult to describe, are decomposing algae. In most cases these will be blue-green algae already in a state of decomposition. (See photo top right.)

The red algae common in marine tanks is not found in freshwater aquariums because the pH is too low, however they could be found in an African Cichlid tank, one with rocky outcroppings, since these fish can tolerate a pH to 9. You can eliminate the problem by reducing the tank's pH to 8.0. The drop will not disturb the Cichlids.

Photo, top right:
Tanks with yellow water and an infestation of algae on both the plants and the glass, requires urgent cleaning along with a complete water change. If not, both the plants and fish will die.

Blue-green algae

Red Algae

2. Duckweed

Most commonly introduced with live food, Duckweed is a popular plant with such herbivores as Silver Dollars (*Metynnis*), *Distichodus, Abramites* and *Leporinus* sp. African Cichlids such as *Pseudotropheus aff. zebra* will eat it if they are hungry. Though it is a sign of good water quality, Duckweed reproduces so quickly it soon reduces the amount of light reaching the bottom, eventually affecting the quality of the plants below. The only way to remove Duckweed is by hand, scooping it into a fine-mesh net.

3. Hydra, leeches and diskworms

These pests are animal not plants and are introduced into a tank with live foods. *Hydra* can be controlled with copper sulfate but, since this is toxic to fish and plants, it is not advised and must be used with great caution. Try a dosage of 0.50-0.80 ppm (parts per million) and remember copper sulfate will not be effective if is used with Tetra's AquaSafe due to the latters high metal ion-binding capacity. *Hydra* are not harmful to aquarium fish, but these freshwater polyps can attack and devour fry. Since they can survive only on live food you can readily control them by adjusting the food you give your fishes. As they lose their source of nourishment, they will slowly die.

Leeches are seldom found in an aquarium, but you may occasionally spot one, like the *Hydra*, introduced through the feeding of live foods. To protect your tank, screen the live food before you feed it. The easiest way is to pass the food through a properly-sized net.

Diskworms are not harmful to fish but can become a nuisance if you have a tendency to overfeed your fish. They are light-brown in color and can be controlled by copper sulfate, though this is not advised. The best solution is to stock the aquarium with a few fish that eat the worms – the Blue Gourami *Trichogaster sumatranus* and Paradise Fish.

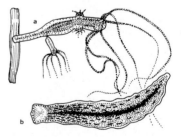

a) *Hydra*; b) diskworm

If diskworms get out of control the only solution is to empty the tank, remove the gravel, filter and decorations and disinfect every part in a saline solution. Everything must be rinsed thoroughly with clean water before the tank can be rebuilt. The worms can also be controlled by increasing the water temperature to 32° C. You must, obviously, remove the fish beforehand though most plants can tolerate the high temperature for a short period of time.

4. Snails

a. Trumpet or Spire Snails

The beautiful Malaysian trumpet snail, with its pretty spiraled, pointed shell, is not harmful to fish and can be considered useful since it burrows through the gravel keeping it open and friable. Many aquarists consider it a good sign when this little snail makes a tank its home. They do not touch plants and come out of the bottom at night to live on the remains of food which has filtered down during the day. Their numbers can be controlled by regulating the amount of food they receive. At night they will collect on the glass just beneath the water line where they can be caught with a net and passed along to other aquarists as a most welcome gift.

Trumpet snail

Ramshorn snail

Small pond snail

Snail spawn

b) Ramshorn Snails

Occasionally found in local ponds, they can be seen in several color forms, red, black and checkered. Over-feeding will cause their numbers to increase and these snails can be a problem since they may eat plants. You can safely leave 10 to 20 in a tank, but more should be removed.

c) Pond Snails

These small snails are found locally and can be introduced with live food. There are both left-spiraled and right-spiraled varieties and the larger ones will eat plants. On this basis alone they should removed and there are two ways to do it:

1. Puffer fish relish these and Ramshorn snails.

2. Place a saucer upside down on the bottom of the tank and just before you turn off the light place two or three food tablets in its center. Within a few hours the tank's snail population will have gathered for their feast and you can remove the saucer along with the unwelcome snails. If you have catfish in the tank you can forget this idea since the fish will reach the food long before the snails. This species will not greatly multiply if you control the amount of food it receives.

d) Apple Snails

The *Ampullaria* or Apple snail grows to the size of a tennis ball and is the pride and joy of many an aquarist. Not everyone can successfully raise them. Do not combine them with larger fish since they could damage their sensitive breathing tube. And be sure to count the snail population daily. A dead and decomposing snail is deadly. It can quickly poison the water, killing all of the fish. If you breed snails, do it in a separate tank.

Their favorite is flake foods scattered on the surface and their eggs are laid in honeycomb-like chalk cells set above the the the water. Apple snails are also helpful allies in breeding tanks since they are scavengers. They will eat dead fry and never attack live fish.

Do not attempt to control snails chemically. As indicated above, the fleshy part of the snail, with its high protein content, will quickly decompose and poison the water. Instead, gather up the snails by hand if there are too many in a tank. Remember, most chemical snail controls contain metal salts which, in turn, are neutralized by water conditioners. You should not be surprised if snails survive happily despite the use of an expensive eraticator.

Ampullaria (Apple snail)

Leaving Your Aquarium Alone

Perhaps the premier advantage of keeping fish, when compared with other domestic pets, is that they can be left alone for periods of time without special attention. A weekend away from home is no problem at all and well-fed adult fish can actually go several weeks without food. Fry, on the other hand, should never go more than one day without feeding. You can solve the problem with an automatic feeder or, better still, with the aid of a helpful neighbor. The most important point is this: to survive an absence your fish must be healthy and sound before you leave. Do not add new fish for at least six weeks prior to your vacation. This is the only way you can be certain a new arrival has not infected your tank.

Before leaving clean the tank thoroughly, replacing at least one third of the water. Be sure to treat the new tap water with a good conditioner and double check the filter. It must be clean and the bacteria which form the "living bilogical filter" must be active and effective. This alone, provides a buffer in case of a power outage. Do not remove the algae since it is a valuable source of supplementary food for many fish.

A community tank with peaceful, undemanding fish can be adequately fed with an automatic feeder. A good one should also control the lights, turning them on in the morning and off at night. This is important for continuous and vigorous plant growth. If you simply leave the light on while you are away it can adversely affect your plants even though they also receive daylight.

Set the feeder to operate once or, at the most, twice each day. The frequency depends on the size and quantity of fish in your tank. Remember, it is easy to over-estimate feedings, even for a small tank and we suggest running a week-long test before you leave. If a feeder costs $25.00 to $50.00 compare that with the cost of your aquarium and fishes, or even with the cost of your vacation, and you'll quickly see a feeder is an effective, indispensible bargain.

If you decide not to buy a feeder you can either leave the fish alone (for no more than two or three weeks) or have them fed by a reliable friend. The basics can be quickly explained to an outsider and the easiest procedure is to write out a "care and feeding" schedule, including points to be checked – water temperature and the tank condition among them. Since people often feel sorry for fish, remind your friends that is is easy to overfeed. Remind them that this is a cardinal sign. The best answer is to pre-measure daily feedings for the time you'll be away. Friends can't go wrong that way.

If all your inexperienced friend need do is shake the contents of an envelope of food into the tank then the only disaster to guard against is overheating. If you cannot avoid hot sun (by moving the tank) ask your friend to check the heater, flourescent tube and water temperatures and if it becomes too warm, have him darken the room. It would be good to have your temporary aquarium-keeper make a practice run before you leave. Incidently, if you use pre-measured food it is a good idea to include a food tablet or two for safety's sake.

If you feel uneasy about either of these proposals there is a third possibility. Remove the fish (tank and all if possible) and leave them in the care of an experienced aquarist-friend (or at a retail store. Some pet shops provide this service.) You need not worry about anything, including proper feeding and daily lighting, but we suggest hooking the tank to a timer switch. These are inexpensive and worth the investment. Whether you move your fish or the entire tank, be sure to continue running the filter to keep the biological filter operating. You can then immediately replace your fish when you return.

Hygiene and Quarantine for Aquarium Fish

In order to prevent the introduction of parasites or infectious diseases to fishes already in an aquarium, or to breeders, all fish to be added should be placed in quarantine. This is usually done in quarantine tanks that are kept in a separate room. Smaller glass or plastic tanks can be used for this purpose. Tropical fish have to be kept in heated tanks. Constant, good aeration is recommended. The quarantine for food, plants, gravel, and stones should be at least three days. Newly bought fish usually are separated for four, but better six weeks. Only after this time is it assured that the tank will not be infested.

Aquatic Diseases

Many beginners take up the hobby only to quit when their fish become ill or die without explanation. It is usually a question of quitting too soon. Generally the disease is unnoticed, incorrectly diagnosed, improperly treated or allowed to progress until little can be done. In some cases not only the fish are gone but the plants as well. It adds up to a frustrating set-back the new aquarist cannot cope with. He has lost confidence and has no desire to try again.

If you find a disease or situation you cannot explain ask your local pet store for help. Many retailers are long-time hobbyists with a wealth of experience. They can tell you instantly how to correct the problem. They know which products to recommend and what dosage to use. A good dealer will never suggest a product that does not work and when a situation is serious or possibly terminal, will explain both the problem and the probable consequences.

There are hundreds of aquatic diseases and it is impossible to attempt an encyclopedic account of them in one chapter. Instead we will discuss the most common diseases, breaking them into five categories — symptoms, methods of diagnosis, the cause, an explanation and corrective action. This approach should help most hobbyists diagnose the common diseases quickly and accurately. In addition you will learn about both the causes and seriousness of the disease as well its prevention.

When approaching the problem of diseases, you should consider conditions which may cause them. In the strictest sense these are the "original cause" even though they may be mistakes, too often overlooked. We will begin by examining the (biotic) or living and (abiotic) or non-living factors found in your aquarium.

Negative factors

The fish in your aquarium live in a close balance between the living and non-living factors in their environment and when one segment varies, the balance is disturbed. The tank may be jeopardized.

Non-living factors include such obvious things as temperature, light, pH and the water quality, that is the nature and quantity of such things as nitrite and nitrate content, carbonate, overall hardness and more. Biotic factors include food, plants, undesirable foreign animal material and plant life (freshwater polyps, planarium worms, green and blue-green algae) and the fish.

Factors which may adversely affect fish can be attributed to such toxic materials as these:

1. Heavy metal ions (iron, lead, copper, etc.). All tend to break down the mucous coating of the fish and destroy the epithelium of the gills producing respiratory problems, paralyzing shock and death. For this reason you should not allow any metal to be introduced into the tank.

2. Chlorine. Free chlorine is highly toxic. Just 0.1 mg per liter can prove fatal. It attacks the gills, leading to a loss of color and death through oxygen starvation. Chlorine can be removed by boiling or the use of sodium thiosulfate though today most hobbyists use prepared chlorine conditioners.

3. Phenol and derivatives. Organic compounds, these are toxins which affect the nerves. They can also damage the gill epithelium, intestine and skin. Liver, muscles and reproduction glands may also be affected and though it is generally incurable, it is rare a hobbyist will find the problem in his tank.

4. Hydrogen sulphide. A gas, it reminds one of rotten eggs. It is highly poisonous, even in small quantities, and generally causes quick death. In an aquarium it is caused by dirt and debris, polluting contaminants found in the gravel. The early signals are an increase growth of algae. Hydrogen sulphide binds the iron in the blood's hemoglobin, blocking the absorption of oxygen. Symptoms include violet gills and respiratory trouble, the fish gasping for air at the surface. The problem can be prevented by using coarser gravel and by cleaning it often.

5. Detergents. Compounds most often used in household cleaning, these reduce the water's surface tension. Detergents destroy the mucous which covers the fish's body, inhibit the resorbent qualities of the gills and destroy the red corpuscles in the blood. To prevent the problem never use household cleaners in your aquarium or to clean any equipment.

6. Nitrogen. Every aquarium contains some nitrogen compounds. They result whenever albumina (metabolic products from fish, decaying remains of plants and food) are broken down. The most common are ammonia (NH_3), ammonium (NH_4^+), nitrite (NO_2^-), nitrate (NO_3^-) and urea. All can only be broken down in the presence of oxygen, which robs the tank of oxygen the fish need to survive. Oxygen starvation slows the decaying process and increases toxic ammonia. For ammonia the fatal dosage is 0.2 mg per liter; for nitrite, 1 mg per liter; for nitrate, 200-300 mg per liter. Nitrogen compounds can kill your fish. For example, the toxic effect of ammonia is largely determined by the pH. It forms most readily in alkaline water.

The quantity of nitrogen can be checked by means of simple tests and manufacturers such as Tetra offer kits. With them you can identify the problem, then correct it (through good aeration to increase the break-down of nitrogen.) We recommend making regular checks of pH and oxygen values. At the same time do not overfeed.

A Lack of Oxygen

Symptoms: The early warnings are increased respiration, restlessness and a continued gasping for air. The fish loose their color and the gills are open. Without relief the fish will die, literally through strangulation. Oxygen starvation is one of the most common causes of death in an aquarium.

Cause: The problem is a shortage of oxygen in the water and oxygen is, if course, vital to the metabolic process. A lack can come about in many ways. First, from decaying food, plants and other things in the tank (which consume oxygen in the process of decaying), secondly, through the nocturnal respiration of plants and finally, from too high temperatures. Less oxygen is dissolved in water at higher temperatures. It is important to remember that the oxygen requirements of fish varies and consequently species which live in fast-flowing (well oxygenated) streams need more oxygen than those found in slow-moving and standing water.

Explanation: Unless the low oxygen level is increased, the fish will die. In addition, a temporary reduction in oxygen will stress the fish, weaken your charges and increase the incidence of disease.

Action: Immediately aerate the water. An effective filter can solve the problem, guaranteeing an adequate supply. Remove all dead vegetation and fish since decomposition requires oxygen. Balanced vegetation will stabilize the oxygen levels and the fish should be kept at a temperature which is best for them. If the problem is acute only immediate action, a quick water change or inmmediate aeration, can help.

Gas Bubble Disease

Symptoms: Blisters are formed beneath the skin and inside the body, the bubbles found most around the head, the eyes and in the eyes. According to SCHUBERT, larger fish affected with the problem give a croaking sound when removed from the water. The disease can easily be seen by the naked eye.

Cause: A specific quantity of gas is always dissolved in liquids, whether water or blood, in relation to such factors as pressure and temperature. When too much gas is dissolved for the relationship it creates a highly unstable condition known as "over saturation". The over saturated liquid will continually attempt to release the excess gas in the form of small bubbles. Over saturation can result from the heavy plant and algeal growth common with too much sun. The plants themselves assimilate and release a lot of oxygen. As a result, the fishes' blood becomes over-saturated as well. If you reduce the sunlight plant growth slows and the situation is alleviated – though excess gas remains in the fish's blood. It is this which produces the bubbles.

Explanation: In extreme cases the problem can lead to death through asphyxiation or gas embolism.

Gas bubble disease in a Damsel fish.
It can be diagnosed by the bubble in the
eye.

Action: The best cure is to return the fish to normal water. Good aeration with an air stone prevents over-saturation and as a precaution avoid placing an aquariuim where it can get too much sun.

Acidosis and Akalosis

Symptoms: Affected fish display an excess of mucous, inflammation of the skin and bleeding and erosion of the gills. Their darting movements can also be a key. They often jump in an attempt to to leave the water. Respiration will increase and they may be seen at the surface, gasping for air.

Cause: The problem stems from fluctuating pH values, that is the concentration of hydrogen ions. Each fish is at home in a certain pH range, which for most aquarium fish is between pH 6.0 (slightly acid) and 8.0 (slightly alkaline). Individual species have varying sensitivities. Many can tolerate wide fluctuations while others can live only within a narrow range. The ideal for some, such as *Rasbora*, is in an acid range (pH 5.0-6.0) while others, such as *Barbus*, prefer alkaline water (pH 7.0-8.5). Dropping the pH below 5.5 is accompanied by skin problems (acidosis) in most cases. An increase in pH above 9.0 can also cause problems, erosion of the skin and gills (Alkalosis) in many fish. Water with too low or too high pH can cause death. Low values in combination with soft water are especially dangerous.

Action: The best remedy is an immediate water change and if you can't do that, transfer the fish to water with a neutral pH. Prevent the problem by checking pH values regularly, once or twice a week. A number of reliable test kits are available.

908

Be sure values never exceed a low of pH 5.5 or a high of 8.5. An exception are the Lake Malawi Cichlids, many of which are at home only in water between pH 8.5 and 9.2. You can also prevent the problem by avoiding too much sun and a heavy growth of plants.

Detrimental live factors

Examples of detrimental living factors are the "pests" outlined previously, freshwater polyps (*Hydra*) and planarians (*Turbellaria*). *Hydra* is a freshwater version of the sea anemone (Coelenterat). It consists of a trunk with tentacles at one end. These include stinging cells with which the *Hydra* paralyzes and catches its prey. While the polyp does little harm in an aquarium, it can multiply quickly and will eat larvae and fry. In quantity it can compete with the fish for food.

Action: You can deal with the problem either biologically, by adding fish which eat *Hydra* (Macropods and species of *Trichogaster*) or chemically, adding copper sulfate, see page 898, 3. The *Hydra* die after a few days. The dosage will not harm the fish and will, in fact, help fertilize any plants.

Planarians or "diskworms" are usually introduced with live foods and if conditions are right they will quickly multiply. They are predators and compete with fish for food. They are partial to fish eggs, greatly reducing the likelihood of successful breeding. Planarians have been been found on young fish.

Action: *Turbellaria* are difficult to control. Baiting is generally the better approach. Fill a small gauze or fabric bag with meat and at night hang it near the bottom of the tank. The worms scent the meat and will gather in quantities. If the bag is removed before morning the worms come with it. They can be destroyed in boiling water. Planarians are also eaten by Macropods.

(Parasitosis) – Visible Diseases

1. Single-celled Organisms

Oodinium or Velvet

Symptoms: The disease is seen as patches of velvety-gray or bluish-gray on the sides of the fish and under a microscope this is found to be numerous single-celled organisms pear-shaped to spherical in form. These will occasionally penetrate the skin causing inflammation. When the gills are affected bleeding, inflammation and tissue degeneration can occur and the fish may be seen gasping for air. When acute, the skin may actually peel off in strips. The fish will rub against rocks and plants and may lose weight.

Diagnosis: If possible examine live material, skin and gill smears are good examples. Segments of the gill and fins can be removed and examined under a microscope at an enlargment between 120 to 600 power.

Cause: The cause of Velvet or *Oodinium* is a dinoflagellate called *Oodinium pillularis* which was discovered and described by SCHAE-PERCLAUS, 1951 on *Colisa lalia*. The disease is most common on aquarium fishes and can vary in form from a rounded oval to a pear shape, 30 to 140 μm in size. The average is 65 μm. With the proper enlargement you can see the chitin envelope which surrounds the animalcule. It is pointed at one end and the parasite uses this to attach itself to the fish. There are three stages to its life cycle: 1) parasitic, a stationary growth stage when it is seen on the body and gills; 2) cyst stage, when the parasite falls away from the host and divides several times; 3) free-swimming stage when the elliptical divisions or dinospores are infectious and dangerous. They have two flagella, one located in annular groove. If the dinospores do not find a new host they die in 12-24 hours.

Explanation: A mass infestation can produce severe damage to the skin and gills. Death, through asphyxia, may occur. The disease is highly infectious.

Dinoflagellate

Oodinium pillularis

Action: The best cure is a prolonged bath in Trypaflavine at a strength of 1 g to 100 liters of water. Increase the water temperature to 30° C. Be sure to use a separate "hospital" tank, one without plants or gravel. For best results it should be darkened. Other remedies include Copper Sulfate (0.3 g to 1000 liters of water), Quinine Hydrochloride (1.5 g to 1000 liters of water) or a 3% solution of table salt. Reliable, pre-mixed, ready-to-use remedies are also available from your local pet store.

Costia (Costiasis)

Symptoms: The body is covered with a veiled, grey coat and a heavy infestation can cause reddish, blood-colored patches on the skin. The fish may swim erratically in see-saw fashion, closing their fins and rubbing against plants, decorations and rocks. They may also be tired, listless and may lose weight.

Diagnosis: The disease can only be identified from living samples, fresh gill or skin smears for example. Place these under a microscope and enlarge them 100 to 120 times. The pathogen can be recognized by its tumbling motion.

Cause: *Costia necatrix* is a bean-shaped flagellate 8 to 20 μm in length and 6 to 10 μm wide, with two flagella which are used for propulsion. The parasite attaches itself to the skin with a suction disc and a pointed end. It reproduces by dividing and can survive only one half to one hour without a suitable host.

Costia generally occurs only in a crowded tank. It will not thrive at temperatures above 25° C and cannot survive above 30° C. Research indicates it reproduces best at or below 25° C in moderately acid water, pH 4.5 - 5.5.

Explanation: The parasite can cause substantial damage and fry are particularly susceptible. The disease is transmitted directly and is highly infectious. It can be fatal for smaller fishes.

Action: Bathe infected fish in a 1-2% salt solution for 20 minutes or a mix of Formol 1:2000 (i.e. 1 ml to 2 liters of water). A 15 minute soak will do the job. A prolonged (two days) immersion in a solution of Trypaflavine has also proven effective (1 g to 100 liters of water). Increasing the water temperature to 30° C is also helpful. Prepared medications are available from pet stores.

Flagellate
Costia (Ichthyobodo) necatrix

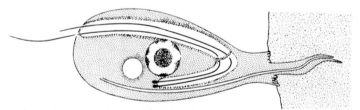

Ichthyophthirius or White Spot (Ichthyophthiriasis) (North America: ICH)

Symptoms: The entire body, fins and gills, are covered with prominent white spots. If the attack is especially heavy the spots may combine into patches of gray. The skin becomes slimy and infected. The fish close their fins, rub their bodies against rocks, plants and decorations and eventually become thin and listless.

Examination: If possible use live fish, making smears from the gills and skin. Combine these with a drop of water and enlarge 50 to 120 times.

Cause: Ich or White-Spot is caused by the ciliate *Ichthyophthirius multifiliis*, an organism with body pear-shaped to spherical in form and 0.2 to 1 mm in size. Their macronucleus is horse-shoe shaped and the micronucleus is spherical.

912

Ichthyophthirius spends much of its life on a host fish, feeding off the skin, digging sealed-off hollows into the flesh. The parasite has a three-stage life cycle: 1) growth, spent on the skin; 2) cyst, when it drops to the bottom of the tank protected by a gelatin covering then dividing and; 3) the infectious stage, when pear-shaped zoospores seek a new host. The cyst can divide into as many as 1000 zoospores which have 70 hours to find a new host.

Explanation: This is a highly infectious disease which can attack all species of fish. The survivors acquire an immunity but may remain dangerous since they may be carriers without showing signs of the disease.

Action: The parasite must be identified then you can handle the problem best by attacking Ich in its third or free-swimming stage. We suggest the use of Malachite Green Chlorooxalate, Trypaflavine, Atebrine, Aureomycin or Quinine. Any of these should used for 15 to 20 days, the length depending on the temperature. It can take as long as 20 days for the three cycles to be completed.
Pet stores stock a number of reliable medications (e.g. Tetra Contra Ick).

A freshwater Pufferfish with *Ichthyophthirius multifiliis*. The parasites can be seen as white spots on the fins.

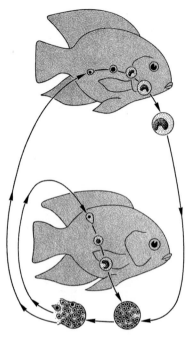

Ciliates

The life cycle of Ich according to AMLACHER.
Top: Zoospores develop in the fish's skin.

Bottom: The zoospores or ciliospores in cyst form (right) and (left) free-swimming.

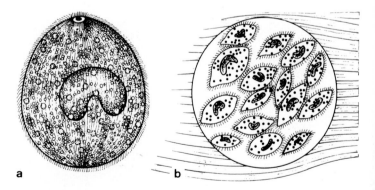

Ichthyophthirius multifiliis: a) single adult; b) cyst stage with numerous zoospores.

Chilodonella (Chilodonelliasis)

Symptoms: The skin and gills become discolored, generally bluish-white to grey in color. The heaviest infection is normally seen in an area from the back of the head to the dorsal. The skin may be discolored and shredded and the fish will rub their bodies against rocks, decorations and plants for relief. Their swimming is impaired.

Diagnosis: Use only live fish since the parasite departs once the host dies. Take smears from the skin and gills and highlight them with dye. Place the slide under a microscope, enlarging it 50 to 120 times.

Cause: The disease is caused by *Chilodonella cyprini*, a holotrichous ciliate. It is oval shaped, between 40 and 70 μm in size. The rear of its head is concave which has given the parasite the name "heart-shaped skin clouder" in Europe. In addition to its size and shape, it can be identified by a grainy appearance. The macronucleus is of uniform shape covering about two-thirds of the parasite's length. The micronucleus is spherical. It reproduces by lateral division. Under certain conditions basal cysts can be formed and we do not yet know how the parasite feeds.

Explanation: When a fish is heavily infected the disease is generally fatal and fish can be damaged in two ways: 1) gill segments are affected, their numbers may be reduced and the fish will have respiratory problems resulting in asphyxiation; 2) the skin is gradually eroded.

Action: Malachite Green, prepared in a commercial remedy, is extremely effective. You can also place the fish in a solution of 1% table salt for 10 minutes followed by a ten hour bath in Trypaflavine. Be sure to increase the water temperature to 28° C. Since overcrowding is a prominent cause, you can minimize the problem by reducing the populations of suspected tanks (allowing five quarts of water per [normal-sized] fish). Be sure the water has plenty of oxygen, has the right temperature and the recommended hardness and pH. Make regular water changes and be sure to quarantine new fish.

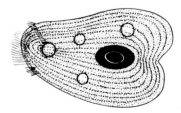

Ciliate
Chilodonella sp.

The disease can also be cured with medication available from your pet store.

Trichodina (Trichodiniasis)

Symptoms: Though generally not visible, an overwhelming attack may be seen as a gray film on the skin and gills. The most common symptoms are that the fish gasp for air at the surface and lose weight. *Trichodina* is commonly found with Ich.

Diagnosis: Examine smears from the sin and gills under a microscope. Enlarge the slide 100 -200 times.

Cause: The disease is caused by peritrichous ciliates of three genera, *Trichodina*, *Trichodinella* and *Tripartiella*. The cell has a spherical body 25-75 μm in diameter. A semi-circular macronucleus can be seen under magnification along with vacuoles. The organism has a suction with rings located on the lower side. It reproduces by lateral division. *Trichodina* can survive in free-swimming form for 24 hours and must find a host within that period. *Trichodina pediculus* may be introduced together with *Hydra* as you feed live food.

Explanation: It rarely causes death but, once it penetrates the skin, the disease becomes dangerous.

Action: You can immerse the fish for short periods (five to ten minutes) in a 1-3% solution of table salt, glacial acetic acid (1 ml to 5 liters of water), Formol (1 ml to 4 liters of water) or Potassium Permanganate (0.1 g to 50 liters of water). We feel the best results come from ten hour immersions in Trypaflavine or Malachite Green (1.5 mg to 10 liters of water). Long baths are the most effective.

Ciliate
Trichodina sp.
Ventral View

Diseases

2. Multicelled Organisms

Dactylogyrus or Gill Worms

Symptoms: The root cause is not visible and there are few external symptoms though it can be identified by these signals: damage to the gills, a redness or inflammation in the gill structure, bleeding of the gills, noticeable growths, and inflamed or slimy gills. With a heavy infestation the fish will lose weight. The pathogen can be readily seen with a microscope. The worms are generally found on the gill leaves.

Diagnosis: Examine a portion of the gills under a microscope at a magnification of 50-120 power. The gill may be taken immediately from the fish or may be fixed in formalin. Remove the flukes by cutting them and observe the slide under a drop of water.

Explanation: The problem is caused by a monogenetic fluke (Trematode), *Dactylogyrus vastator, D. anchoratus. D. minutus, D. extensus, D. crassus, D. lamellatus* or *D. formosus. Dactylogyrus* infections are rare in an aquarium but *Tetraonchus monenteron* and *Cichlidogyrus tilapiae* are more common. The first is found in Angels and Glass Fish. The front segment of *Dactylogyrus* has four conical projections with a black "eye" and a suction cup visible under magnification. The cap on these consists of a suction disk and two hooks. The pathogen lays eggs from which ciliate larvae hatch. The species varies in length from 0.5 to 2.3 mm.

Explanation: The monogenetic fluke is dangerous, particularly in a massive attack, and can cause great damage in a tank. Younger fish should be considered the greatest risk. The infection destroys the gill epithelium and damages blood vessels, resulting in respiratory collapse and, eventually, death through asphyxiation.

Action: The flukes can be controlled by immersion in any of these solutions: a 60-second bath in Ammonium Hydroxide (1 ml of 25% Ammonium Hydroxide for each liter of water). Do not keep the fish in the solution for more than one minute. Try a $2^1/_2$% solution of table salt for 15 minutes or a prolonged immersion (several days) in Trypaflavine (1 g to 100 liters of water). You may also use Quinine Hydrochloride (1 g to 500 liters of water) or Rivanol (1 g to 400 liters.)

Gyrodactylus

Symptoms: Unlike *Dactylogyrus, Gyrodactylus* attacks the skin and can be identified under a microscope. Heavy infestations produce a gray discoloration on the skin with inflammed, reddish patches visible. The eyeless worms can be identified by their typical hooks.

Diagnosis: Prepare smears of the skin adding a drop of water before the slide is placed beneath the scope. Magnify the slide 50 to 120 times. Smears from the tissue of dead fish are not suitable since the parasite leaves upon the death of the host. Smears from preserved fish are also unsuitable.

Cause: The parasite is a monogenetic fluke, a Trematode or sucking worm of the genus *Gyrodactylus* – *G. elegans, G. medius, G. cyprini, G. bullatarudis.* They range in size from 0.25 to 0.8 mm., are without eyes and have a visible adhesive disc with two centrally-located hooks and 16 lateral hooks in the rear. The worm is viviparous, laying no eggs. Instead, it produces an embryo (sometimes called a "daughter") which contains a second embryo (sometimes called a "grandchild"). Up to four generations can be programmed in this way, an extreme example of paedogenesis. The fluke is generally associated with inadequate tank maintenance.

Explanation: An attack of this fluke is harmful, especially to younger fishes. It feeds on the skin, damaging the outer layers.

Action: Your pet store will recommend a prepared remedy.

Diplozoa *(Diplozoon)*

Symptoms: Adult Diplozoa can be seen with the eye, identified as greyish- brown, worm-like organisms found between the fringes of the gills.

Trematode (Sucking Worm)
Monogenea
Dactylogyrus sp.

Monogenea
Gyrodactylus sp.

Diplozoon paradoxum

As the pathogen increases, the gills become inflamed. Eventually they will close. Bleeding may occur and the fish will surface, gasping for air.

Diagnosis: Follow our recommendations for *Dactylogyrus* and *Gyrodactylus*.

Explanation: The cause is a *Diplozoon – D. paradoxum, D. barbi, D. tetragonopterini*. All are monogenetic flukes or trematodes 1 to 5 mm long. They are without eyes and have two suction cups at the front and four pairs of adhesive "arms" at the rear. They lay large, yellowish eggs, each with an attached thread. Freeswimming larvae develop from these and eventually attack fish. As they grow the larvae develop a dorsal cone. When two approach each grips the other with its ventral suction cup. They then grow together forming a "double". In the case of *D. paradoxum* they are attached at the back while in the case of *D. barbi* they are connected along the flat side of the body.

Explanation: A slight attack is seldom dangerous but a massive infestation can be. As the trematodes attack the gills the fish become short of breath. *D. barbi* is found chiefly in Cyprinids *(Barbus* sp.) while *D. tetragonopterini* is limited to Characins.

Action: *Diplozoon* are harder to treat than *Gyrodactylus* or *Dactylogyrus*. We suggest a short bath in a solution of table salt (15 g per liter of water) or longer immersions in Trypaflavine, Rivanol or Atebrin (Mepacrine Hydrochloride) using 1 g per 100 liters of water). Allow the fish to remain in the solution for several days. A few products may prove only marginally effective.

Cercaria and Metacercaria, Black-Spot

Symptoms: Both can be identified as long, yellowish cysts on the fish's head. They may be found in muscles, eyes, gills, blood and internal organs. You will see an opaque film over the lens of the eye. The cysts are often black which results in the common name, Black-Spot disease.

Diagnosis: Prepare a smear from the lens of the eye, or from the muscle of a freshly-killed fish. Examine the slide at a magnification of 50 to 120 power.

Cause: The disease is caused by the larvae of several digenetic worms (Cercaria and Metacercaria). The larvae of two, *Diplostomum spathaceum* and *Clinostomum* deserve special mention. They can lie undetected inside a cyst and their life cycle depends on a change of host. The eggs are laid in the water where the newly-hatched ciliate larvae finds its first host, a water snail. It developes into its second larval form, called a sporocyst, in the snail's liver. By a process called parthenogenesis, it turns into a third larval form called the Redia. The Redia produces larvae (called Cercaria) which must soon go in search of fish. They discard their forked tails and penetrate the host. The fish forms a cyst around the attacking larvae and from this point on the larvae are known as Metacercaria. If an infected fish is captured by a bird the cysted Metacercaria dissolve in the bird's stomach and become mature worms. In all of nature this is one of the longest and most complex life cycles. The organism can reach a length of 0.5 mm.

Explanation: A heavy attack can kill aquarium fish. Damage to the muscles can cause paralysis and, if the eyes are involved, blindness. The metabolism may also be affected. The disease is not infectious.

Action: There is no cure for the problem. Parasites lodged in the skin may be removed with a sterile needle or scalpel but the job is dangerous considering the small size of the fishes involved.

Diseases

Ventral View of a *Trichodina*
species (ciliate)

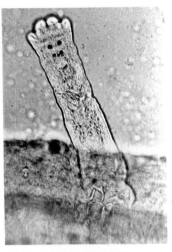

Dactylogyrus lodged in the skin.
The four-lobed front is typical.
The *Gyrodactylus* has only two lobes.

Oodinium pillularis on
Aphyosemion gardneri

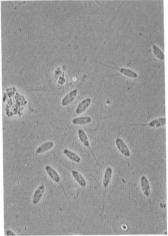

Spironucleus symphysodonis in a
Discus.
These flagellates are closely related to
Hexamita.

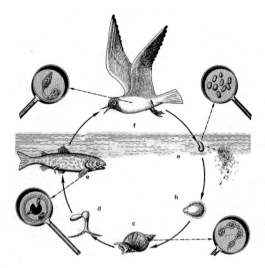

Trematoda or sucking worms
The life cycle of *Proalaria spathaceum* includes: a) eggs; b) miracidium; c) sporocyst; d) cercarium; e) worm "cataract" (*Diplostomum volvens*); f) mature worm in the intenstine of a seagull.

Since an infection of metacercaria is linked to snails, the problem can be effectively prevented by introducing no snail collected from open waters. Many dedicated aquarists insist snails should be avoided on principle since they can carry Redia. Fortunately an infection of metacercaria is rare in an aquarium. The disease is generally seen only in newly introduced imported fishes.

Gill Copepod or *Ergasilus*

Symptoms: There is little external evidence though an infected fish will lose weight and if heavily involved will display the typical "knifeback" look. The parasite can be seen however, when you lift the gill covers – as long, white dots on the gill leaves. The gills may also be slimy and pale.

Diagnosis: If an infection of *Ergasilus* is suspected, you should examine the gill leaves, lifting the gill cover with clean tweezers. If you are in doubt remove one gill raker from a freshly-killed fish and examine it under the microscope, at a magnfication of 50 to 120.

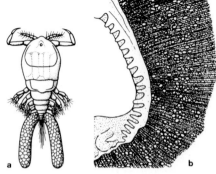

Crustacea (crab)
Copepoda (paddle-foot crab or cyclops)
Ergasilus sieboldii (gill fluke): a) adult female; b) gill fluke or white spots, on a gill.

Cause: The primary cause of gill fluke is the "paddle-footed crab" or copepod *Ergasilus sieboldii*. Only the female is a parasite while the male is a free-swimming plankton. The female is 1.3 to 1.7 mm. in length and 0.4 to 0.7 mm. wide. A second pair of antennae have been tansformed into large clamp-like hooks which help to anchor the copepod to the gills. Older adults can be recognized by their blue color. Nauplii hatch from the eggs and grow quickly into to a mature crab and two generations can be produced in the course of one summer. The copepods generally attack bottom dwelling fish.

Explanation: Fish suffering from a massive attack are difficult to cure. The crab feeds on the gill epithelium and on blood. The clamp-like hooks penetrate the skin and allow the parasite to draw blood from the capillaries. This hinders respiration, causes anemia and the weight lose. Secondary fungal infections from *Saprolegnia* and *Achlya* are common.

Action: The copepod can be removed with medication. We suggest any of these: a five to ten minute bath in Masoten $2^1/_2$% solution **(very poisonous and available only on prescription - you must be very careful)**; Sodium Permanganate 1:10,000, i.e. 1 g per 10 liters – for five to 10 minutes); or Formalin (1:4000 i.e. 1 ml 37% Formalin to four liter of water – for one hour). The parasites can also be killed with the addition of a weak solution of insecticide – DDT **(which is illegal in many areas)**, Lindane **(also very poisonous)** and Gesarol (1:100 million i.e. 1 mg per 100 liters of water). Immerse for several days.

Anchor Worm or *Lernaea*

Symptoms: *Lernaea* are readily visible, though often you can only see the egg sac projecting. The worms usually attack the skin and rarely the gills. They may also penetrate the liver.

Diagnosis: Suspected fish can be examined with a magnifying glass though for a more precise diagnosis you must prepare a smear from the tissue of a freshly-killed fish. Examine the slide at 50 to 120 magnification.

Cause: The disease is caused by a copepod, *Lernaea* and *Lernaeocera*, the Anchor Worm. The most common species are *L. cyprinacea* and *L. carassii*, both typical in form and action. The former is 9 to 22 mm. in length and the latter grows to 4 cm. The female body is cylindrical and worm-like and the head is characterized by a typical anchor-shape which gives the worms their name. Chitinous extensions on the mouth are used to hold onto the host fish. In a sexually mature form the sexual organs are swollen. The egg sac is long and slender. The worms can develop without changing hosts.

Explanation: Anchor worms can cause considerable damage since they penetrate muscle tissue, directly tapping blood vessels. Anemia and loss of weight are the immediate results. Goldfish, Cichlids and *Nandidae* are particularly susceptible.

Action: Try a 10 to 20 minute bath in a solution of table salt (20 g to one liter of water), and a solution of Masoten (2 1/2% solution for 1 to 10 minutes – Masoten is available by prescription only and is extremely poisonous) followed by a longer bath (several days) in Lindane (1 mg to 100 liters of water).

Lernaea attached behind the dorsal fin.

Lernaea cyprinacea. Note the egg sac projecting at the rear.

Argulus or Fish Lice

Symptoms: Fish infected with lice are restless, suffer from pinched fins and often rub against tank decorations, rocks and the glass. The point of attack may be reddened and inflammed. Small red spots can be seen with a pink center.

Diagnosis: The lice are visible, can be seen on the skin and can be removed with tweezers.

Cause: Fish lice belong to the genus *Argulus* and the parasite is a crab, sub-class Branchiura. The most common louse is *Argulus foliaceus*, the carp louse. It reaches a length of 6-7 mm. and has a rounded, thorny abdomen. Argulids can also be identified by their fattened, shield-like shape. They are well adapted to the life of a parasite. Their antenna feature a grasping hook and one pair of maxillaries has been modified to form a suction device. The hooks and suckers are used to attach to the host while the blood is drawn in by the long proboscis. To lay eggs the louse must leave the host, depositing 20 to 250 eggs on rocks or gravel. Lice develop through nine stages to reach sexually maturity.

Explanation: The poisons from *Argulus* can paralyze or kill aquarium fish and the loss of blood causes anemia and weight loss. In addition, the bite can transfer infectious pathogens causing dropsy. Fungus such as *Saprolegnia* often enter raw and reddened bites, causing a secondary infection.

Action: It is easy to treat fish since many lice cannot survive long in warm water. Lice can be destroyed in several additional ways: in a 15 to 60 second bath of dilute Lysol (1 ml to 5 liters of water); An hour

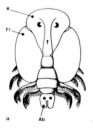

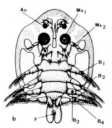

Argulus foliaceus, the fish louse. a) rear view; b) ventral view. AB = Abdominal plate; Au = the complex eye; B₁ - B₄ = thoracopods or swimming legs; F = furca; Fl = wing-like lateral carapace area; C (K) = frontal carapace area.

and one half bath in Sodium Permanganate (1 g to 100 liters); a 10 to 30 minute bath in Neguvon, a poison available only by prescription (be very careful – use a 2-3% solution only); Masoten (also a prescription-only poison – $2^1/_2$% solution – 1-10 minutes); or longer baths, of several days immersion, in DDT and Lindane (1 mg to 100 liters of water). Both of the latter are dangerous poisons, available only by prescription.

3. Fungal Diseases
Saprolegnia and *Achlya*
Symptoms: A cottony, wool-like coating that eventually becomes brownish in color. Its form collapses when the fish is removed from water. Affected areas can include the skin, gills, mouth, fins and even the eyes.

Diagnosis: Try skin smears examined under a microscope at enlargments between 50 and 120 power. Thin, transparent threads called Hyphae can be seen along with the darker Sporangia.

Cause: These are fungii of two genera, *Saprolegnia* and *Achlya*, which belong to the order Oomycetales. When the Hyphae or individual filaments are combined the whole is called a "mycelium", a hose shaped form.

Saprolegnia fungus on a Sumatra Barb, *Barbus tetrazona*. The fungus is concentrated on the fins.

Asexual reproduction is common in single-celled zoospores. After a transitional change in shape, the zoospores settle on a new host, in this case an injured fish, forming new threads or Hyphae.

Explanation: Fungus such as *Saprolegnia* and *Achlya* attack only injured, stressed and weakened fish, fish whose mucous defences are impaired. Healthy fish are not affected. Damage changes the pH of the mucuous membrane, creating the proper conditions for an attack. In a heavy infestation the fungus can penetrate the skin, causing severe damage.

Fungal infections can be caused by several things: 1) Physical injury to the mucous membrane; 2) Water temperatures too low for the species – the most common cause; 3) the mucous membrane is weakened by acid or alkali; 4) previous damage by a bacterial disease; 5) wounds and open sores on skin tissue.

Action: One easy and often successful cure is to increase the temperature the water. Another, to transfer the fish to a hospital tank with clean water. Other possibilities include a 30 minute bath in a solution of Sodium Permanganate (1 g to 100 liters of water). You can also try painting the affected parts with Rivanol. Malachite Green has also been successful and is helpful as a preventative measure since it inhibits the development of fungus. Other, more general remedies, available from pet stores may not control fungus but will attack primary bacterial infections, offering the fish substantial help. Tetra Tonic is one example.

The life cycle of *Saprolegnia* sp.
Upper circle: asexual reproduction; lower circle: sexual reproduction. Generally only the asexual phase is found in fish.
a) Hypha. b) Formation of the sporangium. c) Sporangium with zoospores. d) Zoospores with two flagella or tentacles at one end. e) Spores without tentacles. f) Zoospores with two flagella or lateral tentacles. g) Growing spores. h) sprouting spore. f) and g) die when the fungus cannot find acceptable nourishment.

4. Bacteria and Virus

Infectious Dropsy

Symptom: The disease can be found in two forms, typical dropsy and an ulcerated or "Polish" form. Typical dropsy can be identified by several symptoms, bulging eyes, regressing eyes, a protruding and inflammed anus, and pale gills. You may also see red patches on the skin and extensive fin damage. The body cavity may contain a purulent liquid which inflates the belly. Other symptoms, found only on autopsy, include such internal deformities as a yellow to green discoloration of the liver. The ulcerated form has a characteristic sequence of color changes. The ulcer is red, surrounded by a white ring and, beyond that, blackened skin. Boils can be seen where the scales are missing and defective scales will also be noted.

Diagnosis: You can generally make a diagnosis from external symptoms, but if you are uncertain you will need to dissect the fish. Pay special attention to the liver, which will probably be discolored – greenish, light yellow, rust-red or bluish in tone.

Cause: Researchers cannot agree on identification of the pathogen which causes the illness. Many feel two bacteria, *Aeromonas punctata* and *Pseudomonas fluorescens*, are the causes. *Aeromonas punctata* is a gram-negative flagellate 1-2.2 μm in length and 0.5-0.8 μm wide. The bacterium dies when exposed to temperatures above 50° C for more than two hours. It is also killed by dehydration.

Explanation: Dropsy is extremely infectious. Fish are generally atacked only if they have been stressed by another disease or by environmental conditions. The disease destroys the liver's mucous membrane and causes ulceration. The number of red corpuscles is reduced which leads to circulatory defects. The liver is damaged and eventually destroyed and numerous other problems can develop. Though Cyprinids are commonly affected, the disease is rare in an aquarium.

Action: The disease is difficult to treat and prevention is a more important concern. Measures range from the administration of such

A Cichlid, possibly *Pseudotropheus zebra*, shown with protruding scales. These are generally a symptom of Dropsy though they may also be caused by a swelling of internal organs after feeding on too many Bloodworms.

antibiotics as Chloramphenicol, Streptomycin and Leucomycin (in food) to varying the food input. Foods which burden the liver may create conditions favorable for the disease. Once a fish is affected with Dropsy it should be removed and destroyed.

A typical tubercular fish with bleeding scales and enlarged growths on the fins. The symptoms may also be caused by stress. Battles which lead to injuries of the skin and fins often trigger disease so it is best to remove weakened, ill and injured fish early.

Tuberculosis piscium

Symptoms: A number of symptoms can indicate tuberculosis. Fish often lose appetite, grow thin, have hollow stomachs and "bent" or arched backs. Their colors pale, the skin becomes inflammed, fins are affected and the internal organs may even cease to function, with small growths forming on them. Fish are also lethargic, swimmming eratically. Other symptoms include pop-eyes, the loss of eyes, defective scales, gill deformities and changes in the shape of the spinal column.

Diagnosis: Positive diagnosis comes only by identifying the acidresistent, gram-positive bacillae. Slides can be made of material from the intestine, heart, kidney and liver or from a combination of the kidney and spleen. Smears from the former organs should be examined under a magnification between 120 and 600 power. Those from the latter should be examined in an oil at 1300 magnification.

Cause: *Mycobacterium* bacteria are suspected. These are straight or comma-shaped, are acid-resistent and gram-positive. *Mycobacterium* can apply in a temperature range from 10-37° C. The optimum temperature is around 25° C. They are 1-6 μm long and can affect nearly every species of freshwater fish.

Explanation: *Tuberculosis* is the most dangerous of all aquatic diseases. It is highly infectious and can be readily transferred. Bacteria can also survive in the gravel and thus infect a tank. An attack can quickly destroy all of the fish in an aquarium with little advance warning and few visible symptoms. It can also be latent in some fish, progressing slowly with unseen internal damage (see Symptoms). The primary danger lies in the fact that the affected tissue dies.

Action: Only a few antibiotics such as Tetracycline are successful. Since the disease is the result of stress we prefer an emphasis on prevention. Fish should be fed a varied diet and the tank should not be over-stocked – housing no more than one fish per five quarts of water. The tank should be kept scrupulously clean.

Fin Rot (*Bacteriosis pinnarum*)

Symptoms: The earliest symptoms, discolorations at the edges of the fins, are often so slight that they go unseen but as the disease progresses the fins become visibly ragged and frayed, portions actually sloughing off with time. In the terminal stages only shreds of the rotting tail remain. The disease leaves a fish susceptible to a secondary fungual infection as well and *Saprolegnia* and *Achlya* only accelerate destruction of the fins.

Diagnosis: You must examine a segment of the diseased fin under a high-powered microscope – a 600 x enlargement is recommended.

Cause: Fin rot can be caused by several bacteria: *Pseudomonas fluorescens, Aeromonas* sp. and *Haemophilus piscium.* Gill rot (*Branchiomycosis*) is caused by an algal fungi, *Branchiomyces.*

Explanation: Fin rot is considered highly contagious. STERBA believes that environmental factors are a root cause. Infrequent water changes and a temperature too low for the species, may also introduce the disease. Fin rot sharply hampers manueverability.

Action: Many researchers feel fin rot is among the most difficult of diseases to treat. We suggest a bath with Trypoflavine (1 g per 100 liters) or such Sulphonamides as Albucid and Globucid (1 g per liter of water). Proper care and temperature also have positive effects. A six-day immersion in Chloramphenicol is said to produce a cure. (60 mg per liter of water). Chloramphenicol is available only by prescription.

Bacterial fin rot
a-d) propgressive stages of
the disease: e) tail fin with
rot, greatly enlarged.

Mouth Fungus (Columnaris)

Symptoms: Cotton-like, gray-white patches can be seen on the head, fins, gills and body, primarily around the mouth. In time these develop into open sores.

Diagnosis: Examine a scraping from an affected area under strong magnification, at least 600 x. For a positive identification the pathogen must be incubated, a procedure few hobbyists can duplicate.

Cause: Columnaris is a gram-positive bacteria and can identified by a standard gram-color test. If the bacteria takes color, it is gram-positive and if not, it is gram-negative. The pathogens may be one of two types, *Chondrococcus columnaris* and *Cytophaga columnaris*. The larger is between 0.5 x 5-10 μm in size. The bacteria find weakened skin areas, a scrape or injury, and attack through these.

Explanation: Columnaris is highly infectious and should be considered dangerous. It can destroy an entire aquarium. Muscles can be inflamed and capillaries, gorged with blood, may rupture.

Action: There are several ways to prevent the disease. Do not overstock a tank, be sure the water is properly aerated and remove diseased fish immediately. For treatment follow our suggestions for fungus, *Saprolegnia*.

Lymphocystis

Symptoms: You will see berry-like growths on parts of the body. The fins may show the heaviest infestation. A number of small nodules may be seen together as lines.

Diagnosis: Identification is beyond the means of most hobbyists since the tissue must be examined by an electron microscope.

Cause: Lymphocystis is caused by a DNS virus which lives and multiplies in a cystoplasm. Its size fluctuates from 180 to 220 μm (1 μm = one millionth of a millimeter). It belongs to a group of cubic virus and is hexagonal in shape. At temperatures to 25° C it can become active within two days. Cytoplasmic mutations are evident from the sixth day and the disease becomes virulent by the 15th. The affected cells burst, releasing contagious virus which remain contagious for two months.

Explanation: The disease should be considered dangerous since it can easily reach epidemic proportions, destroying an entire tank. The tumors can reach surprising size and the affected cells are slowly destroyed as the virus multiplies. Fish affected do not seem impaired and may swim and act normally.

Action: There are no known medical remedies, though we have had some success swabbing affected areas with tincture of iodine. If only small parts of a fin are affected these can be removed with a scissors, but fish with more severe infection must be caught and destroyed immediately. Healthy fish should be placed in a separate tank (though not with other fish) and kept there for two months. After this quarantine period they can be regarded as healthy. A contaminated aquarium should be emptied, disinfected with hydrochloric acid, then rinsed and re-assembled.

Invisible Diseases

1. Unicellular organisms
Sleeping Sickness or Cryptobiasis (*Cryptobia*)

Symptoms: The fish become sluggish, their heads are held lower than their tails and in extreme cases they become immobile or "sleeping" and can be picked up by hand. Occasionally they swim in circles. The eyes retract and their bodies become thin. The gills will become pale, a sign of anemia.

Diagnosis: Remove the kidney from a freshly-killed fish and prepare a smear. Place this on a slide. The parasites can be seen in the blood at an enlargment of 150 x.

Cause: The disease is caused by *Cryptobia cyprini* flagellates. These are 20-25 μm in length and live in the intestine of the fish leech *Piscicola*. Fish become infected as they eat the leech. The flagellate can be found in the fish's blood after seven days. The organism has two flagella.

Explanation: *Cryptobia* is a serious disease and can be terminal. The flagella can remove as much as ten percent of the blood, reducing the red blood count by 40%. The good news is that the leech rarely survives in an aquarium environment and is seldom seen in the hobby. It has been diagnosed in goldfish and some Cichlids imported from Lake Malawi.

Action: The disease is incurable. Infected fish should be removed and destroyed. Any leeches found in the tank should also be destroyed.

A Neon (*Paracheirodon innesi*) infected with *Plistophora hyphessobryconis*

Cryptobia sp. Three *Cryptobia* and five red corpuscles, shown with nucelus.

Neon Tetra Disease, or *Plistophora* (Sporozoasis myolytica)

Symptoms: The symptoms can vary and the way a hobbyist may see the disease is far from uniform. Infected fish may lose color and the typical luminous side band is broken, though this is not a definitive symptom. The muscles can become reddish and bright, with a visible milky transparency. The fish become sluggish and lose their equilibrum, swimming in an eratic manner. They may swim with the head erect or even upside down. They try to regain a normal position with jerky movements. Infected fish will separate from their school and will swim through out the night while healthy Neons have a characteristic sleeping position – schooling peacefully just above the bottom. Other symptoms include a loss of weight and collapse of the stomach area.

Diagnosis: For positive identification prepare smears which are placed on slides. The characteristic pansporoblasts can be seen under 150-200 x enlargement. They will be seen as dark, spherical forms.

Cause: The disease is generally caused by the sporozoan *Plistophora hypessobryconis* though other sporozoan of the genus may also be involved. Its life cycle and development is not clearly known. The pathogen was discovered and described in 1941 by SCHAEPERCLAUS on a normal Neon, *Paracheirodon innesi*, which accounts for its common name though today we know that other Characins, carp-like fishes and Cichlids can be affected. The pansporoblasts primarily attack the body's basic muscle units.
These are spherical cysts containing 16 to 32 spores. Several are thought to lie together in a common capsule formed by the host fish. The spores are released when the pansporoblasts burst. Ameoboid nucleii hatch from them, developing into new sporoblasts, a process which leads to continual reinfection and spread of the disease. Since the kidneys can be infected, the spores may leave the body with the urine, entering the intestinal tracts of healthy fish.

Explanation: The disease is highly dangerous since it affects the muscles, splitting the fibers, sometimes destroying them. Wasting muscles may be seen as a lateral distortion or Skoliosis. The spores can reach the liver, kidneys and skin through the blood, creating new centers of infection. Once you think you have the disease controlled it may reccur.

Action: Since there are no known remedies, prevention is basic. Once you have identified the disease infected fish should be quickly removed. The tank, gravel, decorations and catching net should be disinfected with Hydrochloric acid or Chloramin. SCHUBERT claims that a plate with holes placed on the bottom will prevent the fish from absorbing new spores, but the method is doubtful.

Coccidosis (Enteric Coccidosis in Cyprinids)

Symptoms: Sunken eye and substantial weight loss are among the first signals. Fish may try head standing and a yellowish exudate may be seen at the anus, especially when the stomach is pressed. Upon autopsy it will be found the intestines are inflamed.

Diagnosis: Open the intestine of a freshly killed fish, remove some of the contents with a spatula along with a portion of mucous membrane and place on a slide. Combine with water. Examine at a magnification of 150 to 600 x. You should be able to see oocysts 8-14 μm in size along with many oval oospores 5-8 μm in length.

Cause: Coccidosis is caused by *Eimeria cyprini*, a sporozoan which reaches its host through parasites ingested with the excreta of infected fishes.

Explanation: The disease is quite infectious, affecting the intestinal mucous membrane, leading to a severe intestinal inflammation. The diseased segment can be spotted by its yellowish color.

Action: Coccidosis cannot be cured therapeutically but fish can be protected against it. The disease is generally introduced along with *Tubifex* worms and glass worms harvested from local waters home to native fishes. Food from such sources should be avoided. Infected fishes should be removed and the tank thoroughly cleaned and disinfected.

Hexamita or Octomitus

Symptoms: Diseased fish lose weight and color and make erratic, darting movements. On dissection the lower intestine, gall bladder and blood will be found to contain fast-moving, pearshaped, unicellular organisms. The intestine is inflamed and often filled with mucus and blood. The gall bladder may be enlarged and hard.

Diagnosis: The fish should be killed, preferably with a cut across its neck. Open the abdomen and make a smear from portions of the gall bladder and lower intestine. Examine it under a magnification of 120x or more.

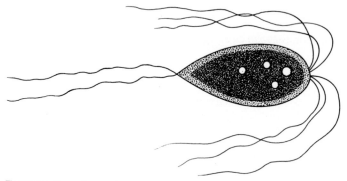

Flagellates: *Hexamita* sp.

Cause: The trouble-maker is a flagellate of the genus *Hexamita* (or *Octomitus*). The most common are *H. salmonis*, *H. symphysodonis* and *H. intestinalis*. Another genus, *Spironucleus* is similar to *Hexamita* and, in an aquarium, cannot be distinguished from it. *H. salmonis* has an oval body with two nucleii, three flagella at the front on either side and two long control flagella at the rear. The species is 7-13 μm in length. All can be distinguished by their jerky, tumbling motion.

Explanation: *Hexamita* causes inflammation of the gall bladder and a hardening of the gall bladder epithelium. As a result fish lose weight and often die. Although the parasite is not common in an aquarium it can attack pet fish and can result in heavy losses among newly imported fishes. Some of the parasites can be found in the intestines of every fish, living in a harmless symbiosis. It becomes dangerous only at times of stress or, as the secondary effect of another disease. It often accompanies tuberculosis.

Action: Since it can be introduced with live foods a basic suggestion is to avoid feeding live foods from questionable sources. Medication is still in experimental stages. Some American writers have suggested mixing 0.2% Calomel (Mercury Chloride) with food for two days or 0.2% Carcasone for four days. We have no reports on their efficacy.

2. Quadricellular Living Organisms

Bloodworm Disease or Sanguinicoliasis

Symptoms: Though it sounds paradoxical, the disease is most obvious after the fish is dead. Affected specimens lack color with pale or colorless gills. Living fishes may also be slow, listless swimmers. Carp-like fishes are particularly prone to this disease.

Diagnosis: Use a smear made from material from the liver, kidney and gills. Place the mix on a slide and examine it under a microscope at 120 to 600 x enlargment. Characteristic cap-shaped eggs can be seen in the blood.

Cause: Bloodworm disease is caused by a digenetic sucking worm, *Sanguinicola.* When sexually mature these worms are 1 to 1.5 mm in length and live in the blood vessels of a host fish. They will most often be found in larger numbers in vessels near the gills and kidneys. Adult *Sanguinicola* have a spindle-shaped body. The eggs are formed in summer and autumn and the female's genital tract contains a single egg. After they are laid the eggs continue to grow in the blood vessel until they are twice their original size. They are carried by the blood flow to the gills, heart, liver, kidney and other organs. Miracida or ciliates hatch from the eggs and literally dig their way out of the host to attack water snails.

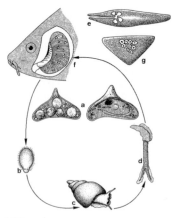

Trematoda or sucking worm
Life cycle of *Sanguinicola inermis:* a) eggs; b) miracidium or planula; c) snail or interim host; d) Cercarie (*Cercaria cristata*); e) sexually mature form; f) egg in the gills; g) degenerate, clumped eggs in the kidneys.

Once inside the snail a sporocyst develops from each miracidium. It contains the second and final larval stages (cercaria). These again infect the fish. After penetrating a host fish the cercaria lose their forked tails and become sexually mature worms.

Explanation: If the worms or their eggs become numerous they can block the flow of blood to the gills and heart leading to thrombosis and death. The eggs are also carried into the kidneys where they become cysts. Gill tissue can be affected, reducing respiration.

Action: No treatment is possible after the disease has broken out. However, it can be overcome in course of time if all snails (intermediate hosts) are removed from the aquarium. A snail-free aquarium is the best preventive measure against blood-worm disease.

Tapeworms or Cestodes

Symptoms: The intestine becomes inflamed and congested and a massive infection may even block it. Fish lose weight and become anemic with pale gills. Tapeworm larvae can be found in the body as whitish or dark lumps.

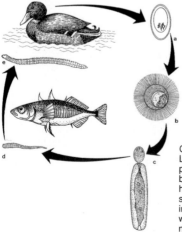

Cestodes or tapeworms.
Life cycle of *Schistocephalus solidas*, a parasite common in Stickelbacks: a) egg; b) coracidium; c) the first intermediate host, procercoid in a copepoda; d) second intermediate host, plerocercoid, in a Stickelback; e) adult worm in a waterbird, its final host. The drawings are not to scale.

The fishes' eyes may become enlarged and cloudy.

Diagnosis: A section from a freshly-killed fish will show the worms as intestinal organisms 8-15 mm in length and can be identified in a slide prepared from portions of the muscles and internal organs. The larvae have heads with suction devices as do the adults.

Cause: Two genera, *Caryophyllaeus* and *Khawia*, are common to the aquarium. Strapworm (Ligulosis) may occasionally be found, generally induced by *Ligula intestinalis*. *Caryophyllaeus* and *Khawia* are commonly seen in the intestines in adult form while *Ligula intestinalis* is seen in larval form.

The life cycle is complex, generally involving a single or double change of hosts. Adult *Khawia sinensis* are 80-170 mm in length and 3.5-5 mm wide, while adult *Caryophyllaeus fimbriceps* are just 15-25 mm long and 1-1.5 mm wide. Both use *Tubifex* worms as their intermediate host, in which the larvae or procercoid develops. When an infected *Tubifex* worm is eaten by a fish the larvae hatches and becomes a sexually mature worm. Adult strapworms live in the intestine of water birds. The eggs of *Ligula* reach the water where a ciliate larva, called the coracidium, hatches. It is eaten by such copepods as *Diaptomus* and *Cyclops*, the first intermediate host. It then develops into its second stage and, if taken by a fish (which becomes the second host), the procercoid changes to its final larval stage (plercocercoid). When the fish is caught by a bird the sexually mature worm developes in the latter's intestine.

Explanation: A heavy infection will damage the intestine's mucous membrane and weight loss and stunted growth result. In an aquarium just a few tapeworms can cause wide-spread death. An infection may cause atrophy, local necrosis and angiorhexis.

Action: The disease is easier to prevent than to cure. The best prevention is to avoid feeding Copepods and *Tubifex* worms – both intermediate hosts. An infestation with tapeworm larvae cannot be treated successfully. Chemical medication is largely impossible since the existing vermicides are also toxic to the fish. Information on treating ponds can be found in AMLACHER (1976).

Threadworms or Nematodes

Symptoms: A light infestation can be present without visible symptoms but when it is severe fish become listless, thin and will not eat. Occasionally worms can be seen hanging from the anus and upon autopsy the liver and intestines will be found to be inflamed.

Diagnosis: The worms can be seen when a freshly-killed fish is autopsied — as thin, 1-2 mm long threads in the intestines. In some cases the worms may be even longer and their eggs can be found in a microscopic study of the excrement. Mix a small amount of the contents of the intestine with a drop of water. Magnify 50 to 120 x. The eggs can be identified by two nodules at each end. When examined under a microscope, larvae can be found in samples taken from the various organs.

Cause: The problem is caused by white to brown Nematodes, round bodied and pointed at the front. The sexes are separate and include egg-layers and live-bearers. The males are generally smaller and have an extendable pointed spine, called a spiculate, at the rear. Fish can be either an intermediate or final host. When they are the intermediate host, Threadworm larvae will be found in the skin, muscle and internal organs. The larvae, 0.5-1 mm in size, are encysted by the fish's own tissue. When a fish is the final host, adults Nematodes can be found in the intestinal tract. Threadworms will attack nearly any aquarium fish though certain species are preferred. The most dangerous to aquarium fishes are Hairworms, *Capillaria* sp. These do not require an intermediate host and are most often found in Catfish, Cichlids and Angelfish.

Explanation: Nematodes cause severe damage, both as Threadworms and larvae. They cause extensive damage to the intestinal wall, leading to inflammation, loss of weight and death.

Action: Threadworms are difficult to combat since available vermicides such as Neguvon, are toxic to fishes as well and can be used only with extreme caution. It is best to remove an infected fish and isolate or destroy it so that it cannot infect healthy tankmates.

Some experts feel that feeding dry food soaked in parachlormetaxylenmol and baths in the same chemical can help. Encysted Nematodes cannot be treated.

Thorn-Head worms

Symptoms: An attack by a few Thorn-Head worms may have little effect on a fish and you may not even be aware of it. A heavier infection is serious. A fish will lose weight and may die. Symptoms include an inflamed anus and, upon autopsy, eggs can be found in the intestinal tract. The tract may be blocked and inflamed.

Diagnosis: Open the abdominal cavity of a dead fish and remove the intestines. On dissection, Thorn-Head worms can be seen with a magnifying glass. They can be identified by their characteristic proboscis.

Cause: *Acanthocephala* is a round, white to yellow or orange colored, parasitic intestinal worm from one millimeter to one centimeter in length. Their most evident feature is the hooked proboscis which gives them their name. They lack a mouth, intestines and anal opening and absorb food over their entire body surface. The sexual organs are pronounced. Thorn-Heads have a complex development cycle with several laval stages. They may need only one host or several. Freshwater shrimps, water lice, the larvae of such water insects as mud flies and fish can act as intermediate hosts. Fish and mammals may also be the final host.

Explanation: An occasional infestation may do little damage, but a heavy attack can cause death, particularly with younger fishes. The intestinal wall is damaged by the hooked nose and internal bleeding weakens the fish. Thorn-Heads inflict further damage by competing for the nutrition found in the food a host fish ingests. In some cases the intestines can be completely blocked with parasites.

Action: The disease is impossible to control since there is no medication which will affect the parasite in either the intestines or in larval form. Fortunately Thorn-Heads are rarely seen in an aquarium though they can be found in freshly-imported specimens. Fish infected with the disease should be destroyed.

The most effective means of preventing an attack is to refrain from feeding freshwater shrimp, water lice and larvae which are their intermediate host.

3. Fungus

Ichthyosporidium

Symptoms: The most common external symptom is a roughness of the scales, known in Europe as the "sandpaper effect". It is caused by many small nodules, generally less than 0.1 mm. in size. These can often be identified by their black color. Destruction of the skin also leads to an obvious loss of scales and patches of dead flesh. Fish may also be affected by swelling, bleeding, open sores and crater-like areas on the skin. Internal symptoms include white nodules on the heart, liver and kidneys. Infected fish may swim erratically, literally staggering. Their bodies may become distended.

Diagnosis: To perform an autopsy, kill an infected fish by a cut across its neck. Remove tissue samples from the heart, liver, kidneys, spleen and brain. Make a combined smear and examine it under a magnification of 50-120 x. The fungus can also be identified from scrapings taken from a fresh site.

Cause: *Ichthyosporidium* is an algae fungus or Phycomycet, called *Ichthyosporidium* or (*Ichthyophonus*) *hoferi*. It can be acquired orally and has a complex life of latent cysts or ameoboblasts partially outlined below:

Ichthyosporidium hoferi: a) latent cyst; b) germinating plasmodium.

As the case surrounding the amoeboblast is slowly digested numbers of amoebid spores are released. These penetrate the intestinal mucous membrane and eventually reach a fish's circulatory system. Spores are carried by the blood to various organs where they develop, surrounding themselves with a protective envelope. The fungus then reproduces quickly through a number of cell divisions and when it matures relinquishes its protective envelope. Division and growth then stop. The host forms a protective capsule around the fungus and after a reprieve of several days, a multi-cored mass called plasma hatches and reproduces, creating new cysts. The secondary reproduction leads to eventual death and still more spores. As the host dies sprouting Hyphae appear. These are absorbed by a new host and, after being broken down by digestive juices, the cycle is complete.

Explanation: The disease is infectious and quickly results in death. It produces chronic inflammation and the formation of granules in the infected tissues. Muscles atrophy. Affected internal organs are covered with small cysts which literally devour living tissue. Muscles and other systems may cease to function, leading to paralysis.

Action: There is no way to currently treat an entrenched case of *Ichthyosporidium* and once an infestation occurs the only solution is to destroy all stock in the tank and thoroughly disinfect the aquarium. In the beginning, however, when only the intestinal wall is affected, it may be treated with Tetracycline added to the food (1 mg to each 50-100 g of fish body weight).

4.Viral diseases

Swim Bladder Inflammation (Aerocystitis)

Symptom: In the early stages fish stop eating, but as the disease progresses gas or pus-filled cysts are formed at the rear of the abdominal cavity, distending the body and producing "head standing".

As the cysts increase in size so will girth of the fish affected and upon dissection the swim bladder will show signs of inflammation and thickening of the wall. As the illness progresses symptoms of degeneration will appear and in the end other organs, the kidney, spleen and liver, become affected.

Diagnosis: Examination of the swim bladder is beyond most of us since it requires extremely high magnification and advanced techniques. The hobbyist must rely on those few visual symptoms outlined above.

Cause: Swim bladder infection is caused by a virus and the temperature in which it can grow ranges between 4 and 33° C. The optimum is between 15 and 28° C.

Explanation: The disease is highly infectious and will cause the uncontrolled growth of tissue in the duct between the swim bladder and the intestine. In time it will also produce severe changes in the spleen, liver and kidney as well as kinetic or nervous disorders.

Action: Though the disease may be slowed through the use of antibiotics, sulphonamides and methyl blue, we suggest that diseased fishes be killed.

5. Non-parasitic problems

Tumors

Symptoms: Skin tumors or epithelioma, will be found on the skin and scales. Malignant tumors can be divided into five categories, cartilage, bone, muscles, nerves and heart or cardiac carcinomas.

Cause: Benign tumors can be caused by irritations and will disappear when the irritant is removed. Malignant tumors are often hereditary but can also be caused by such carcinogens as cancer-producing elements in the food.

Action: Benign tumors often disappear when the irritant is removed. Malignant tumors can only rarely be treated.

Dietary Deficencies

Problems caused by dietary deficiencies can be attributed to two causes, a complete lack of vitamins (avitaminosis) or an inadequate supply of them (Hypovitaminosis). In both cases see our chapter on vitamins for details: pages 874-876.

Index

Index

Index

Index of Commons Names

Index of Commons Names

Index of Commons Names

Index of Synonyma

Index of Synonyma

Index of Synonyma

Index of Synonyma

Index of Synonyma

Index of Synonyma

Index of Synonyma

Index of Synonyma

Index of Scientific Names

974

Index of Scientific Names

Index of Scientific Names

Index of Scientific Names

Index of Scientific Names

Literature

Aldinger, H. (1965): Der Hecht. Verlag Paul Parey, Hamburg.

Amlacher, E. (1976): Taschenbuch der Fischkrankheiten für Veterinärmediziner und Biologen. VEB Gustav Fischer Verlag, Jena.

Arnold, J. P. (ohne Jahr): Alphabetisches Verzeichnis der bisher eingeführten fremdländischen Süßwasserfische. Verlag Gustav Wenzel & Sohn, Braunschweig.

Arnold, J. P. und E. Ahl (1936): Fremdländische Süßwasserfische, Verlag Gustav Wenzel & Sohn, Braunschweig.

Autorenkollektiv (1978): Kosmos-Handbuch Aquarienkunde – Das Süßwasseraquarium. Franckh'sche Verlagshandlung, Stuttgart.

Axelrod, H. & L. Schultz (1971): Handbook of Tropical Aquarium Fishes. T.F.H. Publications, Neptune City, N. J., USA.

Bade, E. (1909): Das Süßwasser-Aquarium. Verlag für Sport und Naturliebhaberei Fritz Pfenningstorff, Berlin; 3. Auflage.

Baensch, U. (1980): Bunte Zierfischkunde. Tetra Verlag, Melle.

Banarescu, P. & T. T. Nalbant (1973): Das Tierreich, Lieferung 93: Subfamilia Gobioninae. Verlag Walter de Gruyter, Berlin.

Bailey, R. M. (1970): A list of common and scientific names of fishes from the United States and Canada, American Fish. Soc., Spec. Publ. No. 6, Washington D. C., USA.

Bauch, G. (1954): Die einheimischen Süßwasserfische. Verlag J. Neumann, Radebeul und Berlin.

Bell-Cross, G. (1976): The fishes of Rhodesia. Trust.Nat.Mus.Monum. Rhodesia, Salisbury.

Berg, L. S. (1958): System der rezenten und fossilen Fischartigen und Fische. VEB Deutscher Verlag der Wissenschaften, Berlin.

Blache, J. (1964): Les poissons du bassin du Tchad et du bassin du Mayo Kebbi. Off. Rech. Scient. Tech. Outre-Mer, Paris.

Blätter für Aquarien- und Terrarienkunde. Illustrierte Zeitschrift für die Interessen der Vivarienkunde. Herausgegeben von Dr. W. Wolterstorff. Stuttgart 1920. Verlag von Julius E. G. Wegner.

Boulenger, G. A. (1901): Les Poissons Du Bassin Du Congo. Publication de l'Etat Indépendant du Congo.

Brittan, M. R. (1954): A revision of the Indo-Malayan fresh-water fish genus Rasbora. Bureau of Printing, Manila.

Daget, J. (1962): Les poissons du Fouta Dialon et de la basse Guines. Mem.IFAN, Dakar.

Daget, J. & A. Iltis (1965): Poissons de Cote d'Ivoire. Mem.IFAN, Dakar.

Dathe, H. (1975): Wirbeltiere I: Pisces, Amphibia, Reptilia. VEB Gustav Fischer Verlag, Jena.

De Wit, H. C. D. (1970): Aquarienpflanzen, Verlag Eugen Ulmer, Stuttgart.

Düringen, B. (um 1896): Fremdländische Zierfische. Zweite Auflage. Creutz'sche Verlags-buchhandlung (R. & M. Kretschmann). Magdeburg.

Duncker, (G. &. W. Ladiges (1960): Die Fische der Nordmark. Kommissionsverlag Cramm de Gruyter & Co., Hamburg.

Eigenmann, C. H. (1918): The American Characidae. Mem.Mus.Comp. Zool. Harvard Coll., Cambridge, USA.

Fowler, H. W. (1941): Contributions to the biology of the Philippine Archipelago and adjacent regions. Smithonian Inst. U. S. Nat. Mus. Bull. 100, Washington, USA.

Fowler, H. W. (1948–1954): Os peixes de agua doce do Brasil, vol. I. + II. Arq. Zool. Est. Sao Paulo, Sao Paulo.

Flauaus, G. (1975): Der Goldfisch. Franckh'sche Verlagshandlung, Stuttgart.

Frey, H. (1971): Zierfisch-Monographien, Band 1: Salmler, Verlag J. Neumann, Radebeul.

Frey, H. (1974): Zierfisch-Monographien, Band 2: Karpfenfische. Verlag J. Neumann, Radebeul.

Frey, H. (1974): Zierfisch-Monographien, Band 3: Welse und andere Sonderlinge. Verlag J. Neumann, Radebeul.

Frey, H. (1978): Zierfisch-Monographien, Band 4: Buntbarsche – Cichliden. Verlag J. Neumann, Melsungen.

Gärtner, G. (1981): Zahnkarpfen – Die Lebendgebärenden im Aquarium. Verlag Eugen Ulmer, Stuttgart.

Géry, J. (1977): Characoids of the world. T. F. H. Publications, Inc. Ltd. Neptune City, N. J., USA.

Gilchrist, J. D. F. & W. W. Thompson (1917): The freshwater fishes of South Africa. Ann. S. Afr. Mus. 11, Kapstadt.

Goldstein, R. J. (1971): Anabantoids, Gouramis and related fishes. T. F. H. Publications, Neptune City, N. J., USA.

Goldstein, R. J. (1973): Cichlids of the world. T. F. H. Publications, Neptune City, N. J., USA.

Gosse, J.-P. (1975): Revision du genre Geophagus. Acad. Roy. Scien. Outre-Mer, Brüssel.

Greenwood, P. H. (1979): Towards a phyletic classification of the genus Haplochromis (Pisces, Cichlidae) and related taxa, part 1. Bull. Br. Mus. nat. Hist. (Zool.) 35, London.

Greenwood, P. H. (1980): Towards a phyletic classification of the genus „Haplochromis" (Pisces, Cichlidae) and related taxa, part II. Bull. Br. Mus. nat. Hist. (Zool.) 39, London.

Heilborn, A. (1949): Der Stichling. A. Ziemsen Verlag, Wittenberg Lutherstadt.

Holly, M., H. Meinken & A. Rachow (o. J.): Die Aquarienfische in Wort und Bild. Alfred Kernen Verlag, Stuttgart.

Inger, R. F. & Ch. P. Kong (1962): The fresh-water fishes of North Borneo. Fieldiana Zool. 45, Chicago, USA.

Jackson, P. B. N. (1961): Checklist of the fishes of Nyassaland. Nat. Mus. S. Rhodesia, Samfya.

Literature

Jackson, P. B. N. & T. Ribbink (1975): Mbuna-rock-dwelling cichlids of lake Malawi. T. F. H. Publications, Neptune City, N. J., USA.

Jacobs, K. (1969): Die lebendgebärenden Fische der Süßgewässer. Edition Leipzig, Leipzig.

Jacobs, K. (1976/1977): Vom Guppy dem Millionenfisch, Band 1 + 2, Landbuch Verlag, Hannover.

Jordan, D. S. & B. W. Evermann (1896): The fishes of North and Middle America. Smithonian Institution, Washington.

Jubb, R. A. (1967): Freshwater fishes of Southern Africa. Gothic Printing Comp., Cape Town–Amsterdam.

Knaack, K. (1970): Killifische im Aquarium. Franckh'sche Verlagshandlung, Stuttgart.

Kramer, K. (1943): Aquarienkunde. Bearbeitet von Hugo Weise. Gustav Wenzel & Sohn, Braunschweig.

Kraus, O. (1970): Internationale Regeln für die zoologische Nomenklatur. Verlag Waldemar Kramer, Frankfurt/M.

Krause, H.-J. (1981): Einführung in die Aquarientechnik. Franckh'sche Verlagshandlung, Stuttgart.

Kuhn, O. (1967): Die vorzeitlichen Fischartigen und Fische. A. Ziemsen Verlag, Wittenberg Lutherstadt.

Kuhnt. M. (ca. 1922): Exotische Zierfische, Illustriertes Handbuch für Aquarianer. Verlag Vereinigte Zierfischzüchtereien Berlin-Rahnsdorf.

Kullander, S. O. (1973): Amerikas Cichlider: Gullänget, Schweden.

Kullander, S. O. (1980): A taxonomic study of the genus Apistogramma Regan, with a revision of Brazilian and Peruvian species (Teleostei; Percoidei; Cichlidae). Bonner Zool. Monograph., Nr. 14; 1–152.

Ladiges, W. (1976): Kaltwasserfische in Haus und Garten. Tetra Verlag, Melle.

Ladiges, W. & D. Vogt (1979): Die Süßwasserfische Europas. Verlag Paul Parey, Hamburg, 2. Auflage.

Lagler, K. F., J. E. Bardach &. R. R. Miller (1962): Ichthyology. John Wiley & Sons, New York, N. Y., USA.

Linke, H. &. W. Staeck (1981): Afrikanische Cichliden, I. West-Afrika, Tetra-Verlag, Melle.

Lowe-McConnell, R. H. (1977): Ecology of fishes in tropical waters. Edward Arnold, London.

Lüling, K. H. (1977): Die Knochenzüngler-Fische. A. Ziemsen Verlag, Wittenberg Lutherstadt.

Matthes, H. (1964): Les poissons de lac Tumba et de la region d'Ikela. Ann. Mus. Roy. Afr. Centrale, Tervuren.

Mayland, H. J. (1978): Große Aquarienpraxis – Band 1–3. Landbuch Verlag, Hannover.

Mayland, H. J. (1981): Diskusfische – Könige Amazoniens. Landbuch Verlag, Hannover.

Müller, A. H. (1966): Lehrbuch der Paläozoologie, Band 3: Vertebraten, Teil 1: Fische im weiteren Sinne und Amphibien. VEB Gustav Fischer Verlag, Jena.

Munro, I. S. R. (1955): The marine and freshwater fishes of Ceylon. Dept. Extern. Affairs. Canberra, Australien.

Munro, I. S. R. (1967): The fishes of New Guinea. Dept. Agriculture, Stock and Fishereis. Port Moresby, New Guinea.

Myers, G. S. (1972): The Piranha book. T. F. H. Publications, Neptune City, N. J., USA.

Nikolski, G. W. (1957): Spezielle Fischkunde. VEB Deutscher Verlag der Wissenschaften, Berlin.

Osetrova, W. S. (1978): Handbuch der Fischkrankheiten. Verlag Kolos, Moskau, USSR.

Paffrath, K. (1978): Bestimmung und Pflege von Aquarienpflanzen. Landbuch-Verlag GmbH, Hannover.

Paepke, H.-J. (1979): Segelflosser – die Gattung Pterophyllum. A. Ziemsen Verlag, Wittenberg Lutherstadt.

Paysan, K. (1970): Welcher Zierfisch ist das? Franckh'sche Verlagshandlung, Stuttgart.

Pellegrin, J. (1903): Contribution a l'etude anatomique, biologique et taxonomique des poissons de la famille Cichlides. Mem. Soc. Zool. France 16, Paris.

Petzold, H.-G. (1968): Der Guppy. A. Ziemsen Verlag, Wittenberg Lutherstadt.

Piechocki, R. (1973): Der Goldfisch. A. Ziemsen Verlag, Wittenberg Lutherstadt.

Pinter, H. (o. J.): Handbuch der Aquarienfischzucht. Alfred Kernen Verlag, Stuttgart.

Pinter, H. (1981): Cichliden – Buntbarsche im Aquarium. Verlag Eugen Ulmer, Stuttgart.

Poll, M. (1957): Les genres des poissons d'eau douce de l'Afrique. Ann. Mus. Roy. Congo Belge 54, Tervuren.

Poll, M. (1953): Poissons non Cichlidae. Explor, Hydrobiol. Lac Tanganika, vol. III, Brüssel.

Poll, M. (1956): Poissons Cichlidae. Explor. Hydrobiol. Lac Tanganika, vol. III. Brüssel.

Poll, M. (1957): Les genres des poissons d'eau douce de l'Afrique. Ann. Mus. Roya. Congo Belge 54, Tervuren.

Poll, M. (1967): Contribution a la faune ichthyologique de l'Angola. Diamang, Publ. Cultur. no. 75, Lissabon.

Puyo, J. (1949): Poissons de la Guyane Francaise. Libraire Larose, Paris.

Reichenbach-Klinke, H. H. (1980): Krankheiten und Schädigungen der Fische. Gustav Fischer Verlag, Stuttgart, 2. Auflage.

Reichenbach-Klinke, H. H. (1968): Krankheiten der Aquarienfische. Kernen Verlag, Stuttgart.

Reichenbach-Klinke, H. H. (1970): Grundzüge der Fischkunde. Gustav Fischer Verlag, Stuttgart.

Reichenbach-Klinke, H. H. (1975): Bestimmungsschlüssel zur Diagnose von Fischkrankheiten. Gustav Fischer Verlag, Stuttgart.

Literature

Ringuelet, R. A., R. H. Aramburu & A. A. Aramburu (1967): Los Peces Argentinos de agua dulce. Comm. Invest. Cientifica, La Plata.

Roman, B. (1966): Les poissons de haute-bassins de la Volta. Ann. Mus. R. Afr. Centrale, Tervuren.

Rosen, D. E. (1979): Fishes from the uplands and intermontane basis of Guatemala: revisionary studies and comparative geography. Bull. Amer. Mus. nat. Hist. 162.

Schäperclaus, W. (1979): Fischkrankheiten, Band 1 + 2. Akademie Verlag, Berlin (4. Auflage).

Scheel, J. J. (1972): Rivulins of the world. T. F. H. Publications, Neptune City, N. J., USA.

Scheel, J. J. (1974): Rivuline studies – taxonomic studies of Rivuline Cyprinodonts from tropical atlantic Africa. Ann. Mus. R. Afr. Centrale no. 211, Tervuren.

Schubert, G. (1971): Krankheiten der Fische. Franckh'sche Verlagshandlung, Stuttgart.

Seegers, L. (1980): Killifische, Eierlegende Zahnkarpfen im Aquarium, Verlag Eugen Ulmer, Stuttgart.

Smith, H. M. (1945): The fresh-water fishes of Siam or Thailand. U. S. Govern. Print. Office, Washington, USA.

Staeck, W. (1974/1977): Cichliden: Verbreitung–Verhalten–Arten, Band 1 + 2. Engelbert Pfriem Verlag, Wuppertal-Elberfeld.

Staeck, W. & H. Linke (1982): Afrikanische Cichliden. II. Ost-Afrika. Tetra-Verlag, Melle.

Stansch, K. (1914): Die exotischen Zierfische in Wort und Bild. Kommissionsverlag: Gustav Wenzel & Sohn, Braunschweig.

Sterba, G. (1968): Süßwasserfische aus aller Welt. Urania Verlag, Leipzig–Jena–Berlin.

Sterba, G. (1975): Aquarienkunde, Band 1+2. Verlag J. Neumann, Melsungen–Berlin–Basel–Wien.

Sterba, G. (1978): Lexikon der Aquaristik und Ichthyologie. Edition Leipzig, Leipzig.

Suworow, J. K. (1959): Allgemeine Fischkunde. VEB Deutscher Verlag der Wissenschaften.

Thorson, T. R. (1976): Investigations to the ichthyofauna of Nicaraguan lakes. University of Nebraska, Lincoln, USA.

Thys van den Audenaerde, D. F. E. (1968): An annotated bibliography of Tilapia. Mus. R. Afr. Centrale no. 14, Tervuren.

Tortonese, E. (1970): Osteichthyes – Pesci Ossei, parte prima. Edizione Calderini, Bologna, Italien.

Trewavas, E. (1935): A synopsis of the cichlid fishes of lake Nyassa. Ann. Mag. nat. Hist. 16, London.

Vierke, J. (1977): Zwergbuntbarsche im Aquarium. Franckh'sche Verlagshandlung, Stuttgart.

Vierke, J. (1978): Labyrinthfische und verwandte Arten. Engelbert Pfriem Verlag, Wuppertal-Elberfeld.

Vogt, C. & B. Hofer (1909): Die Süßwasserfische von Mitteleuropa. Verlag Wilhelm Engelmann, Leipzig.

Weatherly, A. H. (1972): Growth and ecology of fish populations. Academic Press, London + New York.

Whitley, G. P. (1960): Native freshwater fishes of Australia. Jarracanda Press, Brisbane, Australien.

Zukal, R. & S. Frank (1979): Geschlechtsunterschiede der Aquarienfische. Landbuch Verlag, Hannover.

Photografic Sources

Dr. Gerald R. Allen (2): p. 813 t, 851 b.
Aqua Medic (1): p. 19.
Hans A. Baensch (37): p.11, 18, 41, 80, 85,183 t, 187 (2), 191 (2), 193, 195, 291 b.r,
319, 351 t, 461 t.l., 463 m.l., 465 m, 467 t.l.+t.r., 471 t.r. + b.r., 603 t, 660 b, 699 b, 707
b, 719 t + b, 763 t, 765, 895 t.l., 897 (2), 899 (2), 929 (2).
Dr. Ulrich Baensch (1): p. 87.
Heiko Bleher (2): p. 293 t, 279 t.
Gerhard Brünner (1): p. 119 b.l.
Ingo Carstensen (4): p. 535 t, 547 t, 569 m, 577 t.
Horst Dieckhoff (2): p. 683 b, 711 t.
Dr. Walter Foersch (13): p. 481, 489 b, 525 b, 527 b, 533 t, 552, 555 t + b, 607 t, 650,
807t, 820, 851 t.
Dr. Stanislav Frank (3): p. 297 t, 303 t, 387 b.
Hilmar Hansen (13): p. 209, 231 t, 429 b, 461 b, 673 b, 687 t, 737 b, 743 t, 813 b, 841,
844, 849 m, 867 t.
Peter Hoffmann (1): p. 247 b.
Kurt Huwald (6): p. 538 t, 539 t, 545 b, 561 b, 581 b, 583 t.
Heinrich Jung (3): p. 333 t, 675 b, 677 b.
Juwel Aquarium (2): p. 12, 13.
Burkhard Kahl (166): p. 219 t, 223 b, 227 b, 243 b, 257 t, 259 b, 261 t, 263 (2), 265 b,
269 (2), 271 (2), 273 (2), 281 (2), 283 (2), 285 (2), 287 (2), 289 (2), 291 b, 293 b, 295 t,
303 b, 305 b, 309 b, 313 t, 325 t, 327 t, 341 (2), 343 t, 347 b, 350 t + m, 353 b, 355 t,
357 (2), 359 b, 365 m, 367 t, 369 b, 371 b, 373 b, 381 b, 383 b, 385 b, 393 b, 394, 395
t, 399 t + b, 401 t, 405 t, 407 b, 409 (2), 423 t, 427 t, 431, 433 (2), 437 (2), 439 b, 447
t, 451, 463 t, 467 m.r., 471 m + b.l., 472, 475 m.r. + b.l., 477 b, 485, 487 t, 489 t, 499 (2),
505 b, 513, 525 t, 537 b, 541 b, 567 t, 569 b, 571 b, 575 t, 581 t, 585 t, 592 (2), 595 b,
597 t, 601 t.r., 603 b, 607 b, 608 (2), 610, 611 t + b.r., 614, 633 b, 635 t, 637 (2), 639
b, 645 b, 649 t, 653 t, 691 t, 693 b, 701 t, 715 b, 719 m, 721 t, 729 (3), 739 (2), 743 b,
745 t, 755 t, 757 b, 761 t, 762, 764, 766 (2), 767 (2), 769 b, 771 (2), 772, 777 t, 779 t,
783 b, 787, 790, 793 b, 823 t, 837 b, 845, 847 b, 853 t, 855 t, 857 t, 869 t, 880, 885, 893
t.r., 895 t.r. + b, 908, 926.
Horst Kipper, Dupla Aquaristik (3): p. 47, 49, 183 b.
Karl Knaack (1): p. 557 t.
Alexander M. Kochetov (1): p. 811 b.
Ingo Koslowski (1): p. 679 b.
Axel Kulbe (1): p. 770.
Horst Linke (12): p. 425 t, 631 b, 633 t, 643 t, 667 b, 685 b, 695 b, 723 t + m, 747 t, 751
(2).
Anton Lamboj (1): p. 749 b.
K. H. Lübeck (1): p. 421 t.
Meinken-Archiv (3): p. 663 t, 781 b, 782.
Manfred K. Meyer (5): p. 591 b, 602 t, 605 t, 613 t, 759 b.
Arend van den Nieuwenhuizen (59): p. 14, 15, 74/75, 198/199, 213, 221 (2), 253 t, 309
t, 335 t + m, 343 b, 349 (2), 379, 385 t, 389 b, 399 m, 403 t, 407 t, 441 b, 471 t.l., 480,
512, 519, 522, 523 (2), 525 m, 527 t + m, 531 (2), 533 b, 536, 537 t, 539 t, 543 t, 545 t,
547b, 549 (2), 551 t, 553 t, 559 b, 565 t, 573 t + b, 579 b, 583 b, 587, 618, 631 t, 697
b, 833 t, 835 t, 347 t, 363 t, 871 b.
Aaron Norman (157): p. 210 t, 215, 217 b, 219 b, 225 t, 228 t, 233, 235 b, 241(3),
243 t, 245 (3), 249 t, 253 m, 261 b, 265 t, 267 (5), 275 b, 280, 282, 291 m.l. + m.r. + b.l.,
299 t, 301 b, 305 t, 311 (2), 313 b, 315 (2), 321 (2), 323 t, 327 b, 329 t, 331 (2), 335 b,
336, 351 b, 355 b, 387 t, 389 t, 391 (2), 393 t, 395 b, 397 (2), 403 b, 413 (2), 419 t, 427
b, 429 t, 435 b, 439 t, 446, 448, 455, 457 (2), 461 t.r. + 2 m.l + 2. m.r., 463 m.r. + 2 b,
465 t.r. + b.l., 467 m.l. + b, 469 m.l. + m.r. + b.l., 475 m.l. + b.r., 477 t, 478, 479, 483 b,
485 (2), 493 b, 495 b, 497 t, 501 b, 507 b, 508 b, 514, 517, 521, 577 b, 620 t, 627 t, 647
b, 663 m.l. + m.r., 665 (2), 671 t, 680, 681 t, 683 t, 688, 689 b, 694, 695 t, 703 t, 705 b,
709 (2), 712, 713 t, 715 t, 724, 727 b, 731 (2), 733 b, 740, 757 t, 763 b, (2), 773, 778,
785 b, 793 t, 795 b, 797 (2), 799 b, 801 t, 803 t, 805, 810, 827 b, 833 b, 836, 839 t, 843
b, 849 b, 853 b, 855 b, 859 b, 869 b, 871 t.

Photographic Sources

Gerhard Ott (3): p. 365 b, 449 (2)
Kurt Paffrath (103): p. 89 -147, 893 t.l. + b.
Klaus Paysan (13): p. 232, 325 b, 345 b, 359 t, 367 b, 375 t, 383 t, 441 t, 465 m, 543 b, 801 b, 864, 865.
Eduard Pürzl (4): p. 411, 445 b, 529 t, 595 t.
Hans Reinhard (96): p. 205 (2), 207, 208, 210 b, 227 t, 239 b, 251 b, 254, 255, 257 b, 316, 323 b, 356, 361, 365 t, 373 t, 375 t, 381 b, 411 t, 415 (2), 421 b, 423 b, 425 b, 430, 443 (2), 445 t, 459 t, 465 t.l ., 469 t, 473 t, 475 t, 491 (2), 500, 501 t, 503 (2) 505 t, 508 t, 509, 51 1 (2), 516, 551 b, 598, 617, 625 (2), 627 b, 635 b, 645 t, 647 t, 649 b, 655, 663 t. r., 669 b, 671 b, 681 b, 693 t, 711 b, 713 b, 716, 730, 733 t, 735 b, 741 b, 756, 779 b, 783 t, 785 t, 791, 795 t, 799 t, 803 b, 804, 809 t, 821, 825, 826 (2), 827 t, 829 t, 831, 835 b, 839 b, 840, 849 t, 857 b, 859 t, 860, 863 b, 901, 913.
Günter Reitz (2): p. 185 b, 189.
Hans Joachim Richter (107): p. 217 t, 225 b, 229 b, 231 b, 237 (2) 247 t, 249 b, 253 b, 259 t, 295 b, 297 t, 299 b, 301 t, 307, 317, 329 b, 333 b, 347 t, 353 t, 363, 369 t, 371 t, 401 b, 403 b, 408, 417 (2), 419 b, 435 t, 447 b, 454, 459 b, 469 b.l., 473 b, 474, 483 t, 487 b, 493 t, 507t, 515, 541 t, 553 b, 559 t, 561 t, 563 b, 565 b, 567b, 569 t, 575 b, 579 t, 585 b, 591 t, 597 b, 599 (2), 601 all 7 without t.r., 605 b, 609, 611 m.l + m.r., + b.l, 620 b, 622, 623 (2), 639 t, 641 (2) 643 t, 651 t, 653 b, 660 t, 675 t, 679 t, 681 t, 691 b, 697 t, 703 b, 705 t, 717 t, 723 t, 725 b, 727 t, 735 t, 737 t, 741 t, 745 b, 753 t, 755 t, 769 t, 775 (2), 781 t, 807 b, 811 t, 824, 837 t, 843 t, 867 m + b.
Hans Jürgen Rösler (3): p. 651 b, 749 (2).
Mike Sandford (1): p. 497 b.
Gunther Schmida (1): p. 823 b.
Jürgen Schmidt (5): p. 621, 624, 629 (2), 829 b.
Erwin Schraml (1): p. 689 t.
Dr. Gottfried Schubert (6): p. 921 (4), 924, 934.
Lothar Seegers (11): p. 495 t, 529 (2), 535 b, 557 t, 563, 571 t, 633t, 761 b, 777b, 861.
Ernst Sosna (1): p. 275 t.
Andreas Spreinat (7): p. 693 t, 711 b, 717 t, 719 t, 721 (2), 743 t.
Dr. Wolfgang Staeck (4): p. 701 b, 747 b, 753 b, 759 t.
Rainer Stawikowski (9): p. 587 b, 667 (2), 669 t, 673 t, 682, 685 t, 687 b, 721 b.
Tetra Archiv (4): p. 10, 181, 185 t, 306.
Dr. Jörg Vierke (1): p. 830.
Vogelsänger-Studios (1): p. 16/17.
Uwe Werner (4): p. 663 b, 699 t, 707 t, 725 t.
Ruud Wildekamp (2): p. 223 t, 251 t.
Lothar Wischnath (5): p. 375 m, 613 b, 615, 809 b, 815.

The Authors

Ruediger Riehl was born in West Germany in 1949, at Gombeth near Kassel. From early childhood the nearby Schwalm River molded his relationship with fish. By six he was collecting native fish, housing them in small jars. His first aquarium quickly followed and he began keeping tropical and exotic fishes. After graduating from high school in 1967 he studied biology at the University of Giessen. His major was zoology and fishes remained his first love. He received a doctorate in natural science from the university in 1976. His specialty was Oogenesis or the formation of eggs in German freshwater fishes, and involved meticulous high-magnification studies with the electron microscope.

From 1974 to 1979 Dr. Riehl worked as a scientist at the Institute for General and Specific Zoology in Giessen and in 1979 joined the University of Heidelberg's dermatology research group, studying skin cancer in humans. He transferred to Duesseldorf University in 1982 and is now an advisor on electron microscopic procedures at the Biological Institute.

The Authors

Hans A. Baensch was born in 1941 at Flensburg, and grew up near the beautiful West German city of Hannover. A biologist's son, his father introduced him to the local aquatic flora and fauna. After advanced studies in zoological sales, he joined his father's firm which manufactured and marketed internationally known aquarium foods. While with the firm he travelled to nearly every center of the aquarium hobby in the world. He took part in two expeditions to the Amazon, participating in the discovery of three new species of fish and is an experienced diver and underwater photographer. He published his first book, "Kleine Seewasser Praxis" in 1974. It has sold nearly 50,000 copies, is still available and is now in its fourth edition. In 1977 he purchased the internationally known Meinken collection of aquatic books. With more than 3,000 titles it is one of the largest privately owned libraries devoted exclusively to aquatic subjects. In the same year he launched his own publishing firm.

Today, he lives on a small farm near Melle, in West Germany, and is surrounded by woods and water. Here, he actively studies and developes ways to ecologically protect local fishes, amphibians and reptiles. He is internationally known for his publications on these subjects. They are read avidly by nature lovers around the world.